THE QUR'AN SELECTED SURAHS

PATH TO ETERNAL LIFE

COMMENTARY BY
SHAYKH FADHLALLA HAERI

THE QUR'AN SELECTED SURAHS

PATH TO ETERNAL LIFE

COMMENTARY BY
SHAYKH FADHLALLA HAERI

Zahra Publications

Zahra Publications

Selected Surahs Version ISBN: 978-1-776490-20-2

First Published in 2025 by Zahra Publications

Distributed and Published by Zahra Publications
PO Box 50764
Wierda Park, 0149
Centurion
South Africa
Email info@shaykhfadhlallahaeri.com
www.shaykhfadhlallahaeri.com
www.zahrapublications.pub

© 2025 Shaykh Fadhlalla Haeri

All rights reserved. Except for brief quotations in critical articles or reviews, no part of this book may be reproduced or utilised in any form or by any means, electronic or mechanical, without permission in writing from the publisher.

Set in 10 point in Lexicon

Contents

Foreword by Shaykh Fadhlalla Haeri i
Editor's Note vii

1.	Surah 1 al-Fatihah (The Opening)	1
2.	Surah 9 At-Tawbah (Repentance)	1
3.	Surah 11 Hud (Hud)	25
4.	Surah 16 an-Nahl (The Bee)	44
5.	Surah 17 al-Isra' (The Night Journey)	61
6.	Surah 18 al-Kahf (The Cave)	76
7.	Surah 24 an-Nur (The Light)	92
8.	Surah 26 ash-Shu'ara' (The Poets)	104
9.	Surah 27 al-Naml (The Ant)	118
10.	Surah 28 al-Qasas (The Stories)	129
11.	Surah 29 al-'Ankabut (The Spider)	144
12.	Surah 32 as-Sajdah (Prostration)	153
13.	Surah 36 Ya-Seen (Ya-seen)	157
14.	Surah 37 as-Saffat (The Arrayed in Ranks)	165
15.	Surah 38 Saad (Saad)	176
16.	Surah 41 Fussilat (Expounded)	184
17.	Surah 44 ad-Dukhan (Smoke)	193
18.	Surah 46 al-Ahqaf (The Dunes)	197
19.	Surah 50 Qaf (Qaf)	204
20.	Surah 52 at-Tur (The Mount)	208
21.	Surah 53 an-Najm (The Star)	212
22.	Surah 54 al-Qamar (The Moon)	216
23.	Surah 55 ar-Rahman (The Merciful to All)	220
24.	Surah 56 al-Waqi'ah (The Inevitable)	225
25.	Surah 57 al-Hadid (Iron)	230
26.	Surah 62 al-Jumu'ah (Friday)	236
27.	Surah 63 al-Munafiqun (The Hypocrites)	239
28.	Surah 67 al-Mulk (Sovereignty)	241
29.	Surah 74 al-Muddathir (The Cloaked)	245
30.	Surah 75 al-Qiyamah (Resurrection)	248
31.	Surah 76 al-Insan (Humankind)	251
32.	Surah 78 an-Naba' (The Event)	253
33.	Surah 85 al-Buruj (The Constellations)	256
34.	Surah 87 al-A'la (The Most High)	258
35.	Surah 88 al-Ghashiyah (The Overshadowing Event)	259
36.	Surah 90 al-Balad (The City)	261
37.	Surah 93 adh-Duha (Morning Brightness)	262
38.	Surah 94 ash-Sharh (The Expanding)	263
39.	Surah 97 al-Qadr (Determination)	264
40.	Surah 112 al-Ikhlas (Sincerity)	265
41.	Surah 113 al-Falaq (Break of Dawn)	265
42.	Surah 114 al-Nas (Mankind)	266

Foreword By
Shaykh Fadhlalla Haeri

There are numerous challenges and quests in human life. The most powerful drive, however, is to understand and connect with that which is timeless and boundless. Part of this quest is our keen interest in the beginning of creation as well as its end. The Qur'an is the voice of truth that involves what is considered to be rational and shareable consciousness. The majesty of the Qur'an is that it addresses most of our human situation and day-to-day reality whilst connecting these with the absolute and boundless.

At the level of normal, conditioned, human consciousness, the Qur'an can help to reduce suffering and discord, but a point is reached where spiritual insights go beyond the mind and into the realm of the soul, where discernment and differentiations melt away into a zone where energy and matter are not distinguishable. For this reason, most classical scholars of Qur'an refer to this higher level as the divine domain and refrain from commenting upon or discussing it.

Our human drive towards a higher, durable understanding of the meaning and purpose of life is a persistent driving force for all people at all times. From prehistoric times, prophets and seers presented different models and descriptions of the nature of life and death relevant to their people at those times. The Qur'an is a distillation of several revelations regarding human consciousness within cultures and civilisations in South West Asia. The Qur'an encompasses the teachings of most of the Abrahamic prophets and messengers and resonates with numerous other world religions and spiritual paths.

The Qur'an presents us with an entire spectrum of realities and shows how human consciousness is propelled towards the highest accessible level of consciousness. The Qur'an connects the visible and tangible world that we experience through our senses and mind with vast unseen realities. It seamlessly connects physics, chemistry, biology, and other domains with the countless energies and lights that emanate from the original sacred *Reality*. The book presents the truth at numerous stages and levels and thus uses historical examples and stories as well as symbols, metaphors, allegories, and numerous descriptions and prescriptions to show that the universe is permeated by the primal light of *Oneness*.

The prescriptions and recommendations of the Qur'an are all there to enable the human mind to interact appropriately with all the dualities that we experience in life on earth. We naturally try to deal with what is discernible and tangible, but at all times we seek answers from beyond the limitations of the mind. Matter and energy are inseparable. Earth and heavens are within the sacred Unity. Our life of causality, rationality, discernment, and discrimination is completely energized by the power of Unity. All pluralities emanate from the *One* and point towards *Oneness*. Human nature is described as that of an animal with higher consciousness, plus a soul that contains within it the imprint of the ever-present, permanent sacred light. Human consciousness spans the entire spectrum of physical matter, with all of its earthly links through chemistry, biology, changes in temperature, pressure, humidity, and all other factors; at the same time this consciousness is constantly in the quest of greater power, ability, knowledge and acknowledgement of the major forces that are at play in existence. The three primary forces that we are in constant connection with are: consciousness itself (from whence life arises); connections and relationships between entities as they appear, and the drive to experience continuity and timelessness. Whatever endeavours we undertake on earth enhance these three forces. Whatever occupation you have serves one or more of these forces. Indeed, we are all caught in the grip of the creator of it all.

Whatever we experience in life relates to one or two zones of our life. The basic zone is that of conditioned consciousness, including our personal life, biography, and identities. This is the normal human state. It is constantly changing, not always reliable, and is seeking the constancy and stability of the higher zone. This higher zone relates to higher consciousness and perpetual life itself. The Qur'an describes human life on earth as a temporary prelude to our return to the pool of life itself, with its own ultimate return to the origin from whence it emerged.

Every person struggles towards more reliable understanding and knowledge in order to reduce affliction, suffering, and all other lower tendencies of the animal self. Life has been evolving for millennia; however, the human challenge drives everyone towards revolution, instant awakening, and liberation from darkness. The wise person is revolutionary at heart and patiently evolutionary when it comes to creation itself, which has been going on for millennia. The Qur'an demonstrates to us how space and time are relative; for instance, the way many people have the experience that years have passed as if they were a few minutes. A thousand years as we count are like a day in *Reality*. Fifty thousand years as we count are like a day in *Reality*—it is not fixed.

The basic foundation of the Qur'an is the revelation of the map of truth, which is mainly in two sections. One has to do with higher consciousness and *Oneness*, the other with the purpose and meaning of life. Most intelligent people would conclude that day-to-day life and our concern for survival do not lead to real security, contentment, and joy. We are continuously struggling to match the diverse desires and needs of our own self as well as of other beings and situations. This perpetual struggle is within the zone of dualities between our identification with the animal self and the soul within us.

The Qur'an constantly brings in the issue of the afterlife: whatever we intend or act in this world will affect our overall preparedness to live as souls, rather than as evolving animals. The prophetic teachings emphasize the prescription that we be ready to depart from the body and mind. Most human endeavours exist to reduce mental agitation and break through our mental constructs, fears and sorrows. Prophets and enlightened beings naturally broke through the barriers of lower animal consciousness and thus experienced the joy of spiritual awakening and the treasure of the soul within.

Historically, the Qur'an was considered as an unwelcome challenge to the prevailing established religions in the Middle East, especially Christians and Jews. Walls of accusations and assumptions were established, resulting in much suspicion, fear, and distortion. The language of the Qur'an belongs to the cultures of nomadic Arabs, those who were yet hunter-gathers and those living in a few oasis settlements in Arabia. Translations are therefore, at best, attempts to make accessible the meaning of the message. Many of the words used in the Qur'an shifted in meaning over time, just as any language evolves and changes. The numerous stories of peoples and events mentioned in the Qur'an will come to life fully if you can imagine yourself living at that time with the limitations of the human mind and physical ability.

Hundreds of attempts by scholars and investigators over the past centuries have focused upon the unique power and potency of the Qur'anic revelations. In our present time, it is probably one of the books most frequently read with reverence and awe. The amazing combination of descriptions, prescriptions, and foreseen outcomes is magisterial. Acknowledging the local time and place with the wisdom of discrimination, the revelations constantly refer to the timeless origin of the sacred lights that penetrate everything known and unknown. We are given a map of what is appropriate and what is not, what is just, and what is out of balance, and we are shown a path that links all strands of consciousness within the human heart.

The *deen* of Islam, Prophet Muhammad's path, is founded upon reading the maps of existence and accepting them. Then trusting (*Iman*) in our drive towards *Truth* and *Reality*. When one is awakened to the higher self within, the sacred soul, then one cannot but resonate with the divine qualities of generosity, mercy, compassion as well as the highest qualities of humanity. All the virtues and higher qualities attributed to Allah are like ladders that human beings can climb, raising themselves to their highest potential. Every being is on a journey, from the lower basic consciousness of survival to the perfect joy of arrival. The *deen* of Islam prescribes the need for discipline and moral accountability, as well as the restriction and grooming of the lower self. When a young person comes of age, parents and society have the task of allowing the lower self and ego to grow, whilst encouraging reference to the soul and Allah's ways and prescriptions. The list of vices and virtues appears in numerous fashions and ways in the Qur'an. What is most remarkable is that most human beings accept the Qur'anic virtues as being good and necessary. Ultimately, the big door to the virtue of the soul is the constancy of self-awareness and the awareness of one's intentions and actions at the present time and place.

Life in the hereafter is described in numerous ways to help us go beyond the limitations of the mind to a zone where there are only fields of energies, varying in degree from the maximum agitation of hell to the perfect joy of paradise. The Qur'anic description of the state of the perfect garden alludes to the state of perpetual bliss without effort. Body, mind, space, and time vanish.

The Qur'an tells many stories relating to prophets and messengers and the way that at all times they were rejected by their people. The human self, with its illusion and assertion of identity, is reinforced by habits, traditions, and repetitions of rituals that have lost their meaning. It is natural for us to seek that which is continuous, and within our cultures we invent reminders and commemorations to enhance what we consider to be conducive for a better life. Individually and collectively we have a tremendous capacity for self-deception in order to avoid the meaning and purpose of human life and its direction towards awakening.

Whatever we experience, discern, or desire is balanced between acceptance and rejection, relating to a prejudice about what we consider to be good or bad. Every aspect of human life is relative and changeable, and as such not durable or reliable. We are creatures who have emanated from light and higher consciousness, passing through the experience of the confinements of space and time. Our life on earth is a mere prelude to the next life where the physical and metaphysical are in union. All human conflict and crises are due to the lack of clarity of the soul within. The Qur'an prescribes regular reference to Allah – the light of lights. The importance of appropriate companionship is an essential ingredient for spiritual growth, for whomever you encounter is like a mirror who will reflect some aspect upon you, good or bad.

Since the industrial revolution and subsequent technological development, our present day life has progressed to a state of emergency for the spiritual seeker. Humanity has emanated from divinity, and every individual is between what the head and the mind discern and what the heart and soul know. We are on earth but not of earth. Without constant reference to higher awareness with its spiritual replenishment, we end up as confused and depressed beings. The ultimate thrill that any intelligent person can witness has to do with the miracle of life itself and the intricate balancing that goes on in the seen and the unseen worlds. I consider the difficulties and challenges of our present day as a force driving us to break through the limitations of our mental and cultural conditioning in order to experience transformation into the real light within the heart. One brilliant prescription in the Qur'an declares that at all times human beings are at a loss, unless you are secure in your faith and constantly improve in intention, action, and reference to truth, patience, and timelessness (Surah 'Asr).

The Qur'an helps anyone who is sincere to attain a better understanding of normal, conditioned consciousness, and it alludes to supreme Godconsciousness to which evolved human beings aspire. The project of this book began quite a few years ago when I began to experience a considerable rise in the interest of Muslims and others to explore and understand the Qur'an. Hundreds of books have appeared in the last decades on the Qur'an and Islam. My exposure to numerous people of Islamic background who are living in western countries highlighted the need to produce a new introduction and allegorical rendering of the Qur'an for young, educated minds. My comments on the *ayat* point towards higher *Reality* and truth as it is revealed in those verses rather than providing the sort of commentary or interpretation that is already plentiful. For the very serious student of Qur'an and Islam, the Arabic language and all the basics that go with it cannot be bypassed.

This modern interpretation of the Quran is the effort of several friends and associates especially Shaykh Hosam Raouf, Shaykh Saadi Douglas Klotz, Dr Adnan Al Adnani and Leyya Kalla who coordinated and lead the project to its completion.

May this work bring you delight and increase your faith and hope.

Bismillah.

Shaykh Fadhlalla Haeri
Whiteriver
2025

Editor's Note

Dear seeker

Before you journey through the Qur'an and Qur'anic reflections herein, please note a few technicalities that will assist you in understanding the text.

- While it is customary to include invocations of peace and blessings upon the Prophets and more specifically Prophet Muhammad and his family whenever their names are mentioned, these have not been included in the text for reasons of space. Nonetheless such prayers are implicit in the mention of their names and we trust the reader will naturally invoke Allah's blessings upon the Prophets and their families.
- Arabic terms have been italicised.
- In the commentaries, terms that substitute for the name of Allah/ God, that is, pointing beyond the name or activity towards their Source, have been both italicised and capitalised (for instance, *Essence, Reality, The One, Oneness, Divine, Source*). As the Qur'an notes, the name Allah itself refers to a reality that is beyond naming, gendering, languaging or conceiving, although it is what enables all of these human abilities. Capitalising a word ultimately can at best serve to help the mind stop for an instant to take notice of something specific, in this case, specifically to recalibrate to what is beyond human language.
- Likewise in the commentaries all other divine attributes are printed as lower case except where they hold a place where the word "Allah" would occur, as above. The commentator noted that since Allah is everything and everything is Allah, what is there to capitalise? All happenings and beings in the universe are "names" and activities of *Reality*, whether we are able at the moment to witness them as such or not. It is also important to remember that no ancient Semitic language, including Qur'anic Arabic, has any capital letters, so all translations involve a judgment about what is considered "sacred" and what is not. Readers can and undoubtedly will have their own judgments about this question, but the intent of the commentary and subsequent editing is to encourage–at any moment–the higher or greater witnessing (*mushahida*) mentioned above.
- Transliterations of Arabic language *asma'* (names) and other terms are still italicized and, depending on the term, capitalised for ease of identification in the text.
- In four *Surahs* of the Qur'an, there is a verse of *sajdah*, which means that if one recites this verse, he should immediately perform *sajdah* after the verse has finished. If he forgets to do this, he must perform *sajdah* whenever he remembers. The locations are in *Surah al-Sajdah* (32:15); in *Surah Fussilat* (41:37); in *Surah al-Najm* (53:62) and in *Surah al-'Alaq* (96:19). There are

other views on recommended prostrations, we advise the reader follow their usual standard.
- Prophets' names have been rendered in English, however, for ease of use for all readers' preferences, please find a list of the prophets' names in both English and Arabic:
Prophet Isaac/Ishaq; Prophet Abraham/Ibrahim; Prophet Jesus/Issa; Prophet Zachariah/Zakariyya; Prophet Moses/Musa; Prophet Noah/Nuh; Prophet Lot/Lout; Prophet Jethro/ Shu'aib; Prophet Joseph/Yusuf; Prophet John the Baptist/Yahya; Prophet Enoch/Idrees; Prophet Prophet Ishmael/Ismael; Prophet David/Dawud; Prophet Solomon/Sulayman; Prophet Jonah/Yunus; Prophet Muhammad.
- Any reference to 'men', 'man' and 'mankind' in the text has the connotation of humankind and equally refers to women and should be regarded as non-gender specific.
- A number of terms and concepts are used throughout the commentaries. This list defines them for your ease of reference:

   o Consciousness: A field of energy that expresses the manifestation of life. Consciousness comes in many different zones that differ in nature and intensity. Within each zone there are numerous strands of consciousness. Basic sentiency is the most common beginning of consciousness, whereas pure consciousness is the highest. Consciousness is the proof of life.

   o Higher consciousness/Pure consciousness/God consciousness/Supreme consciousness Divine consciousness Boundless Perpetual: This level of consciousness is not subject to the level of consciousness is not subject to the limitations of space or time. It is both the pinnacle and all-encompassing zone of consciousness. Pure consciousness is the first step of the manifestation of the power of consciousness from the Absolute.

   o Absolute/God/Source/Supreme Essence/C/cosmic (C/cosmic sacredess): From whence all emanates and to which all returns.

   o Cosmic Life: From whence all life emanates and to which it returns.

   o Human consciousness/Personal consciousness/ Conditioned consciousness/Normal consciousness /Limited consciousness/ Temporary, Transitory consciousness: These terms have been used interchangeably. They span the common human experience. This consciousness spans several states or zones; within each are numerous strands of consciousness. Sleep, for example, spans a range of twilight zone of consciousness to deep sleep and includes dreams, light, or heavy sleep. It is always inadequate, a cause of suffering, regret, blames, and claims. The realm of duality is within conditioned consciousness; any form, entity, or event that appears in conditioned consciousness is one of two forces and not in the zone of *Oneness*.

- Animal consciousness: More limited than human consciousness, aspires to human consciousness.
- Spectrum of consciousness: The spectrum of consciousness ranges from very basic sentiency to the ultimate discernible Pure consciousness. The spectrum of consciousness depends on the universe in which it appears. In our universe, the ultimate measure or reference is human consciousness.
- R/reality /Higher reality = Reality R/real: Reality (small 'r') is the point of consciousness that is prominent in the moment, for example: fear, pain, pleasure, sleep, sorrow. Reality: The zone from which all realities emanate. It is powered by supreme consciousness and empowers all manifesting consciousnesses.
- D/din (also standardised 'deen' or 'din'): Set of rules, regulations, and boundaries that enable one to act appropriately without causing much regret, fear, sorrow, and suffering. One "owes" it to oneself to follow these rules, regulations and boundaries, as in paying a debt, the "transaction" due for being alive in human, conditioned consciousness.
- Path: The spiritual path, implies adherence to boundaries and moving along towards one's destiny, which is to be at one with the One. It takes one higher in consciousness.
- Essence: Refers to divine spirit or higher Reality.
- Soul essence: The cosmic soul.
- Cosmic soul: The primary force that permeates all the universes, not limited to any space or time or to any culture, is defined as God or the Sacred. All souls are energized by the cosmic soul. The cosmic soul is only one major burst of countless bursts of energy emanating from the Absolute.
- Soul/Ruh: A package of energies that contain within them the attri-butes of the Source/God. It is the portal through which personal life accesses eternal cosmic life.
- Ego (self, self-ego, lower self-ego, ego darkness, ego self, shadow self, animal self, dark self): It is the shadow of the soul. Ever-changing in its intensity, colour, value and use-fulness. Every human experience is part of a duality. The light of life is balanced by its shadow, which is called ego. As long as one breathes, one has an ego.
- Paradise/Garden/Bliss/PerpetualJoy/Jannah/Gardenic: Heavenly equivalent of what we experience on earth as pleasure, happiness, and joy. It is a state of perfect ease and peace, and the experience of timelessness.
- Hell/Jahannam: Heavenly equivalent of what we experience on earth as misery, intense sorrow, helpless, and hopelessness. It is a state of unease and appears endless in time.
- Middle people: Middle people are middle creation between absolute and earthly creation, between divinity and humanity. They range between the highest and lowest levels of con-

sciousness. Human beings are indeed middle people for numerous reasons. We are between birth and death, ignorance and knowledge, fear and security, limited consciousness and the vastness of supreme consciousness.

- Inner/outer garden/gardenic: Outer garden: The literal earthly garden is the nursery for us to practice our desire and love to experience gardens at different metaphorical, experiential, and visible levels—the outer manifestation of the bliss of the inner garden. Inner garden: metaphorical state of inner peace. There is a natural inclination for intelligent human beings to seek outer beauty, harmony and whatever is conducive for inner pleasure. Historically, those who seek enlightenment often refer to this state of joyful contentment as the inner garden.
- Map of Oneness/Domain of Oneness/Zone of Oneness: Whatever indicates the inter-connectedness of existences that lead to the One that encompasses all.
- Definition of the Map: The Qur'an describes and prescribes the keys that will enable us to decode the flow of life, its meaning and purpose. This sacred atlas covers the entire spectrum of consciousness, from that of basic sentiency of life to the fully enlightened and awakened soul. Faith and trust in these maps are necessary to be able to read them, and then be able to commit to them and follow them. A fully awakened being knows that the source of all knowledge lies within the heart, and this is what gives that individual confidence and trust in Reality. This state is complete awakening to the immensity of the present moment, which is inseparable from timelessness.
- Tuned/tune/calibrated: In unison to the flow of, directly connected to, and calibrated with the Source.
- Believing men and women: Those who accept the notion that there is life after death and that life on earth is a preparation for the here-after, and who believe in the perfect governance of Allah/Source/God.
- Evolvement: A change that indicates movement generally towards higher consciousness.
- Shaytanic: Evil and destructive forces, the dark shadow of the light of consciousness. It is one zone of consciousness with varying intensities.
- Sacred books: Sacred books imply a package of revelation of truth that can be used by individuals or communities to maintain quality life and to grow in consciousness.
- Intelligent and Enlightened: The intelligent person is one who reviews cause and effect, reads patterns and events and seeks to understand their meaning and origin; this person is in a state of duality. The enlightened person is a person who is in a state of

Tawhid, not in duality, who has experienced and touched the Absolute.
- o Transaction: No one is spared from the need to transact and connect within conditioned consciousness, benefitting from the connection by moving towards the absolute zone of peace, ease and tranquillity.

- Effort has been made to ensure that punctuation in the English translation of the Qur'an has been approached balancing both the verse by verse structure of this production, its display and accuracy in terms of the English language. The reader may appreciate that quotation marks and general punctuation are more a matter of style as they do not technically exist in the Qur'anic Arabic and may forgive inconsistencies in this regard.
- Translations of verses are in italics and are numbered in the margin to ease reading. This is followed by verse-numbered commentary corresponding to the verses preceding it. Thereafter, two paragraphs then follow which are presented as further reflections as well as prescriptions the aforementioned verses.

The editors,

1. Surah 1 al-Fatihah (The Opening)

This most-often recited Surah declares that whatever we praise refers to a divine attribute. These attributes and other subtle forces hold the universe together and radiate mercy and grace, which link living entities to their origin directly through an illumined path, transmitted from a believing heart.

1-7 بِسْمِ ٱللَّهِ ٱلرَّحْمَٰنِ ٱلرَّحِيمِ ۝ ٱلْحَمْدُ لِلَّهِ رَبِّ ٱلْعَٰلَمِينَ ۝ ٱلرَّحْمَٰنِ ٱلرَّحِيمِ ۝ مَٰلِكِ يَوْمِ ٱلدِّينِ ۝ إِيَّاكَ نَعْبُدُ وَإِيَّاكَ نَسْتَعِينُ ۝ ٱهْدِنَا ٱلصِّرَٰطَ ٱلْمُسْتَقِيمَ ۝ صِرَٰطَ ٱلَّذِينَ أَنْعَمْتَ عَلَيْهِمْ غَيْرِ ٱلْمَغْضُوبِ عَلَيْهِمْ وَلَا ٱلضَّآلِّينَ ۝

In the name of Allah, the Merciful to all, the Compassionate to each! Praise be to Allah, Lord of the Worlds. Merciful to all, the Compassionate to each! Sovereign of the Day of Recompense. It is You we worship, and upon You we call for help. Guide us to the straight path. The path of those You have blessed, those who incur no anger and who have not gone astray.

1-7 Everything emanates from one cosmic Source. All of creation, including its existence and individual experiences themselves, is balanced between attraction and repulsion. The purpose of creation is to interact with manifest realities and to relate them to the original patterns and higher consciousness. The human soul carries the lights and knowledge of heaven and earth. While death ends the illusion of separate and independent identity for many, a few will awaken to this truth before death. Whatever we praise emanates from Allah who is the source of universal mercy, life and consciousness. The direct path between creation and its origin leads from darkness to light.

The lower self or ego is a shadow of the soul, which carries all the great attributes that we aspire toward. The greatest attribute is mercy for all creation and compassion for each and everyone. It is that Reality that we adore and worship.

It is in our nature to praise and whatever we praise is an attribute of us. These attributes enable us to enter worship, and through worship we enter into a complete link between divinity and humanity.

2. Surah 9 At-Tawbah (Repentance)

The challenge of human life on earth can only be resolved if we accept the promise that the divine soul within us is the source of life; and that this is the biggest gift. The appropriate response to having this gift is to acknowledge its origin as well as our need to be in constant reference to that sacred essence.

بَرَآءَةٌ مِّنَ ٱللَّهِ وَرَسُولِهِۦٓ إِلَى ٱلَّذِينَ عَٰهَدتُّم مِّنَ ٱلْمُشْرِكِينَ ۝ فَسِيحُوا۟ فِى ٱلْأَرْضِ ١-٦
أَرْبَعَةَ أَشْهُرٍ وَٱعْلَمُوٓا۟ أَنَّكُمْ غَيْرُ مُعْجِزِى ٱللَّهِ وَأَنَّ ٱللَّهَ مُخْزِى ٱلْكَٰفِرِينَ ۝
وَأَذَٰنٌ مِّنَ ٱللَّهِ وَرَسُولِهِۦٓ إِلَى ٱلنَّاسِ يَوْمَ ٱلْحَجِّ ٱلْأَكْبَرِ أَنَّ ٱللَّهَ بَرِىٓءٌ مِّنَ ٱلْمُشْرِكِينَ
وَرَسُولُهُۥ فَإِن تُبْتُمْ فَهُوَ خَيْرٌ لَّكُمْ وَإِن تَوَلَّيْتُمْ فَٱعْلَمُوٓا۟ أَنَّكُمْ غَيْرُ مُعْجِزِى
ٱللَّهِ وَبَشِّرِ ٱلَّذِينَ كَفَرُوا۟ بِعَذَابٍ أَلِيمٍ ۝ إِلَّا ٱلَّذِينَ عَٰهَدتُّم مِّنَ ٱلْمُشْرِكِينَ ثُمَّ
لَمْ يَنقُصُوكُمْ شَيْـًٔا وَلَمْ يُظَٰهِرُوا۟ عَلَيْكُمْ أَحَدًا فَأَتِمُّوٓا۟ إِلَيْهِمْ عَهْدَهُمْ إِلَىٰ مُدَّتِهِمْ
إِنَّ ٱللَّهَ يُحِبُّ ٱلْمُتَّقِينَ ۝ فَإِذَا ٱنسَلَخَ ٱلْأَشْهُرُ ٱلْحُرُمُ فَٱقْتُلُوا۟ ٱلْمُشْرِكِينَ حَيْثُ
وَجَدتُّمُوهُمْ وَخُذُوهُمْ وَٱحْصُرُوهُمْ وَٱقْعُدُوا۟ لَهُمْ كُلَّ مَرْصَدٍ فَإِن تَابُوا۟ وَأَقَامُوا۟
ٱلصَّلَوٰةَ وَءَاتَوُا۟ ٱلزَّكَوٰةَ فَخَلُّوا۟ سَبِيلَهُمْ إِنَّ ٱللَّهَ غَفُورٌ رَّحِيمٌ ۝ وَإِنْ أَحَدٌ مِّنَ
ٱلْمُشْرِكِينَ ٱسْتَجَارَكَ فَأَجِرْهُ حَتَّىٰ يَسْمَعَ كَلَٰمَ ٱللَّهِ ثُمَّ أَبْلِغْهُ مَأْمَنَهُۥ ذَٰلِكَ بِأَنَّهُمْ
قَوْمٌ لَّا يَعْلَمُونَ ۝

An acquittal, from Allah and His Messenger, unto the idolaters with whom you made covenant: 'Journey freely in the land for four months; and know that you cannot frustrate the will of Allah, and that Allah degrades the unbelievers.' A proclamation from Allah and His Messenger to all mankind on the day of the Greater Pilgrimage. Allah is quite of the polytheists, as is His Messenger. If you repent, this shall be better for you. If you turn away, know that you cannot evade the power of Allah. And announce to the unbelievers a torment most painful. As for those who have honoured the treaty you made with them and who have not supported anyone against you; fulfil your agreement with them to the end of their term. Allah loves those who are conscious of Him. Once the sacred months are passed, kill the polytheists wherever you find them, arrest them, imprison them, besiege them, and lie in wait for them at every site of ambush. If they repent, perform the prayer and pay the alms, let them go on their way. Allah is All-Forgiving, Compassionate to each. And if any of the idolaters seeks of your protection, grant him protection till he hears the words of Allah; then do you convey him to his place of security – that, because they are a people who do not know.

1-6 Human progress towards spiritual fulfilment cannot take place in a combative environment. Law, order, and good governance with reference to divine justice are needed for the maintenance of humanity. The outer world is to be respected and not abused. The inner world too has its rules and regulations for increasing spiritual wisdom by containing the self and following the light of the soul. We hope to realise the governance of the perfect soul through the purified heart and subdued self, or ego. Religious rituals and adherence to codes of correct practices naturally enhance our conduct and wellbeing. It is necessary to be firm with transgressors and those who deny truth and the purpose of human life. Darkened hearts and confused energies naturally affect us adversely.

2. Surah 9 At-Tawbah (Repentance)

The purpose of human life on earth is to rise in consciousness towards awakening to the cosmic *Oneness* and Allah's perfect governance overall. All human suffering and confusion are due to dualities, multiplicities, and pluralities. These do exist in our earthly realm, but they are only shadows of the *Real*.

The nature of human life on earth is based on dualities, pluralities, and multiplicities. Our own state is based on an evolved animal that has been brought to life over billions of years through the mysterious power of the divine life itself within us. So, each one of us is made up of numerous, intricate cells that connect with each other and produce organs and different chemical and physical vehicles, all activated by this light that we call life within the cell. Each one of us is two; if the instrument is damaged by inheritance, bad habits, or wrong thinking, then there is no rise in consciousness or intelligence. That human being is unlikely to be awakened or enlightened.

7-15 كَيْفَ يَكُونُ لِلْمُشْرِكِينَ عَهْدٌ عِندَ ٱللَّهِ وَعِندَ رَسُولِهِۦٓ إِلَّا ٱلَّذِينَ عَٰهَدتُّمْ عِندَ ٱلْمَسْجِدِ ٱلْحَرَامِ ۖ فَمَا ٱسْتَقَٰمُوا۟ لَكُمْ فَٱسْتَقِيمُوا۟ لَهُمْ ۚ إِنَّ ٱللَّهَ يُحِبُّ ٱلْمُتَّقِينَ ۝ كَيْفَ وَإِن يَظْهَرُوا۟ عَلَيْكُمْ لَا يَرْقُبُوا۟ فِيكُمْ إِلًّا وَلَا ذِمَّةً ۚ يُرْضُونَكُم بِأَفْوَٰهِهِمْ وَتَأْبَىٰ قُلُوبُهُمْ وَأَكْثَرُهُمْ فَٰسِقُونَ ۝ ٱشْتَرَوْا۟ بِـَٔايَٰتِ ٱللَّهِ ثَمَنًا قَلِيلًا فَصَدُّوا۟ عَن سَبِيلِهِۦٓ ۚ إِنَّهُمْ سَآءَ مَا كَانُوا۟ يَعْمَلُونَ ۝ لَا يَرْقُبُونَ فِى مُؤْمِنٍ إِلًّا وَلَا ذِمَّةً ۚ وَأُو۟لَٰٓئِكَ هُمُ ٱلْمُعْتَدُونَ ۝ فَإِن تَابُوا۟ وَأَقَامُوا۟ ٱلصَّلَوٰةَ وَءَاتَوُا۟ ٱلزَّكَوٰةَ فَإِخْوَٰنُكُمْ فِى ٱلدِّينِ ۗ وَنُفَصِّلُ ٱلْءَايَٰتِ لِقَوْمٍ يَعْلَمُونَ ۝ وَإِن نَّكَثُوٓا۟ أَيْمَٰنَهُم مِّنۢ بَعْدِ عَهْدِهِمْ وَطَعَنُوا۟ فِى دِينِكُمْ فَقَٰتِلُوٓا۟ أَئِمَّةَ ٱلْكُفْرِ ۙ إِنَّهُمْ لَآ أَيْمَٰنَ لَهُمْ لَعَلَّهُمْ يَنتَهُونَ ۝ أَلَا تُقَٰتِلُونَ قَوْمًا نَّكَثُوٓا۟ أَيْمَٰنَهُمْ وَهَمُّوا۟ بِإِخْرَاجِ ٱلرَّسُولِ وَهُم بَدَءُوكُمْ أَوَّلَ مَرَّةٍ ۚ أَتَخْشَوْنَهُمْ ۚ فَٱللَّهُ أَحَقُّ أَن تَخْشَوْهُ إِن كُنتُم مُّؤْمِنِينَ ۝ قَٰتِلُوهُمْ يُعَذِّبْهُمُ ٱللَّهُ بِأَيْدِيكُمْ وَيُخْزِهِمْ وَيَنصُرْكُمْ عَلَيْهِمْ وَيَشْفِ صُدُورَ قَوْمٍ مُّؤْمِنِينَ ۝ وَيُذْهِبْ غَيْظَ قُلُوبِهِمْ ۗ وَيَتُوبُ ٱللَّهُ عَلَىٰ مَن يَشَآءُ ۗ وَٱللَّهُ عَلِيمٌ حَكِيمٌ ۝

How could there be a treaty with Allah and His Messenger for such idolaters? But as for those with whom you made a treaty at the Sacred Mosque, so long as they remain true to you, be true to them; Allah loves those who are conscious of Him. How can it be, whenever they gain the upper hand over you, they respect neither kinship nor covenant with you! They give you pleasure with their mouths, but their hearts disdain, and most are transgressors. They have sold the signs of Allah for a small price, and have barred from His way; truly evil is that they have been doing. Towards a believer, they respect neither kinship nor covenant. They are truly the aggressors. If they repent, perform the prayer and pay the alms, they are to be your brothers in religion. We make intelligible Our revelations for a people who understand. And if they break their oaths after their agreement and revile your religion, then fight the leaders of unbelief, surely their oaths are nothing, so that they may desist.

Will you not fight a people who broke their oaths and purposed to expel the Messenger, beginning the first time against you? Are you afraid of them? You would do better to be afraid of Allah, if you are believers. Fight them, and Allah will chastise them at your hands and degrade them, and He will help you against them, and bring healing to the breasts of a people who believe, and He will remove the rage within their hearts; and Allah turns towards whomsoever He will; Allah is All-Knowing, All-Wise.

7-15 Whoever believes that life on earth has a purpose and a direction will come to realise that effecting this purpose requires faith, trust, and application. In the same way that outer difficulties and challenges help people grow and evolve, so also the awareness of the supremacy of the soul helps a seeker awaken to higher consciousness. When outer and inner states are in balance and harmony, there will be better progress towards our life's real purpose. To banish inner and outer enemies is a necessary start for inner and outer friendships. Through repentance and adherence to the practices and applications of the prophetic path, we will realise how God's grace is experienced through good will, hope, and good expectations.

To not be awakened to *Oneness* is a deep defect that affects all aspects of one's life and can only be rectified by faith, trust, and the hope to leave behind the confusion of darkness and shadows. Lasting goodness begins when you see the *One's* Hand behind the multitudes.

As humans, a situation may arise that the damage we have caused to ourselves, knowingly or otherwise, is irreversible. In that case, there is no possibility for real help, compassion, or empathy. The situation reaches a point beyond its ability to connect with higher consciousness.

16-23 أَمْ حَسِبْتُمْ أَن تُتْرَكُوا۟ وَلَمَّا يَعْلَمِ ٱللَّهُ ٱلَّذِينَ جَٰهَدُوا۟ مِنكُمْ وَلَمْ يَتَّخِذُوا۟ مِن دُونِ ٱللَّهِ وَلَا رَسُولِهِۦ وَلَا ٱلْمُؤْمِنِينَ وَلِيجَةً ۚ وَٱللَّهُ خَبِيرٌۢ بِمَا تَعْمَلُونَ ۝ مَا كَانَ لِلْمُشْرِكِينَ أَن يَعْمُرُوا۟ مَسَٰجِدَ ٱللَّهِ شَٰهِدِينَ عَلَىٰٓ أَنفُسِهِم بِٱلْكُفْرِ ۚ أُو۟لَٰٓئِكَ حَبِطَتْ أَعْمَٰلُهُمْ وَفِى ٱلنَّارِ هُمْ خَٰلِدُونَ ۝ إِنَّمَا يَعْمُرُ مَسَٰجِدَ ٱللَّهِ مَنْ ءَامَنَ بِٱللَّهِ وَٱلْيَوْمِ ٱلْءَاخِرِ وَأَقَامَ ٱلصَّلَوٰةَ وَءَاتَى ٱلزَّكَوٰةَ وَلَمْ يَخْشَ إِلَّا ٱللَّهَ ۖ فَعَسَىٰٓ أُو۟لَٰٓئِكَ أَن يَكُونُوا۟ مِنَ ٱلْمُهْتَدِينَ ۝ أَجَعَلْتُمْ سِقَايَةَ ٱلْحَآجِّ وَعِمَارَةَ ٱلْمَسْجِدِ ٱلْحَرَامِ كَمَنْ ءَامَنَ بِٱللَّهِ وَٱلْيَوْمِ ٱلْءَاخِرِ وَجَٰهَدَ فِى سَبِيلِ ٱللَّهِ ۚ لَا يَسْتَوُۥنَ عِندَ ٱللَّهِ ۗ وَٱللَّهُ لَا يَهْدِى ٱلْقَوْمَ ٱلظَّٰلِمِينَ ۝ ٱلَّذِينَ ءَامَنُوا۟ وَهَاجَرُوا۟ وَجَٰهَدُوا۟ فِى سَبِيلِ ٱللَّهِ بِأَمْوَٰلِهِمْ وَأَنفُسِهِمْ أَعْظَمُ دَرَجَةً عِندَ ٱللَّهِ ۚ وَأُو۟لَٰٓئِكَ هُمُ ٱلْفَآئِزُونَ ۝ يُبَشِّرُهُمْ رَبُّهُم بِرَحْمَةٍ مِّنْهُ وَرِضْوَٰنٍ وَجَنَّٰتٍ لَّهُمْ فِيهَا نَعِيمٌ مُّقِيمٌ ۝ خَٰلِدِينَ فِيهَآ أَبَدًا ۚ إِنَّ ٱللَّهَ عِندَهُۥٓ أَجْرٌ عَظِيمٌ ۝ يَٰٓأَيُّهَا ٱلَّذِينَ ءَامَنُوا۟ لَا تَتَّخِذُوٓا۟ ءَابَآءَكُمْ وَإِخْوَٰنَكُمْ أَوْلِيَآءَ إِنِ ٱسْتَحَبُّوا۟ ٱلْكُفْرَ عَلَى ٱلْإِيمَٰنِ ۚ وَمَن يَتَوَلَّهُم مِّنكُمْ فَأُو۟لَٰٓئِكَ هُمُ ٱلظَّٰلِمُونَ ۝

Or did you suppose you would be left in peace, and Allah knows not as yet those of you who have struggled, and taken not apart from Allah and His Messenger and the believers any intimate? Allah is aware of what you do. It is not for the idolaters to inhabit Allah's places of worship, witnessing against themselves unbelief; those, their works have failed them, and in the Fire they shall dwell forever. Only he shall inhabit Allah's places of worship who believes in Allah and the Last Day, and performs the prayer, and pays the alms, and fears none but Allah alone; it may be that those will be among the guided. Are you indeed equating provision of water to pilgrims and caring for the Sacred Mosque with one who believes in Allah and the Last Day, and labors hard in the cause of Allah? They are not equal in the sight of Allah, and Allah guides not the evildoers. Those who believe, and have emigrated, and have struggled in the way of Allah with their possessions and their selves are mightier in rank with Allah; and those, they are the triumphant; their Lord gives them good tidings of mercy from Him and good pleasure; for them await gardens wherein is lasting bliss. Therein to dwell forever and ever; surely with Allah is a mighty wage. O you who believe! Do not take your fathers and your brothers for guardians if they love unbelief more than belief; and whoever of you takes them for a guardian, these it is that are the wrongdoers.

16-23 Every human being pursues some desire, interest, or need. Ultimately, the highest desire is to experience and know the prevalence and perfect governance of Allah. A migration towards that objective is the duty of all sincere people seeking spiritual awakening. We always seek renewal and what promises to give us durable security and certainty. Personal will and dedication are necessary to realise the immense divine grace transmitted by the soul within the heart. This is the earthly experience that reflects the paradise of the hereafter. The celestial realities are reflected by terrestrial events and situations. The higher and lower are in perpetual balance.

The prophetic path is to have faith, trust, accountability for actions and a willingness to sacrifice in order to be purified from the lower distractions and the illusions of the ego-self. Once one gives up one's attachments, and the misplaced identification with one's lower self, the light will show itself, leaving one the choice to follow it to awakening.

There may be situations where some of our close family or relatives have been damaged at the human level – physical, chemical, biological, and otherwise – to a point whereby we cannot do anything to help them, nor can any of our hopes and aspirations for them take us anywhere. We must understand that there are natural patterns to existences, whether simple or complex.

24-29 قُلْ إِن كَانَ ءَابَآؤُكُمْ وَأَبْنَآؤُكُمْ وَإِخْوَٰنُكُمْ وَأَزْوَٰجُكُمْ وَعَشِيرَتُكُمْ وَأَمْوَٰلٌ اقْتَرَفْتُمُوهَا وَتِجَٰرَةٌ تَخْشَوْنَ كَسَادَهَا وَمَسَٰكِنُ تَرْضَوْنَهَآ أَحَبَّ إِلَيْكُم مِّنَ

اللَّهِ وَرَسُولِهِ وَجِهَادٍ فِى سَبِيلِهِ فَتَرَبَّصُوا حَتَّىٰ يَأْتِىَ ٱللَّهُ بِأَمْرِهِ ۗ وَٱللَّهُ لَا يَهْدِى ٱلْقَوْمَ ٱلْفَـٰسِقِينَ ۝ لَقَدْ نَصَرَكُمُ ٱللَّهُ فِى مَوَاطِنَ كَثِيرَةٍ ۙ وَيَوْمَ حُنَيْنٍ ۙ إِذْ أَعْجَبَتْكُمْ كَثْرَتُكُمْ فَلَمْ تُغْنِ عَنكُمْ شَيْـًٔا وَضَاقَتْ عَلَيْكُمُ ٱلْأَرْضُ بِمَا رَحُبَتْ ثُمَّ وَلَّيْتُم مُّدْبِرِينَ ۝ ثُمَّ أَنزَلَ ٱللَّهُ سَكِينَتَهُۥ عَلَىٰ رَسُولِهِۦ وَعَلَى ٱلْمُؤْمِنِينَ وَأَنزَلَ جُنُودًا لَّمْ تَرَوْهَا وَعَذَّبَ ٱلَّذِينَ كَفَرُوا ۚ وَذَٰلِكَ جَزَآءُ ٱلْكَـٰفِرِينَ ۝ ثُمَّ يَتُوبُ ٱللَّهُ مِنۢ بَعْدِ ذَٰلِكَ عَلَىٰ مَن يَشَآءُ ۗ وَٱللَّهُ غَفُورٌ رَّحِيمٌ ۝ يَـٰٓأَيُّهَا ٱلَّذِينَ ءَامَنُوٓا إِنَّمَا ٱلْمُشْرِكُونَ نَجَسٌ فَلَا يَقْرَبُوا ٱلْمَسْجِدَ ٱلْحَرَامَ بَعْدَ عَامِهِمْ هَـٰذَا ۚ وَإِنْ خِفْتُمْ عَيْلَةً فَسَوْفَ يُغْنِيكُمُ ٱللَّهُ مِن فَضْلِهِۦٓ إِن شَآءَ ۚ إِنَّ ٱللَّهَ عَلِيمٌ حَكِيمٌ ۝ قَـٰتِلُوا ٱلَّذِينَ لَا يُؤْمِنُونَ بِٱللَّهِ وَلَا بِٱلْيَوْمِ ٱلْءَاخِرِ وَلَا يُحَرِّمُونَ مَا حَرَّمَ ٱللَّهُ وَرَسُولُهُۥ وَلَا يَدِينُونَ دِينَ ٱلْحَقِّ مِنَ ٱلَّذِينَ أُوتُوا ٱلْكِتَـٰبَ حَتَّىٰ يُعْطُوا ٱلْجِزْيَةَ عَن يَدٍ وَهُمْ صَـٰغِرُونَ ۝

Say: 'If your fathers and your sons, your brothers and your spouses and your clans, together with the wealth you acquired and a commerce you fear will find no market, and homes you find pleasing if all these are more dear to you than Allah, His Messenger and the struggle in His cause, then wait and attend until Allah fulfils His decree.' Allah guides not the dissolute. Allah gave you victory on many a battlefield. Recall the Day of Hunayn, when you fancied your great number but it did not help you one whit. So, the earth, for all its wide expanse, narrowed before you, and you turned tail and fled. Then Allah made His serenity descend upon His Messenger and the believers, and sent down troops you did not see, and tormented the unbelievers. Such is the reward of unbelievers. Thereafter Allah will restore to His grace whosoever He wills; Allah is All-Forgiving, Compassionate to each. O believers, the polytheists are indeed a pollution, so let them not approach the Sacred Mosque beyond this year of theirs. If you fear poverty, Allah will supply your needs from His bounty, if He wills. Allah is All-Knowing, All-Wise. Fight those who believe not in Allah and the Last Day and do not forbid what Allah and His Messenger have forbidden; such men as practise not the religion of truth, being of those who have been given the Book, until they pay the tribute out of hand and have been humbled.

24-29 The human journey on earth presents numerous challenges, confrontations, and alliances. The higher the level of connectedness to God's intention, the more durable and reliable the human connection will be. We experience the greatest stability and harmony when our reference is the absolute origin – God. The weakest links between human beings are transient, earthly transactions and connections. Our concerns for survival and security can distract us from following and achieving our duties and obligations towards the absolute *Reality*. Remembrance of and concern regarding the hereafter are important touchstones that help us recharge and renew our direction and focus. We naturally desire a good outcome in our state as experienced after death.

Human life is a process of spiritual delights and openings, distractions, darkness, and suffering. Whoever is not on the path of cosmic Unity has not truly entered the zone of evolution towards awakening. As such, one can regard them as structurally deficient.

The starting point of well-beingness is the understanding of the duality of human nature and the mercy of the divine in every situation. The promise is that, with diligence, patience, and perfecting worship, you will come to know that the light within you is divine, and this light will guide you.

30-36 وَقَالَتِ ٱلْيَهُودُ عُزَيْرٌ ٱبْنُ ٱللَّهِ وَقَالَتِ ٱلنَّصَٰرَى ٱلْمَسِيحُ ٱبْنُ ٱللَّهِ ذَٰلِكَ قَوْلُهُم
بِأَفْوَٰهِهِمْ يُضَٰهِـُٔونَ قَوْلَ ٱلَّذِينَ كَفَرُوا۟ مِن قَبْلُ قَٰتَلَهُمُ ٱللَّهُ أَنَّىٰ يُؤْفَكُونَ ﴿٣٠﴾
ٱتَّخَذُوٓا۟ أَحْبَارَهُمْ وَرُهْبَٰنَهُمْ أَرْبَابًا مِّن دُونِ ٱللَّهِ وَٱلْمَسِيحَ ٱبْنَ مَرْيَمَ وَمَآ أُمِرُوٓا۟
إِلَّا لِيَعْبُدُوٓا۟ إِلَٰهًا وَٰحِدًا لَّآ إِلَٰهَ إِلَّا هُوَ سُبْحَٰنَهُۥ عَمَّا يُشْرِكُونَ ﴿٣١﴾ يُرِيدُونَ أَن
يُطْفِـُٔوا۟ نُورَ ٱللَّهِ بِأَفْوَٰهِهِمْ وَيَأْبَى ٱللَّهُ إِلَّآ أَن يُتِمَّ نُورَهُۥ وَلَوْ كَرِهَ ٱلْكَٰفِرُونَ ﴿٣٢﴾
هُوَ ٱلَّذِىٓ أَرْسَلَ رَسُولَهُۥ بِٱلْهُدَىٰ وَدِينِ ٱلْحَقِّ لِيُظْهِرَهُۥ عَلَى ٱلدِّينِ كُلِّهِۦ وَلَوْ كَرِهَ
ٱلْمُشْرِكُونَ ﴿٣٣﴾ يَٰٓأَيُّهَا ٱلَّذِينَ ءَامَنُوٓا۟ إِنَّ كَثِيرًا مِّنَ ٱلْأَحْبَارِ وَٱلرُّهْبَانِ لَيَأْكُلُونَ
أَمْوَٰلَ ٱلنَّاسِ بِٱلْبَٰطِلِ وَيَصُدُّونَ عَن سَبِيلِ ٱللَّهِ وَٱلَّذِينَ يَكْنِزُونَ ٱلذَّهَبَ
وَٱلْفِضَّةَ وَلَا يُنفِقُونَهَا فِى سَبِيلِ ٱللَّهِ فَبَشِّرْهُم بِعَذَابٍ أَلِيمٍ ﴿٣٤﴾ يَوْمَ يُحْمَىٰ عَلَيْهَا فِى
نَارِ جَهَنَّمَ فَتُكْوَىٰ بِهَا جِبَاهُهُمْ وَجُنُوبُهُمْ وَظُهُورُهُمْ هَٰذَا مَا كَنَزْتُمْ لِأَنفُسِكُمْ
فَذُوقُوا۟ مَا كُنتُمْ تَكْنِزُونَ ﴿٣٥﴾ إِنَّ عِدَّةَ ٱلشُّهُورِ عِندَ ٱللَّهِ ٱثْنَا عَشَرَ شَهْرًا فِى
كِتَٰبِ ٱللَّهِ يَوْمَ خَلَقَ ٱلسَّمَٰوَٰتِ وَٱلْأَرْضَ مِنْهَآ أَرْبَعَةٌ حُرُمٌ ذَٰلِكَ ٱلدِّينُ ٱلْقَيِّمُ فَلَا
تَظْلِمُوا۟ فِيهِنَّ أَنفُسَكُمْ وَقَٰتِلُوا۟ ٱلْمُشْرِكِينَ كَآفَّةً كَمَا يُقَٰتِلُونَكُمْ كَآفَّةً وَٱعْلَمُوٓا۟
أَنَّ ٱللَّهَ مَعَ ٱلْمُتَّقِينَ ﴿٣٦﴾

The Jews say, 'Ezra is the Son of Allah'; the Christians say, 'The Messiah is the Son of Allah.' That is the utterance of their mouths, conforming with the unbelievers before them. Allah assail them! How they are perverted! They have taken their rabbis and their monks as lords apart from Allah, and the Messiah, Mary's son; and they were commanded to serve but One Allah; there is no Allah but He; glory be to Him, above that they associate. Desiring to extinguish with their mouths Allah's light; and Allah refuses but to perfect His light, though the unbelievers be averse. It is He Who sent His Messenger with Guidance and the religion of truth, that He may exalt it above all religions, even if the idolaters find it abhorrent. O believers, many rabbis and monks consume the wealth of people unjustly and bar the way to the path of Allah. And those who hoard gold and silver, and do not spend them in the cause of Allah; warn them of a most painful torment, upon a Day when the fire of hell shall be stoked, and with it shall be scorched their foreheads, sides and backs. 'This is what you hoarded for yourselves, so taste what you used to hoard!' The number of the months, with Allah, is twelve in the Book of Allah, the day that He created the heavens and the earth; four of them are sacred.

That is the right religion. So wrong not each other during them. And fight the unbelievers totally even as they fight you totally and know that Allah is with the cautiously aware.

30-36 It is natural for tribes and groups of people to consider themselves to be better than others. The idea of being special or chosen is deep within us. The soul within is an extraordinary entity. We place more value on whatever is close to us than what is remote. The ultimate proof of this rule is the value of our soul, which is immeasurable. The soul is the source of life itself and is nearer than nearness. The ignorant are in darkness and denial, and they lack the wisdom and ability to differentiate what is appropriate for the journey and what is not. We need to distinguish what is local and human from what is absolute, universal, and true.

All true spiritual messages originated from the same source and emphasized the need for human beings to accept the truth of *Oneness* and to work towards experiencing its power in day-to-day life. However, due to the shadow self, which wants to preserve itself, we find faults and enter into doubts and arguments.

Simply declaring that you are religious or spiritual does not mean that you are able to help others or even yourself. The decrees that brought about this complex creation are such that these patterns link and superimpose upon each other most intricately. All we need is to be observant and reflective enough to see the way of *Reality* manifesting, connecting the visible and the invisible. It is not by claim or hope.

37-42 إِنَّمَا ٱلنَّسِيٓءُ زِيَادَةٌ فِى ٱلْكُفْرِ يُضَلُّ بِهِ ٱلَّذِينَ كَفَرُوا۟ يُحِلُّونَهُۥ عَامًا وَيُحَرِّمُونَهُۥ عَامًا لِّيُوَاطِـُٔوا۟ عِدَّةَ مَا حَرَّمَ ٱللَّهُ فَيُحِلُّوا۟ مَا حَرَّمَ ٱللَّهُ زُيِّنَ لَهُمْ سُوٓءُ أَعْمَٰلِهِمْ وَٱللَّهُ لَا يَهْدِى ٱلْقَوْمَ ٱلْكَٰفِرِينَ ۝ يَٰٓأَيُّهَا ٱلَّذِينَ ءَامَنُوا۟ مَا لَكُمْ إِذَا قِيلَ لَكُمُ ٱنفِرُوا۟ فِى سَبِيلِ ٱللَّهِ ٱثَّاقَلْتُمْ إِلَى ٱلْأَرْضِ أَرَضِيتُم بِٱلْحَيَوٰةِ ٱلدُّنْيَا مِنَ ٱلْءَاخِرَةِ فَمَا مَتَٰعُ ٱلْحَيَوٰةِ ٱلدُّنْيَا فِى ٱلْءَاخِرَةِ إِلَّا قَلِيلٌ ۝ إِلَّا تَنفِرُوا۟ يُعَذِّبْكُمْ عَذَابًا أَلِيمًا وَيَسْتَبْدِلْ قَوْمًا غَيْرَكُمْ وَلَا تَضُرُّوهُ شَيْـًٔا وَٱللَّهُ عَلَىٰ كُلِّ شَىْءٍ قَدِيرٌ ۝ إِلَّا تَنصُرُوهُ فَقَدْ نَصَرَهُ ٱللَّهُ إِذْ أَخْرَجَهُ ٱلَّذِينَ كَفَرُوا۟ ثَانِىَ ٱثْنَيْنِ إِذْ هُمَا فِى ٱلْغَارِ إِذْ يَقُولُ لِصَٰحِبِهِۦ لَا تَحْزَنْ إِنَّ ٱللَّهَ مَعَنَا فَأَنزَلَ ٱللَّهُ سَكِينَتَهُۥ عَلَيْهِ وَأَيَّدَهُۥ بِجُنُودٍ لَّمْ تَرَوْهَا وَجَعَلَ كَلِمَةَ ٱلَّذِينَ كَفَرُوا۟ ٱلسُّفْلَىٰ وَكَلِمَةُ ٱللَّهِ هِىَ ٱلْعُلْيَا وَٱللَّهُ عَزِيزٌ حَكِيمٌ ۝ ٱنفِرُوا۟ خِفَافًا وَثِقَالًا وَجَٰهِدُوا۟ بِأَمْوَٰلِكُمْ وَأَنفُسِكُمْ فِى سَبِيلِ ٱللَّهِ ذَٰلِكُمْ خَيْرٌ لَّكُمْ إِن كُنتُمْ تَعْلَمُونَ ۝ لَوْ كَانَ عَرَضًا قَرِيبًا وَسَفَرًا قَاصِدًا لَّٱتَّبَعُوكَ وَلَٰكِنۢ بَعُدَتْ عَلَيْهِمُ ٱلشُّقَّةُ وَسَيَحْلِفُونَ بِٱللَّهِ لَوِ ٱسْتَطَعْنَا لَخَرَجْنَا مَعَكُمْ يُهْلِكُونَ أَنفُسَهُمْ وَٱللَّهُ يَعْلَمُ إِنَّهُمْ لَكَٰذِبُونَ ۝

Postponing sacred months is another act of disobedience by which those who disregard are led astray; they will allow it one year and forbid it in another in order outwardly to conform with the number of Allah's sacred months, but in doing so they permit what Allah has forbidden. Their evil deeds are made alluring to them; Allah does not guide the unbelievers. O believers, what is amiss with you, that when it is said to you, 'Go forth in the way of Allah,' you sink down heavily to the ground? Are you so content with this present life, rather than the world to come? Yet the enjoyment of this present life, compared with the world to come, is a little thing. If you go not forth, He will chastise you with a painful chastisement, and instead of you He will substitute another people; and you will not hurt Him anything, for Allah is powerful over everything. If you do not rally to his support, Allah has already supported him when the unbelievers drove him out, one of two men in a cave. It was then that he said to his companion: 'Do not grieve, for Allah is with us.' Then Allah made His serenity descend upon him and backed him with troops you did not see. Thus, He abased the word of the unbelievers, and the Word of Allah was supreme. Allah is Almighty, All-Wise. March forth, then, whether light or heavy in armor. Labor hard in the cause of Allah, with your property and persons; this is best for you, if only you knew. Were it a gain near at hand, and an easy journey, they would have followed you; but the distance was too far for them. Still, they will swear by Allah, 'Had we been able, we would have gone out with you,' so destroying their souls; and Allah knows that they are truly liars.

37-42 With faith and trust in the *One* comes clarity on the path and an evolution in consciousness. If there is no spiritual growth, stagnation and decay set in, leading to destruction and an unhappy end to human life. The opportunity to awaken to the power of the soul within can only be revealed through faith, trust, and complete adherence to the prophetic path. With wisdom and spiritual insight come courage as well as the realisation that divine grace and human commitment are ever connected. Grace is always there but will be fully experienced through human will and effort. This was illustrated by the Prophet Muhammad and his companion in the cave, where the Prophet was only a few metres away from his enemies who were searching for him. Allah veils and reveals in ways that the human mind can barely comprehend.

The path of enlightenment requires deep conviction, courage, and steadfastness. With these qualities, wisdom emerges that helps us appreciate what is appropriate and what is not. We require correct references to bring about goodness that lasts.

Through intelligence, one realises that no matter how much you acquire in a worldly sense, of power, wealth, knowledge, and well-being, it is not enough. Because what you are seeking and driving towards is the ultimate absolute, which is the nature of the light within your own heart or soul. This is boundless and eternal, whereas anything we experience in our minds is limited and earthly. Through the light we can naturally connect it all to its source and destiny, which is limitless.

43-51

عَفَا ٱللَّهُ عَنكَ لِمَ أَذِنتَ لَهُمْ حَتَّىٰ يَتَبَيَّنَ لَكَ ٱلَّذِينَ صَدَقُوا۟ وَتَعْلَمَ ٱلْكَٰذِبِينَ ۝ لَا يَسْتَـْٔذِنُكَ ٱلَّذِينَ يُؤْمِنُونَ بِٱللَّهِ وَٱلْيَوْمِ ٱلْـَٔاخِرِ أَن يُجَٰهِدُوا۟ بِأَمْوَٰلِهِمْ وَأَنفُسِهِمْ ۗ وَٱللَّهُ عَلِيمٌۢ بِٱلْمُتَّقِينَ ۝ إِنَّمَا يَسْتَـْٔذِنُكَ ٱلَّذِينَ لَا يُؤْمِنُونَ بِٱللَّهِ وَٱلْيَوْمِ ٱلْـَٔاخِرِ وَٱرْتَابَتْ قُلُوبُهُمْ فَهُمْ فِى رَيْبِهِمْ يَتَرَدَّدُونَ ۝ وَلَوْ أَرَادُوا۟ ٱلْخُرُوجَ لَأَعَدُّوا۟ لَهُۥ عُدَّةً وَلَٰكِن كَرِهَ ٱللَّهُ ٱنۢبِعَاثَهُمْ فَثَبَّطَهُمْ وَقِيلَ ٱقْعُدُوا۟ مَعَ ٱلْقَٰعِدِينَ ۝ لَوْ خَرَجُوا۟ فِيكُم مَّا زَادُوكُمْ إِلَّا خَبَالًا وَلَأَوْضَعُوا۟ خِلَٰلَكُمْ يَبْغُونَكُمُ ٱلْفِتْنَةَ وَفِيكُمْ سَمَّٰعُونَ لَهُمْ ۗ وَٱللَّهُ عَلِيمٌۢ بِٱلظَّٰلِمِينَ ۝ لَقَدِ ٱبْتَغَوُا۟ ٱلْفِتْنَةَ مِن قَبْلُ وَقَلَّبُوا۟ لَكَ ٱلْأُمُورَ حَتَّىٰ جَآءَ ٱلْحَقُّ وَظَهَرَ أَمْرُ ٱللَّهِ وَهُمْ كَٰرِهُونَ ۝ وَمِنْهُم مَّن يَقُولُ ٱئْذَن لِّى وَلَا تَفْتِنِّىٓ ۚ أَلَا فِى ٱلْفِتْنَةِ سَقَطُوا۟ ۗ وَإِنَّ جَهَنَّمَ لَمُحِيطَةٌۢ بِٱلْكَٰفِرِينَ ۝ إِن تُصِبْكَ حَسَنَةٌ تَسُؤْهُمْ ۖ وَإِن تُصِبْكَ مُصِيبَةٌ يَقُولُوا۟ قَدْ أَخَذْنَآ أَمْرَنَا مِن قَبْلُ وَيَتَوَلَّوا۟ وَّهُمْ فَرِحُونَ ۝ قُل لَّن يُصِيبَنَآ إِلَّا مَا كَتَبَ ٱللَّهُ لَنَا هُوَ مَوْلَىٰنَا ۚ وَعَلَى ٱللَّهِ فَلْيَتَوَكَّلِ ٱلْمُؤْمِنُونَ ۝

Allah pardons you! Why did you give them leave, till it was clear to you which of them spoke the truth, and you knew the liars? Those who believe in Allah and the Last Day do not ask your permission to labor with their property and persons. Allah knows full well who the cautiously aware are. They only ask leave of you who do not believe in Allah and the latter day and their hearts are in doubt, so in their doubt do they waver. Had they wanted to march out, they would have made preparations for it, but Allah was averse to their joining the expedition, so He slackened them, and it was said to them: 'Stay behind with those who stay behind.' Had they gone out with you, they would only have added to your difficulties, hastening between your ranks and intending to spread discord among you, while some of you would have lent them an ear. But Allah knows full well who the wrongdoers are. They sought to stir up sedition already before, and turned things up-side down for you, until the truth came, and Allah's command appeared, though they were averse. Among them are some who say: 'Grant me leave, and do not tempt me.' But it is precisely in temptation that they have fallen, and hell shall engulf the unbelievers! If good fortune befalls you, it vexes them; but if thou art visited by an affliction, they say, 'We took our dispositions before', and turn away, rejoicing. Say: 'Naught shall visit us but what Allah has prescribed for us; He is our Protector; in Allah let the believers put all their trust.'

43-51 There are rules for dealing with friends and foes, with those who profess to faith and those who are in denial. The evolving person mistrusts the lower self and questions it until the effects of the ego become negligible. Similarly, those without faith or a path are like the lower self and ego, wayward and untrustworthy. Early in our evolution and growth, we place our attention and concern on the dangers of the ego and lower self, which is the enemy within us. Once the lower self is subdued and contained, then naturally the light of the soul will shine and lead. Denial and hypocrisy form the dark fog that will cause endless confusion, distraction, and loss. There is only one residing master and lord within us, the soul or spirit within; when we follow it, we stop following other illusions.

If we truly believe in Allah's power over everything, then we will flow in this life with inner confidence and outer caution. Mischief and affliction are natural in our day-to day-life on earth but will not touch the believer deeply.

Deception, discord, and warfare exist at many levels, and most of them arise because the people who are perpetrating these activities have not reached a point of realisation that ultimately it is Allah who is in charge. It is that Light that has given us life, and it is that Light that is drawing us to it through higher levels of devotion and conduct.

52-59 قُلْ هَلْ تَرَبَّصُونَ بِنَا إِلَّا إِحْدَى ٱلْحُسْنَيَيْنِ وَنَحْنُ نَتَرَبَّصُ بِكُمْ أَن يُصِيبَكُمُ ٱللَّهُ بِعَذَابٍ مِّنْ عِندِهِ أَوْ بِأَيْدِينَا فَتَرَبَّصُوٓاْ إِنَّا مَعَكُم مُّتَرَبِّصُونَ ۝ قُلْ أَنفِقُواْ طَوْعًا أَوْ كَرْهًا لَّن يُتَقَبَّلَ مِنكُمْ إِنَّكُمْ كُنتُمْ قَوْمًا فَسِقِينَ ۝ وَمَا مَنَعَهُمْ أَن تُقْبَلَ مِنْهُمْ نَفَقَتُهُمْ إِلَّا أَنَّهُمْ كَفَرُواْ بِٱللَّهِ وَبِرَسُولِهِۦ وَلَا يَأْتُونَ ٱلصَّلَوٰةَ إِلَّا وَهُمْ كُسَالَىٰ وَلَا يُنفِقُونَ إِلَّا وَهُمْ كَـٰرِهُونَ ۝ فَلَا تُعْجِبْكَ أَمْوَٰلُهُمْ وَلَآ أَوْلَـٰدُهُمْ إِنَّمَا يُرِيدُ ٱللَّهُ لِيُعَذِّبَهُم بِهَا فِى ٱلْحَيَوٰةِ ٱلدُّنْيَا وَتَزْهَقَ أَنفُسُهُمْ وَهُمْ كَـٰفِرُونَ ۝ وَيَحْلِفُونَ بِٱللَّهِ إِنَّهُمْ لَمِنكُمْ وَمَا هُم مِّنكُمْ وَلَـٰكِنَّهُمْ قَوْمٌ يَفْرَقُونَ ۝ لَوْ يَجِدُونَ مَلْجَـًٔا أَوْ مَغَـٰرَٰتٍ أَوْ مُدَّخَلًا لَّوَلَّوْاْ إِلَيْهِ وَهُمْ يَجْمَحُونَ ۝ وَمِنْهُم مَّن يَلْمِزُكَ فِى ٱلصَّدَقَـٰتِ فَإِنْ أُعْطُواْ مِنْهَا رَضُواْ وَإِن لَّمْ يُعْطَوْاْ مِنْهَآ إِذَا هُمْ يَسْخَطُونَ ۝ وَلَوْ أَنَّهُمْ رَضُواْ مَآ ءَاتَـٰهُمُ ٱللَّهُ وَرَسُولُهُۥ وَقَالُواْ حَسْبُنَا ٱللَّهُ سَيُؤْتِينَا ٱللَّهُ مِن فَضْلِهِۦ وَرَسُولُهُۥٓ إِنَّآ إِلَى ٱللَّهِ رَٰغِبُونَ ۝

Say: 'Are you waiting to see if either of the two most glorious rewards shall be ours? We too are waiting to see whether Allah will inflict His punishment upon you, or else at our hands. So, wait and see, and we are waiting with you!' Say: 'Spend willingly or unwillingly, it shall not be accepted from you; surely you are a transgressing people.' The only thing that prevents what they give from being accepted is the fact that they defy Allah and His Messenger, perform the prayer only lazily, and give only grudgingly. So do not be impressed by their wealth or their progeny; Allah only desires to torment them therewith in this present life, and their souls shall expire while still unbelievers. And they swear by Allah that they do indeed belong to you – the while they do not belong to you, but are people ridden by fear. if they could find a place of refuge, or a cave, or somewhere to crawl into, they would run there with great haste. Among them are some who reproach you regarding voluntary alms; if given a portion thereof, they are content, but if they are not given anything they grow discontented. O were they well-pleased with what Allah and His Messenger have brought them, saying, 'Enough for us is Allah; Allah will bring us of His bounty, and His Messenger; to Allah we humbly turn.'

52-59 Whatever we experience, physically or mentally, is due to a multitude of factors, seen and unseen, which have come together and enabled the microcosm, the 'I', to reflect, relate, and connect with the macrocosm, the outer world. This is how whatever we do – if it is with the right awareness and intention, and the ability to reflect upon and correct it – will eventually take us higher towards pure consciousness. That implies that others, who are not on the same path, will cause themselves and whoever is close to them disturbances, which are distractions in our journey in this life. People who are not on a clear path and don't understand it through mind and heart are already in great inner conflict. They bring about similar or more complex discord and confusion in others. Unless we adhere strictly to the path of self-awareness and self-correction, we can end up in situations that are irreversible, and there will be intense suffering. Trust in Allah. Perseverance and continuity are the marks of those on the path to awakening.

The lower self gets naturally attached to objects and emotional desires. With higher awareness, we can acknowledge the tendency to be attached, but can also leave it behind and move on to higher levels of lights. When we believe in the *One*, the cosmic controller, and refer to its light during difficulties with true devotion and faith, the relief we receive will only increase our faith.

It's natural for us human beings to be impressed by other people's power, wealth, and abilities. But in reality, most of these qualities come to nothing unless they are totally in the way of the divine decree towards improving our worship and being in this world, but not of this world.

60-67 إِنَّمَا ٱلصَّدَقَٰتُ لِلْفُقَرَآءِ وَٱلْمَسَٰكِينِ وَٱلْعَٰمِلِينَ عَلَيْهَا وَٱلْمُؤَلَّفَةِ قُلُوبُهُمْ وَفِى ٱلرِّقَابِ وَٱلْغَٰرِمِينَ وَفِى سَبِيلِ ٱللَّهِ وَٱبْنِ ٱلسَّبِيلِ ۖ فَرِيضَةً مِّنَ ٱللَّهِ ۗ وَٱللَّهُ عَلِيمٌ حَكِيمٌ ۝ وَمِنْهُمُ ٱلَّذِينَ يُؤْذُونَ ٱلنَّبِىَّ وَيَقُولُونَ هُوَ أُذُنٌ ۚ قُلْ أُذُنُ خَيْرٍ لَّكُمْ يُؤْمِنُ بِٱللَّهِ وَيُؤْمِنُ لِلْمُؤْمِنِينَ وَرَحْمَةٌ لِّلَّذِينَ ءَامَنُوا۟ مِنكُمْ ۚ وَٱلَّذِينَ يُؤْذُونَ رَسُولَ ٱللَّهِ لَهُمْ عَذَابٌ أَلِيمٌ ۝ يَحْلِفُونَ بِٱللَّهِ لَكُمْ لِيُرْضُوكُمْ وَٱللَّهُ وَرَسُولُهُۥٓ أَحَقُّ أَن يُرْضُوهُ إِن كَانُوا۟ مُؤْمِنِينَ ۝ أَلَمْ يَعْلَمُوٓا۟ أَنَّهُۥ مَن يُحَادِدِ ٱللَّهَ وَرَسُولَهُۥ فَأَنَّ لَهُۥ نَارَ جَهَنَّمَ خَٰلِدًا فِيهَا ۚ ذَٰلِكَ ٱلْخِزْىُ ٱلْعَظِيمُ ۝ يَحْذَرُ ٱلْمُنَٰفِقُونَ أَن تُنَزَّلَ عَلَيْهِمْ سُورَةٌ تُنَبِّئُهُم بِمَا فِى قُلُوبِهِمْ ۚ قُلِ ٱسْتَهْزِءُوٓا۟ إِنَّ ٱللَّهَ مُخْرِجٌ مَّا تَحْذَرُونَ ۝ وَلَئِن سَأَلْتَهُمْ لَيَقُولُنَّ إِنَّمَا كُنَّا نَخُوضُ وَنَلْعَبُ ۚ قُلْ أَبِٱللَّهِ وَءَايَٰتِهِۦ وَرَسُولِهِۦ كُنتُمْ تَسْتَهْزِءُونَ ۝ لَا تَعْتَذِرُوا۟ قَدْ كَفَرْتُم بَعْدَ إِيمَٰنِكُمْ ۚ إِن نَّعْفُ عَن طَآئِفَةٍ مِّنكُمْ نُعَذِّبْ طَآئِفَةًۢ بِأَنَّهُمْ

كَانُوا۟ مُجْرِمِينَ ۝ ٱلْمُنَٰفِقُونَ وَٱلْمُنَٰفِقَٰتُ بَعْضُهُم مِّنۢ بَعْضٍ يَأْمُرُونَ بِٱلْمُنكَرِ وَيَنْهَوْنَ عَنِ ٱلْمَعْرُوفِ وَيَقْبِضُونَ أَيْدِيَهُمْ نَسُوا۟ ٱللَّهَ فَنَسِيَهُمْ إِنَّ ٱلْمُنَٰفِقِينَ هُمُ ٱلْفَٰسِقُونَ ۝

Voluntary alms are for the poor and wretched, for those who collect them, for those whose hearts have been won over, for slaves to buy their freedom, for those in debt, for the cause of Allah and for the needy wayfarer. This is an ordinance of Allah; Allah is All-Knowing, All-Wise. And some of them hurt the Prophet, saying, 'He is an ear!' Say: 'An ear of good for you; he believes in Allah, and believes the believers, and he is a mercy to the believers among you. Those who hurt Allah's Messenger; for them awaits a painful chastisement.' They swear by Allah in order to please you if they were true believers, it would be more fitting for them to please Allah and His Messenger. Do they not know that he who oversteps the limit with Allah and His Messenger; for him awaits the fire of hell, abiding therein forever? That is the greatest disgrace. The Hypocrites are anxious that a surah might be sent down regarding them, which would reveal to them what lies in their hearts. Say: 'Go ahead and mock! Allah shall reveal what you are anxious about.' If you ask them, they say: 'We were merely gossiping and jesting.' Say: 'Was it Allah, His revelations and His Messenger you were mocking? Do not try to justify yourselves; you have gone from belief to disbelief.' We may forgive some of you, but We will punish others; they are evildoers. Hypocrites, male and female, are all alike; they command what is forbidden and forbid what is virtuous, and clench tight their hands. They have forgotten Allah and so He has forgotten them. The Hypocrites are the dissolute.

60-67 There are numerous levels and degrees of mischief, hypocrisy, and lies. The ultimate is when people who follow their lower nature are exposed to higher-quality beings, especially those more evolved due to being on the prophetic way. Then it becomes a clash between darkness and light. When beings are on the edge of the unseen, constantly reflecting what is known and unknown, themselves in the middle between humanity and divinity, any discord will cause greater disturbance. For pure light the slightest shadow seems a great darkness.

Lies, deceptions, and hypocrisies are natural tendencies of the lower self and ego. It is through reflection and higher awareness that one can avoid these destructive pitfalls. If you are afflicted by such shadows, you will not be able to enter the high potency field of the eternal now.

The path of rising intelligence and awakening is founded upon courage, honesty and service without immediate expectations. Otherwise, we live with our cunning, deceptive humanity and hypocrisy at every level. That is why, with all the attempts for the world to be a healthy place, those who are seriously seeking the meaning of it and serving in that meaning are increasingly despondent. Discordance and enmity prevail over friendship, love, and generosity.

68-72 وَعَدَ ٱللَّهُ ٱلْمُنَٰفِقِينَ وَٱلْمُنَٰفِقَٰتِ وَٱلْكُفَّارَ نَارَ جَهَنَّمَ خَٰلِدِينَ فِيهَا ۚ هِىَ حَسْبُهُمْ ۚ وَلَعَنَهُمُ ٱللَّهُ ۖ وَلَهُمْ عَذَابٌ مُّقِيمٌ ۝ كَٱلَّذِينَ مِن قَبْلِكُمْ كَانُوٓا۟ أَشَدَّ مِنكُمْ قُوَّةً وَأَكْثَرَ أَمْوَٰلًا وَأَوْلَٰدًا فَٱسْتَمْتَعُوا۟ بِخَلَٰقِهِمْ فَٱسْتَمْتَعْتُم بِخَلَٰقِكُمْ كَمَا ٱسْتَمْتَعَ ٱلَّذِينَ مِن قَبْلِكُم بِخَلَٰقِهِمْ وَخُضْتُمْ كَٱلَّذِى خَاضُوٓا۟ ۚ أُو۟لَٰٓئِكَ حَبِطَتْ أَعْمَٰلُهُمْ فِى ٱلدُّنْيَا وَٱلْءَاخِرَةِ ۖ وَأُو۟لَٰٓئِكَ هُمُ ٱلْخَٰسِرُونَ ۝ أَلَمْ يَأْتِهِمْ نَبَأُ ٱلَّذِينَ مِن قَبْلِهِمْ قَوْمِ نُوحٍ وَعَادٍ وَثَمُودَ وَقَوْمِ إِبْرَٰهِيمَ وَأَصْحَٰبِ مَدْيَنَ وَٱلْمُؤْتَفِكَٰتِ ۚ أَتَتْهُمْ رُسُلُهُم بِٱلْبَيِّنَٰتِ ۖ فَمَا كَانَ ٱللَّهُ لِيَظْلِمَهُمْ وَلَٰكِن كَانُوٓا۟ أَنفُسَهُمْ يَظْلِمُونَ ۝ وَٱلْمُؤْمِنُونَ وَٱلْمُؤْمِنَٰتُ بَعْضُهُمْ أَوْلِيَآءُ بَعْضٍ ۚ يَأْمُرُونَ بِٱلْمَعْرُوفِ وَيَنْهَوْنَ عَنِ ٱلْمُنكَرِ وَيُقِيمُونَ ٱلصَّلَوٰةَ وَيُؤْتُونَ ٱلزَّكَوٰةَ وَيُطِيعُونَ ٱللَّهَ وَرَسُولَهُۥٓ ۚ أُو۟لَٰٓئِكَ سَيَرْحَمُهُمُ ٱللَّهُ ۗ إِنَّ ٱللَّهَ عَزِيزٌ حَكِيمٌ ۝ وَعَدَ ٱللَّهُ ٱلْمُؤْمِنِينَ وَٱلْمُؤْمِنَٰتِ جَنَّٰتٍ تَجْرِى مِن تَحْتِهَا ٱلْأَنْهَٰرُ خَٰلِدِينَ فِيهَا وَمَسَٰكِنَ طَيِّبَةً فِى جَنَّٰتِ عَدْنٍ ۚ وَرِضْوَٰنٌ مِّنَ ٱللَّهِ أَكْبَرُ ۚ ذَٰلِكَ هُوَ ٱلْفَوْزُ ٱلْعَظِيمُ ۝

Allah has promised the hypocrites, both men and women – as well as the deniers of the truth, the fire of hell, therein to abide; this shall be their allotted portion. For, Allah has rejected them, and lasting torment awaits them. Like those before you; they were stronger than you in power and more abundant in wealth and children, so they enjoyed their portion; thus, have you enjoyed your portion as those before you enjoyed their portion; and you entered into vain discourses like the vain discourses in which entered those before you. These are they whose works are null in this world and the hereafter, and these are they who are the losers. Has there not come to you the tidings of those who were before you; the people of Noah, Ad, Thamud, the people of Abraham, the men of Midian and the subverted cities? Their Messengers came to them with the clear signs Allah would not wrong them, but themselves they wronged. The believers, male and female, are friends of one another. They command to virtue and forbid vice. They perform the prayers and pay the alms, and they obey Allah and His Messenger. These, Allah shall show them mercy. Allah is Almighty, All-Wise. Allah has promised the believers, men and women, gardens underneath which rivers flow, forever therein to dwell, and goodly dwelling-places in the Gardens of Eden; and greater, Allah's good pleasure; that is the mighty triumph.

68-72 The prophetic path is to realise *Oneness* and be in constant reference to it. Hypocrisy, lies, and ignorance fall under the shadow of conflicting dualities and oppose *Oneness*. Those who are steadfast on the path of trust, faith, and awakening are companions of one another and support each other with trust and love. They know that their ultimate abode is a perpetual garden of perfection, which they are in touch with already. This is the promised victory of the divine spirit within. Wealth and strength in this world can often be detrimental for awakening to the *Truth*. Any attraction is a distraction except the original obsession with life itself.

Reflection upon cultures and nations that have come and gone helps us to not repeat the same mistakes of arrogance, abusiveness, and reliance upon worldly wealth and power. With true faith and trust, with constant presence in the moment, you will experience the bliss of eternal joy and paradise.

As much as hypocrites pretend to be friendly with each other, they are in fact in competition and only concerned about what they think is to their advantage and benefit. As for those who believe they're here to be prepared for the magnificent state of the next life, then they act in a manner that is liberating them from the memory and the behaviour of the animal within us. We are in this world to be prepared for the next phase which is boundless and eternal.

73-80

يَـٰٓأَيُّهَا ٱلنَّبِىُّ جَـٰهِدِ ٱلْكُفَّارَ وَٱلْمُنَـٰفِقِينَ وَٱغْلُظْ عَلَيْهِمْ ۚ وَمَأْوَىٰهُمْ جَهَنَّمُ ۖ وَبِئْسَ ٱلْمَصِيرُ ۝ يَحْلِفُونَ بِٱللَّهِ مَا قَالُوا۟ وَلَقَدْ قَالُوا۟ كَلِمَةَ ٱلْكُفْرِ وَكَفَرُوا۟ بَعْدَ إِسْلَـٰمِهِمْ وَهَمُّوا۟ بِمَا لَمْ يَنَالُوا۟ ۚ وَمَا نَقَمُوٓا۟ إِلَّآ أَنْ أَغْنَىٰهُمُ ٱللَّهُ وَرَسُولُهُۥ مِن فَضْلِهِۦ ۚ فَإِن يَتُوبُوا۟ يَكُ خَيْرًۭا لَّهُمْ ۖ وَإِن يَتَوَلَّوْا۟ يُعَذِّبْهُمُ ٱللَّهُ عَذَابًا أَلِيمًا فِى ٱلدُّنْيَا وَٱلْـَٔاخِرَةِ ۚ وَمَا لَهُمْ فِى ٱلْأَرْضِ مِن وَلِىٍّۢ وَلَا نَصِيرٍۢ ۝ وَمِنْهُم مَّنْ عَـٰهَدَ ٱللَّهَ لَئِنْ ءَاتَىٰنَا مِن فَضْلِهِۦ لَنَصَّدَّقَنَّ وَلَنَكُونَنَّ مِنَ ٱلصَّـٰلِحِينَ ۝ فَلَمَّآ ءَاتَىٰهُم مِّن فَضْلِهِۦ بَخِلُوا۟ بِهِۦ وَتَوَلَّوا۟ وَّهُم مُّعْرِضُونَ ۝ فَأَعْقَبَهُمْ نِفَاقًۭا فِى قُلُوبِهِمْ إِلَىٰ يَوْمِ يَلْقَوْنَهُۥ بِمَآ أَخْلَفُوا۟ ٱللَّهَ مَا وَعَدُوهُ وَبِمَا كَانُوا۟ يَكْذِبُونَ ۝ أَلَمْ يَعْلَمُوٓا۟ أَنَّ ٱللَّهَ يَعْلَمُ سِرَّهُمْ وَنَجْوَىٰهُمْ وَأَنَّ ٱللَّهَ عَلَّـٰمُ ٱلْغُيُوبِ ۝ ٱلَّذِينَ يَلْمِزُونَ ٱلْمُطَّوِّعِينَ مِنَ ٱلْمُؤْمِنِينَ فِى ٱلصَّدَقَـٰتِ وَٱلَّذِينَ لَا يَجِدُونَ إِلَّا جُهْدَهُمْ فَيَسْخَرُونَ مِنْهُمْ ۙ سَخِرَ ٱللَّهُ مِنْهُمْ وَلَهُمْ عَذَابٌ أَلِيمٌ ۝ ٱسْتَغْفِرْ لَهُمْ أَوْ لَا تَسْتَغْفِرْ لَهُمْ إِن تَسْتَغْفِرْ لَهُمْ سَبْعِينَ مَرَّةًۭ فَلَن يَغْفِرَ ٱللَّهُ لَهُمْ ۚ ذَٰلِكَ بِأَنَّهُمْ كَفَرُوا۟ بِٱللَّهِ وَرَسُولِهِۦ ۗ وَٱللَّهُ لَا يَهْدِى ٱلْقَوْمَ ٱلْفَـٰسِقِينَ ۝

O Prophet, exert yourself against the unbelievers and Hypocrites, and deal harshly with them. Their refuge is hell; a wretched destiny. They swear by Allah that they did not, but they certainly did speak words of defiance and became defiant after having submitted; they tried to do something, though they did not achieve it, being spiteful was their only response to Allah and His Messenger enriching them out of His bounty. They would be better off turning back Allah; if they turn away, Allah will torment them in this world and the Hereafter, and there will be no one on earth to protect or help them. And some of them have made covenant with Allah; 'If He gives us of His bounty, we will make offerings and be of the righteous.' Yet when He did give them some of His bounty, they became mean and turned obstinately away. So, as a consequence He put hypocrisy into their hearts, until the day they meet Him, for that they failed Allah in that they promised Him and they were liars. Do they not know that Allah knows their secrets and their most intimate talk? That Allah is Knower of the Unseen. Those who find fault with the believers who volunteer their freewill offerings, and those who find nothing but their endeavour they deride, Allah derides them; for them awaits a painful chastisement. It makes no difference whether you ask forgiveness for them or not; Allah will not forgive them even if you ask seventy times, because they reject Allah and His Messenger. Allah does not guide the rebellious people.

73-80 Human beings face outer dangers, which threaten survival, as well as inner dangers that perpetuate darkness of the heart and confusion. Deception and trickery are dark energy fields that delay insights and spiritual evolution. The love for knowledge, truth, and honesty stems from love of the attributes of Allah. The natural darkness of the lower self will veil access to the light of the soul and thereby enlightenment. Arrogance, vanity, and the love of the lower self are barriers to growth in consciousness, inner illumination, and spiritual guidance. When someone is entrenched in such dark states, no amount of help or prayers will help until they become neutral and receptive. A point of irreversibility may be reached through transgression that is not remediable. And that is what we call *spiritual death*.

If one wants peace, one must be willing to resist and object, sometimes even fight for it. Allah knows what is deep in our hearts and sees and hears everything that occurs; therefore, all that is left for us is to ask forgiveness and pray to accept what is written for us.

It is natural for human beings to be deceptive, because the nature of the soul or the spirit within us is such that it cannot be seen, touched, or described, and yet is the source of our own life. If you live in faith, you know that Allah knows what you are saying, and the extent of your honesty. With that, hypocrisy and lies decrease because you are aware of them. They may stop: then you are present and whatever you say is from your head and heart with no veils to it. This is a healthy state because then you see things more for what they are. Be watchful regarding the honesty of your intention and actions.

81-87 فَرِحَ ٱلْمُخَلَّفُونَ بِمَقْعَدِهِمْ خِلَٰفَ رَسُولِ ٱللَّهِ وَكَرِهُوٓا۟ أَن يُجَٰهِدُوا۟ بِأَمْوَٰلِهِمْ وَأَنفُسِهِمْ فِى سَبِيلِ ٱللَّهِ وَقَالُوا۟ لَا تَنفِرُوا۟ فِى ٱلْحَرِّ قُلْ نَارُ جَهَنَّمَ أَشَدُّ حَرًّا لَّوْ كَانُوا۟ يَفْقَهُونَ ۝ فَلْيَضْحَكُوا۟ قَلِيلًا وَلْيَبْكُوا۟ كَثِيرًا جَزَآءًۢ بِمَا كَانُوا۟ يَكْسِبُونَ ۝ فَإِن رَّجَعَكَ ٱللَّهُ إِلَىٰ طَآئِفَةٍ مِّنْهُمْ فَٱسْتَـْٔذَنُوكَ لِلْخُرُوجِ فَقُل لَّن تَخْرُجُوا۟ مَعِىَ أَبَدًا وَلَن تُقَٰتِلُوا۟ مَعِىَ عَدُوًّا إِنَّكُمْ رَضِيتُم بِٱلْقُعُودِ أَوَّلَ مَرَّةٍ فَٱقْعُدُوا۟ مَعَ ٱلْخَٰلِفِينَ ۝ وَلَا تُصَلِّ عَلَىٰٓ أَحَدٍ مِّنْهُم مَّاتَ أَبَدًا وَلَا تَقُمْ عَلَىٰ قَبْرِهِۦٓ إِنَّهُمْ كَفَرُوا۟ بِٱللَّهِ وَرَسُولِهِۦ وَمَاتُوا۟ وَهُمْ فَٰسِقُونَ ۝ وَلَا تُعْجِبْكَ أَمْوَٰلُهُمْ وَأَوْلَٰدُهُمْ إِنَّمَا يُرِيدُ ٱللَّهُ أَن يُعَذِّبَهُم بِهَا فِى ٱلدُّنْيَا وَتَزْهَقَ أَنفُسُهُمْ وَهُمْ كَٰفِرُونَ ۝ وَإِذَآ أُنزِلَتْ سُورَةٌ أَنْ

ءَامِنُواْ بِٱللَّهِ وَجَٰهِدُواْ مَعَ رَسُولِهِ ٱسْتَـْٔذَنَكَ أُوْلُواْ ٱلطَّوْلِ مِنْهُمْ وَقَالُواْ ذَرْنَا نَكُن مَّعَ ٱلْقَٰعِدِينَ ۝ رَضُواْ بِأَن يَكُونُواْ مَعَ ٱلْخَوَالِفِ وَطُبِعَ عَلَىٰ قُلُوبِهِمْ فَهُمْ لَا يَفْقَهُونَ ۝

Those left behind were pleased with where they squatted, contrary to the wish of the Messenger of Allah. They hated to labor hard with their property and persons in the cause of Allah and said: 'Do not march out in the heat.' Say: 'The fire of hell is far hotter, if only they had understanding.' They shall laugh a little and weep a lot, in recompense for what they have earned. Should Allah bring you back, and you meet a group of them who ask your permission to set out, say: 'You shall never set out with me nor fight an enemy with me. You were content to squat behind the first time, so squat with those who are left behind.' Do not hold prayers for any of them if they die, and do not stand by their graves: they disbelieved in Allah and His Messenger and died rebellious. And let not their wealth and their children excite your admiration; Allah but wants to chastise them by these means in this world, and their selves to depart while they are unbelievers. When a chapter is sent down; 'Believe in Allah and strive with His Messenger,' the men of wealth among them seek your leave and say: 'Let us be with those who squat behind.' They are content to be among those left behind. A seal has been set upon their hearts, so they do not comprehend.

81-87 Those on the path will be challenged in numerous ways and at different levels regarding how passionate and sincere their drive to *Reality* is. Most people succumb to the lower self, which presents every excuse to avoid being confronted or weakened. Ego preservation is most treacherous, as the self will do anything to continue its survival. This situation shows how wasteful and lost most people are. Outer laughter may be a prelude to much weeping, both outward and inward. Outer wealth and power on earth may mean more entanglement and entrapment than freedom and light. Most people are caught in the darkness of their lower self and do not understand the intricate maps and patterns of the path to arrival in *Reality*.

Once the path of destiny has been clearly marked, nothing can change it. Therefore, it is always incumbent upon us to be cautious and not enter an irreversible trajectory. There are people who are on their way to their own hell, and there is nothing one can do about it.

Our animal tendencies, such as giving respect for those who are more powerful, has to be re-evaluated. Many people who we may have come across in this life have found that their wealth, power, or reputation was enabling them to rise only so that their fall became even more damaging or destroying. Often, we do not know the real purpose and the meaning of a situation we are in. It may well be for us to learn a lesson so that we do not repeat it.

لَٰكِنِ ٱلرَّسُولُ وَٱلَّذِينَ ءَامَنُوا۟ مَعَهُۥ جَٰهَدُوا۟ بِأَمْوَٰلِهِمْ وَأَنفُسِهِمْ ۚ وَأُو۟لَٰٓئِكَ لَهُمُ ٱلْخَيْرَٰتُ ۖ وَأُو۟لَٰٓئِكَ هُمُ ٱلْمُفْلِحُونَ ۝ أَعَدَّ ٱللَّهُ لَهُمْ جَنَّٰتٍ تَجْرِى مِن تَحْتِهَا ٱلْأَنْهَٰرُ خَٰلِدِينَ فِيهَا ۚ ذَٰلِكَ ٱلْفَوْزُ ٱلْعَظِيمُ ۝ وَجَآءَ ٱلْمُعَذِّرُونَ مِنَ ٱلْأَعْرَابِ لِيُؤْذَنَ لَهُمْ وَقَعَدَ ٱلَّذِينَ كَذَبُوا۟ ٱللَّهَ وَرَسُولَهُۥ ۚ سَيُصِيبُ ٱلَّذِينَ كَفَرُوا۟ مِنْهُمْ عَذَابٌ أَلِيمٌ ۝ لَّيْسَ عَلَى ٱلضُّعَفَآءِ وَلَا عَلَى ٱلْمَرْضَىٰ وَلَا عَلَى ٱلَّذِينَ لَا يَجِدُونَ مَا يُنفِقُونَ حَرَجٌ إِذَا نَصَحُوا۟ لِلَّهِ وَرَسُولِهِۦ ۚ مَا عَلَى ٱلْمُحْسِنِينَ مِن سَبِيلٍ ۚ وَٱللَّهُ غَفُورٌ رَّحِيمٌ ۝ وَلَا عَلَى ٱلَّذِينَ إِذَا مَآ أَتَوْكَ لِتَحْمِلَهُمْ قُلْتَ لَآ أَجِدُ مَآ أَحْمِلُكُمْ عَلَيْهِ تَوَلَّوا۟ وَّأَعْيُنُهُمْ تَفِيضُ مِنَ ٱلدَّمْعِ حَزَنًا أَلَّا يَجِدُوا۟ مَا يُنفِقُونَ ۝ إِنَّمَا ٱلسَّبِيلُ عَلَى ٱلَّذِينَ يَسْتَـْٔذِنُونَكَ وَهُمْ أَغْنِيَآءُ ۚ رَضُوا۟ بِأَن يَكُونُوا۟ مَعَ ٱلْخَوَالِفِ وَطَبَعَ ٱللَّهُ عَلَىٰ قُلُوبِهِمْ فَهُمْ لَا يَعْلَمُونَ ۝ يَعْتَذِرُونَ إِلَيْكُمْ إِذَا رَجَعْتُمْ إِلَيْهِمْ ۚ قُل لَّا تَعْتَذِرُوا۟ لَن نُّؤْمِنَ لَكُمْ قَدْ نَبَّأَنَا ٱللَّهُ مِنْ أَخْبَارِكُمْ ۚ وَسَيَرَى ٱللَّهُ عَمَلَكُمْ وَرَسُولُهُۥ ثُمَّ تُرَدُّونَ إِلَىٰ عَٰلِمِ ٱلْغَيْبِ وَٱلشَّهَٰدَةِ فَيُنَبِّئُكُم بِمَا كُنتُمْ تَعْمَلُونَ ۝

But the Messenger and the believers with him have labored hard with their properties and persons. These, to them belong the finest rewards. These shall truly gain success. Allah has prepared for them gardens underneath which rivers flow, therein to dwell forever; that is the mighty triumph. And those with excuses from among the dwellers of the desert came that permission may be given to them and they stayed behind who lied to Allah and His Messenger; a painful chastisement shall afflict those of them who disbelieved. No blame attaches to the infirm, nor to the sick, nor to those who find nothing to spend, provided they keep faith with Allah and His Messenger; in no way can the virtuous be faulted. Allah is All-Forgiving, Compassionate to each. Nor are they to be faulted who came to you asking to be mounted for war and to whom you said: 'I find nothing I can mount you upon.' Whereupon they left, their eyes overflowing with tears, in sorrow that they possessed nothing to spend. The way is open only against those who ask leave of you, being rich; they are well-pleased to be with those behind; Allah has set a seal on their hearts, so they know not. They offer excuses to you when you return to them. Say: 'Do not make excuses. We do not trust you. Allah has apprised us of your news. Allah shall see your deeds, as shall His Messenger. You shall then be returned to the Knower of the Invisible and the Visible, And He will inform you of what you used to do.'

88-94 As for those who are on the path, they exert their best and trust completely in Allah's mercy and grace, for Allah is All-Forgiving and understands human weakness and frailty. Those human beings who consider themselves strong and wealthy and do not remember that the purpose of life on earth lies in the hereafter are in serious danger and confusion. The most important purpose and direction of evolution is to awaken to the cosmic immensity of the power that governs all the universes – known and unknown.

2. Surah 9 At-Tawbah (Repentance)

Allah knows our weaknesses and mistakes and is All-Forgiving, provided that we are in a mode of repentance, with honesty and inner resolve. Outer wealth, power, and health can cause distractions through arrogance and vanity, which lead to darkness and loss.

Naturally, there are phases in human life in which we need to recoup and recover physically, chemically, and emotionally. Then we are in a reasonable state again to be finely tuned to our inner intentions and actions. By people simply declaring that they want to embrace Islam or to be enlightened, it does not necessarily mean that they will be on the path that leads them ultimately to the light within their own hearts. Some different stages and steps need to take place; otherwise, you are again at the usual risk and danger of the distraction of the animal-self. We always need to watch out for this, acknowledge it, and transcend it to the light of the soul.

95-101

سَيَحْلِفُونَ بِٱللَّهِ لَكُمْ إِذَا ٱنقَلَبْتُمْ إِلَيْهِمْ لِتُعْرِضُواْ عَنْهُمْ فَأَعْرِضُواْ عَنْهُمْ إِنَّهُمْ رِجْسٌ وَمَأْوَىٰهُمْ جَهَنَّمُ جَزَآءً بِمَا كَانُواْ يَكْسِبُونَ ۝ يَحْلِفُونَ لَكُمْ لِتَرْضَوْاْ عَنْهُمْ فَإِن تَرْضَوْاْ عَنْهُمْ فَإِنَّ ٱللَّهَ لَا يَرْضَىٰ عَنِ ٱلْقَوْمِ ٱلْفَـٰسِقِينَ ۝ ٱلْأَعْرَابُ أَشَدُّ كُفْرًا وَنِفَاقًا وَأَجْدَرُ أَلَّا يَعْلَمُواْ حُدُودَ مَآ أَنزَلَ ٱللَّهُ عَلَىٰ رَسُولِهِۦ وَٱللَّهُ عَلِيمٌ حَكِيمٌ ۝ وَمِنَ ٱلْأَعْرَابِ مَن يَتَّخِذُ مَا يُنفِقُ مَغْرَمًا وَيَتَرَبَّصُ بِكُمُ ٱلدَّوَآئِرَ عَلَيْهِمْ دَآئِرَةُ ٱلسَّوْءِ وَٱللَّهُ سَمِيعٌ عَلِيمٌ ۝ وَمِنَ ٱلْأَعْرَابِ مَن يُؤْمِنُ بِٱللَّهِ وَٱلْيَوْمِ ٱلْأَخِرِ وَيَتَّخِذُ مَا يُنفِقُ قُرُبَـٰتٍ عِندَ ٱللَّهِ وَصَلَوَٰتِ ٱلرَّسُولِ أَلَآ إِنَّهَا قُرْبَةٌ لَّهُمْ سَيُدْخِلُهُمُ ٱللَّهُ فِى رَحْمَتِهِۦٓ إِنَّ ٱللَّهَ غَفُورٌ رَّحِيمٌ ۝ وَٱلسَّـٰبِقُونَ ٱلْأَوَّلُونَ مِنَ ٱلْمُهَـٰجِرِينَ وَٱلْأَنصَارِ وَٱلَّذِينَ ٱتَّبَعُوهُم بِإِحْسَـٰنٍ رَّضِىَ ٱللَّهُ عَنْهُمْ وَرَضُواْ عَنْهُ وَأَعَدَّ لَهُمْ جَنَّـٰتٍ تَجْرِى تَحْتَهَا ٱلْأَنْهَـٰرُ خَـٰلِدِينَ فِيهَآ أَبَدًا ذَٰلِكَ ٱلْفَوْزُ ٱلْعَظِيمُ ۝ وَمِمَّنْ حَوْلَكُم مِّنَ ٱلْأَعْرَابِ مُنَـٰفِقُونَ وَمِنْ أَهْلِ ٱلْمَدِينَةِ مَرَدُواْ عَلَى ٱلنِّفَاقِ لَا تَعْلَمُهُمْ نَحْنُ نَعْلَمُهُمْ سَنُعَذِّبُهُم مَّرَّتَيْنِ ثُمَّ يُرَدُّونَ إِلَىٰ عَذَابٍ عَظِيمٍ ۝

They will swear by Allah to you when you turn back to them, to leave off their reproach. So, leave them alone. They are indeed a pollution; their final place of rest is hell, in recompense for what they earned. They swear to you to forgive them but even if you do, Allah will not forgive the corrupt. The dwellers of the desert are very hard in unbelief and hypocrisy, and more disposed not to know the limits of what Allah has revealed to His Messenger; and Allah is All-Knowing, All-Wise. And of the dwellers of the desert are those who take what they spend to be a fine, and they wait calamities to you; on them the evil calamity; and Allah is All-Hearing, All-Knowing. And of the dwellers of the desert are those who believe in Allah and the latter day and take what they spend to be the nearness of Allah and the Messenger's prayers; surely it shall be means of nearness for them; Allah will make them enter into His mercy; surely Allah is All-Forgiving, Compassionate to each. As for the precursors, the first to believe among the Emigrants, and the Helpers, and those who followed after them and were virtuous, Allah is well pleased with them and they with Him. He has prepared for them Gardens beneath which rivers flow, abiding therein forever. This is the greatest of triumphs. And from among those who are round about you of the dwellers of the desert there are hypocrites, and from among the people of Medina; they are stubborn in hypocrisy; you do not know them; We know them; We will chastise them twice then shall they be turned back to a grievous chastisement.

95-101 People who are perpetually concerned with their comfort, ease, and outer survival, due to the harshness of the conditions of their lives, may not be ready to hear and understand the reality of the message of *Oneness*. Our life on earth is like a ladder, which takes us from the basic survival, selfish mode towards the arc of origin and cosmic *Oneness*. Within each one of us is a crude, lower self that requires grooming in order to transcend to the light of the soul. Then we are able to yield to the higher *Truth* that contains all. Self-realisation is like the drop of the ocean that awakens to the truth that it contains the essence of the whole ocean.

Human beings have been evolving from a very crude level of humanity towards embracing the cosmic light of divinity. There are always people whom we encounter on our journey who are rising in consciousness and require help and assistance in order to have insights in the beginning of their awakening.

It's very helpful for us to know where our empathy, sympathy, and helpfulness must stop. Otherwise, we waste a great deal of time and effort and eventually end up disappointed. If somebody is persisting in their hypocrisy and their lies, with disbelief in the purpose of being on this earth, then it is wise for us to not waste time, energy, and hope in trying to be of assistance. Equally, you will never know how people can turn and be eligible for help and guidance.

102-109 وَءَاخَرُونَ ٱعْتَرَفُواْ بِذُنُوبِهِمْ خَلَطُواْ عَمَلًا صَٰلِحًا وَءَاخَرَ سَيِّئًا عَسَى ٱللَّهُ أَن يَتُوبَ عَلَيْهِمْ إِنَّ ٱللَّهَ غَفُورٌ رَّحِيمٌ ۝ خُذْ مِنْ أَمْوَٰلِهِمْ صَدَقَةً تُطَهِّرُهُمْ وَتُزَكِّيهِم بِهَا وَصَلِّ عَلَيْهِمْ إِنَّ صَلَوٰتَكَ سَكَنٌ لَّهُمْ وَٱللَّهُ سَمِيعٌ عَلِيمٌ ۝ أَلَمْ يَعْلَمُوٓاْ أَنَّ ٱللَّهَ هُوَ يَقْبَلُ ٱلتَّوْبَةَ عَنْ عِبَادِهِۦ وَيَأْخُذُ ٱلصَّدَقَٰتِ وَأَنَّ ٱللَّهَ هُوَ ٱلتَّوَّابُ ٱلرَّحِيمُ ۝ وَقُلِ ٱعْمَلُواْ فَسَيَرَى ٱللَّهُ عَمَلَكُمْ وَرَسُولُهُۥ وَٱلْمُؤْمِنُونَ وَسَتُرَدُّونَ إِلَىٰ عَٰلِمِ ٱلْغَيْبِ وَٱلشَّهَٰدَةِ فَيُنَبِّئُكُم بِمَا كُنتُمْ تَعْمَلُونَ ۝ وَءَاخَرُونَ مُرْجَوْنَ لِأَمْرِ ٱللَّهِ إِمَّا يُعَذِّبُهُمْ وَإِمَّا يَتُوبُ عَلَيْهِمْ وَٱللَّهُ عَلِيمٌ حَكِيمٌ ۝ وَٱلَّذِينَ ٱتَّخَذُواْ مَسْجِدًا ضِرَارًا وَكُفْرًا وَتَفْرِيقًۢا بَيْنَ ٱلْمُؤْمِنِينَ وَإِرْصَادًا لِّمَنْ حَارَبَ ٱللَّهَ وَرَسُولَهُۥ مِن قَبْلُ وَلَيَحْلِفُنَّ إِنْ أَرَدْنَآ إِلَّا ٱلْحُسْنَىٰ وَٱللَّهُ يَشْهَدُ إِنَّهُمْ لَكَٰذِبُونَ ۝ لَا تَقُمْ فِيهِ أَبَدًا لَّمَسْجِدٌ أُسِّسَ عَلَى ٱلتَّقْوَىٰ مِنْ أَوَّلِ يَوْمٍ أَحَقُّ أَن تَقُومَ فِيهِ فِيهِ رِجَالٌ يُحِبُّونَ أَن يَتَطَهَّرُواْ وَٱللَّهُ يُحِبُّ ٱلْمُطَّهِّرِينَ ۝ أَفَمَنْ أَسَّسَ بُنْيَٰنَهُۥ عَلَىٰ تَقْوَىٰ مِنَ ٱللَّهِ

وَرِضْوَانٍ خَيْرٌ أَم مَّنْ أَسَّسَ بُنْيَـٰنَهُۥ عَلَىٰ شَفَا جُرُفٍ هَارٍ فَٱنْهَارَ بِهِۦ فِى نَارِ جَهَنَّمَ ۗ وَٱللَّهُ لَا يَهْدِى ٱلْقَوْمَ ٱلظَّـٰلِمِينَ ۞

Others have admitted their misdeeds they mixed a good deed with another that is evil. Perhaps Allah will pardon them. Allah is All-Forgiving, Compassionate to each. Take of their wealth an offering, to purify them and to cleanse them thereby, and pray for them; your prayers are a comfort for them; Allah is All-Hearing, All-Knowing. Do they not know that Allah accepts repentance from His worshippers, that He accepts freely given alms, that it is Allah Who is All-Pardoning, Compassionate to each. Say: 'Strive, and Allah shall see your striving, as also His Messenger and the believers. You shall be returned to the Knower of the Invisible and the Visible, and He will inform you of what you used to do.' And others are deferred to Allah's commandment, whether He chastises them, or turns towards them; Allah is All-Knowing, All-Wise. And those who have taken a mosque in opposition and unbelief, and to divide the believers, and as a place of ambush for those who fought Allah and His Messenger aforetime; they will swear 'We desired nothing but good'; and Allah testifies they are truly liars. Stand there never. A mosque that was founded upon reverence from the first day is worthier for you to stand in; therein are men who love to purify themselves; and Allah loves those who purify themselves. Is he who builds its foundations upon piety towards Allah and His good pleasure better, or one who builds them upon the edge of a tottering precipice which then collapses with him into the fire of hell? Allah guides not the wrongdoers.

102-109 Life on earth is a journey from our cosmic origin and back to it. The ease of reaching this destiny depends upon the intention of our mind and heart, our attention and action. Every person's state is a result of the past as modified by the present. Time is constantly moving and as such it appears like an arrow from the past to the future. Truth is ever-present, constant, and perfect. If you are truly aware of divine Truth, then you are living fully in the present moment. If you are living in the moment, then you participate in bringing about the next moment with less fear or sorrow. Our inner state now will be more actualised in the next moment and still more fully in the hereafter. The first steps and intentions of any endeavour have a huge influence on the ultimate outcome.

Allah is ever-present and timeless and as such can erase our errors and shortcomings if our hearts are cleansed and genuine in their repentance. The lower self can be weak and meek, but equally arrogant and vain, whereas the soul always transmits the divine light.

Intelligent human beings will reaise that there are all kinds of people around us, most of whom who do not truly evaluate and understand their own tendencies deeply at heart. The majority of human beings live in a very superficial way and are mostly concerned about basic survival. Life is ever continuous anyway. It is only individual life that moves on from the physical, material, earthly level back again to another higher level, but most people have not discerned this reality and truth.

110-116

لَا يَزَالُ بُنْيَـٰنُهُمُ ٱلَّذِى بَنَوْا۟ رِيبَةً فِى قُلُوبِهِمْ إِلَّآ أَن تَقَطَّعَ قُلُوبُهُمْ ۗ وَٱللَّهُ عَلِيمٌ حَكِيمٌ ۝ إِنَّ ٱللَّهَ ٱشْتَرَىٰ مِنَ ٱلْمُؤْمِنِينَ أَنفُسَهُمْ وَأَمْوَٰلَهُم بِأَنَّ لَهُمُ ٱلْجَنَّةَ ۚ يُقَـٰتِلُونَ فِى سَبِيلِ ٱللَّهِ فَيَقْتُلُونَ وَيُقْتَلُونَ ۖ وَعْدًا عَلَيْهِ حَقًّا فِى ٱلتَّوْرَىٰةِ وَٱلْإِنجِيلِ وَٱلْقُرْءَانِ ۚ وَمَنْ أَوْفَىٰ بِعَهْدِهِۦ مِنَ ٱللَّهِ ۚ فَٱسْتَبْشِرُوا۟ بِبَيْعِكُمُ ٱلَّذِى بَايَعْتُم بِهِۦ ۚ وَذَٰلِكَ هُوَ ٱلْفَوْزُ ٱلْعَظِيمُ ۝ ٱلتَّـٰٓئِبُونَ ٱلْعَـٰبِدُونَ ٱلْحَـٰمِدُونَ ٱلسَّـٰٓئِحُونَ ٱلرَّٰكِعُونَ ٱلسَّـٰجِدُونَ ٱلْـَٔامِرُونَ بِٱلْمَعْرُوفِ وَٱلنَّاهُونَ عَنِ ٱلْمُنكَرِ وَٱلْحَـٰفِظُونَ لِحُدُودِ ٱللَّهِ ۗ وَبَشِّرِ ٱلْمُؤْمِنِينَ ۝ مَا كَانَ لِلنَّبِىِّ وَٱلَّذِينَ ءَامَنُوٓا۟ أَن يَسْتَغْفِرُوا۟ لِلْمُشْرِكِينَ وَلَوْ كَانُوٓا۟ أُو۟لِى قُرْبَىٰ مِنۢ بَعْدِ مَا تَبَيَّنَ لَهُمْ أَنَّهُمْ أَصْحَـٰبُ ٱلْجَحِيمِ ۝ وَمَا كَانَ ٱسْتِغْفَارُ إِبْرَٰهِيمَ لِأَبِيهِ إِلَّا عَن مَّوْعِدَةٍ وَعَدَهَآ إِيَّاهُ فَلَمَّا تَبَيَّنَ لَهُۥٓ أَنَّهُۥ عَدُوٌّ لِّلَّهِ تَبَرَّأَ مِنْهُ ۚ إِنَّ إِبْرَٰهِيمَ لَأَوَّٰهٌ حَلِيمٌ ۝ وَمَا كَانَ ٱللَّهُ لِيُضِلَّ قَوْمًۢا بَعْدَ إِذْ هَدَىٰهُمْ حَتَّىٰ يُبَيِّنَ لَهُم مَّا يَتَّقُونَ ۚ إِنَّ ٱللَّهَ بِكُلِّ شَىْءٍ عَلِيمٌ ۝ إِنَّ ٱللَّهَ لَهُۥ مُلْكُ ٱلسَّمَـٰوَٰتِ وَٱلْأَرْضِ ۖ يُحْىِۦ وَيُمِيتُ ۚ وَمَا لَكُم مِّن دُونِ ٱللَّهِ مِن وَلِىٍّ وَلَا نَصِيرٍ ۝

The structure they built shall remain questionable in their hearts until their very hearts are torn asunder. Allah is All-Knowing, All-Wise. Allah has bought from the believers their selves and their possession against the gift of Paradise; they fight in the way of Allah; they kill, and are killed; that is a promise binding upon Allah in the Torah, and the Gospel, and the Koran; and who fulfils his covenant truer than Allah? So, rejoice in the bargain you have made with Him; that is the mighty triumph. The repentant, the worshippers, the thankful, the fasting, they who kneel and prostrate themselves, the bidders to good and forbidders of evil, the respecters of the bounds of Allah; give glad tidings to the believers! It is not for the Prophet and the believers to ask pardon for the idolaters, even though they be near kinsmen, after that it has become clear to them that they will be the inhabitants of Hell. When Abraham asked forgiveness for his father, this was only to fulfil a promise he had promised him. But once it became clear to him that he was an enemy of Allah, he washed his hands of him; Abraham was one who sighed much, and forbearing. Allah would never lead astray a people once He had guided them until He has made clear to them what they are to be cautiously aware. Allah is the Knower of everything. To Allah belongs the kingdom of the heavens and the earth; He gives life and He deals death; Apart from Allah, you have neither friend nor champion.

110-116 The most evolved spiritual beings are those who are aware of their dependence on Allah's mercy, grace, inspiration, and guidance. To experience the inner garden, we need to migrate from the distractions and pitfalls of outer, worldly changes and interactions. To begin with, we need to perceive the darkness and confusion of our lives and actively seek the direction that leads to a more durable destiny. Paradise is accessible, but we do not experience that state due to our preoccupation with the outer entanglements and darkness of the lower self. Migration from our lower tendencies toward higher aspirations, which is more difficult than physical migration, is essential to experiencing this state.

For the true believer on the prophetic path there is no ownership or control, only what has been loaned by Allah. The true believer will have no sorrow or fear, because he or she will know that the author of everything is Allah, and we are simply given different roles at different times in our journey.

The *mu'mins* aim to be in constant communion with the highest light within them. In other words, they want to act in a way that they do not have regrets and cause any suffering or sorrow. That requires total awareness regarding their intention and the direction in which they are heading. An awakened *mu'min* realises that all belongs to Allah, emanating from Allah, returning to Allah. Therefore, they have no fear or anxiety about their achievements and attainment. As such, they are liberated from concerns.

117-122 لَقَد تَّابَ ٱللَّهُ عَلَى ٱلنَّبِيِّ وَٱلْمُهَٰجِرِينَ وَٱلْأَنصَارِ ٱلَّذِينَ ٱتَّبَعُوهُ فِى سَاعَةِ ٱلْعُسْرَةِ مِنۢ بَعْدِ مَا كَادَ يَزِيغُ قُلُوبُ فَرِيقٍ مِّنْهُمْ ثُمَّ تَابَ عَلَيْهِمْ إِنَّهُۥ بِهِمْ رَءُوفٌ رَّحِيمٌ ۝ وَعَلَى ٱلثَّلَٰثَةِ ٱلَّذِينَ خُلِّفُوا۟ حَتَّىٰٓ إِذَا ضَاقَتْ عَلَيْهِمُ ٱلْأَرْضُ بِمَا رَحُبَتْ وَضَاقَتْ عَلَيْهِمْ أَنفُسُهُمْ وَظَنُّوٓا۟ أَن لَّا مَلْجَأَ مِنَ ٱللَّهِ إِلَّآ إِلَيْهِ ثُمَّ تَابَ عَلَيْهِمْ لِيَتُوبُوٓا۟ إِنَّ ٱللَّهَ هُوَ ٱلتَّوَّابُ ٱلرَّحِيمُ ۝ يَٰٓأَيُّهَا ٱلَّذِينَ ءَامَنُوا۟ ٱتَّقُوا۟ ٱللَّهَ وَكُونُوا۟ مَعَ ٱلصَّٰدِقِينَ ۝ مَا كَانَ لِأَهْلِ ٱلْمَدِينَةِ وَمَنْ حَوْلَهُم مِّنَ ٱلْأَعْرَابِ أَن يَتَخَلَّفُوا۟ عَن رَّسُولِ ٱللَّهِ وَلَا يَرْغَبُوا۟ بِأَنفُسِهِمْ عَن نَّفْسِهِۦ ذَٰلِكَ بِأَنَّهُمْ لَا يُصِيبُهُمْ ظَمَأٌ وَلَا نَصَبٌ وَلَا مَخْمَصَةٌ فِى سَبِيلِ ٱللَّهِ وَلَا يَطَـُٔونَ مَوْطِئًا يَغِيظُ ٱلْكُفَّارَ وَلَا يَنَالُونَ مِنْ عَدُوٍّ نَّيْلًا إِلَّا كُتِبَ لَهُم بِهِۦ عَمَلٌ صَٰلِحٌ إِنَّ ٱللَّهَ لَا يُضِيعُ أَجْرَ ٱلْمُحْسِنِينَ ۝ وَلَا يُنفِقُونَ نَفَقَةً صَغِيرَةً وَلَا كَبِيرَةً وَلَا يَقْطَعُونَ وَادِيًا إِلَّا كُتِبَ لَهُمْ لِيَجْزِيَهُمُ ٱللَّهُ أَحْسَنَ مَا كَانُوا۟ يَعْمَلُونَ ۝ وَمَا كَانَ ٱلْمُؤْمِنُونَ لِيَنفِرُوا۟ كَآفَّةً فَلَوْلَا نَفَرَ مِن كُلِّ فِرْقَةٍ مِّنْهُمْ طَآئِفَةٌ لِّيَتَفَقَّهُوا۟ فِى ٱلدِّينِ وَلِيُنذِرُوا۟ قَوْمَهُمْ إِذَا رَجَعُوٓا۟ إِلَيْهِمْ لَعَلَّهُمْ يَحْذَرُونَ ۝

Allah has pardoned the Prophet, the Emigrants and the Helpers, those who followed him in the hour of hardship, after the hearts of a group of them were about to fall into temptation. Then He pardoned them, for to them He is All-Tender, Compassionate to each. Likewise, He pardoned the three who were left behind. Once the earth, so wide in expanse, had become constricted for them, and their very selves were constricted, and they came to believe that there can be no refuge from Allah except with Him, it was then that Allah turned towards them in pardon that they might turn to Him. It is Allah Who is All-Pardoning, Compassionate to each. O believers, be cautiously aware

Allah and keep the company of those who are sincere. It did not beseem the people of Medina and those round about them of the dwellers of the desert to remain behind the Messenger of Allah, nor should they desire for themselves in preference to him; this is because there afflicts them not thirst or fatigue or hunger in Allah's way, nor do they tread a path which enrages the unbelievers, nor do they attain from the enemy what they attain, but a good work is written down to them on account of it; surely Allah does not waste the reward of the doers of good; they shall expend no sum, small or great, nor ever cross a valley but it shall be inscribed for them. And Allah will then reward them for the best of their deeds. It is not for the believers to go forth totally; but why should not a party of every section of them go forth, to become learned in religion, and to warn their people when they return to them, that haply they may beware.

117-122 Allah's mercy is universal and perpetual and engulfs everything known and unknown. The purpose of human life on earth is to differentiate between what is conducive for a better-quality life and what is likely to lead to fear, sorrow, and regret. Appropriate action on earth may lead to action that is inspired by Allah. The best intentions and actions are those with the least concern for personal gain. Self-interest is only an outer link to the light of the soul. To be at one with the inner spirit is to calibrate with *Truth* and *Reality*, and this creates the optimum human state.

Being completely honest and grateful for the light of faith and trust propels one towards higher levels of consciousness and enlightenment. Our mindset and actions can reveal the extent of our inner resolve and honesty.

We are on a journey of rising in intelligence and consciousness. When a person realises that their life has been wasted due to personal ambitions and desires, without referencing the higher intentions behind them, and then repents, they find greater potency in whatever they do from there on and they maintain that state of repentance and presence.

123-129 يَـٰٓأَيُّهَا ٱلَّذِينَ ءَامَنُوا۟ قَـٰتِلُوا۟ ٱلَّذِينَ يَلُونَكُم مِّنَ ٱلْكُفَّارِ وَلْيَجِدُوا۟ فِيكُمْ غِلْظَةً ۚ وَٱعْلَمُوٓا۟ أَنَّ ٱللَّهَ مَعَ ٱلْمُتَّقِينَ ۝ وَإِذَا مَآ أُنزِلَتْ سُورَةٌ فَمِنْهُم مَّن يَقُولُ أَيُّكُمْ زَادَتْهُ هَـٰذِهِۦٓ إِيمَـٰنًا ۚ فَأَمَّا ٱلَّذِينَ ءَامَنُوا۟ فَزَادَتْهُمْ إِيمَـٰنًا وَهُمْ يَسْتَبْشِرُونَ ۝ وَأَمَّا ٱلَّذِينَ فِى قُلُوبِهِم مَّرَضٌ فَزَادَتْهُمْ رِجْسًا إِلَىٰ رِجْسِهِمْ وَمَاتُوا۟ وَهُمْ كَـٰفِرُونَ ۝ أَوَلَا يَرَوْنَ أَنَّهُمْ يُفْتَنُونَ فِى كُلِّ عَامٍ مَّرَّةً أَوْ مَرَّتَيْنِ ثُمَّ لَا يَتُوبُونَ وَلَا هُمْ يَذَّكَّرُونَ ۝ وَإِذَا مَآ أُنزِلَتْ سُورَةٌ نَّظَرَ بَعْضُهُمْ إِلَىٰ بَعْضٍ هَلْ يَرَىٰكُم مِّنْ أَحَدٍ ثُمَّ ٱنصَرَفُوا۟ ۚ صَرَفَ ٱللَّهُ قُلُوبَهُم بِأَنَّهُمْ قَوْمٌ لَّا يَفْقَهُونَ ۝ لَقَدْ جَآءَكُمْ رَسُولٌ مِّنْ أَنفُسِكُمْ عَزِيزٌ عَلَيْهِ مَا عَنِتُّمْ حَرِيصٌ عَلَيْكُم بِٱلْمُؤْمِنِينَ رَءُوفٌ رَّحِيمٌ ۝ فَإِن تَوَلَّوْا۟ فَقُلْ حَسْبِىَ ٱللَّهُ لَآ إِلَـٰهَ إِلَّا هُوَ ۖ عَلَيْهِ تَوَكَّلْتُ ۖ وَهُوَ رَبُّ ٱلْعَرْشِ ٱلْعَظِيمِ ۝

O believers, fight the unbelievers who are near to you; and let them find in you harshness; and know that Allah is with the cautiously aware. When a chapter is sent down, some of them say: 'Which of you has this increased in faith?' Those who believe; it shall increase them in faith, and they shall regard it as auspicious. As for those with sickness in their hearts, it shall increase them in pollution, adding to their pollution, and they shall die as unbelievers. Do they not see that they are tried every year once or twice? Yet still they do not repent, nor do they remember. When a chapter is sent down, they exchange glances: 'Has anyone seen you?' And they turn away. May Allah turn away their hearts! For they are a people who do not understand. To you has come a messenger, from among your number, aggrieved by the hardship you suffer, concerned for you, tender and compassionate towards the believers. If they turn away, say: 'Allah suffices me. There is no deity but He. In Him I trust. Lord of the great throne is He.'

123-129 Once we are on the path, ignorance, darkness, and other aspects of the lower self recede and are replaced with inner reflection and the yearning to transcend earthly limitations. People who deny the prophetic path towards *Reality* will always be in doubt and uncertainty regarding descriptions of the hereafter or states of transcendence beyond body and mind. An awakened prophet is concerned about human awakening to the divine *Presence* that illumines all darkness. The message of truth is to awaken to the voice of conscience that emanates from a pure heart. The *nafs* tends to be dismissive, since it wants to perpetuate its illusion. Allah's ways are inscribed upon every soul, and it is the responsibility of the seeker to discover that treasure and live that grace.

We are on earth in order to participate in completing our work grooming the lower self and being tuned to the divine presence in our own hearts. It is the spiritually enlightened being who cannot do anything without permission from Allah, and is willing to constantly change when new inspirations come. The outer prophet reflects the inner lights.

The rise in human consciousness has been gradual, very smooth, and flowing with ease. People understand others if they talk to them in a language they understand and that has been the case with most messengers and prophets. The same thing applies to us as individuals. We need to be able to link with whoever we are trying to help in a manner that their mind and their intellect can grasp. And then they can internalise it, hopefully, and diligently act upon it. It is all a seamless link from the infinite light at the beginning to all the lights and shadows now, then back again to the original light.

3. Surah 11 Hud (Hud)

The last two *ayat* of Surah Yunus inform us that truth was revealed through prophetic beings so that we may follow a path towards higher consciousness and awaken from earthly darkness. The first ayah of Surah Hud confirms that what has been revealed is decisive and has descended from God-consciousness.

بِسْمِ اللَّهِ الرَّحْمَٰنِ الرَّحِيمِ

الٓر ۚ كِتَٰبٌ أُحْكِمَتْ ءَايَٰتُهُۥ ثُمَّ فُصِّلَتْ مِن لَّدُنْ حَكِيمٍ خَبِيرٍ ۝ أَلَّا تَعْبُدُوٓا۟ إِلَّا اللَّهَ ۚ إِنَّنِى لَكُم مِّنْهُ نَذِيرٌ وَبَشِيرٌ ۝ وَأَنِ ٱسْتَغْفِرُوا۟ رَبَّكُمْ ثُمَّ تُوبُوٓا۟ إِلَيْهِ يُمَتِّعْكُم مَّتَٰعًا حَسَنًا إِلَىٰٓ أَجَلٍ مُّسَمًّى وَيُؤْتِ كُلَّ ذِى فَضْلٍ فَضْلَهُۥ ۖ وَإِن تَوَلَّوْا۟ فَإِنِّىٓ أَخَافُ عَلَيْكُمْ عَذَابَ يَوْمٍ كَبِيرٍ ۝ إِلَى ٱللَّهِ مَرْجِعُكُمْ ۖ وَهُوَ عَلَىٰ كُلِّ شَىْءٍ قَدِيرٌ ۝ أَلَآ إِنَّهُمْ يَثْنُونَ صُدُورَهُمْ لِيَسْتَخْفُوا۟ مِنْهُ ۚ أَلَا حِينَ يَسْتَغْشُونَ ثِيَابَهُمْ يَعْلَمُ مَا يُسِرُّونَ وَمَا يُعْلِنُونَ ۚ إِنَّهُۥ عَلِيمٌۢ بِذَاتِ ٱلصُّدُورِ ۝ وَمَا مِن دَآبَّةٍ فِى ٱلْأَرْضِ إِلَّا عَلَى ٱللَّهِ رِزْقُهَا وَيَعْلَمُ مُسْتَقَرَّهَا وَمُسْتَوْدَعَهَا ۚ كُلٌّ فِى كِتَٰبٍ مُّبِينٍ ۝ وَهُوَ ٱلَّذِى خَلَقَ ٱلسَّمَٰوَٰتِ وَٱلْأَرْضَ فِى سِتَّةِ أَيَّامٍ وَكَانَ عَرْشُهُۥ عَلَى ٱلْمَآءِ لِيَبْلُوَكُمْ أَيُّكُمْ أَحْسَنُ عَمَلًا ۗ وَلَئِن قُلْتَ إِنَّكُم مَّبْعُوثُونَ مِنۢ بَعْدِ ٱلْمَوْتِ لَيَقُولَنَّ ٱلَّذِينَ كَفَرُوٓا۟ إِنْ هَٰذَآ إِلَّا سِحْرٌ مُّبِينٌ ۝

1-7

In the name of Allah, the Merciful to all, the Compassionate to each!

Alif Lam Ra. A Book whose verses are set clear, and then distinguished, from One All-Wise, All-Aware. That you worship none but Allah; I am to you from Him a herald of glad tidings, and a warner. That you call upon your Lord to forgive you, and repent to Him. He will then make you enjoy His good pleasure for a determined period. Upon every doer of good He will bestow good. Should you turn away, I fear for you the torment of a mighty Day. To Allah is your return, and He holds power over all things. And still they slouch, chests bent, meaning to hide from Him! But even as they don their garments, He knows what they conceal, and what they proclaim! He knows full well what lies within breasts. There is not a creature that moves on earth whose provision is not His concern. He knows where it lives and its resting place. It is all in a clear book. And it is He who created the heavens and the earth in six days, and His Throne was upon the waters, that He might try you, which one of you is fairer in works. And if thou sayest, 'you shall surely be raised up after death,' the unbelievers will say, 'This is naught but a manifest sorcery.'

1-7 Through divine consciousness Allah's mercy is revealed to those who are attuned to receive it. Messengers and their books simply illustrate the connection between the origin – the *Essence* – and what appears to us as earthly, experiential reality. Human consciousness yearns for its origin, which is ever-present. Our life is truly worth living when it leads towards the ultimate, timeless *Reality* and *Truth*. All prophetic messages warn against diversion from the path of awakening due to the illusions of lower passions, desires, or animalistic whims. We need to be focused on the ultimate hope, the wish and destiny to be at one with the *Creator* of the heavens, earth, and human consciousness. Our intentions and actions provide the driving force in this journey. Through them, we participate in their outcomes and our ultimate future.

Prophetic messages have the potency of the divine light and power in them. A great declaration is that whatever is alive on earth is progressing towards higher consciousness and awakening to the light within it that is driving it. We are all evolving from a base beginning to the Light of lights.

All that we experience on earth has emerged from a heavenly zone of cosmic oneness, which encompasses every aspect of life on earth, and it prepares us to return to the *Absolute*.

8-16 وَلَئِنْ أَخَّرْنَا عَنْهُمُ ٱلْعَذَابَ إِلَىٰٓ أُمَّةٍ مَّعْدُودَةٍ لَّيَقُولُنَّ مَا يَحْبِسُهُۥٓ أَلَا يَوْمَ يَأْتِيهِمْ لَيْسَ مَصْرُوفًا عَنْهُمْ وَحَاقَ بِهِم مَّا كَانُوا۟ بِهِۦ يَسْتَهْزِءُونَ ۝ وَلَئِنْ أَذَقْنَا ٱلْإِنسَـٰنَ مِنَّا رَحْمَةً ثُمَّ نَزَعْنَـٰهَا مِنْهُ إِنَّهُۥ لَيَـُٔوسٌ كَفُورٌ ۝ وَلَئِنْ أَذَقْنَـٰهُ نَعْمَآءَ بَعْدَ ضَرَّآءَ مَسَّتْهُ لَيَقُولَنَّ ذَهَبَ ٱلسَّيِّـَٔاتُ عَنِّىٓ إِنَّهُۥ لَفَرِحٌ فَخُورٌ ۝ إِلَّا ٱلَّذِينَ صَبَرُوا۟ وَعَمِلُوا۟ ٱلصَّـٰلِحَـٰتِ أُو۟لَـٰٓئِكَ لَهُم مَّغْفِرَةٌ وَأَجْرٌ كَبِيرٌ ۝ فَلَعَلَّكَ تَارِكٌۢ بَعْضَ مَا يُوحَىٰٓ إِلَيْكَ وَضَآئِقٌۢ بِهِۦ صَدْرُكَ أَن يَقُولُوا۟ لَوْلَآ أُنزِلَ عَلَيْهِ كَنزٌ أَوْ جَآءَ مَعَهُۥ مَلَكٌ إِنَّمَآ أَنتَ نَذِيرٌ وَٱللَّهُ عَلَىٰ كُلِّ شَىْءٍ وَكِيلٌ ۝ أَمْ يَقُولُونَ ٱفْتَرَىٰهُ قُلْ فَأْتُوا۟ بِعَشْرِ سُوَرٍ مِّثْلِهِۦ مُفْتَرَيَـٰتٍ وَٱدْعُوا۟ مَنِ ٱسْتَطَعْتُم مِّن دُونِ ٱللَّهِ إِن كُنتُمْ صَـٰدِقِينَ ۝ فَإِلَّمْ يَسْتَجِيبُوا۟ لَكُمْ فَٱعْلَمُوٓا۟ أَنَّمَآ أُنزِلَ بِعِلْمِ ٱللَّهِ وَأَن لَّآ إِلَـٰهَ إِلَّا هُوَ فَهَلْ أَنتُم مُّسْلِمُونَ ۝ مَن كَانَ يُرِيدُ ٱلْحَيَوٰةَ ٱلدُّنْيَا وَزِينَتَهَا نُوَفِّ إِلَيْهِمْ أَعْمَـٰلَهُمْ فِيهَا وَهُمْ فِيهَا لَا يُبْخَسُونَ ۝ أُو۟لَـٰٓئِكَ ٱلَّذِينَ لَيْسَ لَهُمْ فِى ٱلْـَٔاخِرَةِ إِلَّا ٱلنَّارُ وَحَبِطَ مَا صَنَعُوا۟ فِيهَا وَبَـٰطِلٌ مَّا كَانُوا۟ يَعْمَلُونَ ۝

And if we postpone their punishment for a set period of time, they will say: 'What is holding it back?' Indeed, that Day shall come upon them, nor shall it be held back from them! Engulfing them shall be that which before they would mock! And if We let a man taste mercy from Us, and then We wrest it from him, he is desperate, ungrateful. And if We let him taste mercy after some harm has touched him, he is sure to say, 'Misfortune has gone away from me.' He becomes exultant and boastful. All except those who bear with patience and perform good deeds. These, to them belongs forgiveness and a great reward. Perchance you leave part of what is revealed to you, and your breast is straitened by it, because they say, 'Why has a treasure not been sent down upon him, or an angel not come with him?' You are only a warner; and Allah is a Guardian over everything. Or because they say: 'He fabricated it?' Say: 'Bring forth ten chapters like it, fabricated, and call upon whomever you can, apart from Allah, if you speak the truth.' Then, if they do not answer you, know that it has been sent down with Allah's knowledge, and that there is no deity but He. So, have you surrendered? Whoso desires this nether world and its luxuries, to them We pay in full their works therein, and in it they shall not be short-changed. Those are they for whom in the world to come there is only the Fire; their deeds there will have failed, and void will be their works.

8-16 Human nature is fickle. Whenever we are at ease and in comfort, we face the danger of becoming complacent, distracted, and forgetful of the direction towards the One. When we do good, we tend to become proud and want acknowledgment. This tendency arises from the lower self. The higher self is closer to the light of the inner soul and draws from that higher light and energy. Whenever we fall into the trap of the outer world and its attractions, we tend to be swamped by them unless suffering, shocks, or other events propel us towards the remedy of higher awareness. Our earthly experiences provide samples or metaphors of the meanings and light that have originated them. Our earthly experiences prepare us for the hereafter. Earthly disasters and small hells serve as previews of the timeless hell of the hereafter. Similarly, being content and cheerful is a prelude to the timeless paradise of the hereafter.

The lower nature of human beings is to be impatient and assume independence from the original source and destiny. It is through prayers, reflection, and being constantly engaged in good actions and service to others along the path to truth that we can lead healthy lives on earth. We are naturally attracted to beauty and majesty on earth; this can cause destruction or can lead to the divine source.

A human being is a shadow of the cosmic being of the soul itself, and as such there is often the illusion of independence as well as the desire to continue forever, to have the attributes and powers of the divine *Source* within the heart. This is the danger of obsession with life on earth: the lack of transcendence and preparation to experience the eternal light within the heart.

17-24 أَفَمَن كَانَ عَلَىٰ بَيِّنَةٍ مِّن رَّبِّهِۦ وَيَتْلُوهُ شَاهِدٌ مِّنْهُ وَمِن قَبْلِهِۦ كِتَـٰبُ مُوسَىٰٓ إِمَامًا وَرَحْمَةً أُوْلَـٰٓئِكَ يُؤْمِنُونَ بِهِۦ وَمَن يَكْفُرْ بِهِۦ مِنَ ٱلْأَحْزَابِ فَٱلنَّارُ مَوْعِدُهُۥ فَلَا تَكُ فِى مِرْيَةٍ مِّنْهُ إِنَّهُ ٱلْحَقُّ مِن رَّبِّكَ وَلَـٰكِنَّ أَكْثَرَ ٱلنَّاسِ لَا يُؤْمِنُونَ ۝ وَمَنْ أَظْلَمُ مِمَّنِ ٱفْتَرَىٰ عَلَى ٱللَّهِ كَذِبًا أُوْلَـٰٓئِكَ يُعْرَضُونَ عَلَىٰ رَبِّهِمْ وَيَقُولُ ٱلْأَشْهَـٰدُ هَـٰٓؤُلَآءِ ٱلَّذِينَ كَذَبُواْ عَلَىٰ رَبِّهِمْ أَلَا لَعْنَةُ ٱللَّهِ عَلَى ٱلظَّـٰلِمِينَ ۝ ٱلَّذِينَ يَصُدُّونَ عَن سَبِيلِ ٱللَّهِ وَيَبْغُونَهَا عِوَجًا وَهُم بِٱلْـَٔاخِرَةِ هُمْ كَـٰفِرُونَ ۝ أُوْلَـٰٓئِكَ لَمْ يَكُونُواْ مُعْجِزِينَ فِى ٱلْأَرْضِ وَمَا كَانَ لَهُم مِّن دُونِ ٱللَّهِ مِنْ أَوْلِيَآءَ يُضَـٰعَفُ لَهُمُ ٱلْعَذَابُ مَا كَانُواْ يَسْتَطِيعُونَ ٱلسَّمْعَ وَمَا كَانُواْ يُبْصِرُونَ ۝ أُوْلَـٰٓئِكَ ٱلَّذِينَ خَسِرُوٓاْ أَنفُسَهُمْ وَضَلَّ عَنْهُم مَّا كَانُواْ يَفْتَرُونَ ۝ لَا جَرَمَ أَنَّهُمْ فِى ٱلْـَٔاخِرَةِ هُمُ ٱلْأَخْسَرُونَ ۝ إِنَّ ٱلَّذِينَ ءَامَنُواْ وَعَمِلُواْ ٱلصَّـٰلِحَـٰتِ وَأَخْبَتُوٓاْ إِلَىٰ رَبِّهِمْ أُوْلَـٰٓئِكَ أَصْحَـٰبُ ٱلْجَنَّةِ هُمْ فِيهَا

خَٰلِدُونَ ۝ مَثَلُ ٱلْفَرِيقَيْنِ كَٱلْأَعْمَىٰ وَٱلْأَصَمِّ وَٱلْبَصِيرِ وَٱلسَّمِيعِ هَلْ يَسْتَوِيَانِ مَثَلًا ۚ أَفَلَا تَذَكَّرُونَ ۝

And what of him who stands upon a clear sign from his Lord, and a witness from Him recites it, and before him is the Book of Moses for an example and a mercy? Those believe in it; but whosoever disbelieves in it, being one of the partisans, his promised land is the Fire. So be you not in doubt of it; it is the truth from your Lord, but most men do not believe. Who is more wicked than he who fabricates a lie from Allah? These shall be passed in review before their Lord, and the witnesses shall say: 'These are the ones who lied about their Lord; Allah's curse upon the wicked!' Who hinder others from Allah's path, trying to make it crooked, and deny the life to come. These will not escape on earth, and apart from Allah, shall have no protectors. He shall multiply their torment. They were incapable of hearing and could not see. They are those who lost their selves, and that which they fabricated has deserted them. Truly it is they, they who in the life to come shall be the losers! Those who attain to faith and do righteous deeds and humble themselves before their Lord, they are destined for paradise, and there shall they abide. The likeness of the two groups is like the blind and deaf, and the one who sees and hears; are they equal in likeness? Will you not remember.

17-24 With wisdom and intellect, we realise the clear difference between those who have intelligence and insight and those who don't. We need to distinguish between those who are qualified to guide us out of our worldly darkness towards the light of the soul with its divine perfections, and those who are not. Prophets, messengers, and enlightened people navigate by the inner light and are worthy of being followed and emulated. Most people are lost and misguided, some in worse ways than others. As for the heart, the home of the soul, it is like a universe within – what a loss it is if we do not realise this treasure! The path is about containing the lower self to follow the divine light. Confused people are worse than cattle, concerned only about survival, whereas the soul is eternal.

Everyone wants benefit for themselves, but only a few will realise that the self needs to be stabilised and transmuted by the soul, which has offered it the illusion of its independence. Once we have touched the light of the soul and are determined to follow it, we will experience the garden around us. We will know that our own soul is eternal and will lose all fear and sorrow.

With the rise of awareness and basic intelligence, as well as suffering, higher intelligence will lead us to be in constant reference to the divine light of the soul and not fall into and remain in the pitfalls of the animal self.

25-32 وَلَقَدْ أَرْسَلْنَا نُوحًا إِلَىٰ قَوْمِهِۦ إِنِّي لَكُمْ نَذِيرٌ مُّبِينٌ ۝ أَن لَّا تَعْبُدُوٓا۟ إِلَّا ٱللَّهَ ۖ إِنِّىٓ أَخَافُ عَلَيْكُمْ عَذَابَ يَوْمٍ أَلِيمٍ ۝ فَقَالَ ٱلْمَلَأُ ٱلَّذِينَ كَفَرُوا۟ مِن قَوْمِهِۦ مَا

نَرَىٰكَ إِلَّا بَشَرًا مِّثْلَنَا وَمَا نَرَىٰكَ ٱتَّبَعَكَ إِلَّا ٱلَّذِينَ هُمْ أَرَاذِلُنَا بَادِىَ ٱلرَّأْىِ وَمَا نَرَىٰ لَكُمْ عَلَيْنَا مِن فَضْلٍۭ بَلْ نَظُنُّكُمْ كَٰذِبِينَ ۝ قَالَ يَٰقَوْمِ أَرَءَيْتُمْ إِن كُنتُ عَلَىٰ بَيِّنَةٍۢ مِّن رَّبِّى وَءَاتَىٰنِى رَحْمَةًۭ مِّنْ عِندِهِۦ فَعُمِّيَتْ عَلَيْكُمْ أَنُلْزِمُكُمُوهَا وَأَنتُمْ لَهَا كَٰرِهُونَ ۝ وَيَٰقَوْمِ لَآ أَسْـَٔلُكُمْ عَلَيْهِ مَالًا إِنْ أَجْرِىَ إِلَّا عَلَى ٱللَّهِ وَمَآ أَنَا۠ بِطَارِدِ ٱلَّذِينَ ءَامَنُوٓا۟ إِنَّهُم مُّلَٰقُوا۟ رَبِّهِمْ وَلَٰكِنِّىٓ أَرَىٰكُمْ قَوْمًۭا تَجْهَلُونَ ۝ وَيَٰقَوْمِ مَن يَنصُرُنِى مِنَ ٱللَّهِ إِن طَرَدتُّهُمْ أَفَلَا تَذَكَّرُونَ ۝ وَلَآ أَقُولُ لَكُمْ عِندِى خَزَآئِنُ ٱللَّهِ وَلَآ أَعْلَمُ ٱلْغَيْبَ وَلَآ أَقُولُ إِنِّى مَلَكٌۭ وَلَآ أَقُولُ لِلَّذِينَ تَزْدَرِىٓ أَعْيُنُكُمْ لَن يُؤْتِيَهُمُ ٱللَّهُ خَيْرًا ٱللَّهُ أَعْلَمُ بِمَا فِىٓ أَنفُسِهِمْ إِنِّىٓ إِذًۭا لَّمِنَ ٱلظَّٰلِمِينَ ۝ قَالُوا۟ يَٰنُوحُ قَدْ جَٰدَلْتَنَا فَأَكْثَرْتَ جِدَٰلَنَا فَأْتِنَا بِمَا تَعِدُنَآ إِن كُنتَ مِنَ ٱلصَّٰدِقِينَ ۝

We sent Noah to his people, saying: 'I am come to you as a clear warner.' You are not to worship anything but Allah. 'I fear for you the torment of a grievous Day.' Said the Council of the unbelievers of his people, 'We see you not other than a mortal like ourselves, and we see no one is following you but the vilest of us, inconsiderately. We do not see you have over us any superiority; no, rather we think you are liars.' He said: 'My people, tell me this. If I am certain of my Lord, and He has brought me a mercy from Him which was hidden from you, are we to force you to accept it when you are averse to it? O my people, I do not ask of you wealth for this; my wage falls only up- on Allah. I will not drive away those who believe; they shall surely meet their Lord. But I see you are an ignorant people. My people, who will take my side against Allah if I drive them away? Will you not recollect? I do not say to you that I possess the treasures of Allah. I do not know the Unseen, nor do I say I am an angel, nor do I tell those whom your eyes despise that Allah will not bring them good, for Allah knows best what is in their hearts. If I did so I would indeed be wicked.' They said: 'O Noah, you have argued with us; indeed, you have exceeded the limit in argument. So now bring upon us what you threaten us with, if you are truthful.'

25-32 The key message of the prophets has to do with worship of truth and knowledge, as well as the awareness of who and how to worship. Worship implies obsessive love, adoration, and total concern. The act of worship ultimately connects and unifies the worshipper and the worshipped. Prophet Noah exemplifies this state when he warns his people that, due to their confusion, loss, and misconduct, they are bringing disaster upon themselves – not unlike our world today with an irreversible extinction upon us. Prophet Noah understood that the people around him were in deep darkness. He expressed, as other prophets did, his limited ability to change or control events. Our duty is to move from the self-hood of the animal state to the soul-hood of the divine grace within us. Then our earth is a garden, preparing us for Paradise.

An enlightened being has no option other than calling others to rise to their ultimate potential in spiritual awakening. Equally, the awakened person reminds people around him that he or she does not possess anything independent from God's grace. Therefore, the true guides are those who simply point to the truth without implying that they can play any role other than what has been decreed by God.

Every human being has regular connectedness with the higher voice within. As for communities and nations, messengers and enlightened ones have come to them repeatedly to remind them of the ultimate purpose of this short journey on earth as a preparation for the next phase of life. Because of old habits and desire for what is familiar, most people reject and object to such reminders and remain in their darkness and suffering.

33-41 قَالَ إِنَّمَا يَأْتِيكُم بِهِ ٱللَّهُ إِن شَآءَ وَمَآ أَنتُم بِمُعْجِزِينَ ۝ وَلَا يَنفَعُكُمْ نُصْحِىٓ إِنْ أَرَدتُّ أَنْ أَنصَحَ لَكُمْ إِن كَانَ ٱللَّهُ يُرِيدُ أَن يُغْوِيَكُمْ هُوَ رَبُّكُمْ وَإِلَيْهِ تُرْجَعُونَ ۝ أَمْ يَقُولُونَ ٱفْتَرَىٰهُ قُلْ إِنِ ٱفْتَرَيْتُهُ فَعَلَىَّ إِجْرَامِى وَأَنَا۠ بَرِىٓءٌ مِّمَّا تُجْرِمُونَ ۝ وَأُوحِىَ إِلَىٰ نُوحٍ أَنَّهُۥ لَن يُؤْمِنَ مِن قَوْمِكَ إِلَّا مَن قَدْ ءَامَنَ فَلَا تَبْتَئِسْ بِمَا كَانُوا۟ يَفْعَلُونَ ۝ وَٱصْنَعِ ٱلْفُلْكَ بِأَعْيُنِنَا وَوَحْيِنَا وَلَا تُخَٰطِبْنِى فِى ٱلَّذِينَ ظَلَمُوٓا۟ إِنَّهُم مُّغْرَقُونَ ۝ وَيَصْنَعُ ٱلْفُلْكَ وَكُلَّمَا مَرَّ عَلَيْهِ مَلَأٌ مِّن قَوْمِهِۦ سَخِرُوا۟ مِنْهُ قَالَ إِن تَسْخَرُوا۟ مِنَّا فَإِنَّا نَسْخَرُ مِنكُمْ كَمَا تَسْخَرُونَ ۝ فَسَوْفَ تَعْلَمُونَ مَن يَأْتِيهِ عَذَابٌ يُخْزِيهِ وَيَحِلُّ عَلَيْهِ عَذَابٌ مُّقِيمٌ ۝ حَتَّىٰٓ إِذَا جَآءَ أَمْرُنَا وَفَارَ ٱلتَّنُّورُ قُلْنَا ٱحْمِلْ فِيهَا مِن كُلٍّ زَوْجَيْنِ ٱثْنَيْنِ وَأَهْلَكَ إِلَّا مَن سَبَقَ عَلَيْهِ ٱلْقَوْلُ وَمَنْ ءَامَنَ وَمَآ ءَامَنَ مَعَهُۥٓ إِلَّا قَلِيلٌ ۝ وَقَالَ ٱرْكَبُوا۟ فِيهَا بِسْمِ ٱللَّهِ مَجْر۪ىٰهَا وَمُرْسَىٰهَآ إِنَّ رَبِّى لَغَفُورٌ رَّحِيمٌ ۝

He said: 'It is Allah Who will bring it upon you, if He wills. Nor can you escape it. My counsel, should I wish to counsel you, will be of no benefit to you if Allah desires to confound you. He is your Lord, and to Him you shall return.' If they say, 'He has made this up,' say, 'If I have made this up, I am responsible for my own crime, but I am innocent of the crimes you commit.' And it was revealed to Noah, saying, 'None of your people shall believe but he who has already believed; so, do not be distressed by that they may be doing. Build the Ark where We can see you and with Our inspiration, and do not plead with Me regarding those who are wicked. They shall be drowned.' So, he was making the Ark; and whenever a council of his people passed by him they scoffed at him, He said, 'If you scoff at us, we shall surely scoff at you, as you scoff. You will surely know upon whom shall fall a torment that will abase him, upon whom shall fall an everlasting torment.' And so it came to pass that when Our command went out, and water gushed forth to the surface, We said: 'Load up on board two of every kind, and your family, except for those foretold, and those who believed.' But the believers with him were few.

He said: 'Go on board. In the name of Allah may it sail and anchor! My Lord is All-Forgiving, Compassionate to each.'

33-41 Prophet Noah had clearly realised that he could only help those amongst his people who already believed in the purpose and direction of life on earth. As for those who would not or could not heed, there was little he could do for them. The metaphor of the ark refers to the safety and security desired by the self and experienced by the soul within, leaving the tumultuous grounds of confusion and whim for the safety, security, and perfection of the soul. It is the light that can save us from confusing duality and worldly uncertainties. Outwardly, the people of Prophet Noah rode on the physical ark, and inwardly, upon the ark of the divine light. Our human life on earth is like this: either the preparation of an ark-like journey to heaven – or a denial that we are in transit towards the hereafter.

Faith and belief are like the lights that shine upon hope and good expectations. Unless there is already trust and hope, faith will not illuminate the path. The essence of belief emanates from the soul through a purified heart, otherwise, it remains dormant.

It is through intelligence that we desire safety, security, and continuation of life until, through hard work and mercy, we realise that life is ever-continuous, and that my life is not separate from that life itself. With this knowledge, most fears and sorrows vanish. The awakened individual knows that you are carried by divine grace in time and beyond time.

42-49 وَهِيَ تَجْرِي بِهِمْ فِي مَوْجٍ كَالْجِبَالِ وَنَادَىٰ نُوحٌ ٱبْنَهُۥ وَكَانَ فِي مَعْزِلٍ يَٰبُنَيَّ ٱرْكَب مَّعَنَا وَلَا تَكُن مَّعَ ٱلْكَٰفِرِينَ ۞ قَالَ سَـَٔاوِىٓ إِلَىٰ جَبَلٍ يَعْصِمُنِى مِنَ ٱلْمَآءِ ۚ قَالَ لَا عَاصِمَ ٱلْيَوْمَ مِنْ أَمْرِ ٱللَّهِ إِلَّا مَن رَّحِمَ ۚ وَحَالَ بَيْنَهُمَا ٱلْمَوْجُ فَكَانَ مِنَ ٱلْمُغْرَقِينَ ۞ وَقِيلَ يَٰٓأَرْضُ ٱبْلَعِى مَآءَكِ وَيَٰسَمَآءُ أَقْلِعِى وَغِيضَ ٱلْمَآءُ وَقُضِىَ ٱلْأَمْرُ وَٱسْتَوَتْ عَلَى ٱلْجُودِىِّ ۖ وَقِيلَ بُعْدًا لِّلْقَوْمِ ٱلظَّٰلِمِينَ ۞ وَنَادَىٰ نُوحٌ رَّبَّهُۥ فَقَالَ رَبِّ إِنَّ ٱبْنِى مِنْ أَهْلِى وَإِنَّ وَعْدَكَ ٱلْحَقُّ وَأَنتَ أَحْكَمُ ٱلْحَٰكِمِينَ ۞ قَالَ يَٰنُوحُ إِنَّهُۥ لَيْسَ مِنْ أَهْلِكَ ۖ إِنَّهُۥ عَمَلٌ غَيْرُ صَٰلِحٍ ۖ فَلَا تَسْـَٔلْنِ مَا لَيْسَ لَكَ بِهِۦ عِلْمٌ ۖ إِنِّىٓ أَعِظُكَ أَن تَكُونَ مِنَ ٱلْجَٰهِلِينَ ۞ قَالَ رَبِّ إِنِّىٓ أَعُوذُ بِكَ أَنْ أَسْـَٔلَكَ مَا لَيْسَ لِى بِهِۦ عِلْمٌ ۖ وَإِلَّا تَغْفِرْ لِى وَتَرْحَمْنِىٓ أَكُن مِّنَ ٱلْخَٰسِرِينَ ۞ قِيلَ يَٰنُوحُ ٱهْبِطْ بِسَلَٰمٍ مِّنَّا وَبَرَكَٰتٍ عَلَيْكَ وَعَلَىٰٓ أُمَمٍ مِّمَّن مَّعَكَ ۚ وَأُمَمٌ سَنُمَتِّعُهُمْ ثُمَّ يَمَسُّهُم مِّنَّا عَذَابٌ أَلِيمٌ ۞ تِلْكَ مِنْ أَنۢبَآءِ ٱلْغَيْبِ نُوحِيهَآ إِلَيْكَ ۖ مَا كُنتَ تَعْلَمُهَآ أَنتَ وَلَا قَوْمُكَ مِن قَبْلِ هَٰذَا ۖ فَٱصْبِرْ ۖ إِنَّ ٱلْعَٰقِبَةَ لِلْمُتَّقِينَ ۞

And so, it sailed with them amidst waves like mountains. Noah called out to his son, who had kept away: 'My son, embark with us and do not remain among the unbelievers.' He said: 'I shall find refuge on a mountain which shall protect me from the waters.' He said: 'Today there is no protector from the command of Allah, except him to whom Allah shows mercy.' Then the waves came between them and he was among those who were drowned. And it was said, 'Earth, swallow your waters; and, heaven, abate!' And the waters subsided, the affair was accomplished, and the Ark settled on El-Judi, and it was said: 'Away with the people of the evildoers!' Noah then called out to his Lord, saying: 'Lord, my son is of my family. Your promise is the truth, and you are the fairest of judges.' He said: 'O Noah, he is not of your family. It is an act unrighteous. So, ask Me not for that of which you have no knowledge. I counsel you not to be foolish.' He said: 'My Lord, I seek refuge in You lest I be one who asks You for what I have no knowledge of! If You do not forgive me and show me mercy, I shall surely be lost.' It was said: 'O Noah, disembark in Our peace, and with Our blessings upon you and upon the nations with you. Other nations We shall grant prosperity, and then there shall touch them from Us a torment most painful.' These are reports of the Unseen which We reveal to you. You knew them not, neither you nor your people, beforehand. So be patient: the final outcome will vindicate the pious.

42-49 Those who have awakened to *Reality* and the gift of the soul within themselves experience a steadier journey on this earth, whilst they observe the tumultuous changes and upheavals that other ordinary people go through. Riding one's own ark will show us the insane way of others. Biologically we may be related to people for whom we wish goodness and safety, but there is clearly a limit to our help. The darkness of the self, the stubborn mind, and past habits and beliefs are barriers not easy to change. Thus was the case of Prophet Noah and his son. Hence, our real family and clan are those who live their faith and are inspired by the insights and guidelines of the prophetic light and direction.

Natural events on earth have helped humankind to evolve to the point that it is at present. Floods, hurricanes, tsunamis, volcanos, and other disasters have taken their toll on us and are deep in our psyche. The lower self carries aspects of such destructive events.

It is only through grace that we improve through reason and rationality and even improve more in goodness through inspiration and the reflection of the light of the heart. On the surface, we have relations, connections, and family links, but in reality, our links are only through the heart and to those who are at the same stage, if not higher, of awakening to the light of the soul within the heart.

50-59 وَإِلَىٰ عَادٍ أَخَاهُمْ هُودًا قَالَ يَٰقَوْمِ ٱعْبُدُوا۟ ٱللَّهَ مَا لَكُم مِّنْ إِلَٰهٍ غَيْرُهُۥٓ إِنْ أَنتُمْ إِلَّا مُفْتَرُونَ ۝ يَٰقَوْمِ لَآ أَسْـَٔلُكُمْ عَلَيْهِ أَجْرًا إِنْ أَجْرِىَ إِلَّا عَلَى ٱلَّذِى فَطَرَنِىٓ أَفَلَا تَعْقِلُونَ ۝ وَيَٰقَوْمِ ٱسْتَغْفِرُوا۟ رَبَّكُمْ ثُمَّ تُوبُوٓا۟ إِلَيْهِ يُرْسِلِ ٱلسَّمَآءَ عَلَيْكُم مِّدْرَارًا وَيَزِدْكُمْ قُوَّةً إِلَىٰ قُوَّتِكُمْ وَلَا تَتَوَلَّوْا۟ مُجْرِمِينَ ۝ قَالُوا۟ يَٰهُودُ مَا جِئْتَنَا بِبَيِّنَةٍ وَمَا نَحْنُ بِتَارِكِىٓ ءَالِهَتِنَا عَن قَوْلِكَ وَمَا نَحْنُ لَكَ بِمُؤْمِنِينَ ۝ إِن نَّقُولُ إِلَّا ٱعْتَرَىٰكَ بَعْضُ ءَالِهَتِنَا بِسُوٓءٍ قَالَ إِنِّىٓ أُشْهِدُ ٱللَّهَ وَٱشْهَدُوٓا۟ أَنِّى بَرِىٓءٌ مِّمَّا تُشْرِكُونَ ۝ مِن

دُونِهِۦ فَكِيدُونِى جَمِيعًا ثُمَّ لَا تُنظِرُونِ ۝ إِنِّى تَوَكَّلْتُ عَلَى ٱللَّهِ رَبِّى وَرَبِّكُم مَّا مِن دَآبَّةٍ إِلَّا هُوَ ءَاخِذٌۢ بِنَاصِيَتِهَآ إِنَّ رَبِّى عَلَىٰ صِرَٰطٍ مُّسْتَقِيمٍ ۝ فَإِن تَوَلَّوْا۟ فَقَدْ أَبْلَغْتُكُم مَّآ أُرْسِلْتُ بِهِۦٓ إِلَيْكُمْ ۚ وَيَسْتَخْلِفُ رَبِّى قَوْمًا غَيْرَكُمْ وَلَا تَضُرُّونَهُۥ شَيْـًٔا ۚ إِنَّ رَبِّى عَلَىٰ كُلِّ شَىْءٍ حَفِيظٌ ۝ وَلَمَّا جَآءَ أَمْرُنَا نَجَّيْنَا هُودًا وَٱلَّذِينَ ءَامَنُوا۟ مَعَهُۥ بِرَحْمَةٍ مِّنَّا وَنَجَّيْنَٰهُم مِّنْ عَذَابٍ غَلِيظٍ ۝ وَتِلْكَ عَادٌ ۖ جَحَدُوا۟ بِـَٔايَٰتِ رَبِّهِمْ وَعَصَوْا۟ رُسُلَهُۥ وَٱتَّبَعُوٓا۟ أَمْرَ كُلِّ جَبَّارٍ عَنِيدٍ ۝

And to 'Ad their brother Hud; he said, 'O my people, serve Allah! You have no Allah other than He; you are but forgers. O my people, I do not ask of you a wage for this; my wage falls only upon Him who did originate me; will you not understand? My people, ask your Lord's forgiveness and repent to Him and He will pour down the heavens in torrents upon you, and increase you in strength above your strength. Do not turn away and be wicked.' They replied, 'Hud, you have not brought us any clear evidence. We will not forsake our Gods on the strength of your word alone, nor will we believe in you. We say only that one of our deities must have afflicted you with harm.' He said: 'I call Allah to witness, and you too are to witness, that I am innocent of your idolatry apart from Him; so, try your guile on me, all together, then you shall give me no respite. I have put my trust in Allah, my Lord and yours. There is no creature but that He holds tight by its forelock. My Lord is upon a straight path. If they turn away, I have delivered to you what I was sent to you with. My Lord shall choose a people other than you to be your successors. You cannot harm Him one whit. My Lord is Guardian over all things.' And when Our command came, We delivered Hud and those who believed with him by a mercy from Us, and delivered them from a harsh chastisement. Such was Ad! They repudiated the signs of their Lord and disobeyed His messengers, and followed the lead of every obdurate tyrant.

50-59 Human history and evolution occur according to self-organizing patterns and cycles along the arc of rising consciousness. Many awakened prophets and messengers have appeared to different people at different times with similar messages of good news and warnings. The main qualities of these beings were their total reliance on Allah as well as their hope and expectations for human awakening. They knew how to read the map that had saved them from the illusions and limitations of earthly consciousness. They hoped to be guided by higher consciousness toward the destination of *Truth* and *Reality*. The path is to be saved from the darkness of the lower self by grace of the soul.

Faith, trust and total reliance upon Allah for guidance are necessary foundations for the rise towards higher consciousness and awakening. Individuals, as well as groups of people and nations, have the potential drive to live as divine beings on earth. Yet due to the lower tendencies of the dark self, we are still in a battleground of darkness and injustice on earth.

A child has to be helped and groomed to grow up at the physical, chemical, rational, and then higher emotional and spiritual levels. The same thing applies to all of us in terms of awakening to the most amazing gift of the divine light within our hearts. Once you are attuned to that, then you transcend the usual human fears and concern about security and survival. You live now by grace and trust of the *Absolute*, which encompasses all.

60-67 وَأُتْبِعُواْ فِى هَٰذِهِ ٱلدُّنْيَا لَعْنَةً وَيَوْمَ ٱلْقِيَٰمَةِ ۚ أَلَآ إِنَّ عَادًا كَفَرُواْ رَبَّهُمْ ۗ أَلَا بُعْدًا لِّعَادٍ قَوْمِ هُودٍ ۝ وَإِلَىٰ ثَمُودَ أَخَاهُمْ صَٰلِحًا ۚ قَالَ يَٰقَوْمِ ٱعْبُدُواْ ٱللَّهَ مَا لَكُم مِّنْ إِلَٰهٍ غَيْرُهُۥ ۖ هُوَ أَنشَأَكُم مِّنَ ٱلْأَرْضِ وَٱسْتَعْمَرَكُمْ فِيهَا فَٱسْتَغْفِرُوهُ ثُمَّ تُوبُوٓاْ إِلَيْهِ ۚ إِنَّ رَبِّى قَرِيبٌ مُّجِيبٌ ۝ قَالُواْ يَٰصَٰلِحُ قَدْ كُنتَ فِينَا مَرْجُوًّا قَبْلَ هَٰذَا ۖ أَتَنْهَىٰنَآ أَن نَّعْبُدَ مَا يَعْبُدُ ءَابَآؤُنَا وَإِنَّنَا لَفِى شَكٍّ مِّمَّا تَدْعُونَآ إِلَيْهِ مُرِيبٍ ۝ قَالَ يَٰقَوْمِ أَرَءَيْتُمْ إِن كُنتُ عَلَىٰ بَيِّنَةٍ مِّن رَّبِّى وَءَاتَىٰنِى مِنْهُ رَحْمَةً فَمَن يَنصُرُنِى مِنَ ٱللَّهِ إِنْ عَصَيْتُهُۥ ۖ فَمَا تَزِيدُونَنِى غَيْرَ تَخْسِيرٍ ۝ وَيَٰقَوْمِ هَٰذِهِۦ نَاقَةُ ٱللَّهِ لَكُمْ ءَايَةً فَذَرُوهَا تَأْكُلْ فِىٓ أَرْضِ ٱللَّهِ وَلَا تَمَسُّوهَا بِسُوٓءٍ فَيَأْخُذَكُمْ عَذَابٌ قَرِيبٌ ۝ فَعَقَرُوهَا فَقَالَ تَمَتَّعُواْ فِى دَارِكُمْ ثَلَٰثَةَ أَيَّامٍ ۖ ذَٰلِكَ وَعْدٌ غَيْرُ مَكْذُوبٍ ۝ فَلَمَّا جَآءَ أَمْرُنَا نَجَّيْنَا صَٰلِحًا وَٱلَّذِينَ ءَامَنُواْ مَعَهُۥ بِرَحْمَةٍ مِّنَّا وَمِنْ خِزْىِ يَوْمِئِذٍ ۗ إِنَّ رَبَّكَ هُوَ ٱلْقَوِىُّ ٱلْعَزِيزُ ۝ وَأَخَذَ ٱلَّذِينَ ظَلَمُواْ ٱلصَّيْحَةُ فَأَصْبَحُواْ فِى دِيَٰرِهِمْ جَٰثِمِينَ ۝

They were rejected in this life and so they shall be on the Day of Judgement. Yes, the 'Ad denied their Lord; so away with the Ad, the people of Hud! To Thamud We sent their fellow tribesman Salih. He said: 'My people, worship Allah; you have no other deity but He. He it was Who raised you up from the earth and made you build upon it. So, ask your Lord's forgiveness and repent to Him; my Lord is ever at hand, ever ready to respond.' They said: 'O Salih, among us you were one from whom much was expected before this matter. Are you forbidding us to worship what our ancestors worshipped when we are in perplexing doubt about what you call us to?' He said, 'My people, just think: if I did have clear proof from my Lord, and if He had given me mercy of His own, who could protect me from Allah if I disobeyed Him? You would only make my loss greater. My people, here is the she-camel of Allah, a sign for you. Set it free to graze in Allah's earth, and touch it not with harm lest an imminent punishment should overtake you.' But they hamstrung the she-camel. He said: 'Enjoy your homes for three days; that is a promise not to be denied.' When Our command came to pass, We saved Salih and those who believed with him, through a mercy from Us, and from the humiliation of that day. Your Lord is All-Powerful, Almighty. And the scream overtook those who had been bent on evildoing: and then they lay lifeless, in their very homes, on the ground,

60-67 The people of Hud, 'Ad, Thamud, and numerous others were given evidence by their prophets that they were endowed with a higher level of consciousness, as evidenced by miracles they showed. When a miracle occurs, our mind and lower self are briefly subdued and overcome, and we may accept these pieces of evidence as proof of the superiority of a prophet. Soon afterwards the mind tends to dominate once more and bring about doubt and uncertainty. We return to the old habits of mischief and ego. When one is in serious danger, one is willing to do anything to be saved, but once the danger is removed, the self returns to its old habits: asserting its whims, desires, and waywardness.

Allah's mercy is such that no people are left without some enlightened people amongst them. Those who hear the message may also be deviated and corrupted, and the cycle will end up in disintegration. The lower self is so tricky that it gets accustomed to its habits and enjoys that illusion of continuity. This is the most common way to self-destruction; individually or collectively.

There is a big advantage in reflecting upon what happened to individuals who went astray and left this world without any attainment and readiness for the next experience. It is part of the rise in intelligence that once you are in reasonable safety, security and health, you inquire as to the next phase: how can I be ready for a zone of experience that I have no control over or the ability to change (which is after death)? That is a true preparation with complete reliance upon God.

68-77 كَأَن لَّمْ يَغْنَوْا۟ فِيهَآ ۗ أَلَآ إِنَّ ثَمُودَا۟ كَفَرُوا۟ رَبَّهُمْ ۗ أَلَا بُعْدًا لِّثَمُودَ ۝ وَلَقَدْ جَآءَتْ رُسُلُنَآ إِبْرَٰهِيمَ بِٱلْبُشْرَىٰ قَالُوا۟ سَلَـٰمًا ۖ قَالَ سَلَـٰمٌ ۖ فَمَا لَبِثَ أَن جَآءَ بِعِجْلٍ حَنِيذٍ ۝ فَلَمَّا رَءَآ أَيْدِيَهُمْ لَا تَصِلُ إِلَيْهِ نَكِرَهُمْ وَأَوْجَسَ مِنْهُمْ خِيفَةً ۚ قَالُوا۟ لَا تَخَفْ إِنَّآ أُرْسِلْنَآ إِلَىٰ قَوْمِ لُوطٍ ۝ وَٱمْرَأَتُهُۥ قَآئِمَةٌ فَضَحِكَتْ فَبَشَّرْنَـٰهَا بِإِسْحَـٰقَ وَمِن وَرَآءِ إِسْحَـٰقَ يَعْقُوبَ ۝ قَالَتْ يَـٰوَيْلَتَىٰٓ ءَأَلِدُ وَأَنَا۠ عَجُوزٌ وَهَـٰذَا بَعْلِى شَيْخًا ۖ إِنَّ هَـٰذَا لَشَىْءٌ عَجِيبٌ ۝ قَالُوٓا۟ أَتَعْجَبِينَ مِنْ أَمْرِ ٱللَّهِ ۖ رَحْمَتُ ٱللَّهِ وَبَرَكَـٰتُهُۥ عَلَيْكُمْ أَهْلَ ٱلْبَيْتِ ۚ إِنَّهُۥ حَمِيدٌ مَّجِيدٌ ۝ فَلَمَّا ذَهَبَ عَنْ إِبْرَٰهِيمَ ٱلرَّوْعُ وَجَآءَتْهُ ٱلْبُشْرَىٰ يُجَـٰدِلُنَا فِى قَوْمِ لُوطٍ ۝ إِنَّ إِبْرَٰهِيمَ لَحَلِيمٌ أَوَّٰهٌ مُّنِيبٌ ۝ يَـٰٓإِبْرَٰهِيمُ أَعْرِضْ عَنْ هَـٰذَآ ۖ إِنَّهُۥ قَدْ جَآءَ أَمْرُ رَبِّكَ ۖ وَإِنَّهُمْ ءَاتِيهِمْ عَذَابٌ غَيْرُ مَرْدُودٍ ۝ وَلَمَّا جَآءَتْ رُسُلُنَا لُوطًا سِىٓءَ بِهِمْ وَضَاقَ بِهِمْ ذَرْعًا وَقَالَ هَـٰذَا يَوْمٌ عَصِيبٌ ۝

as though they had never lived there. Oh, verily, Thamud denied their Sustainer! Oh, away with Thamud! Our envoys came to Abraham, bearing glad tidings. They said: 'Peace!' He said: 'Peace!' At once he brought forth a roasted calf. When he saw that their hands did not stretch forth to it, he was in doubt about them and harbored some fear of them. They said: 'Fear not. We were sent to the people of Lot.' His wife, standing by, laughed, so We brought her glad tidings of Isaac, and after Isaac, of Jacob. She said: 'Alas for me! Am I to give birth, me an old woman, and here is my husband, an old man? That would indeed be a marvel!' They said: 'Do you marvel at the command of Allah? May the mercy of Allah and His blessings descend upon you, O members of the house! He is All-Praiseworthy, All-Glorious.' When fear left Abraham, and glad tidings came to him, he began to argue with Us regarding the people of Lot. Abraham was gentle, sighing much, penitent. 'O Abraham, make no mention of this matter. The command of your Lord is come and they; there shall come to them a torment irreversible.' And when Our messengers came to Lot, he was troubled on their account and distressed for them, and he said, 'This is a fierce day.'

68-77 The greatest of the famous and known prophets is perhaps the Prophet Abraham. He awoke to the truth that there is one magnificent *Reality* encompassing all that we think is real, including all natural, celestial, or physical deities and objects of worship. When the angels came to visit him, it signified a serious and evident connection between the unseen and the seen. It testified that this great being was forbearing, tender-hearted, and would affect the lives of many human beings for a long time to come. The same significance manifested when the angels went to the Prophet Lot to warn and remind him that it was too late to save his people, including his wife.

When we are struck by something awesome, we take notice and may even realise our old, dark ways. Usually when relief comes, we revert to old habits. These lower tendencies are most dangerous and can only be transcended through deep reflection, repentance, and worship.

Insight and the good news about the ongoingness of life come to us from within us, from our surroundings, from nature, and from the history of others. This life is temporary but exists because of the grace of the permanent. We are to practice, through effort and intelligence, the ability to be in the eternal moment itself. This is the doorway to the cosmic vista that we will experience after death.

78-85 وَجَآءَهُۥ قَوْمُهُۥ يُهْرَعُونَ إِلَيْهِ وَمِن قَبْلُ كَانُوا۟ يَعْمَلُونَ ٱلسَّيِّـَٔاتِ قَالَ يَـٰقَوْمِ هَـٰٓؤُلَآءِ بَنَاتِى هُنَّ أَطْهَرُ لَكُمْ فَٱتَّقُوا۟ ٱللَّهَ وَلَا تُخْزُونِ فِى ضَيْفِىٓ أَلَيْسَ مِنكُمْ رَجُلٌ رَّشِيدٌ ۝ قَالُوا۟ لَقَدْ عَلِمْتَ مَا لَنَا فِى بَنَاتِكَ مِنْ حَقٍّ وَإِنَّكَ لَتَعْلَمُ مَا نُرِيدُ ۝ قَالَ لَوْ أَنَّ لِى بِكُمْ قُوَّةً أَوْ ءَاوِىٓ إِلَىٰ رُكْنٍ شَدِيدٍ ۝ قَالُوا۟ يَـٰلُوطُ إِنَّا رُسُلُ رَبِّكَ لَن يَصِلُوٓا۟ إِلَيْكَ فَأَسْرِ بِأَهْلِكَ بِقِطْعٍ مِّنَ ٱلَّيْلِ وَلَا يَلْتَفِتْ مِنكُمْ أَحَدٌ إِلَّا ٱمْرَأَتَكَ إِنَّهُۥ مُصِيبُهَا مَآ أَصَابَهُمْ إِنَّ مَوْعِدَهُمُ ٱلصُّبْحُ أَلَيْسَ ٱلصُّبْحُ بِقَرِيبٍ ۝ فَلَمَّا جَآءَ أَمْرُنَا جَعَلْنَا عَـٰلِيَهَا سَافِلَهَا وَأَمْطَرْنَا عَلَيْهَا حِجَارَةً مِّن سِجِّيلٍ مَّنضُودٍ ۝ مُّسَوَّمَةً عِندَ رَبِّكَ وَمَا هِىَ مِنَ ٱلظَّـٰلِمِينَ بِبَعِيدٍ ۝ وَإِلَىٰ مَدْيَنَ أَخَاهُمْ شُعَيْبًا قَالَ يَـٰقَوْمِ ٱعْبُدُوا۟ ٱللَّهَ مَا لَكُم مِّنْ إِلَـٰهٍ غَيْرُهُۥ وَلَا تَنقُصُوا۟ ٱلْمِكْيَالَ وَٱلْمِيزَانَ

إِنِّى أَرَىٰكُم بِخَيْرٍ وَإِنِّىٓ أَخَافُ عَلَيْكُمْ عَذَابَ يَوْمٍ مُّحِيطٍ ۝ وَيَٰقَوْمِ أَوْفُوا۟ ٱلْمِكْيَالَ وَٱلْمِيزَانَ بِٱلْقِسْطِ ۖ وَلَا تَبْخَسُوا۟ ٱلنَّاسَ أَشْيَآءَهُمْ وَلَا تَعْثَوْا۟ فِى ٱلْأَرْضِ مُفْسِدِينَ ۝

His people came to him, hurrying in haste; beforehand, they had committed misdeeds. He said: 'My people, here are my daughters; they are more pure for you. So, fear Allah and do not shame me with my guests. Is there not among you a man of discernment?' They said: 'You know we have no right to your daughters, and you know well what we want.' He said: 'If only I had some power against you, or else I could take refuge in a pillar of great strength!' They said: 'O Lot, we are the envoys of your Lord. They shall not reach out to harm you. So set out with your family in the course of the night, and let none of you turn their heads back except your wife. She will be smitten with that which will smite them. Their appointed time shall be the morning: is not the morning close at hand?' So, when Our command came, We turned it uppermost nethermost, and rained on it stones of baked clay, one on another. Marked with your Lord, and never far from the evildoers. To Midian We sent their fellow tribesman Shu'ayb. He said: 'My people, worship Allah; you have no other deity but He. Do not shortchange the measure and the balance. I see you are prosperous, and I fear for you the torment of a Day, All-Encompassing. My people, give full share in the measure and balance, acting justly. Do not cheat people of their goods and do not act wickedly on earth, corrupting it.

78-85 The advice to Prophet Lot from the angels was to leave his place and migrate, as there would be a major upheaval on earth, which may have been earthquakes or volcanoes. What happened to the people of Lot was repeated with other people, who were warned by their messengers about the usual human distractions: disregarding the natural order of the earth and the human duty towards it instead of maintaining boundaries and exemplifying honesty, justice and self-restraint. Thousands of prophets and messengers repeated the same teachings of the human situation within the decree of divine purpose and will. We may be now amongst the last cultures and civilisations on earth.

Within our hearts lies a zone of consciousness of warning, but if we do not take heed early on, we will become arrogant with the illusion that we can overcome anything. Corruption through power and the acclaim of others can bring about destruction to everyone within that field. It is only through awareness of the moment and genuine reference to mortality that self-correction can arise.

Human beings have evolved to such a point that touching the zone of the spirit within, which is beyond cause and effect, has become much easier, provided there is reasonable health and the discipline to stop unhelpful intentions, actions, and mental attitudes.

86-93 بَقِيَّتُ ٱللَّهِ خَيْرٌ لَّكُمْ إِن كُنتُم مُّؤْمِنِينَ وَمَآ أَنَا۠ عَلَيْكُم بِحَفِيظٍ ۝ قَالُوا۟ يَـٰشُعَيْبُ أَصَلَوٰتُكَ تَأْمُرُكَ أَن نَّتْرُكَ مَا يَعْبُدُ ءَابَآؤُنَآ أَوْ أَن نَّفْعَلَ فِىٓ أَمْوَٰلِنَا مَا نَشَـٰٓؤُا۟ إِنَّكَ لَأَنتَ ٱلْحَلِيمُ ٱلرَّشِيدُ ۝ قَالَ يَـٰقَوْمِ أَرَءَيْتُمْ إِن كُنتُ عَلَىٰ بَيِّنَةٍ مِّن رَّبِّى وَرَزَقَنِى مِنْهُ رِزْقًا حَسَنًا وَمَآ أُرِيدُ أَنْ أُخَالِفَكُمْ إِلَىٰ مَآ أَنْهَىٰكُمْ عَنْهُ إِنْ أُرِيدُ إِلَّا ٱلْإِصْلَـٰحَ مَا ٱسْتَطَعْتُ وَمَا تَوْفِيقِىٓ إِلَّا بِٱللَّهِ عَلَيْهِ تَوَكَّلْتُ وَإِلَيْهِ أُنِيبُ ۝ وَيَـٰقَوْمِ لَا يَجْرِمَنَّكُمْ شِقَاقِىٓ أَن يُصِيبَكُم مِّثْلُ مَآ أَصَابَ قَوْمَ نُوحٍ أَوْ قَوْمَ هُودٍ أَوْ قَوْمَ صَـٰلِحٍ وَمَا قَوْمُ لُوطٍ مِّنكُم بِبَعِيدٍ ۝ وَٱسْتَغْفِرُوا۟ رَبَّكُمْ ثُمَّ تُوبُوٓا۟ إِلَيْهِ إِنَّ رَبِّى رَحِيمٌ وَدُودٌ ۝ قَالُوا۟ يَـٰشُعَيْبُ مَا نَفْقَهُ كَثِيرًا مِّمَّا تَقُولُ وَإِنَّا لَنَرَىٰكَ فِينَا ضَعِيفًا وَلَوْلَا رَهْطُكَ لَرَجَمْنَـٰكَ وَمَآ أَنتَ عَلَيْنَا بِعَزِيزٍ ۝ قَالَ يَـٰقَوْمِ أَرَهْطِىٓ أَعَزُّ عَلَيْكُم مِّنَ ٱللَّهِ وَٱتَّخَذْتُمُوهُ وَرَآءَكُمْ ظِهْرِيًّا إِنَّ رَبِّى بِمَا تَعْمَلُونَ مُحِيطٌ ۝ وَيَـٰقَوْمِ ٱعْمَلُوا۟ عَلَىٰ مَكَانَتِكُمْ إِنِّى عَـٰمِلٌ سَوْفَ تَعْلَمُونَ مَن يَأْتِيهِ عَذَابٌ يُخْزِيهِ وَمَنْ هُوَ كَـٰذِبٌ وَٱرْتَقِبُوٓا۟ إِنِّى مَعَكُمْ رَقِيبٌ ۝

What remains from Allah is better for you if you are true believers. But I am not a guardian over you.' They said: 'O Shuʿayb, is it your mode of worship that commands you that we abandon what our ancestors worshipped? Or are we to do with our wealth what we please? For you are gentle and discerning.' He answered, 'My people, can you not see? What if I am acting on clear evidence from my Lord? He Himself has given me good provision; I do not want to do what I am forbidding you to do, I only want to put things right as far as I can. I cannot succeed without Allah's help; I trust in Him, and always turn to Him. My people, let not your enmity towards me bring upon you a calamity such as befell the people of Noah, or of Hud, or of Salih; nor is the example of Lot's people remote from you. Ask your Lord's forgiveness and repent to Him: my Lord is Compassionate to each, All-Tender.' They said, 'Shuʿayb, we do not understand much of what you say, and we find you very weak in our midst. But for your tribe, we would have stoned you, for you have no great status among us.' He said: 'My people, is my clan more powerful against you than Allah, Whom you have cast behind your backs? My Lord encompasses all that you do. O my people, act according to your station; I am acting; and certainly, you will know to whom will come the chastisement degrading him, and who is a liar. And be upon the watch; I shall be with you, watching.'

86-93 The people of the lands east of the Mediterranean all the way to Asia received numerous and often connected streams of revelation and prophets. Geographical connections and similarity of cultures and languages created a melting pot of religious and spiritual paths, which remained alive to our present day. Prophet Shuʿayb's story presents an example of yet another messenger, denied by his own people, who were set in their old ways. Shuʿayb experienced, shared, and followed what was transmitted from his heart, from his inner Lord. He was in true obedience to and worship of God. Indeed, human beings are celestial realities experiencing a terrestrial journey.

To review one's own state of mind and action regularly is to knock at the door of repentance and self-correction. With regular reference to the light of the soul within you, you will know whether you are keeping to the narrow path that takes you from lower levels of consciousness to enlightenment.

We can act haphazardly or we can act with a certain pattern that guides us. We can also act with clear, disciplined guidance that enables us to attain a sure outcome. The same thing applies to your awakening to the higher light within you, until such time you have no option other than listening to your own heart whilst the mind is kept in temporary silence.

94-104

وَلَمَّا جَآءَ أَمْرُنَا نَجَّيْنَا شُعَيْبًا وَٱلَّذِينَ ءَامَنُوا۟ مَعَهُۥ بِرَحْمَةٍ مِّنَّا وَأَخَذَتِ ٱلَّذِينَ ظَلَمُوا۟ ٱلصَّيْحَةُ فَأَصْبَحُوا۟ فِى دِيَٰرِهِمْ جَٰثِمِينَ ۝ كَأَن لَّمْ يَغْنَوْا۟ فِيهَآ أَلَا بُعْدًا لِّمَدْيَنَ كَمَا بَعِدَتْ ثَمُودُ ۝ وَلَقَدْ أَرْسَلْنَا مُوسَىٰ بِـَٔايَٰتِنَا وَسُلْطَٰنٍ مُّبِينٍ ۝ إِلَىٰ فِرْعَوْنَ وَمَلَإِيْهِۦ فَٱتَّبَعُوٓا۟ أَمْرَ فِرْعَوْنَ وَمَآ أَمْرُ فِرْعَوْنَ بِرَشِيدٍ ۝ يَقْدُمُ قَوْمَهُۥ يَوْمَ ٱلْقِيَٰمَةِ فَأَوْرَدَهُمُ ٱلنَّارَ وَبِئْسَ ٱلْوِرْدُ ٱلْمَوْرُودُ ۝ وَأُتْبِعُوا۟ فِى هَٰذِهِۦ لَعْنَةً وَيَوْمَ ٱلْقِيَٰمَةِ بِئْسَ ٱلرِّفْدُ ٱلْمَرْفُودُ ۝ ذَٰلِكَ مِنْ أَنۢبَآءِ ٱلْقُرَىٰ نَقُصُّهُۥ عَلَيْكَ مِنْهَا قَآئِمٌ وَحَصِيدٌ ۝ وَمَا ظَلَمْنَٰهُمْ وَلَٰكِن ظَلَمُوٓا۟ أَنفُسَهُمْ فَمَآ أَغْنَتْ عَنْهُمْ ءَالِهَتُهُمُ ٱلَّتِى يَدْعُونَ مِن دُونِ ٱللَّهِ مِن شَىْءٍ لَّمَّا جَآءَ أَمْرُ رَبِّكَ وَمَا زَادُوهُمْ غَيْرَ تَتْبِيبٍ ۝ وَكَذَٰلِكَ أَخْذُ رَبِّكَ إِذَآ أَخَذَ ٱلْقُرَىٰ وَهِىَ ظَٰلِمَةٌ إِنَّ أَخْذَهُۥٓ أَلِيمٌ شَدِيدٌ ۝ إِنَّ فِى ذَٰلِكَ لَءَايَةً لِّمَنْ خَافَ عَذَابَ ٱلْءَاخِرَةِ ذَٰلِكَ يَوْمٌ مَّجْمُوعٌ لَّهُ ٱلنَّاسُ وَذَٰلِكَ يَوْمٌ مَّشْهُودٌ ۝ وَمَا نُؤَخِّرُهُۥٓ إِلَّا لِأَجَلٍ مَّعْدُودٍ ۝

When what We had ordained came about, in Our mercy We saved Shu'ayb and his fellow believers, but a mighty blast struck the wrongdoers. By morning they lay dead in their homes. As though they had never prospered therein. Away with Midian, as was done away with Thamud! And We sent Moses with Our signs, and a manifest authority, to Pharaoh and his grandees, but they followed the command of Pharaoh, and Pharaoh's command was not guided aright. He shall be at the head of his people on the Day of Resurrection, for he has led them into the Fire, wretched the place he placed them in! And there was sent following after them in this world a curse, and upon the Day of Resurrection; evil the offering to be offered! These are reports of cities which We narrate to you; some are left standing; some have withered away. And We wronged them not, but they wronged themselves; their deities availed them not that they called upon, apart from Allah, anything, when the command of thy Lord came; and they increased them not, save in destruction. Such is the seizing of thy Lord, when He seizes the cities that are evildoing; surely His seizing is painful, terrible. In this is a sign for him who fears *the torment of the hereafter. That will be a Day at which mankind shall be gathered; that will be a Day witnessed by all. And We shall not postpone it, save to a term reckoned;*

94-104 All these messengers, prophets, and enlightened beings were saved, perhaps both physically and in indestructible spirit. When you live as a soul, then you know that life is eternal, and your life is not separate from perpetual life. Death is a natural process for conditioned consciousness, which leads out of the limitations of space and time to timelessness. Death is the beginning of true consciousness, without the illusion of self or ego as a separate entity. There are wonderful examples of the battles of Prophet Moses and Pharaoh, the historical Moses as well as Moses of the heart, and the message of these stories: is that light will overcome the darkness and imperial ego-self of Pharaoh. Every human being experiences to some extent the battle between the Pharaoh of the lower self and ego and the Moses of the higher soul. The metaphor reveals guidelines for how to be saved from the tyranny of the self, individually and collectively. The present moment is always the right time to be in synchronicity with one's soul and the divine light.

There is so much joy and usefulness in looking at the history of the great prophets and the afflictions that they endured with complete patience and trust. The lower self is limited and fickle, and the soul or spirit within is divine, boundless and eternal. If there are enough enlightened people, then the rest of the creation will naturally benefit and rise towards its destiny.

The human desire to learn about the past is very helpful if we are looking for the basic sketches and maps of how to behave with the intelligence that will take us to the zone that prepares us for the next life. We are in ever-changing space and time, and we seek to reference the Source which is beyond space and time, and this is the soul or spirit within our own heart.

105-113 يَوْمَ يَأْتِ لَا تَكَلَّمُ نَفْسٌ إِلَّا بِإِذْنِهِ فَمِنْهُمْ شَقِيٌّ وَسَعِيدٌ ۝ فَأَمَّا ٱلَّذِينَ شَقُواْ فَفِى ٱلنَّارِ لَهُمْ فِيهَا زَفِيرٌ وَشَهِيقٌ ۝ خَٰلِدِينَ فِيهَا مَا دَامَتِ ٱلسَّمَٰوَٰتُ وَٱلْأَرْضُ إِلَّا مَا شَآءَ رَبُّكَ إِنَّ رَبَّكَ فَعَّالٌ لِّمَا يُرِيدُ ۝ وَأَمَّا ٱلَّذِينَ سُعِدُواْ فَفِى ٱلْجَنَّةِ خَٰلِدِينَ فِيهَا مَا دَامَتِ ٱلسَّمَٰوَٰتُ وَٱلْأَرْضُ إِلَّا مَا شَآءَ رَبُّكَ عَطَآءً غَيْرَ مَجْذُوذٍ ۝ فَلَا تَكُ فِى مِرْيَةٍ مِّمَّا يَعْبُدُ هَٰٓؤُلَآءِ مَا يَعْبُدُونَ إِلَّا كَمَا يَعْبُدُ ءَابَآؤُهُم مِّن قَبْلُ وَإِنَّا لَمُوَفُّوهُمْ نَصِيبَهُمْ غَيْرَ مَنقُوصٍ ۝ وَلَقَدْ ءَاتَيْنَا مُوسَى ٱلْكِتَٰبَ فَٱخْتُلِفَ فِيهِ وَلَوْلَا كَلِمَةٌ سَبَقَتْ مِن رَّبِّكَ لَقُضِىَ بَيْنَهُمْ وَإِنَّهُمْ لَفِى شَكٍّ مِّنْهُ مُرِيبٍ ۝ وَإِنَّ كُلًّا لَّمَّا لَيُوَفِّيَنَّهُمْ رَبُّكَ أَعْمَٰلَهُمْ إِنَّهُ بِمَا يَعْمَلُونَ خَبِيرٌ ۝ فَٱسْتَقِمْ كَمَآ أُمِرْتَ وَمَن تَابَ مَعَكَ وَلَا تَطْغَوْاْ إِنَّهُ بِمَا تَعْمَلُونَ بَصِيرٌ ۝ وَلَا تَرْكَنُوٓاْ إِلَى ٱلَّذِينَ ظَلَمُواْ فَتَمَسَّكُمُ ٱلنَّارُ وَمَا لَكُم مِّن دُونِ ٱللَّهِ مِنْ أَوْلِيَآءَ ثُمَّ لَا تُنصَرُونَ ۝

the day it comes, no soul shall speak save by His leave; some of them shall be wretched and some happy. The wretched ones will be in the Fire, sighing and groaning. There to remain for as long as the heavens and earth endure, unless your Lord wills otherwise; your Lord carries out whatever He wills. And as for the happy, they shall be in Paradise, therein dwelling forever, so long as the heavens and earth abide, save as your Lord will; for a gift unbroken. Therefore, be not in any doubt as to what these people worship. They merely worship as their forefathers had worshipped before. We shall pay them their share in full, undiminished. We had brought Moses the Book, and disputes arose concerning it. Were it not for a prior Word from your Lord, judgment would have been passed upon them. They are in perplexing doubt concerning it. Surely each one of them; your Lord will pay them in full for their works; He is aware of the things they do. So, keep to the right course as you have been commanded, together with those who have turned to Allah with you. Do not overstep the limits, for He sees everything you do. Do not incline to those who did wrong, or else the Fire will touch you. You have, apart from Allah, no protectors, nor will you be aided.

105-113 Remembrance of death and the afterlife is both a remedy and an opportunity for all seekers on a spiritual path to learn to silence the mind, to transcend the illusions of memory, and to free themselves from the fantasy of being an entity separate from the divine soul. Conditioned life on earth in its connection with body and mind finally ends, whereas life itself continues, as does the soul in the afterlife. Awakened and enlightened beings knew that life on earth was a work in progress, learning to be fully guided by the divine soul and to avoid the pitfalls of the shadows of the lower self. They found only safe ground in Noah's ark, in the bliss of the soul, whilst in their actions they lived in caution within the natural limitations of conditioned consciousness. Placing our human consciousness within the cosmic infinitude of the divine light is indeed a great gift.

We naturally get carried away in our projects and actions. To stop everything and enter the inner silence enables us to recalibrate and remain on the middle path. There is no end to human ambition, because the light of the soul within is boundless and eternal. We must maintain modesty and curb our ambitions and desires except for the drive for enlightenment.

Those who manage to touch the soul and its light regularly experience happiness, which will continue as long as there are creations that we are part of. The next zone itself has its own eternal perfections.

114-123 وَأَقِمِ ٱلصَّلَوٰةَ طَرَفَىِ ٱلنَّهَارِ وَزُلَفًا مِّنَ ٱلَّيۡلِ إِنَّ ٱلۡحَسَنَٰتِ يُذۡهِبۡنَ ٱلسَّيِّـَٔاتِ ذَٰلِكَ ذِكۡرَىٰ لِلذَّٰكِرِينَ ۝ وَٱصۡبِرۡ فَإِنَّ ٱللَّهَ لَا يُضِيعُ أَجۡرَ ٱلۡمُحۡسِنِينَ ۝ فَلَوۡلَا كَانَ مِنَ ٱلۡقُرُونِ مِن قَبۡلِكُمۡ أُوْلُواْ بَقِيَّةٖ يَنۡهَوۡنَ عَنِ ٱلۡفَسَادِ فِي ٱلۡأَرۡضِ إِلَّا قَلِيلٗا مِّمَّنۡ أَنجَيۡنَا مِنۡهُمۡۗ وَٱتَّبَعَ ٱلَّذِينَ ظَلَمُواْ مَآ أُتۡرِفُواْ فِيهِ وَكَانُواْ مُجۡرِمِينَ ۝ وَمَا كَانَ رَبُّكَ

لِيُهْلِكَ ٱلْقُرَىٰ بِظُلْمٍ وَأَهْلُهَا مُصْلِحُونَ ۝ وَلَوْ شَآءَ رَبُّكَ لَجَعَلَ ٱلنَّاسَ أُمَّةً وَٰحِدَةً ۖ وَلَا يَزَالُونَ مُخْتَلِفِينَ ۝ إِلَّا مَن رَّحِمَ رَبُّكَ ۚ وَلِذَٰلِكَ خَلَقَهُمْ ۗ وَتَمَّتْ كَلِمَةُ رَبِّكَ لَأَمْلَأَنَّ جَهَنَّمَ مِنَ ٱلْجِنَّةِ وَٱلنَّاسِ أَجْمَعِينَ ۝ وَكُلًّا نَّقُصُّ عَلَيْكَ مِنْ أَنۢبَآءِ ٱلرُّسُلِ مَا نُثَبِّتُ بِهِۦ فُؤَادَكَ ۚ وَجَآءَكَ فِى هَٰذِهِ ٱلْحَقُّ وَمَوْعِظَةٌ وَذِكْرَىٰ لِلْمُؤْمِنِينَ ۝ وَقُل لِّلَّذِينَ لَا يُؤْمِنُونَ ٱعْمَلُوا۟ عَلَىٰ مَكَانَتِكُمْ إِنَّا عَٰمِلُونَ ۝ وَٱنتَظِرُوٓا۟ إِنَّا مُنتَظِرُونَ ۝ وَلِلَّهِ غَيْبُ ٱلسَّمَٰوَٰتِ وَٱلْأَرْضِ وَإِلَيْهِ يُرْجَعُ ٱلْأَمْرُ كُلُّهُۥ فَٱعْبُدْهُ وَتَوَكَّلْ عَلَيْهِ ۚ وَمَا رَبُّكَ بِغَٰفِلٍ عَمَّا تَعْمَلُونَ ۝

Perform the prayer at the two ends of the day and for some hours of the night. Good deeds efface bad deeds. This is a Remembrance to those who remember. Bear with patience; Allah neglects not the reward of those who do good. Would that, in ages past before you, there had been a group, a remnant, who forbade corruption on earth! Except for a few, and these We saved. But wrongdoers pursued the luxuries they were plunged in, and grew wicked. And yet your Lord would not have destroyed cities unjustly if their inhabitants had been virtuous. Had your Lord willed, He would have created mankind a single nation. But they continue to differ, except those on whom your Lord has mercy, for He created them to be this way, and the word of your Lord is final: 'I shall definitely fill Hell with both jinn and men.' All that We narrate to you from the tales of messengers is such wherewith We fortify your heart. To you thereby has come the Truth, a Lesson and a Remembrance to the believers. And say to the unbelievers: 'Act you according to your station; we are acting. And watch and wait; we too are watching and waiting.' To Allah belongs the Unseen in the heavens and earth. To Him all matters revert. Worship Him; 67-75 *Trust in Him; Nor is your Lord heedless of what you do.*

114-123 Spiritual seekers need to maintain awareness of boundaries to their thoughts and actions in order to avoid being distracted by the physical, mental, and other challenges of day-to-day life. Good actions can erase the effects of wrong ones. We need to be aware of the depth of our intention and the appropriateness of our actions if we expect goodwill and justice all around. Quality of life improves dramatically if we remember two things: at all times Allah knows what is in our head and heart, and our earthly life is only a prelude to the hereafter. There will always be people who cannot accept real faith or trust in the soul, and there is often little that one can do to change others. Intelligent ones can only refer to the one *Author* from whom all universes emerged and to whom all return. Truly Allah is the one worthy of worship.

Good deeds will efface the wrong ones, and patience always leads to better understanding. Whatever is known and unknown emanates from Allah and is under this perfect governance. It is through intelligence and dedication that we rely entirely on the unseen and do our utmost in intention and action for the goodness of life on earth.

The prescription to save one from the lower self and to be tuned to the higher light within the soul is regular reflection, meditation, and presence in the moment. This rule will not change for any human being, whether a criminal or a prophet. We are all subjected to the same pattern of darkness and light as well as the choice, through intelligence and application, to get out of disturbances and distractions and to remain steadfast in the divine light within the heart.

4. Surah 16 An-Nahl (The Bee)

The ability to believe in the perfection of cosmic interconnectedness and, being neutral, witness the link between the unseen and the visible, is a great gift to us.

بِسْمِ اللَّهِ الرَّحْمَٰنِ الرَّحِيمِ

أَتَىٰ أَمْرُ اللَّهِ فَلَا تَسْتَعْجِلُوهُ ۚ سُبْحَانَهُ وَتَعَالَىٰ عَمَّا يُشْرِكُونَ ۝ يُنَزِّلُ الْمَلَائِكَةَ بِالرُّوحِ مِنْ أَمْرِهِ عَلَىٰ مَنْ يَشَاءُ مِنْ عِبَادِهِ أَنْ أَنْذِرُوا أَنَّهُ لَا إِلَٰهَ إِلَّا أَنَا فَاتَّقُونِ ۝ خَلَقَ السَّمَاوَاتِ وَالْأَرْضَ بِالْحَقِّ ۚ تَعَالَىٰ عَمَّا يُشْرِكُونَ ۝ خَلَقَ الْإِنْسَانَ مِنْ نُطْفَةٍ فَإِذَا هُوَ خَصِيمٌ مُبِينٌ ۝ وَالْأَنْعَامَ خَلَقَهَا ۗ لَكُمْ فِيهَا دِفْءٌ وَمَنَافِعُ وَمِنْهَا تَأْكُلُونَ ۝ وَلَكُمْ فِيهَا جَمَالٌ حِينَ تُرِيحُونَ وَحِينَ تَسْرَحُونَ ۝ وَتَحْمِلُ أَثْقَالَكُمْ إِلَىٰ بَلَدٍ لَمْ تَكُونُوا بَالِغِيهِ إِلَّا بِشِقِّ الْأَنْفُسِ ۚ إِنَّ رَبَّكُمْ لَرَءُوفٌ رَحِيمٌ ۝ وَالْخَيْلَ وَالْبِغَالَ وَالْحَمِيرَ لِتَرْكَبُوهَا وَزِينَةً ۚ وَيَخْلُقُ مَا لَا تَعْلَمُونَ ۝ وَعَلَى اللَّهِ قَصْدُ السَّبِيلِ وَمِنْهَا جَائِرٌ ۚ وَلَوْ شَاءَ لَهَدَاكُمْ أَجْمَعِينَ ۝ هُوَ الَّذِي أَنْزَلَ مِنَ السَّمَاءِ مَاءً ۖ لَكُمْ مِنْهُ شَرَابٌ وَمِنْهُ شَجَرٌ فِيهِ تُسِيمُونَ ۝

In the name of Allah, the Merciful to all, the Compassionate to each!

Allah's command comes; so, seek not to hasten it. Glory be to Him! High be He exalted above that they associate with Him! He sends down the angels with the Spirit of His command upon whomsoever He will among His servants, saying: Give you warning that there is no Allah but I; so, beware of Me! He created the heavens and the earth with the truth, highly exalted be He above what they associate. He created man from a drop of fluid, and yet man openly challenges Him. And cattle He created, from which you derive warmth and other uses, and from which you eat. And there is beauty in them for you, when you rest them or you send them out to pasture. They carry your loads to a land you would not have reached except after much hardship. Your Lord is surely All-Gracious, Compassionate to each. Horses, mules, donkeys are there for you to ride, and an adornment. And He creates what you know not. Allah points out the right path, for some paths lead the wrong way: had He wished, He would have guided you all. He it is Who made water descend from the sky, of which some is for you to drink and some for trees from which you pasture.

1-10 Creation encompasses a wide spectrum, from entities subtle and unseen to those that are physical and material. Life can only exist when these material, physical, and chemical substances connect with the light or spirit, which provides sentience and the experience of life itself. Ultimately, whatever experiences life seeks to realise its origin. This is the direction of evolving, conscious human beings – from duality to *Oneness*. The forces that control and govern our universe are numerous and interlinked, some of which have become visible, like wind and cosmic rays, and others that are not discernible. The creation of the human being combines the seeds of a man and a woman, grown in a complex manner, linked in amazing harmony. Allah's plan is to be known and worshipped, and that is the purpose of the offspring of Adam.

The patterns of creation were already in place before the Big Bang. As such the human soul emerged from the infinite unseen to make its journey to full realisation of the divine light within. The discernible, physical side of creation is only the outer manifestation of numerous interlinked realities, forces, and powers at play.

With the miracle of creation, all of the patterns and designs that relate to governance – beginnings, endings, and everything in between – have already been set in place. Countless souls and spirits have emerged connecting the visible, tangible, and earthly with its origin: the heavenly energy that gave it life and sustenance. For humans, we have the amazing backup of all kinds of other creatures that help us for travel, livelihood, and other things. All of this connects and relates through life and water that is life-sustaining.

11-21 يُنۢبِتُ لَكُم بِهِ ٱلزَّرْعَ وَٱلزَّيْتُونَ وَٱلنَّخِيلَ وَٱلْأَعْنَٰبَ وَمِن كُلِّ ٱلثَّمَرَٰتِۗ إِنَّ فِى ذَٰلِكَ لَءَايَةً لِّقَوْمٍ يَتَفَكَّرُونَ ۝ وَسَخَّرَ لَكُمُ ٱلَّيْلَ وَٱلنَّهَارَ وَٱلشَّمْسَ وَٱلْقَمَرَۖ وَٱلنُّجُومُ مُسَخَّرَٰتٌۢ بِأَمْرِهِۦٓۗ إِنَّ فِى ذَٰلِكَ لَءَايَٰتٍ لِّقَوْمٍ يَعْقِلُونَ ۝ وَمَا ذَرَأَ لَكُمْ فِى ٱلْأَرْضِ مُخْتَلِفًا أَلْوَٰنُهُۥۤۗ إِنَّ فِى ذَٰلِكَ لَءَايَةً لِّقَوْمٍ يَذَّكَّرُونَ ۝ وَهُوَ ٱلَّذِى سَخَّرَ ٱلْبَحْرَ لِتَأْكُلُوا۟ مِنْهُ لَحْمًا طَرِيًّا وَتَسْتَخْرِجُوا۟ مِنْهُ حِلْيَةً تَلْبَسُونَهَاۖ وَتَرَى ٱلْفُلْكَ مَوَاخِرَ فِيهِ وَلِتَبْتَغُوا۟ مِن فَضْلِهِۦ وَلَعَلَّكُمْ تَشْكُرُونَ ۝ وَأَلْقَىٰ فِى ٱلْأَرْضِ رَوَٰسِىَ أَن تَمِيدَ بِكُمْ وَأَنْهَٰرًا وَسُبُلًا لَّعَلَّكُمْ تَهْتَدُونَ ۝ وَعَلَٰمَٰتٍۚ وَبِٱلنَّجْمِ هُمْ يَهْتَدُونَ ۝ أَفَمَن يَخْلُقُ كَمَن لَّا يَخْلُقُۗ أَفَلَا تَذَكَّرُونَ ۝ وَإِن تَعُدُّوا۟ نِعْمَةَ ٱللَّهِ لَا تُحْصُوهَآۗ إِنَّ ٱللَّهَ لَغَفُورٌ رَّحِيمٌ ۝ وَٱللَّهُ يَعْلَمُ مَا تُسِرُّونَ وَمَا تُعْلِنُونَ ۝ وَٱلَّذِينَ يَدْعُونَ مِن دُونِ ٱللَّهِ لَا يَخْلُقُونَ شَيْـًٔا وَهُمْ يُخْلَقُونَ ۝ أَمْوَٰتٌ غَيْرُ أَحْيَآءٍۖ وَمَا يَشْعُرُونَ أَيَّانَ يُبْعَثُونَ ۝

With it He causes vegetation to sprout for your benefit: olives, palms and vines, and all types of fruit. In this is a sign for a people who reflect. He made the night to serve you as also the day, the sun, the moon and the stars – all are made to serve by His command. In these are signs for a people who un-

derstand. *Behold what He created for you on earth, diverse in color. In this is a sign for a people who remember. It is He Who made the sea to serve you so that you may eat from it soft flesh and extract from it jewelry for you to wear. Therein you can see ships ploughing through the waves, that you may seek of His bounty – perchance you will give thanks. He cast upon the earth towering mountains, lest it should shake you violently, and rivers and highways – perhaps you will be guided aright, and waymarks; and by the stars they are guided. Is He who creates as he who does not create? Will you not remember? If you were to count Allah's blessings, you could not take stock of them. Allah is All-Forgiving, Compassionate to each. And Allah knows what you conceal and what you do openly. And those they call upon, apart from Allah, created nothing, and themselves are created, dead, not alive; and are not aware when they shall be raised.*

11-21 Interdependence between humans and animals occurs at the body, heart, and emotional levels. However, earthly desires can never be fully satisfied due to the nature of the ever-discontent lower self. Reflecting upon our earthly life will show us the connection and intricate link between the seen and unseen, heaven and earth: how water gives life to all, the interchange between day and night, and the infinite varieties of plants, colours, and flavours. The purpose of life is to be awakened to the existence of the *One*, to be enlightened by the *One* through the light of our soul. Those who are not on this path of awakening are considered 'spiritually dead', unaware of their true state.

It is a great gift for us to reflect upon all the bounty of goodness around us, including the joy and pleasure that we get from the beauty and majesty of creation. Our drive to understand the smallest entities in creation takes us to a point beyond reason and discernment, which reflects the infinite vastness of the cosmos.

The interactivity of creation – physical, material, earthly, as well as the unseen and heavenly – is beckoning us human beings to experience wonderment about the way they link together and the patterns they set for us.

22-30 إِلَٰهُكُمْ إِلَٰهٌ وَٰحِدٌ فَٱلَّذِينَ لَا يُؤْمِنُونَ بِٱلْآخِرَةِ قُلُوبُهُم مُّنكِرَةٌ وَهُم مُّسْتَكْبِرُونَ ۝ لَا جَرَمَ أَنَّ ٱللَّهَ يَعْلَمُ مَا يُسِرُّونَ وَمَا يُعْلِنُونَ إِنَّهُۥ لَا يُحِبُّ ٱلْمُسْتَكْبِرِينَ ۝ وَإِذَا قِيلَ لَهُم مَّاذَآ أَنزَلَ رَبُّكُمْ قَالُوٓا۟ أَسَٰطِيرُ ٱلْأَوَّلِينَ ۝ لِيَحْمِلُوٓا۟ أَوْزَارَهُمْ كَامِلَةً يَوْمَ ٱلْقِيَٰمَةِ وَمِنْ أَوْزَارِ ٱلَّذِينَ يُضِلُّونَهُم بِغَيْرِ عِلْمٍ أَلَا سَآءَ مَا يَزِرُونَ ۝ قَدْ مَكَرَ ٱلَّذِينَ مِن قَبْلِهِمْ فَأَتَى ٱللَّهُ بُنْيَٰنَهُم مِّنَ ٱلْقَوَاعِدِ فَخَرَّ عَلَيْهِمُ ٱلسَّقْفُ مِن فَوْقِهِمْ وَأَتَىٰهُمُ ٱلْعَذَابُ مِنْ حَيْثُ لَا يَشْعُرُونَ ۝ ثُمَّ يَوْمَ ٱلْقِيَٰمَةِ يُخْزِيهِمْ وَيَقُولُ أَيْنَ شُرَكَآءِىَ ٱلَّذِينَ كُنتُمْ تُشَٰقُّونَ فِيهِمْ قَالَ ٱلَّذِينَ أُوتُوا۟ ٱلْعِلْمَ إِنَّ ٱلْخِزْىَ ٱلْيَوْمَ وَٱلسُّوٓءَ عَلَى ٱلْكَٰفِرِينَ ۝ ٱلَّذِينَ تَتَوَفَّىٰهُمُ ٱلْمَلَٰٓئِكَةُ ظَالِمِىٓ أَنفُسِهِمْ فَأَلْقَوُا۟ ٱلسَّلَمَ مَا كُنَّا نَعْمَلُ مِن سُوٓءٍ بَلَىٰٓ إِنَّ ٱللَّهَ عَلِيمٌۢ بِمَا كُنتُمْ تَعْمَلُونَ ۝ فَٱدْخُلُوٓا۟ أَبْوَٰبَ

$$\text{جَهَنَّمَ خَالِدِينَ فِيهَا ۖ فَلَبِئْسَ مَثْوَى ٱلْمُتَكَبِّرِينَ ۝ وَقِيلَ لِلَّذِينَ ٱتَّقَوْا۟ مَاذَآ أَنزَلَ رَبُّكُمْ ۚ قَالُوا۟ خَيْرًا ۗ لِّلَّذِينَ أَحْسَنُوا۟ فِى هَٰذِهِ ٱلدُّنْيَا حَسَنَةٌ ۚ وَلَدَارُ ٱلْءَاخِرَةِ خَيْرٌ ۚ وَلَنِعْمَ دَارُ ٱلْمُتَّقِينَ ۝}$$

Your Allah is the One Allah. As for those who deny the life to come, their hearts refuse to admit the truth and they are arrogant. There is no doubt that Allah knows what they conceal and what they reveal. He does not love the arrogant. And if it is said to them: 'What has your Lord sent down?' They answer: 'Fables of the ancients.' So let them shoulder their burdens in full on the Day of Resurrection, as also the burdens of those whom they lead astray, without knowledge. Wretched indeed is the burden they carry! Those that were before them contrived; then Allah came upon their building from the foundations, and the roof fell down on them from over them, and the chastisement came upon them from whence they were not aware. Then, on the Day of Resurrection, He shall humiliate them and ask: 'Where are My associates concerning whom you used to dispute?' Those granted knowledge shall say: 'Today humiliation and evil are the lot of the unbelievers.' Those whose lives the angels take while they are wronging themselves will show submission: 'We were doing no evil. Yes, you were: Allah knows fully everything that you have done. So, enter through the gates of hell, dwelling therein eternally. Wretched is the resting place of the arrogant!' And it shall be said to the cautiously aware, 'What has your Lord sent down?' They will say, 'Good!' For those who do good in this world good; and surely the abode of the world to come is better; excellent is the abode of the cautiously aware.

22-30 Through higher consciousness we reach the original Essence – Allah – which permeates the known and unknown in the universe. To realise this divine presence and governance we need to transcend the world and be with the light of the soul within the heart, free of arrogance and pride. Belief in the hereafter as well as a natural awareness and acceptance of death help to reduce pride and arrogance in this life and ignorance of eternal life. Hell is the abode of total darkness, loss and regrets; its doors beckon to those who are not illuminated by God-consciousness.

Numerous peoples and nations have come before. Through their traces we can discover the extent of their contribution to life on earth. The ultimate test of durability and goodness is that which helps creation to rise in consciousness towards its intended destiny. If we do not strive toward the ultimate light, we will be engulfed in darkness in this world and the hereafter.

The nature of human consciousness is such that we need to care for our sustenance and survival, but even more so about the nature of higher consciousness and the unseen towards which we are all travelling after death. We are here on earth to be prepared for the amazing, boundless, intense nature of what we will all face then.

جَنَّٰتُ عَدْنٍ يَدْخُلُونَهَا تَجْرِى مِن تَحْتِهَا ٱلْأَنْهَٰرُ لَهُمْ فِيهَا مَا يَشَآءُونَ كَذَٰلِكَ يَجْزِى ٱللَّهُ ٱلْمُتَّقِينَ ۝ ٱلَّذِينَ تَتَوَفَّىٰهُمُ ٱلْمَلَٰٓئِكَةُ طَيِّبِينَ يَقُولُونَ سَلَٰمٌ عَلَيْكُمُ ٱدْخُلُوا۟ ٱلْجَنَّةَ بِمَا كُنتُمْ تَعْمَلُونَ ۝ هَلْ يَنظُرُونَ إِلَّآ أَن تَأْتِيَهُمُ ٱلْمَلَٰٓئِكَةُ أَوْ يَأْتِىَ أَمْرُ رَبِّكَ كَذَٰلِكَ فَعَلَ ٱلَّذِينَ مِن قَبْلِهِمْ وَمَا ظَلَمَهُمُ ٱللَّهُ وَلَٰكِن كَانُوٓا۟ أَنفُسَهُمْ يَظْلِمُونَ ۝ فَأَصَابَهُمْ سَيِّـَٔاتُ مَا عَمِلُوا۟ وَحَاقَ بِهِم مَّا كَانُوا۟ بِهِۦ يَسْتَهْزِءُونَ ۝ وَقَالَ ٱلَّذِينَ أَشْرَكُوا۟ لَوْ شَآءَ ٱللَّهُ مَا عَبَدْنَا مِن دُونِهِۦ مِن شَىْءٍ نَّحْنُ وَلَآ ءَابَآؤُنَا وَلَا حَرَّمْنَا مِن دُونِهِۦ مِن شَىْءٍ كَذَٰلِكَ فَعَلَ ٱلَّذِينَ مِن قَبْلِهِمْ فَهَلْ عَلَى ٱلرُّسُلِ إِلَّا ٱلْبَلَٰغُ ٱلْمُبِينُ ۝ وَلَقَدْ بَعَثْنَا فِى كُلِّ أُمَّةٍ رَّسُولًا أَنِ ٱعْبُدُوا۟ ٱللَّهَ وَٱجْتَنِبُوا۟ ٱلطَّٰغُوتَ فَمِنْهُم مَّنْ هَدَى ٱللَّهُ وَمِنْهُم مَّنْ حَقَّتْ عَلَيْهِ ٱلضَّلَٰلَةُ فَسِيرُوا۟ فِى ٱلْأَرْضِ فَٱنظُرُوا۟ كَيْفَ كَانَ عَٰقِبَةُ ٱلْمُكَذِّبِينَ ۝ إِن تَحْرِصْ عَلَىٰ هُدَىٰهُمْ فَإِنَّ ٱللَّهَ لَا يَهْدِى مَن يُضِلُّ وَمَا لَهُم مِّن نَّٰصِرِينَ ۝ وَأَقْسَمُوا۟ بِٱللَّهِ جَهْدَ أَيْمَٰنِهِمْ لَا يَبْعَثُ ٱللَّهُ مَن يَمُوتُ بَلَىٰ وَعْدًا عَلَيْهِ حَقًّا وَلَٰكِنَّ أَكْثَرَ ٱلنَّاسِ لَا يَعْلَمُونَ ۝

The gardens of perpetuity, they shall enter them, rivers flowing beneath them; they shall have in them what they please. Thus does Allah reward those who are cautiously aware. Whom the angels take while they are goodly, saying, 'Peace be on you! Enter Paradise for that you were doing.' Do they look for aught but that the angels shall come to them, or your Lord's command shall come? So did those before them, and Allah wronged them not, but themselves they wronged. So, the evil they had done hit them and they were surrounded by the very thing they had mocked. Those who associate others with Allah say: 'Had Allah willed, we would not have worshipped anything apart from Him, neither us nor our ancestors, nor would we have sanctified anything apart from Him.' This too is how men before them used to act. Are messengers enjoined to do anything other than deliver a manifest message? To every nation We sent a messenger: 'Worship Allah and keep away from idol worship.' Some of them Allah guided aright; some deserved to be led astray. So, journey in the land and observe how the fate of the deniers turned out. Even though you may be concerned that they be guided aright, Allah guides not whomever He leads astray, nor shall they have any advocate. They swore a mighty oath that Allah does not resurrect the dead. Yes indeed! Truly a promise He shall keep! But most of mankind do not understand.

31-38 Those who are awakened to truth experience aspects of paradise on earth before dwelling there in the hereafter. This state of joy without needs, desires, fear, or sorrow is only achieved through the divine light of *Oneness* through the perfect soul. To turn away from the lower self towards the soul and divine light is the message of all prophets. To trust in cosmic *Oneness* and divine guidance and avoid the pitfalls of ego-darkness is a precondition for spiritual progress and fulfilment of our earthly duties.

4. Surah 16 An-Nahl (The Bee)

The ultimate step in awakening is to see all dualities and multiplicities clearly emerging from *Oneness* and returning to it. We shall suffer from fears and sorrows if we do not awaken to the truth of *Oneness* that governs the entire universe.

As humans, we are given a certain leeway to act according to what we think is conducive. In reality, unless we connect our will with the divine will, there will always be regret, sorrow, and fear. Our purpose in life is to live with faith, with the trust that Allah is in charge at every level.

39-50 لِيُبَيِّنَ لَهُمُ ٱلَّذِى يَخْتَلِفُونَ فِيهِ وَلِيَعْلَمَ ٱلَّذِينَ كَفَرُوٓاْ أَنَّهُمْ كَانُواْ كَٰذِبِينَ ۞ إِنَّمَا قَوْلُنَا لِشَىْءٍ إِذَآ أَرَدْنَٰهُ أَن نَّقُولَ لَهُۥ كُن فَيَكُونُ ۞ وَٱلَّذِينَ هَاجَرُواْ فِى ٱللَّهِ مِنۢ بَعْدِ مَا ظُلِمُواْ لَنُبَوِّئَنَّهُمْ فِى ٱلدُّنْيَا حَسَنَةً ۖ وَلَأَجْرُ ٱلْءَاخِرَةِ أَكْبَرُ ۚ لَوْ كَانُواْ يَعْلَمُونَ ۞ ٱلَّذِينَ صَبَرُواْ وَعَلَىٰ رَبِّهِمْ يَتَوَكَّلُونَ ۞ وَمَآ أَرْسَلْنَا مِن قَبْلِكَ إِلَّا رِجَالًا نُّوحِىٓ إِلَيْهِمْ ۚ فَسْـَٔلُوٓاْ أَهْلَ ٱلذِّكْرِ إِن كُنتُمْ لَا تَعْلَمُونَ ۞ بِٱلْبَيِّنَٰتِ وَٱلزُّبُرِ ۗ وَأَنزَلْنَآ إِلَيْكَ ٱلذِّكْرَ لِتُبَيِّنَ لِلنَّاسِ مَا نُزِّلَ إِلَيْهِمْ وَلَعَلَّهُمْ يَتَفَكَّرُونَ ۞ أَفَأَمِنَ ٱلَّذِينَ مَكَرُواْ ٱلسَّيِّـَٔاتِ أَن يَخْسِفَ ٱللَّهُ بِهِمُ ٱلْأَرْضَ أَوْ يَأْتِيَهُمُ ٱلْعَذَابُ مِنْ حَيْثُ لَا يَشْعُرُونَ ۞ أَوْ يَأْخُذَهُمْ فِى تَقَلُّبِهِمْ فَمَا هُم بِمُعْجِزِينَ ۞ أَوْ يَأْخُذَهُمْ عَلَىٰ تَخَوُّفٍ فَإِنَّ رَبَّكُمْ لَرَءُوفٌ رَّحِيمٌ ۞ أَوَلَمْ يَرَوْاْ إِلَىٰ مَا خَلَقَ ٱللَّهُ مِن شَىْءٍ يَتَفَيَّؤُاْ ظِلَٰلُهُۥ عَنِ ٱلْيَمِينِ وَٱلشَّمَآئِلِ سُجَّدًا لِّلَّهِ وَهُمْ دَٰخِرُونَ ۞ وَلِلَّهِ يَسْجُدُ مَا فِى ٱلسَّمَٰوَٰتِ وَمَا فِى ٱلْأَرْضِ مِن دَآبَّةٍ وَٱلْمَلَٰٓئِكَةُ وَهُمْ لَا يَسْتَكْبِرُونَ ۞ يَخَافُونَ رَبَّهُم مِّن فَوْقِهِمْ وَيَفْعَلُونَ مَا يُؤْمَرُونَ ۞

He shall make clear to them what once they argued about, and so the unbelievers will come to admit that they are liars. The only words We say to a thing, when We desire it, is that We say to it 'Be,' and it is. As for those who emigrated in the cause of Allah, after they had been wronged, We shall settle them in this world in a good abode, but the reward of the hereafter is greater, if only they knew; those who are patient and on their Lord do they rely. We sent not before you save men to whom We revealed – ask the People who possess the Remembrance, if you yourselves do not know, clear signs and the Psalms. Upon you We sent down the Remembrance, to make clear to mankind what has been sent down to them – perhaps they will reflect. Those who work their cunning in evil deeds – do they feel secure that Allah will not make the earth cave in up- on them? Nor that a torment will seize them from where they had not expected? Nor seize them as they travel to and fro? They cannot escape Him. Or might He seize them while in a state of fearful expectancy? Your Lord is All-Tender, Compassionate to each. Have they not observed all the things Allah has created? How they cast their shadows left and right, bowing to Allah in humility? To Allah prostrate what are in the heavens and earth of things that tread the ground, as also the angels, who display no arrogance. They fear their Lord above them, and they do what they are commanded.

39-50 To become aware of the base human needs for survival and increased awareness is wise, a necessary step towards subduing the lower self in order to access the light of the soul. This journey from the head to heart, or mind to soul, is necessary for everyone on the path of spiritual awakening. Also, we need patience and appropriate conduct, as learnt from wise and illuminated beings. The universe is in a state of utter dependence on local and cosmic forces emanating from the *Source*. Humanity can choose to discard the illusions of independence and choice in action without reference to divine authorship or to follow the narrow and defined path of reference to the *Source* and avoid the pitfalls of the lower self.

Whatever is in heavens and earth follows an intended pattern towards its ultimate destiny. The intelligent human being will always leave behind what was not conducive for a quality life led in a durable and easy way. If we do not flow along the divine, intended light, we will suffer and live in regret.

In childhood we think we can do anything at any time, but with wisdom and experience, we have fewer options, until such time, with awakening, we know there is no option other than doing what is appropriate and has already been decreed so that we have no regrets or fears. That is how we can be at the point of full presence and awareness, in touch with what is eternally present, the divine light.

51-61 وَقَالَ ٱللَّهُ لَا تَتَّخِذُوٓا۟ إِلَٰهَيْنِ ٱثْنَيْنِ إِنَّمَا هُوَ إِلَٰهٌ وَٰحِدٌ فَإِيَّٰىَ فَٱرْهَبُونِ ۞ وَلَهُۥ مَا فِى ٱلسَّمَٰوَٰتِ وَٱلْأَرْضِ وَلَهُ ٱلدِّينُ وَاصِبًا أَفَغَيْرَ ٱللَّهِ تَتَّقُونَ ۞ وَمَا بِكُم مِّن نِّعْمَةٍ فَمِنَ ٱللَّهِ ثُمَّ إِذَا مَسَّكُمُ ٱلضُّرُّ فَإِلَيْهِ تَجْـَٔرُونَ ۞ ثُمَّ إِذَا كَشَفَ ٱلضُّرَّ عَنكُمْ إِذَا فَرِيقٌ مِّنكُم بِرَبِّهِمْ يُشْرِكُونَ ۞ لِيَكْفُرُوا۟ بِمَآ ءَاتَيْنَٰهُمْ فَتَمَتَّعُوا۟ فَسَوْفَ تَعْلَمُونَ ۞ وَيَجْعَلُونَ لِمَا لَا يَعْلَمُونَ نَصِيبًا مِّمَّا رَزَقْنَٰهُمْ تَٱللَّهِ لَتُسْـَٔلُنَّ عَمَّا كُنتُمْ تَفْتَرُونَ ۞ وَيَجْعَلُونَ لِلَّهِ ٱلْبَنَٰتِ سُبْحَٰنَهُۥ وَلَهُم مَّا يَشْتَهُونَ ۞ وَإِذَا بُشِّرَ أَحَدُهُم بِٱلْأُنثَىٰ ظَلَّ وَجْهُهُۥ مُسْوَدًّا وَهُوَ كَظِيمٌ ۞ يَتَوَٰرَىٰ مِنَ ٱلْقَوْمِ مِن سُوٓءِ مَا بُشِّرَ بِهِۦٓ أَيُمْسِكُهُۥ عَلَىٰ هُونٍ أَمْ يَدُسُّهُۥ فِى ٱلتُّرَابِ أَلَا سَآءَ مَا يَحْكُمُونَ ۞ لِلَّذِينَ لَا يُؤْمِنُونَ بِٱلْـَٔاخِرَةِ مَثَلُ ٱلسَّوْءِ وَلِلَّهِ ٱلْمَثَلُ ٱلْأَعْلَىٰ وَهُوَ ٱلْعَزِيزُ ٱلْحَكِيمُ ۞ وَلَوْ يُؤَاخِذُ ٱللَّهُ ٱلنَّاسَ بِظُلْمِهِم مَّا تَرَكَ عَلَيْهَا مِن دَآبَّةٍ وَلَٰكِن يُؤَخِّرُهُمْ إِلَىٰٓ أَجَلٍ مُّسَمًّى فَإِذَا جَآءَ أَجَلُهُمْ لَا يَسْتَـْٔخِرُونَ سَاعَةً وَلَا يَسْتَقْدِمُونَ ۞

Allah says: 'Take not to you two Allah's. He is only One Allah; so, have awe of Me.' Everything in the heavens and earth belongs to Him: everlasting obedience is His right. Will you heed anyone other than Allah. Whatsoever blessing you have it comes from Allah; then when affliction visits you it is unto Him that you groan. Then, when He removes the affliction from you, lo, a party of you assign associates to their Lord, that they may show thanklessness for that We have given them. So, take your joy; certainly, you will soon know! And yet they dedicate to what they know not a portion of what We bestowed upon them! By Allah, you shall be questioned concerning the lies you fabricated! And they ascribe daughters to Allah! Glory be to Him! But they shall have what they desire! When one of them is given news of a female, his face darkens and he is filled with gloom. He keeps out of people's sight, because of the evil news he was greeted with. Will he retain the infant, in disgrace, or will he bury it in haste in the ground? Wretched indeed is their decision! To those who do not believe in the hereafter belongs the evil attribute; to Allah belongs the loftiest of attributes. He is All-Mighty, All-Wise. If Allah were to hold mankind to account for their wrongdoing, He would not leave alive one single creature that treads the earth. He merely defers them until a stated time. When their time arrives, they can neither delay it nor bring it forward, even by an instant.

51-61 Human life spans a wide spectrum of consciousness and states, ranging from complete darkness and animal consciousness to full light, awakening, and supreme consciousness. Suffering and discord are due to ignorance and darkness. What we truly desire is grace, which is due to the lights of God-consciousness. We often wrong ourselves by failing to commit to a clear path of vigilant, accountable conduct and behaviour. Our commitment requires faith, trust, and constant reference to the soul-author and divine guidance. Allah's mercy is such that despite our mistakes, we are given repeated opportunities to leave darkness and suffering for the light of divine offering. Punishment as divine justice for our earthly misdeeds is often postponed to give us the opportunity to repent and improve our intentions and actions.

The nature of the lower self is to experience what is desirable here and now, and this reflects the contentment and joy of the soul itself. We need a clear head, mature emotions, and a pure, illumined heart so that our life on earth will be joyful and lead to the perfection of the hereafter.

With intelligence, each of us realises that the truth is what we are seeking and that this *Truth* is ever-present. All of our hopes and expectations are to be connected totally with the moment that is eternal, without denying the short-term life that we are in. More and more we realise that life is eternal and our personal life is not separate from it.

62-70 وَيَجْعَلُونَ لِلَّهِ مَا يَكْرَهُونَ وَتَصِفُ أَلْسِنَتُهُمُ ٱلْكَذِبَ أَنَّ لَهُمُ ٱلْحُسْنَىٰ لَا جَرَمَ أَنَّ لَهُمُ ٱلنَّارَ وَأَنَّهُم مُّفْرَطُونَ ۝ تَٱللَّهِ لَقَدْ أَرْسَلْنَآ إِلَىٰٓ أُمَمٍ مِّن قَبْلِكَ فَزَيَّنَ لَهُمُ ٱلشَّيْطَٰنُ أَعْمَٰلَهُمْ فَهُوَ وَلِيُّهُمُ ٱلْيَوْمَ وَلَهُمْ عَذَابٌ أَلِيمٌ ۝ وَمَآ أَنزَلْنَا عَلَيْكَ ٱلْكِتَٰبَ إِلَّا لِتُبَيِّنَ لَهُمُ ٱلَّذِى ٱخْتَلَفُوا۟ فِيهِ وَهُدًى وَرَحْمَةً لِّقَوْمٍ يُؤْمِنُونَ ۝ وَٱللَّهُ أَنزَلَ مِنَ ٱلسَّمَآءِ مَآءً فَأَحْيَا بِهِ ٱلْأَرْضَ بَعْدَ مَوْتِهَآ إِنَّ فِى ذَٰلِكَ لَءَايَةً لِّقَوْمٍ يَسْمَعُونَ ۝ وَإِنَّ لَكُمْ فِى ٱلْأَنْعَٰمِ لَعِبْرَةً نُّسْقِيكُم مِّمَّا فِى بُطُونِهِۦ مِنۢ بَيْنِ فَرْثٍ وَدَمٍ لَّبَنًا خَالِصًا سَآئِغًا لِّلشَّٰرِبِينَ ۝ وَمِن ثَمَرَٰتِ ٱلنَّخِيلِ وَٱلْأَعْنَٰبِ تَتَّخِذُونَ مِنْهُ سَكَرًا وَرِزْقًا

حَسَنًا إِنَّ فِى ذَٰلِكَ لَآيَةً لِّقَوْمٍ يَعْقِلُونَ ۝ وَأَوْحَىٰ رَبُّكَ إِلَى ٱلنَّحْلِ أَنِ ٱتَّخِذِى مِنَ ٱلْجِبَالِ بُيُوتًا وَمِنَ ٱلشَّجَرِ وَمِمَّا يَعْرِشُونَ ۝ ثُمَّ كُلِى مِن كُلِّ ٱلثَّمَرَٰتِ فَٱسْلُكِى سُبُلَ رَبِّكِ ذُلُلًا يَخْرُجُ مِنۢ بُطُونِهَا شَرَابٌ مُّخْتَلِفٌ أَلْوَٰنُهُ فِيهِ شِفَآءٌ لِّلنَّاسِ إِنَّ فِى ذَٰلِكَ لَآيَةً لِّقَوْمٍ يَتَفَكَّرُونَ ۝ وَٱللَّهُ خَلَقَكُمْ ثُمَّ يَتَوَفَّىٰكُمْ وَمِنكُم مَّن يُرَدُّ إِلَىٰ أَرْذَلِ ٱلْعُمُرِ لِكَىْ لَا يَعْلَمَ بَعْدَ عِلْمٍ شَيْـًٔا إِنَّ ٱللَّهَ عَلِيمٌ قَدِيرٌ ۝

They assign to Allah that they themselves dislike; and their tongues describe falsehood, that the reward most fair shall be theirs. Without any doubt theirs shall be the Fire, and they are hastened in. By Allah, We sent to nations before you, but Satan embellished their deeds in their eyes; so now he is their patron, and there awaits them a painful torment. We sent down the Book upon you only to make clear to them what they disputed about, as a Guidance and a mercy to a people who have faith. And Allah sends down water from the sky by which He revives the earth after it has died. In this is a sign to a people who listen. In cattle too there is a lesson for you. We give you to drink from their entrails, in between the filth and the blood, pure milk, tasty to those who drink. And from the fruit of palm trees and vines you derive intoxicants as well as a goodly provision. In this is a sign for a people who understand. And your Lord inspired the bee, saying, 'Build yourselves houses in the mountains and trees and what people construct. Then eat of all fruits and follow the paths of your Lord, made easy for you.' From their entrails comes a drink, of diverse colors, in which there is a remedy for mankind. In this is a sign for a people who reflect. It is Allah who has created you and in time will cause you to die. Some of you will be reduced, in old age, to a most abject state, so that, after having knowledge, they will know nothing at all: Allah is truly All-Knowing and All-Powerful.

62-70 Sacred books, revelations of prophetic beings, the amazing variety of life on earth, and the interdependence of creation all demonstrate the grace and generosity of God and provide a reminder for us to be clear in mind and pure at heart. From babyhood to maturity, increased awakening and raised consciousness are guided by our interaction with the outer world, our inner reason and light, and the divine will to be illuminated by *Truth*. Our life on earth is a preparation for the eternal state of the hereafter, where we lose body, mind, and all ability to act or mend our ways.

It is natural that we can often be wrong, and it is divine mercy that we are allowed to carry on before the reaction to our wrong action takes place. Allah's grace is upon all of creation, giving us numerous opportunities to rise in consciousness and touch the higher lights transmitted by our own soul.

Life has emerged from the unseen, bringing to life what was considered to be dead. Once an entity is touched by life, it becomes obsessed with it, because life is the most magnificent, invaluable gift. The truth of that gift is that life is eternal. Once it becomes personalised and identified with an animal with a beginning and an end, then all the other anxieties, fears and concerns arise.

71-77 وَٱللَّهُ فَضَّلَ بَعْضَكُمْ عَلَىٰ بَعْضٍ فِى ٱلرِّزْقِ ۚ فَمَا ٱلَّذِينَ فُضِّلُوا۟ بِرَآدِّى رِزْقِهِمْ عَلَىٰ مَا مَلَكَتْ أَيْمَٰنُهُمْ فَهُمْ فِيهِ سَوَآءٌ ۚ أَفَبِنِعْمَةِ ٱللَّهِ يَجْحَدُونَ ۝ وَٱللَّهُ جَعَلَ لَكُم مِّنْ أَنفُسِكُمْ أَزْوَٰجًا وَجَعَلَ لَكُم مِّنْ أَزْوَٰجِكُم بَنِينَ وَحَفَدَةً وَرَزَقَكُم مِّنَ ٱلطَّيِّبَٰتِ ۚ أَفَبِٱلْبَٰطِلِ يُؤْمِنُونَ وَبِنِعْمَتِ ٱللَّهِ هُمْ يَكْفُرُونَ ۝ وَيَعْبُدُونَ مِن دُونِ ٱللَّهِ مَا لَا يَمْلِكُ لَهُمْ رِزْقًا مِّنَ ٱلسَّمَٰوَٰتِ وَٱلْأَرْضِ شَيْـًٔا وَلَا يَسْتَطِيعُونَ ۝ فَلَا تَضْرِبُوا۟ لِلَّهِ ٱلْأَمْثَالَ ۚ إِنَّ ٱللَّهَ يَعْلَمُ وَأَنتُمْ لَا تَعْلَمُونَ ۝ ضَرَبَ ٱللَّهُ مَثَلًا عَبْدًا مَّمْلُوكًا لَّا يَقْدِرُ عَلَىٰ شَىْءٍ وَمَن رَّزَقْنَٰهُ مِنَّا رِزْقًا حَسَنًا فَهُوَ يُنفِقُ مِنْهُ سِرًّا وَجَهْرًا ۖ هَلْ يَسْتَوُۥنَ ۚ ٱلْحَمْدُ لِلَّهِ ۚ بَلْ أَكْثَرُهُمْ لَا يَعْلَمُونَ ۝ وَضَرَبَ ٱللَّهُ مَثَلًا رَّجُلَيْنِ أَحَدُهُمَآ أَبْكَمُ لَا يَقْدِرُ عَلَىٰ شَىْءٍ وَهُوَ كَلٌّ عَلَىٰ مَوْلَىٰهُ أَيْنَمَا يُوَجِّههُّ لَا يَأْتِ بِخَيْرٍ ۖ هَلْ يَسْتَوِى هُوَ وَمَن يَأْمُرُ بِٱلْعَدْلِ ۙ وَهُوَ عَلَىٰ صِرَٰطٍ مُّسْتَقِيمٍ ۝ وَلِلَّهِ غَيْبُ ٱلسَّمَٰوَٰتِ وَٱلْأَرْضِ ۚ وَمَآ أَمْرُ ٱلسَّاعَةِ إِلَّا كَلَمْحِ ٱلْبَصَرِ أَوْ هُوَ أَقْرَبُ ۚ إِنَّ ٱللَّهَ عَلَىٰ كُلِّ شَىْءٍ قَدِيرٌ ۝

Allah has preferred some of you over others in bounty. Those granted preference will not turn over their bounty to their bondsmen, so as to share it in equity. Do they repudiate the blessing of Allah? And it is Allah who has given you spouses from amongst yourselves and through them He has given you children and grandchildren and provided you with good things. How can they believe in falsehood and deny Allah's blessings? And yet they worship, instead of Allah, that which has no provision whatever to grant them, in heaven or on earth! Nor are they able to do so! So, strike not any similitudes for Allah; surely Allah knows, and you know not. Allah strikes a simile: a bonded slave who has no power over anything, and a person whom We granted a goodly provision, from which he expends in secret and in the open. Are these two equal? Praise be to Allah! But most of them have no knowledge. Allah strikes a simile of two men: one is dumb with no power over anything, and is a burden to his guardian. Wherever he sends him, he brings back nothing good. Is such the equal of one who commands justice and is set upon a straight path? To Allah belongs the Unseen in the heavens and in the earth. And the matter of the Hour is as a twinkling of the eye, or nearer. Surely Allah is powerful over everything.

71-77 In the outer world, no two beings or two moments are ever the same. There is always change. Our inner state is also in flux according to its clarity and purity. We experience the situation we are according to how our inner state interacts with the outer world. Our sensory experiences and mind offer us only a small sample of the patterns of *Reality* emanating from the divine light of the *Real*. Whoever refers to supreme consciousness and God's light will move from the usual confusion of discordant signals towards better understanding of creational patterns and limits. To be free from the ever-changing demands and desires of the lower self and ego, we need to commit to the prophetic path.

We cannot survive without other people, though we also suffer from the enmity, envy, and jealousy of others. When one truly follows the light of one's own heart, then one is spared from being confused about one's direction due to opposing attractions and fears.

Life is absolute and timeless and not confined to any space. But once it has emerged on earth within time and space, it always appears in dualities, as one of two. Whoever experiences life with higher intelligence, desires to reach a point of its original *Oneness*. This stops the possible confusion of dualities, which are always complimentary and in opposition. The nature of the *ruh* is one and divine, and the nature of the *nafs* is twos. So, our life is a challenging process of connecting our humanity with what gives us life – connecting through patience, compassion, and all of the other qualities and attributes of the divine.

78-86

وَٱللَّهُ أَخْرَجَكُم مِّنۢ بُطُونِ أُمَّهَٰتِكُمْ لَا تَعْلَمُونَ شَيْـًٔا وَجَعَلَ لَكُمُ ٱلسَّمْعَ وَٱلْأَبْصَٰرَ وَٱلْأَفْـِٔدَةَ لَعَلَّكُمْ تَشْكُرُونَ ۝ أَلَمْ يَرَوْاْ إِلَى ٱلطَّيْرِ مُسَخَّرَٰتٍ فِى جَوِّ ٱلسَّمَآءِ مَا يُمْسِكُهُنَّ إِلَّا ٱللَّهُ إِنَّ فِى ذَٰلِكَ لَءَايَٰتٍ لِّقَوْمٍ يُؤْمِنُونَ ۝ وَٱللَّهُ جَعَلَ لَكُم مِّنۢ بُيُوتِكُمْ سَكَنًا وَجَعَلَ لَكُم مِّن جُلُودِ ٱلْأَنْعَٰمِ بُيُوتًا تَسْتَخِفُّونَهَا يَوْمَ ظَعْنِكُمْ وَيَوْمَ إِقَامَتِكُمْ وَمِنْ أَصْوَافِهَا وَأَوْبَارِهَا وَأَشْعَارِهَآ أَثَٰثًا وَمَتَٰعًا إِلَىٰ حِينٍ ۝ وَٱللَّهُ جَعَلَ لَكُم مِّمَّا خَلَقَ ظِلَٰلًا وَجَعَلَ لَكُم مِّنَ ٱلْجِبَالِ أَكْنَٰنًا وَجَعَلَ لَكُمْ سَرَٰبِيلَ تَقِيكُمُ ٱلْحَرَّ وَسَرَٰبِيلَ تَقِيكُم بَأْسَكُمْ كَذَٰلِكَ يُتِمُّ نِعْمَتَهُۥ عَلَيْكُمْ لَعَلَّكُمْ تُسْلِمُونَ ۝ فَإِن تَوَلَّوْاْ فَإِنَّمَا عَلَيْكَ ٱلْبَلَٰغُ ٱلْمُبِينُ ۝ يَعْرِفُونَ نِعْمَتَ ٱللَّهِ ثُمَّ يُنكِرُونَهَا وَأَكْثَرُهُمُ ٱلْكَٰفِرُونَ ۝ وَيَوْمَ نَبْعَثُ مِن كُلِّ أُمَّةٍ شَهِيدًا ثُمَّ لَا يُؤْذَنُ لِلَّذِينَ كَفَرُواْ وَلَا هُمْ يُسْتَعْتَبُونَ ۝ وَإِذَا رَءَا ٱلَّذِينَ ظَلَمُواْ ٱلْعَذَابَ فَلَا يُخَفَّفُ عَنْهُمْ وَلَا هُمْ يُنظَرُونَ ۝ وَإِذَا رَءَا ٱلَّذِينَ أَشْرَكُواْ شُرَكَآءَهُمْ قَالُواْ رَبَّنَا هَٰٓؤُلَآءِ شُرَكَآؤُنَا ٱلَّذِينَ كُنَّا نَدْعُواْ مِن دُونِكَ فَأَلْقَوْاْ إِلَيْهِمُ ٱلْقَوْلَ إِنَّكُمْ لَكَٰذِبُونَ ۝

It is Allah who brought you out of your mothers' wombs knowing nothing, and gave you hearing and sight and hearts, so that you might be thankful. Have they not observed the birds, made subservient in the sphere of the sky, whom only Allah can control? In this are signs for a people of faith. It is Allah Who made your homes to be places of rest, Who made for you of cattle-skins tents you find light to carry when you travel and where you put up; and from their wool, furs, and hair furnishings and enjoyment, for a while. It is Allah Who made for you, among what He created, the shades, and made the mountains for you places wherein to hide, and made for you shirts to protect you from the heat, and other shirts to protect you in battle. Thus, does He complete His bounty upon you; perhaps you will submit to Him. If they turn away, yours is only to convey a manifest message. They are fully aware of Allah's blessings, but none the less they refuse to acknowledge them, since most of them are given to denying the truth. But one Day We shall raise up a witness out of every community, whereupon they who were bent on denying the truth will not be allowed to plead, and neither will they be allowed to make amends. And when the evildoers behold the chastisement, it shall not be lightened for them, and no respite shall be given them. When those who associate catch sight of their associates, they shall say: 'Our Lord, these are our associates whom we used to worship instead of You.' And these shall retort: 'You are indeed liars.'

78-86 The foundation of the journey in higher consciousness is to connect mind and heart, the light of reason with the light of the soul. We must practice reflecting upon our earthly existence, how everything has a beginning and an end, and how all creation is equipped with what it needs to support its life on earth. This may lead us to trust in the perfection and completion of the patterns that rule existence and the universe. Our life on earth is the practice to live either a life of goodness and joy or a life of fear, sorrow, and discord. Our physical earthly life drives us to care and provide for survival, as well as to avoid suffering and sorrow in anticipation of the perfect state of the hereafter.

It is a big gift upon us to reflect upon and draw meaning from events that occur in our journey on earth. We receive comfort, ease, and food from material life and sustenance as well as the emotional pleasure from other more subtle experiences.

Human life emerges from the unseen in numerous stages, the last one of which is the emergence from the mother's womb. Then comes the rise of consciousness during the first few years of one's life followed by the rise of numerous other levels of intelligence, such as reason and perspective. Finally, we awaken to the truth that all we experience are shadows illuminated by the light of the soul itself, which is divine.

87-93 وَأَلْقَوْاْ إِلَى ٱللَّهِ يَوْمَئِذٍ ٱلسَّلَمَ وَضَلَّ عَنْهُم مَّا كَانُواْ يَفْتَرُونَ ۝ ٱلَّذِينَ كَفَرُواْ وَصَدُّواْ عَن سَبِيلِ ٱللَّهِ زِدْنَٰهُمْ عَذَابًا فَوْقَ ٱلْعَذَابِ بِمَا كَانُواْ يُفْسِدُونَ ۝ وَيَوْمَ نَبْعَثُ فِى كُلِّ أُمَّةٍ شَهِيدًا عَلَيْهِم مِّنْ أَنفُسِهِمْ وَجِئْنَا بِكَ شَهِيدًا عَلَىٰ هَٰٓؤُلَآءِ وَنَزَّلْنَا عَلَيْكَ ٱلْكِتَٰبَ تِبْيَٰنًا لِّكُلِّ شَىْءٍ وَهُدًى وَرَحْمَةً وَبُشْرَىٰ لِلْمُسْلِمِينَ ۝ إِنَّ ٱللَّهَ يَأْمُرُ بِٱلْعَدْلِ وَٱلْإِحْسَٰنِ وَإِيتَآئِ ذِى ٱلْقُرْبَىٰ وَيَنْهَىٰ عَنِ ٱلْفَحْشَآءِ وَٱلْمُنكَرِ وَٱلْبَغْىِ يَعِظُكُمْ لَعَلَّكُمْ تَذَكَّرُونَ ۝ وَأَوْفُواْ بِعَهْدِ ٱللَّهِ إِذَا عَٰهَدتُّمْ وَلَا تَنقُضُواْ ٱلْأَيْمَٰنَ بَعْدَ تَوْكِيدِهَا وَقَدْ جَعَلْتُمُ ٱللَّهَ عَلَيْكُمْ كَفِيلًا إِنَّ ٱللَّهَ يَعْلَمُ مَا تَفْعَلُونَ ۝ وَلَا تَكُونُواْ كَٱلَّتِى نَقَضَتْ غَزْلَهَا مِنۢ بَعْدِ قُوَّةٍ أَنكَٰثًا تَتَّخِذُونَ أَيْمَٰنَكُمْ دَخَلًۢا بَيْنَكُمْ أَن تَكُونَ أُمَّةٌ هِىَ أَرْبَىٰ مِنْ أُمَّةٍ إِنَّمَا يَبْلُوكُمُ ٱللَّهُ بِهِۦ

وَلِيُبَيِّنَ لَكُمْ يَوْمَ ٱلْقِيَٰمَةِ مَا كُنتُمْ فِيهِ تَخْتَلِفُونَ ۝ وَلَوْ شَآءَ ٱللَّهُ لَجَعَلَكُمْ أُمَّةً وَٰحِدَةً وَلَٰكِن يُضِلُّ مَن يَشَآءُ وَيَهْدِى مَن يَشَآءُ وَلَتُسْـَٔلُنَّ عَمَّا كُنتُمْ تَعْمَلُونَ ۝

And they will offer Allah surrender that day, and there shall go astray from them that they were forging. Upon all who were bent on denying the truth and who turned others away from the path of Allah will We heap suffering upon suffering in return for all the corruption that they wrought. And the day We shall raise up from every nation a witness against them from amongst them, and We shall bring you as a witness against those. And We have sent down on you the Book making clear everything, and as a guidance and a mercy, and as good tidings to those who surrender. Allah commands justice, virtue and generosity to kin. He forbids debauchery, abomination and injustice. He counsels you; perhaps you will remember. Fulfil Allah's covenant, when you make covenant, and break not the oaths after they have been confirmed, and you have made Allah your surety; surely Allah knows the things you do. And be not like her who unravels her yarn, disintegrating it into pieces after she has spun it strongly. You make your oaths to be means of deceit between you because one nation is more numerous than another nation. Allah only tries you by this; and He will most certainly make clear to you on the resurrection day that about which you differed. Had Allah willed, He would have made you a single nation. But He leads astray whom He wills and guides whom He wills, and you will surely be questioned concerning that which you used to do.

87-93 A healthy earthly journey means to become aware of our thoughts and actions, to be accountable at all times, and to aim for the best intentions and outer actions, referencing the divine justice and governance transmitted by our divine soul. Every soul is encoded with the knowledge of its sacred origin, but we need to recognise and deal with its shadow self or ego. Earthly dualities and differences can serve as an incentive to trace their origin to *Oneness*, if we look for the light of grace. Diversity and differences within humanity are only on the surface. In reality, all of us seek the same goodness of the divine attributes, such as peace, tranquillity, security, and the prophetic path.

It is through intelligence that we rise in consciousness towards the original light of it all. It is due to a lack of intelligence that we remain in confusion and darkness. To be fair, generous, and in balance are necessary conditions for goodness and harmony amongst people.

Various peoples, cultures, religions, and nations are essentially emerging from the same *Oneness*, but diversity is the nature of our worldly duality. This shows us all of the amazing possibilities that exist, whose nature and destiny is the same.

وَلَا تَتَّخِذُوٓاْ أَيْمَٰنَكُمْ دَخَلًۢا بَيْنَكُمْ فَتَزِلَّ قَدَمٌۢ بَعْدَ ثُبُوتِهَا وَتَذُوقُواْ ٱلسُّوٓءَ بِمَا صَدَدتُّمْ عَن سَبِيلِ ٱللَّهِ وَلَكُمْ عَذَابٌ عَظِيمٌ ۝ وَلَا تَشْتَرُواْ بِعَهْدِ ٱللَّهِ ثَمَنًا 94-102

قَلِيلًا إِنَّمَا عِندَ ٱللَّهِ هُوَ خَيْرٌ لَّكُمْ إِن كُنتُمْ تَعْلَمُونَ ۝ مَا عِندَكُمْ يَنفَدُ وَمَا عِندَ ٱللَّهِ بَاقٍ وَلَنَجْزِيَنَّ ٱلَّذِينَ صَبَرُوٓا۟ أَجْرَهُم بِأَحْسَنِ مَا كَانُوا۟ يَعْمَلُونَ ۝ مَنْ عَمِلَ صَٰلِحًا مِّن ذَكَرٍ أَوْ أُنثَىٰ وَهُوَ مُؤْمِنٌ فَلَنُحْيِيَنَّهُۥ حَيَوٰةً طَيِّبَةً وَلَنَجْزِيَنَّهُمْ أَجْرَهُم بِأَحْسَنِ مَا كَانُوا۟ يَعْمَلُونَ ۝ فَإِذَا قَرَأْتَ ٱلْقُرْءَانَ فَٱسْتَعِذْ بِٱللَّهِ مِنَ ٱلشَّيْطَٰنِ ٱلرَّجِيمِ ۝ إِنَّهُۥ لَيْسَ لَهُۥ سُلْطَٰنٌ عَلَى ٱلَّذِينَ ءَامَنُوا۟ وَعَلَىٰ رَبِّهِمْ يَتَوَكَّلُونَ ۝ إِنَّمَا سُلْطَٰنُهُۥ عَلَى ٱلَّذِينَ يَتَوَلَّوْنَهُۥ وَٱلَّذِينَ هُم بِهِۦ مُشْرِكُونَ ۝ وَإِذَا بَدَّلْنَآ ءَايَةً مَّكَانَ ءَايَةٍ وَٱللَّهُ أَعْلَمُ بِمَا يُنَزِّلُ قَالُوٓا۟ إِنَّمَآ أَنتَ مُفْتَرٍۭ بَلْ أَكْثَرُهُمْ لَا يَعْلَمُونَ ۝ قُلْ نَزَّلَهُۥ رُوحُ ٱلْقُدُسِ مِن رَّبِّكَ بِٱلْحَقِّ لِيُثَبِّتَ ٱلَّذِينَ ءَامَنُوا۟ وَهُدًى وَبُشْرَىٰ لِلْمُسْلِمِينَ ۝

Take not your oaths as mere mutual deceit, lest any foot should slip after it has stood firm, and you should taste evil, for that you barred from the way of Allah, and lest there should await you a mighty chastisement. Do not barter the covenant of Allah for a paltry sum. What is with Allah is better for you, if only you knew. What is with you comes to an end, but what is with Allah abides; and surely, We shall recompense those who were patient their wage, according to the best of what they did. Whoever does good, male or female, while having faith, We shall make him live a decent life, and We shall recompense them with their wages, in accordance with the best of their deeds. When you recite the Qur'an, seek Allah's protection from the outcast, Satan. He has no authority over those who believe and trust in their Lord, His authority is over those who take him for their friend and ascribe to him associates. When We substitute one sign for another sign – and Allah knows best what He sends down – they say, 'You are just making it up,' but most of them have no knowledge. Say: 'The Holy Spirit sent it down from thy Lord in truth, and to confirm those who believe, and to be a guidance and good tidings to those who surrender.'

94-102 Our intentions and actions lead us towards higher or lower consciousness. Our hope for a better life can only be realised if we are evolving towards higher knowledge, light, and awareness constantly. Everything we experience on earth will pass; what remains is Allah's domain, which includes the spirit within the heart. The soul knows divine perfection and understands the extent of the lower self and its distractions. Our connection to God is via our soul, which is the doorway to paradise. The more we refer to the ever-present light, the more aligned we are to the path of truth.

In essence, all human beings have the same hope and aspiration: to live the highest quality of life on earth without fear and anxiety about the hereafter. To have faith and belief and then act as best as one can is the correct foundation from which to ascend in consciousness towards enlightenment.

Human consciousness has been touched by the divine light, and as such it can deal with the limitations that come with our normal human nature as well as with the original absolute Light itself, which can only be experienced when everything stops and we disconnect our sensory faculties from the world outside, simply remaining in the sacred silence from which everything emerges.

103-111 وَلَقَدْ نَعْلَمُ أَنَّهُمْ يَقُولُونَ إِنَّمَا يُعَلِّمُهُ بَشَرٌ ۗ لِسَانُ ٱلَّذِى يُلْحِدُونَ إِلَيْهِ أَعْجَمِىٌّ وَهَٰذَا لِسَانٌ عَرَبِىٌّ مُّبِينٌ ۝ إِنَّ ٱلَّذِينَ لَا يُؤْمِنُونَ بِـَٔايَٰتِ ٱللَّهِ لَا يَهْدِيهِمُ ٱللَّهُ وَلَهُمْ عَذَابٌ أَلِيمٌ ۝ إِنَّمَا يَفْتَرِى ٱلْكَذِبَ ٱلَّذِينَ لَا يُؤْمِنُونَ بِـَٔايَٰتِ ٱللَّهِ ۖ وَأُو۟لَٰٓئِكَ هُمُ ٱلْكَٰذِبُونَ ۝ مَن كَفَرَ بِٱللَّهِ مِنۢ بَعْدِ إِيمَٰنِهِۦٓ إِلَّا مَنْ أُكْرِهَ وَقَلْبُهُۥ مُطْمَئِنٌّۢ بِٱلْإِيمَٰنِ وَلَٰكِن مَّن شَرَحَ بِٱلْكُفْرِ صَدْرًا فَعَلَيْهِمْ غَضَبٌ مِّنَ ٱللَّهِ وَلَهُمْ عَذَابٌ عَظِيمٌ ۝ ذَٰلِكَ بِأَنَّهُمُ ٱسْتَحَبُّوا۟ ٱلْحَيَوٰةَ ٱلدُّنْيَا عَلَى ٱلْءَاخِرَةِ وَأَنَّ ٱللَّهَ لَا يَهْدِى ٱلْقَوْمَ ٱلْكَٰفِرِينَ ۝ أُو۟لَٰٓئِكَ ٱلَّذِينَ طَبَعَ ٱللَّهُ عَلَىٰ قُلُوبِهِمْ وَسَمْعِهِمْ وَأَبْصَٰرِهِمْ ۖ وَأُو۟لَٰٓئِكَ هُمُ ٱلْغَٰفِلُونَ ۝ لَا جَرَمَ أَنَّهُمْ فِى ٱلْءَاخِرَةِ هُمُ ٱلْخَٰسِرُونَ ۝ ثُمَّ إِنَّ رَبَّكَ لِلَّذِينَ هَاجَرُوا۟ مِنۢ بَعْدِ مَا فُتِنُوا۟ ثُمَّ جَٰهَدُوا۟ وَصَبَرُوٓا۟ إِنَّ رَبَّكَ مِنۢ بَعْدِهَا لَغَفُورٌ رَّحِيمٌ ۝ يَوْمَ تَأْتِى كُلُّ نَفْسٍ تُجَٰدِلُ عَن نَّفْسِهَا وَتُوَفَّىٰ كُلُّ نَفْسٍ مَّا عَمِلَتْ وَهُمْ لَا يُظْلَمُونَ ۝

We know that they say: 'A mere human is teaching him.' The speech of him to whom they allude is foreign, but this is clear Arabic speech. Those that believe not in the signs of Allah, Allah will not guide; there awaits them a painful chastisement. They only forge falsehood, who believe not in the signs of Allah, and those – they are the liars. As for anyone who denies Allah after having once attained to faith – and this, to be sure, does not apply to one who does it under duress, the while his heart remains true to his faith, but him who willingly opens up his heart to a denial of the truth: upon all such falls Allah's condemnation, and tremendous suffering awaits them: all this, because they hold this world's life in greater esteem than the life to come, and because Allah does not bestow His guidance upon people who deny. It is they whom Allah has put a seal upon their hearts, their hearing and their sight. They are the heedless. No doubt that in the hereafter they will be the losers. Then your Lord – to those who emigrated following the ordeal they suffered, then exerted themselves and bore with patience – to them your Lord shall henceforth be All-Forgiving, Compassionate to each. The day that every soul shall come disputing in its own behalf; and every soul shall be paid in full for what it wrought, and they shall not be wronged.

103-111 Witnessing *Oneness*, with genuine faith and trust in the meaning and purpose of life, we can discern through our own earthly experiences the outer signs as well as their inner meanings. If you love the illusions of the transitory world and its attractions, you are unlikely to access the keys needed to evolve towards higher consciousness. A clear mind and pure heart are necessary for spiritual progress; otherwise, we become distracted and remain in the darkness of ignorance and confusion. With death, one awakens to one's self-inflicted waste and barrenness. That sorrow or regret may be too late for any agreeable outcome. Earthly life is a preparation for an agreeable hereafter.

There will be no guidance without faith, trust, and good action. Without faith, one falls prey to worldly distractions and infatuations that will bring darkness upon the heart, leaving only frivolous pleasures usually accompanied with pain. Allah is All-Forgiving, but it is true repentance that we need to display.

It is through real education in this world that we come to the point of doing our best but trusting in the rest: knowing that the *Master* of the known and the unknown universes is ever-present, and that the perfections of this mastery are always here in this instant. This is faith and trust, by which we live well on this earth and return to the original garden from which we emerged.

112-120 وَضَرَبَ ٱللَّهُ مَثَلًا قَرْيَةً كَانَتْ ءَامِنَةً مُّطْمَئِنَّةً يَأْتِيهَا رِزْقُهَا رَغَدًا مِّن كُلِّ مَكَانٍ فَكَفَرَتْ بِأَنْعُمِ ٱللَّهِ فَأَذَٰقَهَا ٱللَّهُ لِبَاسَ ٱلْجُوعِ وَٱلْخَوْفِ بِمَا كَانُوا۟ يَصْنَعُونَ ۝ وَلَقَدْ جَآءَهُمْ رَسُولٌ مِّنْهُمْ فَكَذَّبُوهُ فَأَخَذَهُمُ ٱلْعَذَابُ وَهُمْ ظَٰلِمُونَ ۝ فَكُلُوا۟ مِمَّا رَزَقَكُمُ ٱللَّهُ حَلَٰلًا طَيِّبًا وَٱشْكُرُوا۟ نِعْمَتَ ٱللَّهِ إِن كُنتُمْ إِيَّاهُ تَعْبُدُونَ ۝ إِنَّمَا حَرَّمَ عَلَيْكُمُ ٱلْمَيْتَةَ وَٱلدَّمَ وَلَحْمَ ٱلْخِنزِيرِ وَمَآ أُهِلَّ لِغَيْرِ ٱللَّهِ بِهِۦ فَمَنِ ٱضْطُرَّ غَيْرَ بَاغٍ وَلَا عَادٍ فَإِنَّ ٱللَّهَ غَفُورٌ رَّحِيمٌ ۝ وَلَا تَقُولُوا۟ لِمَا تَصِفُ أَلْسِنَتُكُمُ ٱلْكَذِبَ هَٰذَا حَلَٰلٌ وَهَٰذَا حَرَامٌ لِّتَفْتَرُوا۟ عَلَى ٱللَّهِ ٱلْكَذِبَ إِنَّ ٱلَّذِينَ يَفْتَرُونَ عَلَى ٱللَّهِ ٱلْكَذِبَ لَا يُفْلِحُونَ ۝ مَتَٰعٌ قَلِيلٌ وَلَهُمْ عَذَابٌ أَلِيمٌ ۝ وَعَلَى ٱلَّذِينَ هَادُوا۟ حَرَّمْنَا مَا قَصَصْنَا عَلَيْكَ مِن قَبْلُ وَمَا ظَلَمْنَٰهُمْ وَلَٰكِن كَانُوٓا۟ أَنفُسَهُمْ يَظْلِمُونَ ۝ ثُمَّ إِنَّ رَبَّكَ لِلَّذِينَ عَمِلُوا۟ ٱلسُّوٓءَ بِجَهَٰلَةٍ ثُمَّ تَابُوا۟ مِنۢ بَعْدِ ذَٰلِكَ وَأَصْلَحُوٓا۟ إِنَّ رَبَّكَ مِنۢ بَعْدِهَا لَغَفُورٌ رَّحِيمٌ ۝ إِنَّ إِبْرَٰهِيمَ كَانَ أُمَّةً قَانِتًا لِّلَّهِ حَنِيفًا وَلَمْ يَكُ مِنَ ٱلْمُشْرِكِينَ ۝

Allah strikes a simile: a town, once secure and content, its livelihood coming to it in plenty from all directions, which then denied the blessings of Allah. He made it taste the raiment of hunger and fear because of what they did. There came indeed to them a Messenger from amongst them, but they cried him lies; so, they were seized by the chastisement while they were evildoers. Therefore, eat from what Allah provided you with, licit and tasty, and give thanks for Allah's blessings if it is Him you worship. He has forbidden you only these things: carrion, blood, pig's meat, and animals over which any name other than Allah's has been invoked. But if anyone is forced by hunger, not desiring it nor exceeding their immediate need, Allah is forgiving and merciful. And do not say, as to what your tongues falsely describe, 'This is lawful; and this is forbidden,' so that you may forge against Allah falsehood; surely those who forge against Allah falsehood shall not prosper. A little en-

joyment and they shall have a painful torment. For the Jews We pronounced illicit what We related to you beforehand. We wronged them not; it was their own selves they wronged. But then your Lord – to those who committed evil unknowingly and later repented and made good – your Lord shall thereafter be All-Forgiving, Compassionate to each. Abraham was himself a nation, devoted to Allah, of pristine faith, and was not an idol worshipper.

112-120 Individuals and communities generally follow similar patterns along their journey on earth. A human being's consciousness remains limited and conditioned, although it may expand and deepen and occasionally break through to a higher zone of awakening to the absolute *Truth*. The soul is ever content and tranquil, but its shadow-self brings about distraction and destruction. Reviewing human history, we repeatedly recognise the flow of this cycle. The great prophets and enlightened beings were connected to the inner light of their souls and were driven to help people and communities to awaken to their own full potential. The one divine light appears as countless souls within hearts; when followed faithfully, goodness prevails.

Grace always bestows its nature upon everyone, and it is through our wrong intention and action that we move out of its flow. The lower nature of human beings succumbs to distractions and mistakes, but the presence of the inner light can be accessed at any time if one is in a neutral state.

As humans we have to accept boundaries, limitations, and accountabilities. With constant calibration with the ever-present eternal light of life itself within us, we are able to transcend serious obstacles, difficulties, and suffering.

121-128

شَاكِرًا لِّأَنْعُمِهِ ٱجْتَبَىٰهُ وَهَدَىٰهُ إِلَىٰ صِرَٰطٍ مُّسْتَقِيمٍ ۝ وَءَاتَيْنَٰهُ فِى ٱلدُّنْيَا حَسَنَةً ۖ وَإِنَّهُۥ فِى ٱلْءَاخِرَةِ لَمِنَ ٱلصَّٰلِحِينَ ۝ ثُمَّ أَوْحَيْنَآ إِلَيْكَ أَنِ ٱتَّبِعْ مِلَّةَ إِبْرَٰهِيمَ حَنِيفًا ۖ وَمَا كَانَ مِنَ ٱلْمُشْرِكِينَ ۝ إِنَّمَا جُعِلَ ٱلسَّبْتُ عَلَى ٱلَّذِينَ ٱخْتَلَفُوا۟ فِيهِ ۚ وَإِنَّ رَبَّكَ لَيَحْكُمُ بَيْنَهُمْ يَوْمَ ٱلْقِيَٰمَةِ فِيمَا كَانُوا۟ فِيهِ يَخْتَلِفُونَ ۝ ٱدْعُ إِلَىٰ سَبِيلِ رَبِّكَ بِٱلْحِكْمَةِ وَٱلْمَوْعِظَةِ ٱلْحَسَنَةِ ۖ وَجَٰدِلْهُم بِٱلَّتِى هِىَ أَحْسَنُ ۚ إِنَّ رَبَّكَ هُوَ أَعْلَمُ بِمَن ضَلَّ عَن سَبِيلِهِۦ ۖ وَهُوَ أَعْلَمُ بِٱلْمُهْتَدِينَ ۝ وَإِنْ عَاقَبْتُمْ فَعَاقِبُوا۟ بِمِثْلِ مَا عُوقِبْتُم بِهِۦ ۖ وَلَئِن صَبَرْتُمْ لَهُوَ خَيْرٌ لِّلصَّٰبِرِينَ ۝ وَٱصْبِرْ وَمَا صَبْرُكَ إِلَّا بِٱللَّهِ ۚ وَلَا تَحْزَنْ عَلَيْهِمْ وَلَا تَكُ فِى ضَيْقٍ مِّمَّا يَمْكُرُونَ ۝ إِنَّ ٱللَّهَ مَعَ ٱلَّذِينَ ٱتَّقَوا۟ وَّٱلَّذِينَ هُم مُّحْسِنُونَ ۝

He rendered thanks for his blessings, and Allah chose him and guided him to a straight path. And We gave him in this world good, and in the world to come he shall be among the righteous. Then We revealed to you: follow the religion of Abraham, of pristine faith, who was not an idol worshipper. The Sabbath was merely appointed for those who disputed concerning it, and your Lord shall pass judgment on the Day of Resurrection concerning that over which they used to dispute. Call to the way of your Lord with wisdom and fair counsel, and debate with them in the fairest manner. Your Lord knows best who has strayed from His path; He knows best who are guided aright. And if you punish, you are to punish with the like of what you were punished; but if you bear with patience, then best it is for the patient. And be patient; yet is your patience only with the help of Allah. And do not sorrow for them, nor be your straitened for what they devise. Surely, Allah is with those who are cautiously aware and those who are virtuous.

121-128 The great prophets were content and obsessed with the awareness of the divine presence within their hearts. They transmitted their knowledge, wisdom and light to others without restriction. They described the appropriate way of living to their people, the path that leads out of the darkness of the self to the enlightened soul. They were not afflicted by fear or grief, and they exercised considerable patience, tolerance, and forbearance. Our drive to speed up time to achieve what we passionately desire is a natural attempt to bring a story to its end. In this world we are restricted by space and time, while the nature of our soul is perpetual and boundless. This is what we aspire for.

Goodness begets goodness, and wrong actions bring about their equal and opposite reactions. Grace is tangible for those who are fully aware, doing their utmost in good deeds with generosity.

Our life on earth is an exercise of practising the virtues of generosity, goodness, patience, and justice, of hoping and expecting the best for everyone else, because in reality, all souls are the same. It is only our outer, human side that differs and changes with time and dies, whereas the soul will continue.

5. Surah 17 Al-Isra' (The Night Journey)

If you touch the beam of the sacred light, you lose the experience of distance and time. They only exist within limited earthly consciousness. That divine grace is experienced when consciousness of your body and mind have transcended to soul and spirit. That transcendence is exemplified by the Prophet Muhammad's night journey, which goes beyond distance, time, and mental understanding.

بِسْمِ اللَّـهِ الرَّحْمَـٰنِ الرَّحِيمِ

1-8 سُبْحَانَ الَّذِي أَسْرَىٰ بِعَبْدِهِ لَيْلًا مِنَ الْمَسْجِدِ الْحَرَامِ إِلَى الْمَسْجِدِ الْأَقْصَا الَّذِي بَرَكْنَا حَوْلَهُ لِنُرِيَهُ مِنْ ءَايَٰتِنَا إِنَّهُ هُوَ السَّمِيعُ الْبَصِيرُ ۞ وَءَاتَيْنَا مُوسَى الْكِتَٰبَ وَجَعَلْنَٰهُ هُدًى لِبَنِي إِسْرَٰءِيلَ أَلَّا تَتَّخِذُوا مِنْ دُونِي وَكِيلًا ۞ ذُرِّيَّةَ مَنْ حَمَلْنَا مَعَ نُوحٍ إِنَّهُ كَانَ عَبْدًا شَكُورًا ۞ وَقَضَيْنَا إِلَىٰ بَنِي إِسْرَٰءِيلَ فِي الْكِتَٰبِ

لَتُفْسِدُنَّ فِى ٱلْأَرْضِ مَرَّتَيْنِ وَلَتَعْلُنَّ عُلُوًّا كَبِيرًا ۞ فَإِذَا جَآءَ وَعْدُ أُولَىٰهُمَا بَعَثْنَا عَلَيْكُمْ عِبَادًا لَّنَآ أُوْلِى بَأْسٍ شَدِيدٍ فَجَاسُواْ خِلَـٰلَ ٱلدِّيَارِ ۚ وَكَانَ وَعْدًا مَّفْعُولًا ۞ ثُمَّ رَدَدْنَا لَكُمُ ٱلْكَرَّةَ عَلَيْهِمْ وَأَمْدَدْنَـٰكُم بِأَمْوَٰلٍ وَبَنِينَ وَجَعَلْنَـٰكُمْ أَكْثَرَ نَفِيرًا ۞ إِنْ أَحْسَنتُمْ أَحْسَنتُمْ لِأَنفُسِكُمْ ۖ وَإِنْ أَسَأْتُمْ فَلَهَا ۚ فَإِذَا جَآءَ وَعْدُ ٱلْـَٔاخِرَةِ لِيَسُـۥٓـُٔواْ وُجُوهَكُمْ وَلِيَدْخُلُواْ ٱلْمَسْجِدَ كَمَا دَخَلُوهُ أَوَّلَ مَرَّةٍ وَلِيُتَبِّرُواْ مَا عَلَوْاْ تَتْبِيرًا ۞ عَسَىٰ رَبُّكُمْ أَن يَرْحَمَكُمْ ۚ وَإِنْ عُدتُّمْ عُدْنَا ۘ وَجَعَلْنَا جَهَنَّمَ لِلْكَـٰفِرِينَ حَصِيرًا ۞

In the name of Allah, the Merciful to all, the Compassionate to each!

Glory be to Him Who carried His servant by night from the Sacred Mosque to the Furthest Mosque, whose precincts We have blessed, to show him of Our wonders! He it is Who is All-Hearing, All-Seeing! We brought Moses the Book and made it a guidance to the Children of Israel: 'Take none for protector instead of Me.' They were the progeny of those We made to embark with Noah. He was in truth a thankful servant. And We decreed to the Children of Israel in the Book: 'You shall corrupt the earth twice, and shall soar to a great height.' So, when the promise of the first of these came to pass, We sent against you servants of Ours, men of great might, and they went through the habitat- ions, and it was a promise performed. Then We gave you back the turn to prevail against them, and aided you with wealth and children and made you a numerous band. 'If you do good, it is your own souls you do good to, and if you do evil it is to them likewise.' Then, when the promise of the second came to pass, We sent against you Our servants to discountenance you, and to enter the Temple, as they entered it the first time, and to destroy utterly that which they ascended to. 'Perhaps your Lord will show you mercy; but if you begin again, We too shall begin again. We have made hell a dungeon for the unbelievers.'

1-8 Our earthly limitations within space and time are one reality, contrasted with other realities whose nature is of higher dimensions, such as angels and prophetic visions and experiences. Beings who have achieved higher consciousness and live in constant reference to it occasionally experience events in the past or in the future, or movement within space-time, in a different manner to the average person within the limitations of conditioned consciousness. Most people are given the opportunity to reflect on the ultimate *Truth*, which encompasses all relative truths and short-lived events.

Our origin is the heavenly abode of the infinite and the eternal. All experiences on earth aim us toward that point of evolution and consciousness that confirms our true identity. Whatever goodness we do is towards our own self, so that the self realises its reality is only the soul and everything else is shadows. In this realisation lies clear divine mercy.

It is natural for us human beings to be driven towards any goodness we experience that takes us higher in consciousness and intelligence. Essentially, we are heavenly creatures, journeying within dualities that connect with us through our senses. We have to deal with these dualities in the best way we can, which ultimately is to reference the origin and destiny of everything, *Unity*.

17-9 وَإِنَّ هَٰذَا ٱلْقُرْءَانَ يَهْدِى لِلَّتِى هِىَ أَقْوَمُ وَيُبَشِّرُ ٱلْمُؤْمِنِينَ ٱلَّذِينَ يَعْمَلُونَ ٱلصَّٰلِحَٰتِ أَنَّ لَهُمْ أَجْرًا كَبِيرًا ۞ وَأَنَّ ٱلَّذِينَ لَا يُؤْمِنُونَ بِٱلْءَاخِرَةِ أَعْتَدْنَا لَهُمْ عَذَابًا أَلِيمًا ۞ وَيَدْعُ ٱلْإِنسَٰنُ بِٱلشَّرِّ دُعَآءَهُۥ بِٱلْخَيْرِ وَكَانَ ٱلْإِنسَٰنُ عَجُولًا ۞ وَجَعَلْنَا ٱلَّيْلَ وَٱلنَّهَارَ ءَايَتَيْنِ فَمَحَوْنَآ ءَايَةَ ٱلَّيْلِ وَجَعَلْنَآ ءَايَةَ ٱلنَّهَارِ مُبْصِرَةً لِّتَبْتَغُوا۟ فَضْلًا مِّن رَّبِّكُمْ وَلِتَعْلَمُوا۟ عَدَدَ ٱلسِّنِينَ وَٱلْحِسَابَ وَكُلَّ شَىْءٍ فَصَّلْنَٰهُ تَفْصِيلًا ۞ وَكُلَّ إِنسَٰنٍ أَلْزَمْنَٰهُ طَٰٓئِرَهُۥ فِى عُنُقِهِۦ وَنُخْرِجُ لَهُۥ يَوْمَ ٱلْقِيَٰمَةِ كِتَٰبًا يَلْقَىٰهُ مَنشُورًا ۞ ٱقْرَأْ كِتَٰبَكَ كَفَىٰ بِنَفْسِكَ ٱلْيَوْمَ عَلَيْكَ حَسِيبًا ۞ مَّنِ ٱهْتَدَىٰ فَإِنَّمَا يَهْتَدِى لِنَفْسِهِۦ وَمَن ضَلَّ فَإِنَّمَا يَضِلُّ عَلَيْهَا وَلَا تَزِرُ وَازِرَةٌ وِزْرَ أُخْرَىٰ وَمَا كُنَّا مُعَذِّبِينَ حَتَّىٰ نَبْعَثَ رَسُولًا ۞ وَإِذَآ أَرَدْنَآ أَن نُّهْلِكَ قَرْيَةً أَمَرْنَا مُتْرَفِيهَا فَفَسَقُوا۟ فِيهَا فَحَقَّ عَلَيْهَا ٱلْقَوْلُ فَدَمَّرْنَٰهَا تَدْمِيرًا ۞ وَكَمْ أَهْلَكْنَا مِنَ ٱلْقُرُونِ مِنۢ بَعْدِ نُوحٍ وَكَفَىٰ بِرَبِّكَ بِذُنُوبِ عِبَادِهِۦ خَبِيرًۢا بَصِيرًا ۞

This Qur'an does indeed show the straightest way. It gives the faithful who do right the good news that they will have a great reward that for them who believe not in the hereafter We have prepared a torment most painful. Mankind prays for evil, as he prays for good; mankind is ever hasty. We made night and day to be two signs, and We erase the sign of night and cause the sign of day to appear to the eyes, so that you may seek bounty from your Lord, and learn the computation of years and accounts. All things have We clarified most clearly. And every man – We have fastened to him his bird of omen upon his neck; and We shall bring forth for him, on the Day of Resurrection, a book he shall find spread wide open. Read your Book. Let your own self suffice you now as accountant. Whosoever is guided, is only guided to his own gain, and whosoever goes astray, it is only to his own loss; no soul laden bears the load of another. We never chastise, until We send forth a Messenger. If We desire to destroy a town, We order its men of luxury, and they indulge in transgression, so Our just decree comes to pass upon it, and We destroy it utterly. How many a generation We destroyed after Noah! Let your Lord suffice as One All-Versed, All-Seeing, as to the misdeeds of His servants!

9-17 Those on the prophetic path may awaken to the infinite presence of the divine before death, after which their abode will be in perfect bliss. This path presents a prescription for self-reflection, acceptance of boundaries and accountability for all our actions and thoughts. What we experience in nature, such as the variations between day and night, light and dark, good and bad, indicate the natural balance between opposites. Human beings are also balanced between humanity and divinity. The purpose of life is to discover the inner spiritual source, to yield to it and live by it. If this search is not followed and attained, disappointment and regret will be the outcome. People and towns decay and are destroyed when they follow misguided leaders who desire wealth, power, and control of earthly situations without moral and spiritual references.

An intelligent person desires to avoid suffering and pain and to experience a higher quality life that brings about greater contentment and happiness. Guidance begets guidance, and awareness is based on being present in the moment. Most of our suffering is due to distraction and waywardness – the soul is ever present.

Every human being is driven towards a realisation that gives reliable, constant contentment and security. This can only come through the light of the heart and the soul. Every other experience of goodness and happiness is transitory and not as good as the calibration and reference to the eternal light within the heart.

18-27

مَّن كَانَ يُرِيدُ ٱلْعَاجِلَةَ عَجَّلْنَا لَهُۥ فِيهَا مَا نَشَآءُ لِمَن نُّرِيدُ ثُمَّ جَعَلْنَا لَهُۥ جَهَنَّمَ يَصْلَىٰهَا مَذْمُومًا مَّدْحُورًا ۝ وَمَنْ أَرَادَ ٱلْءَاخِرَةَ وَسَعَىٰ لَهَا سَعْيَهَا وَهُوَ مُؤْمِنٌ فَأُوْلَٰٓئِكَ كَانَ سَعْيُهُم مَّشْكُورًا ۝ كُلًّا نُّمِدُّ هَٰٓؤُلَآءِ وَهَٰٓؤُلَآءِ مِنْ عَطَآءِ رَبِّكَ وَمَا كَانَ عَطَآءُ رَبِّكَ مَحْظُورًا ۝ ٱنظُرْ كَيْفَ فَضَّلْنَا بَعْضَهُمْ عَلَىٰ بَعْضٍ وَلَلْءَاخِرَةُ أَكْبَرُ دَرَجَٰتٍ وَأَكْبَرُ تَفْضِيلًا ۝ لَّا تَجْعَلْ مَعَ ٱللَّهِ إِلَٰهًا ءَاخَرَ فَتَقْعُدَ مَذْمُومًا مَّخْذُولًا ۝ وَقَضَىٰ رَبُّكَ أَلَّا تَعْبُدُوٓاْ إِلَّآ إِيَّاهُ وَبِٱلْوَٰلِدَيْنِ إِحْسَٰنًا إِمَّا يَبْلُغَنَّ عِندَكَ ٱلْكِبَرَ أَحَدُهُمَآ أَوْ كِلَاهُمَا فَلَا تَقُل لَّهُمَآ أُفٍّ وَلَا تَنْهَرْهُمَا وَقُل لَّهُمَا قَوْلًا كَرِيمًا ۝ وَٱخْفِضْ لَهُمَا جَنَاحَ ٱلذُّلِّ مِنَ ٱلرَّحْمَةِ وَقُل رَّبِّ ٱرْحَمْهُمَا كَمَا رَبَّيَانِى صَغِيرًا ۝ رَّبُّكُمْ أَعْلَمُ بِمَا فِى نُفُوسِكُمْ إِن تَكُونُواْ صَٰلِحِينَ فَإِنَّهُۥ كَانَ لِلْأَوَّٰبِينَ غَفُورًا ۝ وَءَاتِ ذَا ٱلْقُرْبَىٰ حَقَّهُۥ وَٱلْمِسْكِينَ وَٱبْنَ ٱلسَّبِيلِ وَلَا تُبَذِّرْ تَبْذِيرًا ۝ إِنَّ ٱلْمُبَذِّرِينَ كَانُوٓاْ إِخْوَٰنَ ٱلشَّيَٰطِينِ وَكَانَ ٱلشَّيْطَٰنُ لِرَبِّهِۦ كَفُورًا ۝

He who desires this fleeting world, We fleetingly grant him therein whatever We please, to whomever We desire, and then We consign him to hell – there to be scorched, disgraced, confuted! And he who desires the hereafter, and pursues it as it should be pursued, being a man of faith, these – their pursuit shall be worthy of all praise. All do We provide these as well as those – out of the bounty of your Lord, and the bounty of your Lord is not confined. Consider how We preferred some to others; but the hereafter is assuredly higher in degree, and greatly to be preferred. Take not with Allah another deity, or you will end up disgraced, thwarted. Your Lord decrees: that you worship none but Him, and graciousness to parents. If they attain old age with you, either or both, say not to them: 'Phew!' and do not scold them but speak to them words of kindness. And lower to them the wing of humility, out of compassion, and say: 'My Lord, grant them mercy, as they raised me up when I was young.' Your Lord knows best what lies in your selves; if you are virtuous, He is All-Forgiving to those who return. Give kinsmen their due, as also the poor and the wayfarer. But do not squander and dissipate, for squanderers are the brothers of devils. And Satan has ever been ungrateful to his Lord.

18-27 Human beings are always challenged to choose between what benefits them immediately and what will help them later. We enjoy immediate relief and pleasure, and we equally value long-term, durable goodness, which may come later if we are patient in the short-term. Awareness of the hereafter may help to postpone immediate and short-term pleasures, which are always accompanied by some pain or disappointment. Belief, knowledge, and some experience of the timelessness of the hereafter give us a taste of a different zone of consciousness, that is, if we are determined, focused, and fortunate. This boundless realm was before time, before space; it has given rise to what is now to prepare us for the return to the original, absolute *Oneness*.

The nature of the soul is timeless. It transmits that light to the self, which is a mere shadow. Impatience causes much suffering, but its origin is the timeless soul. The self needs to be groomed and contained until it is transcended.

Our life on earth enables us to have the illusion of independent action and an ability to perform A, B, or C. In reality all of these drives emanate from the *ruh* itself, which is ever constant, ever content, and inseparable from its divine origin. It is as though you have to be shown that no matter what choices and powers you have, you return to being subservient to the perfect destiny prescribed for you, which is a continuation of the state that you have in your mind and heart.

28-38 وَإِمَّا تُعْرِضَنَّ عَنْهُمُ ٱبْتِغَآءَ رَحْمَةٍ مِّن رَّبِّكَ تَرْجُوهَا فَقُل لَّهُمْ قَوْلًا مَّيْسُورًا ۝ وَلَا تَجْعَلْ يَدَكَ مَغْلُولَةً إِلَىٰ عُنُقِكَ وَلَا تَبْسُطْهَا كُلَّ ٱلْبَسْطِ فَتَقْعُدَ مَلُومًا مَّحْسُورًا ۝ إِنَّ رَبَّكَ يَبْسُطُ ٱلرِّزْقَ لِمَن يَشَآءُ وَيَقْدِرُ إِنَّهُۥ كَانَ بِعِبَادِهِۦ خَبِيرًۢا بَصِيرًا ۝ وَلَا تَقْتُلُوٓا۟ أَوْلَٰدَكُمْ خَشْيَةَ إِمْلَٰقٍ نَّحْنُ نَرْزُقُهُمْ وَإِيَّاكُمْ إِنَّ قَتْلَهُمْ كَانَ خِطْـًٔا كَبِيرًا ۝ وَلَا تَقْرَبُوا۟ ٱلزِّنَىٰٓ إِنَّهُۥ كَانَ فَٰحِشَةً وَسَآءَ سَبِيلًا ۝ وَلَا تَقْتُلُوا۟ ٱلنَّفْسَ ٱلَّتِى حَرَّمَ ٱللَّهُ إِلَّا بِٱلْحَقِّ وَمَن قُتِلَ مَظْلُومًا فَقَدْ جَعَلْنَا لِوَلِيِّهِۦ سُلْطَٰنًا فَلَا يُسْرِف فِّى ٱلْقَتْلِ إِنَّهُۥ كَانَ مَنصُورًا ۝ وَلَا تَقْرَبُوا۟ مَالَ ٱلْيَتِيمِ إِلَّا بِٱلَّتِى هِىَ أَحْسَنُ حَتَّىٰ يَبْلُغَ أَشُدَّهُۥ وَأَوْفُوا۟ بِٱلْعَهْدِ إِنَّ ٱلْعَهْدَ كَانَ مَسْـُٔولًا ۝ وَأَوْفُوا۟ ٱلْكَيْلَ إِذَا كِلْتُمْ وَزِنُوا۟ بِٱلْقِسْطَاسِ ٱلْمُسْتَقِيمِ ذَٰلِكَ خَيْرٌ وَأَحْسَنُ تَأْوِيلًا ۝ وَلَا تَقْفُ مَا لَيْسَ لَكَ بِهِۦ عِلْمٌ إِنَّ ٱلسَّمْعَ وَٱلْبَصَرَ وَٱلْفُؤَادَ كُلُّ أُو۟لَٰٓئِكَ كَانَ عَنْهُ مَسْـُٔولًا ۝ وَلَا تَمْشِ فِى ٱلْأَرْضِ مَرَحًا إِنَّكَ لَن تَخْرِقَ ٱلْأَرْضَ وَلَن تَبْلُغَ ٱلْجِبَالَ طُولًا ۝ كُلُّ ذَٰلِكَ كَانَ سَيِّئُهُۥ عِندَ رَبِّكَ مَكْرُوهًا ۝

And if you turn away from them, seeking a mercy from your Lord which you hope for, speak to them words of comfort. Let not your hand be chained to your neck, nor spread it out as far as it extends, or else you will end up worthy of blame, regretful. Your Lord spreads out His bounty to whomever He wills – and withholds it. In respect of His servants, He is All-Versed, All-Seeing. And do not kill your children for fear of poverty; We give them sustenance and yourselves surely to kill them is a great wrong. Do not come near to adultery; it is debauchery and a wretched path to follow. Do not kill the self which Allah declares hallowed except in justice. Whoever is killed unjustly, We have granted authority to his guardian. But he should not exceed the limit in killing, for he has already obtained divine support. And do not approach the property of the orphan save in the fairest manner, until he is of age. And fulfil the covenant; surely the covenant shall be questioned of. Be fair in measures when you measure out, and weigh with a balance that is true: that would be better and more rewarding. Follow not what you have no knowledge of: hearing, sight and the heart – all of these a person shall be questioned about. Do not stride forth jauntily on earth: you will not thereby traverse the earth, nor reach up to the mountains in height. All this – the evil of it – is hateful in the sight of your Lord.

28-38 Self-awareness and referencing the inner light bring about modesty, efficiency, generosity, kindness, and compassion, all necessary to groom the self to allow the light of the soul to lead. Then we are liberated from fear, anxiety, sorrow, anguish, over-concern, and other stresses, which automatically come to the surface and dissipate. Higher efficiency and quality of life will prevail. This faith and belief require us to accept limitations and responsibilities in our relationships with other living creatures, so we exercise cautious awareness, which is a necessary condition for spiritual progress. To grow out of the limitations of ordinary consciousness, we need stillness, silence, and transcendence of unhealthy expressions of the norm.

Our responsibilities include acting correctly to ensure a healthy body and mind as well as engaging in appropriate relationships with others. From these responsibilities also arises a negative side: concern for provision and reputation. The soul is ever-generous due to its divine origin, and by acting generously we bring about grace and unknown provisions.

As worldly creatures, we have no option other than to improve our intentions, actions, and conduct, so that our humanity becomes so refined that it links smoothly with its divine source. All of the virtues that emanate from the soul itself are accepted by human beings as being desirable and good. These enable us to have less ego, fewer fears, and more reliance on the inner light itself.

39-48 ذَٰلِكَ مِمَّآ أَوْحَىٰٓ إِلَيْكَ رَبُّكَ مِنَ ٱلْحِكْمَةِ ۗ وَلَا تَجْعَلْ مَعَ ٱللَّهِ إِلَٰهًا ءَاخَرَ فَتُلْقَىٰ فِى جَهَنَّمَ مَلُومًا مَّدْحُورًا ۝ أَفَأَصْفَىٰكُمْ رَبُّكُم بِٱلْبَنِينَ وَٱتَّخَذَ مِنَ ٱلْمَلَٰٓئِكَةِ إِنَٰثًا

إِنَّكُمْ لَتَقُولُونَ قَوْلًا عَظِيمًا ۝ وَلَقَدْ صَرَّفْنَا فِى هَٰذَا ٱلْقُرْءَانِ لِيَذَّكَّرُوا۟ وَمَا يَزِيدُهُمْ إِلَّا نُفُورًا ۝ قُل لَّوْ كَانَ مَعَهُۥٓ ءَالِهَةٌ كَمَا يَقُولُونَ إِذًا لَّٱبْتَغَوْا۟ إِلَىٰ ذِى ٱلْعَرْشِ سَبِيلًا ۝ سُبْحَٰنَهُۥ وَتَعَٰلَىٰ عَمَّا يَقُولُونَ عُلُوًّا كَبِيرًا ۝ تُسَبِّحُ لَهُ ٱلسَّمَٰوَٰتُ ٱلسَّبْعُ وَٱلْأَرْضُ وَمَن فِيهِنَّ وَإِن مِّن شَىْءٍ إِلَّا يُسَبِّحُ بِحَمْدِهِۦ وَلَٰكِن لَّا تَفْقَهُونَ تَسْبِيحَهُمْ إِنَّهُۥ كَانَ حَلِيمًا غَفُورًا ۝ وَإِذَا قَرَأْتَ ٱلْقُرْءَانَ جَعَلْنَا بَيْنَكَ وَبَيْنَ ٱلَّذِينَ لَا يُؤْمِنُونَ بِٱلْءَاخِرَةِ حِجَابًا مَّسْتُورًا ۝ وَجَعَلْنَا عَلَىٰ قُلُوبِهِمْ أَكِنَّةً أَن يَفْقَهُوهُ وَفِىٓ ءَاذَانِهِمْ وَقْرًا وَإِذَا ذَكَرْتَ رَبَّكَ فِى ٱلْقُرْءَانِ وَحْدَهُۥ وَلَّوْا۟ عَلَىٰٓ أَدْبَٰرِهِمْ نُفُورًا ۝ نَّحْنُ أَعْلَمُ بِمَا يَسْتَمِعُونَ بِهِۦٓ إِذْ يَسْتَمِعُونَ إِلَيْكَ وَإِذْ هُمْ نَجْوَىٰٓ إِذْ يَقُولُ ٱلظَّٰلِمُونَ إِن تَتَّبِعُونَ إِلَّا رَجُلًا مَّسْحُورًا ۝ ٱنظُرْ كَيْفَ ضَرَبُوا۟ لَكَ ٱلْأَمْثَالَ فَضَلُّوا۟ فَلَا يَسْتَطِيعُونَ سَبِيلًا ۝

This is some of the wisdom your Lord has revealed to you: do not set up another Allah beside Allah, or you will be thrown into Hell, blamed and rejected. Did Allah favour you with boys and made the angels female? You are uttering an enormity! We have detailed in this Qur'an all manner of things, that they might ponder and remember, but it only increases them in their distaste of it. Say: 'Had there been with Him other Gods, as they allege, then they would have sought access to the Master of the throne.' Glory be to Him and exalted be He in high exaltation above what they say. The seven heavens and the earth sing His praises, and all who are therein. There is nothing that does not sing His praise, but you do not understand their songs of praise. Surely, He is All-Forbearing, All-Forgiving. And when you recite the Qur'an, We place between you and those who do not believe in the hereafter a hidden barrier. Upon their hearts We draped veils lest they understand it, and in their ears heaviness. Should you happen to mention in the Qur'an that your Lord is One, they turn tail, and withdraw in aversion. We know best what they listen to, when they listen to you, conspiring together, and when the wicked say: 'You are merely following a man bewitched.' Look how they strike similes for you and go astray, unable to find the right path.

39-48 Sacred books are powerful but unless we approach them with trust, respect, and humility, their content will elude us. The Qur'an reveals that everything in existence is connected to God through attributes and qualities that humanity pursues. In order to understand how this cosmic interconnectedness encompasses everything, we need insight, deep reflection, and clear reference to the light of our soul. The alchemy of the Qur'an is such that, when recited, some hearts will open and respond, while others, immersed within the darkness of the ego, will reject its message. Belief in the hereafter and continuation of life after death is a key test as to whether one is on a spiritual path or not.

Correct conduct is always necessary, including appropriate thought, action, and presence in the moment, as well as other virtues such as kindness, generosity, and positivity. Faith and trust increase only when there is a basic foundation of belief; otherwise, the lower self blocks the light.

One of our main duties towards our welfare is to be clear in the head, not confused and noisy, as well as pure at heart. Then we can use reason and rationality as well as intuition and the higher insight that comes to us through a pure heart.

49-57 وَقَالُوٓاْ أَءِذَا كُنَّا عِظَٰمًا وَرُفَٰتًا أَءِنَّا لَمَبْعُوثُونَ خَلْقًا جَدِيدًا ۞ قُلْ كُونُواْ حِجَارَةً أَوْ حَدِيدًا ۞ أَوْ خَلْقًا مِّمَّا يَكْبُرُ فِى صُدُورِكُمْ ۚ فَسَيَقُولُونَ مَن يُعِيدُنَا ۖ قُلِ ٱلَّذِى فَطَرَكُمْ أَوَّلَ مَرَّةٍ ۚ فَسَيُنْغِضُونَ إِلَيْكَ رُءُوسَهُمْ وَيَقُولُونَ مَتَىٰ هُوَ ۖ قُلْ عَسَىٰٓ أَن يَكُونَ قَرِيبًا ۞ يَوْمَ يَدْعُوكُمْ فَتَسْتَجِيبُونَ بِحَمْدِهِۦ وَتَظُنُّونَ إِن لَّبِثْتُمْ إِلَّا قَلِيلًا ۞ وَقُل لِّعِبَادِى يَقُولُواْ ٱلَّتِى هِىَ أَحْسَنُ ۚ إِنَّ ٱلشَّيْطَٰنَ يَنزَغُ بَيْنَهُمْ ۚ إِنَّ ٱلشَّيْطَٰنَ كَانَ لِلْإِنسَٰنِ عَدُوًّا مُّبِينًا ۞ رَّبُّكُمْ أَعْلَمُ بِكُمْ ۖ إِن يَشَأْ يَرْحَمْكُمْ أَوْ إِن يَشَأْ يُعَذِّبْكُمْ ۚ وَمَآ أَرْسَلْنَٰكَ عَلَيْهِمْ وَكِيلًا ۞ وَرَبُّكَ أَعْلَمُ بِمَن فِى ٱلسَّمَٰوَٰتِ وَٱلْأَرْضِ ۗ وَلَقَدْ فَضَّلْنَا بَعْضَ ٱلنَّبِيِّۦنَ عَلَىٰ بَعْضٍ ۖ وَءَاتَيْنَا دَاوُۥدَ زَبُورًا ۞ قُلِ ٱدْعُواْ ٱلَّذِينَ زَعَمْتُم مِّن دُونِهِۦ فَلَا يَمْلِكُونَ كَشْفَ ٱلضُّرِّ عَنكُمْ وَلَا تَحْوِيلًا ۞ أُوْلَٰٓئِكَ ٱلَّذِينَ يَدْعُونَ يَبْتَغُونَ إِلَىٰ رَبِّهِمُ ٱلْوَسِيلَةَ أَيُّهُمْ أَقْرَبُ وَيَرْجُونَ رَحْمَتَهُۥ وَيَخَافُونَ عَذَابَهُۥٓ ۚ إِنَّ عَذَابَ رَبِّكَ كَانَ مَحْذُورًا ۞

They say: 'Are we, having turned into bones and dust, to be resurrected as a new creation?' Say: 'Let you be stones, or iron, or any other created thing which looms large in your minds!' They will say: 'Who shall bring us back to life?' Say: 'He Who created you in the first place.' They will shake their heads at you in disbelief, and say: 'When will this be?' Say: 'Perhaps it will be soon; it will be the Day when He calls you, and you answer by praising Him, and you think you have stayed only a little while.' Tell My servants to say only what is right and proper, for Satan stirs dissension among them; assuredly Satan is to man a manifest enemy. Your Lord knows you very well; if He will, He will have mercy on you, or, if He will, He will chastise you. We sent you not to be a guardian over them. Your Lord knows best who is in the heavens and on earth. We preferred some prophets over others and brought David the Psalms. Say: 'Call upon those you allege are Gods apart from Allah, but they shall have no power to remove harm from you, nor turn it away.' Those they call upon are themselves seeking the means to come to their Lord, which of them shall be nearer; they hope for His mercy, and fear His chastisement. Surely thy Lord's chastisement is a thing to beware of.

49-57 The mind, limited by dualities and earthly conditioning, finds it difficult to imagine resurrection and a different state of life in the hereafter. Such mental limitations and earthly darkness set up obstacles to our awakening to the soul's divine nature. To be aware of these limitations and boundaries is a necessary step; it precedes transcending them and experiencing the higher knowledge contained within the heart. Our earthly life is a work in progress, preparing us for a higher zone of consciousness that functions without the illusions of independence or separation from *Truth* and its universal governance and control.

The dark lower self always acts to preserve itself; therefore, it presents every possible argument to avoid it being transcended and left aside. It is through prayers, good intentions, and good actions that we experience the grace of knowing the divine soul's presence.

Our journey on earth is in the zone of duality, plurality, and multiplicity. Our origin is total mercy and grace, but once we appear on earth, our choices can be one of two, either acceptable or rejectable. It is here that wisdom and referencing to the ultimate outcome helps us to either act appropriately, or on many occasions, to not act, respond, or waste time.

58-66 وَإِن مِّن قَرْيَةٍ إِلَّا نَحْنُ مُهْلِكُوهَا قَبْلَ يَوْمِ ٱلْقِيَٰمَةِ أَوْ مُعَذِّبُوهَا عَذَابًا شَدِيدًا كَانَ ذَٰلِكَ فِى ٱلْكِتَٰبِ مَسْطُورًا ۝ وَمَا مَنَعَنَآ أَن نُّرْسِلَ بِٱلْءَايَٰتِ إِلَّآ أَن كَذَّبَ بِهَا ٱلْأَوَّلُونَ وَءَاتَيْنَا ثَمُودَ ٱلنَّاقَةَ مُبْصِرَةً فَظَلَمُوا۟ بِهَا وَمَا نُرْسِلُ بِٱلْءَايَٰتِ إِلَّا تَخْوِيفًا ۝ وَإِذْ قُلْنَا لَكَ إِنَّ رَبَّكَ أَحَاطَ بِٱلنَّاسِ وَمَا جَعَلْنَا ٱلرُّءْيَا ٱلَّتِىٓ أَرَيْنَٰكَ إِلَّا فِتْنَةً لِّلنَّاسِ وَٱلشَّجَرَةَ ٱلْمَلْعُونَةَ فِى ٱلْقُرْءَانِ وَنُخَوِّفُهُمْ فَمَا يَزِيدُهُمْ إِلَّا طُغْيَٰنًا كَبِيرًا ۝ وَإِذْ قُلْنَا لِلْمَلَٰٓئِكَةِ ٱسْجُدُوا۟ لِءَادَمَ فَسَجَدُوٓا۟ إِلَّآ إِبْلِيسَ قَالَ ءَأَسْجُدُ لِمَنْ خَلَقْتَ طِينًا ۝ قَالَ أَرَءَيْتَكَ هَٰذَا ٱلَّذِى كَرَّمْتَ عَلَىَّ لَئِنْ أَخَّرْتَنِ إِلَىٰ يَوْمِ ٱلْقِيَٰمَةِ لَأَحْتَنِكَنَّ ذُرِّيَّتَهُۥٓ إِلَّا قَلِيلًا ۝ قَالَ ٱذْهَبْ فَمَن تَبِعَكَ مِنْهُمْ فَإِنَّ جَهَنَّمَ جَزَآؤُكُمْ جَزَآءً مَّوْفُورًا ۝ وَٱسْتَفْزِزْ مَنِ ٱسْتَطَعْتَ مِنْهُم بِصَوْتِكَ وَأَجْلِبْ عَلَيْهِم بِخَيْلِكَ وَرَجِلِكَ وَشَارِكْهُمْ فِى ٱلْأَمْوَٰلِ وَٱلْأَوْلَٰدِ وَعِدْهُمْ وَمَا يَعِدُهُمُ ٱلشَّيْطَٰنُ إِلَّا غُرُورًا ۝ إِنَّ عِبَادِى لَيْسَ لَكَ عَلَيْهِمْ سُلْطَٰنٌ وَكَفَىٰ بِرَبِّكَ وَكِيلًا ۝ رَّبُّكُمُ ٱلَّذِى يُزْجِى لَكُمُ ٱلْفُلْكَ فِى ٱلْبَحْرِ لِتَبْتَغُوا۟ مِن فَضْلِهِۦٓ إِنَّهُۥ كَانَ بِكُمْ رَحِيمًا ۝

No city is there, but We shall destroy it before the Day of Resurrection, or We shall chastise it with a terrible chastisement; that is in the Book inscribed. Nothing prevented us from sending down miracles except that the ancients called them lies. We brought Thamud the she-camel, an evident miracle, but they repudiated it. We send down miracles only to inspire awe. Remember when We said to you that your Lord encompasses mankind in His knowledge. Nor did We make the vision We showed you except as a test to people, as also the accursed tree in the Qur'an. We frighten them, but this renders them ever more arrogant. And We said unto the angels, 'Prostrate yourselves before Adam' – whereupon they all prostrated themselves, save Iblis. Said he: 'Shall I prostrate myself before one whom you have created out of clay?' He said: 'Do You see this creature You honoured above me? If You defer me till the Day of Resurrection, I will seize up his progeny, except for a few.' He said: 'Depart! Whoso follows you of their number, hell will be your reward, a reward unstinted. And startle whomsoever of them you can with your voice; and rally against them your horsemen and your foot, and share with them in their wealth and their children, and promise them! But Satan promises them naught, except delusion. Over My servants you shall have no dominion: let your Lord suffice as guardian.' It is your Lord Who drives on ships at sea for your sake, that you may seek of His bounty. To you He has ever been Compassionate.

58-66 Individuals and communities alike are subjected to the inevitable end of life on earth. They either journey in ignorance and disgrace or with ease and harmony back to origin. The rise of Adamic consciousness, a great mystery and miracle, provided the possibility of accessing the entire spectrum of consciousness, from the physical and material to the sublime and cosmic. This mystery will be clarified on the Day of Reckoning, when each soul will realise that its earthly purpose was to prepare for the next phase of life after death. The experiences of hell or paradise are natural consequences of our earthly awareness of our intentions and actions. Purgatory and the responsibility of rendering an account after death become insignificant if during one's life one practiced constant reflection and accountability of one's actions.

Individuals can move from darkness and misery to light and awakening, and so can communities. The reverse is also true: we bring destruction upon ourselves individually or collectively. The spiritual origin of Adam was higher than all angels, and the downfall of Adam's offspring can be lower than the lowest.

It is in the nature of the mind to be rebellious and reject the ultimate goodness itself. That goodness implies transcending the mind. Like anything that exists and has been touched by life, the ego-mind wants to continue. It is for this reason you can never completely get rid of your ego. All you can do is to refer it to the light that has caused it, which is from your soul. In itself, the mind is a shadow of the soul, but can also cause such entanglement that the light becomes dim, and the mind ends up being almost evil.

67-75 وَإِذَا مَسَّكُمُ ٱلضُّرُّ فِى ٱلْبَحْرِ ضَلَّ مَن تَدْعُونَ إِلَّا إِيَّاهُ فَلَمَّا نَجَّىٰكُمْ إِلَى ٱلْبَرِّ أَعْرَضْتُمْ وَكَانَ ٱلْإِنسَٰنُ كَفُورًا ۝ أَفَأَمِنتُمْ أَن يَخْسِفَ بِكُمْ جَانِبَ ٱلْبَرِّ أَوْ يُرْسِلَ عَلَيْكُمْ حَاصِبًا ثُمَّ لَا تَجِدُوا۟ لَكُمْ وَكِيلًا ۝ أَمْ أَمِنتُمْ أَن يُعِيدَكُمْ فِيهِ تَارَةً أُخْرَىٰ فَيُرْسِلَ عَلَيْكُمْ قَاصِفًا مِّنَ ٱلرِّيحِ فَيُغْرِقَكُم بِمَا كَفَرْتُمْ ثُمَّ لَا تَجِدُوا۟ لَكُمْ عَلَيْنَا بِهِۦ تَبِيعًا ۝ وَلَقَدْ كَرَّمْنَا بَنِىٓ ءَادَمَ وَحَمَلْنَٰهُمْ فِى ٱلْبَرِّ وَٱلْبَحْرِ وَرَزَقْنَٰهُم مِّنَ ٱلطَّيِّبَٰتِ وَفَضَّلْنَٰهُمْ عَلَىٰ كَثِيرٍ مِّمَّنْ خَلَقْنَا تَفْضِيلًا ۝ يَوْمَ نَدْعُوا۟ كُلَّ أُنَاسٍۭ بِإِمَٰمِهِمْ فَمَنْ أُوتِىَ كِتَٰبَهُۥ بِيَمِينِهِۦ فَأُو۟لَٰٓئِكَ يَقْرَءُونَ كِتَٰبَهُمْ وَلَا يُظْلَمُونَ فَتِيلًا ۝ وَمَن كَانَ فِى هَٰذِهِۦٓ أَعْمَىٰ فَهُوَ فِى ٱلْءَاخِرَةِ أَعْمَىٰ وَأَضَلُّ سَبِيلًا ۝ وَإِن كَادُوا۟

لَيَفْتِنُونَكَ عَنِ ٱلَّذِىٓ أَوْحَيْنَآ إِلَيْكَ لِتَفْتَرِىَ عَلَيْنَا غَيْرَهُۥ ۖ وَإِذًا لَّٱتَّخَذُوكَ خَلِيلًا ۝ وَلَوْلَآ أَن ثَبَّتْنَـٰكَ لَقَدْ كِدتَّ تَرْكَنُ إِلَيْهِمْ شَيْـًٔا قَلِيلًا ۝ إِذًا لَّأَذَقْنَـٰكَ ضِعْفَ ٱلْحَيَوٰةِ وَضِعْفَ ٱلْمَمَاتِ ثُمَّ لَا تَجِدُ لَكَ عَلَيْنَا نَصِيرًا ۝

When calamity touches you at sea, they are nowhere to be found – those you call upon instead of Him. And if He should deliver you safely to shore, you turn away from Him. Mankind is truly ungrateful. Can you be sure that Allah will not have you cave in swallowed up into the earth when you are back on land, or that He will not send a sandstorm against you? Then you will find no one to protect you. Or are you so secure He will not, once more, send you back to sea, where He will unleash upon you a devastating hurricane, drowning you for your ingratitude, whereupon you will find none to plead your case before Us? We honoured the progeny of Adam and carried them on land and sea. We provisioned them with delicacies and preferred them far above many whom We had created. On the day when We shall call all men with their record, and whoso is given his book in his right hand – those shall read their book, and they shall not be wronged a single date-thread. Whoso is blind in this world, in the hereafter he shall be even more blind and more astray from the path. There was a time when they almost beguiled you away from what We had revealed to you, to falsely ascribe to Us something different, whereupon they would have taken you for an intimate. If We had not made you stand firm, you would almost have inclined a little towards them. Had you done so, We would have made you taste a double torment in this world, and double after death, and then you would have found no one to help you against Us.

67-75 Humanity's highest potential is to flow with harmony in life and to act as a steward over what we relate to on earth and in our environment. We need constant reference to the *Source* of existence to avoid transgression and arrogance. Our earthly experiences should move from sight to insight, from outer power to being at unison with the divine power and will that encompass the whole universe. If we do not awaken to the light of the soul in this world, we may experience the darkness of hell in the afterlife. The highest state we reach on earth becomes the foundation of our state in the hereafter. Whoever is blind to realities and truth in this world will be more blind in the next.

It is natural for a healthy human being to rise in consciousness and understand both what is near and what is far. This is the way to receive greater insights and achieve awakening. This process continues until full awakening and enlightenment after death.

Human nature, in its own earthly sense, is very weak and fickle. But what energises and gives it life is from the divine itself. Therefore, if we want to have no fear, sorrow or regret, we need to stop all other motives in our activities and refer to the original light with complete neutrality. We need to be able to stop or retract what we are doing that can cause us much harm.

وَإِن كَادُواْ لَيَسْتَفِزُّونَكَ مِنَ ٱلْأَرْضِ لِيُخْرِجُوكَ مِنْهَا ۖ وَإِذًا لَّا يَلْبَثُونَ خِلَٰفَكَ إِلَّا قَلِيلًا ۝ سُنَّةَ مَن قَدْ أَرْسَلْنَا قَبْلَكَ مِن رُّسُلِنَا ۖ وَلَا تَجِدُ لِسُنَّتِنَا تَحْوِيلًا ۝ أَقِمِ ٱلصَّلَوٰةَ لِدُلُوكِ ٱلشَّمْسِ إِلَىٰ غَسَقِ ٱلَّيْلِ وَقُرْءَانَ ٱلْفَجْرِ ۖ إِنَّ قُرْءَانَ ٱلْفَجْرِ كَانَ مَشْهُودًا ۝ وَمِنَ ٱلَّيْلِ فَتَهَجَّدْ بِهِۦ نَافِلَةً لَّكَ عَسَىٰٓ أَن يَبْعَثَكَ رَبُّكَ مَقَامًا مَّحْمُودًا ۝ وَقُل رَّبِّ أَدْخِلْنِى مُدْخَلَ صِدْقٍ وَأَخْرِجْنِى مُخْرَجَ صِدْقٍ وَٱجْعَل لِّى مِن لَّدُنكَ سُلْطَٰنًا نَّصِيرًا ۝ وَقُلْ جَآءَ ٱلْحَقُّ وَزَهَقَ ٱلْبَٰطِلُ ۚ إِنَّ ٱلْبَٰطِلَ كَانَ زَهُوقًا ۝ وَنُنَزِّلُ مِنَ ٱلْقُرْءَانِ مَا هُوَ شِفَآءٌ وَرَحْمَةٌ لِّلْمُؤْمِنِينَ ۙ وَلَا يَزِيدُ ٱلظَّٰلِمِينَ إِلَّا خَسَارًا ۝ وَإِذَآ أَنْعَمْنَا عَلَى ٱلْإِنسَٰنِ أَعْرَضَ وَنَـَٔا بِجَانِبِهِۦ ۖ وَإِذَا مَسَّهُ ٱلشَّرُّ كَانَ يَـُٔوسًا ۝ قُلْ كُلٌّ يَعْمَلُ عَلَىٰ شَاكِلَتِهِۦ فَرَبُّكُمْ أَعْلَمُ بِمَنْ هُوَ أَهْدَىٰ سَبِيلًا ۝ وَيَسْـَٔلُونَكَ عَنِ ٱلرُّوحِ ۖ قُلِ ٱلرُّوحُ مِنْ أَمْرِ رَبِّى وَمَآ أُوتِيتُم مِّنَ ٱلْعِلْمِ إِلَّا قَلِيلًا ۝ وَلَئِن شِئْنَا لَنَذْهَبَنَّ بِٱلَّذِىٓ أَوْحَيْنَآ إِلَيْكَ ثُمَّ لَا تَجِدُ لَكَ بِهِۦ عَلَيْنَا وَكِيلًا ۝

Again, they were about to provoke you so as to drive you away from the land; but had they succeeded, they would not have lasted after you except for a short while. Such was the course among those of Our messengers We sent before you – and never will you find Our course to vary! Perform the prayer at the setting of the sun and until darkness of night and the Recitation of dawn – the Recitation of dawn is always witnessed. And as for the night, keep vigil a part of it, as a work of supererogation for you; it may be that your Lord will raise you up to a laudable station. And say: 'My Lord, lead me in with a just ingoing, and lead me out with a just outgoing; grant me authority from Thee, to help me.' And say: 'The Truth has come and falsehood is stifled – falsehood shall ever be stifled.' We send down the Qur'an as healing and mercy to those who believe; as for those who disbelieve, it only increases their loss. When We send down Our blessings upon man, he turns away, and moves to the side, but when evil touches him he becomes despondent. Say: 'Every one acts according to his manner; but your Lord best knows who is best guided in the path.' They ask you about the soul. Say: 'The soul belongs to the realm of my Lord, and of knowledge you have been granted but little.' If We wish, We can do away with what We revealed to you, whereupon you will find none to champion you before Us in this matter,

76-86 Allah's ways and designs are always perfect. The human being needs to remain in constant awareness and remembrance of Allah and His light in order to live a quality life, one that leads to Truth in the hereafter. The lower nature of human beings causes us to forget and succumb to deviations and distractions from a joyful, spiritual way of life. Human responses to the outer world express their inner state and condition – of body, mind, and the light of the soul. Every living creature reveals its state and condition by its actions and behaviour. With spiritual wisdom you understand the nature of other living entities and the destiny towards which they are heading.

The most important duty, responsibility, and reward for a human being is regular prayers and transcendence of anything within space-time. The essential Qur'anic teaching is to attend to our humanity with constant reference to and recharge from our soul within, which carries divine grace and lights.

Each one of us has two sides in our existence: one is the evolving human, whose origin is an animal, and the other is a light that is ever constant and eternal, not bound by space or time. Our journey on earth is to enable these two sides to relate to each other in a seamlessly harmonious way.

87-96 [Arabic Qur'anic text of verses 87–96 of Surah Al-Isra']

unless it be a mercy from your Lord. His grace towards you has indeed been abundant. Say: 'Were humans and Jinn to band together to produce a semblance of this Qur'an, they could not do so, even if they back one another up.' And certainly, We have explained for men in this Qur'an every kind of similitude, but most men do not consent to aught but denying. They say: 'We will not trust you unless you cause a spring to gush forth for us from the ground; or else you come to own a garden of palm trees and vines, and you cause rivers to gush forth in torrents through it all; or make the sky fall on us in pieces, as you claimed will happen; or bring Allah and the angels before us face to face; or else you come to own a house made of gold; or you ascend to the sky – nor will we trust your ascent unless you bring down upon us a book we can read.' Say: 'Glory be to my Lord! Am I anything other than a human being, a Messenger?' Nothing prevented mankind from believing, when Guidance came to them, except their saying: 'Did Allah really send a mere human as Messenger?' Say: 'Had there been in the earth angels walking at peace, We would have sent down upon them out of heaven an angel as Messenger.' Say: 'Allah suffices as a witness between me and you; surely He is aware of and sees His servants.'

The Qur'an - Selected Surahs

87-96 The Qur'an is the greatest mercy that has descended upon humanity. It reveals appropriate patterns that are both seen and unseen, as well as the direction and the end of all stories. It reveals how the physical world is inseparable from higher spiritual energies and lights. Multitudes of energy fields, and states emerge from the cosmic divine light. We experience them, either by choice or inadvertently. Our purpose is to acknowledge and witness what we experience and then to connect to the original *Source*. No story is complete without an end. The end of everything is where it began, and that is Allah – not subject to definition or confined to a place or time. God is ever present, ever was, and ever will be.

It is a basic structural defect for a human being not to have a higher intelligence that desires the ultimate state of awakening; even animals attempt to rise in consciousness and awareness. Yet, there are human beings who are blind, deaf, and dumb.

It is natural for the human side of us to be occasionally arrogant and proud of possessions, abilities, or powers. But ultimately, through reference to the higher light within the soul, we realise that humanity is only a precursor to living and being at one with the divinity within.

97-105

وَمَن يَهْدِ ٱللَّهُ فَهُوَ ٱلْمُهْتَدِ وَمَن يُضْلِلْ فَلَن تَجِدَ لَهُمْ أَوْلِيَآءَ مِن دُونِهِۦ وَنَحْشُرُهُمْ يَوْمَ ٱلْقِيَٰمَةِ عَلَىٰ وُجُوهِهِمْ عُمْيًا وَبُكْمًا وَصُمًّا مَّأْوَىٰهُمْ جَهَنَّمُ كُلَّمَا خَبَتْ زِدْنَٰهُمْ سَعِيرًا ۝ ذَٰلِكَ جَزَآؤُهُم بِأَنَّهُمْ كَفَرُوا۟ بِـَٔايَٰتِنَا وَقَالُوٓا۟ أَءِذَا كُنَّا عِظَٰمًا وَرُفَٰتًا أَءِنَّا لَمَبْعُوثُونَ خَلْقًا جَدِيدًا ۝ أَوَلَمْ يَرَوْا۟ أَنَّ ٱللَّهَ ٱلَّذِى خَلَقَ ٱلسَّمَٰوَٰتِ وَٱلْأَرْضَ قَادِرٌ عَلَىٰٓ أَن يَخْلُقَ مِثْلَهُمْ وَجَعَلَ لَهُمْ أَجَلًا لَّا رَيْبَ فِيهِ فَأَبَى ٱلظَّٰلِمُونَ إِلَّا كُفُورًا ۝ قُل لَّوْ أَنتُمْ تَمْلِكُونَ خَزَآئِنَ رَحْمَةِ رَبِّىٓ إِذًا لَّأَمْسَكْتُمْ خَشْيَةَ ٱلْإِنفَاقِ وَكَانَ ٱلْإِنسَٰنُ قَتُورًا ۝ وَلَقَدْ ءَاتَيْنَا مُوسَىٰ تِسْعَ ءَايَٰتٍۭ بَيِّنَٰتٍ فَسْـَٔلْ بَنِىٓ إِسْرَٰٓءِيلَ إِذْ جَآءَهُمْ فَقَالَ لَهُۥ فِرْعَوْنُ إِنِّى لَأَظُنُّكَ يَٰمُوسَىٰ مَسْحُورًا ۝ قَالَ لَقَدْ عَلِمْتَ مَآ أَنزَلَ هَٰٓؤُلَآءِ إِلَّا رَبُّ ٱلسَّمَٰوَٰتِ وَٱلْأَرْضِ بَصَآئِرَ وَإِنِّى لَأَظُنُّكَ يَٰفِرْعَوْنُ مَثْبُورًا ۝ فَأَرَادَ أَن يَسْتَفِزَّهُم مِّنَ ٱلْأَرْضِ فَأَغْرَقْنَٰهُ وَمَن مَّعَهُۥ جَمِيعًا ۝ وَقُلْنَا مِنۢ بَعْدِهِۦ لِبَنِىٓ إِسْرَٰٓءِيلَ ٱسْكُنُوا۟ ٱلْأَرْضَ فَإِذَا جَآءَ وَعْدُ ٱلْأَخِرَةِ جِئْنَا بِكُمْ لَفِيفًا ۝ وَبِٱلْحَقِّ أَنزَلْنَٰهُ وَبِٱلْحَقِّ نَزَلَ وَمَآ أَرْسَلْنَٰكَ إِلَّا مُبَشِّرًا وَنَذِيرًا ۝

He whom Allah guides is truly guided; he whom He leads astray, for him you shall find no protectors apart from Him. We shall herd them, tumbled upon their faces, on the Day of Resurrection – blind, dumb and deaf. Their refuge will be hell; whenever its flames subside, We intensify the blaze upon them. This is what they will get for rejecting Our signs and saying, 'What? When we are turned to bones and dust, how can we be raised in a new act of creation?' Do they not consider that Allah, Who created the heavens and the earth, is able to create their like, and He has appointed for them a doom about which there is no doubt? But the unjust do not consent to aught but denying. Say: 'Had you possessed the treasures of my Lord's mercy, you would have held them back, for fear of spending; man has always been miserly.' To Moses We brought nine clear wonders – ask the Children of Israel. When he came to them, Pharaoh said to him: 'O Moses, I believe you are a man bewitched.' He said, 'You know very well that only the Lord of the heavens and earth could have sent these signs as clear proof. I think that you, Pharaoh, are doomed.' So, he planned to drive them out of the land, but We drowned him, he and all who were with him. Thereafter, We said to the Children of Israel: 'Inhabit the land, and when the promise of the hereafter is fulfilled, We shall summon you forth, all in a swarm.' With the Truth We sent it down, and with the Truth it descended. We sent you only as a herald of glad tidings, and a warner.

97-105 It is natural for balanced, healthy human beings to seek guidance and hope for a fulfilled life on earth. We need appropriate guidance and direction in order to journey with less drama. To establish higher connections and receive spiritual nourishment, we need to understand our lower nature, fears, meanness, and grief, as well as learn the art of avoiding these selfish tendencies. It is human nature to desire personal wealth, power, and control, and to dismiss the signs that are essential for higher spiritual heavenly control. The Prophet's role is to remind and warn, without being responsible for people's progress or regression. It is through fear and hope that spiritual progress along the prophetic pathway takes place.

A most useful exercise is to reflect upon creation and its numerous levels: how it all arose from nothing discernible and will eventually return to that state. The true miracle is the soul within the heart, connecting all that is in the heavens with our limited earthly reality.

Good intentions, right conduct, and wisdom are all preliminary stages towards higher consciousness, which will give us exactly what we need when it is needed. This is the ultimate victory and liberation of those who fully live their faith and trust in the divine presence within them.

106-111 وَقُرْءَانًا فَرَقْنَٰهُ لِتَقْرَأَهُۥ عَلَى ٱلنَّاسِ عَلَىٰ مُكْثٍ وَنَزَّلْنَٰهُ تَنزِيلًا ۝ قُلْ ءَامِنُوا۟ بِهِۦٓ أَوْ لَا تُؤْمِنُوٓا۟ إِنَّ ٱلَّذِينَ أُوتُوا۟ ٱلْعِلْمَ مِن قَبْلِهِۦٓ إِذَا يُتْلَىٰ عَلَيْهِمْ يَخِرُّونَ لِلْأَذْقَانِ سُجَّدًا ۝ وَيَقُولُونَ سُبْحَٰنَ رَبِّنَآ إِن كَانَ وَعْدُ رَبِّنَا لَمَفْعُولًا ۝ وَيَخِرُّونَ لِلْأَذْقَانِ يَبْكُونَ وَيَزِيدُهُمْ خُشُوعًا ۝ قُلِ ٱدْعُوا۟ ٱللَّهَ أَوِ ٱدْعُوا۟ ٱلرَّحْمَٰنَ أَيًّا مَّا تَدْعُوا۟ فَلَهُ ٱلْأَسْمَآءُ ٱلْحُسْنَىٰ وَلَا تَجْهَرْ بِصَلَاتِكَ وَلَا تُخَافِتْ بِهَا وَٱبْتَغِ بَيْنَ ذَٰلِكَ سَبِيلًا ۝ وَقُلِ ٱلْحَمْدُ لِلَّهِ ٱلَّذِى لَمْ يَتَّخِذْ وَلَدًا وَلَمْ يَكُن لَّهُۥ شَرِيكٌ فِى ٱلْمُلْكِ وَلَمْ يَكُن لَّهُۥ وَلِىٌّ مِّنَ ٱلذُّلِّ وَكَبِّرْهُ تَكْبِيرًۢا ۝

And a Qur'an We have divided, for you to recite it to mankind at intervals, and We have sent it down successively. Say: 'Believe in it, or believe not; those who were given the knowledge before it when it is recited to them, fall down upon their faces prostrating, saying: "Glory be to our Lord! The promise of our Lord will surely come about." And they fall down upon their faces weeping; and it increases them in humility.' Say: 'Call upon Allah or call upon the All-Merciful: whichever you call upon, to Him belong the names most glorious.' Do not raise your voice in prayer, nor whisper it, but seek a middle way between. And say: 'Praise belongs to Allah, who has not taken to Him a child, and who has not any associate in the Kingdom, nor any protector out of humbleness.' And magnify Him with all magnificence."

106-111 To progress from the darkness of the lower self to the light of the soul within, we need trust and faith in the divine governance and perfection of everything in its essence. Allah's desirable attributes, such as generosity, patience, and mercy, are manifestations of the sacred, original light within us. Emulating these higher attributes projects us towards the ultimate spiritual light. Wealth, knowledge, power, patience, compassion, generosity, and steadfastness are all desirable qualities that our higher nature beams towards us, attracting us to its *Source*.

Truth is absolute and ever constant. This is why it appears that the Qur'an is fairly repetitive. Ultimately, truth emanates from the absolute divine precinct, but the way to it is to ascend in consciousness and leave behind all that is discernible.

The Adamic consciousness is embedded within all of the divine attributes that we as human beings respect, admire, and love. There is a big difference between admiring generosity and being generous due to the knowledge that you own nothing. At best, you are a connector and a guardian of whatever good comes into your life. There is a huge difference between believing and accepting that the divine attributes are a desirable objective and actually living them, being liberated from the illusion of otherness, and evolving as human beings.

6. Surah 18 Al-Kahf (The Cave)

When the heart is still and in a state of gratitude, it may read the perfection of the creational pattern and witness what is described comprehensively in the Book of Creation.

بِسْمِ اللَّـهِ الرَّحْمَـٰنِ الرَّحِيمِ

1-10 ٱلْحَمْدُ لِلَّـهِ ٱلَّذِى أَنزَلَ عَلَىٰ عَبْدِهِ ٱلْكِتَـٰبَ وَلَمْ يَجْعَل لَّهُۥ عِوَجَاۜ ۝ قَيِّمًا لِّيُنذِرَ بَأْسًا شَدِيدًا مِّن لَّدُنْهُ وَيُبَشِّرَ ٱلْمُؤْمِنِينَ ٱلَّذِينَ يَعْمَلُونَ ٱلصَّـٰلِحَـٰتِ أَنَّ لَهُمْ أَجْرًا حَسَنًا ۝ مَّـٰكِثِينَ فِيهِ أَبَدًا ۝ وَيُنذِرَ ٱلَّذِينَ قَالُوا۟ ٱتَّخَذَ ٱللَّـهُ وَلَدًا ۝ مَّا لَهُم بِهِۦ مِنْ عِلْمٍ وَلَا لِـَٔابَآئِهِمْ ۚ كَبُرَتْ كَلِمَةً تَخْرُجُ مِنْ أَفْوَٰهِهِمْ ۚ إِن يَقُولُونَ إِلَّا كَذِبًا ۝ فَلَعَلَّكَ بَـٰخِعٌ نَّفْسَكَ عَلَىٰٓ ءَاثَـٰرِهِمْ إِن لَّمْ يُؤْمِنُوا۟ بِهَـٰذَا ٱلْحَدِيثِ أَسَفًا ۝ إِنَّا جَعَلْنَا

مَا عَلَى ٱلْأَرْضِ زِينَةً لَّهَا لِنَبْلُوَهُمْ أَيُّهُمْ أَحْسَنُ عَمَلًا ۝ وَإِنَّا لَجَاعِلُونَ مَا عَلَيْهَا صَعِيدًا جُرُزًا ۝ أَمْ حَسِبْتَ أَنَّ أَصْحَٰبَ ٱلْكَهْفِ وَٱلرَّقِيمِ كَانُوا۟ مِنْ ءَايَٰتِنَا عَجَبًا ۝ إِذْ أَوَى ٱلْفِتْيَةُ إِلَى ٱلْكَهْفِ فَقَالُوا۟ رَبَّنَآ ءَاتِنَا مِن لَّدُنكَ رَحْمَةً وَهَيِّئْ لَنَا مِنْ أَمْرِنَا رَشَدًا ۝

In the name of Allah, the Merciful to all, the Compassionate to each!

Praise be to Allah, Who brought down the Book upon His servant, and rendered it free, from distortion, unswerving, to give warning of grievous wrath from on high, and announce glad tidings to the faithful who perform good deeds, that a fair reward awaits them, therein dwelling for ever. And to warn those who claim that Allah took a child to Himself. They have no knowledge of it, nor had their fathers; a grievous word it is that comes out of their mouths; they speak nothing but a lie. Yet perchance, if they believe not in this tiding, you will consume yourself, following after them, of grief. We have appointed all that is on the earth for an adornment for it, and that We may try which of them is fairest in works; and We shall surely make all that is on it barren dust. Or do you think the Men of the Cave and Er-Rakeem were among Our signs a wonder? When the youths took refuge in the Cave saying, 'Our lord, give us mercy from You, and furnish us with rectitude in our affair.'

1-10 We require faith and trust in the fact that our life on earth has purpose and that its direction is to the ultimate *Source*. This process, as well as its higher meaning and guidance, are fully described in the Qur'an. Earthly attractions and beauties are metaphors for the perfect design behind them. Falling under their allure and distraction hampers the movement towards higher consciousness and awakening to the divine *Truth*. Our curiosity about the nature of time and its distractions provides a good starting point to meditate and reflect upon timelessness and the boundless *Reality*. The Men of the Cave were seekers of truth and the nature of time and eternity. That is why they were rejected from the established community.

Our life on earth is a preliminary introduction to the divine majesty and beauty that becomes much more powerful after death. Like gazing at the intensity of sunlight, one needs to practice and shield one's sight and move from sight to insight.

Creation occurred by divine decree and follows patterns within space and time that will continue until the end of creation. A believer is he or she who accepts there is a perfect path to live joyfully on earth in readiness for the next experience of higher consciousness after death.

11-18 فَضَرَبْنَا عَلَىٰٓ ءَاذَانِهِمْ فِى ٱلْكَهْفِ سِنِينَ عَدَدًا ۝ ثُمَّ بَعَثْنَٰهُمْ لِنَعْلَمَ أَىُّ ٱلْحِزْبَيْنِ أَحْصَىٰ لِمَا لَبِثُوٓا۟ أَمَدًا ۝ نَّحْنُ نَقُصُّ عَلَيْكَ نَبَأَهُم بِٱلْحَقِّ إِنَّهُمْ فِتْيَةٌ ءَامَنُوا۟ بِرَبِّهِمْ وَزِدْنَٰهُمْ هُدًى ۝ وَرَبَطْنَا عَلَىٰ قُلُوبِهِمْ إِذْ قَامُوا۟ فَقَالُوا۟ رَبُّنَا رَبُّ ٱلسَّمَٰوَٰتِ وَٱلْأَرْضِ

لَن نَّدْعُوَاْ مِن دُونِهِۦٓ إِلَٰهًا لَّقَدْ قُلْنَآ إِذًا شَطَطًا ۝ هَٰٓؤُلَآءِ قَوْمُنَا ٱتَّخَذُواْ مِن دُونِهِۦٓ ءَالِهَةً لَّوْلَا يَأْتُونَ عَلَيْهِم بِسُلْطَٰنٍۭ بَيِّنٍ فَمَنْ أَظْلَمُ مِمَّنِ ٱفْتَرَىٰ عَلَى ٱللَّهِ كَذِبًا ۝ وَإِذِ ٱعْتَزَلْتُمُوهُمْ وَمَا يَعْبُدُونَ إِلَّا ٱللَّهَ فَأْوُۥٓاْ إِلَى ٱلْكَهْفِ يَنشُرْ لَكُمْ رَبُّكُم مِّن رَّحْمَتِهِۦ وَيُهَيِّئْ لَكُم مِّنْ أَمْرِكُم مِّرْفَقًا ۝ وَتَرَى ٱلشَّمْسَ إِذَا طَلَعَت تَّزَٰوَرُ عَن كَهْفِهِمْ ذَاتَ ٱلْيَمِينِ وَإِذَا غَرَبَت تَّقْرِضُهُمْ ذَاتَ ٱلشِّمَالِ وَهُمْ فِى فَجْوَةٍ مِّنْهُ ذَٰلِكَ مِنْ ءَايَٰتِ ٱللَّهِ مَن يَهْدِ ٱللَّهُ فَهُوَ ٱلْمُهْتَدِ وَمَن يُضْلِلْ فَلَن تَجِدَ لَهُۥ وَلِيًّا مُّرْشِدًا ۝ وَتَحْسَبُهُمْ أَيْقَاظًا وَهُمْ رُقُودٌ وَنُقَلِّبُهُمْ ذَاتَ ٱلْيَمِينِ وَذَاتَ ٱلشِّمَالِ وَكَلْبُهُم بَٰسِطٌ ذِرَاعَيْهِ بِٱلْوَصِيدِ لَوِ ٱطَّلَعْتَ عَلَيْهِمْ لَوَلَّيْتَ مِنْهُمْ فِرَارًا وَلَمُلِئْتَ مِنْهُمْ رُعْبًا ۝

So, We sealed their ears in the cave for a number of years, then We brought them forth in order to know which of the two groups was more accurate as to the time they spent. We shall now narrate to you their story, in truth. They were youths who believed in their Lord, and whom We increased in guidance. And We strengthened their hearts when they rose up, saying: 'Our Lord, Lord of the heavens and earth! We shall call upon no other Allah besides Him, else we utter a falsehood. These our people have taken to themselves Gods apart from Him. If only they could show some manifest proof for them! But who is more wicked than he who fabricates lies against Allah? And now, having abandoned them and what they worship other than Allah, let us take refuge in a cave, and your lord will spread out His mercy and make it easy for you to find the prudent path to follow in this matter.' And you would have seen the sun, as it arose, veering away from their cave on the right, and, as it set, cutting them out of its path on the left, they being in a cavity therein. That was one of the signs of Allah. He whom Allah guides is truly guided; he whom He leads astray, for him you shall find no protector, no mentor. You would have thought them awake, as they lay sleeping, while We turned them now to the right, now to the left, and their dog stretching its paws on the threshold. Had you observed them surely you would have turned your back on them in flight, and been filled with terror of them.

11-18 A group of believers who were chosen to experience the relativity of time were put in a cave for 309 years. Outer changes occurred around them, but this did not affect them nor were they aware of the swift passage of many years. This band of people in the cave had escaped from their people, who were in darkness and denial about the *Real*. Time is an illusion that reinforces the transient nature of our earthly life, providing a resemblance of continuity and its hazy reality: a manifest flow of the creative *Author* – Allah.

It may be necessary for a seeker to occasionally take refuge from the usual habits of day-to-day life to enhance inner reflectiveness and to rise in consciousness. Throughout our history some individuals and peoples have preferred to retreat from material and commercial activities.

6. Surah 18 Al-Kahf (The Cave)

Some people are always looking for signs as to the next phase of life and do not accept that our earthly experience is the only thing that exists. This is a sign of higher intelligence regarding a reality that's eternal, rather than short-lived, as human life is on earth. Historically every people have had individuals or certain groups who wanted to spend time and effort to reflect upon the nature of reality after death.

19-24 وَكَذَٰلِكَ بَعَثْنَٰهُمْ لِيَتَسَآءَلُوا۟ بَيْنَهُمْ ۚ قَالَ قَآئِلٌ مِّنْهُمْ كَمْ لَبِثْتُمْ ۖ قَالُوا۟ لَبِثْنَا يَوْمًا أَوْ بَعْضَ يَوْمٍ ۚ قَالُوا۟ رَبُّكُمْ أَعْلَمُ بِمَا لَبِثْتُمْ فَٱبْعَثُوٓا۟ أَحَدَكُم بِوَرِقِكُمْ هَٰذِهِۦٓ إِلَى ٱلْمَدِينَةِ فَلْيَنظُرْ أَيُّهَآ أَزْكَىٰ طَعَامًا فَلْيَأْتِكُم بِرِزْقٍ مِّنْهُ وَلْيَتَلَطَّفْ وَلَا يُشْعِرَنَّ بِكُمْ أَحَدًا ۝ إِنَّهُمْ إِن يَظْهَرُوا۟ عَلَيْكُمْ يَرْجُمُوكُمْ أَوْ يُعِيدُوكُمْ فِى مِلَّتِهِمْ وَلَن تُفْلِحُوٓا۟ إِذًا أَبَدًا ۝ وَكَذَٰلِكَ أَعْثَرْنَا عَلَيْهِمْ لِيَعْلَمُوٓا۟ أَنَّ وَعْدَ ٱللَّهِ حَقٌّ وَأَنَّ ٱلسَّاعَةَ لَا رَيْبَ فِيهَآ إِذْ يَتَنَٰزَعُونَ بَيْنَهُمْ أَمْرَهُمْ ۖ فَقَالُوا۟ ٱبْنُوا۟ عَلَيْهِم بُنْيَٰنًا ۖ رَّبُّهُمْ أَعْلَمُ بِهِمْ ۚ قَالَ ٱلَّذِينَ غَلَبُوا۟ عَلَىٰٓ أَمْرِهِمْ لَنَتَّخِذَنَّ عَلَيْهِم مَّسْجِدًا ۝ سَيَقُولُونَ ثَلَٰثَةٌ رَّابِعُهُمْ كَلْبُهُمْ وَيَقُولُونَ خَمْسَةٌ سَادِسُهُمْ كَلْبُهُمْ رَجْمًۢا بِٱلْغَيْبِ ۖ وَيَقُولُونَ سَبْعَةٌ وَثَامِنُهُمْ كَلْبُهُمْ ۚ قُل رَّبِّىٓ أَعْلَمُ بِعِدَّتِهِم مَّا يَعْلَمُهُمْ إِلَّا قَلِيلٌ ۗ فَلَا تُمَارِ فِيهِمْ إِلَّا مِرَآءً ظَٰهِرًا وَلَا تَسْتَفْتِ فِيهِم مِّنْهُمْ أَحَدًا ۝ وَلَا تَقُولَنَّ لِشَا۟ىْءٍ إِنِّى فَاعِلٌ ذَٰلِكَ غَدًا ۝ إِلَّآ أَن يَشَآءَ ٱللَّهُ ۚ وَٱذْكُر رَّبَّكَ إِذَا نَسِيتَ وَقُلْ عَسَىٰٓ أَن يَهْدِيَنِ رَبِّى لِأَقْرَبَ مِنْ هَٰذَا رَشَدًا ۝

Thus, did We make them rise up again, to question one another. Said one of them: 'How long did you remain thus?' They said: 'We remained for a day, or a part thereof.' He said: 'Your Lord knows best how long you remained. So, send out one of you, with this your silver money, to the city, and let him find out which is the tastiest of food, and let him bring back to you a provision of it. Let him be discreet, and let no one know of your presence. If they should get knowledge of you, they will stone you, or restore you to their creed, then you will not prosper ever.' And even so We made them stumble upon them, that they might know that Allah's promise is true, and that the Hour – there is no doubt of it. When they were contending among themselves of their affair then they said, 'Build over them a building; their Lord knows of them very well.' Said those who prevailed over their affair, 'We will raise over them a place of worship.' They will say, 'Three; and their dog was the fourth of them.' They will say, 'Five; and their dog was the sixth of them,' guessing at the Unseen. They will say, 'Seven; and their dog was the eighth of them.' Say: 'My Lord knows very well their number, and none knows them, except a few.' So do not dispute with them, except in outward disputation, and ask not any of them for a pronouncement on them. And do not say, regarding anything, 'I am going to do that tomorrow,' but only, 'If Allah wills'; and mention your Lord, when you forget, and say, 'It may be that my Lord will guide me unto something nearer to rectitude than this.'

19-24 This group of believers had experienced many years as a few hours, and they imagined having been in the cave for just part of a day. As this unusual event came to be known to common people, they discussed and argued as to how many were in the cave – three, six or seven people – as well as the number of years that they dwelled therein. Our human experience and senses provide us with one strand of consciousness, which is only relative in its reality. Our measure of time becomes confused with deep sleep, under anaesthesia, or in a coma. The example of the people in the cave is a sample of how time is relative and hazy, and eternity relates to higher consciousness and the nature of God.

In both the East and West, humanity had people who were not in the mainstream. These people were often tolerated and respected because of their ability to turn away from more typical, usual, worldly ambitions.

Our experiences on earth have a temporary reality, which continuously changes in clarity. Absolute certainty belongs to the soul and higher consciousness, not to our conditioned consciousness. Therefore, we pray for more durable light and knowledge, which is ever there but requires us to lay aside our mental and emotional distractions.

25-31 وَلَبِثُوا۟ فِى كَهْفِهِمْ ثَلَـٰثَ مِا۟ئَةٍ سِنِينَ وَٱزْدَادُوا۟ تِسْعًا ۝ قُلِ ٱللَّهُ أَعْلَمُ بِمَا لَبِثُوا۟ لَهُۥ غَيْبُ ٱلسَّمَـٰوَٰتِ وَٱلْأَرْضِ أَبْصِرْ بِهِۦ وَأَسْمِعْ مَا لَهُم مِّن دُونِهِۦ مِن وَلِىٍّ وَلَا يُشْرِكُ فِى حُكْمِهِۦٓ أَحَدًا ۝ وَٱتْلُ مَآ أُوحِىَ إِلَيْكَ مِن كِتَابِ رَبِّكَ لَا مُبَدِّلَ لِكَلِمَـٰتِهِۦ وَلَن تَجِدَ مِن دُونِهِۦ مُلْتَحَدًا ۝ وَٱصْبِرْ نَفْسَكَ مَعَ ٱلَّذِينَ يَدْعُونَ رَبَّهُم بِٱلْغَدَوٰةِ وَٱلْعَشِىِّ يُرِيدُونَ وَجْهَهُۥ وَلَا تَعْدُ عَيْنَاكَ عَنْهُمْ تُرِيدُ زِينَةَ ٱلْحَيَوٰةِ ٱلدُّنْيَا وَلَا تُطِعْ مَنْ أَغْفَلْنَا قَلْبَهُۥ عَن ذِكْرِنَا وَٱتَّبَعَ هَوَىٰهُ وَكَانَ أَمْرُهُۥ فُرُطًا ۝ وَقُلِ ٱلْحَقُّ مِن رَّبِّكُمْ فَمَن شَآءَ فَلْيُؤْمِن وَمَن شَآءَ فَلْيَكْفُرْ إِنَّآ أَعْتَدْنَا لِلظَّـٰلِمِينَ نَارًا أَحَاطَ بِهِمْ سُرَادِقُهَا وَإِن يَسْتَغِيثُوا۟ يُغَاثُوا۟ بِمَآءٍ كَٱلْمُهْلِ يَشْوِى ٱلْوُجُوهَ بِئْسَ ٱلشَّرَابُ وَسَآءَتْ مُرْتَفَقًا ۝ إِنَّ ٱلَّذِينَ ءَامَنُوا۟ وَعَمِلُوا۟ ٱلصَّـٰلِحَـٰتِ إِنَّا لَا نُضِيعُ أَجْرَ مَنْ أَحْسَنَ عَمَلًا ۝ أُو۟لَـٰٓئِكَ لَهُمْ جَنَّـٰتُ عَدْنٍ تَجْرِى مِن تَحْتِهِمُ ٱلْأَنْهَـٰرُ يُحَلَّوْنَ فِيهَا مِنْ أَسَاوِرَ مِن ذَهَبٍ وَيَلْبَسُونَ ثِيَابًا خُضْرًا مِّن سُندُسٍ وَإِسْتَبْرَقٍ مُّتَّكِـِٔينَ فِيهَا عَلَى ٱلْأَرَآئِكِ نِعْمَ ٱلثَّوَابُ وَحَسُنَتْ مُرْتَفَقًا ۝

They remained in their cave for three hundred years, to which were added nine. Say: 'Allah knows how long they remained. To Him belongs the Unseen in the heavens and earth. How He sees all! How He hears all! Apart from Him they have no protector, nor does He associate anyone with Him in His judgment.' Recite what has been revealed to you of the Book of your Lord; no change to His words. Apart from Him, you will find no refuge. And restrain yourself with those who call upon their Lord at morning and evening, desir-

ing His countenance, and let not your eyes turn away from them, desiring the adornment of the present life; and obey not him whose heart We have made neglectful of Our remembrance so that he follows his own whim, and his affair has become all excess. Say, 'Now the truth has come from your Lord: let those who wish to believe in it do so, and let those who wish to reject it do so.' We have prepared a Fire for the wrongdoers that will envelop them from all sides. If they call for relief, they will be relieved with water like molten metal, scalding their faces. What a terrible drink! What a painful resting place! As for those who believed and performed good deeds – We waste not the wage of one righteous in works. These it is for whom are gardens of perpetuity beneath which rivers flow, ornaments shall be given to them therein of bracelets of gold, and they shall wear green robes of fine silk and thick silk brocade interwoven with gold, reclining therein on raised couches; excellent the recompense and goodly the resting place.

25-31 Human knowledge, understanding, and mental rationale are limited and relative. Human sight and outer senses are just samples of modified divine sight and *Reality*. A believer who experiences life on earth as a gradual awakening to the eternal *Truth* will exercise patience and constant reference to the light within the heart. The ultimate good deed is to accept the temporary, approximate nature of our earthly reality with trust and faith in what is true. This is the path to the divine energy field of paradise, ever-present, for whomsoever is graced to access it within the heart.

To rise in higher consciousness, it is useful to be in the company of others with a similar ambition; otherwise, the norm, to be enamoured with the world and its glitter, will naturally distract one from the goal towards light. It is most important for people on the path to partake in activities of joyful service.

The ultimate duty, respect, and responsibility of an intelligent human being are to do what we can with accountability and transparency and then leave the rest, as part of the natural drive to have faith and trust in the divine Light. As such, you combine your interaction with the world of duality with the full acknowledgement and grasp of the eternal light of divinity within the heart.

32-40 وَٱضْرِبْ لَهُم مَّثَلًا رَّجُلَيْنِ جَعَلْنَا لِأَحَدِهِمَا جَنَّتَيْنِ مِنْ أَعْنَٰبٍ وَحَفَفْنَٰهُمَا بِنَخْلٍ وَجَعَلْنَا بَيْنَهُمَا زَرْعًا ۝ كِلْتَا ٱلْجَنَّتَيْنِ ءَاتَتْ أُكُلَهَا وَلَمْ تَظْلِم مِّنْهُ شَيْـًٔا وَفَجَّرْنَا خِلَٰلَهُمَا نَهَرًا ۝ وَكَانَ لَهُۥ ثَمَرٌ فَقَالَ لِصَٰحِبِهِۦ وَهُوَ يُحَاوِرُهُۥٓ أَنَا۠ أَكْثَرُ مِنكَ مَالًا وَأَعَزُّ نَفَرًا ۝ وَدَخَلَ جَنَّتَهُۥ وَهُوَ ظَالِمٌ لِّنَفْسِهِۦ قَالَ مَآ أَظُنُّ أَن تَبِيدَ هَٰذِهِۦٓ أَبَدًا ۝ وَمَآ أَظُنُّ ٱلسَّاعَةَ قَآئِمَةً وَلَئِن رُّدِدتُّ إِلَىٰ رَبِّى لَأَجِدَنَّ خَيْرًا مِّنْهَا مُنقَلَبًا ۝ قَالَ لَهُۥ صَاحِبُهُۥ وَهُوَ يُحَاوِرُهُۥٓ أَكَفَرْتَ بِٱلَّذِى خَلَقَكَ مِن تُرَابٍ ثُمَّ مِن نُّطْفَةٍ ثُمَّ سَوَّىٰكَ رَجُلًا ۝ لَّٰكِنَّا۠ هُوَ ٱللَّهُ رَبِّى وَلَآ أُشْرِكُ بِرَبِّىٓ أَحَدًا ۝ وَلَوْلَآ إِذْ دَخَلْتَ

جَنَّتَكَ قُلْتَ مَا شَاءَ ٱللَّهُ لَا قُوَّةَ إِلَّا بِٱللَّهِ إِن تَرَنِ أَنَا۠ أَقَلَّ مِنكَ مَالًا وَوَلَدًا ۞ فَعَسَىٰ رَبِّىٓ أَن يُؤْتِيَنِ خَيْرًا مِّن جَنَّتِكَ وَيُرْسِلَ عَلَيْهَا حُسْبَانًا مِّنَ ٱلسَّمَآءِ فَتُصْبِحَ صَعِيدًا زَلَقًا ۞

Strike for them a parable of two men. To one of them We allotted two gardens of vine, which We surrounded with palms, and We placed a cultivated field in between. Both gardens produced their harvest in full, diminishing it not one bit. Through them both We caused a river to gush forth. One of them gathered his fruit and said to his companion, in conversation: 'I am greater in wealth than you are and more powerful in kin.' And he entered his garden, wronging himself; he said, 'I do not think that this will ever perish; I do not think that the Hour is coming; and if I am indeed returned to my Lord, I shall surely find a better resort than this.' His companion retorted, 'Have you no faith in Him who created you from dust, from a small drop of fluid, then shaped you into a man? But lo, He is Allah, my Lord, and I will not associate with my Lord anyone. If only you had entered your garden and said: "This is the will of Allah! There is no strength save in Allah!" If you see me inferior to you in wealth and offspring, perhaps my Lord will bring me what is better than your garden. Or perhaps He will cast down upon it thunderbolts from the sky, and it will become a slippery plain,

32-40 It is a natural human tendency to be competitive and acquisitive, as well as envious and jealous. These attributes reflect our earthly, animal nature revealed through the lower self and ego. The source of these behaviour patterns reflects the divine majesty that is transmitted by the soul and that the shadow self wants to acquire. We are attracted to that which is powerful, beautiful, or bigger than normal, because the *Source* is most powerful, most strong, and bigger than all. Our experience of life on earth is a sample of the perfection of life itself as well as the divine attributes and qualities that emanate from the essence of life.

Meanness and greed are natural vices for those who mostly pursue earthly acquisitions. Once a seeker has tasted the joy of inner light and the immensity of the present moment, then their commitment to pursue that state deepens.

As humans, sometimes we win or lose, but ultimately death will put an end to any idea of success. Only by constant referencing to the timeless, which is transmitted from our own heart, will we have a balanced way of life with no regrets, fears, or sorrows.

41-49 أَوْ يُصْبِحَ مَآؤُهَا غَوْرًا فَلَن تَسْتَطِيعَ لَهُۥ طَلَبًا ۞ وَأُحِيطَ بِثَمَرِهِۦ فَأَصْبَحَ يُقَلِّبُ كَفَّيْهِ عَلَىٰ مَآ أَنفَقَ فِيهَا وَهِىَ خَاوِيَةٌ عَلَىٰ عُرُوشِهَا وَيَقُولُ يَٰلَيْتَنِى لَمْ أُشْرِكْ بِرَبِّىٓ أَحَدًا ۞ وَلَمْ تَكُن لَّهُۥ فِئَةٌ يَنصُرُونَهُۥ مِن دُونِ ٱللَّهِ وَمَا كَانَ مُنتَصِرًا ۞ هُنَالِكَ ٱلْوَلَٰيَةُ لِلَّهِ ٱلْحَقِّ هُوَ خَيْرٌ ثَوَابًا وَخَيْرٌ عُقْبًا ۞ وَٱضْرِبْ لَهُم مَّثَلَ ٱلْحَيَوٰةِ ٱلدُّنْيَا

كَمَآءٍ أَنزَلْنَٰهُ مِنَ ٱلسَّمَآءِ فَٱخْتَلَطَ بِهِۦ نَبَاتُ ٱلْأَرْضِ فَأَصْبَحَ هَشِيمًا تَذْرُوهُ ٱلرِّيَٰحُ ۗ وَكَانَ ٱللَّهُ عَلَىٰ كُلِّ شَىْءٍ مُّقْتَدِرًا ۝ ٱلْمَالُ وَٱلْبَنُونَ زِينَةُ ٱلْحَيَوٰةِ ٱلدُّنْيَا ۖ وَٱلْبَٰقِيَٰتُ ٱلصَّٰلِحَٰتُ خَيْرٌ عِندَ رَبِّكَ ثَوَابًا وَخَيْرٌ أَمَلًا ۝ وَيَوْمَ نُسَيِّرُ ٱلْجِبَالَ وَتَرَى ٱلْأَرْضَ بَارِزَةً وَحَشَرْنَٰهُمْ فَلَمْ نُغَادِرْ مِنْهُمْ أَحَدًا ۝ وَعُرِضُواْ عَلَىٰ رَبِّكَ صَفًّا لَّقَدْ جِئْتُمُونَا كَمَا خَلَقْنَٰكُمْ أَوَّلَ مَرَّةٍ ۚ بَلْ زَعَمْتُمْ أَلَّن نَّجْعَلَ لَكُم مَّوْعِدًا ۝ وَوُضِعَ ٱلْكِتَٰبُ فَتَرَى ٱلْمُجْرِمِينَ مُشْفِقِينَ مِمَّا فِيهِ وَيَقُولُونَ يَٰوَيْلَتَنَا مَالِ هَٰذَا ٱلْكِتَٰبِ لَا يُغَادِرُ صَغِيرَةً وَلَا كَبِيرَةً إِلَّآ أَحْصَىٰهَا ۚ وَوَجَدُواْ مَا عَمِلُواْ حَاضِرًا ۗ وَلَا يَظْلِمُ رَبُّكَ أَحَدًا ۝

or in the morning the water of it will be sunk into the earth, so that you will not be able to seek it out.' And his fruit was all encompassed, and in the morning, he was wringing his hands for that he had expended upon it, and it was fallen down upon its trellises, and he was saying, 'Would I had not associated with my Lord any one!' But there was no host to help him, apart from Allah, and he was helpless. In that situation, the only protection is that of Allah, the True. He gives the best rewards and the best outcome. Strike for them a parable of this present life. It is like water We caused to descend from the sky, with which the vegetation of the earth was mingled. But it turned into chaff, scattered by the winds. Allah has power over all things. Property and progeny are the ornament of this present life, but those things that abide, virtuous deeds, are better in reward with your Lord, and better in prospect. And on the day, We shall set the mountains in motion, and you see the earth coming forth, and We muster them so that We leave not so much as one of them behind; they shall be passed in review before your Lord, in line: 'So now you come to Us just as We created you the first time. Or do you claim that We have not assigned an appointed time for you?' The record of their deeds will be laid open and you will see the guilty, dismayed at what they contain, saying, 'Woe to us! What a record this is! It does not leave any deed, small or large, unaccounted for!' They will find everything they ever did laid in front of them: your Lord will not be unjust to anyone.

41-49 Our journey of experiences on earth propels us towards higher awareness, consciousness, and connectedness to the essence of Godhood. Our perspective of time and our fear of the end of time both can expedite our journey in consciousness towards timeless, supreme consciousness. If we are not on this path, we will inevitably be despondent and depressed. Our pursuit of wealth and our desire for a comfortable life on earth reflect our pursuit of truth, which transcends all these qualities. Awareness of the temporary nature of life on earth and the eventual collapse of the universe helps us to keep a balanced spiritual perspective. With this perspective the believer may deal with worldly matters without great emotional attachment or upheaval. Only a few people will understand the immensity of *Truth* and divine prevalence.

Humans are naturally attracted to earthly wealth, power, and relationships. With reflection, we will realise that what we truly seek is a state that is constant and eternal. To reflect upon natural events will alter our perspective on time. Mountains, viewed over a timescale of a million years, will appear to move as clouds.

We have been given enough reason and ability to reflect that we can rise higher in intelligence to realise that no matter how much power, wealth, and ability we accumulate in this world, it will never be sufficient. It will end with death. This is why we always want to transcend the limitations of our minds and be recalibrated with the eternal light transmitted from the heart.

50-57 وَإِذْ قُلْنَا لِلْمَلَٰٓئِكَةِ ٱسْجُدُوا۟ لِـَٔادَمَ فَسَجَدُوٓا۟ إِلَّآ إِبْلِيسَ كَانَ مِنَ ٱلْجِنِّ فَفَسَقَ عَنْ أَمْرِ رَبِّهِۦٓ ۗ أَفَتَتَّخِذُونَهُۥ وَذُرِّيَّتَهُۥٓ أَوْلِيَآءَ مِن دُونِى وَهُمْ لَكُمْ عَدُوٌّۢ ۚ بِئْسَ لِلظَّٰلِمِينَ بَدَلًا ۝ مَّآ أَشْهَدتُّهُمْ خَلْقَ ٱلسَّمَٰوَٰتِ وَٱلْأَرْضِ وَلَا خَلْقَ أَنفُسِهِمْ وَمَا كُنتُ مُتَّخِذَ ٱلْمُضِلِّينَ عَضُدًا ۝ وَيَوْمَ يَقُولُ نَادُوا۟ شُرَكَآءِىَ ٱلَّذِينَ زَعَمْتُمْ فَدَعَوْهُمْ فَلَمْ يَسْتَجِيبُوا۟ لَهُمْ وَجَعَلْنَا بَيْنَهُم مَّوْبِقًا ۝ وَرَءَا ٱلْمُجْرِمُونَ ٱلنَّارَ فَظَنُّوٓا۟ أَنَّهُم مُّوَاقِعُوهَا وَلَمْ يَجِدُوا۟ عَنْهَا مَصْرِفًا ۝ وَلَقَدْ صَرَّفْنَا فِى هَٰذَا ٱلْقُرْءَانِ لِلنَّاسِ مِن كُلِّ مَثَلٍ ۚ وَكَانَ ٱلْإِنسَٰنُ أَكْثَرَ شَىْءٍ جَدَلًا ۝ وَمَا مَنَعَ ٱلنَّاسَ أَن يُؤْمِنُوٓا۟ إِذْ جَآءَهُمُ ٱلْهُدَىٰ وَيَسْتَغْفِرُوا۟ رَبَّهُمْ إِلَّآ أَن تَأْتِيَهُمْ سُنَّةُ ٱلْأَوَّلِينَ أَوْ يَأْتِيَهُمُ ٱلْعَذَابُ قُبُلًا ۝ وَمَا نُرْسِلُ ٱلْمُرْسَلِينَ إِلَّا مُبَشِّرِينَ وَمُنذِرِينَ ۚ وَيُجَٰدِلُ ٱلَّذِينَ كَفَرُوا۟ بِٱلْبَٰطِلِ لِيُدْحِضُوا۟ بِهِ ٱلْحَقَّ ۖ وَٱتَّخَذُوٓا۟ ءَايَٰتِى وَمَآ أُنذِرُوا۟ هُزُوًا ۝ وَمَنْ أَظْلَمُ مِمَّن ذُكِّرَ بِـَٔايَٰتِ رَبِّهِۦ فَأَعْرَضَ عَنْهَا وَنَسِىَ مَا قَدَّمَتْ يَدَاهُ ۚ إِنَّا جَعَلْنَا عَلَىٰ قُلُوبِهِمْ أَكِنَّةً أَن يَفْقَهُوهُ وَفِىٓ ءَاذَانِهِمْ وَقْرًا ۖ وَإِن تَدْعُهُمْ إِلَى ٱلْهُدَىٰ فَلَن يَهْتَدُوٓا۟ إِذًا أَبَدًا ۝

Then We told the angels, 'Prostrate yourselves before Adam,' they all prostrated themselves, save Iblis: he was one of those hidden, but then he turned away from his lord's command. Will you, then, take him and his seed for, masters instead of Me, although they are your foe? How vile an exchange for the evil-doers. I made them not witnesses of the creation of the heavens and earth, neither of the creation of themselves; I would not ever take those who lead others astray to be My supporters. And on the day, He shall say, 'Call on My associates whom you asserted;' and then they shall call on them, but they will not answer them, and We shall set a gulf between them. The evil-doers will see the Fire and they will realize that they are about to fall into it: they will find no escape from it. In this Qur'an, We have elucidated to mankind every sort of parable, and man is, of all beings, the most argumentative. What prevents mankind from believing, now that Guidance has come to them, or from seeking the forgiveness of their Lord, unless it be the example of the ancients that will overwhelm them, or else they be overwhelmed by imminent torment? We send messengers only as heralds of glad tidings and warners. But those who disbelieve use false arguments in order to refute the truth. They have taken My signs, and the warnings in mockery. And who does greater evil than he who, being reminded of the signs of his Lord, turns away from them and forgets what his hands have forwarded? Surely, We have laid veils on their hearts lest they understand it, and in their ears heaviness; and though you call them to the guidance, yet they will not be guided ever.

50-57 Everything in existence expresses an aspect of duality, as does the human mind with its acceptance or rejection of both trust and doubt. Revealed knowledge from the great prophets confirms that our life experience on earth is a sample of life experience after death. The revelations provide descriptions of the perfect soul, as well as warnings about the distraction of the love of *dunya* with its desires, which darken the soul. When the heart is veiled with the darkness of fear and insecurity, the senses remain at a low, earthly level; rather than pointing towards higher truths, they then disable spiritual growth to higher consciousness and awakening.

In our world of dualities, there will always be dark shadows with lights, pain with pleasure. The good news is that the soul is divine and eternal, and its shadow, that the lower self, is earthly and deceptive. We need to have healthy bodies, senses, and most importantly pure, untarnished hearts free from enmity and hatred.

It is human nature to question, argue, and doubt, but it is also the divine nature within our own heart that drives us towards a reliable state that is ever there to guide us and give us the stability we look for. It is for that reason we need to be in a constant state of worship of that which is absolute. Then we can deal with that which is relative and changeable with greater ease.

58-68 وَرَبُّكَ ٱلْغَفُورُ ذُو ٱلرَّحْمَةِ لَوْ يُؤَاخِذُهُم بِمَا كَسَبُواْ لَعَجَّلَ لَهُمُ ٱلْعَذَابَ بَل لَّهُم مَّوْعِدٌ لَّن يَجِدُواْ مِن دُونِهِۦ مَوْئِلًا ۝ وَتِلْكَ ٱلْقُرَىٰٓ أَهْلَكْنَٰهُمْ لَمَّا ظَلَمُواْ وَجَعَلْنَا لِمَهْلِكِهِم مَّوْعِدًا ۝ وَإِذْ قَالَ مُوسَىٰ لِفَتَىٰهُ لَآ أَبْرَحُ حَتَّىٰٓ أَبْلُغَ مَجْمَعَ ٱلْبَحْرَيْنِ أَوْ أَمْضِىَ حُقُبًا ۝ فَلَمَّا بَلَغَا مَجْمَعَ بَيْنِهِمَا نَسِيَا حُوتَهُمَا فَٱتَّخَذَ سَبِيلَهُۥ فِى ٱلْبَحْرِ سَرَبًا ۝ فَلَمَّا جَاوَزَا قَالَ لِفَتَىٰهُ ءَاتِنَا غَدَآءَنَا لَقَدْ لَقِينَا مِن سَفَرِنَا هَٰذَا نَصَبًا ۝ قَالَ أَرَءَيْتَ إِذْ أَوَيْنَآ إِلَى ٱلصَّخْرَةِ فَإِنِّى نَسِيتُ ٱلْحُوتَ وَمَآ أَنسَىٰنِيهُ إِلَّا ٱلشَّيْطَٰنُ أَنْ أَذْكُرَهُۥ وَٱتَّخَذَ سَبِيلَهُۥ فِى ٱلْبَحْرِ عَجَبًا ۝ قَالَ ذَٰلِكَ مَا كُنَّا نَبْغِ فَٱرْتَدَّا عَلَىٰٓ ءَاثَارِهِمَا قَصَصًا ۝ فَوَجَدَا عَبْدًا مِّنْ عِبَادِنَآ ءَاتَيْنَٰهُ رَحْمَةً مِّنْ عِندِنَا وَعَلَّمْنَٰهُ مِن لَّدُنَّا عِلْمًا ۝ قَالَ لَهُۥ مُوسَىٰ هَلْ أَتَّبِعُكَ عَلَىٰٓ أَن تُعَلِّمَنِ مِمَّا عُلِّمْتَ رُشْدًا ۝ قَالَ إِنَّكَ لَن تَسْتَطِيعَ مَعِىَ صَبْرًا ۝ وَكَيْفَ تَصْبِرُ عَلَىٰ مَا لَمْ تُحِطْ بِهِۦ خُبْرًا ۝

Your Lord, All-Forgiving, Abounding in mercy – were He to hold them to account for what they earned, He would hasten torment upon them. Indeed, an appointed time is set for them, and they shall find no escape from it. These cities We destroyed when they wronged, and set an appointed time for their destruction. And when Moses said to his page, 'I will not give up until I reach the meeting of the two seas, though I go on for many years.' When they arrived at the place where two seas meet, they forgot their fish, which headed for the sea, slinking away. When they had passed beyond, Moses said to his attendant: 'Bring us our food, for we have met with much toil on our journey.' He said: 'Do you recall when we sheltered by the rock? I forgot the fish and none but Satan made me forget it. And so, it headed into the sea, a wonder to behold.' He said: 'This is just what we were seeking.' So, they turned back, retracing their steps. And found one of Our servants – whom We had granted Our mercy and whom We had given knowledge of Our own. Moses said to him, 'Shall I follow you so that you teach me, of what you have been taught, right judgment.' Said he, 'Assuredly you will not be able to bear with me patiently. And how would you bear patiently what you have not encompassed in knowledge?'

58-68 Life on earth is a process of evolution in consciousness, from visible, discernible concerns for survival towards the subtler realms of higher consciousness and the lights of the unseen – a journey from the tangible sights to insights. The story of Khidr and Prophet Moses reflects the experience and dialogue between the soul of Khidr and the lower self and ego of Prophet Moses, who was warned that he would not understand nor be patient with that which his mind did not comprehend. This is a great lesson for seekers to heed on their spiritual path. When one discovers the real meaning of an event or situation, the mind stops its concerns and enquiry.

Patience begins with a reluctant postponement to an action in time and ends with the ability to transcend time. Initially, we experience patience as difficult and not desirable, due to our immaturity. Later, when one takes on the mantle of the soul, patience becomes most enjoyable, sweet as the timeless soul itself.

It is in human nature to be forgetful, and quite often, not reliable. But equally it is in human nature to be in reference to the zone of consciousness that is perfectly stable, always here, transmitted by one's own heart. The more we calibrate with the inner light, the more beautiful, attractive, and friendly our humanity becomes.

69-78 قَالَ سَتَجِدُنِي إِن شَآءَ ٱللَّهُ صَابِرًا وَلَآ أَعْصِى لَكَ أَمْرًا ۝ قَالَ فَإِنِ ٱتَّبَعْتَنِي فَلَا تَسْـَٔلْنِى عَن شَىْءٍ حَتَّىٰٓ أُحْدِثَ لَكَ مِنْهُ ذِكْرًا ۝ فَٱنطَلَقَا حَتَّىٰٓ إِذَا رَكِبَا فِى ٱلسَّفِينَةِ خَرَقَهَا قَالَ أَخَرَقْتَهَا لِتُغْرِقَ أَهْلَهَا لَقَدْ جِئْتَ شَيْـًٔا إِمْرًا ۝ قَالَ أَلَمْ أَقُلْ إِنَّكَ لَن تَسْتَطِيعَ مَعِىَ صَبْرًا ۝ قَالَ لَا تُؤَاخِذْنِى بِمَا نَسِيتُ وَلَا تُرْهِقْنِى مِنْ أَمْرِى عُسْرًا ۝ فَٱنطَلَقَا حَتَّىٰٓ إِذَا لَقِيَا غُلَـٰمًا فَقَتَلَهُۥ قَالَ أَقَتَلْتَ نَفْسًا زَكِيَّةً بِغَيْرِ نَفْسٍ لَّقَدْ جِئْتَ شَيْـًٔا نُّكْرًا ۝ قَالَ أَلَمْ أَقُل لَّكَ إِنَّكَ لَن تَسْتَطِيعَ مَعِىَ صَبْرًا ۝ قَالَ إِن سَأَلْتُكَ عَن شَىْءٍۭ بَعْدَهَا فَلَا تُصَـٰحِبْنِى قَدْ بَلَغْتَ مِن لَّدُنِّى عُذْرًا ۝ فَٱنطَلَقَا حَتَّىٰٓ إِذَآ أَتَيَآ أَهْلَ قَرْيَةٍ ٱسْتَطْعَمَآ أَهْلَهَا فَأَبَوْاْ أَن يُضَيِّفُوهُمَا فَوَجَدَا فِيهَا

$$\text{جِدَارًا يُرِيدُ أَن يَنقَضَّ فَأَقَامَهُۥ ۖ قَالَ لَوْ شِئْتَ لَتَّخَذْتَ عَلَيْهِ أَجْرًا ۝ قَالَ هَٰذَا فِرَاقُ بَيْنِى وَبَيْنِكَ ۚ سَأُنَبِّئُكَ بِتَأْوِيلِ مَا لَمْ تَسْتَطِع عَّلَيْهِ صَبْرًا ۝}$$

He said: 'You will find me, Allah willing, enduring; nor will I ever disobey your command.' He said: 'If you follow me, you are not to ask me about anything until I make mention of it to you.' So they departed; until, when they embarked upon the ship, he made a hole in it. He said, 'What, have you made a hole in it so as to drown its passengers? You have indeed done a grievous thing.' Said he, 'Did I not say that you could never bear with me patiently?' He said: 'Take me not to task for what I forgot, and do not overburden me with difficulties.' So they set off until, meeting with a youth, he killed him. He said: 'Did you kill an innocent self, and not in retaliation for another? You have done an execrable deed!' Said he, 'Did I not say that you could never bear with me patiently?' He said, 'If I question you on any- thing after this, then keep me company no more; you have already experienced excuse sufficient on my part.' So they set off until, reaching the people of a town, they asked its people for food, but they refused to offer them hospitality. In it they found a wall about to collapse and he repaired it. He said: 'Had you wished, you could have obtained a wage for it.' Said he, 'This is the parting between me and you. Now I will tell you the interpretation of that you have not bear patiently.'

69-78 When Prophet Moses was confused by Khidr's behaviour in breaking the boat, Khidr reminded him about his impatience and explained to Prophet Moses that patience is due to understanding a situation and knowing the nature of the events linked to it. Then Khidr shocked Moses by killing a boy who appeared to be innocent. It was when Khidr built the wall and Moses raised his objections regarding the compensation that was due that Khidr was prompted to explain how his actions were inspired from the unseen.

One can only accept patience if one realises its meaning and gains knowledge as to its inner perfection. As humans, we continuously seek to know the end of events, because we live in a world of cycles, of beginnings and endings. An end to a story brings short-term tranquillity until the next endeavour begins.

Like anything else, the faculty of memory and remembrance, has a useful, important, positive side, but it can also cause distress and regrets. It only connects us with something that has happened already, which may or may not indicate what can happen in the future. The ultimate connectedness is between self and soul. The self is short-lived and uncertain within space and time, and the soul is constantly connected with the eternal light of the divine.

$$\text{79-86 أَمَّا ٱلسَّفِينَةُ فَكَانَتْ لِمَسَٰكِينَ يَعْمَلُونَ فِى ٱلْبَحْرِ فَأَرَدتُّ أَنْ أَعِيبَهَا وَكَانَ وَرَآءَهُم مَّلِكٌ يَأْخُذُ كُلَّ سَفِينَةٍ غَصْبًا ۝ وَأَمَّا ٱلْغُلَٰمُ فَكَانَ أَبَوَاهُ مُؤْمِنَيْنِ فَخَشِينَآ أَن}$$

يُرْهِقَهُمَا طُغْيَـٰنًا وَكُفْرًا ۝ فَأَرَدْنَآ أَن يُبْدِلَهُمَا رَبُّهُمَا خَيْرًا مِّنْهُ زَكَوٰةً وَأَقْرَبَ رُحْمًا ۝ وَأَمَّا ٱلْجِدَارُ فَكَانَ لِغُلَـٰمَيْنِ يَتِيمَيْنِ فِى ٱلْمَدِينَةِ وَكَانَ تَحْتَهُۥ كَنزٌ لَّهُمَا وَكَانَ أَبُوهُمَا صَـٰلِحًا فَأَرَادَ رَبُّكَ أَن يَبْلُغَآ أَشُدَّهُمَا وَيَسْتَخْرِجَا كَنزَهُمَا رَحْمَةً مِّن رَّبِّكَ ۚ وَمَا فَعَلْتُهُۥ عَنْ أَمْرِى ۚ ذَٰلِكَ تَأْوِيلُ مَا لَمْ تَسْطِع عَّلَيْهِ صَبْرًا ۝ وَيَسْـَٔلُونَكَ عَن ذِى ٱلْقَرْنَيْنِ ۖ قُلْ سَأَتْلُواْ عَلَيْكُم مِّنْهُ ذِكْرًا ۝ إِنَّا مَكَّنَّا لَهُۥ فِى ٱلْأَرْضِ وَءَاتَيْنَـٰهُ مِن كُلِّ شَىْءٍ سَبَبًا ۝ فَأَتْبَعَ سَبَبًا ۝ حَتَّىٰٓ إِذَا بَلَغَ مَغْرِبَ ٱلشَّمْسِ وَجَدَهَا تَغْرُبُ فِى عَيْنٍ حَمِئَةٍ وَوَجَدَ عِندَهَا قَوْمًا ۗ قُلْنَا يَـٰذَا ٱلْقَرْنَيْنِ إِمَّآ أَن تُعَذِّبَ وَإِمَّآ أَن تَتَّخِذَ فِيهِمْ حُسْنًا ۝

'Regarding the ship, it belonged to poor people working in the sea, and I wanted to make it defective; beyond them was a king who seized every ship, unlawfully. And as for that young man, his parents were [true] believers – whereas we had every reason to fear that he would bring bitter grief upon them by [his] overweening wickedness and denial of all truth: So we wished that their Lord would give them in exchange one more pure than him in character, and more caring towards his kin. The wall belonged to two young orphans in the town and there was buried treasure beneath it belonging to them. Their father had been a righteous man, so your Lord intended them to reach maturity and then dig up their treasure as a mercy from your Lord. I did not act of my own accord: these are the explanations for those things you could not bear with patience.' They ask you about the two-horned, Dhu'l Qarnayn. Say: 'I shall recite to you some mention of him.' Behold, We established him securely on earth, and endowed him with [the knowledge of] the right means to achieve anything [that he might set out to achieve]; We had established him firmly on earth, and granted him a path to the knowledge of all things. So, he followed a path, [and he marched westwards] till, when he came to the setting of the sun, it appeared to him that it was setting in a dark, turbid sea; and nearby he found a people [given to every kind of wrongdoing]. We said: 'O thou Two-Horned One! You may either cause [them] to suffer or treat them with kindness!' Until, when he reached the place of the sun's setting, he found it setting in a pool of hot water, and there he found a people. We said: 'O Dhu'l Qarnayn, either you torment them or you follow with them the way of virtue.'

79-86 The breaking of the boat was done to save its owners from losing it to a tyrant who was confiscating all seaworthy boats. The killing of the young man was to save his parents from his future tyranny. The wall hid a chest of treasure, which would be discovered later by two deserving orphans, who were descendants of pious parents. Khidr received his instructions from a much higher zone of consciousness than Moses could understand. Higher knowledge of reality emanates from the divine *Source*. It occasionally reaches those who are clear in head, pure at heart and directly receptive to divine inspiration and guidance. The channels of divine revelation regarding the mysteries of past, present, and future are there for those qualified to tap into them.

Earthly and spiritual wisdom brings its recipients compassion and understanding for those who are less endowed. Access to the ultimate truth in one's own heart will enable one to understand anything that seems to others most strange or shocking.

Our experiences, knowledge, and wisdom help us not to digress too far beyond the middle path, but equally, they are limited in that we don't know more than what has been conveyed to us by our senses. Therefore, we need to be respectful of events whose real nature and cause are not known to us. We only know the superficial aspects of why a storm has occurred or not.

87-97 قَالَ أَمَّا مَن ظَلَمَ فَسَوْفَ نُعَذِّبُهُ ثُمَّ يُرَدُّ إِلَىٰ رَبِّهِۦ فَيُعَذِّبُهُۥ عَذَابًا نُّكْرًا ۝ وَأَمَّا مَنْ ءَامَنَ وَعَمِلَ صَٰلِحًا فَلَهُۥ جَزَآءً ٱلْحُسْنَىٰ وَسَنَقُولُ لَهُۥ مِنْ أَمْرِنَا يُسْرًا ۝ ثُمَّ أَتْبَعَ سَبَبًا ۝ حَتَّىٰٓ إِذَا بَلَغَ مَطْلِعَ ٱلشَّمْسِ وَجَدَهَا تَطْلُعُ عَلَىٰ قَوْمٍ لَّمْ نَجْعَل لَّهُم مِّن دُونِهَا سِتْرًا ۝ كَذَٰلِكَ وَقَدْ أَحَطْنَا بِمَا لَدَيْهِ خُبْرًا ۝ ثُمَّ أَتْبَعَ سَبَبًا ۝ حَتَّىٰٓ إِذَا بَلَغَ بَيْنَ ٱلسَّدَّيْنِ وَجَدَ مِن دُونِهِمَا قَوْمًا لَّا يَكَادُونَ يَفْقَهُونَ قَوْلًا ۝ قَالُوا۟ يَٰذَا ٱلْقَرْنَيْنِ إِنَّ يَأْجُوجَ وَمَأْجُوجَ مُفْسِدُونَ فِى ٱلْأَرْضِ فَهَلْ نَجْعَلُ لَكَ خَرْجًا عَلَىٰٓ أَن تَجْعَلَ بَيْنَنَا وَبَيْنَهُمْ سَدًّا ۝ قَالَ مَا مَكَّنِّى فِيهِ رَبِّى خَيْرٌ فَأَعِينُونِى بِقُوَّةٍ أَجْعَلْ بَيْنَكُمْ وَبَيْنَهُمْ رَدْمًا ۝ ءَاتُونِى زُبَرَ ٱلْحَدِيدِ حَتَّىٰٓ إِذَا سَاوَىٰ بَيْنَ ٱلصَّدَفَيْنِ قَالَ ٱنفُخُوا۟ حَتَّىٰٓ إِذَا جَعَلَهُۥ نَارًا قَالَ ءَاتُونِىٓ أُفْرِغْ عَلَيْهِ قِطْرًا ۝ فَمَا ٱسْطَٰعُوٓا۟ أَن يَظْهَرُوهُ وَمَا ٱسْتَطَٰعُوا۟ لَهُۥ نَقْبًا ۝

He said: 'Whoso is wicked we shall torment. Then he will be turned over to his Lord, Who will torment him with grievous torment. Whoso is faithful and does good deeds, to him belongs a reward most fair, and to him we shall teach some of what we know.' Then he followed a path, until, when he reached the rising of the sun, he found it to rise on a people for whom We had provided no shelter from it. Thus, did We encompass in our knowledge all that he achieved. Then he followed a path, then, when he reached a place between two mountain barriers, he found beside them a people who could barely understand speech. They said, 'O Dhu'l Qarnayn, behold, Gog and Magog are doing corruption in the earth; so, shall we assign to you a tribute, against you setting up a barrier between us and between them?' He said, 'That wherein my Lord has established me is better; so, aid me forcefully, and I will set up a rampart between you and between them. Bring me ingots of iron!' Until, when he had made all level between the two cliffs, he said, 'Blow!' Until, when he had made it a fire, he said, 'Bring me, that I may pour molten brass on it.' So, they were unable either to scale it or pierce it.

87-97 Every human being will experience ease or hardship in life, according and proportionate to their intentions, actions, and evolution in higher consciousness, which reveals the unseen and unknown. The One with Two Horns, who was inspired by higher knowledge and intuition, saved people from those who caused mischief on earth. He used molten metal to create a dam to block a narrow mountain passage, which prevented the regular descent of the mischief-makers from the mountains onto the poorer people. There was, historically, much controversy about the One with Two Horns, as there was about the people of the cave.

Throughout history prophetic beings have possessed great insights, dazzling those among them. For the awakened and enlightened being, the ultimate miracle of all is the human state – being in this world but of heavenly eternal origin. Heroic feats occur when one can transcend the norms of time.

It is a sign of maturity and wisdom that we want to act according to boundaries and limitations, with a view toward a longer path that does not cause us regrets and suffering later on. This is why we have been given indications of our own limitations as well as our constant duty towards awareness and presence in the moment, so that we do not get distracted.

98-108

قَالَ هَٰذَا رَحْمَةٌ مِّن رَّبِّى فَإِذَا جَآءَ وَعْدُ رَبِّى جَعَلَهُۥ دَكَّآءَ وَكَانَ وَعْدُ رَبِّى حَقًّا ۝ وَتَرَكْنَا بَعْضَهُمْ يَوْمَئِذٍ يَمُوجُ فِى بَعْضٍ وَنُفِخَ فِى ٱلصُّورِ فَجَمَعْنَٰهُمْ جَمْعًا ۝ وَعَرَضْنَا جَهَنَّمَ يَوْمَئِذٍ لِّلْكَٰفِرِينَ عَرْضًا ۝ ٱلَّذِينَ كَانَتْ أَعْيُنُهُمْ فِى غِطَآءٍ عَن ذِكْرِى وَكَانُوا۟ لَا يَسْتَطِيعُونَ سَمْعًا ۝ أَفَحَسِبَ ٱلَّذِينَ كَفَرُوٓا۟ أَن يَتَّخِذُوا۟ عِبَادِى مِن دُونِىٓ أَوْلِيَآءَ إِنَّآ أَعْتَدْنَا جَهَنَّمَ لِلْكَٰفِرِينَ نُزُلًا ۝ قُلْ هَلْ نُنَبِّئُكُم بِٱلْأَخْسَرِينَ أَعْمَٰلًا ۝ ٱلَّذِينَ ضَلَّ سَعْيُهُمْ فِى ٱلْحَيَوٰةِ ٱلدُّنْيَا وَهُمْ يَحْسَبُونَ أَنَّهُمْ يُحْسِنُونَ صُنْعًا ۝ أُو۟لَٰٓئِكَ ٱلَّذِينَ كَفَرُوا۟ بِـَٔايَٰتِ رَبِّهِمْ وَلِقَآئِهِۦ فَحَبِطَتْ أَعْمَٰلُهُمْ فَلَا نُقِيمُ لَهُمْ يَوْمَ ٱلْقِيَٰمَةِ وَزْنًا ۝ ذَٰلِكَ جَزَآؤُهُمْ جَهَنَّمُ بِمَا كَفَرُوا۟ وَٱتَّخَذُوٓا۟ ءَايَٰتِى وَرُسُلِى هُزُوًا ۝ إِنَّ ٱلَّذِينَ ءَامَنُوا۟ وَعَمِلُوا۟ ٱلصَّٰلِحَٰتِ كَانَتْ لَهُمْ جَنَّٰتُ ٱلْفِرْدَوْسِ نُزُلًا ۝ خَٰلِدِينَ فِيهَا لَا يَبْغُونَ عَنْهَا حِوَلًا ۝

He said: 'This is an act of grace from my Lord, but when the promise of my Lord is fulfilled, He shall level it to the ground – my Lord's promise is ever true.' Upon that day We shall leave them surging on one another, and the Trumpet shall he blown, and We shall gather them together. On that Day, We shall open hell to the unbelievers view, all in one view. It is they whose eyes were veiled from My remembrance, and who were incapable of hearing. Did they who disbelieved imagine that they could adopt My servants as protectors instead of Me? To the unbelievers, We have prepared hell as a resting place. Say: 'Shall We inform you who are the greatest losers in works?' Those whose striving goes astray in the present life, while they think that they are working good deeds. Those are they that disbelieve in the signs of their Lord and the encounter with Him; their works have failed, and on the Day of Resurrection We shall not assign to them any weight. That is their recompense Jahannam for that they were unbelievers and took My signs and My messengers in mockery. [But,] verily, as for those who attain to faith and do righteous deeds – the gardens of paradise will be there to welcome them, therein will they abide, [and] never will they desire any change therefrom.

98-108 The way we live and our state of wellbeing mirror our intentions and actions. In the hereafter there can be no blame or claim as all will be obvious and clear. Those who have no clarity of this truth on earth will be even more disappointed and confused when they reach the natural end of this short earthly life. Humans have received abundant messages, signs, and actual events, all of which show clearly the urgent need to be on a clear, well-defined path of conduct and to realise God's designs and intentions.

Our personal choice of actions appears attractive to us; therefore, it is most important to have references that may save us from the abyss of darkness of the lower self. It is through faith and good actions that we become open and honest and will experience a way to paradise.

Human actions on earth can only be meaningful and have longevity if they are along the path of the divine decree: to increasingly know more and be attuned to the divine light that is ever-present at all times. Good intentions and good actions, together with calibrating with what is acceptable by the divine decree, are our true references in this life. Anything other than that will just disappear like everything else.

109-110 قُل لَّوْ كَانَ ٱلْبَحْرُ مِدَادًا لِّكَلِمَٰتِ رَبِّى لَنَفِدَ ٱلْبَحْرُ قَبْلَ أَن تَنفَدَ كَلِمَٰتُ رَبِّى وَلَوْ جِئْنَا بِمِثْلِهِۦ مَدَدًا ۝ قُلْ إِنَّمَآ أَنَا۠ بَشَرٌ مِّثْلُكُمْ يُوحَىٰٓ إِلَىَّ أَنَّمَآ إِلَٰهُكُمْ إِلَٰهٌ وَٰحِدٌ فَمَن كَانَ يَرْجُوا۟ لِقَآءَ رَبِّهِۦ فَلْيَعْمَلْ عَمَلًا صَٰلِحًا وَلَا يُشْرِكْ بِعِبَادَةِ رَبِّهِۦٓ أَحَدًۢا ۝

Say: 'If the sea were ink for the Words of my Lord, the sea would be spent before the Words of my Lord are spent, though We brought replenishment the like of it.' Say: 'I am but a human being like you, to whom revelation is sent. Your Allah is in truth One Allah. Whoso hopes to meet his Lord, let him perform deeds of righteousness, and associate none with the worship of his Lord.'

109-110 No two moments are the same, nor can they ever be repeated exactly as before. What we experience in a material or an allegorical sense is in a constant state of flux. Unless we turn from sight to insight, to higher subtler unveilings, we will remain confused and discontent. To see life's experiences through the lens of the *One* is the fruit of the prescribed path. The truth of *Oneness* is absolute as well as relative in our earthly experiences. If we do not awaken in this realm, all will be revealed in the hereafter.

Our worldly experiences demonstrate the endless varieties of what can appear and disappear through our senses. What remains ever-constant is the divine power that governs everything known and the unknown.

The ways and means whereby things combine and change are endless. The *Source* is one, the manifestations innumerable. As human beings, we are all driven towards a level of consciousness that is ever- constant, ever-reliable, and ever-joyful. For this, we need to do our utmost to have less of the darkness of the ego-self and more of the guidance of the soul's light. All of this means perfecting one's worship.

7. Surah 24 An-Nur (The Light)

The last ayah of the previous surah links to this surah and gives us a hint as to its overall message. The last ayah asks us to seek forgiveness and mercy from Allah and declare Allah the source of all mercy and goodness. The first ayah of this surah shows us the bounty and mercy in these Revelations: unless we transcend our mind and instead use our heart and the light of the soul, we will not realise the guidance that comes to us from faith and awakening.

بِسْمِ اللَّهِ الرَّحْمَٰنِ الرَّحِيمِ

سُورَةٌ أَنزَلْنَٰهَا وَفَرَضْنَٰهَا وَأَنزَلْنَا فِيهَآ ءَايَٰتٍ بَيِّنَٰتٍ لَّعَلَّكُمْ تَذَكَّرُونَ ۝ ٱلزَّانِيَةُ وَٱلزَّانِي فَٱجْلِدُوا۟ كُلَّ وَٰحِدٍ مِّنْهُمَا مِا۟ئَةَ جَلْدَةٍ وَلَا تَأْخُذْكُم بِهِمَا رَأْفَةٌ فِى دِينِ ٱللَّهِ إِن كُنتُمْ تُؤْمِنُونَ بِٱللَّهِ وَٱلْيَوْمِ ٱلْءَاخِرِ وَلْيَشْهَدْ عَذَابَهُمَا طَآئِفَةٌ مِّنَ ٱلْمُؤْمِنِينَ ۝ ٱلزَّانِى لَا يَنكِحُ إِلَّا زَانِيَةً أَوْ مُشْرِكَةً وَٱلزَّانِيَةُ لَا يَنكِحُهَآ إِلَّا زَانٍ أَوْ مُشْرِكٌ وَحُرِّمَ ذَٰلِكَ عَلَى ٱلْمُؤْمِنِينَ ۝ وَٱلَّذِينَ يَرْمُونَ ٱلْمُحْصَنَٰتِ ثُمَّ لَمْ يَأْتُوا۟ بِأَرْبَعَةِ شُهَدَآءَ فَٱجْلِدُوهُمْ ثَمَٰنِينَ جَلْدَةً وَلَا تَقْبَلُوا۟ لَهُمْ شَهَٰدَةً أَبَدًا وَأُو۟لَٰٓئِكَ هُمُ ٱلْفَٰسِقُونَ ۝ إِلَّا ٱلَّذِينَ تَابُوا۟ مِنۢ بَعْدِ ذَٰلِكَ وَأَصْلَحُوا۟ فَإِنَّ ٱللَّهَ غَفُورٌ رَّحِيمٌ ۝ وَٱلَّذِينَ يَرْمُونَ أَزْوَٰجَهُمْ وَلَمْ يَكُن لَّهُمْ شُهَدَآءُ إِلَّآ أَنفُسُهُمْ فَشَهَٰدَةُ أَحَدِهِمْ أَرْبَعُ شَهَٰدَٰتٍ بِٱللَّهِ إِنَّهُۥ لَمِنَ ٱلصَّٰدِقِينَ ۝

1-6

In the name of Allah, the Merciful to all, the Compassionate to each!

A sura that We have sent down and appointed; and We have sent down in it signs, clear signs, that haply you will remember. The adulteress and the adulterer: flog each of them a hundred lashes. And let not pity for them overcome you in regard to the law of Allah, provided you believe in Allah and the Last Day. And let their punishment be witnessed by a group of believers. The adulterer shall marry none but an adulteress or an idolatress; and the adulteress shall marry none but an adulterer or an idolater. But this is forbidden to believers. Those who falsely accuse chaste women of adultery, and fail to produce four witnesses, flog them eighty lashes and never thereafter accept their witness. These are the dissolute. Except for those who later repent and reform their ways, for Allah is All-Forgiving, Compassionate to each. Those who accuse their spouses of adultery, and have no witnesses but themselves, let each of them witness four times by Allah that he is telling the truth,

1-6 Human life is growth and progress in consciousness based on our human reality and its limitations. Our life is balanced between the outer and the inner, the higher and the lower. Understanding this balance allows us to accept boundaries and responsibilities in order to experience goodness and peace. Since the body is the abode of the sacred heart and soul, we must regard it with immense respect and deference to the *Creator*. There must be considerable respect and dignity for the sexual and procreative drive and acts. It is important to be clear regarding the boundaries between what is allowed and what is not, in order to bring about stability amongst human beings in a community. We are alive because of the light of the ever-living God within us. It is in human nature to want to discover and apply the best rules and regulations for individuals and communities to thrive. Without stability and safety there will be very little progress and development in life. A healthy community is a foundation for the individuals within it, as well as for its leadership, to evolve to the highest state of conduct and consciousness.

During the past few thousand years we human beings have evolved from a very base animal state to possess the ability to realise our dual nature – that of earth and of heaven. We can recognize the sanctity of our humanity and the reverence that we must give to every aspect of us including our body. We are indeed stewards of the kingdom of body and mind.

Consciousness moves in different steps and stages. It starts from non-discernible consciousness and ends up at pure consciousness. In between, we act according to the level of our state – as a child, a mature person, a grown-up, and a responsible being with accountability, honesty, and courage. That is how it takes us through different roles–men, women, fathers, mothers – to the light within our hearts.

7-15 وَٱلْخَٰمِسَةُ أَنَّ لَعْنَتَ ٱللَّهِ عَلَيْهِ إِن كَانَ مِنَ ٱلْكَٰذِبِينَ ۝ وَيَدْرَؤُا۟ عَنْهَا ٱلْعَذَابَ أَن تَشْهَدَ أَرْبَعَ شَهَٰدَٰتٍۭ بِٱللَّهِ إِنَّهُۥ لَمِنَ ٱلْكَٰذِبِينَ ۝ وَٱلْخَٰمِسَةَ أَنَّ غَضَبَ ٱللَّهِ عَلَيْهَآ إِن كَانَ مِنَ ٱلصَّٰدِقِينَ ۝ وَلَوْلَا فَضْلُ ٱللَّهِ عَلَيْكُمْ وَرَحْمَتُهُۥ وَأَنَّ ٱللَّهَ تَوَّابٌ حَكِيمٌ ۝ إِنَّ ٱلَّذِينَ جَآءُو بِٱلْإِفْكِ عُصْبَةٌ مِّنكُمْ لَا تَحْسَبُوهُ شَرًّا لَّكُم بَلْ هُوَ خَيْرٌ لَّكُمْ لِكُلِّ ٱمْرِئٍ مِّنْهُم مَّا ٱكْتَسَبَ مِنَ ٱلْإِثْمِ وَٱلَّذِى تَوَلَّىٰ كِبْرَهُۥ مِنْهُمْ لَهُۥ عَذَابٌ عَظِيمٌ ۝ لَّوْلَآ إِذْ سَمِعْتُمُوهُ ظَنَّ ٱلْمُؤْمِنُونَ وَٱلْمُؤْمِنَٰتُ بِأَنفُسِهِمْ خَيْرًا وَقَالُوا۟ هَٰذَآ إِفْكٌ مُّبِينٌ ۝ لَّوْلَا جَآءُو عَلَيْهِ بِأَرْبَعَةِ شُهَدَآءَ فَإِذْ لَمْ يَأْتُوا۟ بِٱلشُّهَدَآءِ فَأُو۟لَٰٓئِكَ عِندَ ٱللَّهِ هُمُ ٱلْكَٰذِبُونَ ۝ وَلَوْلَا فَضْلُ ٱللَّهِ عَلَيْكُمْ وَرَحْمَتُهُۥ فِى ٱلدُّنْيَا وَٱلْءَاخِرَةِ لَمَسَّكُمْ فِى مَآ أَفَضْتُمْ فِيهِ عَذَابٌ عَظِيمٌ ۝ إِذْ تَلَقَّوْنَهُۥ بِأَلْسِنَتِكُمْ وَتَقُولُونَ بِأَفْوَاهِكُم مَّا لَيْسَ لَكُم بِهِۦ عِلْمٌ وَتَحْسَبُونَهُۥ هَيِّنًا وَهُوَ عِندَ ٱللَّهِ عَظِيمٌ ۝

and a fifth time that the curse of Allah shall fall upon him if he is a liar. They are then to ward off punishment from her if she testifies four times by Allah that he is a liar, and a fifth time that Allah's wrath shall fall upon her if he is telling the truth. Were it not for Allah's favour upon you and His mercy – and that Allah is All-Forgiving, All-Wise! Those who made up that libel were a gang among you. Count it not as an evil that befell you, but rather as something good. To every one of them is due what he earned of misdeeds, and to him among them who had most to do with magnifying that libel, there awaits a terrible torment. Why is it that, when you heard it, the believers, men and women, did not think well of each other, and say: 'This is a manifest libel?' If only they had produced four witnesses! But since they did not produce witnesses, these people, in Allah's sight, are indeed liars. Were it not for Allah's favor and mercy upon you, in this world and the next, terrible torment would have touched you in regard to the libel that you spread about. You would lap it up with your tongues, and utter with your mouths what you had no knowledge of. You imagined it was a simple matter, but it is momentous with Allah.

7-15 Life is based upon reward and punishment, and these must be acceptable to intelligent beings. All aspects of law must have a sanction of the ultimate Lawgiver – God – and we cannot force the prophetic path upon anyone unless they are willing to embrace it. It is in human nature to occasionally be distracted and commit errors and mistakes. It is Allah's mercy and forgiveness that will enable us to continue learning and growing by accessing the ever-present light within our hearts. Our life on earth has a semblance of the perpetual life of the hereafter; that state comes as a consequence of death. Disagreements and enmity between human beings result from the illusion of distance and separation from the eternal *Truth*; this illusion brings about the idea of 'them and us.' In truth, we are all the same, hoping for sustainable goodness. Those who live their faith and pursue the prescribed path in life will focus their maximum attention upon their thoughts, intentions, and actions, with constant reference to God's acceptance.

The discipline important to our path includes accountability for what we think and say and then for the intention and action behind it. Indeed, it is only by Allah's grace that we can rise to the highest level in consciousness, which is the light of our own spirit within. Without the grace of our soul, we are worse than being dead.

All human souls have the same original pattern, but the ultimate human beings are not only different from each other, they change all the time – from babyhood to maturity, old age, and on to the next zone of consciousness of the hereafter. We have to travel with respect and understand the map of reality as it unfolds.

16-23 وَلَوْلَآ إِذْ سَمِعْتُمُوهُ قُلْتُم مَّا يَكُونُ لَنَآ أَن نَّتَكَلَّمَ بِهَٰذَا سُبْحَٰنَكَ هَٰذَا بُهْتَٰنٌ عَظِيمٌ ۝ يَعِظُكُمُ ٱللَّهُ أَن تَعُودُوا۟ لِمِثْلِهِۦٓ أَبَدًا إِن كُنتُم مُّؤْمِنِينَ ۝ وَيُبَيِّنُ ٱللَّهُ لَكُمُ ٱلْءَايَٰتِ

وَٱللَّهُ عَلِيمٌ حَكِيمٌ ۝ إِنَّ ٱلَّذِينَ يُحِبُّونَ أَن تَشِيعَ ٱلْفَٰحِشَةُ فِى ٱلَّذِينَ ءَامَنُواْ لَهُمْ عَذَابٌ أَلِيمٌ فِى ٱلدُّنْيَا وَٱلْءَاخِرَةِ وَٱللَّهُ يَعْلَمُ وَأَنتُمْ لَا تَعْلَمُونَ ۝ وَلَوْلَا فَضْلُ ٱللَّهِ عَلَيْكُمْ وَرَحْمَتُهُۥ وَأَنَّ ٱللَّهَ رَءُوفٌ رَّحِيمٌ ۝ يَٰٓأَيُّهَا ٱلَّذِينَ ءَامَنُواْ لَا تَتَّبِعُواْ خُطُوَٰتِ ٱلشَّيْطَٰنِ وَمَن يَتَّبِعْ خُطُوَٰتِ ٱلشَّيْطَٰنِ فَإِنَّهُۥ يَأْمُرُ بِٱلْفَحْشَآءِ وَٱلْمُنكَرِ وَلَوْلَا فَضْلُ ٱللَّهِ عَلَيْكُمْ وَرَحْمَتُهُۥ مَا زَكَىٰ مِنكُم مِّنْ أَحَدٍ أَبَدًا وَلَٰكِنَّ ٱللَّهَ يُزَكِّى مَن يَشَآءُ وَٱللَّهُ سَمِيعٌ عَلِيمٌ ۝ وَلَا يَأْتَلِ أُوْلُواْ ٱلْفَضْلِ مِنكُمْ وَٱلسَّعَةِ أَن يُؤْتُوٓاْ أُوْلِى ٱلْقُرْبَىٰ وَٱلْمَسَٰكِينَ وَٱلْمُهَٰجِرِينَ فِى سَبِيلِ ٱللَّهِ وَلْيَعْفُواْ وَلْيَصْفَحُوٓاْ أَلَا تُحِبُّونَ أَن يَغْفِرَ ٱللَّهُ لَكُمْ وَٱللَّهُ غَفُورٌ رَّحِيمٌ ۝ إِنَّ ٱلَّذِينَ يَرْمُونَ ٱلْمُحْصَنَٰتِ ٱلْغَٰفِلَٰتِ ٱلْمُؤْمِنَٰتِ لُعِنُواْ فِى ٱلدُّنْيَا وَٱلْءَاخِرَةِ وَلَهُمْ عَذَابٌ عَظِيمٌ ۝

Why is that, when you heard it, you did not say: 'It is not fitting for us to speak of such matters. Glory be to You! This is a dreadful falsehood?' Allah admonishes you never to return to its like again if you are true believers. Allah makes clear to you the signs; and Allah is All-Knowing, All-Wise. As for those who enjoy spreading obscenities about the believers, painful torment awaits them in this world and the next. Allah knows and you do not. Were it not for Allah's favor upon you and His mercy – and that Allah is All-Tender, Compassionate to each! O believers, follow not the steps of Satan; for whosoever follows the steps of Satan, assuredly he bids to indecency and dishonour. But for Allah's bounty to you and His mercy not one of you would have been pure ever; but Allah purifies whom He will; and Allah is All-Hearing, All-Knowing. Let not those among you, virtuous and affluent, forswear from giving to kinsmen, to the poor and to emigrants in the cause of Allah. Let them pardon, and let them forgive. Do you not want Allah to pardon you? Allah is All-Forgiving, Compassionate to each! Those who falsely accuse women who are chaste, unwary and possessed of faith shall be cursed in this world and the next. Awaiting them is a terrible torment.

16-23 When clear boundaries for appropriate conduct are established and accepted, we then begin to notice and desire better conduct, greater generosity, and increased goodness. The more human beings act for goodness and transcend ego limitations, the more they experience the grace of the most generous God. We are all guests on this earth, in transit to another state of life after death where God alone is the most magnificent host. We are middle people on earth; our heavenly soul is balanced by the earthly self or ego. The prophetic path will lead us out of countless levels of fog and darkness toward the ultimate light of God. In all our conduct and relationships, we need to be vigilant, accountable, willing to admit faults and to repent cheerfully in the knowledge that God is the All-Forgiving. One's own lower self and ego is often encouraged by the other ambitious egos around one, which can lead an entire community to self-destructiveness through meanness and the love of acquisition, power, and wealth.

Our human nature exists between the material and the spiritual; as such, we are on a path disclosing signs and directions that will lead us out of darkness towards brilliant lights. We are driven to look for these hints and signs, which will speed up our progress towards awakening to the realisation of divine presence within the heart.

It is all by the grace of Allah, whose light radiates from our heart, that we can traverse the zone of duality and uncertainty on this earth, back to the zone of *tawhid* and oneness, without any other shadows.

24-30 يَوْمَ تَشْهَدُ عَلَيْهِمْ أَلْسِنَتُهُمْ وَأَيْدِيهِمْ وَأَرْجُلُهُم بِمَا كَانُوا۟ يَعْمَلُونَ ۝ يَوْمَئِذٍ يُوَفِّيهِمُ ٱللَّهُ دِينَهُمُ ٱلْحَقَّ وَيَعْلَمُونَ أَنَّ ٱللَّهَ هُوَ ٱلْحَقُّ ٱلْمُبِينُ ۝ ٱلْخَبِيثَٰتُ لِلْخَبِيثِينَ وَٱلْخَبِيثُونَ لِلْخَبِيثَٰتِ وَٱلطَّيِّبَٰتُ لِلطَّيِّبِينَ وَٱلطَّيِّبُونَ لِلطَّيِّبَٰتِ أُو۟لَٰٓئِكَ مُبَرَّءُونَ مِمَّا يَقُولُونَ لَهُم مَّغْفِرَةٌ وَرِزْقٌ كَرِيمٌ ۝ يَٰٓأَيُّهَا ٱلَّذِينَ ءَامَنُوا۟ لَا تَدْخُلُوا۟ بُيُوتًا غَيْرَ بُيُوتِكُمْ حَتَّىٰ تَسْتَأْنِسُوا۟ وَتُسَلِّمُوا۟ عَلَىٰٓ أَهْلِهَا ذَٰلِكُمْ خَيْرٌ لَّكُمْ لَعَلَّكُمْ تَذَكَّرُونَ ۝ فَإِن لَّمْ تَجِدُوا۟ فِيهَآ أَحَدًا فَلَا تَدْخُلُوهَا حَتَّىٰ يُؤْذَنَ لَكُمْ وَإِن قِيلَ لَكُمُ ٱرْجِعُوا۟ فَٱرْجِعُوا۟ هُوَ أَزْكَىٰ لَكُمْ وَٱللَّهُ بِمَا تَعْمَلُونَ عَلِيمٌ ۝ لَّيْسَ عَلَيْكُمْ جُنَاحٌ أَن تَدْخُلُوا۟ بُيُوتًا غَيْرَ مَسْكُونَةٍ فِيهَا مَتَٰعٌ لَّكُمْ وَٱللَّهُ يَعْلَمُ مَا تُبْدُونَ وَمَا تَكْتُمُونَ ۝ قُل لِّلْمُؤْمِنِينَ يَغُضُّوا۟ مِنْ أَبْصَٰرِهِمْ وَيَحْفَظُوا۟ فُرُوجَهُمْ ذَٰلِكَ أَزْكَىٰ لَهُمْ إِنَّ ٱللَّهَ خَبِيرٌۢ بِمَا يَصْنَعُونَ ۝

On that Day, there shall testify against them their own tongues, hands and feet concerning what they used to do. On that Day, Allah shall pay them in full their just reward, and they shall know that Allah is the Manifest Truth. Vile women for vile men, and vile men for vile women; good women for good men, and good men for good women – these are declared innocent of what they say; theirs shall be forgiveness and generous provision. O believers, do not enter houses other than your own until you make your presence known and greet their inhabitants. This is better for you; perhaps you will remember. If you find no one therein, do not enter unless granted leave. If you are asked to leave, then leave; this would be more seemly for you, and Allah knows best what you do. But no blame attaches to you if you enter uninhabited houses for which you might find some use. And Allah knows best what you reveal and what you hide. Say to the believers, that they cast down their eyes and guard their private parts; that is purer for them. Allah is aware of the things they work.

24-30 The mystery of life is such that every cell acts and reacts in unison with our entire body and mind. The ultimate mystery is that God's light penetrates all that is known and unknown in the universe, and as such everything is God's domain. The state of the hereafter, the infinite, is already here; our need for balance reflects our need for the infinite to replenish and revitalise us. The enlightened human being realises how crucial it is to be clear in mind and pure at heart; this enables us to connect efficiently with the environment through our senses, receiving its constant impact upon our well-beingness. Our sensory faculties need constant recalibration and repair, which often take place in deep sleep. Living with other people is a normal condition for human development, and as such we must exercise respect and much consideration towards those around us.

It is with intelligence that we realise the ceaseless connection between the outer and the inner as well as between the past moment, the present time, and the next moment. Everything in existence vibrates and reverberates with the divine origin and as such reflects aspects of that truth.

Truth is timeless. Anything that happens within time emanates from the zone of timelessness and leaves its traces there. Nothing is ever lost. For that reason, we need to be cautious as to what we think and what we do, because they leave their effect upon us.

31-34 وَقُل لِّلْمُؤْمِنَٰتِ يَغْضُضْنَ مِنْ أَبْصَٰرِهِنَّ وَيَحْفَظْنَ فُرُوجَهُنَّ وَلَا يُبْدِينَ زِينَتَهُنَّ إِلَّا مَا ظَهَرَ مِنْهَا وَلْيَضْرِبْنَ بِخُمُرِهِنَّ عَلَىٰ جُيُوبِهِنَّ وَلَا يُبْدِينَ زِينَتَهُنَّ إِلَّا لِبُعُولَتِهِنَّ أَوْ ءَابَآئِهِنَّ أَوْ ءَابَآءِ بُعُولَتِهِنَّ أَوْ أَبْنَآئِهِنَّ أَوْ أَبْنَآءِ بُعُولَتِهِنَّ أَوْ إِخْوَٰنِهِنَّ أَوْ بَنِىٓ إِخْوَٰنِهِنَّ أَوْ بَنِىٓ أَخَوَٰتِهِنَّ أَوْ نِسَآئِهِنَّ أَوْ مَا مَلَكَتْ أَيْمَٰنُهُنَّ أَوِ ٱلتَّٰبِعِينَ غَيْرِ أُو۟لِى ٱلْإِرْبَةِ مِنَ ٱلرِّجَالِ أَوِ ٱلطِّفْلِ ٱلَّذِينَ لَمْ يَظْهَرُوا۟ عَلَىٰ عَوْرَٰتِ ٱلنِّسَآءِ وَلَا يَضْرِبْنَ بِأَرْجُلِهِنَّ لِيُعْلَمَ مَا يُخْفِينَ مِن زِينَتِهِنَّ وَتُوبُوٓا۟ إِلَى ٱللَّهِ جَمِيعًا أَيُّهَ ٱلْمُؤْمِنُونَ لَعَلَّكُمْ تُفْلِحُونَ ۝ وَأَنكِحُوا۟ ٱلْأَيَٰمَىٰ مِنكُمْ وَٱلصَّٰلِحِينَ مِنْ عِبَادِكُمْ وَإِمَآئِكُمْ إِن يَكُونُوا۟ فُقَرَآءَ يُغْنِهِمُ ٱللَّهُ مِن فَضْلِهِۦ وَٱللَّهُ وَٰسِعٌ عَلِيمٌ ۝ وَلْيَسْتَعْفِفِ ٱلَّذِينَ لَا يَجِدُونَ نِكَاحًا حَتَّىٰ يُغْنِيَهُمُ ٱللَّهُ مِن فَضْلِهِۦ وَٱلَّذِينَ يَبْتَغُونَ ٱلْكِتَٰبَ مِمَّا مَلَكَتْ أَيْمَٰنُكُمْ فَكَاتِبُوهُمْ إِنْ عَلِمْتُمْ فِيهِمْ خَيْرًا وَءَاتُوهُم مِّن مَّالِ ٱللَّهِ ٱلَّذِىٓ ءَاتَىٰكُمْ وَلَا تُكْرِهُوا۟ فَتَيَٰتِكُمْ عَلَى ٱلْبِغَآءِ إِنْ أَرَدْنَ تَحَصُّنًا لِّتَبْتَغُوا۟ عَرَضَ ٱلْحَيَوٰةِ ٱلدُّنْيَا وَمَن يُكْرِههُّنَّ فَإِنَّ ٱللَّهَ مِنۢ بَعْدِ إِكْرَٰهِهِنَّ غَفُورٌ رَّحِيمٌ ۝ وَلَقَدْ أَنزَلْنَآ إِلَيْكُمْ ءَايَٰتٍ مُّبَيِّنَٰتٍ وَمَثَلًا مِّنَ ٱلَّذِينَ خَلَوْا۟ مِن قَبْلِكُمْ وَمَوْعِظَةً لِّلْمُتَّقِينَ ۝

And say to the believing women, that they cast down their eyes' and guard their private parts, and reveal not their adornment save such as is outward; and let them cast their veils over their bosoms, and not reveal their adornment save to their husbands, or their fathers, or their husbands' fathers, or their sons, or their husbands' sons, or their brothers, or their brothers' sons, or their sisters' sons, or their women, or what their right hands own, or such men as attend them, not having sexual desire, or children who have not yet attained knowledge of women's private parts; nor let them stamp their feet, so that their hidden ornament may be known. And turn all together to Allah, O you believers; haply so you will prosper. Marry the spouseless among you, and your slaves and handmaidens that are righteous; if they are poor, Allah will enrich them of His bounty; Allah is All-Embracing, All-Knowing.

And let those who find not the means to marry have recourse to chastity until Allah enriches them from His bounty. Whoso from among your slaves seeks a contract of manumission, contract with them accordingly, if you know of any talent in them, and grant them of the wealth that Allah has granted you. Do not force your female slaves into prostitution, if they desire chastity, in order to gain some advantage in this present world. If forced, Allah, once they are forced, is towards them All-Forgiving, Compassionate to each. We have sent signs down to you making all clear, examples of those who passed away before you, and advice for those who are cautiously aware.

31-34 Human consciousness today has emerged from millions of years of evolutionary development and carries the traces of our historical backgrounds. We cannot act anymore like animals in terms of using force to control other people's minds and bodies. We need to exercise special kindness and consideration for the weak ones amongst us. Gender issues can cause considerable confusion and emotional disturbances, and therefore, we need to give special attention to the delicate balance and courtesies in that respect. Many of our desires and ambitions cannot be legitimately fulfilled, so we need to exercise self-control and patience, waiting for the joys and thrills that follow spiritual awakening in this lifetime or the realisation of *Truth* after death.

The prophetic path begins with serious attention to outer courtesies and correct conduct, so that we limit distractions that waste our time and energy. With intelligence we build upon the clear signs we have already experienced, rather than being constantly on the lookout for new insights and lights. Through trusting the heart and being patient, we realise the treasure within the heart.

The nature of the human being is confused and lost, but the light that enables the human being to be alive and reflective is divine and permanent. And it is this that we need to refer to at all times, regarding the extent of our faith, trust, and reliance upon the *Truth*.

35-40 ٱللَّهُ نُورُ ٱلسَّمَٰوَٰتِ وَٱلْأَرْضِ ۚ مَثَلُ نُورِهِۦ كَمِشْكَوٰةٍ فِيهَا مِصْبَاحٌ ۖ ٱلْمِصْبَاحُ فِى زُجَاجَةٍ ۖ ٱلزُّجَاجَةُ كَأَنَّهَا كَوْكَبٌ دُرِّىٌّ يُوقَدُ مِن شَجَرَةٍ مُّبَٰرَكَةٍ زَيْتُونَةٍ لَّا شَرْقِيَّةٍ وَلَا غَرْبِيَّةٍ يَكَادُ زَيْتُهَا يُضِىٓءُ وَلَوْ لَمْ تَمْسَسْهُ نَارٌ ۚ نُّورٌ عَلَىٰ نُورٍ ۗ يَهْدِى ٱللَّهُ لِنُورِهِۦ مَن يَشَآءُ ۚ وَيَضْرِبُ ٱللَّهُ ٱلْأَمْثَٰلَ لِلنَّاسِ ۗ وَٱللَّهُ بِكُلِّ شَىْءٍ عَلِيمٌ ۝ فِى بُيُوتٍ أَذِنَ ٱللَّهُ أَن تُرْفَعَ وَيُذْكَرَ فِيهَا ٱسْمُهُۥ يُسَبِّحُ لَهُۥ فِيهَا بِٱلْغُدُوِّ وَٱلْءَاصَالِ ۝ رِجَالٌ لَّا تُلْهِيهِمْ تِجَٰرَةٌ وَلَا بَيْعٌ عَن ذِكْرِ ٱللَّهِ وَإِقَامِ ٱلصَّلَوٰةِ وَإِيتَآءِ ٱلزَّكَوٰةِ ۙ يَخَافُونَ يَوْمًا تَتَقَلَّبُ فِيهِ ٱلْقُلُوبُ وَٱلْأَبْصَٰرُ ۝ لِيَجْزِيَهُمُ ٱللَّهُ أَحْسَنَ مَا عَمِلُوا۟ وَيَزِيدَهُم مِّن فَضْلِهِۦ ۗ وَٱللَّهُ يَرْزُقُ مَن يَشَآءُ بِغَيْرِ حِسَابٍ ۝ وَٱلَّذِينَ كَفَرُوٓا۟ أَعْمَٰلُهُمْ كَسَرَابٍۭ بِقِيعَةٍ يَحْسَبُهُ ٱلظَّمْـَٔانُ مَآءً حَتَّىٰٓ إِذَا جَآءَهُۥ لَمْ يَجِدْهُ شَيْـًٔا وَوَجَدَ ٱللَّهَ عِندَهُۥ فَوَفَّىٰهُ حِسَابَهُۥ ۗ وَٱللَّهُ سَرِيعُ ٱلْحِسَابِ ۝ أَوْ كَظُلُمَٰتٍ فِى بَحْرٍ لُّجِّىٍّ يَغْشَىٰهُ مَوْجٌ

مِّن فَوْقِهِۦ مَوْجٌ مِّن فَوْقِهِۦ سَحَابٌ ظُلُمَٰتٌۢ بَعْضُهَا فَوْقَ بَعْضٍ إِذَآ أَخْرَجَ يَدَهُۥ لَمْ يَكَدْ يَرَىٰهَا وَمَن لَّمْ يَجْعَلِ ٱللَّهُ لَهُۥ نُورًا فَمَا لَهُۥ مِن نُّورٍ ۝

Allah is the light of the heavens and the earth. A parable of his light is a niche in which is a lantern, The lantern in a glass, The glass like a shimmering star, Kindled from a blessed tree, An olive, neither of the East nor of the West, Its oil almost aglow, though untouched by fire. Light upon light! Allah guides to His light whomever He wills, and strikes parables for mankind. Allah has knowledge of all things. In houses which Allah permits to be raised, And His name to be mentioned therein, There He is glorified, morning and evening, by men whom neither commerce nor trade distracts from the remembrance of Allah, from constant prayer, and from giving alms. They fear a Day when hearts and eyes will turn and turn again, when Allah shall reward them for their best deeds, and multiply His favours upon them. And Allah bestows His bounty, uncountable, upon whomsoever He wills. As for the unbelievers, their works are like a mirage in a far-flung plain, that a thirsty man imagines to be water, until, when he arrives thereto, he finds it to be nothing, but there he finds Allah, Who pays him his account in full, And Allah is swift to settle accounts. Or else they are like shades obscure over a vast ocean, enveloped by the waves, above which are waves, above which is fog; darkest shades, piled one upon the other. If he stretches forth his hand, he can scarcely see it. He on whom Allah sheds no light, no light has he.

35-40 The human heart is where the inner soul resides and emits the life force that helps to maintain the health and goodness that we desire. The visible light outside is the outer manifestation balanced by our inner light of life, as alluded to by the metaphor that God's light within our own heart is illumined without any oil or physical entity. The entire universe is permeated by God's power, and the human heart is permeated with that universality. Our life becomes richer, of a higher quality, when we more frequently reference the soul within, not being distracted by the lower self. Those on the path of awakening realise the constant mercy and generosity of God, while those who are not remain confused and move from states of difficulty and uncertainty to those of sorrow and fear. We either move higher in consciousness or lower.

It is a great miracle that a human being can have consciousness of consciousness and contain the divine light within the inner heart. This light is cosmic, and if followed will lead to the understanding of the inner meaning of all our experiences. Without belief, without constant connectedness to inner *Oneness*, our life is indeed a waste. With old age, we will then only become more anxious about death.

Truth, *Reality*, or God are all names given to the radiation of experience that we call life. Everybody shares that touch, and everyone is obsessed with it, because its nature is continuity and eternity. We know that the human side of us is temporary and is only a cover for that light to enable it to transit through the zone of duality on earth. The quality of human life on earth is as good as our referencing to the inner light within our hearts. This referencing enables the self to live with patience, generosity, kindness, and all the virtues.

41-49 أَلَمْ تَرَ أَنَّ ٱللَّهَ يُسَبِّحُ لَهُۥ مَن فِى ٱلسَّمَٰوَٰتِ وَٱلْأَرْضِ وَٱلطَّيْرُ صَٰٓفَّٰتٍۖ كُلٌّ قَدْ عَلِمَ صَلَاتَهُۥ وَتَسْبِيحَهُۥۗ وَٱللَّهُ عَلِيمٌۢ بِمَا يَفْعَلُونَ ۝ وَلِلَّهِ مُلْكُ ٱلسَّمَٰوَٰتِ وَٱلْأَرْضِۖ وَإِلَى ٱللَّهِ ٱلْمَصِيرُ ۝ أَلَمْ تَرَ أَنَّ ٱللَّهَ يُزْجِى سَحَابًا ثُمَّ يُؤَلِّفُ بَيْنَهُۥ ثُمَّ يَجْعَلُهُۥ رُكَامًا فَتَرَى ٱلْوَدْقَ يَخْرُجُ مِنْ خِلَٰلِهِۦ وَيُنَزِّلُ مِنَ ٱلسَّمَآءِ مِن جِبَالٍ فِيهَا مِنۢ بَرَدٍ فَيُصِيبُ بِهِۦ مَن يَشَآءُ وَيَصْرِفُهُۥ عَن مَّن يَشَآءُۖ يَكَادُ سَنَا بَرْقِهِۦ يَذْهَبُ بِٱلْأَبْصَٰرِ ۝ يُقَلِّبُ ٱللَّهُ ٱلَّيْلَ وَٱلنَّهَارَۚ إِنَّ فِى ذَٰلِكَ لَعِبْرَةً لِّأُو۟لِى ٱلْأَبْصَٰرِ ۝ وَٱللَّهُ خَلَقَ كُلَّ دَآبَّةٍ مِّن مَّآءٍۖ فَمِنْهُم مَّن يَمْشِى عَلَىٰ بَطْنِهِۦ وَمِنْهُم مَّن يَمْشِى عَلَىٰ رِجْلَيْنِ وَمِنْهُم مَّن يَمْشِى عَلَىٰٓ أَرْبَعٍۚ يَخْلُقُ ٱللَّهُ مَا يَشَآءُۚ إِنَّ ٱللَّهَ عَلَىٰ كُلِّ شَىْءٍ قَدِيرٌ ۝ لَّقَدْ أَنزَلْنَآ ءَايَٰتٍ مُّبَيِّنَٰتٍۚ وَٱللَّهُ يَهْدِى مَن يَشَآءُ إِلَىٰ صِرَٰطٍ مُّسْتَقِيمٍ ۝ وَيَقُولُونَ ءَامَنَّا بِٱللَّهِ وَبِٱلرَّسُولِ وَأَطَعْنَا ثُمَّ يَتَوَلَّىٰ فَرِيقٌ مِّنْهُم مِّنۢ بَعْدِ ذَٰلِكَۚ وَمَآ أُو۟لَٰٓئِكَ بِٱلْمُؤْمِنِينَ ۝ وَإِذَا دُعُوٓا۟ إِلَى ٱللَّهِ وَرَسُولِهِۦ لِيَحْكُمَ بَيْنَهُمْ إِذَا فَرِيقٌ مِّنْهُم مُّعْرِضُونَ ۝ وَإِن يَكُن لَّهُمُ ٱلْحَقُّ يَأْتُوٓا۟ إِلَيْهِ مُذْعِنِينَ ۝

Do you not see how all that is in the heavens and earth glorifies Allah, And the birds with wings outspread? Each has learnt his prayer and his glorification. And Allah knows full well what they do. To Allah belongs the kingdom of the heavens and the earth, and to Allah is the journey's end. Do you not see how Allah drives the clouds? Then blends them together, then turns them into billowing masses, and you can see the rain coming down from their crevices? How He sends from the sky, from mountains therein, hailstones, with which He strikes whomever He wishes, and averts it from whomever He wishes? The flash of its lightning almost blinds the eyes. Allah turns over the night and the day; most surely there is a lesson in this for those who have sight. Allah created every creature from water. Some walk on their bellies, some walk on two legs, some walk on four. Allah creates what He pleases, and Allah is powerful over everything. Now We have sent down signs making all clear; Allah guides whomsoever He will to a straight path. They say: 'We believe in Allah and in the Messenger, and we obey.' But a band of them turns away thereafter, and these are not believers. And when they are summoned to Allah and His Messenger in order for him to judge between them, some of them turn away. But if they are in the right, they will come to him submissively.

41-49 Ultimate contentment and joy result from surrendering our will to the owner of it all – Allah. All that there is in the heavens and earth follows interactive patterns and designs that have emanated from God. Every living creature has one major, constant obsession: the continuity of life within them. Ultimately every one of us is loyal to the life-source within ourselves; this is loyalty to God and the way God manifests in us. With good intentions, hope, and prayers we begin to realise the countless signs and signals around us, reminding us what to avoid and guiding us to that which is durable and real. Our soul is eternal, so in all the activities that we are happy with, we desire continuity and longevity. In truth the soul in essence is timeless and boundless.

It is a big gift of insight to be able to see that everything in the heavens and on earth resonates with cosmic *Oneness* according to its limitations. The plants grow and continue through their seeds, and thereby glorify ongoing timelessness. The amazing dance of dualities around us, such as night leading to day and vice versa, when sped up becomes a dot from which all emerged. *Truth* encompasses all that is known and unknown.

Life in all its forms displays miracles and amazing links between entities, which otherwise would not have seemed to relate to each other. The physical, material, and natural world all show us amazing connectedness emerging from the light of reality itself, enabling individualities to appear and then disappear.

50-57
أَفِى قُلُوبِهِم مَّرَضٌ أَمِ ٱرْتَابُوٓا۟ أَمْ يَخَافُونَ أَن يَحِيفَ ٱللَّهُ عَلَيْهِمْ وَرَسُولُهُۥ بَلْ أُو۟لَٰٓئِكَ هُمُ ٱلظَّٰلِمُونَ ۞ إِنَّمَا كَانَ قَوْلَ ٱلْمُؤْمِنِينَ إِذَا دُعُوٓا۟ إِلَى ٱللَّهِ وَرَسُولِهِۦ لِيَحْكُمَ بَيْنَهُمْ أَن يَقُولُوا۟ سَمِعْنَا وَأَطَعْنَا وَأُو۟لَٰٓئِكَ هُمُ ٱلْمُفْلِحُونَ ۞ وَمَن يُطِعِ ٱللَّهَ وَرَسُولَهُۥ وَيَخْشَ ٱللَّهَ وَيَتَّقْهِ فَأُو۟لَٰٓئِكَ هُمُ ٱلْفَآئِزُونَ ۞ وَأَقْسَمُوا۟ بِٱللَّهِ جَهْدَ أَيْمَٰنِهِمْ لَئِنْ أَمَرْتَهُمْ لَيَخْرُجُنَّ قُل لَّا تُقْسِمُوا۟ طَاعَةٌ مَّعْرُوفَةٌ إِنَّ ٱللَّهَ خَبِيرٌۢ بِمَا تَعْمَلُونَ ۞ قُلْ أَطِيعُوا۟ ٱللَّهَ وَأَطِيعُوا۟ ٱلرَّسُولَ فَإِن تَوَلَّوْا۟ فَإِنَّمَا عَلَيْهِ مَا حُمِّلَ وَعَلَيْكُم مَّا حُمِّلْتُمْ وَإِن تُطِيعُوهُ تَهْتَدُوا۟ وَمَا عَلَى ٱلرَّسُولِ إِلَّا ٱلْبَلَٰغُ ٱلْمُبِينُ ۞ وَعَدَ ٱللَّهُ ٱلَّذِينَ ءَامَنُوا۟ مِنكُمْ وَعَمِلُوا۟ ٱلصَّٰلِحَٰتِ لَيَسْتَخْلِفَنَّهُمْ فِى ٱلْأَرْضِ كَمَا ٱسْتَخْلَفَ ٱلَّذِينَ مِن قَبْلِهِمْ وَلَيُمَكِّنَنَّ لَهُمْ دِينَهُمُ ٱلَّذِى ٱرْتَضَىٰ لَهُمْ وَلَيُبَدِّلَنَّهُم مِّنۢ بَعْدِ خَوْفِهِمْ أَمْنًا يَعْبُدُونَنِى لَا يُشْرِكُونَ بِى شَيْـًٔا وَمَن كَفَرَ بَعْدَ ذَٰلِكَ فَأُو۟لَٰٓئِكَ هُمُ ٱلْفَٰسِقُونَ ۞ وَأَقِيمُوا۟ ٱلصَّلَوٰةَ وَءَاتُوا۟ ٱلزَّكَوٰةَ وَأَطِيعُوا۟ ٱلرَّسُولَ لَعَلَّكُمْ تُرْحَمُونَ ۞ لَا تَحْسَبَنَّ ٱلَّذِينَ كَفَرُوا۟ مُعْجِزِينَ فِى ٱلْأَرْضِ وَمَأْوَىٰهُمُ ٱلنَّارُ وَلَبِئْسَ ٱلْمَصِيرُ ۞

Is there sickness in their hearts? Or did they have doubts? Or were they afraid that Allah and His Messenger would do them an injustice? Rather, it is they who are unjust. The believers, in contrast, when summoned to Allah and His Messenger to judge between them, will merely say: 'We hear and obey.' These are the prosperous. Whoso obeys Allah and His Messenger, and fears Allah and is pious before Him – these are the victors. They have sworn by Allah the most earnest oaths, if you command them, they will go forth. Say: 'Do not swear; honourable obedience is sufficient. Surely Allah is aware of the things you do.' Say: 'Obey Allah and obey the Messenger.' If they turn and go, upon him rests his burden, and upon you your own. If you obey Him, you will be guided aright. The Messenger is enjoined only to deliver the clear message. Allah has promised those among you who believed and did righteous deeds to make them inherit the earth, as He caused those before them to inherit, and to establish their religion on firm foundations – the religion He sanctioned for them – and to instil peace of mind following their fear. And let them worship Me, and associate nothing with Me. Thereafter, whoso disbelieves, these are the dissolute. And keep up the prayer, pay the prescribed alms, and obey the Messenger, so that you may be given mercy. Do not imagine that the unbelievers can evade the power of Allah on earth. Their refuge is hell, and a wretched destiny it is.

50-57 We are naturally concerned about health and give attention to our overall physical wellbeing. The health and clarity of our mind is also crucial for our welfare. More important than all of these is our spiritual state, the purity of our heart resulting from regular referencing to the soul. Physical ailments are easier to cure than mental ones, and the most challenging need is to be spiritually sound, with a heart that is pure, not blocked or diseased. The heart of a criminal is so dark that it justifies the worst of actions to its wretched possessor. Countless communities in the past have initially thrived and expanded, only to ultimately fail and disintegrate. We are naturally driven to understand why these collapses take place. Ultimately, they are all caused by loss of direction towards awakening and God-consciousness.

The animal in us makes us give our attention to our mental, physical, and other discernible illnesses and sicknesses. The worst of these is the sickness of the heart, which prevents the spirit from leading and guiding us. It is only through faith, trust, and constant watchfulness of our intentions and actions, that we may truly act as God's stewards on earth. This includes self-accountability. The biggest gift is to experience mercy upon oneself in every situation.

Hope is an aspect of faith, the belief that there will be goodness awaiting us both in this world as well as in the hereafter. To live with trust, faith, and accountability is the healthy way of journeying on this earth.

58-64 يَٰٓأَيُّهَا ٱلَّذِينَ ءَامَنُوا۟ لِيَسْتَـْٔذِنكُمُ ٱلَّذِينَ مَلَكَتْ أَيْمَٰنُكُمْ وَٱلَّذِينَ لَمْ يَبْلُغُوا۟ ٱلْحُلُمَ مِنكُمْ ثَلَٰثَ مَرَّٰتٍ مِّن قَبْلِ صَلَوٰةِ ٱلْفَجْرِ وَحِينَ تَضَعُونَ ثِيَابَكُم مِّنَ ٱلظَّهِيرَةِ وَمِنۢ بَعْدِ صَلَوٰةِ ٱلْعِشَآءِ ثَلَٰثُ عَوْرَٰتٍ لَّكُمْ لَيْسَ عَلَيْكُمْ وَلَا عَلَيْهِمْ جُنَاحٌۢ بَعْدَهُنَّ طَوَّٰفُونَ عَلَيْكُم بَعْضُكُمْ عَلَىٰ بَعْضٍ كَذَٰلِكَ يُبَيِّنُ ٱللَّهُ لَكُمُ ٱلْءَايَٰتِ وَٱللَّهُ عَلِيمٌ حَكِيمٌ ۝ وَإِذَا بَلَغَ ٱلْأَطْفَٰلُ مِنكُمُ ٱلْحُلُمَ فَلْيَسْتَـْٔذِنُوا۟ كَمَا ٱسْتَـْٔذَنَ ٱلَّذِينَ مِن قَبْلِهِمْ كَذَٰلِكَ يُبَيِّنُ ٱللَّهُ لَكُمْ ءَايَٰتِهِۦ وَٱللَّهُ عَلِيمٌ حَكِيمٌ ۝ وَٱلْقَوَٰعِدُ مِنَ ٱلنِّسَآءِ ٱلَّٰتِى لَا يَرْجُونَ نِكَاحًا فَلَيْسَ عَلَيْهِنَّ جُنَاحٌ أَن يَضَعْنَ ثِيَابَهُنَّ غَيْرَ مُتَبَرِّجَٰتٍۭ بِزِينَةٍ وَأَن يَسْتَعْفِفْنَ خَيْرٌ لَّهُنَّ وَٱللَّهُ سَمِيعٌ عَلِيمٌ ۝ لَّيْسَ عَلَى ٱلْأَعْمَىٰ حَرَجٌ وَلَا عَلَى ٱلْأَعْرَجِ حَرَجٌ وَلَا عَلَى

الْمَرِيضِ حَرَجٌ وَلَا عَلَىٰ أَنفُسِكُمْ أَن تَأْكُلُوا مِنْ بُيُوتِكُمْ أَوْ بُيُوتِ ءَابَآئِكُمْ أَوْ بُيُوتِ أُمَّهَٰتِكُمْ أَوْ بُيُوتِ إِخْوَٰنِكُمْ أَوْ بُيُوتِ أَخَوَٰتِكُمْ أَوْ بُيُوتِ أَعْمَٰمِكُمْ أَوْ بُيُوتِ عَمَّٰتِكُمْ أَوْ بُيُوتِ أَخْوَٰلِكُمْ أَوْ بُيُوتِ خَٰلَٰتِكُمْ أَوْ مَا مَلَكْتُم مَّفَاتِحَهُۥٓ أَوْ صَدِيقِكُمْ ۚ لَيْسَ عَلَيْكُمْ جُنَاحٌ أَن تَأْكُلُوا جَمِيعًا أَوْ أَشْتَاتًا ۚ فَإِذَا دَخَلْتُم بُيُوتًا فَسَلِّمُوا عَلَىٰٓ أَنفُسِكُمْ تَحِيَّةً مِّنْ عِندِ ٱللَّهِ مُبَٰرَكَةً طَيِّبَةً ۚ كَذَٰلِكَ يُبَيِّنُ ٱللَّهُ لَكُمُ ٱلْءَايَٰتِ لَعَلَّكُمْ تَعْقِلُونَ ۝ إِنَّمَا ٱلْمُؤْمِنُونَ ٱلَّذِينَ ءَامَنُوا بِٱللَّهِ وَرَسُولِهِۦ وَإِذَا كَانُوا مَعَهُۥ عَلَىٰٓ أَمْرٍ جَامِعٍ لَّمْ يَذْهَبُوا حَتَّىٰ يَسْتَـْٔذِنُوهُ ۚ إِنَّ ٱلَّذِينَ يَسْتَـْٔذِنُونَكَ أُو۟لَٰٓئِكَ ٱلَّذِينَ يُؤْمِنُونَ بِٱللَّهِ وَرَسُولِهِۦ ۚ فَإِذَا ٱسْتَـْٔذَنُوكَ لِبَعْضِ شَأْنِهِمْ فَأْذَن لِّمَن شِئْتَ مِنْهُمْ وَٱسْتَغْفِرْ لَهُمُ ٱللَّهَ ۚ إِنَّ ٱللَّهَ غَفُورٌ رَّحِيمٌ ۝ لَّا تَجْعَلُوا دُعَآءَ ٱلرَّسُولِ بَيْنَكُمْ كَدُعَآءِ بَعْضِكُم بَعْضًا ۚ قَدْ يَعْلَمُ ٱللَّهُ ٱلَّذِينَ يَتَسَلَّلُونَ مِنكُمْ لِوَاذًا ۚ فَلْيَحْذَرِ ٱلَّذِينَ يُخَالِفُونَ عَنْ أَمْرِهِۦٓ أَن تُصِيبَهُمْ فِتْنَةٌ أَوْ يُصِيبَهُمْ عَذَابٌ أَلِيمٌ ۝ أَلَآ إِنَّ لِلَّهِ مَا فِى ٱلسَّمَٰوَٰتِ وَٱلْأَرْضِ ۖ قَدْ يَعْلَمُ مَآ أَنتُمْ عَلَيْهِ وَيَوْمَ يُرْجَعُونَ إِلَيْهِ فَيُنَبِّئُهُم بِمَا عَمِلُوا ۗ وَٱللَّهُ بِكُلِّ شَىْءٍ عَلِيمٌ ۝

O you who believe! Let those whom your right hands possess and those of you who have not attained to puberty ask permission of you three times; before the morning prayer, and when you put off your clothes at midday in summer, and after the prayer of the nightfall; these are three times of privacy for you; neither is it a fault on you nor on them besides these, some of you must go round about upon others; thus does Allah make clear to you the communications, and Allah is All-Knowing, All-Wise. When your children reach the age of puberty, they are to ask permission as did others before them. Thus, does Allah clarify His signs to you, and Allah is All-Knowing, All-Wise. Such women as are past child-bearing and have no hope of marriage – there is no fault in them that they put off their clothes, so be it that they flaunt no ornament; but to abstain is better for them; and Allah is All-Hearing, All-Knowing. No blame attaches to the blind; no blame attaches to the lame; no blame attaches to the sick; and no blame attaches to you if you eat at your own houses, or at the houses of your fathers and your mothers, your brothers or your sisters, or the houses of your paternal uncles or aunts, or your maternal uncles and aunts, or any house whose keys you own, or at the house of a friend. No blame attaches to you if you eat all together or scattered in groups. When entering a house, greet each other with the greeting of peace, a greeting blessed and seemly from Allah. Thus, does Allah clarify His signs to you; perhaps you will understand. The believers are those who believe in Allah and His Messenger. If they are with him on some common endeavor, they should not depart until they ask his permission. Those who ask your permission are the ones who believe in Allah and His Messenger. If they ask your permission to attend to some affair of theirs, grant permission to whomever of them you wish, and ask Allah's forgiveness for them. Allah is All-Forgiving, Compassionate to each. Do not address the Messenger in your midst as you address one another. Allah knows those of you who slink away, hiding behind each other. Let those who defy his orders beware lest some ordeal should befall them, or else a pain-

ful torment. To Allah belongs what is in the heavens and on earth. He knows what you are about, and on the Day they are returned to Him, He shall inform them of what they did. And Allah has knowledge of all things.

58-64 We experience two parallel stages of growth: one is biological and physiological, the other spiritual. By acknowledging limitations and being fully accountable, a community needs to enforce these boundaries and accept the gifts of punishment and reward. The prophetic path requires total sincerity, commitment, and clear attention if it is to yield the fruit of transcending the earthly trap. Whatever is known and unknown belongs to the *One*, who knows all. The prophetic path leads to this realisation.

As humans we must possess the correct courtesy regarding our limitations on earth. As a divine spirit, however, we are given the opportunity to recharge from the original divine light. At every level that we encompass, appropriate courtesy exists. We cannot treat a child in the same way that we treat an accomplished adult, nor can we talk to someone who is totally worldly as though we are in the company of a pious person devoted to truth.

Through human wisdom, we will understand limitations and incapacities that we may be subjected to. It is the earthly wisdom that enables us to forgive and forget, but it is the higher divine wisdom that recharges us beyond the mind and reason.

8. Surah 26 Ash-Shu'ara' (The Poets)

Due to the light of intelligence, consciousness climbs toward the original zone of divine manifestations. There is a natural barrier between the basic, conditioned human consciousness and this boundless zone, which we refer to as divine or sacred. Yet the two zones are seamlessly connected, since conditioned consciousness is totally dependent on cosmic consciousness.

بِسْمِ اللَّهِ الرَّحْمَٰنِ الرَّحِيمِ

1-15 طسم ۝ تِلْكَ ءَايَٰتُ ٱلْكِتَٰبِ ٱلْمُبِينِ ۝ لَعَلَّكَ بَٰخِعٌ نَّفْسَكَ أَلَّا يَكُونُوا۟ مُؤْمِنِينَ ۝ إِن نَّشَأْ نُنَزِّلْ عَلَيْهِم مِّنَ ٱلسَّمَآءِ ءَايَةً فَظَلَّتْ أَعْنَٰقُهُمْ لَهَا خَٰضِعِينَ ۝ وَمَا يَأْتِيهِم مِّن ذِكْرٍ مِّنَ ٱلرَّحْمَٰنِ مُحْدَثٍ إِلَّا كَانُوا۟ عَنْهُ مُعْرِضِينَ ۝ فَقَدْ كَذَّبُوا۟ فَسَيَأْتِيهِمْ أَنۢبَٰٓؤُا۟ مَا كَانُوا۟ بِهِۦ يَسْتَهْزِءُونَ ۝ أَوَلَمْ يَرَوْا۟ إِلَى ٱلْأَرْضِ كَمْ أَنۢبَتْنَا فِيهَا مِن كُلِّ زَوْجٍ كَرِيمٍ ۝ إِنَّ فِى ذَٰلِكَ لَءَايَةً ۖ وَمَا كَانَ أَكْثَرُهُم مُّؤْمِنِينَ ۝ وَإِنَّ رَبَّكَ لَهُوَ ٱلْعَزِيزُ ٱلرَّحِيمُ ۝ وَإِذْ نَادَىٰ رَبُّكَ مُوسَىٰٓ أَنِ ٱئْتِ ٱلْقَوْمَ ٱلظَّٰلِمِينَ ۝ قَوْمَ فِرْعَوْنَ ۚ أَلَا يَتَّقُونَ ۝ قَالَ رَبِّ إِنِّىٓ أَخَافُ أَن يُكَذِّبُونِ ۝ وَيَضِيقُ صَدْرِى وَلَا يَنطَلِقُ لِسَانِى فَأَرْسِلْ إِلَىٰ هَٰرُونَ ۝ وَلَهُمْ عَلَىَّ ذَنۢبٌ فَأَخَافُ أَن يَقْتُلُونِ ۝ قَالَ كَلَّا ۖ فَٱذْهَبَا بِـَٔايَٰتِنَآ ۖ إِنَّا مَعَكُم مُّسْتَمِعُونَ ۝

8. Surah 26 Ash-Shu'ara (The Poets)

In the name of Allah, the Merciful to all, the Compassionate to each!

Ta Sin Mim. Those are the signs of the Manifest Book. And will you perchance torture yourself because they are not believers? If We will, We shall send down on them out of heaven a sign, so their necks will stay humbled to it. There comes not to them any remembrance anew, from the All-Merciful, but they turn away from it. They have cried lies! But there shall come to them the true import of what they used to mock. Have they not observed the earth and how many We planted therein of every beauteous species? Surely in that is a sign, yet most of them are not believers. It is your Lord Who is Almighty, Compassionate to each. Remember when your Lord called out to Moses: 'Go forth to that wicked people, the people of Pharaoh. Will they not take heed?' He said: 'My Lord, I fear they will call me a liar, and my breast will be straitened, and my tongue will not be loosed; so, send to Aaron. Besides, they hold me accountable for a crime, and I fear they will kill me.' He said: 'No, they shall not, so go forth, you two, with Our signs, and We shall be with you, listening.

1-15 It is natural for human beings to have empathy and interact with other beings in order to experience healthy relationships. Parents try to pass their personal experience to their offspring to help them reduce errors and suffering, but sometimes this is futile. Everyone tries to push the boundaries, and they sometimes commit mistakes or errors that are irreversible. Individuals and communities succeed according to the extent of their cautious awareness. We need to acknowledge the limitations of our temporary earthly experiences.

It is natural for us humans to want to share any interesting and exciting experiences that we may have had with others. In terms of spiritual insights, unless the person practices belief and accountability, they are unlikely to be touched by higher experiences that are beyond the mind and the ego.

For the past few thousand years, the evolution of human beings and the rise of spiritual intelligence has been repeatedly enhanced by great individuals and prophets who have revealed the true essence of the timeless, unique, eternal *Oneness*. They also pointed out that all dualities and pluralities lead to the same *Oneness*, because they have emanated from the same. Most of our human experience fits within space, time, and duality, but always has a touch of the unique timelessness of *Essence*.

16-32 فَأْتِيَا فِرْعَوْنَ فَقُولَآ إِنَّا رَسُولُ رَبِّ ٱلْعَٰلَمِينَ ۝ أَنْ أَرْسِلْ مَعَنَا بَنِىٓ إِسْرَٰٓءِيلَ ۝ قَالَ أَلَمْ نُرَبِّكَ فِينَا وَلِيدًا وَلَبِثْتَ فِينَا مِنْ عُمُرِكَ سِنِينَ ۝ وَفَعَلْتَ فَعْلَتَكَ ٱلَّتِى فَعَلْتَ وَأَنتَ مِنَ ٱلْكَٰفِرِينَ ۝ قَالَ فَعَلْتُهَآ إِذًا وَأَنَا۠ مِنَ ٱلضَّآلِّينَ ۝ فَفَرَرْتُ مِنكُمْ لَمَّا خِفْتُكُمْ فَوَهَبَ لِى رَبِّى حُكْمًا وَجَعَلَنِى مِنَ ٱلْمُرْسَلِينَ ۝ وَتِلْكَ نِعْمَةٌ تَمُنُّهَا عَلَىَّ أَنْ عَبَّدتَّ بَنِىٓ إِسْرَٰٓءِيلَ ۝ قَالَ فِرْعَوْنُ وَمَا رَبُّ ٱلْعَٰلَمِينَ ۝

قَالَ رَبُّ ٱلسَّمَٰوَٰتِ وَٱلْأَرْضِ وَمَا بَيْنَهُمَآ إِن كُنتُم مُّوقِنِينَ ۝ قَالَ لِمَنْ حَوْلَهُۥٓ أَلَا تَسْتَمِعُونَ ۝ قَالَ رَبُّكُمْ وَرَبُّ ءَابَآئِكُمُ ٱلْأَوَّلِينَ ۝ قَالَ إِنَّ رَسُولَكُمُ ٱلَّذِىٓ أُرْسِلَ إِلَيْكُمْ لَمَجْنُونٌ ۝ قَالَ رَبُّ ٱلْمَشْرِقِ وَٱلْمَغْرِبِ وَمَا بَيْنَهُمَآ إِن كُنتُمْ تَعْقِلُونَ ۝ قَالَ لَئِنِ ٱتَّخَذْتَ إِلَٰهًا غَيْرِى لَأَجْعَلَنَّكَ مِنَ ٱلْمَسْجُونِينَ ۝ قَالَ أَوَلَوْ جِئْتُكَ بِشَىْءٍ مُّبِينٍ ۝ قَالَ فَأْتِ بِهِۦٓ إِن كُنتَ مِنَ ٱلصَّٰدِقِينَ ۝ فَأَلْقَىٰ عَصَاهُ فَإِذَا هِىَ ثُعْبَانٌ مُّبِينٌ ۝

Go to Pharaoh and say to him: 'We are the messenger of the Lord of the Worlds.' So send out with us the Children of Israel. He said: 'Did we not raise you up among us as an infant? Did you not remain with us some years of your life? And then you went and committed your crime! You are indeed an ingrate!' Said he, 'Indeed I did it then, being one of those that stray; so I fled from you in fear of you. But My Lord has granted me right judgment and made me a messenger. And is this the favor you reproach me with: that you enslaved the Children of Israel?' Pharaoh said: 'What is the Lord of the Worlds?' He said: 'The Lord of the heavens and the earth and what is between them, if you would be sure.' To those around him he said: 'Are you listening?' He said: 'He is your Lord and the Lord of your ancient forefathers.' He said: 'This, your messenger who has been sent to you, is mad.' He said: 'Lord of the East and the West, if you possess understanding.' Said he, 'If you take a Allah other than me, I shall surely make thee one of the imprisoned.' He said: 'What? Even if I bring to you something manifest?' He said: 'Bring it on if you speak the truth.' So he cast his staff, and behold, it was a serpent manifest.

16-32 The higher voice spoke to Prophet Moses, encouraging him that his duty was to warn the people due to their transgressions and to pray that his tribe be saved from the tyranny of Pharaoh. The messenger in Prophet Moses followed the command without concern or fear of consequences. Naturally humans tend to ignore whatever they are not familiar with. Moses was labelled as a madman and was threatened with imprisonment or worse. Then came the request for a miracle to prove that he was not an ordinary liar. It is in our nature to always look for the supernatural. The usual and familiar becomes ordinary and loses our attention.

Life has evolved on earth from the simplest self-aware state to the most complex Adamic consciousness over many eras. The human being is now capable of accepting its earthly limitations, while constantly yearning for evidence of the miracle of life within the heart.

We have had individuals amongst us throughout our history who imagined themselves as supreme, and people have been depressed and oppressed because of this. Time has passed and all of this was forgotten; people returned to the original question: where is God? And where are his power and influence? And where do I fit within that?

33-49 وَنَزَعَ يَدَهُ فَإِذَا هِيَ بَيْضَاءُ لِلنَّاظِرِينَ ۝ قَالَ لِلْمَلَإِ حَوْلَهُ إِنَّ هَٰذَا لَسَاحِرٌ عَلِيمٌ ۝ يُرِيدُ أَن يُخْرِجَكُم مِّنْ أَرْضِكُم بِسِحْرِهِ فَمَاذَا تَأْمُرُونَ ۝ قَالُوا أَرْجِهْ وَأَخَاهُ وَابْعَثْ فِي الْمَدَائِنِ حَاشِرِينَ ۝ يَأْتُوكَ بِكُلِّ سَحَّارٍ عَلِيمٍ ۝ فَجُمِعَ السَّحَرَةُ لِمِيقَاتِ يَوْمٍ مَّعْلُومٍ ۝ وَقِيلَ لِلنَّاسِ هَلْ أَنتُم مُّجْتَمِعُونَ ۝ لَعَلَّنَا نَتَّبِعُ السَّحَرَةَ إِن كَانُوا هُمُ الْغَالِبِينَ ۝ فَلَمَّا جَاءَ السَّحَرَةُ قَالُوا لِفِرْعَوْنَ أَئِنَّ لَنَا لَأَجْرًا إِن كُنَّا نَحْنُ الْغَالِبِينَ ۝ قَالَ نَعَمْ وَإِنَّكُمْ إِذًا لَّمِنَ الْمُقَرَّبِينَ ۝ قَالَ لَهُم مُّوسَىٰ أَلْقُوا مَا أَنتُم مُّلْقُونَ ۝ فَأَلْقَوْا حِبَالَهُمْ وَعِصِيَّهُمْ وَقَالُوا بِعِزَّةِ فِرْعَوْنَ إِنَّا لَنَحْنُ الْغَالِبُونَ ۝ فَأَلْقَىٰ مُوسَىٰ عَصَاهُ فَإِذَا هِيَ تَلْقَفُ مَا يَأْفِكُونَ ۝ فَأُلْقِيَ السَّحَرَةُ سَاجِدِينَ ۝ قَالُوا آمَنَّا بِرَبِّ الْعَالَمِينَ ۝ رَبِّ مُوسَىٰ وَهَارُونَ ۝ قَالَ آمَنتُمْ لَهُ قَبْلَ أَنْ آذَنَ لَكُمْ إِنَّهُ لَكَبِيرُكُمُ الَّذِي عَلَّمَكُمُ السِّحْرَ فَلَسَوْفَ تَعْلَمُونَ لَأُقَطِّعَنَّ أَيْدِيَكُمْ وَأَرْجُلَكُم مِّنْ خِلَافٍ وَلَأُصَلِّبَنَّكُمْ أَجْمَعِينَ ۝

And he drew forth his hand, and lo, it was white to the beholders. Pharaoh said to the counsellors around him, 'This man is a learned sorcerer! Who desires to expel you from your land by his sorcery; what do you command?' They said, 'Put him and his brother off a while, and send among the cities musterers, who shall assemble before you all sorcerers of great knowledge.' The sorcerers were then summoned for an appointment on a day made known. The people were asked, 'Will you assemble? We might follow the sorcerers if they are the victors.' When the sorcerers arrived, they said to Pharaoh: 'Are we to have our wage if we are the victors?' He said, 'Yes indeed; and you shall then be among the near-stationed.' Moses said to them, 'Cast you down what you will cast.' So, they cast their ropes and their staffs, and said, 'By the might of Pharaoh we shall be the victors.' Then Moses cast his staff and lo, it forthwith swallowed up their lying invention. The sorcerers were thrown to the ground, prostrate. They said: 'We believe in the Lord of the Worlds. The Lord of Musa and Haroun.' He said: 'You believe in Him before I grant you leave? He is merely the greatest among you, who taught you sorcery. You will surely know! I shall cut off your hands and legs, on opposite sides, and then crucify you all.'

33-49 It is a most sublime act when the actors are self-aware and do not consider their conduct to emanate from their own volition or power. This is where the flow of events seems miraculous. Such was the triumph of Prophet Moses. The events that led to Pharaoh's magicians submitting to Prophet Moses resulted in Pharaoh's anger and threats. The dual nature of our self and soul enables us to connect with all earthly realities whilst still yearning for the timeless, perfect state. A divinely-inspired person, acting entirely upon inspiration and without any ego-darkness, is most potent. Free from the lower self and completely oriented towards the divine spirit within, the conduct of enlightened beings and prophets who are regarded to have unusual power sometimes appears in the form of miracles.

Numerous great prophets and enlightened beings were clearly given the ability to live in a way that was considered miraculous by others. A true prophet lives according to divine inspiration and does not perform miracles as such, but they come through him.

The rise of the great Pharaohs was one of the numerous events in human history where individuals got tuned to the source of power within the heart and they imagined themselves being human gods. Then their cycle ended and people were left in wonderment and shock. Once anything manifests, it has a beginning and an end. It has emerged from the power of God, but it is not God.

50-68 قَالُواْ لَا ضَيْرَ إِنَّآ إِلَىٰ رَبِّنَا مُنقَلِبُونَ ۝ إِنَّا نَطْمَعُ أَن يَغْفِرَ لَنَا رَبُّنَا خَطَـٰيَـٰنَآ أَن كُنَّآ أَوَّلَ ٱلْمُؤْمِنِينَ ۝ وَأَوْحَيْنَآ إِلَىٰ مُوسَىٰٓ أَنْ أَسْرِ بِعِبَادِىٓ إِنَّكُم مُّتَّبَعُونَ ۝ فَأَرْسَلَ فِرْعَوْنُ فِى ٱلْمَدَآئِنِ حَـٰشِرِينَ ۝ إِنَّ هَـٰٓؤُلَآءِ لَشِرْذِمَةٌ قَلِيلُونَ ۝ وَإِنَّهُمْ لَنَا لَغَآئِظُونَ ۝ وَإِنَّا لَجَمِيعٌ حَـٰذِرُونَ ۝ فَأَخْرَجْنَـٰهُم مِّن جَنَّـٰتٍ وَعُيُونٍ ۝ وَكُنُوزٍ وَمَقَامٍ كَرِيمٍ ۝ كَذَٰلِكَ وَأَوْرَثْنَـٰهَا بَنِىٓ إِسْرَٰٓءِيلَ ۝ فَأَتْبَعُوهُم مُّشْرِقِينَ ۝ فَلَمَّا تَرَٰٓءَا ٱلْجَمْعَانِ قَالَ أَصْحَـٰبُ مُوسَىٰٓ إِنَّا لَمُدْرَكُونَ ۝ قَالَ كَلَّآ إِنَّ مَعِىَ رَبِّى سَيَهْدِينِ ۝ فَأَوْحَيْنَآ إِلَىٰ مُوسَىٰٓ أَنِ ٱضْرِب بِّعَصَاكَ ٱلْبَحْرَ فَٱنفَلَقَ فَكَانَ كُلُّ فِرْقٍ كَٱلطَّوْدِ ٱلْعَظِيمِ ۝ وَأَزْلَفْنَا ثَمَّ ٱلْءَاخَرِينَ ۝ وَأَنجَيْنَا مُوسَىٰ وَمَن مَّعَهُۥٓ أَجْمَعِينَ ۝ ثُمَّ أَغْرَقْنَا ٱلْءَاخَرِينَ ۝ إِنَّ فِى ذَٰلِكَ لَءَايَةً وَمَا كَانَ أَكْثَرُهُم مُّؤْمِنِينَ ۝ وَإِنَّ رَبَّكَ لَهُوَ ٱلْعَزِيزُ ٱلرَّحِيمُ ۝

They said: 'No harm in that, for we shall return to our Lord. We are eager that our Lord should forgive us our offences, for that we are the first of the believers.' Then We revealed Our will to Moses, 'Leave with My servants by night, for you will be pursued!' Then Pharaoh sent among the cities musterers: 'They are but a few band, but they are a nuisance to us. We are all to be as one, and on alert.' So, We expelled them from gardens and fountains, and treasures and a noble station. Thus, did We bequeath them upon the Children of Israel. Then they followed them at the sunrise; and, when the two hosts sighted each other, the companions of Moses said, 'We are overtaken!' Said he, 'No indeed; surely my Lord is with me; He will guide me.' We inspired Moses: 'Strike the sea with your staff,' and it split open, each side like a towering mountain. Then We brought the others near, and We delivered Moses and those with him all together; then We drowned the others. Surely in that is a sign, yet most of them are not believers. It is your Lord Who is Almighty, Compassionate to each.

50-68 Prophet Moses was inspired to leave Egypt with his followers, protected from the fear of Pharaoh's soldiers who followed behind them. He heard the voice within him say that Allah is their saviour and that he needs to act in the physical sense by striking the sea with his staff. Then the supernatural occurred and enabled them to walk across safely and quickly. Pharaoh and his followers were drowned. No wealth or power, unless it is connected to the divine origin, can last or be of durable goodness. It is with trust, sincerity, and reliance upon God alone that the ocean of difficulties and miseries can open for us to cross over. With humility, faith, and trust in the grace of God, life on earth becomes a pleasant passage to the state of paradise.

The highest gift to a prophet is the total knowledge that guidance will come whenever it is needed and decreed by God. Ordinary human beings sometimes put themselves into impossibly difficult situations and, if they have faith, they may see the hand of the unseen help them. Only those who are living their faith will benefit from this.

Human beings are constantly engaged in a quest for the greatest meaning, for what is boundless and longer-lasting. We fall into so many existential traps because we measure and count; we find this nation greater and these people more powerful. Finally, we find that in truth the only real power, boundless and everlasting, is that of God.

69-90 وَٱتْلُ عَلَيْهِمْ نَبَأَ إِبْرَهِيمَ ۞ إِذْ قَالَ لِأَبِيهِ وَقَوْمِهِ مَا تَعْبُدُونَ ۞ قَالُوا۟ نَعْبُدُ أَصْنَامًا فَنَظَلُّ لَهَا عَـٰكِفِينَ ۞ قَالَ هَلْ يَسْمَعُونَكُمْ إِذْ تَدْعُونَ ۞ أَوْ يَنفَعُونَكُمْ أَوْ يَضُرُّونَ ۞ قَالُوا۟ بَلْ وَجَدْنَآ ءَابَآءَنَا كَذَٰلِكَ يَفْعَلُونَ ۞ قَالَ أَفَرَءَيْتُم مَّا كُنتُمْ تَعْبُدُونَ ۞ أَنتُمْ وَءَابَآؤُكُمُ ٱلْأَقْدَمُونَ ۞ فَإِنَّهُمْ عَدُوٌّ لِّى إِلَّا رَبَّ ٱلْعَـٰلَمِينَ ۞ ٱلَّذِى خَلَقَنِى فَهُوَ يَهْدِينِ ۞ وَٱلَّذِى هُوَ يُطْعِمُنِى وَيَسْقِينِ ۞ وَإِذَا مَرِضْتُ فَهُوَ يَشْفِينِ ۞ وَٱلَّذِى يُمِيتُنِى ثُمَّ يُحْيِينِ ۞ وَٱلَّذِىٓ أَطْمَعُ أَن يَغْفِرَ لِى خَطِيٓــَٔتِى يَوْمَ ٱلدِّينِ ۞ رَبِّ هَبْ لِى حُكْمًا وَأَلْحِقْنِى بِٱلصَّـٰلِحِينَ ۞ وَٱجْعَل لِّى لِسَانَ صِدْقٍ فِى ٱلْءَاخِرِينَ ۞ وَٱجْعَلْنِى مِن وَرَثَةِ جَنَّةِ ٱلنَّعِيمِ ۞ وَٱغْفِرْ لِأَبِىٓ إِنَّهُۥ كَانَ مِنَ ٱلضَّآلِّينَ ۞ وَلَا تُخْزِنِى يَوْمَ يُبْعَثُونَ ۞ يَوْمَ لَا يَنفَعُ مَالٌ وَلَا بَنُونَ ۞ إِلَّا مَنْ أَتَى ٱللَّهَ بِقَلْبٍ سَلِيمٍ ۞ وَأُزْلِفَتِ ٱلْجَنَّةُ لِلْمُتَّقِينَ ۞

And recite to them the story of Abraham. When he said to his father and people: 'What is it that you worship?' They said: 'We worship idols and minister diligently to them.' He said, 'Do they hear you when you call, or benefit you or do you harm?' They said: 'Rather, we found our forefathers so doing.' He said: 'Do you realize what you have been worshipping, you and your ancient forefathers? Surely, they are enemies to me, but not (so) the Lord of the worlds; He is who created me, and He is who guides me; and Himself gives me to eat and drink. When I am sick, He cures me; who makes me to die, then gives me life. He who I sincerely hope will forgive my mistakes on the Day of Reckoning. My Lord, give me Judgment, and join me with the righteous, and appoint me a tongue of truthfulness among the others. And make me of the heirs of the garden of bliss and forgive my father, for he is one of those astray. Do not disgrace me the Day they are resurrected, a Day when neither wealth nor progeny shall be of any worth, except one who approaches Allah with a pure heart.' The Garden shall be drawn near to the pious,

69-90 The great Prophet Abraham was totally in tune with the divine light in his heart. This was the source of his immense courage when he challenged his people regarding their idol worship. He revealed to them that his lord is the *Creator*, who gives guidance, and shows us how to obtain our provisions and to seek healing and health. It is also God who causes us to die and be resurrected again, who is the All-Forgiving that we need to turn to with humility and sincerity, who causes one to realise the closeness of paradise. It is ingrained in all of us to desire the best outcome in our life, which is ultimately a state where we have no fear, sorrow, needs, or desires because our own state is perfect and timeless. All our earthly attempts are to experience this state even for short periods.

Faith always enhances itself towards a higher level of realisation and trust in divine mercy in all situations. Our duty in this life is to have a clear mind, healthy body, and pure heart so that we see perfections at every level of consciousness.

The path of guidance and truth brings in this high level of self-reflection: that God prevails over everything and is the source of guidance in all situations. God is the source of bringing anything alive to neutrality and well-beingness, forgiving all, available to all at all times and in all circumstances. Tuning to the power of God enables us to deal with all existential connectedness with appropriate wisdom and correct balance.

91-111 وَبُرِّزَتِ ٱلْجَحِيمُ لِلْغَاوِينَ ۞ وَقِيلَ لَهُمْ أَيْنَ مَا كُنتُمْ تَعْبُدُونَ ۞ مِن دُونِ ٱللَّهِ هَلْ يَنصُرُونَكُمْ أَوْ يَنتَصِرُونَ ۞ فَكُبْكِبُوا۟ فِيهَا هُمْ وَٱلْغَاوُۥنَ ۞ وَجُنُودُ إِبْلِيسَ أَجْمَعُونَ ۞ قَالُوا۟ وَهُمْ فِيهَا يَخْتَصِمُونَ ۞ تَٱللَّهِ إِن كُنَّا لَفِى ضَلَٰلٍ مُّبِينٍ ۞ إِذْ نُسَوِّيكُم بِرَبِّ ٱلْعَٰلَمِينَ ۞ وَمَآ أَضَلَّنَآ إِلَّا ٱلْمُجْرِمُونَ ۞ فَمَا لَنَا مِن شَٰفِعِينَ ۞ وَلَا صَدِيقٍ حَمِيمٍ ۞ فَلَوْ أَنَّ لَنَا كَرَّةً فَنَكُونَ مِنَ ٱلْمُؤْمِنِينَ ۞ إِنَّ فِى ذَٰلِكَ لَءَايَةً وَمَا كَانَ أَكْثَرُهُم مُّؤْمِنِينَ ۞ وَإِنَّ رَبَّكَ لَهُوَ ٱلْعَزِيزُ ٱلرَّحِيمُ ۞ كَذَّبَتْ قَوْمُ نُوحٍ ٱلْمُرْسَلِينَ ۞ إِذْ قَالَ لَهُمْ أَخُوهُمْ نُوحٌ أَلَا تَتَّقُونَ ۞ إِنِّى لَكُمْ رَسُولٌ أَمِينٌ ۞ فَٱتَّقُوا۟ ٱللَّهَ وَأَطِيعُونِ ۞ وَمَآ أَسْـَٔلُكُمْ عَلَيْهِ مِنْ أَجْرٍ إِنْ أَجْرِىَ إِلَّا عَلَىٰ رَبِّ ٱلْعَٰلَمِينَ ۞ فَٱتَّقُوا۟ ٱللَّهَ وَأَطِيعُونِ ۞ قَالُوٓا۟ أَنُؤْمِنُ لَكَ وَٱتَّبَعَكَ ٱلْأَرْذَلُونَ ۞

And hell shall be revealed to the fiendish. And it shall be said to them: 'Where are those that you used to worship; Will they come to your aid, or can they themselves prevail?' Into it they shall be bundled, they and the fiendish, and the hosts of Iblis, all together. They shall say, as they bicker therein: 'By Allah, we were indeed in manifest error, when we held you equal to the Lord of the Worlds. None led us astray but the wicked, so now we have no intercessors, nor have we an intimate friend. If only we could have a second chance, we would join the faithful.' In this was a sign, but most of them were not believers. It is your Lord Who is Almighty, Compassionate to each. Noah's people cried lies to the messengers. When their brother Noah said to them: 'Will you not beware?' To you I am a trustworthy messenger; therefore, revere Allah and obey me. I ask you no wage for it; my wage falls solely upon the Lord of the Worlds. Therefore, be cautiously aware of Allah and obey me. They said, 'Shall we believe you, whom the vilest follow?'

91-111 Occasionally we experience immense difficulties and hardships; these are like small fires. Experiences of paradise and hell on earth are temporary preludes to the perpetuity of the hereafter. On the Day of Reckoning we realise to what extent we have been misguided on earth and have failed to give due consideration to the *Giver* of all life. In most cases, leadership on earth was arrogant, often accusing prophets and messengers of weakness, madness, or total inadequacy. The Prophet Noah was a great example: centuries of teaching and weeping without any visible effect upon his people. In the end all he could do was save himself, a few followers, and the other living creatures on the ark.

Our life on earth is bracketed between the experiences of birth and death but is a preparation to experience the eternal light of the soul within after death. We can only progress spiritually if we have real faith and trust and are always reflective; this way we do not slip down into the abyss of the darkness of the illusory self.

Human intelligence has risen to such a point that most people with the right guidance and grace can realise that, apart from earthly, useful, helpful wisdom, the spiritual light accessible through the purified heart is greater than all other wisdom.

112-131 قَالَ وَمَا عِلْمِي بِمَا كَانُوا يَعْمَلُونَ ۝ إِنْ حِسَابُهُمْ إِلَّا عَلَىٰ رَبِّي لَوْ تَشْعُرُونَ ۝ وَمَا أَنَا بِطَارِدِ ٱلْمُؤْمِنِينَ ۝ إِنْ أَنَا إِلَّا نَذِيرٌ مُّبِينٌ ۝ قَالُوا لَئِن لَّمْ تَنتَهِ يَٰنُوحُ لَتَكُونَنَّ مِنَ ٱلْمَرْجُومِينَ ۝ قَالَ رَبِّ إِنَّ قَوْمِي كَذَّبُونِ ۝ فَٱفْتَحْ بَيْنِي وَبَيْنَهُمْ فَتْحًا وَنَجِّنِي وَمَن مَّعِيَ مِنَ ٱلْمُؤْمِنِينَ ۝ فَأَنجَيْنَٰهُ وَمَن مَّعَهُۥ فِي ٱلْفُلْكِ ٱلْمَشْحُونِ ۝ ثُمَّ أَغْرَقْنَا بَعْدُ ٱلْبَاقِينَ ۝ إِنَّ فِي ذَٰلِكَ لَءَايَةً وَمَا كَانَ أَكْثَرُهُم مُّؤْمِنِينَ ۝ وَإِنَّ رَبَّكَ لَهُوَ ٱلْعَزِيزُ ٱلرَّحِيمُ ۝ كَذَّبَتْ عَادٌ ٱلْمُرْسَلِينَ ۝ إِذْ قَالَ لَهُمْ أَخُوهُمْ هُودٌ أَلَا تَتَّقُونَ ۝ إِنِّي لَكُمْ رَسُولٌ أَمِينٌ ۝ فَٱتَّقُوا ٱللَّهَ وَأَطِيعُونِ ۝ وَمَا أَسْـَٔلُكُمْ عَلَيْهِ مِنْ أَجْرٍ إِنْ أَجْرِيَ إِلَّا عَلَىٰ رَبِّ ٱلْعَٰلَمِينَ ۝ أَتَبْنُونَ بِكُلِّ رِيعٍ ءَايَةً تَعْبَثُونَ ۝ وَتَتَّخِذُونَ مَصَانِعَ لَعَلَّكُمْ تَخْلُدُونَ ۝ وَإِذَا بَطَشْتُم بَطَشْتُمْ جَبَّارِينَ ۝ فَٱتَّقُوا ٱللَّهَ وَأَطِيعُونِ ۝

He said, 'What knowledge have I of that they have been doing? Their account falls only upon my Lord, were you but aware? I am not one who drives away believers. I am solely a manifest warner.' They said: 'If you do not desist, O Noah, you shall be stoned.' He said, 'My Lord, my people have cried me lies, so give true deliverance between me and them, and deliver me and the believers that are with me.' So, We delivered him, and those with him, in the laden ship, then afterwards We drowned the rest. In this was a sign, but most of them were not believers. It is your Lord Who is Almighty, Compassionate to each. 'Ad cried lies to the messengers. When their brother Hud said to them: 'Will you not guard (against evil) beware? I am for you a faithful Messenger; therefore, be cautiously aware of Allah and obey me. I ask you no wage for it; my wage falls solely upon the Lord of the Worlds. Do you build on every height a marvelous mansion for your revelry? And erect palaces, trusting to win immortality? When you rage, you rage like tyrants. Therefore, be cautiously aware of Allah and obey me.

112-131 The enlightened being or messenger does not impose the message upon others. An important qualification of the messenger is to realise the natural lower tendencies of the human being and to be completely reliant upon God, without any expectation of earthly reward or payment from other beings. Once a religion becomes structured, the love of power and its maintenance may lead to a priestly class that wishes to monopolise power. This leads to decadence and the corruption of a structured religion. To maintain wholesome humanity with access to the light of divinity, we need cautious awareness of supreme consciousness.

We have beautiful stories from the past that are always meaningful metaphorically. The story of Noah is a prominent one. If we do not save ourselves by boarding an ark of certainty, we will naturally find ourselves drowning in illusions and confusions.

An enlightened prophet or messenger does not claim any power or wisdom to himself or herself, only to what touches them from the divine light. They are only here, at best, as pointers to the perfect message: you are here to discover the light of God that is here, there, and everywhere, and yet cannot be defined.

132-151 وَٱتَّقُوا۟ ٱلَّذِىٓ أَمَدَّكُم بِمَا تَعْلَمُونَ ۝ أَمَدَّكُم بِأَنْعَٰمٍ وَبَنِينَ ۝ وَجَنَّٰتٍ وَعُيُونٍ ۝ إِنِّىٓ أَخَافُ عَلَيْكُمْ عَذَابَ يَوْمٍ عَظِيمٍ ۝ قَالُوا۟ سَوَآءٌ عَلَيْنَآ أَوَعَظْتَ أَمْ لَمْ تَكُن مِّنَ ٱلْوَٰعِظِينَ ۝ إِنْ هَٰذَآ إِلَّا خُلُقُ ٱلْأَوَّلِينَ ۝ وَمَا نَحْنُ بِمُعَذَّبِينَ ۝ فَكَذَّبُوهُ فَأَهْلَكْنَٰهُمْ إِنَّ فِى ذَٰلِكَ لَءَايَةً وَمَا كَانَ أَكْثَرُهُم مُّؤْمِنِينَ ۝ وَإِنَّ رَبَّكَ لَهُوَ ٱلْعَزِيزُ ٱلرَّحِيمُ ۝ كَذَّبَتْ ثَمُودُ ٱلْمُرْسَلِينَ ۝ إِذْ قَالَ لَهُمْ أَخُوهُمْ صَٰلِحٌ أَلَا تَتَّقُونَ ۝ إِنِّى لَكُمْ رَسُولٌ أَمِينٌ ۝ فَٱتَّقُوا۟ ٱللَّهَ وَأَطِيعُونِ ۝ وَمَآ أَسْـَٔلُكُمْ عَلَيْهِ مِنْ أَجْرٍ إِنْ أَجْرِىَ إِلَّا عَلَىٰ رَبِّ ٱلْعَٰلَمِينَ ۝ أَتُتْرَكُونَ فِى مَا هَٰهُنَآ ءَامِنِينَ ۝ فِى جَنَّٰتٍ وَعُيُونٍ ۝ وَزُرُوعٍ وَنَخْلٍ طَلْعُهَا هَضِيمٌ ۝ وَتَنْحِتُونَ مِنَ ٱلْجِبَالِ بُيُوتًا فَٰرِهِينَ ۝ فَٱتَّقُوا۟ ٱللَّهَ وَأَطِيعُونِ ۝ وَلَا تُطِيعُوٓا۟ أَمْرَ ٱلْمُسْرِفِينَ ۝

And be cautiously aware of (your duty to) Him Who has given you abundance of what you know. He has given you abundance of cattle and children, and gardens and fountains; I fear for you the torment of a mighty Day.' They said: 'It is all the same to us whether you admonish or do not admonish. This is nothing but the habit of the ancients, nor shall we be tormented.' So, they cried him lies; then We destroyed them. Surely in that is a sign, yet most of them are not believers. It is your Lord Who is Almighty, Compassionate to each. Thamud cried lies to the messengers. When their brother Salih said to them: 'Will you beware? To you I am a trustworthy Messenger. Therefore, be cautiously aware of Allah and obey me. I ask you no wage for it; my wage falls solely upon the Lord of the Worlds. Will you be left secure in this here, in gardens and fountains, plantations and palms, their fruits full-ripe? And do you carve your homes from the mountains, exulting in them? Therefore, be cautiously aware of Allah and obey me. Do not obey the commands of the prodigal,

132-151 It is in the nature of human beings to get carried away with needs, desires, and the love for survival. These are important activities to be undertaken, but often they end up occupying much of our energy and time. An intelligent person would conclude that earthly distractions and lower consciousness cause imbalance and deny one the potential afforded to awaken to *Truth*. So many flourishing civilizations reached their peak and declined rapidly. Early Muslim historians realised that patterns of rise and fall generally span four to six generations. We start off humble and well-meaning, then end up arrogant and haughty, entering a self-destructive loop.

The nature of the mind is habitual; if it is filled with doubt and expectations then it will lead one to the abyss of darkness. Equally, the mind can help us transcend to the perfect abode of the soul. It is only by watchful awareness and constant prayers, meditation, and good deeds that we develop the inner taste of the ever-present divine grace and mercy.

Individuals and nations of the past have often denied their subservience to the divine presence. As such they rose in arrogance and hubris and were recycled and forgotten. It is truly by cautious awareness and constant reference to the absolute light within that we can maintain the modesty, honesty, and courage to realise the boundless light of the soul itself.

152-168 ٱلَّذِينَ يُفْسِدُونَ فِى ٱلْأَرْضِ وَلَا يُصْلِحُونَ ۝ قَالُوٓاْ إِنَّمَآ أَنتَ مِنَ ٱلْمُسَحَّرِينَ ۝ مَآ أَنتَ إِلَّا بَشَرٌ مِّثْلُنَا فَأْتِ بِـَٔايَةٍ إِن كُنتَ مِنَ ٱلصَّـٰدِقِينَ ۝ قَالَ هَـٰذِهِۦ نَاقَةٌ لَّهَا شِرْبٌ وَلَكُمْ شِرْبُ يَوْمٍ مَّعْلُومٍ ۝ وَلَا تَمَسُّوهَا بِسُوٓءٍ فَيَأْخُذَكُمْ عَذَابُ يَوْمٍ عَظِيمٍ ۝ فَعَقَرُوهَا فَأَصْبَحُواْ نَـٰدِمِينَ ۝ فَأَخَذَهُمُ ٱلْعَذَابُ إِنَّ فِى ذَٰلِكَ لَءَايَةً وَمَا كَانَ أَكْثَرُهُم مُّؤْمِنِينَ ۝ وَإِنَّ رَبَّكَ لَهُوَ ٱلْعَزِيزُ ٱلرَّحِيمُ ۝ كَذَّبَتْ قَوْمُ لُوطٍ

$$\text{ٱلْمُرْسَلِينَ ۝ إِذْ قَالَ لَهُمْ أَخُوهُمْ لُوطٌ أَلَا تَتَّقُونَ ۝ إِنِّي لَكُمْ رَسُولٌ أَمِينٌ ۝}$$
$$\text{فَٱتَّقُوا۟ ٱللَّهَ وَأَطِيعُونِ ۝ وَمَآ أَسْـَٔلُكُمْ عَلَيْهِ مِنْ أَجْرٍ ۖ إِنْ أَجْرِيَ إِلَّا عَلَىٰ رَبِّ}$$
$$\text{ٱلْعَـٰلَمِينَ ۝ أَتَأْتُونَ ٱلذُّكْرَانَ مِنَ ٱلْعَـٰلَمِينَ ۝ وَتَذَرُونَ مَا خَلَقَ لَكُمْ رَبُّكُم مِّنْ}$$
$$\text{أَزْوَٰجِكُم ۚ بَلْ أَنتُمْ قَوْمٌ عَادُونَ ۝ قَالُوا۟ لَئِن لَّمْ تَنتَهِ يَـٰلُوطُ لَتَكُونَنَّ مِنَ ٱلْمُخْرَجِينَ ۝}$$
$$\text{قَالَ إِنِّي لِعَمَلِكُم مِّنَ ٱلْقَالِينَ ۝}$$

who do corruption in the earth, and set not things aright.' They said: 'You are but a man who succumbed to sorcery. You are naught but a mortal, like us; then produce a sign, if thou art one of the truthful.' He said, 'This is a she-camel; to her a draught and to you a draught, on a day appointed, and do not touch her with malice so that there seize you the chastisement of a dreadful day.' But they hamstrung her and rose the following morning, repentant. And the torment seized them. In this was a sign, but most of them were not believers. It is your Lord Who is Almighty, Compassionate to each. The people of Lot cried lies to the messengers. When their brother Lot said to them: 'Will you not have reverence? To you I am a trustworthy messenger. Therefore, be cautiously aware of Allah and obey me: I ask you no wage for it; my wage falls solely upon the Lord of the Worlds. Do you cohabit only with males among mankind, and abandon what your Lord created for you of wives? You are a people who have truly overstepped the limit.' They said: 'If you do not desist, O Lot, you will be driven out.' He said: 'I detest your practice.

152-168 Whenever decadence and corruption became rampant, the leaders of a community boasted of their superiority. An awakened being reads the sign that such a period indicates the end of a cycle. Even though miracles and unexpected events occasionally shake people out of their spiritual lethargy, mostly the lower self offers its arguments, denials, and distractions to avoid the truth. The breeze of mercy and goodness from God continues for all creation, at all times and all places; however, unless humanity in its various faces is prepared to receive this grace, no goodness will grow or thrive. When the earth is solid rock, no matter how much you plead with it and pour water on it, you will not harvest a crop.

A child needs protection and guidance so that they do not fall into a way of life that is disagreeable and irreversible. With maturity, both self- awareness and discipline will lead one to live the moment fully, with trust and reliance upon the spirit within.

Individuals are naturally influenced by others, especially by larger numbers and powers. This is where destruction and loss can occur in a manner that was never imagined or expected. Remembrance of the death of the body and the mind is a great reminder of our human vulnerability and the supremacy of the soul within.

169-187
$$\text{رَبِّ نَجِّنِي وَأَهْلِي مِمَّا يَعْمَلُونَ ۝ فَنَجَّيْنَـٰهُ وَأَهْلَهُۥٓ أَجْمَعِينَ ۝ إِلَّا عَجُوزًا فِي}$$
$$\text{ٱلْغَـٰبِرِينَ ۝ ثُمَّ دَمَّرْنَا ٱلْـَٔاخَرِينَ ۝ وَأَمْطَرْنَا عَلَيْهِم مَّطَرًا ۖ فَسَآءَ مَطَرُ ٱلْمُنذَرِينَ}$$

8. Surah 26 Ash-Shu'ara (The Poets)

إِنَّ فِى ذَٰلِكَ لَءَايَةً ۖ وَمَا كَانَ أَكْثَرُهُم مُّؤْمِنِينَ ۝ وَإِنَّ رَبَّكَ لَهُوَ ٱلْعَزِيزُ ٱلرَّحِيمُ ۝ كَذَّبَ أَصْحَـٰبُ لْـَٔيْكَةِ ٱلْمُرْسَلِينَ ۝ إِذْ قَالَ لَهُمْ شُعَيْبٌ أَلَا تَتَّقُونَ ۝ إِنِّى لَكُمْ رَسُولٌ أَمِينٌ ۝ فَٱتَّقُوا۟ ٱللَّهَ وَأَطِيعُونِ ۝ وَمَآ أَسْـَٔلُكُمْ عَلَيْهِ مِنْ أَجْرٍ ۖ إِنْ أَجْرِىَ إِلَّا عَلَىٰ رَبِّ ٱلْعَـٰلَمِينَ ۝ أَوْفُوا۟ ٱلْكَيْلَ وَلَا تَكُونُوا۟ مِنَ ٱلْمُخْسِرِينَ ۝ وَزِنُوا۟ بِٱلْقِسْطَاسِ ٱلْمُسْتَقِيمِ ۝ وَلَا تَبْخَسُوا۟ ٱلنَّاسَ أَشْيَآءَهُمْ وَلَا تَعْثَوْا۟ فِى ٱلْأَرْضِ مُفْسِدِينَ ۝ وَٱتَّقُوا۟ ٱلَّذِى خَلَقَكُمْ وَٱلْجِبِلَّةَ ٱلْأَوَّلِينَ ۝ قَالُوٓا۟ إِنَّمَآ أَنتَ مِنَ ٱلْمُسَحَّرِينَ ۝ وَمَآ أَنتَ إِلَّا بَشَرٌ مِّثْلُنَا وَإِن نَّظُنُّكَ لَمِنَ ٱلْكَـٰذِبِينَ ۝ فَأَسْقِطْ عَلَيْنَا كِسَفًا مِّنَ ٱلسَّمَآءِ إِن كُنتَ مِنَ ٱلصَّـٰدِقِينَ ۝

My Lord, deliver me and my family from what they do.' So, We delivered him and all his family, except for an old woman, who remained behind. Then We destroyed the others, and We rained on them a rain; and evil is the rain of them that are warned. In this was a sign, but most of them were not believers. It is your Lord Who is Almighty, Compassionate to each. The People of the Thicket cried lies to the messengers. When Shu'ayb said to them: 'Will you not guard (against evil)? To you I am a trustworthy messenger. Therefore, be cautiously aware of Allah and obey me: I ask you no wage for it; my wage falls solely upon the Lord of the Worlds. Be fair in weights and measures, and do not shortchange, and weigh with the straight balance, and diminish not the goods of the people, and do not mischief in the earth, working corruption. And guard against (the punishment of) Him who created you and the former nations.' They said, 'You are merely one of those that are bewitched; you are merely a human being, like us, and we reckon you are a liar. So, make the sky fall upon us in fragments, if you speak the truth.'

169-187 To learn from the historical cycles of growth and destruction, we need to clear our minds and hearts, focusing on the extent of a people's faith or trust in God. Without belief in the cosmic *Oneness* and the hereafter, our learning remains superficial. Guarding against our lower tendencies, trusting sincerely and faithfully in the presence of the cosmic light – this is the rope that can save us from impending personal or collective disasters. The danger of the ego becomes more severe when an individual has gained power and strength in the material world in the view of other people. In these situations, *Shaytanic* influences take over, and any action becomes justified. Spiritual blindness is the common cause for most of our self-destructiveness.

When we progress along the path of awakening, we may reach a point where our dealings and connections with other beings will become most restricted, until such time that we will be saved from the nonsense and affliction that others perpetrate. The grace of Allah embraces everything within the universe, but within our humanity, we need a direct individual commitment to move toward awakening to the divine light.

The cycles of emergence, growth, recycling, and ending are numerous. Some of these can be very dramatic and some very slow before we realise that we are being engulfed by them. There is no day without a night. There is no birth without death. As long as we are constantly aware of the total connectedness between these two opposites, then we maintain a good human spiritual balance in this life.

188-207

قَالَ رَبِّى أَعْلَمُ بِمَا تَعْمَلُونَ ۝ فَكَذَّبُوهُ فَأَخَذَهُمْ عَذَابُ يَوْمِ ٱلظُّلَّةِ إِنَّهُۥ كَانَ عَذَابَ يَوْمٍ عَظِيمٍ ۝ إِنَّ فِى ذَٰلِكَ لَءَايَةً وَمَا كَانَ أَكْثَرُهُم مُّؤْمِنِينَ ۝ وَإِنَّ رَبَّكَ لَهُوَ ٱلْعَزِيزُ ٱلرَّحِيمُ ۝ وَإِنَّهُۥ لَتَنزِيلُ رَبِّ ٱلْعَٰلَمِينَ ۝ نَزَلَ بِهِ ٱلرُّوحُ ٱلْأَمِينُ ۝ عَلَىٰ قَلْبِكَ لِتَكُونَ مِنَ ٱلْمُنذِرِينَ ۝ بِلِسَانٍ عَرَبِىٍّ مُّبِينٍ ۝ وَإِنَّهُۥ لَفِى زُبُرِ ٱلْأَوَّلِينَ ۝ أَوَلَمْ يَكُن لَّهُمْ ءَايَةً أَن يَعْلَمَهُۥ عُلَمَٰٓؤُاْ بَنِىٓ إِسْرَٰٓءِيلَ ۝ وَلَوْ نَزَّلْنَٰهُ عَلَىٰ بَعْضِ ٱلْأَعْجَمِينَ ۝ فَقَرَأَهُۥ عَلَيْهِم مَّا كَانُواْ بِهِۦ مُؤْمِنِينَ ۝ كَذَٰلِكَ سَلَكْنَٰهُ فِى قُلُوبِ ٱلْمُجْرِمِينَ ۝ لَا يُؤْمِنُونَ بِهِۦ حَتَّىٰ يَرَوُاْ ٱلْعَذَابَ ٱلْأَلِيمَ ۝ فَيَأْتِيَهُم بَغْتَةً وَهُمْ لَا يَشْعُرُونَ ۝ فَيَقُولُواْ هَلْ نَحْنُ مُنظَرُونَ ۝ أَفَبِعَذَابِنَا يَسْتَعْجِلُونَ ۝ أَفَرَءَيْتَ إِن مَّتَّعْنَٰهُمْ سِنِينَ ۝ ثُمَّ جَآءَهُم مَّا كَانُواْ يُوعَدُونَ ۝ مَآ أَغْنَىٰ عَنْهُم مَّا كَانُواْ يُمَتَّعُونَ ۝

He said: 'My Lord knows best what you do.' They called him a liar, and there seized them the torment of the Day of the Shadow – it was indeed the torment of a mighty Day! In this was a sign, but most of them were not believers. It is your Lord Who is Almighty, Compassionate to each. It is indeed a Revelation from the Lord of the Worlds, brought down by the Trustworthy Spirit, upon your heart, so that you may be a warner, in a clear, Arabic tongue. It is also in the Books of the ancients. Was it not a sign for them, that it is known to the learned of the Children of Israel? Had We sent it down upon a foreigner and he recited it to them, they would still not believe in it. So, We make it pass straight through the hearts of the guilty: they do not believe in it until they witness the painful torment. It comes upon them suddenly, unawares. They say: 'Will we be granted some respite?' Do they wish to hasten Our Punishment? But consider this. If We grant them enjoyment for a number of years, then there comes on them that they were promised, what use will it be to them – that which they were granted to enjoy?

188-207 Throughout the development of human communities, thousands of enlightened beings, prophets and messengers helped to uplift the normal, animal consciousness in us towards the divine *Source*. The most commonly repeated message is to have faith and trust in the *One* God and to be accountable to that *Reality*, while safeguarding against the lower tendencies in us. Altogether, human history enforces the truth of this message. The good news is that within us lies a divine treasure. The warning is that the lower self is the dark shadow that can only lead to distraction and destruction.

Situations may arise in which a person on the prophetic path of enlightenment may have to be less involved with other beings, especially those with bad leadership and other destructive tendencies. When wrong actions and evil become a habit, people do not realise its effect upon themselves. This situation is not that different from our present-day reality.

It is through living faith, trust and belief that we end up being accomplished human beings, with complete and total resonance and connectedness with the divine spirit within. Otherwise, we get carried away by the illusion of our abilities, powers, and knowledge. All of these are insignificant compared to the light of the soul. It is through increased faith and trust that we end up living completely and utterly in the moment, which is eternal in its own way.

208-227

وَمَآ أَهْلَكْنَا مِن قَرْيَةٍ إِلَّا لَهَا مُنذِرُونَ ۝ ذِكْرَىٰ وَمَا كُنَّا ظَٰلِمِينَ ۝ وَمَا تَنَزَّلَتْ بِهِ ٱلشَّيَٰطِينُ ۝ وَمَا يَنۢبَغِى لَهُمْ وَمَا يَسْتَطِيعُونَ ۝ إِنَّهُمْ عَنِ ٱلسَّمْعِ لَمَعْزُولُونَ ۝ فَلَا تَدْعُ مَعَ ٱللَّهِ إِلَٰهًا ءَاخَرَ فَتَكُونَ مِنَ ٱلْمُعَذَّبِينَ ۝ وَأَنذِرْ عَشِيرَتَكَ ٱلْأَقْرَبِينَ ۝ وَٱخْفِضْ جَنَاحَكَ لِمَنِ ٱتَّبَعَكَ مِنَ ٱلْمُؤْمِنِينَ ۝ فَإِنْ عَصَوْكَ فَقُلْ إِنِّى بَرِىٓءٌ مِّمَّا تَعْمَلُونَ ۝ وَتَوَكَّلْ عَلَى ٱلْعَزِيزِ ٱلرَّحِيمِ ۝ ٱلَّذِى يَرَىٰكَ حِينَ تَقُومُ ۝ وَتَقَلُّبَكَ فِى ٱلسَّٰجِدِينَ ۝ إِنَّهُ هُوَ ٱلسَّمِيعُ ٱلْعَلِيمُ ۝ هَلْ أُنَبِّئُكُمْ عَلَىٰ مَن تَنَزَّلُ ٱلشَّيَٰطِينُ ۝ تَنَزَّلُ عَلَىٰ كُلِّ أَفَّاكٍ أَثِيمٍ ۝ يُلْقُونَ ٱلسَّمْعَ وَأَكْثَرُهُمْ كَٰذِبُونَ ۝ وَٱلشُّعَرَآءُ يَتَّبِعُهُمُ ٱلْغَاوُۥنَ ۝ أَلَمْ تَرَ أَنَّهُمْ فِى كُلِّ وَادٍ يَهِيمُونَ ۝ وَأَنَّهُمْ يَقُولُونَ مَا لَا يَفْعَلُونَ ۝ إِلَّا ٱلَّذِينَ ءَامَنُوا۟ وَعَمِلُوا۟ ٱلصَّٰلِحَٰتِ وَذَكَرُوا۟ ٱللَّهَ كَثِيرًا وَٱنتَصَرُوا۟ مِنۢ بَعْدِ مَا ظُلِمُوا۟ وَسَيَعْلَمُ ٱلَّذِينَ ظَلَمُوٓا۟ أَىَّ مُنقَلَبٍ يَنقَلِبُونَ ۝

Never a city We destroyed, but it had warners for a reminder; and never did We wrong. Not by the Satans has it been brought down; it befits them not, nor are they able to do so. They are barred from hearing it. So, call you not upon another Allah with Allah, unless you should be one of those that are chastised. And warn thy clan, thy nearest kin. Lower the wing of your humility to those who have followed you from among the faithful; then, if they disobey you, say, 'I am quit of that you do.' And put your trust in the Almighty, the Compassionate to each, who sees you when you stand and (sees) your behaviour among those who prostrate themselves [before Him]: He is the All-Hearing, the All-Knowing. Shall I tell you on whom the Satans come down? They come down on every guilty impostor. They give ear, but most of them are liars. And the poets – the tempters follow them. Do you not see how they wander in every valley, and how they say that which they do not? Except for those who believe and do good deeds, Who mention the name of Allah often, And who win through, after being wronged. Wrongdoers will surely know what adversity they shall fall upon!

208-227 Our lives on earth are bracketed between the good and the bad, the short term and the long term, the selfless and the selfish.

When injustices and distractions become common amongst people, we experience a breakdown and often a complete annihilation of the system. Recent human history provides dozens of situations where the people in power could not even imagine the rapidity of their destitution and annihilation. Unless the mind is clear and focused, and the light of the soul shines, human beings both individually and collectively fall into darkness and a loss that often ends up in devastation.

The divine mercy is such that we receive good news from within ourselves as well as from outside. Equally, if we are intelligent enough, we will be given warnings from both outside and inside. With clarity of mind and heart, the human instrument represents the most intricate entity in existence, with the capacity to resonate with a full range of cosmic messages.

To acknowledge our humanity, we need to maintain modesty and an awareness that at any minute the body and mind can vanish. The living soul will remain, carrying on as life continues in its own way. It is through trust and faith, correct and accountable actions, and awareness and remembrance of the divine *Presence* that we will truly maintain the most glorious, stable, reliable, and trustworthy life.

9. Surah 27 Al-Naml (The Ant)

The Qur'an reminds us regularly to be aware of our intentions and actions so that we do not cause unnecessary disturbances and changes on earth. We need to act wisely, with accountability towards our duties, and with reference to God. The ultimate gift to humanity is the divine soul within the heart. This precious gift enables us to awaken to the perpetual *Truth* that engulfs the whole universe, which we will experience, if not in this world, then after death.

بِسْمِ اللَّهِ الرَّحْمَٰنِ الرَّحِيمِ

1-11 طسٓ ۚ تِلْكَ ءَايَٰتُ ٱلْقُرْءَانِ وَكِتَابٍ مُّبِينٍ ۝ هُدًى وَبُشْرَىٰ لِلْمُؤْمِنِينَ ۝ ٱلَّذِينَ يُقِيمُونَ ٱلصَّلَوٰةَ وَيُؤْتُونَ ٱلزَّكَوٰةَ وَهُم بِٱلْءَاخِرَةِ هُمْ يُوقِنُونَ ۝ إِنَّ ٱلَّذِينَ لَا يُؤْمِنُونَ بِٱلْءَاخِرَةِ زَيَّنَّا لَهُمْ أَعْمَٰلَهُمْ فَهُمْ يَعْمَهُونَ ۝ أُوْلَٰٓئِكَ ٱلَّذِينَ لَهُمْ سُوٓءُ ٱلْعَذَابِ وَهُمْ فِى ٱلْءَاخِرَةِ هُمُ ٱلْأَخْسَرُونَ ۝ وَإِنَّكَ لَتُلَقَّى ٱلْقُرْءَانَ مِن لَّدُنْ حَكِيمٍ عَلِيمٍ ۝ إِذْ قَالَ مُوسَىٰ لِأَهْلِهِۦٓ إِنِّىٓ ءَانَسْتُ نَارًا سَـَٔاتِيكُم مِّنْهَا بِخَبَرٍ أَوْ ءَاتِيكُم بِشِهَابٍ قَبَسٍ لَّعَلَّكُمْ تَصْطَلُونَ ۝ فَلَمَّا جَآءَهَا نُودِىَ أَنۢ بُورِكَ مَن فِى ٱلنَّارِ وَمَنْ حَوْلَهَا وَسُبْحَٰنَ ٱللَّهِ رَبِّ ٱلْعَٰلَمِينَ ۝ يَٰمُوسَىٰٓ إِنَّهُۥٓ أَنَا ٱللَّهُ ٱلْعَزِيزُ ٱلْحَكِيمُ ۝ وَأَلْقِ عَصَاكَ ۚ فَلَمَّا رَءَاهَا تَهْتَزُّ كَأَنَّهَا جَآنٌّ وَلَّىٰ مُدْبِرًا وَلَمْ يُعَقِّبْ ۚ يَٰمُوسَىٰ لَا تَخَفْ إِنِّى لَا يَخَافُ لَدَىَّ ٱلْمُرْسَلُونَ ۝ إِلَّا مَن ظَلَمَ ثُمَّ بَدَّلَ حُسْنًۢا بَعْدَ سُوٓءٍ فَإِنِّى غَفُورٌ رَّحِيمٌ ۝

9. Surah 27 Al-Naml (The Ant)

In the name of Allah, the Merciful to all, the Compassionate to each!

Ta Sin! These are the verses of the Qur'an and a Book manifest. A Guidance and glad tidings to the faithful, who perform the prayer, hand out alms and are certain of the hereafter. As for those who do not believe in the hereafter, We have made their deeds appear attractive in their sight, so they stumble aimlessly. It is they whom a terrible torment awaits, who shall be the greatest losers in the hereafter. You receive the Qur'an from One All-Wise, All-Knowing. When Moses said to his people 'I glimpsed a fire, and will bring you news of it, or I will bring you a flaming brand, that haply you shall warm yourselves.' When he drew near it, a voice called out to him: 'Blessed be He Who is in the fire and around it! Glory be to Allah, Lord of the Worlds! O Moses, it is I, Allah, Almighty, All-Wise. Cast down thy staff.' And when he saw it quivering like a serpent he turned about, retreating, and turned not back. 'Moses, fear not; surely the Envoys do not fear in My presence. Except one, who did wrong, then exchanged good for evil. I am All-Forgiving, Compassionate to each.

1-11 It is with faith and belief that we can be illumined by the message of *Truth*, which is strengthened by religious duties, especially prayers and other transformative rituals. Trust and faith in the hereafter provide important safeguards from corruption and loss. All enlightened beings and prophets were seekers of knowledge and guidance, following all the signs that came to them. When Prophet Moses crossed over the Sinai desert, he was inspired to embark on a thirty-day pilgrimage leaving his people under the charge of his brother Harun. Ten days later he was given his wish, which confirmed to him the light of *Truth* and the need for humans to pursue it. The Moses within each of us is always searching for the burning bush, with its confirmation of divine presence.

The foundation of spiritual intelligence is to believe that our life on earth is a mere prelude to the hereafter. All our diverse experiences, all the challenges of dualities and diversities, are training us to see the light of unity that shines upon them all.

Due to the rise of intelligence and the upward drive in consciousness, human beings always look for reassurance that the essence of the original, life-giving light continues; this is where all our hopes and our desires lie. It is this state that the seen and the unseen is experienced as a seamless connection.

12-19 وَأَدْخِلْ يَدَكَ فِي جَيْبِكَ تَخْرُجْ بَيْضَاءَ مِنْ غَيْرِ سُوءٍ فِي تِسْعِ ءَايَٰتٍ إِلَىٰ فِرْعَوْنَ وَقَوْمِهِۦٓ إِنَّهُمْ كَانُوا۟ قَوْمًا فَٰسِقِينَ ۝ فَلَمَّا جَآءَتْهُمْ ءَايَٰتُنَا مُبْصِرَةً قَالُوا۟ هَٰذَا سِحْرٌ مُّبِينٌ ۝ وَجَحَدُوا۟ بِهَا وَٱسْتَيْقَنَتْهَآ أَنفُسُهُمْ ظُلْمًا وَعُلُوًّا فَٱنظُرْ كَيْفَ كَانَ عَٰقِبَةُ ٱلْمُفْسِدِينَ ۝ وَلَقَدْ ءَاتَيْنَا دَاوُۥدَ وَسُلَيْمَٰنَ عِلْمًا وَقَالَا ٱلْحَمْدُ لِلَّهِ ٱلَّذِى فَضَّلَنَا عَلَىٰ كَثِيرٍ مِّنْ عِبَادِهِ ٱلْمُؤْمِنِينَ ۝ وَوَرِثَ سُلَيْمَٰنُ دَاوُۥدَ وَقَالَ يَٰٓأَيُّهَا ٱلنَّاسُ عُلِّمْنَا مَنطِقَ ٱلطَّيْرِ وَأُوتِينَا مِن كُلِّ شَىْءٍ إِنَّ هَٰذَا لَهُوَ ٱلْفَضْلُ ٱلْمُبِينُ ۝ وَحُشِرَ لِسُلَيْمَٰنَ

جُنُودُهُۥ مِنَ ٱلْجِنِّ وَٱلْإِنسِ وَٱلطَّيْرِ فَهُمْ يُوزَعُونَ ۝ حَتَّىٰٓ إِذَآ أَتَوْاْ عَلَىٰ وَادِ ٱلنَّمْلِ قَالَتْ نَمْلَةٌ يَٰٓأَيُّهَا ٱلنَّمْلُ ٱدْخُلُواْ مَسَٰكِنَكُمْ لَا يَحْطِمَنَّكُمْ سُلَيْمَٰنُ وَجُنُودُهُۥ وَهُمْ لَا يَشْعُرُونَ ۝ فَتَبَسَّمَ ضَاحِكًا مِّن قَوْلِهَا وَقَالَ رَبِّ أَوْزِعْنِىٓ أَنْ أَشْكُرَ نِعْمَتَكَ ٱلَّتِىٓ أَنْعَمْتَ عَلَىَّ وَعَلَىٰ وَٰلِدَىَّ وَأَنْ أَعْمَلَ صَٰلِحًا تَرْضَىٰهُ وَأَدْخِلْنِى بِرَحْمَتِكَ فِى عِبَادِكَ ٱلصَّٰلِحِينَ ۝

Put your hand inside your sleeve and it will come out white, but without harm.' This was among nine other wonders done before Pharaoh and his people – they were indeed a people depraved.' When Our wonders came to them, for all to see, they said: 'This is sorcery manifest.' And they denied them, though their selves acknowledged them, wrongfully and out of pride. Behold, how was the end of the workers of corruption! We bestowed knowledge on David and Solomon. They said: 'Praise be to Allah Who preferred us above many of His believing worshippers.' And Solomon was David's heir, and he said, 'Men, we have been taught the speech of the birds, and we have been given of everything; surely this is indeed the manifest bounty.' To Solomon were mustered his troops of Jinn, humans and birds, all held in strict order, till, when they came on the Valley of Ants, an ant said, 'Ants, enter your dwelling-places, lest Solomon and his hosts crush you, being unaware!' He smiled in amusement at its words and said: 'My Lord, inspire me to offer thanks for the bounty You bestowed upon me and upon my parents, and to do a good deed of which You will approve, and admit me, through Your mercy, into the company of your virtuous servants.'

12-19 We yearn for openings that prove to us the connection between our individual self, which changes all the time, and the light of our soul, which beams perfect life upon us. The story of the great prophets and messengers demonstrate to us how to create a conducive situation that enables the strong and the weak to be on the same path, seeking constant connectedness with the ever-present divine light. It is within human possibility to extend our senses far beyond the limitations of sight and hearing. The Prophet Solomon could communicate with many seen and unseen creatures including the ants, which warned each other upon the approach of Solomon and his army. They made him smile, then he expressed gratitude and prayed that he might continue doing good and be fully accepted by God.

When the shadow of the ego is least intense, the light of the spirit reflects unusual insights and events. The joy of the prophet Solomon when he heard the ant warning its clan is a wonderful example.

When our intentions are clear, and there is total honesty and courage, then whatever the hand does, has a very long term, potent effect. It is no longer just an individual's wish and hope. It connects with a much higher zone of reality.

20-32 وَتَفَقَّدَ ٱلطَّيْرَ فَقَالَ مَا لِيَ لَا أَرَى ٱلْهُدْهُدَ أَمْ كَانَ مِنَ ٱلْغَآئِبِينَ ۞ لَأُعَذِّبَنَّهُۥ عَذَابًا شَدِيدًا أَوْ لَأَا۟ذْبَحَنَّهُۥٓ أَوْ لَيَأْتِيَنِّى بِسُلْطَٰنٍ مُّبِينٍ ۞ فَمَكَثَ غَيْرَ بَعِيدٍ فَقَالَ أَحَطتُ بِمَا لَمْ تُحِطْ بِهِۦ وَجِئْتُكَ مِن سَبَإٍۭ بِنَبَإٍ يَقِينٍ ۞ إِنِّى وَجَدتُّ ٱمْرَأَةً تَمْلِكُهُمْ وَأُوتِيَتْ مِن كُلِّ شَىْءٍ وَلَهَا عَرْشٌ عَظِيمٌ ۞ وَجَدتُّهَا وَقَوْمَهَا يَسْجُدُونَ لِلشَّمْسِ مِن دُونِ ٱللَّهِ وَزَيَّنَ لَهُمُ ٱلشَّيْطَٰنُ أَعْمَٰلَهُمْ فَصَدَّهُمْ عَنِ ٱلسَّبِيلِ فَهُمْ لَا يَهْتَدُونَ ۞ أَلَّا يَسْجُدُوا۟ لِلَّهِ ٱلَّذِى يُخْرِجُ ٱلْخَبْءَ فِى ٱلسَّمَٰوَٰتِ وَٱلْأَرْضِ وَيَعْلَمُ مَا تُخْفُونَ وَمَا تُعْلِنُونَ ۞ ٱللَّهُ لَآ إِلَٰهَ إِلَّا هُوَ رَبُّ ٱلْعَرْشِ ٱلْعَظِيمِ ۞ قَالَ سَنَنظُرُ أَصَدَقْتَ أَمْ كُنتَ مِنَ ٱلْكَٰذِبِينَ ۞ ٱذْهَب بِّكِتَٰبِى هَٰذَا فَأَلْقِهْ إِلَيْهِمْ ثُمَّ تَوَلَّ عَنْهُمْ فَٱنظُرْ مَاذَا يَرْجِعُونَ ۞ قَالَتْ يَٰٓأَيُّهَا ٱلْمَلَؤُا۟ إِنِّى أُلْقِىَ إِلَىَّ كِتَٰبٌ كَرِيمٌ ۞ إِنَّهُۥ مِن سُلَيْمَٰنَ وَإِنَّهُۥ بِسْمِ ٱللَّهِ ٱلرَّحْمَٰنِ ٱلرَّحِيمِ ۞ أَلَّا تَعْلُوا۟ عَلَىَّ وَأْتُونِى مُسْلِمِينَ ۞ قَالَتْ يَٰٓأَيُّهَا ٱلْمَلَؤُا۟ أَفْتُونِى فِىٓ أَمْرِى مَا كُنتُ قَاطِعَةً أَمْرًا حَتَّىٰ تَشْهَدُونِ ۞

And he inspected the birds. He said: 'Why do I not see the hoopoe? Or is he among the absent? I shall punish him most harshly or even slit his throat, unless he brings me a clear justification.' But the bird was not absent for long. He said: 'I have learnt what you have not. I come to you from Saba, with a sure report. I found a woman ruling over them, and one granted of all gifts, with a magnificent throne. I found her and her people bowing in worship to the sun, instead of Allah. Satan has made their works appear attractive to them, and barred them from the way; thus, they are not guided aright. If only they would prostrate in worship to Allah, Who reveals whatever is hidden in the heavens and on earth, Who knows what you conceal and what you openly declare! Allah, there is no Allah but He, Lord of the mighty throne!' He said: 'We shall wait and see if you speak the truth or you are a liar. Take this letter of mine and deliver it to them, then turn aside and observe what answer they return.' She said: 'O council, a noble letter has been delivered to me'. It is from Solomon and begins 'In the name of Allah, Merciful to all, Compassionate to each.' It says: 'Hold not your head high against me, and come to me in surrender.' She said, 'O Council, pronounce to me concerning my affair; I am not used to decide an affair until you bear me witness.'

20-32 It is in our nature to investigate, search, and discover new openings and knowledges. Numerous lessons from the various prophets can be applied in various times and situations. The self is often a barrier that prevents a clear reading of these events as historical or mythical. It is in human nature to doubt and be uncertain as well as to believe and be secure in the ultimate *Truth*. Many peoples, past and present, have relayed the story of the Prophet Solomon and the Queen of Sheba. Both these wise beings have left many legacies in different cultures, which reinforced each other. Our love for power and access to the All-Powerful is incessant; it reflects the natural connection between the lower self and the soul.

Our normal day-to-day life offers a certain measure of stability, enabling us to connect well with our earthly landing. Yet, it will be insufficient and considered boring unless we experience higher connections in consciousness along with a regular recharge from the divine soul within.

Due to the consciousness of life, all creatures are obsessed to preserve life and its experience. The highest order of intelligence is that we connect with what is boundless, eternal, and timeless. It is for this reason that time is the most precious thing we have because it links us to that which is divine and perpetual. People who have awakened to this truth are regarded as great seers, prophets, messengers, and other illumined beings.

33-41

قَالُوا۟ نَحْنُ أُو۟لُوا۟ قُوَّةٍ وَأُو۟لُوا۟ بَأْسٍ شَدِيدٍ وَٱلْأَمْرُ إِلَيْكِ فَٱنظُرِى مَاذَا تَأْمُرِينَ ۝ قَالَتْ إِنَّ ٱلْمُلُوكَ إِذَا دَخَلُوا۟ قَرْيَةً أَفْسَدُوهَا وَجَعَلُوٓا۟ أَعِزَّةَ أَهْلِهَآ أَذِلَّةً ۖ وَكَذَٰلِكَ يَفْعَلُونَ ۝ وَإِنِّى مُرْسِلَةٌ إِلَيْهِم بِهَدِيَّةٍ فَنَاظِرَةٌۢ بِمَ يَرْجِعُ ٱلْمُرْسَلُونَ ۝ فَلَمَّا جَآءَ سُلَيْمَٰنَ قَالَ أَتُمِدُّونَنِ بِمَالٍ فَمَآ ءَاتَىٰنِۦَ ٱللَّهُ خَيْرٌ مِّمَّآ ءَاتَىٰكُم بَلْ أَنتُم بِهَدِيَّتِكُمْ تَفْرَحُونَ ۝ ٱرْجِعْ إِلَيْهِمْ فَلَنَأْتِيَنَّهُم بِجُنُودٍ لَّا قِبَلَ لَهُم بِهَا وَلَنُخْرِجَنَّهُم مِّنْهَآ أَذِلَّةً وَهُمْ صَٰغِرُونَ ۝ قَالَ يَٰٓأَيُّهَا ٱلْمَلَؤُا۟ أَيُّكُمْ يَأْتِينِى بِعَرْشِهَا قَبْلَ أَن يَأْتُونِى مُسْلِمِينَ ۝ قَالَ عِفْرِيتٌ مِّنَ ٱلْجِنِّ أَنَا۠ ءَاتِيكَ بِهِۦ قَبْلَ أَن تَقُومَ مِن مَّقَامِكَ ۖ وَإِنِّى عَلَيْهِ لَقَوِىٌّ أَمِينٌ ۝ قَالَ ٱلَّذِى عِندَهُۥ عِلْمٌ مِّنَ ٱلْكِتَٰبِ أَنَا۠ ءَاتِيكَ بِهِۦ قَبْلَ أَن يَرْتَدَّ إِلَيْكَ طَرْفُكَ ۚ فَلَمَّا رَءَاهُ مُسْتَقِرًّا عِندَهُۥ قَالَ هَٰذَا مِن فَضْلِ رَبِّى لِيَبْلُوَنِىٓ ءَأَشْكُرُ أَمْ أَكْفُرُ ۖ وَمَن شَكَرَ فَإِنَّمَا يَشْكُرُ لِنَفْسِهِۦ ۖ وَمَن كَفَرَ فَإِنَّ رَبِّى غَنِىٌّ كَرِيمٌ ۝ قَالَ نَكِّرُوا۟ لَهَا عَرْشَهَا نَنظُرْ أَتَهْتَدِىٓ أَمْ تَكُونُ مِنَ ٱلَّذِينَ لَا يَهْتَدُونَ ۝

They said, 'We possess force and we possess great might. The affair rests with thee; so, consider what thou wilt command.' She said: 'When kings enter a city they corrupt it, and reduce its grandees to abject misery. This is how they act. I am sending them a gift, and will see what the messengers bring back.' When her envoy came to Solomon, Solomon said, 'What! Are you offering me wealth? What Allah has given me is better than what He has given you, though you rejoice in this gift of yours. Go back to them and tell them that we shall advance against them with troops they cannot resist, and shall drive them out, abject and humbled.' He said, 'O Council, which one of you will bring me her throne, before they come to me in surrender?' One audacious among the jinn said: 'I will bring it to you before you rise up from your place.' Said he who possessed knowledge from the Book, 'I will bring it to you, before ever your glance returns to you.' Then, when he saw it settled before him, he said, 'This is of my Lord's bounty that He may try me, whether I am thankful or ungrateful. Whosoever gives thanks gives thanks only for his own soul's good, and whosoever is ungrateful – my Lord is surely All-Sufficient,

All-Generous.' He said: *'Disguise her throne and let us see whether she will be guided to it, or unguided.'*

33-41 The Queen of Sheba was aware of the tragedy that can afflict people at war. She also knew that arrogance and haughtiness often follow powerful kings who, as conquerors, can destroy the vanquished. The Queen of Sheba's connection with the Prophet Solomon was such that his power and connection with the *jinn* was so superior that it diffused a potentially confrontational situation. She realised that she was witnessing another level of power, and as such she accepted the great Prophet. If it were not for that prophetic wisdom and light, warfare and destruction could have ensued instead of an increase in goodness on earth and beyond. When you have the power and ability to force a change, it is great wisdom to be gentle, considerate, compassionate, and patient.

When a being is least concerned with the outer world, then new insights and spiritual openings from other universes may occur. Extra sensory perceptions and clear connections with angels are examples of these openings.

Human love for power can often lead individuals and communities to warfare and disaster. Only through subduing the ego-self and allowing the light of the soul to lead and guide us can we travel joyfully in this world back to the origin with its infinitude of grace.

42-51 فَلَمَّا جَآءَتْ قِيلَ أَهَٰكَذَا عَرْشُكِ قَالَتْ كَأَنَّهُ هُوَ وَأُوتِينَا ٱلْعِلْمَ مِن قَبْلِهَا وَكُنَّا مُسْلِمِينَ ۝ وَصَدَّهَا مَا كَانَت تَّعْبُدُ مِن دُونِ ٱللَّهِ إِنَّهَا كَانَتْ مِن قَوْمٍ كَٰفِرِينَ ۝ قِيلَ لَهَا ٱدْخُلِى ٱلصَّرْحَ فَلَمَّا رَأَتْهُ حَسِبَتْهُ لُجَّةً وَكَشَفَتْ عَن سَاقَيْهَا قَالَ إِنَّهُ صَرْحٌ مُّمَرَّدٌ مِّن قَوَارِيرَ قَالَتْ رَبِّ إِنِّى ظَلَمْتُ نَفْسِى وَأَسْلَمْتُ مَعَ سُلَيْمَٰنَ لِلَّهِ رَبِّ ٱلْعَٰلَمِينَ ۝ وَلَقَدْ أَرْسَلْنَآ إِلَىٰ ثَمُودَ أَخَاهُمْ صَٰلِحًا أَنِ ٱعْبُدُوا۟ ٱللَّهَ فَإِذَا هُمْ فَرِيقَانِ يَخْتَصِمُونَ ۝ قَالَ يَٰقَوْمِ لِمَ تَسْتَعْجِلُونَ بِٱلسَّيِّئَةِ قَبْلَ ٱلْحَسَنَةِ لَوْلَا تَسْتَغْفِرُونَ ٱللَّهَ لَعَلَّكُمْ تُرْحَمُونَ ۝ قَالُوا۟ ٱطَّيَّرْنَا بِكَ وَبِمَن مَّعَكَ قَالَ طَٰٓئِرُكُمْ عِندَ ٱللَّهِ بَلْ أَنتُمْ قَوْمٌ تُفْتَنُونَ ۝ وَكَانَ فِى ٱلْمَدِينَةِ تِسْعَةُ رَهْطٍ يُفْسِدُونَ فِى ٱلْأَرْضِ وَلَا يُصْلِحُونَ ۝ قَالُوا۟ تَقَاسَمُوا۟ بِٱللَّهِ لَنُبَيِّتَنَّهُ وَأَهْلَهُ ثُمَّ لَنَقُولَنَّ لِوَلِيِّهِ مَا شَهِدْنَا مَهْلِكَ أَهْلِهِ وَإِنَّا لَصَٰدِقُونَ ۝ وَمَكَرُوا۟ مَكْرًا وَمَكَرْنَا مَكْرًا وَهُمْ لَا يَشْعُرُونَ ۝ فَٱنظُرْ كَيْفَ كَانَ عَٰقِبَةُ مَكْرِهِمْ أَنَّا دَمَّرْنَٰهُمْ وَقَوْمَهُمْ أَجْمَعِينَ ۝

When she arrived, she was asked: *'Is this what your throne looks like?'* She said: *'It is nearly so.'* He said: *'We were granted Knowledge before her, and became Muslims.'* Barring her from right guidance is that which she worships instead of Allah. She belongs to a disbelieving nation. Then it was said to her, *'Enter the hall,'* but when she saw it, she thought it was a deep pool of water, and bared her legs. He said, *'It is a hall paved with glass,'* and she said,

'My Lord, I have wronged myself: I devote myself, with Solomon, to Allah, the Lord of the Worlds.' To the people of Thamud We sent their brother, Salih, saying, 'Worship Allah alone,' but they split into two rival factions. He said: 'My people, why are you quick to do evil rather than good? If only you would ask for Allah's forgiveness, you may be shown mercy.' They said, 'We see you and your followers as an evil omen.' He replied, 'Allah will decide on any omen you may see: you people are being put to the test.' Inside the city was a band of nine who corrupted the land and did no good. They said, 'Swear you, one to another, by Allah, We will attack him and his family by night, then we will tell his protector, We were not witnesses of the destruction of his family; and assuredly we are truthful men.' And they worked their cunning, and We worked Our cunning, of which they were unaware. Behold the outcome of their cunning! We destroyed them and their people, outright.

42-51 The outer physical world is often seductive and can lead us to an irreversible path of loss and destruction. Our love for power is simply a beam from the all-powerful soul within us. Instead of our usual egotistic ambition to acquire and dominate, we should be obsessed to know more about the divine light of the soul. It is one thing to assume power and exercise it, another thing entirely to reference the source of power and simply act as a steward in order to bring about goodness for the longest time and for as many as possible. The ego is a most deceptive shadow; unless we turn away from it and take refuge in Allah's grace, following the prophetic path, we lose the great opportunity that God has given us. The self tries to plot and plan, only an echo of the ability of the divine light whose plans and designs have brought about the whole universe. Allah is the ultimate plotter, and the self simply deceives us, leading to confusion and possible pain.

Deception and concealment are natural in our world and can be helpful and useful as well as destructive. It is our intention and honesty in what we are doing that matters most in our evolution along the spiritual path.

People of the past were given numerous signs, such as miracles, to follow an individual prophet or messenger. As consciousness grows, more people begin to realise that the divine Presence is the foundation of all existence, and that its transmission is through every living heart.

52-61 فَتِلْكَ بُيُوتُهُمْ خَاوِيَةً بِمَا ظَلَمُوٓاْ إِنَّ فِى ذَٰلِكَ لَءَايَةً لِّقَوْمٍ يَعْلَمُونَ ۝ وَأَنجَيْنَا ٱلَّذِينَ ءَامَنُواْ وَكَانُواْ يَتَّقُونَ ۝ وَلُوطًا إِذْ قَالَ لِقَوْمِهِۦٓ أَتَأْتُونَ ٱلْفَٰحِشَةَ وَأَنتُمْ تُبْصِرُونَ ۝ أَئِنَّكُمْ لَتَأْتُونَ ٱلرِّجَالَ شَهْوَةً مِّن دُونِ ٱلنِّسَآءِ بَلْ أَنتُمْ قَوْمٌ تَجْهَلُونَ ۝ فَمَا كَانَ جَوَابَ قَوْمِهِۦٓ إِلَّآ أَن قَالُوٓاْ أَخْرِجُوٓاْ ءَالَ لُوطٍ مِّن قَرْيَتِكُمْ إِنَّهُمْ أُنَاسٌ يَتَطَهَّرُونَ ۝ فَأَنجَيْنَٰهُ وَأَهْلَهُۥٓ إِلَّا ٱمْرَأَتَهُۥ قَدَّرْنَٰهَا مِنَ ٱلْغَٰبِرِينَ ۝ وَأَمْطَرْنَا عَلَيْهِم مَّطَرًا فَسَآءَ مَطَرُ ٱلْمُنذَرِينَ ۝ قُلِ ٱلْحَمْدُ لِلَّهِ وَسَلَٰمٌ عَلَىٰ عِبَادِهِ ٱلَّذِينَ ٱصْطَفَىٰٓ ءَآللَّهُ خَيْرٌ أَمَّا

$$\text{بِهِۦ حَدَآئِقَ ذَاتَ بَهْجَةٍ مَّا كَانَ لَكُمْ أَن تُنۢبِتُوا۟ شَجَرَهَآ ۗ أَءِلَٰهٌ مَّعَ ٱللَّهِ ۚ بَلْ هُمْ قَوْمٌ يَعْدِلُونَ ۝ أَمَّن جَعَلَ ٱلْأَرْضَ قَرَارًا وَجَعَلَ خِلَٰلَهَآ أَنْهَٰرًا وَجَعَلَ لَهَا رَوَٰسِىَ وَجَعَلَ بَيْنَ ٱلْبَحْرَيْنِ حَاجِزًا ۗ أَءِلَٰهٌ مَّعَ ٱللَّهِ ۚ بَلْ أَكْثَرُهُمْ لَا يَعْلَمُونَ ۝}$$

There stand their habitations, desolate because of their wickedness. In this is a sign to a people who understand. And We saved those who believed and were cautiously aware. And Lot, when he said to his people: 'Do you commit debauchery with open eyes? Do you really lust after men instead of women? You are indeed a vicious people.' No answer did his people give but to say: 'Drive out Lot's family from your town, for they are a people determined to be chaste.' So, We delivered him and his family, except for his wife, whom We destined to remain behind. And We rained upon them a rain – baleful the rain that fell upon those who had been warned! Praise be to Allah, and peace upon His servants whom He elected! Is Allah better or is it what they say associate with Him? Is it not He Who created the heavens and the earth? Who brought down water for you from the sky, from which We caused to sprout gardens most pleasing, whose trees you could not have planted? Is there to be another Allah with Allah? Indeed, they are a people who deviate. Is it not He Who made the earth be at rest, and made rivers run through it, and erected mountains therein, and built a barrier between the two seas? Is there to be another Allah with Allah? Truly, most of them have no understanding.

52-61 History tells of the deadly consequences to individuals, people, or kingdoms that were haughty, arrogant, and only inclined towards outer power and wealth. It also relates stories of those few saved who were modest, believing, and well-behaved. The lower self always rebels, rejects, and finds fault with the message of the good of higher consciousness. Not unless we transcend all the natural shadowy tendencies of the lower self and ego, can we catch a glimpse of *Reality* through the light of the soul. The ultimate mystery is that the entire universe has come about as an interim stage between the lower animal consciousness and the highest consciousness of the mystery of cosmic *Unity*. There is a natural drive within human beings to be liberated from the limitation of conditioned consciousness within space-time. Through a strong passion to know the truth and to live honourably and enjoyably on earth, we can realise the temporary nature of our earthly journey as a prelude to the soul's perpetual life and reality. Awakening fully to this *Truth* is not very common on earth, but Allah's justice and generosity to everyone is such that everyone will know this state and experience it after death.

Our life on earth is very brief. This drives us to wake up with urgency to the light of the one Creator, which will give us the best in this world and the next. Outer diversity will lead an intelligent, enquiring mind to the heavenly light in the heart.

Many of our experiences emerge and return to the unseen. As such, we are always looking to resolve the unknown, discover secrets, or even reveal situations of deception and veiling regarding ourselves. What is unseen is far greater in intensity and volume than that which is visible, discernible, and shareable due to our senses.

62-72 أَمَّن يُجِيبُ ٱلْمُضْطَرَّ إِذَا دَعَاهُ وَيَكْشِفُ ٱلسُّوٓءَ وَيَجْعَلُكُمْ خُلَفَآءَ ٱلْأَرْضِ أَءِلَٰهٌ مَّعَ ٱللَّهِ قَلِيلًا مَّا تَذَكَّرُونَ ۝ أَمَّن يَهْدِيكُمْ فِى ظُلُمَٰتِ ٱلْبَرِّ وَٱلْبَحْرِ وَمَن يُرْسِلُ ٱلرِّيَٰحَ بُشْرًۢا بَيْنَ يَدَىْ رَحْمَتِهِۦٓ أَءِلَٰهٌ مَّعَ ٱللَّهِ تَعَٰلَى ٱللَّهُ عَمَّا يُشْرِكُونَ ۝ أَمَّن يَبْدَؤُا۟ ٱلْخَلْقَ ثُمَّ يُعِيدُهُۥ وَمَن يَرْزُقُكُم مِّنَ ٱلسَّمَآءِ وَٱلْأَرْضِ أَءِلَٰهٌ مَّعَ ٱللَّهِ قُلْ هَاتُوا۟ بُرْهَٰنَكُمْ إِن كُنتُمْ صَٰدِقِينَ ۝ قُل لَّا يَعْلَمُ مَن فِى ٱلسَّمَٰوَٰتِ وَٱلْأَرْضِ ٱلْغَيْبَ إِلَّا ٱللَّهُ وَمَا يَشْعُرُونَ أَيَّانَ يُبْعَثُونَ ۝ بَلِ ٱدَّٰرَكَ عِلْمُهُمْ فِى ٱلْءَاخِرَةِ بَلْ هُمْ فِى شَكٍّ مِّنْهَا بَلْ هُم مِّنْهَا عَمُونَ ۝ وَقَالَ ٱلَّذِينَ كَفَرُوٓا۟ أَءِذَا كُنَّا تُرَٰبًا وَءَابَآؤُنَآ أَئِنَّا لَمُخْرَجُونَ ۝ لَقَدْ وُعِدْنَا هَٰذَا نَحْنُ وَءَابَآؤُنَا مِن قَبْلُ إِنْ هَٰذَآ إِلَّآ أَسَٰطِيرُ ٱلْأَوَّلِينَ ۝ قُلْ سِيرُوا۟ فِى ٱلْأَرْضِ فَٱنظُرُوا۟ كَيْفَ كَانَ عَٰقِبَةُ ٱلْمُجْرِمِينَ ۝ وَلَا تَحْزَنْ عَلَيْهِمْ وَلَا تَكُن فِى ضَيْقٍ مِّمَّا يَمْكُرُونَ ۝ وَيَقُولُونَ مَتَىٰ هَٰذَا ٱلْوَعْدُ إِن كُنتُمْ صَٰدِقِينَ ۝ قُلْ عَسَىٰٓ أَن يَكُونَ رَدِفَ لَكُم بَعْضُ ٱلَّذِى تَسْتَعْجِلُونَ ۝

Is it not He Who answers the one in need when he prays to Him, Who draws away evil and makes you successors in the earth? Is there to be another Allah with Allah? Little do you remember! Is it not He Who guides you in the darknesses of land and sea, Who sends the winds as glad tidings ahead of His mercy? Is there to be another Allah with Allah? May Allah be exalted far above what they associate with Him! Is it not He Who originates creation then restores it? Who grants you a livelihood from sky or earth? Is there to be another Allah with Allah? Say: 'Show me your proof if you speak the truth.' Say: 'None in the heavens or on earth know the Unseen save Allah.' They know not when they shall be resurrected. Indeed, they have no knowledge of the hereafter; or rather they are in doubt thereof; or rather they are blind to it. The unbelievers say, 'What, when we are dust, and our fathers, shall we indeed be brought forth? We were promised this before, we and our forefathers. This is nothing but legends of the ancients.' Say: 'Journey in the land, then be- hold how was the end of the wicked.' Do not grieve for them, nor be anxious about that which they are plotting. They say: 'When will this promise come about if you people speak the truth?' Say: 'Perhaps there comes near to you some of what you wish to hasten.'

62-72 The natural world contains all interlinks and connectedness with the upper atmosphere and sub-oceanic energies, including events such as tsunamis, volcanoes, and other activities at molecular and sub-molecular levels. When the self and the soul are in a correct balance, and conditioned consciousness draws from higher consciousness, there is much goodness in human life. Whatever we discern with our senses and mind are according to divine patterns and designs. However, what we perceive of the unseen is a minute fraction of what there is in the universe. It is in our nature to be in constant awe and amazement. Whoever has benefited from prayers and meditation and has transcended the norm is naturally keen to share it with others. In truth, it is one humanity in different stages of its evolutionary progress towards its original divinity.

Our earthly journey will complete the story of evolution in consciousness and awakening to the cosmic light that engulfs all. This journey includes the exercise of interacting with the rest of creation responsibly, accountably, and as stewards.

The ultimate injustice against oneself is to deny the prevalence of the divine light and the fact that as human beings we are always groping to know a bit more, reduce suffering, and increase our hope and presence in the moment. This is the direction of faith, trust, and belief, as opposed to denial and darkness.

73-84

وَإِنَّ رَبَّكَ لَذُو فَضْلٍ عَلَى ٱلنَّاسِ وَلَـٰكِنَّ أَكْثَرَهُمْ لَا يَشْكُرُونَ ۝ وَإِنَّ رَبَّكَ لَيَعْلَمُ مَا تُكِنُّ صُدُورُهُمْ وَمَا يُعْلِنُونَ ۝ وَمَا مِنْ غَآئِبَةٍ فِى ٱلسَّمَآءِ وَٱلْأَرْضِ إِلَّا فِى كِتَـٰبٍ مُّبِينٍ ۝ إِنَّ هَـٰذَا ٱلْقُرْءَانَ يَقُصُّ عَلَىٰ بَنِىٓ إِسْرَٰٓءِيلَ أَكْثَرَ ٱلَّذِى هُمْ فِيهِ يَخْتَلِفُونَ ۝ وَإِنَّهُۥ لَهُدًى وَرَحْمَةٌ لِّلْمُؤْمِنِينَ ۝ إِنَّ رَبَّكَ يَقْضِى بَيْنَهُم بِحُكْمِهِۦ وَهُوَ ٱلْعَزِيزُ ٱلْعَلِيمُ ۝ فَتَوَكَّلْ عَلَى ٱللَّهِ إِنَّكَ عَلَى ٱلْحَقِّ ٱلْمُبِينِ ۝ إِنَّكَ لَا تُسْمِعُ ٱلْمَوْتَىٰ وَلَا تُسْمِعُ ٱلصُّمَّ ٱلدُّعَآءَ إِذَا وَلَّوْا۟ مُدْبِرِينَ ۝ وَمَآ أَنتَ بِهَـٰدِى ٱلْعُمْىِ عَن ضَلَـٰلَتِهِمْ إِن تُسْمِعُ إِلَّا مَن يُؤْمِنُ بِـَٔايَـٰتِنَا فَهُم مُّسْلِمُونَ ۝ وَإِذَا وَقَعَ ٱلْقَوْلُ عَلَيْهِمْ أَخْرَجْنَا لَهُمْ دَآبَّةً مِّنَ ٱلْأَرْضِ تُكَلِّمُهُمْ أَنَّ ٱلنَّاسَ كَانُوا۟ بِـَٔايَـٰتِنَا لَا يُوقِنُونَ ۝ وَيَوْمَ نَحْشُرُ مِن كُلِّ أُمَّةٍ فَوْجًا مِّمَّن يُكَذِّبُ بِـَٔايَـٰتِنَا فَهُمْ يُوزَعُونَ ۝ حَتَّىٰٓ إِذَا جَآءُو قَالَ أَكَذَّبْتُم بِـَٔايَـٰتِى وَلَمْ تُحِيطُوا۟ بِهَا عِلْمًا أَمَّاذَا كُنتُمْ تَعْمَلُونَ ۝

Your Lord is gracious to mankind, but most do not offer thanks. Your Lord knows what their hearts conceal and what they declare. There is no hidden matter in heaven or on earth except it being a Manifest Book. This Qur'an narrates to the Children of Israel most of what they dispute about. It is a guidance and a mercy to the faithful. Surely thy Lord will decide between them by His Judgment; He is the All-Mighty, the All-Knowing. Put your trust in Allah, for you are upon a manifest truth. You cannot make the dead hear, nor make the deaf hear the call if they turn their backs and depart. You shall not guide the blind out of their error neither shall you make any to hear, save such as believe in Our signs, and so surrender. When the verdict is given against them, We shall bring a creature out of the earth, which will tell them that people had no faith in Our signs. Upon the day when We shall muster out of every nation a troop of those that cried lies to Our signs, duly disposed. When they arrive, He will say: 'Did you cry lies to My signs [revelations], and were unable to comprehend them? Or what else were you doing?'

73-84 It is in our nature to investigate, explore, and discover what we do not know. Indeed, we are in constant pursuit of the nature of the *Divine*, who knows and hears all. Those who are in faith and have complete trust in God's will are naturally guided more clearly than others; as such, they experience God's mercy and grace more often than others. The extent to which we rely on God, without ignoring our sense of reason, rationality, and intellect, determines the clarity of our path and our contentment. The same way that a blind person cannot see obstacles on a road, one who has no faith and trust in the unseen will not be able to hear warnings or encouragement. To submit and accept the truth that the supreme *Reality* and *Truth* governs the entire universe shows us the first step towards spiritual growth and awakening. On the other hand, individual and collective denials of this unveiling are causing havoc with human life on earth.

It is natural for us to wish the best for others, and it is wisdom to know the limitations of whether we can help or not. Many of us in this world cause damage to our faculties that are not repairable and this may hinder our flow toward higher consciousness.

Revealed pieces of knowledge, especially those like the Qur'an, provide considerable guidance and direction along the path from childhood ignorance towards maturity, knowledge, and light.

85-93 وَوَقَعَ ٱلْقَوْلُ عَلَيْهِم بِمَا ظَلَمُوا۟ فَهُمْ لَا يَنطِقُونَ ۝ أَلَمْ يَرَوْا۟ أَنَّا جَعَلْنَا ٱلَّيْلَ لِيَسْكُنُوا۟ فِيهِ وَٱلنَّهَارَ مُبْصِرًا إِنَّ فِى ذَٰلِكَ لَـَٔايَـٰتٍ لِّقَوْمٍ يُؤْمِنُونَ ۝ وَيَوْمَ يُنفَخُ فِى ٱلصُّورِ فَفَزِعَ مَن فِى ٱلسَّمَـٰوَٰتِ وَمَن فِى ٱلْأَرْضِ إِلَّا مَن شَآءَ ٱللَّهُ وَكُلٌّ أَتَوْهُ دَٰخِرِينَ ۝ وَتَرَى ٱلْجِبَالَ تَحْسَبُهَا جَامِدَةً وَهِىَ تَمُرُّ مَرَّ ٱلسَّحَابِ صُنْعَ ٱللَّهِ ٱلَّذِىٓ أَتْقَنَ كُلَّ شَىْءٍ إِنَّهُۥ خَبِيرٌۢ بِمَا تَفْعَلُونَ ۝ مَن جَآءَ بِٱلْحَسَنَةِ فَلَهُۥ خَيْرٌ مِّنْهَا وَهُم مِّن فَزَعٍ يَوْمَئِذٍ ءَامِنُونَ ۝ وَمَن جَآءَ بِٱلسَّيِّئَةِ فَكُبَّتْ وُجُوهُهُمْ فِى ٱلنَّارِ هَلْ تُجْزَوْنَ إِلَّا مَا كُنتُمْ تَعْمَلُونَ ۝ إِنَّمَآ أُمِرْتُ أَنْ أَعْبُدَ رَبَّ هَـٰذِهِ ٱلْبَلْدَةِ ٱلَّذِى حَرَّمَهَا وَلَهُۥ كُلُّ شَىْءٍ وَأُمِرْتُ أَنْ أَكُونَ مِنَ ٱلْمُسْلِمِينَ ۝ وَأَنْ أَتْلُوَا۟ ٱلْقُرْءَانَ فَمَنِ ٱهْتَدَىٰ فَإِنَّمَا يَهْتَدِى لِنَفْسِهِۦ وَمَن ضَلَّ فَقُلْ إِنَّمَآ أَنَا۠ مِنَ ٱلْمُنذِرِينَ ۝ وَقُلِ ٱلْحَمْدُ لِلَّهِ سَيُرِيكُمْ ءَايَـٰتِهِۦ فَتَعْرِفُونَهَا وَمَا رَبُّكَ بِغَـٰفِلٍ عَمَّا تَعْمَلُونَ ۝

The verdict will be given against them because of their wrongdoing: they will not speak. Have they not observed that We created the night for them to rest therein, and created the luminous day? In this surely are signs for a people of faith. On the day the Trumpet is blown, and terrified is whosoever is in the heavens and earth, excepting whom Allah wills, and every one shall come to Him, all utterly abject. And thou shalt see the mountains, that you suppose fixed, passing by like clouds – Allah's handiwork, who has created everything very well. He is aware of the things you do. Whoso brings with him a righteous deed shall receive one better than it. That Day they shall be secure from fright. Whoso brings with him an evil deed – their faces shall be tumbled into the Fire. Will you be rewarded other than how you acted? I have only been commanded to serve the Lord of this territory which He has made sacred; to Him belongs everything. And I have been commanded to be of those that surrender, and to recite the Qur'an. Whoso is guided, is guided for his own good. Whoso strays into error, say: 'I am merely a warner.' Praise be to Allah! He shall show you His wonders, and you shall recognize them; nor is your Lord heedless of what you do.

85-93 After death no one can correct earthly physical or mental habits, or patterns of thoughts and actions. On earth we experience movement and change all around us. These changes are natural, but they may take some time to be noticed or understood. We live in conditioned consciousness, within limited space and time. Our soul, the source of life within us, is from timelessness, which is seamlessly connected to the *Absolute* as well as to our relative personal life. With deep insight, we may catch a glimpse of what is timeless and boundless. True religions try to help us connect self and soul, mind and heart, seen and unseen, in preparation for the time when the soul relegates the body to its earthly origin. Yet few are able to celebrate this wonderful, natural event called death, where the soul is no longer confined to body, mind, and space-time.

Our life on earth is full of wonders, such as the mountains that we see as fixed, which are travelling at very high speeds in geological time. When we begin to awaken to the absolute *Truth* of the source of our changing world, we feel the direct guidance of our own soul.

Creation began due to the coalescence of different energy levels, according to interconnected patterns; after a few billion years it will return to that. In the meantime, there may be many other creational realities of which we are not aware. All we can do is be present in the moment, with total honesty, courage, and accountability. Then we find that we have the joy of peace and contentment as well as the delights of whatever is unfolding upon us in the outer world.

10. Surah 28 Al-Qasas (The Stories)

Allah is the governor of whatever occurs in the heavens and earth; all powers inclusive of creation and knowledge emanate from the *Reality*. We need to use our minds to transcend the limitations of causality in order to realise the perfection within all that happens, whether we like it or not. With glimpses of this amazing truth, we may become more cautious and reflective regarding our intentions and actions.

بِسْمِ اللَّهِ الرَّحْمَٰنِ الرَّحِيمِ

1-9 طسم ۚ تِلْكَ ءَايَٰتُ ٱلْكِتَٰبِ ٱلْمُبِينِ ۚ نَتْلُوا۟ عَلَيْكَ مِن نَّبَإِ مُوسَىٰ وَفِرْعَوْنَ

بِٱلْحَقِّ لِقَوْمٍ يُؤْمِنُونَ ۝ إِنَّ فِرْعَوْنَ عَلَا فِى ٱلْأَرْضِ وَجَعَلَ أَهْلَهَا شِيَعًا يَسْتَضْعِفُ طَآئِفَةً مِّنْهُمْ يُذَبِّحُ أَبْنَآءَهُمْ وَيَسْتَحْىِۦ نِسَآءَهُمْ إِنَّهُۥ كَانَ مِنَ ٱلْمُفْسِدِينَ ۝ وَنُرِيدُ أَن نَّمُنَّ عَلَى ٱلَّذِينَ ٱسْتُضْعِفُوا۟ فِى ٱلْأَرْضِ وَنَجْعَلَهُمْ أَئِمَّةً وَنَجْعَلَهُمُ ٱلْوَٰرِثِينَ ۝ وَنُمَكِّنَ لَهُمْ فِى ٱلْأَرْضِ وَنُرِىَ فِرْعَوْنَ وَهَٰمَٰنَ وَجُنُودَهُمَا مِنْهُم مَّا كَانُوا۟ يَحْذَرُونَ ۝ وَأَوْحَيْنَآ إِلَىٰٓ أُمِّ مُوسَىٰٓ أَنْ أَرْضِعِيهِ فَإِذَا خِفْتِ عَلَيْهِ فَأَلْقِيهِ فِى ٱلْيَمِّ وَلَا تَخَافِى وَلَا تَحْزَنِىٓ إِنَّا رَآدُّوهُ إِلَيْكِ وَجَاعِلُوهُ مِنَ ٱلْمُرْسَلِينَ ۝ فَٱلْتَقَطَهُۥٓ ءَالُ فِرْعَوْنَ لِيَكُونَ لَهُمْ عَدُوًّا وَحَزَنًا إِنَّ فِرْعَوْنَ وَهَٰمَٰنَ وَجُنُودَهُمَا كَانُوا۟ خَٰطِـِٔينَ ۝ وَقَالَتِ ٱمْرَأَتُ فِرْعَوْنَ قُرَّتُ عَيْنٍ لِّى وَلَكَ لَا تَقْتُلُوهُ عَسَىٰٓ أَن يَنفَعَنَآ أَوْ نَتَّخِذَهُۥ وَلَدًا وَهُمْ لَا يَشْعُرُونَ ۝

In the name of Allah, the Merciful to all, the Compassionate to each!

Ta Sin Mim. Behold the revelations of a Manifest Book! We are reciting to you some reports of Moses and Pharaoh, the very truth to a people who believe. Pharaoh had grown high and mighty on earth. He had turned its inhabitants into diverse classes, holding a group among them to be weak, slaughtering their progeny and debauching their womenfolk. He truly was a corrupter. We, however, wish to bestow Our favor on those held to be weak on earth. We intend to make them leaders to mankind, and make them the inheritors. We intend to establish them firmly on earth, and to make Pharaoh, Haman and their troops witness at their hands what once they feared. We inspired Moses' mother, saying, 'Suckle him, and then, when you fear for his safety, put him in the river: do not be afraid, and do not grieve, for We shall return him to you and make him a messenger.' The family of Pharaoh picked him up, to be for them an enemy and a source of grief. Pharaoh, Haman and their troops were indeed in error. The wife of Pharaoh said: 'May he be a comfort to the eye, for me and you. Do not kill him; perhaps he might benefit us, or we adopt him as a son' – all unawares.

1-9 We experience human duality clearly in the visible and invisible senses. In a child's mind, ambitions and hopes grow to admiring power, strength, and social status. Real progress takes place when the lower self has been contained and humbled, and when the heart has been purified so that the light of the soul shines and leads. There are many who can offer guidance, but on emotional and spiritual issues our own soul, if approached appropriately, will give us what is needed. There is a natural balance or imbalance in the connection between self and soul. The Prophet Moses of light was harboured and nurtured by the dark Pharaoh himself. Such is Allah's plan, beyond the comprehension of our minds.

All our earthly experiences are based on dualities, some of which are important for our worldly existence and others for the hereafter. If one harnesses one's health, strength, and power on earth, one can do a lot of good. For easier access to higher consciousness, we need to give up our earthly interest, even at the cost of being accused of being weak and meek.

Many of the events around us do not reveal their true inner meaning and impact. We are guided by our minds and our senses, the first entry into consciousness; this leads to timeless consciousness.

10-18 وَأَصْبَحَ فُؤَادُ أُمِّ مُوسَىٰ فَٰرِغًا إِن كَادَتْ لَتُبْدِى بِهِۦ لَوْلَآ أَن رَّبَطْنَا عَلَىٰ قَلْبِهَا لِتَكُونَ مِنَ ٱلْمُؤْمِنِينَ ۝ وَقَالَتْ لِأُخْتِهِۦ قُصِّيهِ فَبَصُرَتْ بِهِۦ عَن جُنُبٍ وَهُمْ لَا يَشْعُرُونَ ۝ وَحَرَّمْنَا عَلَيْهِ ٱلْمَرَاضِعَ مِن قَبْلُ فَقَالَتْ هَلْ أَدُلُّكُمْ عَلَىٰٓ أَهْلِ بَيْتٍ يَكْفُلُونَهُۥ لَكُمْ وَهُمْ لَهُۥ نَٰصِحُونَ ۝ فَرَدَدْنَٰهُ إِلَىٰٓ أُمِّهِۦ كَىْ تَقَرَّ عَيْنُهَا وَلَا تَحْزَنَ وَلِتَعْلَمَ أَنَّ وَعْدَ ٱللَّهِ حَقٌّ وَلَٰكِنَّ أَكْثَرَهُمْ لَا يَعْلَمُونَ ۝ وَلَمَّا بَلَغَ أَشُدَّهُۥ وَٱسْتَوَىٰٓ ءَاتَيْنَٰهُ حُكْمًا وَعِلْمًا وَكَذَٰلِكَ نَجْزِى ٱلْمُحْسِنِينَ ۝ وَدَخَلَ ٱلْمَدِينَةَ عَلَىٰ حِينِ غَفْلَةٍ مِّنْ أَهْلِهَا فَوَجَدَ فِيهَا رَجُلَيْنِ يَقْتَتِلَانِ هَٰذَا مِن شِيعَتِهِۦ وَهَٰذَا مِنْ عَدُوِّهِۦ فَٱسْتَغَٰثَهُ ٱلَّذِى مِن شِيعَتِهِۦ عَلَى ٱلَّذِى مِنْ عَدُوِّهِۦ فَوَكَزَهُۥ مُوسَىٰ فَقَضَىٰ عَلَيْهِ قَالَ هَٰذَا مِنْ عَمَلِ ٱلشَّيْطَٰنِ إِنَّهُۥ عَدُوٌّ مُّضِلٌّ مُّبِينٌ ۝ قَالَ رَبِّ إِنِّى ظَلَمْتُ نَفْسِى فَٱغْفِرْ لِى فَغَفَرَ لَهُۥٓ إِنَّهُۥ هُوَ ٱلْغَفُورُ ٱلرَّحِيمُ ۝ قَالَ رَبِّ بِمَآ أَنْعَمْتَ عَلَىَّ فَلَنْ أَكُونَ ظَهِيرًا لِّلْمُجْرِمِينَ ۝ فَأَصْبَحَ فِى ٱلْمَدِينَةِ خَآئِفًا يَتَرَقَّبُ فَإِذَا ٱلَّذِى ٱسْتَنصَرَهُۥ بِٱلْأَمْسِ يَسْتَصْرِخُهُۥ قَالَ لَهُۥ مُوسَىٰٓ إِنَّكَ لَغَوِىٌّ مُّبِينٌ ۝

On the morrow the heart of Moses's mother became empty, and she well nigh disclosed him had We not strengthened her heart, that she might be among the believers. She said to her sister: 'Follow his tracks.' Her sister espied him from a distance, while they were unaware. We had already forbidden him suckling by wet-nurses, so she said: 'Shall I point out to you a household who would look after him for you and raise him well?' So We returned him to his mother, that her eye might be comforted and not grieve, and that she might know that Allah's promise is true. But most of them do not understand. When he reached full maturity, consummate in form, We endowed him with right judgment and knowledge. Thus, do We reward those who do good. And he entered the city, at a time when its people were unheeding, and found there two men fighting; the one was of his own party, and the other was of his enemies. Then the one that was of his party cried to him to aid him against the other that was of his enemies; so, Moses struck him, and despatched him, and said, 'This is of Satan's doing; he is surely an enemy misleading, manifest.' He said: 'My Lord, I have wronged myself, so forgive me.' And He forgave him – He is All-Forgiving, Compassionate to each. He said: 'My Lord, because of Your favors to me, I shall never make common cause with criminals.' The following day, he went about the city in fear and looking about him, when the man who the day before had called out to him for assistance was now screaming for his help. Moses said to him: 'You are clearly unregenerate.'

10-18 There are of all kinds of reasons and rationalities by which to understand events on earth, but with deep reflectiveness you will realise that there were often hidden reasons that caused a seemingly obvious event. Prophet Moses, in his infancy, did not accept any of the wet nurses they brought for him, and that is how Pharaoh's household were obliged to plead with his mother to nurse him. As humans we are caught between cause and effect. If we put this aside and look at that which is beyond the mind, we may catch glimpses of higher lights. Prophet Moses responded to the cry of his tribesman begging him for help as he was being attacked by an enemy. Moses overwhelmed the attacker and killed him. His fear for the consequences of his action eventually caused him to leave the town and ultimately to join the Prophet Jethro and be groomed by him.

Pharaoh, who tried to kill every male infant, ended up hosting his future enemy Moses. What little we know about Allah's plot other than a minor shadow of it in our feeble minds! Sometimes our good deeds can be a big source of trouble; other times our silence can be what saves us.

Many stories and events in the past can reveal alternate meanings of things that happen to us. We may have considered some things to be agreeable and valuable; however, these may turn out to be the reverse. Indeed, we can only judge by the visible, short-term, realities with which our mind and memory serve us. The rise in consciousness proceeds higher and higher, towards that which is beyond reason and meaning, to the lights that have originated the whole story.

19-25 فَلَمَّآ أَنۡ أَرَادَ أَن يَبۡطِشَ بِٱلَّذِى هُوَ عَدُوٌّ لَّهُمَا قَالَ يَٰمُوسَىٰٓ أَتُرِيدُ أَن تَقۡتُلَنِى كَمَا قَتَلۡتَ نَفۡسًۢا بِٱلۡأَمۡسِۖ إِن تُرِيدُ إِلَّآ أَن تَكُونَ جَبَّارًا فِى ٱلۡأَرۡضِ وَمَا تُرِيدُ أَن تَكُونَ مِنَ ٱلۡمُصۡلِحِينَ ۝ وَجَآءَ رَجُلٌ مِّنۡ أَقۡصَا ٱلۡمَدِينَةِ يَسۡعَىٰ قَالَ يَٰمُوسَىٰٓ إِنَّ ٱلۡمَلَأَ يَأۡتَمِرُونَ بِكَ لِيَقۡتُلُوكَ فَٱخۡرُجۡ إِنِّى لَكَ مِنَ ٱلنَّٰصِحِينَ ۝ فَخَرَجَ مِنۡهَا خَآئِفًا يَتَرَقَّبُۖ قَالَ رَبِّ نَجِّنِى مِنَ ٱلۡقَوۡمِ ٱلظَّٰلِمِينَ ۝ وَلَمَّا تَوَجَّهَ تِلۡقَآءَ مَدۡيَنَ قَالَ عَسَىٰ رَبِّىٓ أَن يَهۡدِيَنِى سَوَآءَ ٱلسَّبِيلِ ۝ وَلَمَّا وَرَدَ مَآءَ مَدۡيَنَ وَجَدَ عَلَيۡهِ أُمَّةً مِّنَ ٱلنَّاسِ يَسۡقُونَ وَوَجَدَ مِن دُونِهِمُ ٱمۡرَأَتَيۡنِ تَذُودَانِۖ قَالَ مَا خَطۡبُكُمَاۖ قَالَتَا لَا نَسۡقِى حَتَّىٰ يُصۡدِرَ ٱلرِّعَآءُۖ وَأَبُونَا شَيۡخٌ كَبِيرٌ ۝ فَسَقَىٰ لَهُمَا ثُمَّ تَوَلَّىٰٓ إِلَى ٱلظِّلِّ فَقَالَ رَبِّ إِنِّى لِمَآ أَنزَلۡتَ إِلَىَّ مِنۡ خَيۡرٍ فَقِيرٌ ۝ فَجَآءَتۡهُ إِحۡدَىٰهُمَا تَمۡشِى عَلَى ٱسۡتِحۡيَآءٍ قَالَتۡ إِنَّ أَبِى يَدۡعُوكَ لِيَجۡزِيَكَ أَجۡرَ مَا سَقَيۡتَ لَنَاۚ فَلَمَّا جَآءَهُۥ وَقَصَّ عَلَيۡهِ ٱلۡقَصَصَ قَالَ لَا تَخَفۡۖ نَجَوۡتَ مِنَ ٱلۡقَوۡمِ ٱلظَّٰلِمِينَ ۝

When he was about to strike down the man who was an enemy to them both, he said: 'O Moses, do you intend to kill me as you killed a soul yesterday? You only want to be a despot in the land, and have no desire to do good.' A man came running from the other end of the city, saying: 'O Moses, the council are planning to kill you, so depart. I give you good counsel.' So, he left the city, fearful and looking about him. He said: 'My Lord, deliver me from a wicked people.' When he set out in the direction of Midian, he said: 'Perchance my

Lord will guide me to a straight path.' Arriving at the waters of Midian, he found there at a concourse of people drawing water and, to one side of them, two women tending flocks. He said: 'What is the matter with the two of you?' They said: 'We cannot give to drink until the shepherds have departed, and our father is an old man.' So he drew water for them and retired to the shade, saying: 'My Lord, I am in dire need of some goodness that You send down upon me.' One of the two women approached him, walking shyly, and said: 'My father invites you in order to reward you with a wage for drawing us water.' When he came to him and narrated to him the story, he said: 'Fear not; you have been saved from an evil people.'

19-25 The human mind, memory, and reason provide a certain amount of connectedness and knowledge. The truth is that everything emanates from Allah and that at every level of consciousness Allah is in charge. At all times we are driven towards full enlightenment and awakening. An enlightened person has a clear mind, pure heart, and complete trust in Allah's ways and governance. The kindness of Prophet Moses towards the two ladies when he helped them water their thirsty sheep led him to their father, the Prophet Jethro. Thus, began his apprenticeship towards prophethood. His past fears and anxieties were preludes for this ultimate enlightenment. The door of the future opened for him as a living example of how a good deed wipes out the wrong ones.

Moses' awakening to prophethood began when he was serving an older prophet, imbibing his wisdom. We can only rise above our limited consciousness through selfless generosity and service. To be gentle and kind to other humans is the beginning of the path of experiencing the constant flow of divine generosity.

Many events in the last three or four thousand years have affected people's view of the nature of this short-term. earthly reality. As such, many of these stories and events have entered into people's cultures as history or even as myth. They have helped people realise that our knowledge and insights are very limited. The overall direction is a rise in consciousness to the highest level, which brings us to the present moment with all its intensity, when the least importance is given to the ups and downs of our desires and judgment.

26-32 قَالَتْ إِحْدَىٰهُمَا يَٰٓأَبَتِ ٱسْتَـْٔجِرْهُ ۖ إِنَّ خَيْرَ مَنِ ٱسْتَـْٔجَرْتَ ٱلْقَوِىُّ ٱلْأَمِينُ ۝ قَالَ إِنِّىٓ أُرِيدُ أَنْ أُنكِحَكَ إِحْدَى ٱبْنَتَىَّ هَٰتَيْنِ عَلَىٰٓ أَن تَأْجُرَنِى ثَمَٰنِىَ حِجَجٍ ۖ فَإِنْ أَتْمَمْتَ عَشْرًا فَمِنْ عِندِكَ ۖ وَمَآ أُرِيدُ أَنْ أَشُقَّ عَلَيْكَ ۚ سَتَجِدُنِىٓ إِن شَآءَ ٱللَّهُ مِنَ ٱلصَّٰلِحِينَ ۝ قَالَ ذَٰلِكَ بَيْنِى وَبَيْنَكَ ۖ أَيَّمَا ٱلْأَجَلَيْنِ قَضَيْتُ فَلَا عُدْوَٰنَ عَلَىَّ ۖ وَٱللَّهُ عَلَىٰ مَا نَقُولُ وَكِيلٌ ۝ فَلَمَّا قَضَىٰ مُوسَى ٱلْأَجَلَ وَسَارَ بِأَهْلِهِۦٓ ءَانَسَ مِن جَانِبِ ٱلطُّورِ نَارًا قَالَ لِأَهْلِهِ ٱمْكُثُوٓا۟ إِنِّىٓ ءَانَسْتُ نَارًا لَّعَلِّىٓ ءَاتِيكُم مِّنْهَا بِخَبَرٍ أَوْ جَذْوَةٍ مِّنَ ٱلنَّارِ لَعَلَّكُمْ تَصْطَلُونَ ۝ فَلَمَّآ أَتَىٰهَا نُودِىَ مِن شَٰطِئِ ٱلْوَادِ ٱلْأَيْمَنِ فِى ٱلْبُقْعَةِ ٱلْمُبَٰرَكَةِ

مِنَ ٱلشَّجَرَةِ أَن يَٰمُوسَىٰٓ إِنِّىٓ أَنَا ٱللَّهُ رَبُّ ٱلْعَٰلَمِينَ ۝ وَأَنْ أَلْقِ عَصَاكَ فَلَمَّا رَءَاهَا تَهْتَزُّ كَأَنَّهَا جَآنٌّ وَلَّىٰ مُدْبِرًا وَلَمْ يُعَقِّبْ يَٰمُوسَىٰٓ أَقْبِلْ وَلَا تَخَفْ إِنَّكَ مِنَ ٱلْءَامِنِينَ ۝ ٱسْلُكْ يَدَكَ فِى جَيْبِكَ تَخْرُجْ بَيْضَآءَ مِنْ غَيْرِ سُوٓءٍ وَٱضْمُمْ إِلَيْكَ جَنَاحَكَ مِنَ ٱلرَّهْبِ فَذَٰنِكَ بُرْهَٰنَانِ مِن رَّبِّكَ إِلَىٰ فِرْعَوْنَ وَمَلَإِيْهِۦٓ إِنَّهُمْ كَانُوا۟ قَوْمًا فَٰسِقِينَ ۝

One of the women said: 'Father, hire him; the best person to hire is one strong and trustworthy.' He said: 'I wish to marry you to one of these two daughters of mine, provided you hire yourself to me for eight years. If you complete ten years, that would be a charitable act on your part. I do not wish to overburden you. And, Allah willing, you shall find me a man of righteousness.' He said: 'Let this be the understanding between you and me. Whichever of the two terms I fulfill, let me suffer no injustice, and may Allah be a witness of what we speak.' When Moses fulfilled the allotted term, he departed with his family. He espied a fire upon the side of the mountain and said to his family: 'Stay behind. I have glimpsed a fire; perhaps I will bring you news of it or a brand from it, to warm yourselves thereby.' Arriving at the fire, a voice called out to him from the right side of the valley, at a blessed spot, and coming from the tree: 'O Moses, it is I, Allah, Lord of the Worlds. Throw down your staff!' When he saw it twitching like a serpent he turned and fled, and did not look back. 'O Moses, come near and be not afraid; you are safe from harm. Put your hand inside your sleeve and it shall come out white, but without harm. And press tight your hand to yourself to ward off fear. These are two wonders from your Lord to Pharaoh and his council – a people depraved.'

26-32 The less selfish our conduct, the deeper and greater our reward. Human light is as good as intention, attention, action and constant reference to the Source of all these powers – God Himself. Every one of us has inherited seeds and patterns of past events in human experience. We share with Prophet Moses, the fear of his enemies chasing him and occasionally we find the sea opens and we are on safe grounds. We sometimes also find ourselves in search of Prophet Musa's God in the Sinai desert until we find a clear light of the Divine Light within the burning bush. We often experience how our *nafs* takes over and anger, fear and rancour distract us, causing regrets and repentance. If we live as a soul, we may be able to reflect on our miracles and thereby understand how the staff of Prophet Moses became the miraculous serpent.

The honesty and clarity of Moses opened for him numerous channels, which were considered as great miracles. The ultimate miracle of all is that the infinite, eternal divine light resides in our own hearts. The life of Moses involved constant reference to the *Absolute*.

Correct conduct and accountability, with total honesty, is the foundation for moving along the path of awakening and enlightenment. Without these, we will be confusing ourselves adding to the deceptions and camouflage that nature provides other creational entities to survive and carry on.

33-41 قَالَ رَبِّ إِنِّي قَتَلْتُ مِنْهُمْ نَفْسًا فَأَخَافُ أَن يَقْتُلُونِ ۝ وَأَخِي هَٰرُونُ هُوَ أَفْصَحُ مِنِّي لِسَانًا فَأَرْسِلْهُ مَعِيَ رِدْءًا يُصَدِّقُنِي ۖ إِنِّي أَخَافُ أَن يُكَذِّبُونِ ۝ قَالَ سَنَشُدُّ عَضُدَكَ بِأَخِيكَ وَنَجْعَلُ لَكُمَا سُلْطَانًا فَلَا يَصِلُونَ إِلَيْكُمَا ۚ بِآيَاتِنَا أَنتُمَا وَمَنِ اتَّبَعَكُمَا الْغَالِبُونَ ۝ فَلَمَّا جَاءَهُم مُّوسَىٰ بِآيَاتِنَا بَيِّنَاتٍ قَالُوا مَا هَٰذَا إِلَّا سِحْرٌ مُّفْتَرًى وَمَا سَمِعْنَا بِهَٰذَا فِي آبَائِنَا الْأَوَّلِينَ ۝ وَقَالَ مُوسَىٰ رَبِّي أَعْلَمُ بِمَن جَاءَ بِالْهُدَىٰ مِنْ عِندِهِ وَمَن تَكُونُ لَهُ عَاقِبَةُ الدَّارِ ۖ إِنَّهُ لَا يُفْلِحُ الظَّالِمُونَ ۝ وَقَالَ فِرْعَوْنُ يَا أَيُّهَا الْمَلَأُ مَا عَلِمْتُ لَكُم مِّنْ إِلَٰهٍ غَيْرِي فَأَوْقِدْ لِي يَا هَامَانُ عَلَى الطِّينِ فَاجْعَل لِّي صَرْحًا لَّعَلِّي أَطَّلِعُ إِلَىٰ إِلَٰهِ مُوسَىٰ وَإِنِّي لَأَظُنُّهُ مِنَ الْكَاذِبِينَ ۝ وَاسْتَكْبَرَ هُوَ وَجُنُودُهُ فِي الْأَرْضِ بِغَيْرِ الْحَقِّ وَظَنُّوا أَنَّهُمْ إِلَيْنَا لَا يُرْجَعُونَ ۝ فَأَخَذْنَاهُ وَجُنُودَهُ فَنَبَذْنَاهُمْ فِي الْيَمِّ ۖ فَانظُرْ كَيْفَ كَانَ عَاقِبَةُ الظَّالِمِينَ ۝ وَجَعَلْنَاهُمْ أَئِمَّةً يَدْعُونَ إِلَى النَّارِ ۖ وَيَوْمَ الْقِيَامَةِ لَا يُنصَرُونَ ۝

He said: 'My Lord, I killed one of them and fear they might kill me. My brother Aaron is more eloquent in tongue than me, so send him with me to back me up and verify my words. I fear they will call me a liar.' Said He, 'We will strengthen your arm by means of thy brother, and We shall appoint to you an authority, so that they shall not reach you because of Our signs; you, and whoso follows you, shall be the victors.' So, when Moses came to them with Our signs, clear signs, they said, 'This is nothing but a forged sorcery. We never heard of this among our fathers, the ancients.' Moses said: 'My Lord knows best who comes with guidance from Him, and who shall inherit the Final Abode. The wicked shall not prosper.' And Pharaoh said, 'Council, I know not that you have any Allah but me. Kindle me, Haman, a fire upon the clay, and make me a tower, that I may mount up to Moses' Allah; for I think that he is one of the liars.' And he and his troops grew arrogant in the land, unjustly, imagining they would not be restored to Us. So, We seized him and his troops and flung them into the sea – behold what end they met, those evildoers! And We turned them into guides who summon to the Fire. On the Day of Resurrection, they shall find no support.

33-41 To rise towards higher consciousness, we need total honesty in our own state of mind and heart. The Moses of the higher self manifests according to the extent of our good intentions and actions, with loyalty and sincerity towards others, especially those close to us. The kindness and empathy of Moses towards the needy ladies at the well caused him to reach Prophet Jethro and benefit from years of guidance and experience with him. When one cares for the rest of humanity, consciousness is lifted to a much higher zone. To move out of conditioned consciousness, one easy path is to take on a bigger cause, such as to relieve the misery and suffering of others. Pride, arrogance and selfishness are clear recipes for personal and communal disasters. Kindness, gentleness, generosity, and empathy with others help us to get out of self-pity and other miseries caused by the ego.

The shadow of Pharaoh and his haughtiness may occur in many people's minds; this can be the cause of personal destruction as well as for the destruction of those who follow these shadows. The soul is so mighty and great that the *nafs* tries to imitate it and thrives on vanity.

Any creature that is aware of life is concerned with preserving that life in every possible way. Experience of life is the highest treasure ever; therefore, everything else is sacrificed to continue that link, until such time – through grace, meditation, and prayer – you will come to know that life is eternal, and your life is not separate from that which is eternal. Therefore, the personal link to it will not have the same intensity and all the spectacular fear and desire that normally comes with it. People who are constantly leaving their minds behind and entering into communion with the light of the heart are certain that liberation and awakening are written for everyone after death.

42-49 وَأَتْبَعْنَٰهُمْ فِى هَٰذِهِ ٱلدُّنْيَا لَعْنَةً ۖ وَيَوْمَ ٱلْقِيَٰمَةِ هُم مِّنَ ٱلْمَقْبُوحِينَ ۝ وَلَقَدْ ءَاتَيْنَا مُوسَى ٱلْكِتَٰبَ مِنۢ بَعْدِ مَآ أَهْلَكْنَا ٱلْقُرُونَ ٱلْأُولَىٰ بَصَآئِرَ لِلنَّاسِ وَهُدًى وَرَحْمَةً لَّعَلَّهُمْ يَتَذَكَّرُونَ ۝ وَمَا كُنتَ بِجَانِبِ ٱلْغَرْبِىِّ إِذْ قَضَيْنَآ إِلَىٰ مُوسَى ٱلْأَمْرَ وَمَا كُنتَ مِنَ ٱلشَّٰهِدِينَ ۝ وَلَٰكِنَّآ أَنشَأْنَا قُرُونًا فَتَطَاوَلَ عَلَيْهِمُ ٱلْعُمُرُ ۚ وَمَا كُنتَ ثَاوِيًا فِىٓ أَهْلِ مَدْيَنَ تَتْلُوا۟ عَلَيْهِمْ ءَايَٰتِنَا وَلَٰكِنَّا كُنَّا مُرْسِلِينَ ۝ وَمَا كُنتَ بِجَانِبِ ٱلطُّورِ إِذْ نَادَيْنَا وَلَٰكِن رَّحْمَةً مِّن رَّبِّكَ لِتُنذِرَ قَوْمًا مَّآ أَتَىٰهُم مِّن نَّذِيرٍ مِّن قَبْلِكَ لَعَلَّهُمْ يَتَذَكَّرُونَ ۝ وَلَوْلَآ أَن تُصِيبَهُم مُّصِيبَةٌۢ بِمَا قَدَّمَتْ أَيْدِيهِمْ فَيَقُولُوا۟ رَبَّنَا لَوْلَآ أَرْسَلْتَ إِلَيْنَا رَسُولًا فَنَتَّبِعَ ءَايَٰتِكَ وَنَكُونَ مِنَ ٱلْمُؤْمِنِينَ ۝ فَلَمَّا جَآءَهُمُ ٱلْحَقُّ مِنْ عِندِنَا قَالُوا۟ لَوْلَآ أُوتِىَ مِثْلَ مَآ أُوتِىَ مُوسَىٰٓ ۚ أَوَلَمْ يَكْفُرُوا۟ بِمَآ أُوتِىَ مُوسَىٰ مِن قَبْلُ ۖ قَالُوا۟ سِحْرَانِ تَظَٰهَرَا وَقَالُوٓا۟ إِنَّا بِكُلٍّ كَٰفِرُونَ ۝ قُلْ فَأْتُوا۟ بِكِتَٰبٍ مِّنْ عِندِ ٱللَّهِ هُوَ أَهْدَىٰ مِنْهُمَآ أَتَّبِعْهُ إِن كُنتُمْ صَٰدِقِينَ ۝

We made Our rejection pursue them in this world, and on the Day of Resurrection they will be among the despised. To Moses We brought the Book, after having destroyed earlier generations, as an illumination to mankind, a guidance and a mercy, that they might remember. You were not upon the western side when We decreed to Moses the commandment, nor were you of those witnessing; but We raised up generations, and long their lives continued. Neither was thou a dweller among the Midianites, reciting to them Our signs; but We were sending Messengers. You were not upon the side of the Mount when We called; but for a mercy from thy Lord, that you warn a people to whom no warner came before thee, and that haply they may remember. If some calamity befalls them for their past misdeeds, they would say: 'Our Lord, if only You had sent us a messenger, so we could abide by Your revelations and be among the faithful.' Even now that Our truth has come to them, they say, 'Why has he not been given signs like those given to Moses?' Did they not also deny the truth that was given to Moses before? They say, 'Two kinds of sorcery, helping each other,' and, 'We refuse to accept either of them.' Say: 'Bring a Book from Allah, more conducive to guidance than both, and I shall follow it, if you speak the truth.'

42-49 The Book of *Truth* resides within every soul, but it does not radiate with the same intensity. This is due to the cover of the darkness and shadows of the lower self, which differs from one person to another. An enlightened being or a prophet who can transcend the lower self and its darkness obviously sees and realises the truth clearer than others. The unseen and the *Truth* reveal themselves to those who live as soul or spirit. The normal progress in spirituality begins with a healthy and balanced body, mind, and heart and then progresses with reason and rationality towards a higher zone of consciousness, to the original sacred light of pure consciousness. By understanding this process and having faith and trust in its authenticity, we will be occasionally given evidences and encouragements to continue our spiritual journey. We are often challenged with uncertainties and choices in our life, and it is here that we need to listen to our inner heart rather than the mind.

Like many prophets before him, Moses had insights regarding the past as well as the future, but his loyalty always remained constant to the divine *Presence*. His inner divine scripture gave rise to the outer book.

Those who think that they are in control of their destiny and that this life on earth is all there is for them, are certainly heading for a much darker period after they leave behind the control mechanism that is the body and the mind. The shock of this is much greater for them and causes them a great deal of anxiety.

50-59 فَإِن لَّمْ يَسْتَجِيبُوا۟ لَكَ فَٱعْلَمْ أَنَّمَا يَتَّبِعُونَ أَهْوَآءَهُمْ وَمَنْ أَضَلُّ مِمَّنِ ٱتَّبَعَ هَوَىٰهُ بِغَيْرِ هُدًى مِّنَ ٱللَّهِ إِنَّ ٱللَّهَ لَا يَهْدِى ٱلْقَوْمَ ٱلظَّـٰلِمِينَ ۝ وَلَقَدْ وَصَّلْنَا لَهُمُ ٱلْقَوْلَ لَعَلَّهُمْ يَتَذَكَّرُونَ ۝ ٱلَّذِينَ ءَاتَيْنَـٰهُمُ ٱلْكِتَـٰبَ مِن قَبْلِهِۦ هُم بِهِۦ يُؤْمِنُونَ ۝ وَإِذَا يُتْلَىٰ عَلَيْهِمْ قَالُوٓا۟ ءَامَنَّا بِهِۦٓ إِنَّهُ ٱلْحَقُّ مِن رَّبِّنَآ إِنَّا كُنَّا مِن قَبْلِهِۦ مُسْلِمِينَ ۝ أُو۟لَـٰٓئِكَ يُؤْتَوْنَ أَجْرَهُم مَّرَّتَيْنِ بِمَا صَبَرُوا۟ وَيَدْرَءُونَ بِٱلْحَسَنَةِ ٱلسَّيِّئَةَ وَمِمَّا رَزَقْنَـٰهُمْ يُنفِقُونَ ۝ وَإِذَا سَمِعُوا۟ ٱللَّغْوَ أَعْرَضُوا۟ عَنْهُ وَقَالُوا۟ لَنَآ أَعْمَـٰلُنَا وَلَكُمْ أَعْمَـٰلُكُمْ سَلَـٰمٌ عَلَيْكُمْ لَا نَبْتَغِى ٱلْجَـٰهِلِينَ ۝ إِنَّكَ لَا تَهْدِى مَنْ أَحْبَبْتَ وَلَـٰكِنَّ ٱللَّهَ يَهْدِى مَن يَشَآءُ وَهُوَ أَعْلَمُ بِٱلْمُهْتَدِينَ ۝ وَقَالُوٓا۟ إِن نَّتَّبِعِ ٱلْهُدَىٰ مَعَكَ نُتَخَطَّفْ مِنْ أَرْضِنَآ أَوَلَمْ نُمَكِّن لَّهُمْ حَرَمًا ءَامِنًا يُجْبَىٰٓ إِلَيْهِ ثَمَرَٰتُ كُلِّ شَىْءٍ رِّزْقًا مِّن لَّدُنَّا وَلَـٰكِنَّ أَكْثَرَهُمْ لَا يَعْلَمُونَ ۝ وَكَمْ أَهْلَكْنَا مِن قَرْيَةٍۭ بَطِرَتْ مَعِيشَتَهَا فَتِلْكَ مَسَـٰكِنُهُمْ لَمْ تُسْكَن مِّنۢ بَعْدِهِمْ إِلَّا قَلِيلًا وَكُنَّا نَحْنُ ٱلْوَٰرِثِينَ ۝ وَمَا كَانَ رَبُّكَ مُهْلِكَ ٱلْقُرَىٰ حَتَّىٰ يَبْعَثَ فِىٓ أُمِّهَا رَسُولًا يَتْلُوا۟ عَلَيْهِمْ ءَايَـٰتِنَا وَمَا كُنَّا مُهْلِكِى ٱلْقُرَىٰٓ إِلَّا وَأَهْلُهَا ظَـٰلِمُونَ ۝

If they do not respond to you, know that they merely follow their caprice – and who is more lost than he who follows his caprice, without guidance from Allah? Allah guides not those who are wicked. We revealed to them Our Speech, without interruption, that they might remember. Those to whom We gave the Book before this believe in it. And, when it is recited to them, they say, 'We believe in it; surely it is the truth from our Lord. Indeed, even before' it we had surrendered.' These shall be paid their wages twice for their steadfastness; they ward off evil by doing good, and expend from what We provided them. When they hear idle talk, they turn away from it and say, 'We have our deeds, and you your deeds. Peace be upon your We desire not the ignorant.' You do not guide those whom you love; rather, Allah guides whom He wishes, and He knows best who are guided aright. They say: 'If we follow guidance with you we will be uprooted from our land.' Did We not establish them firmly in a safe and sacred place, to which are conveyed crops of all varieties, as a provision from Us on high? But post of them are ignorant. How many a town, grown excessively luxurious in manner of life, have We destroyed! Behold their habitations, uninhabited after them except for a few! It was We Who were their heirs. Nor would your Lord have destroyed these towns unless He had first sent a messenger to their capital city, reciting Our revelations. Nor would We have destroyed these towns had not their inhabitants been wicked.

50-59 When one begins to obey and follow the inspiration from the heart, fresh energy and lights will provide encouragement and guidance. The prophetic path connects and unifies the numerous strands of consciousness and lights of awareness. Every human being interacts with the outer world constantly, and as such we are actors following an often-confusing script of duality until we employ our higher referencing and not our selfish whims. With higher awareness and better intentions and actions, we experience the rewards of presence, accountability, and goodness that emanate from connectedness with the soul and the cosmic master – Allah. We are all on a journey from a lower level of consciousness towards supreme consciousness, and when guided by divine grace it is a most beautiful journey. Through patience and generous actions, we move closer to the inner soul. We cannot, however, guide anyone we wish, because the lower self and its darkness can block the light of the soul.

Faith and trust in the divine light is the beginning of one's progress along spiritual awakening. The rules of this path are numerous; most of them are based on appropriate courtesy and appropriate perspective. So many great civilisations reverted to dust. The cycle of creation and destruction continues in every aspect of life.

There are certain clear, natural boundaries and rules regarding the move towards higher consciousness. One is that you cannot push people to desire it simply because of your emotional connections with or hope for them. People must be ready to give up some things they have been concerned with and realise that these are not that important. If you are content with what is in front of you, then that is what will remain. Through discontentment as well as through hope and desire for a higher level of awareness you will see that you have already lost many previous interests that you may have had.

60-70 وَمَآ أُوتِيتُم مِّن شَىۡءٍ فَمَتَـٰعُ ٱلۡحَيَوٰةِ ٱلدُّنۡيَا وَزِينَتُهَا ۚ وَمَا عِندَ ٱللَّهِ خَيۡرٌ وَأَبۡقَىٰٓ ۚ أَفَلَا تَعۡقِلُونَ ۝ أَفَمَن وَعَدۡنَـٰهُ وَعۡدًا حَسَنًا فَهُوَ لَـٰقِيهِ كَمَن مَّتَّعۡنَـٰهُ مَتَـٰعَ ٱلۡحَيَوٰةِ ٱلدُّنۡيَا ثُمَّ هُوَ يَوۡمَ ٱلۡقِيَـٰمَةِ مِنَ ٱلۡمُحۡضَرِينَ ۝ وَيَوۡمَ يُنَادِيهِمۡ فَيَقُولُ أَيۡنَ شُرَكَآءِىَ ٱلَّذِينَ كُنتُمۡ تَزۡعُمُونَ ۝ قَالَ ٱلَّذِينَ حَقَّ عَلَيۡهِمُ ٱلۡقَوۡلُ رَبَّنَا هَـٰٓؤُلَآءِ ٱلَّذِينَ أَغۡوَيۡنَا أَغۡوَيۡنَـٰهُمۡ كَمَا غَوَيۡنَا ۖ تَبَرَّأۡنَآ إِلَيۡكَ ۖ مَا كَانُوٓا۟ إِيَّانَا يَعۡبُدُونَ ۝ وَقِيلَ ٱدۡعُوا۟ شُرَكَآءَكُمۡ فَدَعَوۡهُمۡ فَلَمۡ يَسۡتَجِيبُوا۟ لَهُمۡ وَرَأَوُا۟ ٱلۡعَذَابَ ۚ لَوۡ أَنَّهُمۡ كَانُوا۟ يَهۡتَدُونَ ۝ وَيَوۡمَ يُنَادِيهِمۡ فَيَقُولُ مَاذَآ أَجَبۡتُمُ ٱلۡمُرۡسَلِينَ ۝ فَعَمِيَتۡ عَلَيۡهِمُ ٱلۡأَنۢبَآءُ يَوۡمَئِذٍ فَهُمۡ لَا يَتَسَآءَلُونَ ۝ فَأَمَّا مَن تَابَ وَءَامَنَ وَعَمِلَ صَـٰلِحًا فَعَسَىٰٓ أَن يَكُونَ مِنَ ٱلۡمُفۡلِحِينَ ۝ وَرَبُّكَ يَخۡلُقُ مَا يَشَآءُ وَيَخۡتَارُ ۗ مَا كَانَ لَهُمُ ٱلۡخِيَرَةُ ۚ سُبۡحَـٰنَ ٱللَّهِ وَتَعَـٰلَىٰ عَمَّا يُشۡرِكُونَ ۝ وَرَبُّكَ يَعۡلَمُ مَا تُكِنُّ صُدُورُهُمۡ وَمَا يُعۡلِنُونَ ۝ وَهُوَ ٱللَّهُ لَآ إِلَـٰهَ إِلَّا هُوَ ۖ لَهُ ٱلۡحَمۡدُ فِى ٱلۡأُولَىٰ وَٱلۡـَٔاخِرَةِ ۖ وَلَهُ ٱلۡحُكۡمُ وَإِلَيۡهِ تُرۡجَعُونَ ۝

Whatever you have been granted are merely the joys of this present life and its adornments, but what is with Allah is better and more lasting. Will you not understand? Is he to whom We made a wonderful promise, which he will surely attain, the equal of one whom We allowed to savour the joys of this present life and then, on the Day of Resurrection, is among those summoned to judgement? A Day shall come when He shall call out to them and say: 'Where are My associates whom you falsely avowed?' Said they upon whom sentence was justly pronounced: 'Our Lord, here are the ones whom we tempted to unbelief. We tempted them as we too were tempted. We beg Your forgiveness. It was not us they worshipped.' It was said: 'Summon your partners.' They summoned them but they did not answer their call. And then they caught sight of the torment! If only they had followed the path of guidance! A Day shall come when He shall call out to them and say: 'What answer did you give to the messengers?' All discourse shall be indistinct to them that Day, and they cannot question one another. But he who repents, has faith and does a good deed might perhaps be among the prosperous. It is your Lord Who creates what He wills, and it is He Who chooses – the choice is not theirs. Glory be to Allah! High be He exalted above that they associate! Your Lord knows what their breasts conceal and what they openly declare. He is Allah: there is no Allah but He. To Him be praise in this life and the hereafter! To Him is the final judgment. To Him you shall be returned.

60-70 Our life on earth is a mere preparation for the soul to return to the higher zone of consciousness from which it emanated. Nothing material or emotional is enough to content a human being on the brief journey on earth. Every one of us seeks endless goodness and benefits. Our real contentment and happiness lie in the knowledge of and regular calibration with the divine light of the soul within. Earthly distractions and deviations may on rare occasions bring us more forcefully to the straight path of containment and commitment, but more often mislead us towards darkness and loss. It is not unusual for most human beings to experience the tricky nature of the lower self and ego and its deceptions resulting from short-lived worldly pleasures, which are often accompanied by pain. Seeking visible goodness and wellbeing provides an early step towards entering the zone of perpetual goodness and ultimately permanent joy, due to experiencing the presence of the divine light within.

Spiritual wisdom leads us to recognise that all our desirable earthly experiences are transitory samples of life in paradise. We are offered the illusion of choice and the ability to act. This illusion is a divine mercy that can lead whoever believes in it towards realising that Allah is the only doer.

All the ups and downs that we experience in this world are small samples and metaphors of what happens in a broader sense in the universe. Finally, we realise that all of these movements, changes, and values are within a very narrow band of consciousness, which is defined by space and time on earth. Consciousness itself is vast and emanates from cosmic consciousness, which is boundless and gradually ends up where we are now. As such, we need to respond to the ups and downs of day-to-day existence with perspective and move on to the consciousness that is ever constant, ever eternal, and already transmitted by the light within our own heart.

71-77 قُلْ أَرَءَيْتُمْ إِن جَعَلَ ٱللَّهُ عَلَيْكُمُ ٱلَّيْلَ سَرْمَدًا إِلَىٰ يَوْمِ ٱلْقِيَٰمَةِ مَنْ إِلَٰهٌ غَيْرُ ٱللَّهِ يَأْتِيكُم بِضِيَآءٍ أَفَلَا تَسْمَعُونَ ۝ قُلْ أَرَءَيْتُمْ إِن جَعَلَ ٱللَّهُ عَلَيْكُمُ ٱلنَّهَارَ سَرْمَدًا إِلَىٰ يَوْمِ ٱلْقِيَٰمَةِ مَنْ إِلَٰهٌ غَيْرُ ٱللَّهِ يَأْتِيكُم بِلَيْلٍ تَسْكُنُونَ فِيهِ أَفَلَا تُبْصِرُونَ ۝ وَمِن رَّحْمَتِهِۦ جَعَلَ لَكُمُ ٱلَّيْلَ وَٱلنَّهَارَ لِتَسْكُنُوا۟ فِيهِ وَلِتَبْتَغُوا۟ مِن فَضْلِهِۦ وَلَعَلَّكُمْ تَشْكُرُونَ ۝ وَيَوْمَ يُنَادِيهِمْ فَيَقُولُ أَيْنَ شُرَكَآءِىَ ٱلَّذِينَ كُنتُمْ تَزْعُمُونَ ۝ وَنَزَعْنَا مِن كُلِّ أُمَّةٍ شَهِيدًا فَقُلْنَا هَاتُوا۟ بُرْهَٰنَكُمْ فَعَلِمُوٓا۟ أَنَّ ٱلْحَقَّ لِلَّهِ وَضَلَّ عَنْهُم مَّا كَانُوا۟ يَفْتَرُونَ ۝ إِنَّ قَٰرُونَ كَانَ مِن قَوْمِ مُوسَىٰ فَبَغَىٰ عَلَيْهِمْ وَءَاتَيْنَٰهُ مِنَ ٱلْكُنُوزِ مَآ إِنَّ مَفَاتِحَهُۥ لَتَنُوٓأُ بِٱلْعُصْبَةِ أُو۟لِى ٱلْقُوَّةِ إِذْ قَالَ لَهُۥ قَوْمُهُۥ لَا تَفْرَحْ إِنَّ ٱللَّهَ لَا يُحِبُّ ٱلْفَرِحِينَ ۝ وَٱبْتَغِ فِيمَآ ءَاتَىٰكَ ٱللَّهُ ٱلدَّارَ ٱلْءَاخِرَةَ وَلَا تَنسَ نَصِيبَكَ مِنَ ٱلدُّنْيَا وَأَحْسِن كَمَآ أَحْسَنَ ٱللَّهُ إِلَيْكَ وَلَا تَبْغِ ٱلْفَسَادَ فِى ٱلْأَرْضِ إِنَّ ٱللَّهَ لَا يُحِبُّ ٱلْمُفْسِدِينَ ۝

Say: 'Consider. Had Allah made the night descend upon you without cease, and up to the Day of Resurrection, which Allah other than Allah can bring you light? Can you not hear?' Say: 'Consider. Had Allah made the day shine upon you without cease, and up to the Day of Resurrection, which Allah other than Allah can bring you the night in which you may find rest? Can you not see?' It is a mercy from Him that He created for you the night and the day, in which you may find rest or seek His bounty; perhaps you will give thanks. Upon the day when He shall call to them, and He shall say, 'Where now are My associates whom you were asserting?' And We shall draw out from every nation a witness, and say, 'Produce your proof!' Then will they know that Truth is Allah's, and there shall go astray from them that they were forging. Qarun was one of Moses' people, but he oppressed them. We had given him such treasures that even their keys would have weighed down a whole company of strong men. His people said to him, 'Do not gloat, for Allah does not like people who gloat, but seek, amidst that which Allah has given you, the Last Abode, and forget not your portion of the present world; and do good, as Allah has been good to you. And seek not to work corruption in the earth; surely Allah loves not the workers of corruption.'

71-77 All the changes we experience on earth are samples and metaphors that emanate from the permanent zone of *Truth* itself and reflects that reality. No two minutes in our daily life are ever experienced in the same way, yet each moment is the same as any other. We experience speed and change in time itself, which can only be possible due to the timelessness of our soul, the source of all experiences. We are always challenged by polarity, duality, and plurality, which can only be resolved with reference to the ever-present unity in our own heart. All our senses and the intricate physical, mental, and nervous connections have emanated from the seamless *Oneness* Itself. To accept and honour our human limitations is an expression of gratitude and an acknowledgment of the soul's limitlessness. In the Abrahamic traditions the human soul is regarded as God's shadow on earth. Our life on earth is a preparation for the perpetual hereafter.

All of life's experiences are based on numerous levels of vibrations, which are received by different receptors and minds. Responses to these experiences take place to ensure a hierarchy of needs. The first of these is to survive and continuously experience life.

Our life on earth is based on constant, often recurring, cycles of change. All of these cycles show us that within space and time, much is repeated with only a slight variation in intensity, colour, or flavour. This demonstrates how from pure energy all kinds of matter and events occur and return to the original nothingness.

78-85 قَالَ إِنَّمَآ أُوتِيتُهُۥ عَلَىٰ عِلْمٍ عِندِىٓ أَوَلَمْ يَعْلَمْ أَنَّ ٱللَّهَ قَدْ أَهْلَكَ مِن قَبْلِهِۦ مِنَ ٱلْقُرُونِ مَنْ هُوَ أَشَدُّ مِنْهُ قُوَّةً وَأَكْثَرُ جَمْعًا وَلَا يُسْـَٔلُ عَن ذُنُوبِهِمُ ٱلْمُجْرِمُونَ ۝ فَخَرَجَ عَلَىٰ قَوْمِهِۦ فِى زِينَتِهِۦ قَالَ ٱلَّذِينَ يُرِيدُونَ ٱلْحَيَوٰةَ ٱلدُّنْيَا يَٰلَيْتَ لَنَا مِثْلَ مَآ أُوتِىَ قَٰرُونُ إِنَّهُۥ لَذُو حَظٍّ عَظِيمٍ ۝ وَقَالَ ٱلَّذِينَ أُوتُوا۟ ٱلْعِلْمَ وَيْلَكُمْ ثَوَابُ ٱللَّهِ خَيْرٌ لِّمَنْ ءَامَنَ وَعَمِلَ صَٰلِحًا وَلَا يُلَقَّىٰهَآ إِلَّا ٱلصَّٰبِرُونَ ۝ فَخَسَفْنَا بِهِۦ وَبِدَارِهِ ٱلْأَرْضَ فَمَا كَانَ لَهُۥ مِن فِئَةٍ يَنصُرُونَهُۥ مِن دُونِ ٱللَّهِ وَمَا كَانَ مِنَ ٱلْمُنتَصِرِينَ ۝ وَأَصْبَحَ ٱلَّذِينَ

تَمَنَّوْا۟ مَكَانَهُۥ بِٱلْأَمْسِ يَقُولُونَ وَيْكَأَنَّ ٱللَّهَ يَبْسُطُ ٱلرِّزْقَ لِمَن يَشَآءُ مِنْ عِبَادِهِۦ وَيَقْدِرُ ۖ لَوْلَآ أَن مَّنَّ ٱللَّهُ عَلَيْنَا لَخَسَفَ بِنَا ۖ وَيْكَأَنَّهُۥ لَا يُفْلِحُ ٱلْكَٰفِرُونَ ۝ تِلْكَ ٱلدَّارُ ٱلْءَاخِرَةُ نَجْعَلُهَا لِلَّذِينَ لَا يُرِيدُونَ عُلُوًّا فِى ٱلْأَرْضِ وَلَا فَسَادًا ۚ وَٱلْعَٰقِبَةُ لِلْمُتَّقِينَ ۝ مَن جَآءَ بِٱلْحَسَنَةِ فَلَهُۥ خَيْرٌ مِّنْهَا ۖ وَمَن جَآءَ بِٱلسَّيِّئَةِ فَلَا يُجْزَى ٱلَّذِينَ عَمِلُوا۟ ٱلسَّيِّـَٔاتِ إِلَّا مَا كَانُوا۟ يَعْمَلُونَ ۝ إِنَّ ٱلَّذِى فَرَضَ عَلَيْكَ ٱلْقُرْءَانَ لَرَآدُّكَ إِلَىٰ مَعَادٍ ۚ قُل رَّبِّىٓ أَعْلَمُ مَن جَآءَ بِٱلْهُدَىٰ وَمَنْ هُوَ فِى ضَلَٰلٍ مُّبِينٍ ۝

He said: 'I was granted all this because of a knowledge I possessed.' Is that so? Did he not know that Allah destroyed many generations before him, men more powerful than he, more heaped with wealth? But the guilty shall not be questioned about their misdeeds. So, he came out to his people in all his finery. Said those who preferred this present life: 'If only we possessed what Korah was granted! He is assuredly a man of immense good fortune.' Those granted knowledge said: 'You wretches! Allah's reward is better for one who believes and does good deeds. Only the steadfast shall encounter it.' Then We caused the earth to cave in upon him and his house, and no group came to his rescue, apart from Allah, nor was he among those who won through. And those who, the day before, had coveted his position, rose up and said: 'Alas for us! It is Allah Who spreads forth His bounty to whom He wills among His servants, and He Who holds it back. Had Allah not shown us His favor, He would have caused the earth to cave in beneath us.' Alas! The unbelievers shall not win through. There stands the Abode of the Hereafter, which We have assigned to those who do not seek exaltation on earth, nor corruption. The final outcome belongs to the pious. Whoso comes forth with a good deed shall obtain one better than it. Whoso comes forth with an evil deed, the evildoers shall be recompensed only in accordance with what they committed. He Who ordained the Qur'an upon you shall bring you back to the place of origin. Say: 'My Lord knows best who brings guidance and who is in manifest error.'

78-85 Whatever knowledge we have comes to us through higher consciousness and the *Source* of life itself. Our natural childish drive for earthly power, wealth, and control provides only a glimpse of the colour of the mighty knower and controller of it all. To be absorbed and in constant reference to our soul and its cosmic origin, we must enter the energy field that carries the divine will. Reflecting upon the infinite and the unseen enables us to deal with what we experience of the finite and visible world without being overwhelmed. If we believe that the soul has emerged from sacred vastness and will return to it, we can witness the beautiful zones of consciousness that will encourage us along the way. *Truth* and *Reality* are beyond any measure of comprehension, and this truth will be realised when followed sincerely with trust and good expectations. Goodness begets goodness, and a wrong deed will equally be balanced by its equivalent.

Our short life on earth is like a practice school to improve our intentions and actions, producing goodness that endures and helps others. Any goodness will bring upon its doer tenfold more benefit, and any wrong action will be met by its equivalent. We love boundless wealth and provision. The nature of our own soul is that it is secure in the infinity and eternity of goodness.

Whoever acts with the illusion that he or she is in charge will only experience shocks and disappointments in order to come to the point of humbleness. They need to focus on what is coming to them in destiny rather than what they are carving of destiny for themselves. No doubt there are certain matters we can bring about, but much of what is of value and concern to us is not in our hands. It is the culmination of numerous forces and factors that bring about this moment now, along with our fear, anxiety, contentment, or lack thereof.

86-88 وَمَا كُنتَ تَرْجُوٓاْ أَن يُلْقَىٰٓ إِلَيْكَ ٱلْكِتَٰبُ إِلَّا رَحْمَةً مِّن رَّبِّكَ فَلَا تَكُونَنَّ ظَهِيرًا لِّلْكَٰفِرِينَ ۝ وَلَا يَصُدُّنَّكَ عَنْ ءَايَٰتِ ٱللَّهِ بَعْدَ إِذْ أُنزِلَتْ إِلَيْكَ وَٱدْعُ إِلَىٰ رَبِّكَ وَلَا تَكُونَنَّ مِنَ ٱلْمُشْرِكِينَ ۝ وَلَا تَدْعُ مَعَ ٱللَّهِ إِلَٰهًا ءَاخَرَ لَآ إِلَٰهَ إِلَّا هُوَ كُلُّ شَىْءٍ هَالِكٌ إِلَّا وَجْهَهُۥ لَهُ ٱلْحُكْمُ وَإِلَيْهِ تُرْجَعُونَ ۝

You had not expected the Book to be delivered to you, were it not for a mercy from your Lord. So do not give aid to the disbelievers. Let them not distract you from the signs of Allah, now that they have been sent down upon you. And call to the way of your Lord and be not among those who associate others with Him. And call not upon another Allah with Allah; there is no Allah but He. All things perish, except His Face. His is the Judgment, and unto Him you shall be returned.

86-88 The prophetic advice is to not be affected or afflicted by those who are at a loss and have no faith or trust in the purpose and direction of human life on earth. Those on the prophetic path always have good expectations from the Creator of it all, even though on occasion they are perplexed and may suffer. Through patience, trust, and insight, our ups and downs will constantly point towards awakening to the perpetual divine presence. With regular practice of prayers, supplications, reflections, and meditations we may view existence through the lens of *Oneness*, and this is the key to enlightenment and awakening. In truth, there is only God's light and power; nothing exists in the universe unless it is within that governance and control. In order to give in to that truth fully, you need to have had experience and understanding of it, so that it does not become a sacrifice. In fact, you celebrate by acknowledging its supremacy.

Progressing along the spiritual path has many pitfalls and dangers that accompany it, which include spiritual arrogance and complacency. Our journey on earth is fraught with dangers and pitfalls, and the higher we progress along the path, the more dangerous and fatal they become.

Ultimate success, well-being, and goodness are based initially on faith, trust, and belief and later on through direct knowledge that God is in charge of everything. God occasionally gives us a bit of a role to play, and if we perform it with sincerity, honesty, and humility, then we do not suffer from it. Otherwise, any illusion that I am in charge, or that I can dictate to others how they have to be, will only bring individual and collective disappointment and misery.

11. Surah 29 Al-'Ankabut (The Spider)

Truth is everlasting, beyond the limitations of time and space. We are constantly challenged with situations that we can only understand by transcending the temporary and the limited. Truth permeates the entire universe to different degrees of clarity – the pure light or only a spark.

بِسْمِ اللَّهِ الرَّحْمَٰنِ الرَّحِيمِ

الٓمٓ ۝ أَحَسِبَ ٱلنَّاسُ أَن يُتْرَكُوٓا۟ أَن يَقُولُوٓا۟ ءَامَنَّا وَهُمْ لَا يُفْتَنُونَ ۝ وَلَقَدْ فَتَنَّا ١-٩
ٱلَّذِينَ مِن قَبْلِهِمْ ۖ فَلَيَعْلَمَنَّ ٱللَّهُ ٱلَّذِينَ صَدَقُوا۟ وَلَيَعْلَمَنَّ ٱلْكَٰذِبِينَ ۝ أَمْ حَسِبَ
ٱلَّذِينَ يَعْمَلُونَ ٱلسَّيِّـَٔاتِ أَن يَسْبِقُونَا ۚ سَآءَ مَا يَحْكُمُونَ ۝ مَن كَانَ يَرْجُوا۟ لِقَآءَ
ٱللَّهِ فَإِنَّ أَجَلَ ٱللَّهِ لَءَاتٍ ۚ وَهُوَ ٱلسَّمِيعُ ٱلْعَلِيمُ ۝ وَمَن جَٰهَدَ فَإِنَّمَا يُجَٰهِدُ لِنَفْسِهِۦٓ ۚ
إِنَّ ٱللَّهَ لَغَنِىٌّ عَنِ ٱلْعَٰلَمِينَ ۝ وَٱلَّذِينَ ءَامَنُوا۟ وَعَمِلُوا۟ ٱلصَّٰلِحَٰتِ لَنُكَفِّرَنَّ عَنْهُمْ
سَيِّـَٔاتِهِمْ وَلَنَجْزِيَنَّهُمْ أَحْسَنَ ٱلَّذِى كَانُوا۟ يَعْمَلُونَ ۝ وَوَصَّيْنَا ٱلْإِنسَٰنَ بِوَٰلِدَيْهِ
حُسْنًا ۖ وَإِن جَٰهَدَاكَ لِتُشْرِكَ بِى مَا لَيْسَ لَكَ بِهِۦ عِلْمٌ فَلَا تُطِعْهُمَآ ۚ إِلَىَّ مَرْجِعُكُمْ
فَأُنَبِّئُكُم بِمَا كُنتُمْ تَعْمَلُونَ ۝ وَٱلَّذِينَ ءَامَنُوا۟ وَعَمِلُوا۟ ٱلصَّٰلِحَٰتِ لَنُدْخِلَنَّهُمْ فِى
ٱلصَّٰلِحِينَ ۝

In the name of Allah, the Merciful to all, the Compassionate to each!

Alif Lam Mim. Do people imagine they will be left to say 'We believe', and are not put to the test? We put to the test those who came before them, that Allah may know who were sincere and who were lying. Do the evildoers think they can escape us? How ill they judge! Whoso desires the encounter with Allah, Allah's final destiny shall arrive. He is All-Hearing, All-Knowing. Who so exerts himself does so for his own benefit. And Allah has no need of the worlds. And those who believe, and do righteous deeds, We shall surely acquit them of their evil deeds, and shall recompense them the best of what they were doing. And We have enjoined on man goodness to his parents, and if they contend with you that you should associate others with Me, of which you have no knowledge, do not obey them, to Me is your return, so I will inform you of what you did. And those who believe and perform righteous deeds, these We shall admit among the virtuous.

1-9 No human being is excluded from the divine mercy of being encouraged, challenged, and helped to rise in consciousness in order to overcome natural difficulties and obstacles. Our earthly consciousness is contained within space and time; it is relative and limited. We can only be secure and content when we access higher consciousness and realise that our earthly conditioned state is only an aspect of higher consciousness. It is through striving, hoping, and praying, through faith and trust in God, that we can save ourselves from the lower self. Trust and faith in our awakening are the foundation upon which we can build good intentions, selfless actions, kindness, and generosity to everyone, including enemies, until we realise that God's grace and mercy is upon all unconditionally.

Allah's mercy is so immense that everything in existence is within its governance and grace. Our earthly journey is for us to practice fine tuning our orientation towards the cosmic light and to do our best in resonating with it, until we lose the darkness of the ego. The ultimate good actions are to transcend the illusion of separation from the cosmic light.

The human drive is towards higher intelligence, from the darkness of nothingness towards the shining light of the permanency of the divine presence. How can we ever think that this amazing story is not part of a perfect pattern and design? It is through faith and trust that benefit will increase to us until we arrive to the zone of the *Presence* of life itself. To get to this point, we need to do our best with what is in front of us with total honesty, love, and courage.

10-18 وَمِنَ ٱلنَّاسِ مَن يَقُولُ ءَامَنَّا بِٱللَّهِ فَإِذَآ أُوذِىَ فِى ٱللَّهِ جَعَلَ فِتْنَةَ ٱلنَّاسِ كَعَذَابِ ٱللَّهِ وَلَئِن جَآءَ نَصْرٌ مِّن رَّبِّكَ لَيَقُولُنَّ إِنَّا كُنَّا مَعَكُمْ أَوَلَيْسَ ٱللَّهُ بِأَعْلَمَ بِمَا فِى صُدُورِ ٱلْعَٰلَمِينَ ۝ وَلَيَعْلَمَنَّ ٱللَّهُ ٱلَّذِينَ ءَامَنُوا۟ وَلَيَعْلَمَنَّ ٱلْمُنَٰفِقِينَ ۝ وَقَالَ ٱلَّذِينَ كَفَرُوا۟ لِلَّذِينَ ءَامَنُوا۟ ٱتَّبِعُوا۟ سَبِيلَنَا وَلْنَحْمِلْ خَطَٰيَٰكُمْ وَمَا هُم بِحَٰمِلِينَ مِنْ خَطَٰيَٰهُم مِّن شَىْءٍ إِنَّهُمْ لَكَٰذِبُونَ ۝ وَلَيَحْمِلُنَّ أَثْقَالَهُمْ وَأَثْقَالًا مَّعَ أَثْقَالِهِمْ وَلَيُسْـَٔلُنَّ يَوْمَ ٱلْقِيَٰمَةِ عَمَّا كَانُوا۟ يَفْتَرُونَ ۝ وَلَقَدْ أَرْسَلْنَا نُوحًا إِلَىٰ قَوْمِهِۦ فَلَبِثَ فِيهِمْ أَلْفَ سَنَةٍ إِلَّا خَمْسِينَ عَامًا فَأَخَذَهُمُ ٱلطُّوفَانُ وَهُمْ ظَٰلِمُونَ ۝ فَأَنجَيْنَٰهُ وَأَصْحَٰبَ ٱلسَّفِينَةِ وَجَعَلْنَٰهَآ ءَايَةً لِّلْعَٰلَمِينَ ۝ وَإِبْرَٰهِيمَ إِذْ قَالَ لِقَوْمِهِ ٱعْبُدُوا۟ ٱللَّهَ وَٱتَّقُوهُ ذَٰلِكُمْ خَيْرٌ لَّكُمْ إِن كُنتُمْ تَعْلَمُونَ ۝ إِنَّمَا تَعْبُدُونَ مِن دُونِ ٱللَّهِ أَوْثَٰنًا وَتَخْلُقُونَ إِفْكًا إِنَّ ٱلَّذِينَ تَعْبُدُونَ مِن دُونِ ٱللَّهِ لَا يَمْلِكُونَ لَكُمْ رِزْقًا فَٱبْتَغُوا۟ عِندَ ٱللَّهِ ٱلرِّزْقَ وَٱعْبُدُوهُ وَٱشْكُرُوا۟ لَهُۥٓ إِلَيْهِ تُرْجَعُونَ ۝ وَإِن تُكَذِّبُوا۟ فَقَدْ كَذَّبَ أُمَمٌ مِّن قَبْلِكُمْ وَمَا عَلَى ٱلرَّسُولِ إِلَّا ٱلْبَلَٰغُ ٱلْمُبِينُ ۝

There are people who say: 'We believe in Allah.' If he meets harm in the cause of Allah, he considers harm done by other people as the equal of Allah's punishment. However, a victory comes from Allah, he would say: 'We were always on your side.' Does not Allah know best what lies in the breasts of mankind? Allah shall surely know those who truly believe and those who are hypocrites. The unbelievers say to the believers, 'Follow our path, and let us carry your offences;' yet they cannot carry anything, even of their own offences; they are truly liars. They shall certainly carry their loads, and other loads along with their loads, and upon the Day of Resurrection they shall surely be questioned concerning that they were forging. We sent Noah to his people, and he remained among them for a thousand years, less fifty. And the Deluge swept them away, being wicked. Yet We delivered him, and those who were in the ship, and appointed it for a sign unto all beings. And Abraham, when he said unto his people: 'Worship Allah, and be conscious of Him: this is the best for you, if you but knew it! It is mere idols you worship, instead of Allah, thereby engendering falsehood. Those you worship, instead of Allah, cannot provide you with livelihood; so, seek your livelihood with Allah Worship Him and give thanks to Him, for to Him you shall return. If you deny the truth, other nations before you also denied it. The Messenger is bound only to deliver the message with total clarity.'

10-18 We need to cultivate the habit of personal reflection in order to rise in consciousness and realise that the essence of higher consciousness is within our own heart. With deep reflection we can discern the extent of our own sincerity, as well as our personal station, with regards to consciousness itself. The last few thousand years saw an immensely rapid rise in human awareness and realisation of *Truth*. During this period, thousands of enlightened beings have emerged to help numerous different cultures and peoples. Individual denial and suspicion, as well as collective dismissal of the message of *Truth*, are the natural state of the lower self and ego. Our life on earth is balanced between truth and falsehood, acceptance and rejection, the animal self and the divine soul. It is through personal choice and commitment that we begin to realise the ever-present perfection of everything, including what appears as imperfect. Real prophets realised this truth and preached it.

Allah is the source and origin of anything that occurs in existence, but human beings are also given some limited authority to act and read the results of their actions. Growth in consciousness and goodness can only occur by regular reference to Allah's will and learning what is acceptable to providence and what is not.

We experience life within space and time as the duration between our birth and death. During this period, we need to tune ourselves to that which is timeless, which will be the only experience available after death. We are here undergoing a practice that will benefit us after death whilst also very helpful and useful while alive on earth.

11. Surah 29 Al-'Ankabut (The Spider)

19-27

أَوَلَمْ يَرَوْاْ كَيْفَ يُبْدِئُ ٱللَّهُ ٱلْخَلْقَ ثُمَّ يُعِيدُهُۥٓ إِنَّ ذَٰلِكَ عَلَى ٱللَّهِ يَسِيرٌ ۝ قُلْ سِيرُواْ فِى ٱلْأَرْضِ فَٱنظُرُواْ كَيْفَ بَدَأَ ٱلْخَلْقَ ثُمَّ ٱللَّهُ يُنشِئُ ٱلنَّشْأَةَ ٱلْأَخِرَةَ إِنَّ ٱللَّهَ عَلَىٰ كُلِّ شَىْءٍ قَدِيرٌ ۝ يُعَذِّبُ مَن يَشَآءُ وَيَرْحَمُ مَن يَشَآءُ وَإِلَيْهِ تُقْلَبُونَ ۝ وَمَآ أَنتُم بِمُعْجِزِينَ فِى ٱلْأَرْضِ وَلَا فِى ٱلسَّمَآءِ وَمَا لَكُم مِّن دُونِ ٱللَّهِ مِن وَلِىٍّ وَلَا نَصِيرٍ ۝ وَٱلَّذِينَ كَفَرُواْ بِـَٔايَٰتِ ٱللَّهِ وَلِقَآئِهِۦٓ أُوْلَٰٓئِكَ يَئِسُواْ مِن رَّحْمَتِى وَأُوْلَٰٓئِكَ لَهُمْ عَذَابٌ أَلِيمٌ ۝ فَمَا كَانَ جَوَابَ قَوْمِهِۦٓ إِلَّآ أَن قَالُواْ ٱقْتُلُوهُ أَوْ حَرِّقُوهُ فَأَنجَىٰهُ ٱللَّهُ مِنَ ٱلنَّارِ إِنَّ فِى ذَٰلِكَ لَءَايَٰتٍ لِّقَوْمٍ يُؤْمِنُونَ ۝ وَقَالَ إِنَّمَا ٱتَّخَذْتُم مِّن دُونِ ٱللَّهِ أَوْثَٰنًا مَّوَدَّةَ بَيْنِكُمْ فِى ٱلْحَيَوٰةِ ٱلدُّنْيَا ثُمَّ يَوْمَ ٱلْقِيَٰمَةِ يَكْفُرُ بَعْضُكُم بِبَعْضٍ وَيَلْعَنُ بَعْضُكُم بَعْضًا وَمَأْوَىٰكُمُ ٱلنَّارُ وَمَا لَكُم مِّن نَّٰصِرِينَ ۝ فَـَٔامَنَ لَهُۥ لُوطٌ وَقَالَ إِنِّى مُهَاجِرٌ إِلَىٰ رَبِّىٓ إِنَّهُۥ هُوَ ٱلْعَزِيزُ ٱلْحَكِيمُ ۝ وَوَهَبْنَا لَهُۥٓ إِسْحَٰقَ وَيَعْقُوبَ وَجَعَلْنَا فِى ذُرِّيَّتِهِ ٱلنُّبُوَّةَ وَٱلْكِتَٰبَ وَءَاتَيْنَٰهُ أَجْرَهُۥ فِى ٱلدُّنْيَا وَإِنَّهُۥ فِى ٱلْأَخِرَةِ لَمِنَ ٱلصَّٰلِحِينَ ۝

Have they not observed how Allah originates creation and then revives it? Such is an easy matter for Allah. Say: 'Journey in the land and observe how He began His creation, and how Allah then brings into being the life hereafter. Allah has power over all things, chastising whom He will, and having mercy on whomsoever He will, and unto Him you shall be turned. Nor can you escape His power, on earth or in heaven. Apart from Allah, you have no protector, no champion.' Those who deny Allah's signs and the encounter with Him – these have despaired of My mercy, and there waits them a painful torment. No answer did his people give but to say: 'Kill him, or burn him!' But Allah delivered him from the fire. In this are signs for a people who believe. He said: 'You took up the worship of idols, instead of Allah, only to please one another in this present life. However, on the Day of Resurrection, you shall charge one another with unbelief, and shall curse one another, and your refuge shall be the Fire. None shall come to your aid.' Lot believed him; and he said, 'I will flee to my Lord; He is the All-Mighty, the All-Wise.' We bestowed on him Isaac and Jacob, and made prophecy and the Book descend in his progeny, and granted him his reward in this life while in the hereafter he shall be among the righteous.

19-27 All our experiences on earth follow patterns and cycles within conditioned consciousness. Our physical world appears to be real, but in terms of space and time, it is in flux and change. Therefore, delusion regarding this so-called reality can only lead to disappointment and failure. When we go beyond the form of the event itself, we can understand the meaning and the values that occurred before, during, and after the event. It is with sincere application of our senses and intellect, with trust in divine guidance at a higher level than our earthly reality, that we experience the amazing truth of the seamless connection between the infinite and the finite. An intelligent person is always looking for the ways and means to be saved from the regular self-inflicted disasters and darkness that often engulf us. Noah's ark is always at hand; this is the light of the soul itself. If you hang onto it, all is saved.

Our ability to travel and experience different lands and cultures is a great gift for us to see outer differences, covering original sameness in hope and expectations. We all seek a better life and the best life is to acquire a state within your heart that is eternal and infinite.

Intelligent reflection will lead us to have trust and faith in life after death, as well as the truth that our earthly life is only a preparation for us to be ready for a much higher consciousness. Awakened beings focus more on the life to come than being preoccupied with transitory life on earth. The present moment is eternal if one excludes distractions.

28-36 وَلُوطًا إِذْ قَالَ لِقَوْمِهِ إِنَّكُمْ لَتَأْتُونَ ٱلْفَٰحِشَةَ مَا سَبَقَكُم بِهَا مِنْ أَحَدٍ مِّنَ ٱلْعَٰلَمِينَ ۝ أَئِنَّكُمْ لَتَأْتُونَ ٱلرِّجَالَ وَتَقْطَعُونَ ٱلسَّبِيلَ وَتَأْتُونَ فِى نَادِيكُمُ ٱلْمُنكَرَ فَمَا كَانَ جَوَابَ قَوْمِهِ إِلَّآ أَن قَالُوا۟ ٱئْتِنَا بِعَذَابِ ٱللَّهِ إِن كُنتَ مِنَ ٱلصَّٰدِقِينَ ۝ قَالَ رَبِّ ٱنصُرْنِى عَلَى ٱلْقَوْمِ ٱلْمُفْسِدِينَ ۝ وَلَمَّا جَآءَتْ رُسُلُنَآ إِبْرَٰهِيمَ بِٱلْبُشْرَىٰ قَالُوٓا۟ إِنَّا مُهْلِكُوٓا۟ أَهْلِ هَٰذِهِ ٱلْقَرْيَةِ إِنَّ أَهْلَهَا كَانُوا۟ ظَٰلِمِينَ ۝ قَالَ إِنَّ فِيهَا لُوطًا قَالُوا۟ نَحْنُ أَعْلَمُ بِمَن فِيهَا لَنُنَجِّيَنَّهُۥ وَأَهْلَهُۥٓ إِلَّا ٱمْرَأَتَهُۥ كَانَتْ مِنَ ٱلْغَٰبِرِينَ ۝ وَلَمَّآ أَن جَآءَتْ رُسُلُنَا لُوطًا سِىٓءَ بِهِمْ وَضَاقَ بِهِمْ ذَرْعًا وَقَالُوا۟ لَا تَخَفْ وَلَا تَحْزَنْ إِنَّا مُنَجُّوكَ وَأَهْلَكَ إِلَّا ٱمْرَأَتَكَ كَانَتْ مِنَ ٱلْغَٰبِرِينَ ۝ إِنَّا مُنزِلُونَ عَلَىٰٓ أَهْلِ هَٰذِهِ ٱلْقَرْيَةِ رِجْزًا مِّنَ ٱلسَّمَآءِ بِمَا كَانُوا۟ يَفْسُقُونَ ۝ وَلَقَد تَّرَكْنَا مِنْهَآ ءَايَةًۢ بَيِّنَةً لِّقَوْمٍ يَعْقِلُونَ ۝ وَإِلَىٰ مَدْيَنَ أَخَاهُمْ شُعَيْبًا فَقَالَ يَٰقَوْمِ ٱعْبُدُوا۟ ٱللَّهَ وَٱرْجُوا۟ ٱلْيَوْمَ ٱلْءَاخِرَ وَلَا تَعْثَوْا۟ فِى ٱلْأَرْضِ مُفْسِدِينَ ۝

And Lot, when he said to his people 'Surely you commit such indecency as never any being in all the world committed before you. What, do you approach men, and cut the way, and commit in your assembly dishonour?' But the only answer of his people was that they said, 'Then bring us the chastisement of Allah, if you speak truly.' He said: 'My Lord, help me against a people who work corruption.' When Our heralds brought Abraham the good news, they said: 'We are about to destroy the inhabitants of this town, for its people are wicked.' He said: 'But Lot lives there.' They said: 'We know best who lives therein. We shall deliver him and his family, all but his wife, who shall remain behind.' When Our heralds came to Lot, he was distressed and grew impatient with them. They said: 'Fear not, and do not grieve. We are about to save you and your family, except for your wife who shall remain behind. We are about to send down on the inhabitants of this town a terrible torment from heaven because of their depravity.' We left behind a clear trace of it to a people who understand. To Midian was sent their fellow tribes-man, Shu'ayb. He said: 'My people, worship Allah and keep the Last Day in view, and do not work corruption on earth.'

28-36 The stories of prophets and messengers in the past are not just historical events that have no direct impact in our own lives today. If we approach them with sincere humility, we will find that they repeat themselves very clearly in today's world. A regular feature of these stories is that before the destruction of a people or empire, clear warnings and events give indications of the impending disaster. However, since we love continuity, we lose sight of the situation we are in, unless we step outside of it to see the forest instead of the trees. The heavens and earth are seamlessly ever-connected, and so are natural events, disasters, grace, and mercy. It is not easy to discern cause and effect regarding human tragedies. On our little earth there are hundreds of signs of how great nations of the past have risen to a peak in terms of culture, power, and civilisation, then plummeted and vanished. Myths about Atlantis and Lemuria tell of such civilisations and are pointers to the future.

Numerous nations have risen to great levels of civilisation and material strength; equally quickly, they vanished. We are fortunate to have discovered many of these occurrences during the past few thousand years through archaeology and research. Our real success relates to following the light of our own heart and subduing the lower ego-self.

During the past few thousand years, we have been reminded repeatedly to be aware of our intentions and actions in order to be able to correct them. This need continues until we live the moment fully, with total accountability to the origin of the moment, which is eternal.

37-45 فَكَذَّبُوهُ فَأَخَذَتْهُمُ ٱلرَّجْفَةُ فَأَصْبَحُوا۟ فِى دَارِهِمْ جَٰثِمِينَ ۝ وَعَادًا وَثَمُودَا۟ وَقَد تَّبَيَّنَ لَكُم مِّن مَّسَٰكِنِهِمْ ۖ وَزَيَّنَ لَهُمُ ٱلشَّيْطَٰنُ أَعْمَٰلَهُمْ فَصَدَّهُمْ عَنِ ٱلسَّبِيلِ وَكَانُوا۟ مُسْتَبْصِرِينَ ۝ وَقَٰرُونَ وَفِرْعَوْنَ وَهَٰمَٰنَ ۖ وَلَقَدْ جَآءَهُم مُّوسَىٰ بِٱلْبَيِّنَٰتِ فَٱسْتَكْبَرُوا۟ فِى ٱلْأَرْضِ وَمَا كَانُوا۟ سَٰبِقِينَ ۝ فَكُلًّا أَخَذْنَا بِذَنۢبِهِۦ ۖ فَمِنْهُم مَّنْ أَرْسَلْنَا عَلَيْهِ حَاصِبًا وَمِنْهُم مَّنْ أَخَذَتْهُ ٱلصَّيْحَةُ وَمِنْهُم مَّنْ خَسَفْنَا بِهِ ٱلْأَرْضَ وَمِنْهُم مَّنْ أَغْرَقْنَا ۚ وَمَا كَانَ ٱللَّهُ لِيَظْلِمَهُمْ وَلَٰكِن كَانُوٓا۟ أَنفُسَهُمْ يَظْلِمُونَ ۝ مَثَلُ ٱلَّذِينَ ٱتَّخَذُوا۟ مِن دُونِ ٱللَّهِ أَوْلِيَآءَ كَمَثَلِ ٱلْعَنكَبُوتِ ٱتَّخَذَتْ بَيْتًا ۖ وَإِنَّ أَوْهَنَ ٱلْبُيُوتِ لَبَيْتُ ٱلْعَنكَبُوتِ ۖ لَوْ كَانُوا۟ يَعْلَمُونَ ۝ إِنَّ ٱللَّهَ يَعْلَمُ مَا يَدْعُونَ مِن دُونِهِۦ مِن شَىْءٍ ۚ وَهُوَ ٱلْعَزِيزُ ٱلْحَكِيمُ ۝ وَتِلْكَ ٱلْأَمْثَٰلُ نَضْرِبُهَا لِلنَّاسِ ۖ وَمَا يَعْقِلُهَآ إِلَّا ٱلْعَٰلِمُونَ ۝ خَلَقَ ٱللَّهُ ٱلسَّمَٰوَٰتِ وَٱلْأَرْضَ بِٱلْحَقِّ ۚ إِنَّ فِى ذَٰلِكَ لَءَايَةً لِّلْمُؤْمِنِينَ ۝ ٱتْلُ مَآ أُوحِىَ إِلَيْكَ مِنَ ٱلْكِتَٰبِ وَأَقِمِ ٱلصَّلَوٰةَ ۖ إِنَّ ٱلصَّلَوٰةَ تَنْهَىٰ عَنِ ٱلْفَحْشَآءِ وَٱلْمُنكَرِ ۗ وَلَذِكْرُ ٱللَّهِ أَكْبَرُ ۗ وَٱللَّهُ يَعْلَمُ مَا تَصْنَعُونَ ۝

They called him a liar, and a great quake seized them and, on the morrow, they lay dead in their houses. So, also with 'Ad and Thamud: you can see this clearly in their habitations. Satan had made their deeds attractive in their eyes, and barred them from the right path, even though they were a discerning nation. So, also with Qarun, Pharaoh and Haman: Moses had brought them manifest signs, but they grew arrogant on earth, and could not escape torment. Each We seized for his misdeeds: upon some We sent down a fire storm; some were seized by the Scream; some We caused the earth to cave in beneath them, and some We drowned. Nor would Allah have wronged them; rather, it was themselves they wronged. The likeness of those who took to themselves patrons instead of Allah is like the spider that builds a house for itself. But surely the most fragile of houses is the spider's house, if only they knew! Allah knows what they call upon beside Him: He is the Mighty, the Wise. And those parables – We strike them for the people, but none understands them save those who know. Allah created the Heavens and earth in truth. In this is a sign to people who have faith. Recite what has been revealed to you of the Book, and perform the prayer; prayer forbids indecency and unacceptable behaviour. Allah's remembrance is greater; and Allah knows the things you work.

37-45 The natural tunnel vision that often possesses us results from the darkness of the lower self and our inner Satan. For this reason, we need regular prayers, meditation and repentance to enable us to step out of our blind spots. Our love for timelessness translates into a love of continuity, and this is where we fall into our own tsunamis. No one wrongs us except our own self, due to the ignorance of the shadow ego. We all look for security in our homes, cities, and other so-called safe havens, which are as flimsy as the web of a spider. More important than earthly safety and wellbeing is access to our spiritual light through reflections, meditation, and selfless acts done with transparency and accountability.

We all seek reliability and lasting security. Whatever we consider durable is really as flimsy as a spider's web. It is only by reliance upon the infinite Absolute that we will be able to journey on earth with delight and dignity. To live immersed in faith and to act well will always ensure safe passage.

It is natural for us to try and rely on someone, something, some power or wealth. Ultimately all reliance and dependence emanate from the *Nur* of Allah. All these intermediate loyalties become insignificant in comparison to that which is eternally there.

46-54 وَلَا تُجَٰدِلُوٓا۟ أَهْلَ ٱلْكِتَٰبِ إِلَّا بِٱلَّتِى هِىَ أَحْسَنُ إِلَّا ٱلَّذِينَ ظَلَمُوا۟ مِنْهُمْ وَقُولُوٓا۟ ءَامَنَّا بِٱلَّذِىٓ أُنزِلَ إِلَيْنَا وَأُنزِلَ إِلَيْكُمْ وَإِلَٰهُنَا وَإِلَٰهُكُمْ وَٰحِدٌ وَنَحْنُ لَهُۥ مُسْلِمُونَ ۝ وَكَذَٰلِكَ أَنزَلْنَآ إِلَيْكَ ٱلْكِتَٰبَ فَٱلَّذِينَ ءَاتَيْنَٰهُمُ ٱلْكِتَٰبَ يُؤْمِنُونَ بِهِۦ وَمِنْ هَٰٓؤُلَآءِ مَن يُؤْمِنُ بِهِۦ وَمَا يَجْحَدُ بِـَٔايَٰتِنَآ إِلَّا ٱلْكَٰفِرُونَ ۝ وَمَا كُنتَ تَتْلُوا۟ مِن قَبْلِهِۦ مِن كِتَٰبٍ وَلَا تَخُطُّهُۥ بِيَمِينِكَ إِذًا لَّٱرْتَابَ ٱلْمُبْطِلُونَ ۝ بَلْ هُوَ ءَايَٰتٌۢ بَيِّنَٰتٌ فِى صُدُورِ ٱلَّذِينَ أُوتُوا۟ ٱلْعِلْمَ وَمَا يَجْحَدُ بِـَٔايَٰتِنَآ إِلَّا ٱلظَّٰلِمُونَ ۝ وَقَالُوا۟ لَوْلَآ أُنزِلَ

عَلَيْهِ ءَايَتٌ مِّن رَّبِّهِۦ ۖ قُلْ إِنَّمَا ٱلْءَايَتُ عِندَ ٱللَّهِ وَإِنَّمَآ أَنَا۠ نَذِيرٌ مُّبِينٌ ۝ أَوَلَمْ يَكْفِهِمْ أَنَّآ أَنزَلْنَا عَلَيْكَ ٱلْكِتَبَ يُتْلَىٰ عَلَيْهِمْ ۚ إِنَّ فِى ذَٰلِكَ لَرَحْمَةً وَذِكْرَىٰ لِقَوْمٍ يُؤْمِنُونَ ۝ قُلْ كَفَىٰ بِٱللَّهِ بَيْنِى وَبَيْنَكُمْ شَهِيدًا ۖ يَعْلَمُ مَا فِى ٱلسَّمَٰوَٰتِ وَٱلْأَرْضِ ۗ وَٱلَّذِينَ ءَامَنُوا۟ بِٱلْبَٰطِلِ وَكَفَرُوا۟ بِٱللَّهِ أُو۟لَٰٓئِكَ هُمُ ٱلْخَٰسِرُونَ ۝ وَيَسْتَعْجِلُونَكَ بِٱلْعَذَابِ ۚ وَلَوْلَآ أَجَلٌ مُّسَمًّى لَّجَآءَهُمُ ٱلْعَذَابُ وَلَيَأْتِيَنَّهُم بَغْتَةً وَهُمْ لَا يَشْعُرُونَ ۝ يَسْتَعْجِلُونَكَ بِٱلْعَذَابِ وَإِنَّ جَهَنَّمَ لَمُحِيطَةٌۢ بِٱلْكَٰفِرِينَ ۝

Do not argue with the People of the Book except in the best manner, save the wicked among them, and say: 'We believe in what has been sent down upon us, and sent down upon you. Our Allah and yours is One Allah, and to Him we submit.' So too did We send down the Book upon you. Those to whom We brought the Book believe in it, as do some of them here present. None but the unbelievers repudiate Our revelations. You never recited any Book before it, nor ever wrote it down with your right hand. Otherwise, the impious would have had their doubts. Rather, it contains revelations most clear in the hearts of those granted knowledge, and none repudiates Our revelations save the wicked. They say, 'Why have signs not been sent down upon him from his Lord?' Say: 'The signs are only with Allah, and I am only a plain warner.' Was it not enough for them that We sent down the Book on you to be recited to them? In this is a mercy and a remembrance to a people who have faith. Say: 'Allah suffices as witness bet- ween you and me. He knows what is in the heavens and on earth. And those who believe in falsehood and repudiate Allah – these are truly the losers.' They ask you to hasten the torment upon them. Were it not for a stated term, the torment would have befallen them. It will indeed fall upon them suddenly, unawares. They ask you to hasten the torment upon them, but hell shall surely engulf the unbelievers.

46-54 Most world religions and scriptures have their origins with enlightened individuals who were exposed to higher levels of consciousness and awakening. In many situations the message loses its universal impact and becomes structured or exclusive to a class of priests and specialist interpretations. The light of the soul within every heart contains the sacred divine spark that will enable us to attain transformation, if we manage to leave behind the natural darkness of the self that veils this light. The essence of most world religions and paths is the same. The differences in cosmology and practice have their roots in the culture of the people of that religion. When illumination transforms a being to full enlightenment, a high potency balance takes place between the individual's humanity and the light of *Divinity* within. It is in this world, within our confinement of space and time, that we can fully awaken to the boundlessness nature of the soul within.

Thousands of prophets and enlightened beings have come to humanity speaking a language suitable for those times and cultures, but whose essence is the same. We are most fortunate to be the recipients of great strides in spiritual evolution and progress in terms of enlightenment.

The soul is ever pure, ever clear, and everlasting. It gives rise to an ever-shifting shadow, which is the ego-self that cannot be relied upon since it has no independent origin or power. For this reason, we often end up in argument, denial, or accusation. With wisdom, we reduce all these wastages and only deal with people from whom we can benefit and they benefit from us in a durable manner.

55-69

يَوْمَ يَغْشَىٰهُمُ ٱلْعَذَابُ مِن فَوْقِهِمْ وَمِن تَحْتِ أَرْجُلِهِمْ وَيَقُولُ ذُوقُوا۟ مَا كُنتُمْ تَعْمَلُونَ ۝ يَٰعِبَادِىَ ٱلَّذِينَ ءَامَنُوٓا۟ إِنَّ أَرْضِى وَٰسِعَةٌ فَإِيَّـٰىَ فَٱعْبُدُونِ ۝ كُلُّ نَفْسٍ ذَآئِقَةُ ٱلْمَوْتِ ثُمَّ إِلَيْنَا تُرْجَعُونَ ۝ وَٱلَّذِينَ ءَامَنُوا۟ وَعَمِلُوا۟ ٱلصَّـٰلِحَـٰتِ لَنُبَوِّئَنَّهُم مِّنَ ٱلْجَنَّةِ غُرَفًا تَجْرِى مِن تَحْتِهَا ٱلْأَنْهَـٰرُ خَـٰلِدِينَ فِيهَا ۚ نِعْمَ أَجْرُ ٱلْعَـٰمِلِينَ ۝ ٱلَّذِينَ صَبَرُوا۟ وَعَلَىٰ رَبِّهِمْ يَتَوَكَّلُونَ ۝ وَكَأَيِّن مِّن دَآبَّةٍ لَّا تَحْمِلُ رِزْقَهَا ٱللَّهُ يَرْزُقُهَا وَإِيَّاكُمْ ۚ وَهُوَ ٱلسَّمِيعُ ٱلْعَلِيمُ ۝ وَلَئِن سَأَلْتَهُم مَّنْ خَلَقَ ٱلسَّمَـٰوَٰتِ وَٱلْأَرْضَ وَسَخَّرَ ٱلشَّمْسَ وَٱلْقَمَرَ لَيَقُولُنَّ ٱللَّهُ ۖ فَأَنَّىٰ يُؤْفَكُونَ ۝ ٱللَّهُ يَبْسُطُ ٱلرِّزْقَ لِمَن يَشَآءُ مِنْ عِبَادِهِۦ وَيَقْدِرُ لَهُۥٓ ۚ إِنَّ ٱللَّهَ بِكُلِّ شَىْءٍ عَلِيمٌ ۝ وَلَئِن سَأَلْتَهُم مَّن نَّزَّلَ مِنَ ٱلسَّمَآءِ مَآءً فَأَحْيَا بِهِ ٱلْأَرْضَ مِنۢ بَعْدِ مَوْتِهَا لَيَقُولُنَّ ٱللَّهُ ۚ قُلِ ٱلْحَمْدُ لِلَّهِ ۚ بَلْ أَكْثَرُهُمْ لَا يَعْقِلُونَ ۝ وَمَا هَـٰذِهِ ٱلْحَيَوٰةُ ٱلدُّنْيَآ إِلَّا لَهْوٌ وَلَعِبٌ ۚ وَإِنَّ ٱلدَّارَ ٱلْـَٔاخِرَةَ لَهِىَ ٱلْحَيَوَانُ ۚ لَوْ كَانُوا۟ يَعْلَمُونَ ۝ فَإِذَا رَكِبُوا۟ فِى ٱلْفُلْكِ دَعَوُا۟ ٱللَّهَ مُخْلِصِينَ لَهُ ٱلدِّينَ فَلَمَّا نَجَّىٰهُمْ إِلَى ٱلْبَرِّ إِذَا هُمْ يُشْرِكُونَ ۝ لِيَكْفُرُوا۟ بِمَآ ءَاتَيْنَـٰهُمْ وَلِيَتَمَتَّعُوا۟ ۖ فَسَوْفَ يَعْلَمُونَ ۝ أَوَلَمْ يَرَوْا۟ أَنَّا جَعَلْنَا حَرَمًا ءَامِنًا وَيُتَخَطَّفُ ٱلنَّاسُ مِنْ حَوْلِهِمْ ۚ أَفَبِٱلْبَـٰطِلِ يُؤْمِنُونَ وَبِنِعْمَةِ ٱللَّهِ يَكْفُرُونَ ۝ وَمَنْ أَظْلَمُ مِمَّنِ ٱفْتَرَىٰ عَلَى ٱللَّهِ كَذِبًا أَوْ كَذَّبَ بِٱلْحَقِّ لَمَّا جَآءَهُۥٓ ۚ أَلَيْسَ فِى جَهَنَّمَ مَثْوًى لِّلْكَـٰفِرِينَ ۝ وَٱلَّذِينَ جَـٰهَدُوا۟ فِينَا لَنَهْدِيَنَّهُمْ سُبُلَنَا ۚ وَإِنَّ ٱللَّهَ لَمَعَ ٱلْمُحْسِنِينَ ۝

A Day shall come when the torment overshadows them from above them and from below their feet, and He shall say: 'Taste that which you used to commit!' O worshippers of Mine who believe, My earth is wide. It is Me you must worship. Every self shall taste death and then to Us you shall revert. And those who believe and do good deeds – We shall lodge them in the Garden, in lofty chambers, beneath which rivers flow, abiding therein for ever. Excellent indeed is the wage of those who do good, those who stand fast, and who put their trust in their Lord! How many a creature beast of burden there is that stores not its provisions. Rather, it is Allah Who provides for it – and for you. He is All-Hearing, All-Knowing, Omniscient. If you ask them, 'Who created the heavens and the earth and subjected the sun and the moon?' They will say, 'Allah.' How then are they perverted? Allah spreads wide His bounty to whomever He wishes among His servants, but He also withholds it. Allah has knowledge of all things. And if you ask them: 'Who brings water down from the sky and therewith revives the earth after it is dead?' They will answer: 'It is Allah.' Say: 'Thanks be to Allah!' But most of them have no understanding. This present life is nothing but frivolity and amusement. But the Abode of the Hereafter is the real life, if only they knew! And when they Embarked on a ship, they pray to Allah, sincere of faith. Once He delivers them safely to shore, behold, they ascribe partners to Him! That they may be ungrateful for what We have given them, and take their enjoyment; they will soon know! Do they not see that We established a peaceful sanctuary while all around them people are rent by violence? And yet they believe in falsehood and disown the bounty of Allah! Who is more wicked than he who fabricates lies from Allah, or calls the Truth a lie once it has come to him? Is not hell the final berth of unbelievers. But those who exerted themselves in Our cause – these We shall guide to Our ways. and Allah is assuredly with the righteous.

55-69 Our universe has come about due to the amazing interaction between matter and energy, the visible within the vast unseen. Every person's state at any moment results from a mixture of nature and nurture and past experiences with environment. These experiences are all samples of the infinite possibilities that will become clear to us in the hereafter.

To seek a better-quality life with sufficient safety and tranquillity in our day-to- day existence is necessary and meaningful if we are preparing for the hereafter by transcending the self. With wisdom, we will discover that our earthly life is only a minor preparation for the soul to soar to its higher level in the hereafter rather than being encumbered by the body and mind.

Human life on earth resembles the story of Noah and his people. We all want to be safe. We all want to be in the ark that relieves us from fear, sorrow, and suffering. For this reason, we need to constantly be aware of what we are doing – the right time, the right place, the right intention – and be able to return to the shore with safety, repentance, and admittance.

12. Surah 32 As-Sajdah (Prostration)

Birth and death are part of nature's cycles, and every living entity will experience death, which highlights the desirability of life. The last ayah of the surah before reminds us that no one knows in which land he or she will die, and the first ayah in this surah says that this knowledge is in the sublime book from the Lord of all the worlds.

بِسْمِ اللَّـهِ الرَّحْمَـٰنِ الرَّحِيمِ

1-10 الٓمٓ ۝ تَنزِيلُ ٱلْكِتَـٰبِ لَا رَيْبَ فِيهِ مِن رَّبِّ ٱلْعَـٰلَمِينَ ۝ أَمْ يَقُولُونَ ٱفْتَرَىٰهُ ۚ بَلْ هُوَ ٱلْحَقُّ مِن رَّبِّكَ لِتُنذِرَ قَوْمًا مَّآ أَتَىٰهُم مِّن نَّذِيرٍ مِّن قَبْلِكَ لَعَلَّهُمْ يَهْتَدُونَ ۝ ٱللَّـهُ ٱلَّذِى خَلَقَ ٱلسَّمَـٰوَٰتِ وَٱلْأَرْضَ وَمَا بَيْنَهُمَا فِى سِتَّةِ أَيَّامٍ ثُمَّ ٱسْتَوَىٰ عَلَى ٱلْعَرْشِ

مَا لَكُم مِّن دُونِهِۦ مِن وَلِىٍّ وَلَا شَفِيعٍ أَفَلَا تَتَذَكَّرُونَ ۝ يُدَبِّرُ ٱلْأَمْرَ مِنَ ٱلسَّمَآءِ إِلَى ٱلْأَرْضِ ثُمَّ يَعْرُجُ إِلَيْهِ فِى يَوْمٍ كَانَ مِقْدَارُهُۥٓ أَلْفَ سَنَةٍ مِّمَّا تَعُدُّونَ ۝ ذَٰلِكَ عَٰلِمُ ٱلْغَيْبِ وَٱلشَّهَٰدَةِ ٱلْعَزِيزُ ٱلرَّحِيمُ ۝ ٱلَّذِىٓ أَحْسَنَ كُلَّ شَىْءٍ خَلَقَهُۥ وَبَدَأَ خَلْقَ ٱلْإِنسَٰنِ مِن طِينٍ ۝ ثُمَّ جَعَلَ نَسْلَهُۥ مِن سُلَٰلَةٍ مِّن مَّآءٍ مَّهِينٍ ۝ ثُمَّ سَوَّىٰهُ وَنَفَخَ فِيهِ مِن رُّوحِهِۦ وَجَعَلَ لَكُمُ ٱلسَّمْعَ وَٱلْأَبْصَٰرَ وَٱلْأَفْـِٔدَةَ قَلِيلًا مَّا تَشْكُرُونَ ۝ وَقَالُوٓا۟ أَءِذَا ضَلَلْنَا فِى ٱلْأَرْضِ أَءِنَّا لَفِى خَلْقٍ جَدِيدٍ بَلْ هُم بِلِقَآءِ رَبِّهِمْ كَٰفِرُونَ ۝

In the name of Allah, the Merciful to all, the Compassionate to each!

Alif Lam Mim. The sending down of the Book, wherein no doubt is, from the Lord of all Being. Or do they say: 'He forged it?' Rather, it is the Truth from your Lord, to warn a people to whom no warner had been sent before you, that they may be guided. It is Allah who created the heavens and the earth and everything between them in six Days. Then He established Himself on the Throne. You have no one but Him to protect you and no one to intercede for you, so why do you not take heed? He governs creation from the heavens to the earth, and it ascends back to Him in one day, the length of which is a thousand years by your reckoning. Such is the Knower of the Unseen and the Seen, Almighty, Compassionate to each! Who has created all things well. And He originated the creation of man out of clay, then He fashioned his progeny of an extraction of mean water, then gave him shape and breathed into him of His spirit, then granted you hearing, eyesight and hearts – but little thanks do you give in return. They say: 'So then, once consigned to earth, are we to be created anew?' In fact, they disavow the encounter with their Lord.

1-10 Our universe was created in numerous stages and facets. Various physical, chemical, biological, and other activities took place on earth to enable life to occur in the ocean. Human consciousness is the pinnacle of the drives towards supreme consciousness on earth. Our beginning was from earth and water. Sentiency from our soul gave us our intricate senses, leading to a complex brain and numerous interconnections with the energies radiating around us. Ultimately, life emanates from our own soul, which is on a journey returning to the timeless zone after death.

The infinite varieties of this magnificent creation within the limitations of space-time all occurred as a proof of the divine mercy and honour of the soul to witness and be delighted with the possibilities that are within the Creator's domain.

Whatever we experience on earth is squeezed between the limitations of space and time, so that whatever higher lights of consciousness come through to us are part of the design for us to act as best as we can, so that light can engulf us fully. Then we cannot think, act, or do anything unless we are in reference to the eternal life within our own heart.

12. Surah 32 As-Sajdah (Prostration)

11-20

قُلْ يَتَوَفَّىٰكُم مَّلَكُ ٱلْمَوْتِ ٱلَّذِى وُكِّلَ بِكُمْ ثُمَّ إِلَىٰ رَبِّكُمْ تُرْجَعُونَ ۝ وَلَوْ تَرَىٰٓ إِذِ ٱلْمُجْرِمُونَ نَاكِسُواْ رُءُوسِهِمْ عِندَ رَبِّهِمْ رَبَّنَآ أَبْصَرْنَا وَسَمِعْنَا فَٱرْجِعْنَا نَعْمَلْ صَٰلِحًا إِنَّا مُوقِنُونَ ۝ وَلَوْ شِئْنَا لَءَاتَيْنَا كُلَّ نَفْسٍ هُدَىٰهَا وَلَٰكِنْ حَقَّ ٱلْقَوْلُ مِنِّى لَأَمْلَأَنَّ جَهَنَّمَ مِنَ ٱلْجِنَّةِ وَٱلنَّاسِ أَجْمَعِينَ ۝ فَذُوقُواْ بِمَا نَسِيتُمْ لِقَآءَ يَوْمِكُمْ هَٰذَآ إِنَّا نَسِينَٰكُمْ وَذُوقُواْ عَذَابَ ٱلْخُلْدِ بِمَا كُنتُمْ تَعْمَلُونَ ۝ إِنَّمَا يُؤْمِنُ بِـَٔايَٰتِنَا ٱلَّذِينَ إِذَا ذُكِّرُواْ بِهَا خَرُّواْ سُجَّدًا وَسَبَّحُواْ بِحَمْدِ رَبِّهِمْ وَهُمْ لَا يَسْتَكْبِرُونَ ۝ تَتَجَافَىٰ جُنُوبُهُمْ عَنِ ٱلْمَضَاجِعِ يَدْعُونَ رَبَّهُمْ خَوْفًا وَطَمَعًا وَمِمَّا رَزَقْنَٰهُمْ يُنفِقُونَ ۝ فَلَا تَعْلَمُ نَفْسٌ مَّآ أُخْفِىَ لَهُم مِّن قُرَّةِ أَعْيُنٍ جَزَآءًۢ بِمَا كَانُواْ يَعْمَلُونَ ۝ أَفَمَن كَانَ مُؤْمِنًا كَمَن كَانَ فَاسِقًا لَّا يَسْتَوُۥنَ ۝ أَمَّا ٱلَّذِينَ ءَامَنُواْ وَعَمِلُواْ ٱلصَّٰلِحَٰتِ فَلَهُمْ جَنَّٰتُ ٱلْمَأْوَىٰ نُزُلًۢا بِمَا كَانُواْ يَعْمَلُونَ ۝ وَأَمَّا ٱلَّذِينَ فَسَقُواْ فَمَأْوَىٰهُمُ ٱلنَّارُ كُلَّمَآ أَرَادُوٓاْ أَن يَخْرُجُواْ مِنْهَآ أُعِيدُواْ فِيهَا وَقِيلَ لَهُمْ ذُوقُواْ عَذَابَ ٱلنَّارِ ٱلَّذِى كُنتُم بِهِۦ تُكَذِّبُونَ ۝

Say, 'The Angel of Death put in charge of you will reclaim you, and then you will be brought back to your Lord.' And could you but see when the guilty shall hang down their heads before their Lord: 'Our Lord! We have seen and we have heard, therefore send us back, we will do good; surely, we are certain.' Yet had We so willed, We could indeed have imposed 'Our guidance upon every human being: but that word of Mine has come true: Most certainly will I fill hell with invisible beings as well as with humans, all together!' So, taste it – and since you forgot the encounter of this your Day, We have forgotten you – taste the punishment of eternity for what you have committed. They only believe in Our revelations who, when reminded of them, fall down in prostration, glorifying the praise of their Lord; nor are they too proud to do so. Their sides shun their couches as they call on their Lord in fear and hope; and they expend of that We have provided them. No self knows what lies in wait for them to comfort the eye, as a reward for what they did. Is he who was faithful to be the equal of one who was dissolute? They are indeed unequal. As for those who believed and did righteous deeds, to them belong the Gardens of Refuge as abodes, as a reward for their works. The dissolute, however, shall have the Fire as their refuge: each time they purpose to leave it, they are turned back to it, and it is said to them: 'Taste the torment of the Fire, which once you disowned.'

11-20 The earthly life for most human beings is very superficial and based on conditioned consciousness which connects our senses, mind, and value systems with the outer world in order for survival to become well-rooted. To simply be well and outwardly content is never enough for a fulfilled life. Remembrance of death is a great reminder that in truth we all seek a perpetual *Reality*, as opposed to a temporary and short life. With deep meditation and regular practice of prayers and transcendence of the limitations of our mind and senses, we realise that within us lies the map of the origin of all creation and the story of emergence and return to our origin. This sublime memory is within every soul, but it cannot be attained by mere effort. Intentions and disciplined actions are needed to drop the veil of the mind and identity. Then it is only up to God's grace if supreme consciousness touches us with the light of its infinitude. Most human beings on earth desire more time and more space, but in truth, what we really long for is to touch the other boundless zone of consciousness, as opposed to our present, conditioned and limited one. Simply hoping for more time and space may lead to further distractions, existential problems, and concerns.

Our earthly experiences and apparent choices prepare us for the leap into higher consciousness after death. Our duty towards our own self is not to be distracted by its lower aspects and countless demands and whims. Rather, our ultimate good action is one that liberates us from our lower self.

There are numerous intermediate zones of consciousness that we all go through. The more obvious are being awake or asleep, in a daze or very clear. This includes situations where consciousness appears in one way or another, or disappears. The event of death and the departure of life from the body and the mind is caused by unknown powers and entities, which we refer to as angels. This example or metaphor repeats in countless ways, in our life and other lives as well.

21-30 وَلَنُذِيقَنَّهُم مِّنَ ٱلْعَذَابِ ٱلْأَدْنَىٰ دُونَ ٱلْعَذَابِ ٱلْأَكْبَرِ لَعَلَّهُمْ يَرْجِعُونَ ۝ وَمَنْ أَظْلَمُ مِمَّن ذُكِّرَ بِـَٔايَٰتِ رَبِّهِۦ ثُمَّ أَعْرَضَ عَنْهَآ إِنَّا مِنَ ٱلْمُجْرِمِينَ مُنتَقِمُونَ ۝ وَلَقَدْ ءَاتَيْنَا مُوسَى ٱلْكِتَٰبَ فَلَا تَكُن فِى مِرْيَةٍ مِّن لِّقَآئِهِۦ وَجَعَلْنَٰهُ هُدًى لِّبَنِىٓ إِسْرَٰٓءِيلَ ۝ وَجَعَلْنَا مِنْهُمْ أَئِمَّةً يَهْدُونَ بِأَمْرِنَا لَمَّا صَبَرُوا۟ وَكَانُوا۟ بِـَٔايَٰتِنَا يُوقِنُونَ ۝ إِنَّ رَبَّكَ هُوَ يَفْصِلُ بَيْنَهُمْ يَوْمَ ٱلْقِيَٰمَةِ فِيمَا كَانُوا۟ فِيهِ يَخْتَلِفُونَ ۝ أَوَلَمْ يَهْدِ لَهُمْ كَمْ أَهْلَكْنَا مِن قَبْلِهِم مِّنَ ٱلْقُرُونِ يَمْشُونَ فِى مَسَٰكِنِهِمْ إِنَّ فِى ذَٰلِكَ لَـَٔايَٰتٍ أَفَلَا يَسْمَعُونَ ۝ أَوَلَمْ يَرَوْا۟ أَنَّا نَسُوقُ ٱلْمَآءَ إِلَى ٱلْأَرْضِ ٱلْجُرُزِ فَنُخْرِجُ بِهِۦ زَرْعًا تَأْكُلُ مِنْهُ أَنْعَٰمُهُمْ وَأَنفُسُهُمْ أَفَلَا يُبْصِرُونَ ۝ وَيَقُولُونَ مَتَىٰ هَٰذَا ٱلْفَتْحُ إِن كُنتُمْ صَٰدِقِينَ ۝ قُلْ يَوْمَ ٱلْفَتْحِ لَا يَنفَعُ ٱلَّذِينَ كَفَرُوٓا۟ إِيمَٰنُهُمْ وَلَا هُمْ يُنظَرُونَ ۝ فَأَعْرِضْ عَنْهُمْ وَٱنتَظِرْ إِنَّهُم مُّنتَظِرُونَ ۝

We shall make them taste the lesser torment rather than the greater – perchance they might return. Who does more wrong than someone who, when messages from his Lord are recited to him, turns away from them? We shall inflict retribution on the guilty. We brought Moses the Book – so do not be in doubt regarding His encounter – and We made him a guide to the Children of Israel. And We appointed from among them leaders guiding by Our command, when they endured patiently, and had sure faith in Our signs. Your

Lord shall decide between them on the Day of Resurrection as to that over which they differed. Is it not a guidance to them, how many generations We destroyed before them in whose dwelling-places they walk? Surely in that are signs; what, will they not hear? Do they not observe how We drive water to a land without vegetation, and bring forth therewith crops on which their cattle and they themselves feed? Can they not see? They say: 'When will this Verdict come to pass if you speak the truth?' Say: 'On the Day of Verdict their faith shall not profit the unbelievers, nor shall they be respited.' So turn you away from them, and wait; they too are waiting.

21-30 The seeker on the prophetic path regards earthly afflictions and difficulties as small fires and gifts from the unseen to lift our consciousness higher towards the zone of perpetual bliss, beyond space and time. This earthly life is our kindergarten from which we graduate into life after death. Most prophetic messages have emphasized that our earthly journey is a short transit to help us to evolve in consciousness and spiritual intelligence, which will give us the appropriate discrimination and choice. To begin with, faith and trust is shaky but with practice and sincerity, it becomes the main reality in a person's life. The awakened person is always in refence to the *Absolute* and as such they touch the zone of prostration to the divine (the title of this surah is that of prostration). Those who have not had this nourishment are in doubt and confusion.

It is natural for us to seek liberation and freedom from darkness and suffering, but it is due to our lower self and cultural background and biographies that we bring afflictions, fear, and sorrow upon ourselves. The soul is ever-joyful, content, and within the divine perfect order.

Our experiences on earth are a prelude to what comes after the departure of the veils of the self and the ego-self, as well as the desires, hopes, and fears that we have. All of these emanate from the power of life itself in order for us to be completely obsessed with preserving and serving life. Our suffering and miseries on this earth are a prelude to a timeless state of suffering and confusion after death, unless the self has been transcended to the soul.

13. Surah 36 Ya-Seen (Ya-Seen)

The last ayah of the previous surah informs us that Allah sees and kn-ows all. This connects to the first two to three ayat of this surah confirming that the revelation of the Qur'an is full of wisdom and that the Prophet Muhammad is a messenger of Allah and on the right path.

بِسْمِ اللَّهِ الرَّحْمَٰنِ الرَّحِيمِ

1-12 يس ۝ وَالْقُرْآنِ الْحَكِيمِ ۝ إِنَّكَ لَمِنَ الْمُرْسَلِينَ ۝ عَلَىٰ صِرَاطٍ مُّسْتَقِيمٍ ۝

تَنزِيلَ ٱلْعَزِيزِ ٱلرَّحِيمِ ۝ لِتُنذِرَ قَوْمًا مَّآ أُنذِرَ ءَابَآؤُهُمْ فَهُمْ غَٰفِلُونَ ۝ لَقَدْ حَقَّ ٱلْقَوْلُ عَلَىٰٓ أَكْثَرِهِمْ فَهُمْ لَا يُؤْمِنُونَ ۝ إِنَّا جَعَلْنَا فِىٓ أَعْنَٰقِهِمْ أَغْلَٰلًا فَهِىَ إِلَى ٱلْأَذْقَانِ فَهُم مُّقْمَحُونَ ۝ وَجَعَلْنَا مِنۢ بَيْنِ أَيْدِيهِمْ سَدًّا وَمِنْ خَلْفِهِمْ سَدًّا فَأَغْشَيْنَٰهُمْ فَهُمْ لَا يُبْصِرُونَ ۝ سَوَآءٌ عَلَيْهِمْ ءَأَنذَرْتَهُمْ أَمْ لَمْ تُنذِرْهُمْ لَا يُؤْمِنُونَ ۝ إِنَّمَا تُنذِرُ مَنِ ٱتَّبَعَ ٱلذِّكْرَ وَخَشِىَ ٱلرَّحْمَٰنَ بِٱلْغَيْبِ فَبَشِّرْهُ بِمَغْفِرَةٍ وَأَجْرٍ كَرِيمٍ ۝ إِنَّا نَحْنُ نُحْىِ ٱلْمَوْتَىٰ وَنَكْتُبُ مَا قَدَّمُوا۟ وَءَاثَٰرَهُمْ وَكُلَّ شَىْءٍ أَحْصَيْنَٰهُ فِىٓ إِمَامٍ مُّبِينٍ ۝

In the name of Allah, the Merciful to all, the Compassionate to each!

Ya Seen. By the Wise Qur'an, you are indeed one of the messengers upon a straight path. This is the Revelation of the Almighty, Compassionate to each in order that you warn a people whose ancestors were not warned, and thus are heedless. Upon most of them the Word has come true, and they do not believe. We have placed collars on their necks, reaching to their chins, so their heads are upraised, and We have set a barrier before them and a barrier behind them, and We have enshrouded them in veils so that they cannot see. It is all the same to them whether you warn or do not warn them – they have no faith. You only warn him who follows the Remembrance and fears the All-Merciful in the Unseen. To him give glad tidings of forgiveness and a noble wage. It is We Who revive the dead, We Who register what deeds they committed, what traces they left behind. All things have We tallied in a Manifest Record.

1-12 Our earthly consciousness is balanced between dualities and pluralities, all of which will end where they all began – cosmic *Unity*. An enlightened human being realises the limitations of space and time and yearns to be touched by that which is absolute and timeless. Everyone is constrained by some uncertainty about their future end. A person living in faith and following a disciplined path is reassured that life after death is far greater in value and goodness. As for those who do not trust in the revelation, their darkness will increase until they are submerged in it fully after death. Most of these people miss the benefit from the spiritual message of our duty towards awakening to truth.

The human soul carries the light of the *Absolute* and its reflections. As such, it has the potential to awaken to full consciousness and deal with conditioned, limited consciousness. We understand the greatest news of the cosmic gift, as well as the limitations and warnings regarding our earthly journey.

The Qur'an reveals numerous aspects of the eternal *Truth*, which is everlasting. An important aspect of its revelation is that you will only wake up to the real you according to the extent of your faith, belief, and trust in the light in your own heart. That pre-memory light can only occur if you are on the path to be at one with the miraculous event of the creation.

13-25

وَاضْرِبْ لَهُم مَّثَلًا أَصْحَٰبَ ٱلْقَرْيَةِ إِذْ جَآءَهَا ٱلْمُرْسَلُونَ ۝ إِذْ أَرْسَلْنَآ إِلَيْهِمُ ٱثْنَيْنِ فَكَذَّبُوهُمَا فَعَزَّزْنَا بِثَالِثٍ فَقَالُوٓا۟ إِنَّآ إِلَيْكُم مُّرْسَلُونَ ۝ قَالُوا۟ مَآ أَنتُمْ إِلَّا بَشَرٌ مِّثْلُنَا وَمَآ أَنزَلَ ٱلرَّحْمَٰنُ مِن شَىْءٍ إِنْ أَنتُمْ إِلَّا تَكْذِبُونَ ۝ قَالُوا۟ رَبُّنَا يَعْلَمُ إِنَّآ إِلَيْكُمْ لَمُرْسَلُونَ ۝ وَمَا عَلَيْنَآ إِلَّا ٱلْبَلَٰغُ ٱلْمُبِينُ ۝ قَالُوٓا۟ إِنَّا تَطَيَّرْنَا بِكُمْ لَئِن لَّمْ تَنتَهُوا۟ لَنَرْجُمَنَّكُمْ وَلَيَمَسَّنَّكُم مِّنَّا عَذَابٌ أَلِيمٌ ۝ قَالُوا۟ طَٰٓئِرُكُم مَّعَكُمْ أَئِن ذُكِّرْتُم بَلْ أَنتُمْ قَوْمٌ مُّسْرِفُونَ ۝ وَجَآءَ مِنْ أَقْصَا ٱلْمَدِينَةِ رَجُلٌ يَسْعَىٰ قَالَ يَٰقَوْمِ ٱتَّبِعُوا۟ ٱلْمُرْسَلِينَ ۝ ٱتَّبِعُوا۟ مَن لَّا يَسْـَٔلُكُمْ أَجْرًا وَهُم مُّهْتَدُونَ ۝ وَمَا لِىَ لَآ أَعْبُدُ ٱلَّذِى فَطَرَنِى وَإِلَيْهِ تُرْجَعُونَ ۝ ءَأَتَّخِذُ مِن دُونِهِۦٓ ءَالِهَةً إِن يُرِدْنِ ٱلرَّحْمَٰنُ بِضُرٍّ لَّا تُغْنِ عَنِّى شَفَٰعَتُهُمْ شَيْـًٔا وَلَا يُنقِذُونِ ۝ إِنِّىٓ إِذًا لَّفِى ضَلَٰلٍ مُّبِينٍ ۝ إِنِّىٓ ءَامَنتُ بِرَبِّكُمْ فَٱسْمَعُونِ ۝

Strike for them the parable of the people of the town, when messengers arrived. We had sent them two but they called them liars, so We backed them with a third, and they said: 'We are messengers to you.' They said: 'You are merely human beings like us. The All-Merciful has revealed nothing. You are nothing but liars.' They said: 'Our Lord knows that we are sent as messengers to you, is only to convey a manifest declaration.' They said: 'We hold you to be an evil omen. If you do not desist, we will stone you and a most painful torment will touch you from us.' They said: 'Your evil omen is upon you. Is it because you have been reminded of Allah? You are indeed a people far gone in transgression.' Then, from the furthest part of the city, a man came running. He said, 'My people, follow the messengers. Follow him who asks you no wage. These men are guided aright. And why should I not serve Him who originated me, and unto whom you shall be returned? Am I to take other Gods instead of Him? If the All-Merciful wishes me ill, their intercession will not benefit me in the least, nor will they be able to save me I would then be in manifest error. I believe in your Lord, so listen to me.'

13-25 We can witness numerous signs and hints as to our existing state, as well as our likely state after death. This is why some people become very superstitious, while others deny everything other than the material. To benefit from signs and signals from the unseen, our mind needs to be receptive and clear, the heart open and pure. It is not always easy for an individual to be tuned to the unseen, even less easy for a group of people. A true teacher, guide, or awakened person will not expect any tangible benefits nor will they demand obedience or total commitment from their pupils. It is by free will and higher intelligence that every one of us can be guided to the ultimate realisation that the divine light resides within the soul.

Individually we often hear an inner voice that warns us. The same applies to us collectively. There are beings who reveal the truth, both good news as well as warnings. It is due to our distraction by the lower self that we remain in ignorance and confusion.

Our humanity exists because of the light and the power of divinity within our heart. Through humanity and a purified mind, we can realise the amazing power of the heart itself and the need for it to remain pure.

26-38

قِيلَ ٱدْخُلِ ٱلْجَنَّةَ قَالَ يَٰلَيْتَ قَوْمِى يَعْلَمُونَ ۝ بِمَا غَفَرَ لِى رَبِّى وَجَعَلَنِى مِنَ ٱلْمُكْرَمِينَ ۝ وَمَآ أَنزَلْنَا عَلَىٰ قَوْمِهِۦ مِنۢ بَعْدِهِۦ مِن جُندٍ مِّنَ ٱلسَّمَآءِ وَمَا كُنَّا مُنزِلِينَ ۝ إِن كَانَتْ إِلَّا صَيْحَةً وَٰحِدَةً فَإِذَا هُمْ خَٰمِدُونَ ۝ يَٰحَسْرَةً عَلَى ٱلْعِبَادِ مَا يَأْتِيهِم مِّن رَّسُولٍ إِلَّا كَانُوا۟ بِهِۦ يَسْتَهْزِءُونَ ۝ أَلَمْ يَرَوْا۟ كَمْ أَهْلَكْنَا قَبْلَهُم مِّنَ ٱلْقُرُونِ أَنَّهُمْ إِلَيْهِمْ لَا يَرْجِعُونَ ۝ وَإِن كُلٌّ لَّمَّا جَمِيعٌ لَّدَيْنَا مُحْضَرُونَ ۝ وَءَايَةٌ لَّهُمُ ٱلْأَرْضُ ٱلْمَيْتَةُ أَحْيَيْنَٰهَا وَأَخْرَجْنَا مِنْهَا حَبًّا فَمِنْهُ يَأْكُلُونَ ۝ وَجَعَلْنَا فِيهَا جَنَّٰتٍ مِّن نَّخِيلٍ وَأَعْنَٰبٍ وَفَجَّرْنَا فِيهَا مِنَ ٱلْعُيُونِ ۝ لِيَأْكُلُوا۟ مِن ثَمَرِهِۦ وَمَا عَمِلَتْهُ أَيْدِيهِمْ أَفَلَا يَشْكُرُونَ ۝ سُبْحَٰنَ ٱلَّذِى خَلَقَ ٱلْأَزْوَٰجَ كُلَّهَا مِمَّا تُنۢبِتُ ٱلْأَرْضُ وَمِنْ أَنفُسِهِمْ وَمِمَّا لَا يَعْلَمُونَ ۝ وَءَايَةٌ لَّهُمُ ٱلَّيْلُ نَسْلَخُ مِنْهُ ٱلنَّهَارَ فَإِذَا هُم مُّظْلِمُونَ ۝ وَٱلشَّمْسُ تَجْرِى لِمُسْتَقَرٍّ لَّهَا ذَٰلِكَ تَقْدِيرُ ٱلْعَزِيزِ ٱلْعَلِيمِ ۝

It was said to him: 'Enter the Garden.' He said: 'If only my people knew that my Lord has forgiven me and that He has placed me among the honoured.' After him, We sent no troops from heaven against his people, nor did We intend to do so. It was but a single Scream and, behold, they were lifeless. Alas for humanity! No messenger comes to them but they mock him. Have they not observed how many generations We destroyed before them, and that they do not return to them? They shall every one of them be arraigned before Us. Here is a sign for them: a dead land which We revive, and from which We sprout grains for them to eat. In it We planted gardens of palms and vines, and caused fountains to burst forth, that they may eat of its fruits and the work of their hands – will they not render thanks? Glory be to Him, who created all the pairs of what the earth produces, and of themselves, and of what they know not. And a sign for them is the night; We strip it of the day and lo, they are in darkness. And the sun runs its own course, unchanging, such is the disposition of the Almighty, the All-Knowing.

26-38 Ultimate success comes when a healthy individual adheres to qualities such as reason, rationality, and commonality with others, whilst at the same time calibrating with pure consciousness, beyond reason or causality. With awakening to the two zones of consciousness within us, one realises that life is a preparation for a higher quality experience after death, one is beyond our normal understanding as confined by space and time. Deep in our hearts we seek wholesome, beautiful environments such as earthly gardens, hence the metaphors of a garden-like paradise in the hereafter. Nature around us provides numerous examples of dualities, and natural human drives motivate us to choose what is appropriate for a durable quality of life, interconnected with nature and other beings. The earth has countless wonders, patterns, interchanges, and exchanges, and the celestial realities present the most awesome samples of creations and existences.

Life on earth is balanced between dualities. We are challenged constantly to choose between what is inappropriate and what is appropriate, as well as the extent of that appropriate behaviour. Our life on earth prepares us to realise the perfection from which we emerged and to which we return to after death.

Whatever appears will also disappear. Whoever has been experiencing perfections in this world will flow with greater ease to the ultimate state of the garden after death.

39-51 وَٱلْقَمَرَ قَدَّرْنَٰهُ مَنَازِلَ حَتَّىٰ عَادَ كَٱلْعُرْجُونِ ٱلْقَدِيمِ ۞ لَا ٱلشَّمْسُ يَنۢبَغِى لَهَآ أَن تُدْرِكَ ٱلْقَمَرَ وَلَا ٱلَّيْلُ سَابِقُ ٱلنَّهَارِ وَكُلٌّ فِى فَلَكٍ يَسْبَحُونَ ۞ وَءَايَةٌ لَّهُمْ أَنَّا حَمَلْنَا ذُرِّيَّتَهُمْ فِى ٱلْفُلْكِ ٱلْمَشْحُونِ ۞ وَخَلَقْنَا لَهُم مِّن مِّثْلِهِۦ مَا يَرْكَبُونَ ۞ وَإِن نَّشَأْ نُغْرِقْهُمْ فَلَا صَرِيخَ لَهُمْ وَلَا هُمْ يُنقَذُونَ ۞ إِلَّا رَحْمَةً مِّنَّا وَمَتَٰعًا إِلَىٰ حِينٍ ۞ وَإِذَا قِيلَ لَهُمُ ٱتَّقُوا۟ مَا بَيْنَ أَيْدِيكُمْ وَمَا خَلْفَكُمْ لَعَلَّكُمْ تُرْحَمُونَ ۞ وَمَا تَأْتِيهِم مِّنْ ءَايَةٍ مِّنْ ءَايَٰتِ رَبِّهِمْ إِلَّا كَانُوا۟ عَنْهَا مُعْرِضِينَ ۞ وَإِذَا قِيلَ لَهُمْ أَنفِقُوا۟ مِمَّا رَزَقَكُمُ ٱللَّهُ قَالَ ٱلَّذِينَ كَفَرُوا۟ لِلَّذِينَ ءَامَنُوٓا۟ أَنُطْعِمُ مَن لَّوْ يَشَآءُ ٱللَّهُ أَطْعَمَهُۥٓ إِنْ أَنتُمْ إِلَّا فِى ضَلَٰلٍ مُّبِينٍ ۞ وَيَقُولُونَ مَتَىٰ هَٰذَا ٱلْوَعْدُ إِن كُنتُمْ صَٰدِقِينَ ۞ مَا يَنظُرُونَ إِلَّا صَيْحَةً وَٰحِدَةً تَأْخُذُهُمْ وَهُمْ يَخِصِّمُونَ ۞ فَلَا يَسْتَطِيعُونَ تَوْصِيَةً وَلَآ إِلَىٰٓ أَهْلِهِمْ يَرْجِعُونَ ۞ وَنُفِخَ فِى ٱلصُّورِ فَإِذَا هُم مِّنَ ٱلْأَجْدَاثِ إِلَىٰ رَبِّهِمْ يَنسِلُونَ ۞

And the moon We disposed in phases until it comes back like a withered stalk of palm. Neither the sun may outstrip the moon nor the night the day: each plies its own orbit. And a sign for them is that We carried their seed in the laden ship, and We have created for them the like of it whereon they ride; if We wish We can drown them – no screaming to be heard from them, nor can they be saved, unless it be a mercy from Us and a brief enjoyment of life. And when it is said to them: 'Beware of the present and the future that you may obtain mercy,' there comes to them no sign from the signs of their Lord but they turn their back upon it. And when it is said to them: 'Expend from what Allah in His bounty has provided you,' the unbelievers say to the believers: 'Are we to feed one whom Allah can feed if He so wishes?' In truth you have strayed far in error. They say: 'When will this promise be fulfilled if you speak the truth?' All they can expect is a single Scream, which shall seize them while they dispute, so that they have no time to make a bequest, nor return home to their families. And the Trumpet shall be sounded and, behold, from their graves and to their Lord they shall hurry.

39-51 In our own solar system, we can study with amazement the interrelated movement of numerous planets and their unique star, the Sun. It is difficult for the mind to conceive that every second the Sun releases four million tons of hydrogen, which are converted to helium, releasing the energy that provides life's experiences. Millions of entities follow most intricate directions in total interconnectedness with what is around them. To be liberated from the fear and anxiety of the mind we need to give up that which we are most attached to and want to keep. This is not easy for most human beings. Only those awakened to the truth will realise that there is nothing we can take with us to the next realm, and that the more we are liberated from fears, sorrows, and attachments, the more we are prepared for an honourable, cheerful death. No living individual possesses any independent power, strength, knowledge, or ability. We are totally dependent upon the divine *Reality*.

Our earthly experiences prepare us to improve upon and become aware of our intentions and actions, so that ultimately, we are fully conscious of the precious present moment. Life is eternal; transcending the fear of death and other sorrows allows us to realise this.

All of the earthly phenomena that we observe and try to understand follow certain patterns, movements, and interactions, until they reach their ultimate destiny and revert to what they were before. The same thing happens to us as human beings: we die, we will be resurrected, and through that, we will discover the miracle of divine *Presence*.

52-65 قَالُوا۟ يَٰوَيْلَنَا مَنۢ بَعَثَنَا مِن مَّرْقَدِنَا ۗ هَٰذَا مَا وَعَدَ ٱلرَّحْمَٰنُ وَصَدَقَ ٱلْمُرْسَلُونَ ۝ إِن كَانَتْ إِلَّا صَيْحَةً وَٰحِدَةً فَإِذَا هُمْ جَمِيعٌ لَّدَيْنَا مُحْضَرُونَ ۝ فَٱلْيَوْمَ لَا تُظْلَمُ نَفْسٌ شَيْـًٔا وَلَا تُجْزَوْنَ إِلَّا مَا كُنتُمْ تَعْمَلُونَ ۝ إِنَّ أَصْحَٰبَ ٱلْجَنَّةِ ٱلْيَوْمَ فِى شُغُلٍ فَٰكِهُونَ ۝ هُمْ وَأَزْوَٰجُهُمْ فِى ظِلَٰلٍ عَلَى ٱلْأَرَآئِكِ مُتَّكِـُٔونَ ۝ لَهُمْ فِيهَا فَٰكِهَةٌ وَلَهُم مَّا يَدَّعُونَ ۝ سَلَٰمٌ قَوْلًا مِّن رَّبٍّ رَّحِيمٍ ۝ وَٱمْتَٰزُوا۟ ٱلْيَوْمَ أَيُّهَا ٱلْمُجْرِمُونَ ۝ أَلَمْ أَعْهَدْ إِلَيْكُمْ يَٰبَنِىٓ ءَادَمَ أَن لَّا تَعْبُدُوا۟ ٱلشَّيْطَٰنَ ۖ إِنَّهُۥ لَكُمْ عَدُوٌّ مُّبِينٌ ۝ وَأَنِ ٱعْبُدُونِى ۚ هَٰذَا صِرَٰطٌ مُّسْتَقِيمٌ ۝ وَلَقَدْ أَضَلَّ مِنكُمْ جِبِلًّا كَثِيرًا ۖ أَفَلَمْ تَكُونُوا۟ تَعْقِلُونَ ۝ هَٰذِهِۦ جَهَنَّمُ ٱلَّتِى كُنتُمْ تُوعَدُونَ ۝ ٱصْلَوْهَا ٱلْيَوْمَ بِمَا كُنتُمْ تَكْفُرُونَ ۝ ٱلْيَوْمَ نَخْتِمُ عَلَىٰٓ أَفْوَٰهِهِمْ وَتُكَلِّمُنَآ أَيْدِيهِمْ وَتَشْهَدُ أَرْجُلُهُم بِمَا كَانُوا۟ يَكْسِبُونَ ۝

They shall say: 'Alas for us! Who resurrected us from our resting place?' This is what the All-Merciful promised, and the messengers spoke the truth. It shall be but a single Scream and, behold, they will all be conducted before Us. Today no soul shall be wronged one jot, and you will be recompensed only for the deeds you committed. Today the denizens of the Garden are preoccupied with joy, they and their spouses, reclining on cushions under the shade. therein they have fruits, and they have all that they call for. 'Peace' shall be *the word from a Compassionate Lord. Today, O guilty, keep yourselves apart! Made I not covenant with you, Children of Adam, that you should not serve Satan – surely, he is a manifest foe to you – and to worship Me? This is the path that is straight. He has led astray so many of you! Were you incapable of reasoning? Here is the hell you were promised. Endure it today as an outcome of your persistent denial of the truth! Today We shall seal their mouths and it will be their hands that shall speak to Us and their feet that shall testify as to what they earned.*

52-65 Due to the mind's deceptiveness, we can lie, conceal, and hide what we wish or desire. Believers who know that Allah knows all, and who have a clear connection with that light, need to be utterly truthful, honest, and accountable. Everything will be revealed in the hereafter, and each one of us will face what we tried to conceal. Our life on earth is experienced through our senses and mind, which are only vague and hazy with regard to what is real. Lying makes the whole issue even more complex. Everything we witness has some truth as well as much illusion, delusion, and confusion. To lie, deliberately complicates and confuses our lives. The straight path prescribed by prophets implies readiness to experience higher consciousness and transcend to other zones of realities. The state of God-consciousness is beyond all duality, differentiations, or shadows, except that absolute light and *Reality*. This state is the ultimate sanctuary that we yearn for.

Our life is a preparation for the next phase of consciousness after death, which will be akin to the eternal garden for those who were in constant reference to full consciousness while on earth. For those who lived in darkness and ignorance, the next phase will feel like perpetual death or hell.

This world of plurality leads us to experience a touch of unity and oneness. We are obsessed with prolonging the experience of life, because life is eternal and forever. Once I have experienced life in a personal way, then I am obsessed to try to prolong it and survive as long as possible.

66-83 وَلَوْ نَشَآءُ لَطَمَسْنَا عَلَىٰٓ أَعْيُنِهِمْ فَٱسْتَبَقُوا۟ ٱلصِّرَٰطَ فَأَنَّىٰ يُبْصِرُونَ ۝ وَلَوْ نَشَآءُ لَمَسَخْنَٰهُمْ عَلَىٰ مَكَانَتِهِمْ فَمَا ٱسْتَطَٰعُوا۟ مُضِيًّا وَلَا يَرْجِعُونَ ۝ وَمَن نُّعَمِّرْهُ نُنَكِّسْهُ فِى ٱلْخَلْقِ أَفَلَا يَعْقِلُونَ ۝ وَمَا عَلَّمْنَٰهُ ٱلشِّعْرَ وَمَا يَنۢبَغِى لَهُۥٓ إِنْ هُوَ إِلَّا ذِكْرٌ وَقُرْءَانٌ مُّبِينٌ ۝ لِّيُنذِرَ مَن كَانَ حَيًّا وَيَحِقَّ ٱلْقَوْلُ عَلَى ٱلْكَٰفِرِينَ ۝ أَوَلَمْ يَرَوْا۟ أَنَّا خَلَقْنَا لَهُم مِّمَّا عَمِلَتْ أَيْدِينَآ أَنْعَٰمًا فَهُمْ لَهَا مَٰلِكُونَ ۝ وَذَلَّلْنَٰهَا لَهُمْ فَمِنْهَا رَكُوبُهُمْ وَمِنْهَا يَأْكُلُونَ ۝ وَلَهُمْ فِيهَا مَنَٰفِعُ وَمَشَارِبُ أَفَلَا يَشْكُرُونَ ۝ وَٱتَّخَذُوا۟ مِن دُونِ ٱللَّهِ ءَالِهَةً لَّعَلَّهُمْ يُنصَرُونَ ۝ لَا يَسْتَطِيعُونَ نَصْرَهُمْ وَهُمْ لَهُمْ جُندٌ مُّحْضَرُونَ ۝ فَلَا يَحْزُنكَ قَوْلُهُمْ إِنَّا نَعْلَمُ مَا يُسِرُّونَ وَمَا يُعْلِنُونَ ۝ أَوَلَمْ يَرَ ٱلْإِنسَٰنُ أَنَّا خَلَقْنَٰهُ مِن نُّطْفَةٍ فَإِذَا هُوَ خَصِيمٌ مُّبِينٌ ۝ وَضَرَبَ لَنَا مَثَلًا

وَنَسِىَ خَلْقَهُۥ قَالَ مَن يُحْىِ ٱلْعِظَٰمَ وَهِىَ رَمِيمٌ ۝ قُلْ يُحْيِيهَا ٱلَّذِىٓ أَنشَأَهَآ أَوَّلَ مَرَّةٍ وَهُوَ بِكُلِّ خَلْقٍ عَلِيمٌ ۝ ٱلَّذِى جَعَلَ لَكُم مِّنَ ٱلشَّجَرِ ٱلْأَخْضَرِ نَارًا فَإِذَآ أَنتُم مِّنْهُ تُوقِدُونَ ۝ أَوَلَيْسَ ٱلَّذِى خَلَقَ ٱلسَّمَٰوَٰتِ وَٱلْأَرْضَ بِقَٰدِرٍ عَلَىٰٓ أَن يَخْلُقَ مِثْلَهُم بَلَىٰ وَهُوَ ٱلْخَلَّٰقُ ٱلْعَلِيمُ ۝ إِنَّمَآ أَمْرُهُۥٓ إِذَآ أَرَادَ شَيْـًٔا أَن يَقُولَ لَهُۥ كُن فَيَكُونُ ۝ فَسُبْحَٰنَ ٱلَّذِى بِيَدِهِۦ مَلَكُوتُ كُلِّ شَىْءٍ وَإِلَيْهِ تُرْجَعُونَ ۝

Today We shall seal their mouths and it will be their hands that shall speak to Us and their feet that shall testify as to what they earned. Did We will, We would have changed them where they were, then they could not go on, nor could they return. Whomever We grant old age, We cause to droop in figure: will they not be reasonable? We did not teach him poetry, nor does this befit him. It is nothing but a Remembrance, and a Manifest Qur'an. Therewith to warn him who is living, and to fulfill the Word against the unbelievers. Have they not observed that We created for them, from Our handiwork, cattle which they come to possess? That We tamed them for their benefit, that upon them they ride and from them they eat? That they have other uses for them, and draughts to drink? Will they not render thanks? And yet, instead of Allah, they take to themselves Gods, hoping for success. These cannot grant them success, though they possess troops massed in their service. Therefore, let not their speech sadden you: We know what they conceal and what declare. Has not man observed that We created him from a sperm drop but, behold, he becomes a determined adversary? And he has struck for Us a similitude and forgotten his creation; he says, 'Who shall quicken the bones when they are decayed?' Say: 'He will give life to them Who brought them into existence at first, and He is cognizant of all creation who has made for you out of the green tree fire and lo, from it you kindle. Is not He, who created the heavens and earth, able to create the like of them? Yes indeed; He is the All-Creator, the All-Knowing. His command, when He desires a thing, is to say to it "Be," and it is. So, glory be to Him, in whose hand is the dominion of everything, and unto whom you shall be returned.'

66-83 Most people who pursue earthly power and wealth cannot give a clear answer as to how much is enough for them. The light of God within the heart is beyond measure, and this is what we are consciously or unconsciously aspiring for. The divine light gets diluted so that it can energise and empower us to live on earth in transit towards a more permanent abode. With reflection, we begin to discover how all elements within us support each other and how the main substances of fire, earth, air, and water are interconnected.

Our earthly life is balanced between high and low, good and bad. We must engage with these changes in such a manner that we are not overcome by darkness, which blocks the guiding light of the soul. It requires earthly and spiritual wisdom to be exposed to gossip and confusion without being afflicted by it.

Our human side has been evolving over billions of years and interacting beneficially so that we have reasonable comfort and ease to perfect our worship and still be in the moment, whose nature is eternal anyway. For this reason, we are driven towards a higher zone of consciousness where we lose our specific identity and sense of separation.

14. Surah 37 As-Saffat (The Arrayed in Ranks)

Allah is the sovereign governor of all known and unknown, whose cosmic control is through numerous powers and energy fields, including entities that we name angels. The divine governance is ever perfect and complete.

بِسْمِ اللَّـهِ الرَّحْمَـٰنِ الرَّحِيمِ

1-15 وَالصَّافَّاتِ صَفًّا ۝ فَالزَّاجِرَاتِ زَجْرًا ۝ فَالتَّالِيَاتِ ذِكْرًا ۝ إِنَّ إِلَـٰهَكُمْ لَوَاحِدٌ ۝ رَبُّ السَّمَاوَاتِ وَالْأَرْضِ وَمَا بَيْنَهُمَا وَرَبُّ الْمَشَارِقِ ۝ إِنَّا زَيَّنَّا السَّمَاءَ الدُّنْيَا بِزِينَةٍ الْكَوَاكِبِ ۝ وَحِفْظًا مِّن كُلِّ شَيْطَانٍ مَّارِدٍ ۝ لَا يَسَّمَّعُونَ إِلَى الْمَلَإِ الْأَعْلَىٰ وَيُقْذَفُونَ مِن كُلِّ جَانِبٍ ۝ دُحُورًا ۖ وَلَهُمْ عَذَابٌ وَاصِبٌ ۝ إِلَّا مَنْ خَطِفَ الْخَطْفَةَ فَأَتْبَعَهُ شِهَابٌ ثَاقِبٌ ۝ فَاسْتَفْتِهِمْ أَهُمْ أَشَدُّ خَلْقًا أَم مَّنْ خَلَقْنَا ۚ إِنَّا خَلَقْنَاهُم مِّن طِينٍ لَّازِبٍ ۝ بَلْ عَجِبْتَ وَيَسْخَرُونَ ۝ وَإِذَا ذُكِّرُوا لَا يَذْكُرُونَ ۝ وَإِذَا رَأَوْا آيَةً يَسْتَسْخِرُونَ ۝ وَقَالُوا إِنْ هَـٰذَا إِلَّا سِحْرٌ مُّبِينٌ ۝

In the name of Allah, the Merciful to all, the Compassionate to each!

By those arrayed in ranks! By those who loudly clamor! By those who recite the Remembrance, your Allah is One, Lord of the heavens and earth and what is in between, Lord of all sunrises! We adorned the lower sky with the adornment of stars, a protection against every rebellious demon, they listen not to the High Council, for they are pelted from every side, rejected, and theirs is an everlasting chastisement, except such as snatches a fragment, and he is pursued by a piercing flame. So, sound them out: 'Are they more difficult to create, or those others We created?' We created them from viscous clay. You are filled with wonder but they mock, and when reminded they do not remember. If they see a sign, they gather around to mock. They say: 'This is nothing but flagrant sorcery.

1-15 All material and physical entities have emerged from energies of enormous variety, power, and durability. What we human beings discern is only the surface of what exists in the universe. We can discriminate between different forms of matter and radiation, as well as various fields of energies, including electromagnetic and numerous others, all of which emanate from the same *Source* and are subject to pre-determined designs, patterns, and self-regulation.

Our universe is bounded by space and time; within it is the vast unseen, beyond it exists the infinite unknown. We are perched in a very precarious way on the tiny planet earth, turning on itself and around the Sun and being hurtled through space. Our soul has been exposed to the divine cosmic *Truth* and its vastness, and as such has a latent knowledge of everything. It is quite natural for us to have the desire to transcend all patterns – of body, mind, and emotions.

It is beyond our mind to comprehend the history of the divine control and governance over the entire cosmos. We can, however, imagine other living entities such as angels and *jinn* that are at the lower end of consciousness and who are agents of this governance.

The links in the universe of consciousness are so complex that our mind can only comprehend what connects us with what is close to us in space and time. There are countless forces and powers, many of which are referred to as angels. They repeat, relate, and reconnect for this amazing thing called consciousness to be on the rise at all times. The nature of the human mind is to be limited and contained within what it perceives as being so-called real and as a result of this, it denies or dismisses anything that lifts the consciousness higher up to zones beyond the mind.

16-35

أَءِذَا مِتْنَا وَكُنَّا تُرَابًا وَعِظَٰمًا أَءِنَّا لَمَبْعُوثُونَ ۝ أَوَءَابَآؤُنَا ٱلْأَوَّلُونَ ۝ قُلْ نَعَمْ وَأَنتُمْ دَٰخِرُونَ ۝ فَإِنَّمَا هِيَ زَجْرَةٌ وَٰحِدَةٌ فَإِذَا هُمْ يَنظُرُونَ ۝ وَقَالُوا۟ يَٰوَيْلَنَا هَٰذَا يَوْمُ ٱلدِّينِ ۝ هَٰذَا يَوْمُ ٱلْفَصْلِ ٱلَّذِى كُنتُم بِهِۦ تُكَذِّبُونَ ۝ ٱحْشُرُوا۟ ٱلَّذِينَ ظَلَمُوا۟ وَأَزْوَٰجَهُمْ وَمَا كَانُوا۟ يَعْبُدُونَ ۝ مِن دُونِ ٱللَّهِ فَٱهْدُوهُمْ إِلَىٰ صِرَٰطِ ٱلْجَحِيمِ ۝ وَقِفُوهُمْ إِنَّهُم مَّسْـُٔولُونَ ۝ مَا لَكُمْ لَا تَنَاصَرُونَ ۝ بَلْ هُمُ ٱلْيَوْمَ مُسْتَسْلِمُونَ ۝ وَأَقْبَلَ بَعْضُهُمْ عَلَىٰ بَعْضٍ يَتَسَآءَلُونَ ۝ قَالُوٓا۟ إِنَّكُمْ كُنتُمْ تَأْتُونَنَا عَنِ ٱلْيَمِينِ ۝ قَالُوا۟ بَل لَّمْ تَكُونُوا۟ مُؤْمِنِينَ ۝ وَمَا كَانَ لَنَا عَلَيْكُم مِّن سُلْطَٰنٍۭ بَلْ كُنتُمْ قَوْمًا طَٰغِينَ ۝ فَحَقَّ عَلَيْنَا قَوْلُ رَبِّنَآ إِنَّا لَذَآئِقُونَ ۝ فَأَغْوَيْنَٰكُمْ إِنَّا كُنَّا غَٰوِينَ ۝ فَإِنَّهُمْ يَوْمَئِذٍ فِى ٱلْعَذَابِ مُشْتَرِكُونَ ۝ إِنَّا كَذَٰلِكَ نَفْعَلُ بِٱلْمُجْرِمِينَ ۝ إِنَّهُمْ كَانُوٓا۟ إِذَا قِيلَ لَهُمْ لَآ إِلَٰهَ إِلَّا ٱللَّهُ يَسْتَكْبِرُونَ ۝

When we are dead and turned into dust and bones, are we to be resurrected? Our forefathers too?' Say: 'Yes indeed, and utterly humbled.' For it is only a single scaring, then behold, they are watching. And they shall say: 'O woe to us! This is the day of requital.' This indeed is the Day of Division, which you used to impugn. Muster those who did evil, their wives, and that they were worshiping. Apart from Allah, and guide them unto the path of Hell! Seize them, for they are account- able! Why help you not one another? Ah, but today they are in total surrender, and advance one upon another, asking each other questions, some saying: 'You used the right arm of power to lord it over us,' they will reply: 'Nay, you yourselves were bereft of all faith! We had no power over you – and you were already exceeding all limits. *The Word of our Lord has come true upon us, and we shall taste it. We seduced you, for we were indeed seducers.' So, all of them on that day are sharers in the chastisement. Thus, do We deal with wrongdoers. Whenever it was said to them, 'There is no deity but Allah,' they became arrogant.*

16-35 Individuals whose cosmology of life is limited to the body and mind are naturally unable to imagine life after death and may reckon that all will end with death. Those who have faith, belief, and the experience of transcendental states, know that death is a natural and appropriate redefinition of our human composition. Whatever was material within us reverts to the world of matter, and our soul continues its journey towards light but carries with it traces of this earthly life. With spiritual intelligence and God's grace, many people on earth do their best to be prepared for this natural eventuality, without fear, apprehension, or regret. Such people will experience a natural flow and ease of transfer from this life to the next. Individuals who have lived and practiced arrogance, vanity, pride, and the illusion of independence will naturally experience the big shock of death.

It is not easy to rise in consciousness to the point where we transcend our human limitations; this is why most human beings are in doubt and confusion. It is like a pyramid where the pinnacle is one point with a very wide base. Most human beings live in confusion and darkness.

The human natural habit is to follow what was beforehand, what was learned from parents and our culture, and deny things that are beyond the limitations of our mind and perception. The biggest gateway of opening up the heart towards higher levels of consciousness is total belief and trust in life in the hereafter, which means there are no more filters, value judgments, and other constraints that we live by in this world.

36-56 وَيَقُولُونَ أَئِنَّا لَتَارِكُوٓاْ ءَالِهَتِنَا لِشَاعِرٍ مَّجْنُونٍۭ ۝ بَلْ جَآءَ بِٱلْحَقِّ وَصَدَّقَ ٱلْمُرْسَلِينَ ۝ إِنَّكُمْ لَذَآئِقُواْ ٱلْعَذَابِ ٱلْأَلِيمِ ۝ وَمَا تُجْزَوْنَ إِلَّا مَا كُنتُمْ تَعْمَلُونَ ۝ إِلَّا عِبَادَ ٱللَّهِ ٱلْمُخْلَصِينَ ۝ أُوْلَٰٓئِكَ لَهُمْ رِزْقٌ مَّعْلُومٌ ۝ فَوَٰكِهُ وَهُم مُّكْرَمُونَ ۝ فِى جَنَّٰتِ ٱلنَّعِيمِ ۝ عَلَىٰ سُرُرٍ مُّتَقَٰبِلِينَ ۝ يُطَافُ عَلَيْهِم بِكَأْسٍ مِّن مَّعِينٍۭ ۝ بَيْضَآءَ لَذَّةٍ لِّلشَّٰرِبِينَ ۝ لَا فِيهَا غَوْلٌ وَلَا هُمْ عَنْهَا يُنزَفُونَ ۝ وَعِندَهُمْ قَٰصِرَٰتُ ٱلطَّرْفِ عِينٌ ۝ كَأَنَّهُنَّ بَيْضٌ مَّكْنُونٌ ۝ فَأَقْبَلَ بَعْضُهُمْ عَلَىٰ بَعْضٍ يَتَسَآءَلُونَ ۝ قَالَ قَآئِلٌ مِّنْهُمْ إِنِّى كَانَ لِى قَرِينٌ ۝ يَقُولُ أَءِنَّكَ لَمِنَ ٱلْمُصَدِّقِينَ ۝ أَءِذَا مِتْنَا وَكُنَّا تُرَابًا وَعِظَٰمًا أَءِنَّا لَمَدِينُونَ ۝ قَالَ هَلْ أَنتُم مُّطَّلِعُونَ ۝ فَٱطَّلَعَ فَرَءَاهُ فِى سَوَآءِ ٱلْجَحِيمِ ۝ قَالَ تَٱللَّهِ إِن كِدتَّ لَتُرْدِينِ ۝

Saying, 'What, shall we forsake our Gods for a poet possessed?' Rather, he came with the Truth, corroborating the messengers. You shall surely taste the most painful torment, nor will you be recompensed except for what you used to do. Except for the worshippers of Allah in all sincerity, for them awaits a known provision, fruits – and they high-honoured. In Gardens of Bliss, on couches, face to face, a cup from a spring being passed round to them, crystal clear, a delight to those who drink it. In it there is neither delirium nor are they intoxicated. And with them will be mates of modest gaze, most beautiful of eye, as if they were hidden pearls. And they shall approach each other and begin to question. One of them says, 'I had a comrade,' who would say, 'Are you a confirmer?' When we are dead and turned into dust and bones, will we be held to account? He will then say: 'Will you look down?' Then he looks, and sees him in the midst of Hell. And he will say: 'By Allah, you were about to destroy me!

36-56 Whenever a messenger expounded the pattern of life on earth and the hereafter, the majority of people were in denial, preferring what they were used to from past belief. It is in human nature to flow smoothly with a culture and way of life that we are used to. Our experience of the outer world is dependent on our inner state, which is very much a function of habits, culture, and religion. Our spiritual state dictates our state of mind and body. It is quite normal for a human being to make sense out of opposing dualities by seeking the easiest apparent flow and harmony. The awakened person will experience the interconnectedness of everything in existence, viewing the ever-changing world through the lens of timelessness and unity, as transmitted from the heart. The awakened person views the troubles of other peoples as gifts of warning from the unseen to help them to avoid the cause of their own trouble. The awakened person also sees wealth as a trial, because most distractions come from an excess of luxury and ease. Balanced, healthy connectedness between body, mind, and heart is a great fortune.

For thousands of years, prophets, seers, and enlightened beings were mocked, and people turned away from them, led by those who were wise in earthly dealings. Earthly darkness will be followed by total bleakness after death.

The light transmitted from the heart is so powerful that it can only be used through the mediation of the mind and other filters. But for us to get closer to the *Truth* and *Reality*, we need to turn away from all such limitations and distractions. This can only happen if we are regularly reminded, and connected with the light of the soul itself.

57-78 وَلَوْلَا نِعْمَةُ رَبِّي لَكُنتُ مِنَ ٱلْمُحْضَرِينَ ۝ أَفَمَا نَحْنُ بِمَيِّتِينَ ۝ إِلَّا مَوْتَتَنَا ٱلْأُولَىٰ وَمَا نَحْنُ بِمُعَذَّبِينَ ۝ إِنَّ هَٰذَا لَهُوَ ٱلْفَوْزُ ٱلْعَظِيمُ ۝ لِمِثْلِ هَٰذَا فَلْيَعْمَلِ ٱلْعَٰمِلُونَ ۝ أَذَٰلِكَ خَيْرٌ نُّزُلًا أَمْ شَجَرَةُ ٱلزَّقُّومِ ۝ إِنَّا جَعَلْنَٰهَا فِتْنَةً لِّلظَّٰلِمِينَ ۝

إِنَّهَا شَجَرَةٌ تَخْرُجُ فِىٓ أَصْلِ ٱلْجَحِيمِ ۝ طَلْعُهَا كَأَنَّهُۥ رُءُوسُ ٱلشَّيَٰطِينِ ۝ فَإِنَّهُمْ لَءَاكِلُونَ مِنْهَا فَمَالِـُٔونَ مِنْهَا ٱلْبُطُونَ ۝ ثُمَّ إِنَّ لَهُمْ عَلَيْهَا لَشَوْبًا مِّنْ حَمِيمٍ ۝ ثُمَّ إِنَّ مَرْجِعَهُمْ لَإِلَى ٱلْجَحِيمِ ۝ إِنَّهُمْ أَلْفَوْا۟ ءَابَآءَهُمْ ضَآلِّينَ ۝ فَهُمْ عَلَىٰٓ ءَاثَٰرِهِمْ يُهْرَعُونَ ۝ وَلَقَدْ ضَلَّ قَبْلَهُمْ أَكْثَرُ ٱلْأَوَّلِينَ ۝ وَلَقَدْ أَرْسَلْنَا فِيهِم مُّنذِرِينَ ۝ فَٱنظُرْ كَيْفَ كَانَ عَٰقِبَةُ ٱلْمُنذَرِينَ ۝ إِلَّا عِبَادَ ٱللَّهِ ٱلْمُخْلَصِينَ ۝ وَلَقَدْ نَادَىٰنَا نُوحٌ فَلَنِعْمَ ٱلْمُجِيبُونَ ۝ وَنَجَّيْنَٰهُ وَأَهْلَهُۥ مِنَ ٱلْكَرْبِ ٱلْعَظِيمِ ۝ وَجَعَلْنَا ذُرِّيَّتَهُۥ هُمُ ٱلْبَاقِينَ ۝ وَتَرَكْنَا عَلَيْهِ فِى ٱلْءَاخِرِينَ ۝

Were it not for the grace of my Lord, I would have been among those summoned to damnation. What, do we then not die except for our first death, and are we not chastised? This is truly the greatest of triumphs!' For such a reward let labourers labour. Is this a better welcome or the tree of Bitterness, which We set as an ordeal for the wicked? It is a tree that comes forth in the root of Hell; its spathes are as the heads of Satans, they shall eat from it and fill their bellies; then, in addition, they shall have a scalding drink, then will they be returned to hell. They found their forefathers astray, and rush along in their footsteps. Thus, indeed, most of the people of old went astray before them, to them We sent warners: behold the end of those who were warned! Except for those who worshipped Allah in all devotion. Noah called out to Us: how excellent were Those who answered! And We delivered him and his family from a mighty calamity, and We made his seed the survivors, and conferred honour upon him among later generations.

57-78 Time moves from its inception of timelessness back again to timelessness through an experienced destiny. We are driven in our worldly experience to move from lower levels of consciousness towards the highest. Our worldly journey involves many uncertainties, concerns, doubts, and darknesses, yet what we desire is a deep sense of trust and goodness, the realisation that we are in truth, a divine soul confined temporarily to a body and mind. To imagine that one is in charge of one's life or that we are independent from other entities on earth or heaven is a clear sign of a deficient mind and intellect. Most of us experience disappointment with others or with situations that we hoped would offer us reliability and goodness. Everything in this world is subject to change, balanced between desirables and undesirables, whereas pure joy and contentment belong to our soul. We need the mind to struggle with uncertainty and change, and we need constant referencing to our perfect soul.

The main obstacle to the ascent of human consciousness is the question of death and what comes after it. For this reason, most religions and spiritual paths advocate regular prayers, meditation, and attempts to transcend day-to-day consciousness.

The so-called normal life on earth can often cause considerable distractions, sorrow, and regrets. The only way to be recharged again by the *Source* of life within us is to still the mind, quieten the memory and all of the other noises, and then be at one with the constancy of the light transmitted from the heart. With this, you recalibrate and deal with the ups and downs of the world rationally and correctly.

79-100 سَلَٰمٌ عَلَىٰ نُوحٍ فِى ٱلْعَٰلَمِينَ ۝ إِنَّا كَذَٰلِكَ نَجْزِى ٱلْمُحْسِنِينَ ۝ إِنَّهُۥ مِنْ عِبَادِنَا ٱلْمُؤْمِنِينَ ۝ ثُمَّ أَغْرَقْنَا ٱلْءَاخَرِينَ ۝ وَإِنَّ مِن شِيعَتِهِۦ لَإِبْرَٰهِيمَ ۝ إِذْ جَآءَ رَبَّهُۥ بِقَلْبٍ سَلِيمٍ ۝ إِذْ قَالَ لِأَبِيهِ وَقَوْمِهِۦ مَاذَا تَعْبُدُونَ ۝ أَئِفْكًا ءَالِهَةً دُونَ ٱللَّهِ تُرِيدُونَ ۝ فَمَا ظَنُّكُم بِرَبِّ ٱلْعَٰلَمِينَ ۝ فَنَظَرَ نَظْرَةً فِى ٱلنُّجُومِ ۝ فَقَالَ إِنِّى سَقِيمٌ ۝ فَتَوَلَّوْا۟ عَنْهُ مُدْبِرِينَ ۝ فَرَاغَ إِلَىٰٓ ءَالِهَتِهِمْ فَقَالَ أَلَا تَأْكُلُونَ ۝ مَا لَكُمْ لَا تَنطِقُونَ ۝ فَرَاغَ عَلَيْهِمْ ضَرْبًۢا بِٱلْيَمِينِ ۝ فَأَقْبَلُوٓا۟ إِلَيْهِ يَزِفُّونَ ۝ قَالَ أَتَعْبُدُونَ مَا تَنْحِتُونَ ۝ وَٱللَّهُ خَلَقَكُمْ وَمَا تَعْمَلُونَ ۝ قَالُوا۟ ٱبْنُوا۟ لَهُۥ بُنْيَٰنًا فَأَلْقُوهُ فِى ٱلْجَحِيمِ ۝ فَأَرَادُوا۟ بِهِۦ كَيْدًا فَجَعَلْنَٰهُمُ ٱلْأَسْفَلِينَ ۝ وَقَالَ إِنِّى ذَاهِبٌ إِلَىٰ رَبِّى سَيَهْدِينِ ۝ رَبِّ هَبْ لِى مِنَ ٱلصَّٰلِحِينَ ۝

'Peace be upon Noah throughout all the worlds!' Thus, do We reward the virtuous. He was truly one of Our faithful servants. Then We drowned the others. Of his party was Abraham, when he came unto his Lord with a pure heart, he said to his father and his people, 'What are you worshipping? A delusion? Is it Gods you desire rather than Allah? How then do you regard the Lord of the Worlds?' So, he cast a glance at the stars and he said, 'Surely I am sick.' They turned from him and fled. He then secretly approached their Gods and asked: 'Will you not eat? What is it with you that you do not speak?' And he turned upon them, smiting them with his right hand. His people came to him in a hurry. He said: Do you worship what you sculpt with your own hands when it is Allah Who created you and all that you do?' They said: 'Build him a structure and hurl him into the raging flame.' They intended him mischief but We brought them low. He said: 'I shall go to my Lord and He shall guide me. My Lord, grant me a virtuous progeny.'

79-100 Thousands of messengers, prophets, and enlightened beings have come amongst human beings to expound upon the map of life as well as the human responsibility and duty to achieve the best. Most of these beings were denied serious consideration and were often subjected to resistance and harm. The one thread throughout these messages is: keep a clear head and a pure heart, maintain justice and equanimity through respect of others, and become accountable for one's own as well as others' progress on earth. It is God's generosity for us to experience needs and shortages in order to help us become more reflective, humble, and less wasteful. It is the enlightened being who realises that whatever situation they are in is best for their spiritual evolution and ascent upon the ladder of consciousness. Trusting in God's infinite mercy is a necessary step for those who want to understand it at all times, and so to live the moment fully.

14. Surah 37 As-Saffat (The Arrayed in Ranks)

With maturity, we seek a clearer mind and reason. With wisdom, we also try to have a purer heart with no anger or hatred. With a clear head and a pure heart, we occasionally experience an epiphany, which is like touching the gate of paradise. A determined seeker will regularly leave behind old habits to enter a higher zone of consciousness.

In our recent history, we had numerous beings who have been awakened to the truth of the wholesome heart. The influences of some of these people have been global. At the same time, we have seen many denials, people turning away from things that are not to do with space and time, which is all they are familiar with.

101-118

فَبَشَّرْنَٰهُ بِغُلَٰمٍ حَلِيمٍ ۝ فَلَمَّا بَلَغَ مَعَهُ ٱلسَّعْىَ قَالَ يَٰبُنَىَّ إِنِّىٓ أَرَىٰ فِى ٱلْمَنَامِ أَنِّىٓ أَذْبَحُكَ فَٱنظُرْ مَاذَا تَرَىٰ ۚ قَالَ يَٰٓأَبَتِ ٱفْعَلْ مَا تُؤْمَرُ ۖ سَتَجِدُنِىٓ إِن شَآءَ ٱللَّهُ مِنَ ٱلصَّٰبِرِينَ ۝ فَلَمَّآ أَسْلَمَا وَتَلَّهُۥ لِلْجَبِينِ ۝ وَنَٰدَيْنَٰهُ أَن يَٰٓإِبْرَٰهِيمُ ۝ قَدْ صَدَّقْتَ ٱلرُّءْيَآ ۚ إِنَّا كَذَٰلِكَ نَجْزِى ٱلْمُحْسِنِينَ ۝ إِنَّ هَٰذَا لَهُوَ ٱلْبَلَٰٓؤُا۟ ٱلْمُبِينُ ۝ وَفَدَيْنَٰهُ بِذِبْحٍ عَظِيمٍ ۝ وَتَرَكْنَا عَلَيْهِ فِى ٱلْءَاخِرِينَ ۝ سَلَٰمٌ عَلَىٰٓ إِبْرَٰهِيمَ ۝ كَذَٰلِكَ نَجْزِى ٱلْمُحْسِنِينَ ۝ إِنَّهُۥ مِنْ عِبَادِنَا ٱلْمُؤْمِنِينَ ۝ وَبَشَّرْنَٰهُ بِإِسْحَٰقَ نَبِيًّا مِّنَ ٱلصَّٰلِحِينَ ۝ وَبَٰرَكْنَا عَلَيْهِ وَعَلَىٰٓ إِسْحَٰقَ ۚ وَمِن ذُرِّيَّتِهِمَا مُحْسِنٌ وَظَالِمٌ لِّنَفْسِهِۦ مُبِينٌ ۝ وَلَقَدْ مَنَنَّا عَلَىٰ مُوسَىٰ وَهَٰرُونَ ۝ وَنَجَّيْنَٰهُمَا وَقَوْمَهُمَا مِنَ ٱلْكَرْبِ ٱلْعَظِيمِ ۝ وَنَصَرْنَٰهُمْ فَكَانُوا۟ هُمُ ٱلْغَٰلِبِينَ ۝ وَءَاتَيْنَٰهُمَا ٱلْكِتَٰبَ ٱلْمُسْتَبِينَ ۝ وَهَدَيْنَٰهُمَا ٱلصِّرَٰطَ ٱلْمُسْتَقِيمَ ۝

And We gave him glad tidings of a wise and forbearing son. When the son was old enough to accompany him, he said: 'My son, I saw in a dream that I was sacrificing you, so reflect and give me your opinion.' He said: 'Father, do as you are commanded and you shall find me, Allah willing, steadfast.' When both submitted, he bent his head down and on its side. And We called out to him: 'O Abraham. you have made your vision come true.' Thus, do We reward the virtuous. That was indeed a conspicuous ordeal. And We ransomed him with a tremendous sacrifice, and conferred for him among later generations. 'Peace be upon Abraham!' Thus, do We reward the virtuous. He was one of our faithful worshippers. Then We gave him the good tidings of Isaac, a Prophet, one of the righteous. And blessed him and Isaac too: some of their offspring were good, but some clearly wronged themselves. And We were gracious to Moses and Aaron, and We delivered them and their people from the great distress. And We came to their aid, and they were the victors. And We brought them both the Clarifying Book, guiding them to the straight path,

101-118 It is natural for an intelligent person to seek more knowledge and access to higher consciousness, in order to read the relevant signs and transcend limitations. Everyone is driven to have a better-quality life. This means a healthy body, clear mind, and pure heart. Our earthly journey is uncertain most of the time, yet we muddle through our daily living, blaming others or claiming our inadequacies are due to bad luck. The great Prophets Abraham, Noah, and many others were determined. They committed themselves to follow the divine light that had come to them through signs and indications. Their main strength was their ability to shut out the mental noise and listen to their soul. Awakened beings will always be afflicted with some doubts and outer uncertainties. They must rise with their faith, learn to be patient, and exercise total trust in God's guidance and perfect ways. Most people are concerned with survival and the thin veneer of comfort, ease, and earthly security. It's only a few who can truly live an enlightened way of life.

The ways of great prophets illumined the path for all humanity. The ultimate example and teaching of sacrifice comes to us from the Prophet Abraham, who was challenged by his soul to sever his worldly attachment to his son. Once he was willing to do that, his liberation was celebrated when the unseen and the visible worlds connected by displacing the sacrifice to that of an animal.

All worldly experiences come with their opposites. Good news or success can often be carrying the seeds of regret and sorrow. We have seen examples of great awakened ones who rose above the normal value judgments of good and bad and followed what the heart told them that had to be done, given up, or ignored.

119-140

وَتَرَكْنَا عَلَيْهِمَا فِى ٱلْءَاخِرِينَ ۝ سَلَـٰمٌ عَلَىٰ مُوسَىٰ وَهَـٰرُونَ ۝ إِنَّا كَذَٰلِكَ نَجْزِى ٱلْمُحْسِنِينَ ۝ إِنَّهُمَا مِنْ عِبَادِنَا ٱلْمُؤْمِنِينَ ۝ وَإِنَّ إِلْيَاسَ لَمِنَ ٱلْمُرْسَلِينَ ۝ إِذْ قَالَ لِقَوْمِهِۦٓ أَلَا تَتَّقُونَ ۝ أَتَدْعُونَ بَعْلًا وَتَذَرُونَ أَحْسَنَ ٱلْخَـٰلِقِينَ ۝ ٱللَّهَ رَبَّكُمْ وَرَبَّ ءَابَآئِكُمُ ٱلْأَوَّلِينَ ۝ فَكَذَّبُوهُ فَإِنَّهُمْ لَمُحْضَرُونَ ۝ إِلَّا عِبَادَ ٱللَّهِ ٱلْمُخْلَصِينَ ۝ وَتَرَكْنَا عَلَيْهِ فِى ٱلْءَاخِرِينَ ۝ سَلَـٰمٌ عَلَىٰٓ إِلْ يَاسِينَ ۝ إِنَّا كَذَٰلِكَ نَجْزِى ٱلْمُحْسِنِينَ ۝ إِنَّهُۥ مِنْ عِبَادِنَا ٱلْمُؤْمِنِينَ ۝ وَإِنَّ لُوطًا لَّمِنَ ٱلْمُرْسَلِينَ ۝ إِذْ نَجَّيْنَـٰهُ وَأَهْلَهُۥٓ أَجْمَعِينَ ۝ إِلَّا عَجُوزًا فِى ٱلْغَـٰبِرِينَ ۝ ثُمَّ دَمَّرْنَا ٱلْءَاخَرِينَ ۝ وَإِنَّكُمْ لَتَمُرُّونَ عَلَيْهِم مُّصْبِحِينَ ۝ وَبِٱلَّيْلِ أَفَلَا تَعْقِلُونَ ۝ وَإِنَّ يُونُسَ لَمِنَ ٱلْمُرْسَلِينَ ۝ إِذْ أَبَقَ إِلَى ٱلْفُلْكِ ٱلْمَشْحُونِ ۝

conferring on both among later generations. Peace be upon Moses and Aaron! Thus, do We reward the virtuous. Both were among our faithful worshippers. Elias too was a messenger. 'When he said to his people: Will you not have reverence? Do you call on Baal, and abandon the Best of creators? Allah is your Lord and the Lord of your ancient forefathers.' But they cried him lies; so they will be among the arraigned, all except the sincere worshippers of Allah. And We conferred upon him among later generations. Peace be upon the House of Elias! Thus, do We reward the virtuous. He was one of our faithful worshippers. Lot too was a messenger. Remember when We delivered him and all his household, save an old woman among those that tarried; then We destroyed the others, and you pass by them in the morning. and by night. Will you not, then, use your reason? Jonah too was a messenger. When he ran away to the laden ship,

119-140 Like the rest of humanity, the great awakened beings and prophets lived in the usual conditioned consciousness but with clear access to the divine light and the *Absolute*. Every human being experiences the limitations of body and mind; only a few were graced to transcend these limitations to the divine light transmitted from the heart. Patience implies timelessness. Whenever an awakened being is subjected to complete inability to act or change anything, they switch to supreme consciousness, where there is no time or space. It is natural for all of us to seek a certain measure of outer security, stability, and wellbeing; all of these are enhanced if our reference to supreme consciousness and the soul is frequent and clear. The quality of earthly life is as good as the quality of your spiritual state.

Total sincerity and loyalty are the most difficult tasks for human beings because of the illusion that one is merely a physical entity bracketed between birth and death. Only those who truly live as heavenly souls or spirits will not be confused by earthly afflictions and changes.

Human beings will remain confused, in doubt and darkness, suffering, unless they start climbing the ladder of consciousness by faith, trust, and constant reference to light within the soul. Otherwise, since we have evolved from the lowest of animal states, we can easily slip back into those darknesses. Through living faith, we become more and more connected with the eternal moment in the now: timeless, boundless, divine.

141-161 فَسَاهَمَ فَكَانَ مِنَ ٱلْمُدْحَضِينَ ۝ فَٱلْتَقَمَهُ ٱلْحُوتُ وَهُوَ مُلِيمٌ ۝ فَلَوْلَآ أَنَّهُۥ كَانَ مِنَ ٱلْمُسَبِّحِينَ ۝ لَلَبِثَ فِى بَطْنِهِۦٓ إِلَىٰ يَوْمِ يُبْعَثُونَ ۝ فَنَبَذْنَٰهُ بِٱلْعَرَآءِ وَهُوَ سَقِيمٌ ۝ وَأَنۢبَتْنَا عَلَيْهِ شَجَرَةً مِّن يَقْطِينٍ ۝ وَأَرْسَلْنَٰهُ إِلَىٰ مِا۟ئَةِ أَلْفٍ أَوْ يَزِيدُونَ ۝ فَـَٔامَنُوا۟ فَمَتَّعْنَٰهُمْ إِلَىٰ حِينٍ ۝ فَٱسْتَفْتِهِمْ أَلِرَبِّكَ ٱلْبَنَاتُ وَلَهُمُ ٱلْبَنُونَ ۝ أَمْ خَلَقْنَا ٱلْمَلَٰٓئِكَةَ إِنَٰثًا وَهُمْ شَٰهِدُونَ ۝ أَلَآ إِنَّهُم مِّنْ إِفْكِهِمْ لَيَقُولُونَ ۝ وَلَدَ ٱللَّهُ وَإِنَّهُمْ لَكَٰذِبُونَ ۝ أَصْطَفَى ٱلْبَنَاتِ عَلَى ٱلْبَنِينَ ۝ مَا لَكُمْ كَيْفَ تَحْكُمُونَ ۝ أَفَلَا تَذَكَّرُونَ ۝ أَمْ لَكُمْ سُلْطَٰنٌ مُّبِينٌ ۝ فَأْتُوا۟ بِكِتَٰبِكُمْ إِن كُنتُمْ صَٰدِقِينَ ۝ وَجَعَلُوا۟ بَيْنَهُۥ وَبَيْنَ ٱلْجِنَّةِ نَسَبًا وَلَقَدْ عَلِمَتِ ٱلْجِنَّةُ إِنَّهُمْ لَمُحْضَرُونَ ۝ سُبْحَٰنَ ٱللَّهِ عَمَّا يَصِفُونَ ۝ إِلَّا عِبَادَ ٱللَّهِ ٱلْمُخْلَصِينَ ۝ فَإِنَّكُمْ وَمَا تَعْبُدُونَ ۝

he cast lots and was bested. Then the whale swallowed him down, and he blameworthy. Had he not been one who glorified, he would have tarried in its belly until the day they shall be raised; We then cast him out into the wilderness, ailing. And We caused to sprout over him a tree of gourd, and sent him to a hundred thousand, or more. They believed, so We granted them enjoyment of life for a while. So, sound them out: 'To your Lord daughters are born, and to them sons? Or did We create the angels females, while they were witnesses?' Oh, verily, it is out of their own falsehood that some people assert, 'Allah has begotten.' How they lie! Has He chosen daughters above sons? What is it with you and your judgments? Will you not remember? Or have you a clear authority? Bring your Book, if you speak truly! They have set up a kinship between Him and the jinn; and the jinn know that they shall be arraigned. Glory be to Allah above that they describe, save for the devout worshippers of Allah. you, and what you worship,

141-161 Prophet Jonah being swallowed by a whale is a great metaphor. Every human being is subjected to difficult periods of darkness and doubt without knowing how and when their suffering will end. A difficult situation in which you don't know what to do or where to look for an answer is a great opportunity to fully surrender to God and trust that the *One* who caused you this difficulty will also be the *One* who will bring you relief. The animal in us panics when confronted by intense difficulty or the fear of death, losing the opportunity to corner the lower self. With God's grace, if you are on a prophetic path, you can switch off the mind's confusion and enter into a reflective state, transcending the animal condition that has fallen upon you. Transcendence is best practiced when your humanity – body and mind – is in a reasonable state, not confused by fear and other emergencies. Not until you constantly tap into the light of the soul within your heart will you experience the thrill of the lights of higher consciousness and your heavenly destiny. Indeed, we are here to practice the seamless perfect balance between humanity and divinity.

Our soul can understand and connect with the absolute infinitude and, via the mind, the relative changes within space and time. It is only through higher awareness that we can touch upon the original memory of pre-creation that resides in our heart.

Many of the great prophets and awakened ones had occasions when they also touched upon the darkness with regrets and repentance; this is the nature of the climb towards the ultimate light. None of us are spared such situations so that we do not become spiritually arrogant. We have to be vigilant, diligent, always willing to give up whatever mindset we are in, and return to the light within our hearts. This requires total commitment in sincerity, honesty, loyalty, and courage.

162-182 مَآ أَنتُمْ عَلَيْهِ بِفَٰتِنِينَ ۝ إِلَّا مَنْ هُوَ صَالِ ٱلْجَحِيمِ ۝ وَمَا مِنَّآ إِلَّا لَهُۥ مَقَامٌ مَّعْلُومٌ ۝ وَإِنَّا لَنَحْنُ ٱلصَّآفُّونَ ۝ وَإِنَّا لَنَحْنُ ٱلْمُسَبِّحُونَ ۝ وَإِن كَانُوا۟ لَيَقُولُونَ ۝ لَوْ أَنَّ عِندَنَا ذِكْرًا مِّنَ ٱلْأَوَّلِينَ ۝ لَكُنَّا عِبَادَ ٱللَّهِ ٱلْمُخْلَصِينَ ۝ فَكَفَرُوا۟ بِهِۦ فَسَوْفَ يَعْلَمُونَ ۝ وَلَقَدْ سَبَقَتْ كَلِمَتُنَا لِعِبَادِنَا ٱلْمُرْسَلِينَ ۝

إِنَّهُمْ لَهُمُ ٱلْمَنصُورُونَ ۝ وَإِنَّ جُندَنَا لَهُمُ ٱلْغَٰلِبُونَ ۝ فَتَوَلَّ عَنْهُمْ حَتَّىٰ حِينٍ ۝ وَأَبْصِرْهُمْ فَسَوْفَ يُبْصِرُونَ ۝ أَفَبِعَذَابِنَا يَسْتَعْجِلُونَ ۝ فَإِذَا نَزَلَ بِسَاحَتِهِمْ فَسَآءَ صَبَاحُ ٱلْمُنذَرِينَ ۝ وَتَوَلَّ عَنْهُمْ حَتَّىٰ حِينٍ ۝ وَأَبْصِرْ فَسَوْفَ يُبْصِرُونَ ۝ سُبْحَٰنَ رَبِّكَ رَبِّ ٱلْعِزَّةِ عَمَّا يَصِفُونَ ۝ وَسَلَٰمٌ عَلَى ٱلْمُرْسَلِينَ ۝ وَٱلْحَمْدُ لِلَّهِ رَبِّ ٱلْعَٰلَمِينَ ۝

shall not lead any astray from Him, save those to be scorched in hell. None of us is there, but has a known station; We are indeed arrayed in ranks; We are indeed the glorifiers. What though they would say, 'If only we had had a Reminder from the ancients, we would be devout servants of Allah.' Yet now they disbelieve. They will soon know Our Word has already passed to Our servants the messengers, that they shall be granted victory, that Our troops shall prevail. So, leave them alone for a while, and observe them, and their eyes shall be opened. Is it Our torment they wish to hasten? When it descends on their courtyards, how terrible that morning will be for those who were warned! So, leave them alone for a while, and observe, and their eyes shall be opened. Glory be to thy Lord, the Lord of Glory, above that they describe! Peace be upon the messengers! Praise be to Allah, Lord of the Worlds.

162-182 We can perform our duties and responsibilities in a wholesome way when we are in reasonable balance and in a heathy state. If we are ill or overly concerned about survival or afflicted by old age or illness, we are naturally less able to connect with higher consciousness. An enlightened person is often in touch with the timelessness and boundlessness of higher consciousness, and is recharged. Our soul is graced with the lights of all the divine qualities and attributes. If you know that within you lies a boundless treasure that carries all the divine qualities, you will want to fulfil your duty towards your own self, which is to awaken to your soul. This essential duty toward your real self will not detract from your earthly duties but will bestow a higher potency of goodness and success in all that you do in the outer world. You begin to experience joyful living, with gratitude to all the great ones and prophets who have travelled along this path, and to share this great privilege and responsibility on earth.

Sincerity will eventually lead us to the realisation that we are not a body and a mind and that our life is due to a soul which is eternal. It is natural for us to want to rise in knowledge and consciousness, which means moving from sight to insight. This path is paved with grace and is for those who truly deserve it.

The divine creation is so immense and vast that it is like an iceberg; we only see the tip of it, if at all. Many forces and powers in the unseen drive this creation of ours over billions of years towards higher awareness and consciousness until everything reaches its original point of eternal boundlessness. This is the destiny that anything alive leads towards. Some of us are more fortunate than others in being in the constancy of that higher state; many others are in the turmoil of the warfare between the higher and the lower within ourselves.

15. Surah 38 Saad (Saad)

The divine light is ever continuous and boundless. The human heart and soul carry traces of that cosmic *Reality*, which manifests as reminders and memories in our heart. The soul is eternal, and the human mind, body, and form are transitory; they connect the celestial soul with the terrestrial self.

بِسْمِ اللَّهِ الرَّحْمَٰنِ الرَّحِيمِ

1-11 صٓ وَٱلْقُرْءَانِ ذِى ٱلذِّكْرِ ۝ بَلِ ٱلَّذِينَ كَفَرُواْ فِى عِزَّةٍ وَشِقَاقٍ ۝ كَمْ أَهْلَكْنَا مِن قَبْلِهِم مِّن قَرْنٍ فَنَادَواْ وَّلَاتَ حِينَ مَنَاصٍ ۝ وَعَجِبُوٓاْ أَن جَآءَهُم مُّنذِرٌ مِّنْهُمْ وَقَالَ ٱلْكَٰفِرُونَ هَٰذَا سَٰحِرٌ كَذَّابٌ ۝ أَجَعَلَ ٱلْءَالِهَةَ إِلَٰهًا وَٰحِدًا إِنَّ هَٰذَا لَشَىْءٌ عُجَابٌ ۝ وَٱنطَلَقَ ٱلْمَلَأُ مِنْهُمْ أَنِ ٱمْشُواْ وَٱصْبِرُواْ عَلَىٰٓ ءَالِهَتِكُمْ إِنَّ هَٰذَا لَشَىْءٌ يُرَادُ ۝ مَا سَمِعْنَا بِهَٰذَا فِى ٱلْمِلَّةِ ٱلْءَاخِرَةِ إِنْ هَٰذَآ إِلَّا ٱخْتِلَٰقٌ ۝ أَءُنزِلَ عَلَيْهِ ٱلذِّكْرُ مِنۢ بَيْنِنَا بَلْ هُمْ فِى شَكٍّ مِّن ذِكْرِى بَل لَّمَّا يَذُوقُواْ عَذَابِ ۝ أَمْ عِندَهُمْ خَزَآئِنُ رَحْمَةِ رَبِّكَ ٱلْعَزِيزِ ٱلْوَهَّابِ ۝ أَمْ لَهُم مُّلْكُ ٱلسَّمَٰوَٰتِ وَٱلْأَرْضِ وَمَا بَيْنَهُمَا فَلْيَرْتَقُواْ فِى ٱلْأَسْبَٰبِ ۝ جُندٌ مَّا هُنَالِكَ مَهْزُومٌ مِّنَ ٱلْأَحْزَابِ ۝

In the name of Allah, the Merciful to all, the Compassionate to each!

Saad. By the Qur'an of Remembrance. But those who disbelieve are in pride and dissension. How many a generation We destroyed before them! They cried for help, but there was no time for escape. They find it strange that a warner has come to them, of their number; and the disbelievers say: 'He is a lying sorcerer. Does he reduce the Gods to One Allah? This is surely a thing most bizarre!' And the Council of them depart, saying 'Go! Be steadfast to your Gods; this is a thing to be desired. We never heard of this in the latter faiths. This is nothing but fabrication. Was the Remembrance sent down on him – from among us all?' No indeed! Rather, they are in doubt regarding My Remembrance. Or rather, they have yet to taste torment! Or is it that they possess the treasures of your Lord's mercy, mighty and All-Giving? Or the dominion over the heavens and the earth and all that is between them is theirs? Why, then, let them try to ascend by all means! An army of Confederates will therein be put to rout!

1-11 The human mind discriminates, discerns, and differentiates; this allows us to maintain our natural drive for survival, as well as our drive towards greater knowledge and understanding within the confinement and boundaries of space and time. Every human being is driven to choose what they consider to be most durable and conducive to contentment; these are necessary experiences for higher consciousness. For thousands of years, the quest of human beings has been to discover ways and means that lead us to a higher, finer quality of life individually and collectively. Our soul is in a zone where these dualities do not cause the usual disturbances that the mind experiences. Being present in mind and heart implies understanding what is relative and varies in each moment, as well as calibrating and recharging with a constant light transmitted from our soul and spirit.

All of creation emanates from the infinite unseen, and everything is interconnected. Sound and language are very important means of linking and communicating. The rise in consciousness begins with the realisation of the immensity of *Reality* and *Truth* and the insignificance of individuality and identity.

The human challenge boils down to one major issue to do with duality. We either accept the truth that we have emanated from *Oneness* and return to it or we remain in doubt, denial, and confusion. Due to the light of intelligence, the former is the natural conclusion of an evolution towards the highest level of consciousness. Our job is to rise higher and higher along towards that level.

12-23 كَذَّبَتْ قَبْلَهُمْ قَوْمُ نُوحٍ وَعَادٌ وَفِرْعَوْنُ ذُو ٱلْأَوْتَادِ ۝ وَثَمُودُ وَقَوْمُ لُوطٍ وَأَصْحَٰبُ لْـَٔيْكَةِ أُوْلَٰٓئِكَ ٱلْأَحْزَابُ ۝ إِن كُلٌّ إِلَّا كَذَّبَ ٱلرُّسُلَ فَحَقَّ عِقَابِ ۝ وَمَا يَنظُرُ هَٰٓؤُلَآءِ إِلَّا صَيْحَةً وَٰحِدَةً مَّا لَهَا مِن فَوَاقٍ ۝ وَقَالُوا۟ رَبَّنَا عَجِّل لَّنَا قِطَّنَا قَبْلَ يَوْمِ ٱلْحِسَابِ ۝ ٱصْبِرْ عَلَىٰ مَا يَقُولُونَ وَٱذْكُرْ عَبْدَنَا دَاوُۥدَ ذَا ٱلْأَيْدِ إِنَّهُۥٓ أَوَّابٌ ۝ إِنَّا سَخَّرْنَا ٱلْجِبَالَ مَعَهُۥ يُسَبِّحْنَ بِٱلْعَشِيِّ وَٱلْإِشْرَاقِ ۝ وَٱلطَّيْرَ مَحْشُورَةً كُلٌّۭ لَّهُۥٓ أَوَّابٌ ۝ وَشَدَدْنَا مُلْكَهُۥ وَءَاتَيْنَٰهُ ٱلْحِكْمَةَ وَفَصْلَ ٱلْخِطَابِ ۝ وَهَلْ أَتَىٰكَ نَبَؤُا۟ ٱلْخَصْمِ إِذْ تَسَوَّرُوا۟ ٱلْمِحْرَابَ ۝ إِذْ دَخَلُوا۟ عَلَىٰ دَاوُۥدَ فَفَزِعَ مِنْهُمْ قَالُوا۟ لَا تَخَفْ خَصْمَانِ بَغَىٰ بَعْضُنَا عَلَىٰ بَعْضٍ فَٱحْكُم بَيْنَنَا بِٱلْحَقِّ وَلَا تُشْطِطْ وَٱهْدِنَآ إِلَىٰ سَوَآءِ ٱلصِّرَٰطِ ۝ إِنَّ هَٰذَآ أَخِى لَهُۥ تِسْعٌ وَتِسْعُونَ نَعْجَةً وَلِىَ نَعْجَةٌ وَٰحِدَةٌ فَقَالَ أَكْفِلْنِيهَا وَعَزَّنِى فِى ٱلْخِطَابِ ۝

Before them lied the people of Noah, of Ad, and of Pharaoh, he of the pegs, as too Thamud, the people of Lot and the People of the Thicket – these are the Confederates. Not one, that cried not lies to the Messengers, so My retribution was just. These can only expect a single Scream, from which there is no recovery. They say, 'Our Lord, hasten to us our share before the Day of Reckoning.' Bear their words patiently. Remember Our servant David, a man of strength who always turned to Us: with him We subjected the mountains to give glory at evening and sunrise, and the birds, duly mustered, everyone to him reverting; We strengthened his kingdom, and gave him wisdom and speech decisive. Has the tiding of the dispute come to you? When they scaled the Sanctuary, when they reached David, he took fright, but they said, 'Do not be afraid. We are two litigants, one of whom has wronged the other: judge between us fairly – do not be unjust – and guide us to the right path. This, my brother, has ninety-nine ewes and I have but one. And yet he says to me: 'Place her in my charge,' and he overcomes me in argument.'

12-23 The normal mental processes cannot comprehend the state of consciousness and *Reality*. This is why most people and nations to whom this message was given, remained in denial and resisted and opposed its content, discord, agitation, and opposition are natural phenomena in the world of duality; they are aspects of the natural drive for creation to dominate, survive, and control others. Life on earth is a mere shadow of the real and perpetual life towards which everything is travelling and will arrive. The lower nature of humanity creates wickedness, discord, and confusion, causing individual and collective suffering until the light of *Truth* dispels all these darknesses. The soul and divine light always triumph.

The lower self naturally denies and asserts its shadowy identity. Anything that exists wants to continue, since the entire universe has emerged from what is eternal and infinite. The awakened being is exposed to numerous levels of consciousness and realities; the so-called normal reality we know on earth is only one of them.

For the last few thousand years, we had repeated reminders through prophets or enlightened people, showing that our world of duality has its laws and regulations. Yet these are only manifestations of the timeless, boundless *Truth* of the divine light towards which we are aspiring.

24-32 قَالَ لَقَدْ ظَلَمَكَ بِسُؤَالِ نَعْجَتِكَ إِلَىٰ نِعَاجِهِۦ ۖ وَإِنَّ كَثِيرًا مِّنَ ٱلْخُلَطَآءِ لَيَبْغِى بَعْضُهُمْ عَلَىٰ بَعْضٍ إِلَّا ٱلَّذِينَ ءَامَنُوا۟ وَعَمِلُوا۟ ٱلصَّٰلِحَٰتِ وَقَلِيلٌ مَّا هُمْ ۗ وَظَنَّ دَاوُۥدُ أَنَّمَا فَتَنَّٰهُ فَٱسْتَغْفَرَ رَبَّهُۥ وَخَرَّ رَاكِعًا وَأَنَابَ ۩ ۝ فَغَفَرْنَا لَهُۥ ذَٰلِكَ ۖ وَإِنَّ لَهُۥ عِندَنَا لَزُلْفَىٰ وَحُسْنَ مَـَٔابٍ ۝ يَٰدَاوُۥدُ إِنَّا جَعَلْنَٰكَ خَلِيفَةً فِى ٱلْأَرْضِ فَٱحْكُم بَيْنَ ٱلنَّاسِ بِٱلْحَقِّ وَلَا تَتَّبِعِ ٱلْهَوَىٰ فَيُضِلَّكَ عَن سَبِيلِ ٱللَّهِ ۚ إِنَّ ٱلَّذِينَ يَضِلُّونَ عَن سَبِيلِ ٱللَّهِ لَهُمْ عَذَابٌ شَدِيدٌۢ بِمَا نَسُوا۟ يَوْمَ ٱلْحِسَابِ ۝ وَمَا خَلَقْنَا ٱلسَّمَآءَ وَٱلْأَرْضَ وَمَا بَيْنَهُمَا بَٰطِلًا ۚ ذَٰلِكَ ظَنُّ ٱلَّذِينَ كَفَرُوا۟ ۚ فَوَيْلٌ لِّلَّذِينَ كَفَرُوا۟ مِنَ ٱلنَّارِ ۝ أَمْ نَجْعَلُ ٱلَّذِينَ ءَامَنُوا۟ وَعَمِلُوا۟ ٱلصَّٰلِحَٰتِ كَٱلْمُفْسِدِينَ فِى ٱلْأَرْضِ أَمْ نَجْعَلُ ٱلْمُتَّقِينَ كَٱلْفُجَّارِ ۝ كِتَٰبٌ أَنزَلْنَٰهُ إِلَيْكَ مُبَٰرَكٌ لِّيَدَّبَّرُوٓا۟ ءَايَٰتِهِۦ وَلِيَتَذَكَّرَ أُو۟لُوا۟ ٱلْأَلْبَٰبِ ۝ وَوَهَبْنَا لِدَاوُۥدَ سُلَيْمَٰنَ ۚ نِعْمَ ٱلْعَبْدُ ۖ إِنَّهُۥٓ أَوَّابٌ ۝ إِذْ عُرِضَ عَلَيْهِ بِٱلْعَشِىِّ ٱلصَّٰفِنَٰتُ ٱلْجِيَادُ ۝ فَقَالَ إِنِّىٓ أَحْبَبْتُ حُبَّ ٱلْخَيْرِ عَن ذِكْرِ رَبِّى حَتَّىٰ تَوَارَتْ بِٱلْحِجَابِ ۝

He said: 'He has done you wrong by badgering you to add your ewe to his. Indeed, many who own in common transgress against one another – save those who believe and do good deeds, and they are few in number.' And David imagined that We had put him to the test. So, he sought his Lord's forgiveness, fell in prostration and repented. Accordingly, We forgave him that, and he has a near place in Our presence and a fair resort. 'David, behold, We have appointed you a viceroy in the earth; therefore judge between men justly, and follow not caprice, lest it lead you astray from the way of Allah. Surely those who go astray from the way of Allah – there awaits them a terrible chastisement, for that they have forgotten the Day of Reckoning.' We have not created the heavens and earth, and what between them is, for vanity; such is the thought of the unbelievers, wherefore woe unto the unbelievers because of the Fire! But would We treat those who believe and do good deeds and those who spread corruption on earth as equal? Would We treat those who are aware of Allah and those who recklessly break all bounds in the same way? Here is a Book We brought down upon you, blessed, that they might ponder its verses and that men possessed of mind might remember. And on David We bestowed Solomon – excellent was he as servant, and ever repentant! Remember when, on an evening, were displayed before him horses frisky and fleet. He kept saying, 'My love of fine things is part of my remembering my Lord!' until they [the horses] disappeared from sight.

24-32 It is the lower nature of a person that wants to acquire more wealth, power, and knowledge than others. We disturb the natural balance of kindness, friendship, and cooperation when the lower self desires to dominate others, mimicking the power of the soul within. The only way to address the imbalance of our lower nature is to contain it, accepting limitations and boundaries for the lower self. An awakened person is always aware of the lurking, lower shadow of the self; by this awareness, attention is always focused upon the higher nature of the light of the soul within. Those with this knowledge act with the best intentions and have a naturally higher state and better-quality life than others. The nature and conduct of thousands of previous prophets demonstrates the superiority of this balance between the best of humanity and the light of divinity. When that calibration is optimised, then the intensity with which we experience the moment is at its optimum best. That is what is often described as the treasure of the mercy of the Lord of Creation.

The human journey is from the lowest, smallest entity with very limited consciousness towards supreme consciousness. What was revealed to some of the great beings is passed onto us in books and scriptures, but we can only progress according to our capacity and discipline, leaving everything behind for the inner light.

Whatever is known and unknown follows patterns and designs that have their own perfection and justice. This implies that we too need to do our utmost to maintain balance, fairness, and justice in our worldly affairs. We are, at best, practising stewardship so as to not have any regrets or deviations from the path of rising consciousness. The more we live our duty, the more we are prepared for the next phase of experience after death.

33-47 رُدُّوهَا عَلَىَّ فَطَفِقَ مَسْحًا بِالسُّوقِ وَالْأَعْنَاقِ ۝ وَلَقَدْ فَتَنَّا سُلَيْمَانَ وَأَلْقَيْنَا عَلَىٰ كُرْسِيِّهِ جَسَدًا ثُمَّ أَنَابَ ۝ قَالَ رَبِّ اغْفِرْ لِي وَهَبْ لِي مُلْكًا لَّا يَنبَغِي لِأَحَدٍ مِّنْ بَعْدِي إِنَّكَ أَنتَ الْوَهَّابُ ۝ فَسَخَّرْنَا لَهُ الرِّيحَ تَجْرِي بِأَمْرِهِ رُخَاءً حَيْثُ أَصَابَ ۝ وَالشَّيَاطِينَ كُلَّ بَنَّاءٍ وَغَوَّاصٍ ۝ وَآخَرِينَ مُقَرَّنِينَ فِي الْأَصْفَادِ ۝ هَٰذَا عَطَاؤُنَا فَامْنُنْ أَوْ أَمْسِكْ بِغَيْرِ حِسَابٍ ۝ وَإِنَّ لَهُ عِندَنَا لَزُلْفَىٰ وَحُسْنَ مَآبٍ ۝ وَاذْكُرْ عَبْدَنَا أَيُّوبَ إِذْ نَادَىٰ رَبَّهُ أَنِّي مَسَّنِيَ الشَّيْطَانُ بِنُصْبٍ وَعَذَابٍ ۝ ارْكُضْ بِرِجْلِكَ هَٰذَا مُغْتَسَلٌ بَارِدٌ وَشَرَابٌ ۝ وَوَهَبْنَا لَهُ أَهْلَهُ وَمِثْلَهُم مَّعَهُمْ رَحْمَةً مِّنَّا وَذِكْرَىٰ لِأُولِي الْأَلْبَابِ ۝ وَخُذْ بِيَدِكَ ضِغْثًا فَاضْرِب بِّهِ وَلَا تَحْنَثْ إِنَّا وَجَدْنَاهُ صَابِرًا نِّعْمَ الْعَبْدُ إِنَّهُ أَوَّابٌ ۝ وَاذْكُرْ عِبَادَنَا إِبْرَاهِيمَ وَإِسْحَاقَ وَيَعْقُوبَ أُولِي الْأَيْدِي وَالْأَبْصَارِ ۝ إِنَّا أَخْلَصْنَاهُم بِخَالِصَةٍ ذِكْرَى الدَّارِ ۝ وَإِنَّهُمْ عِندَنَا لَمِنَ الْمُصْطَفَيْنَ الْأَخْيَارِ ۝

'Bring them back!' and started to stroke their legs and necks. Certainly, We tried Solomon, and We cast upon his throne a mere body; then he repented, and said: 'My Lord, forgive me, and grant me a kingship which no one after me shall possess; it is You Who are All-Giving.' We placed the wind at his service to blow at his command, mildly, and wherever he pleased; as well as all the rebellious forces – every kind of builder and diver and others linked together in fetters. 'This is Our gift; bestow or withhold without reckoning.' And he had a near place in Our presence and a fair resort. And mention too Our servant Job, when he called out to his Lord: 'Satan has touched me with hardship and torment.' [So, he was told], 'Kick with your foot: this is a place for washing, cool, and for drinking.' And We restored to him his family, and their like with them, as a mercy from Us, and a remembrance to men possessed of minds. 'Clasp a bunch of grass with your hand, and strike with it, and do not break your oath.' We found him to be patient – excellent was he as servant, and ever repentant. Remember also Our servants Abraham, Isaac and Jacob – men of might they and of vision. Assuredly We purified them with a quality most pure, the remembrance of the Abode, with Us they shall be among the most virtuous of the elect.

33-47 An awakened person knows that in truth no creature can take him out of darkness and mistakes except the divine light acting through numerous agencies, seen or unseen. Ordinary people desire more power, wealth, and knowledge, which can also bring harm due to the nature of the lower self. Numerous prophets and messengers were given access to natural and supernatural powers, which they only exercised with God's approval. To have access to that much power without clear boundaries and accountability to God is a big danger, individually and collectively. Many people have been killed and many more have suffered from destruction and impoverishment due to the most dangerous human weapons, the armaments industry, and the powerful drives of those who manufacture and invest in these evil weapons. We have become used to the hypocrisy of waging wars, small and big, yet pretend that we want peace and friendship.

We are so privileged as human beings to have received numerous waves of reminders about who we really are and the direction we are meant to follow. Thousands of prophets and awakened beings have left their traces for us, reminders that there is a higher purpose to everything, which we can reach only by transcending everything else other than it.

According to our attunement with the light in our own soul, we will be able to see how everything flows in its own perfect way according to prescribed patterns. Yet, because of our personal hopes and desires, we do not always read the situation as it is, and quite often act against the flow of nature. The result of that deviation can only be failure and regret.

48-63 وَاذْكُرْ إِسْمَٰعِيلَ وَالْيَسَعَ وَذَا الْكِفْلِ ۖ وَكُلٌّ مِّنَ الْأَخْيَارِ ۝ هَٰذَا ذِكْرٌ ۚ وَإِنَّ لِلْمُتَّقِينَ لَحُسْنَ مَـَٔابٍ ۝ جَنَّٰتِ عَدْنٍ مُّفَتَّحَةً لَّهُمُ الْأَبْوَٰبُ ۝ مُتَّكِـِٔينَ فِيهَا يَدْعُونَ فِيهَا بِفَٰكِهَةٍ كَثِيرَةٍ وَشَرَابٍ ۝ وَعِندَهُمْ قَٰصِرَٰتُ الطَّرْفِ أَتْرَابٌ ۝ هَٰذَا مَا تُوعَدُونَ لِيَوْمِ الْحِسَابِ ۝ إِنَّ هَٰذَا لَرِزْقُنَا مَا لَهُ مِن نَّفَادٍ ۝ هَٰذَا ۚ وَإِنَّ لِلطَّٰغِينَ لَشَرَّ مَـَٔابٍ ۝ جَهَنَّمَ يَصْلَوْنَهَا فَبِئْسَ الْمِهَادُ ۝ هَٰذَا فَلْيَذُوقُوهُ حَمِيمٌ وَغَسَّاقٌ ۝ وَءَاخَرُ مِن شَكْلِهِۦٓ أَزْوَٰجٌ ۝ هَٰذَا فَوْجٌ مُّقْتَحِمٌ مَّعَكُمْ ۖ لَا مَرْحَبًۢا بِهِمْ ۚ إِنَّهُمْ صَالُوا۟ النَّارِ ۝ قَالُوا۟ بَلْ أَنتُمْ لَا مَرْحَبًۢا بِكُمْ ۖ أَنتُمْ قَدَّمْتُمُوهُ لَنَا ۖ فَبِئْسَ الْقَرَارُ ۝ قَالُوا۟ رَبَّنَا مَن قَدَّمَ لَنَا هَٰذَا فَزِدْهُ عَذَابًا ضِعْفًا فِى النَّارِ ۝ وَقَالُوا۟ مَا لَنَا لَا نَرَىٰ رِجَالًا كُنَّا نَعُدُّهُم مِّنَ الْأَشْرَارِ ۝ أَتَّخَذْنَٰهُمْ سِخْرِيًّا أَمْ زَاغَتْ عَنْهُمُ الْأَبْصَٰرُ ۝

And mention too Ishmael, Elisha and Dhu'l Kifl: all most worthy. This is a reminder; and most surely there is an excellent resort for those who are cautiously aware. Gardens of perpetual bliss, with gates wide-open to them, they shall recline therein, and shall call therein for fruits in abundance, and drink, having beside them well-matched mates of modest gaze. This is what you are promised for the Day of Reckoning: such is Our bounty, inexhaustible. But then, the worst homecoming awaits transgressors: Hell – with which they shall be scorched – wretched is that berth! That is so. Let them taste it: scalding water and pus, and other torments of the like kind coupled together. 'Here is a batch of people plunging into it with you! No "Welcome" to them: they shall be scorched by the Fire'. They will say: 'It is you rather who are not welcome. It is you who led us to it – wretched is this destination!' They will say: 'Our Lord, whoever led us into this, multiply his torment in the Fire.' They will say: 'Why is it that we do not see men we used to regard as evil? What, did we take them for a laughing-stock? Or have our eyes swerved away from them?'

48-63 God's provisions and gifts are endless, but our experience on earth is limited and coloured by our mental state and judgments.

Our intentions and actions in this world are the assets that will be our main provision in the hereafter. Indeed, the meek and the weak will inherit the everlasting state in the hereafter and in the zone of timelessness. Their minds and hearts may be less darkened by earthly desire and greed. The great, mysterious life consciousness that we experience carries traces of the ancient past as well as that which existed prior to creation. Through this pre-time consciousness, we can reach a point of sublime connectedness between the seen and the unseen, between our life on earth and in the hereafter.

Paradise is open to all, but most people are preoccupied with their own illusions and the distractions of afflictions and suffering that they have created themselves. We must remember and know that there are two zones of consciousness that are transmitted from our own soul: one deals with the body, mind, and world; the other is light upon light.

Arrogance and ignorance may cause us to consider others inferior to ourselves and to think that we deserve more than they do. In truth, we are as good as our trust in the perfection of the moment, our caution about the darkness of the lower self and the ego, and our desire to be in constant calibration with the divine light in our hearts.

64-78 إِنَّ ذَٰلِكَ لَحَقٌّ تَخَاصُمُ أَهْلِ ٱلنَّارِ ۝ قُلْ إِنَّمَآ أَنَا۠ مُنذِرٌ وَمَا مِنْ إِلَٰهٍ إِلَّا ٱللَّهُ ٱلْوَٰحِدُ ٱلْقَهَّارُ ۝ رَبُّ ٱلسَّمَٰوَٰتِ وَٱلْأَرْضِ وَمَا بَيْنَهُمَا ٱلْعَزِيزُ ٱلْغَفَّٰرُ ۝ قُلْ هُوَ نَبَؤٌاْ عَظِيمٌ ۝ أَنتُمْ عَنْهُ مُعْرِضُونَ ۝ مَا كَانَ لِىَ مِنْ عِلْمٍۭ بِٱلْمَلَإِ ٱلْأَعْلَىٰٓ إِذْ يَخْتَصِمُونَ ۝ إِن يُوحَىٰٓ إِلَىَّ إِلَّآ أَنَّمَآ أَنَا۠ نَذِيرٌ مُّبِينٌ ۝ إِذْ قَالَ رَبُّكَ لِلْمَلَٰٓئِكَةِ إِنِّى خَٰلِقٌۢ بَشَرًا مِّن طِينٍ ۝ فَإِذَا سَوَّيْتُهُۥ وَنَفَخْتُ فِيهِ مِن رُّوحِى فَقَعُواْ لَهُۥ سَٰجِدِينَ ۝ فَسَجَدَ ٱلْمَلَٰٓئِكَةُ كُلُّهُمْ أَجْمَعُونَ ۝ إِلَّآ إِبْلِيسَ ٱسْتَكْبَرَ وَكَانَ مِنَ ٱلْكَٰفِرِينَ ۝ قَالَ يَٰٓإِبْلِيسُ مَا مَنَعَكَ أَن تَسْجُدَ لِمَا خَلَقْتُ بِيَدَىَّ أَسْتَكْبَرْتَ أَمْ كُنتَ مِنَ ٱلْعَالِينَ ۝ قَالَ أَنَا۠ خَيْرٌ مِّنْهُ خَلَقْتَنِى مِن نَّارٍ وَخَلَقْتَهُۥ مِن طِينٍ ۝ قَالَ فَٱخْرُجْ مِنْهَا فَإِنَّكَ رَجِيمٌ ۝ وَإِنَّ عَلَيْكَ لَعْنَتِىٓ إِلَىٰ يَوْمِ ٱلدِّينِ ۝

Surely that is true – the disputing of the inhabitants of the Fire. Say: 'I am but a warner, and there is no Allah but the One, All-Conquering Allah; Lord of the heavens and earth and what is in between, Almighty, Ever-Forgiving.' Say: 'It is a mighty tiding from which you are turning away. I had no knowledge of the High Council when they disputed. I am merely one who receives inspiration, merely a clear warner.' When your Lord said to the angels, 'See, I am creating a mortal of a clay. And when I have formed him fully and breathed into him of My spirit, fall you down before him in prostration!' Thereupon the angels prostrated themselves, all of them together, save Iblis: he gloried in his arrogance, and is one of those who deny. He said: 'O Iblis, what prevented you from bowing to what I created with My hands? Are you too proud or are you too exalted?' He said: 'I am better than him; You created *me of fire, but him You created of clay.' Said He, 'Then go you forth hence; you are accursed. And My rejection shall be thy due until the Day of Judgment!'*

64-78 No story is ever complete until it ends, and we are always curious about how a situation may end. The rational mind may accept the idea that the end is as good as the beginning. The great news is that we are naturally driven towards greater knowledge, power, wealth, health, and other conditions, both within and beyond the possible limits. Ordinarily we look for news as a safeguard for survival. Consequently, popular news is generally associated with fear and destructiveness. The constant news we seek is what reassures us that the end will be as good as our journey towards it, if we conduct our life with genuine concern and accountability. The mind, which is a discriminating faculty, cannot be used productively at the spiritual level where pure consciousness is dominant. Awakening means accessing a state of consciousness beyond the mind's boundaries, where only lights without shadows exist.

It is not until we move seriously towards full consciousness that the lower self and its limited horizons will cease to dominate our journey and so cause their usual sufferings and depressions. The human soul has taken on the qualities of the divine, and if we do not learn how to refer to and be calibrated by the *Absolute*, we will remain in the darkness that we resent.

The great news is that there is only *Oneness*, which will be realised by everyone after death. For us to live in this world, with the grace of the light of *Oneness*, we need to accept the fact that everything emanates from that *Oneness* and that our power and ability are so insignificant that they amount to nothing when we truly refer to the original power of life within our own hearts.

79-88 قَالَ رَبِّ فَأَنظِرْنِى إِلَىٰ يَوْمِ يُبْعَثُونَ ۝ قَالَ فَإِنَّكَ مِنَ ٱلْمُنظَرِينَ ۝ إِلَىٰ يَوْمِ ٱلْوَقْتِ ٱلْمَعْلُومِ ۝ قَالَ فَبِعِزَّتِكَ لَأُغْوِيَنَّهُمْ أَجْمَعِينَ ۝ إِلَّا عِبَادَكَ مِنْهُمُ ٱلْمُخْلَصِينَ ۝ قَالَ فَٱلْحَقُّ وَٱلْحَقَّ أَقُولُ ۝ لَأَمْلَأَنَّ جَهَنَّمَ مِنكَ وَمِمَّن تَبِعَكَ مِنْهُمْ أَجْمَعِينَ ۝ قُلْ مَا أَسْأَلُكُمْ عَلَيْهِ مِنْ أَجْرٍ وَمَا أَنَا۠ مِنَ ٱلْمُتَكَلِّفِينَ ۝ إِنْ هُوَ إِلَّا ذِكْرٌ لِّلْعَٰلَمِينَ ۝ وَلَتَعْلَمُنَّ نَبَأَهُۥ بَعْدَ حِينٍ ۝

Said he, 'My Lord, respite me till the day they shall be raised.' Said He, 'You are among the ones that are respited until the day of the known time.' Said he, 'Now, by your glory, I shall pervert them all together, excepting those your servants among them that are sincere.' Said He, 'This is the truth, and the truth I say; I shall assuredly fill Gehenna with you, and with whosoever of them follows thee, all together.' say, 'I ask no reward from you for this, nor do I claim to be what I am not: This is but a Remembrance to mankind. In time you will certainly come to know its truth.'

79-88 Our conditioned consciousness and the limitations to which we are all subjected are a necessary prelude to the zone of higher consciousness and transcendence. Children need to exercise their limbs, minds, coordination, basic discrimination, and intelligence. Adults need to exercise higher levels of discrimination along the spiritual path, whereby all attachments and desires for power, status, or other unhealthy tendencies need to be lessened. After death, the soul and the traces of the self leave the limitation of space-time consciousness and enter, often with a shock, into another zone, one entirely new and different from what one is used to. A baby is born with a cry into this world, and often the new birth into the hereafter also occurs with fear and tribulation due to its unknown nature. The true religion and its practices help us to be prepared for this natural eventuality, where no one can exercise any will or power. Those who are prepared, are cheerful about the departure from body and mind; those who are not, leave this world with great reluctance and fear.

From the beginning of creation, dualities and pluralities were set in place, and the glorious lights of the All-Merciful were balanced by the shadow of Shaytan. The lower tendencies and darkness afflict those who are not totally focused with sincerity upon the goal of creation, which is transcendence to the eternal light.

Deviation from this truth is a dark power that needs to exist in the world of duality, because of the beam of the truth of *Reality* itself. In the world of duality there has to be a downside, which we need to recognize and avoid whenever it arises. If people do not manage to avoid it in this life, after death they will come to realise their mistake and the truth of the dominance of the grace of *Oneness*.

16. Surah 41 Fussilat (Expounded)

The human experience and project on earth is like a seed that is meant to germinate and grow into its fruition and completion through the nourishment of faith, belief, and good deeds. If an individual does not accept this responsibility, then the seed will simply die before it has expressed its life.

بِسْمِ اللَّـهِ الرَّحْمَـٰنِ الرَّحِيمِ

1-10 حمٓ ۝ تَنزِيلٌ مِّنَ الرَّحْمَـٰنِ الرَّحِيمِ ۝ كِتَـٰبٌ فُصِّلَتْ ءَايَـٰتُهُۥ قُرْءَانًا عَرَبِيًّا لِّقَوْمٍ يَعْلَمُونَ ۝ بَشِيرًا وَنَذِيرًا فَأَعْرَضَ أَكْثَرُهُمْ فَهُمْ لَا يَسْمَعُونَ ۝ وَقَالُوا۟ قُلُوبُنَا فِىٓ أَكِنَّةٍ مِّمَّا تَدْعُونَآ إِلَيْهِ وَفِىٓ ءَاذَانِنَا وَقْرٌ وَمِنۢ بَيْنِنَا وَبَيْنِكَ حِجَابٌ فَٱعْمَلْ إِنَّنَا عَـٰمِلُونَ ۝ قُلْ إِنَّمَآ أَنَا۠ بَشَرٌ مِّثْلُكُمْ يُوحَىٰٓ إِلَىَّ أَنَّمَآ إِلَـٰهُكُمْ إِلَـٰهٌ وَٰحِدٌ فَٱسْتَقِيمُوٓا۟ إِلَيْهِ وَٱسْتَغْفِرُوهُ وَوَيْلٌ لِّلْمُشْرِكِينَ ۝ ٱلَّذِينَ لَا يُؤْتُونَ ٱلزَّكَوٰةَ وَهُم بِٱلْءَاخِرَةِ هُمْ كَـٰفِرُونَ ۝ إِنَّ ٱلَّذِينَ ءَامَنُوا۟ وَعَمِلُوا۟ ٱلصَّـٰلِحَـٰتِ لَهُمْ أَجْرٌ غَيْرُ مَمْنُونٍ ۝ قُلْ

16. Surah 41 Fussilat (Expounded)

أَئِنَّكُمْ لَتَكْفُرُونَ بِالَّذِي خَلَقَ الْأَرْضَ فِي يَوْمَيْنِ وَتَجْعَلُونَ لَهُ أَندَادًا ذَٰلِكَ رَبُّ الْعَالَمِينَ ۝ وَجَعَلَ فِيهَا رَوَاسِيَ مِن فَوْقِهَا وَبَارَكَ فِيهَا وَقَدَّرَ فِيهَا أَقْوَاتَهَا فِي أَرْبَعَةِ أَيَّامٍ سَوَاءً لِّلسَّائِلِينَ ۝

In the name of Allah, the Merciful to all, the Compassionate to each!

Ha Mim. A Revelation from the All-Merciful, Compassionate to each! Behold a Book whose verses are made distinct: an Arabic Qur'an, to a people who have knowledge. A Herald of glad tidings and a Warner. But most have turned away, for they cannot hear. They say, 'Our hearts are encased against what you call us to; our ears are heavy; there is a barrier between us and you. So, you do whatever you want, and so shall we.' Say: 'I am but a human being like you, to whom inspiration is sent. Your Allah is in truth One Allah. Act righteously in His sight and seek His forgiveness. And woe to the polytheists, who do not pay alms and who, moreover, repudiate the hereafter. Surely those who believe, and do righteous deeds shall have a wage unfailing.' Say: 'do you disbelieve in Him who created the earth in two days, and do you set up compeers to Him? That is the Lord of all worlds.' And He set therein firm mountains over it, and He blessed it, and He ordained therein its diverse sustenance in four days, equal to those who ask.

1-10 The human heart is the most precious and delicate faculty we have. As with everything else two hearts exist: one is the biological one, which provides one of the key functions necessary for our life; the other one is the metaphorical heart, where the divine soul or spirit lies. Many of our emotions, such as hatred, fear, guilt, and obsession, cause darkness to the metaphorical heart and therefore block the light of the soul from guiding us. Our mind, intellect, and reason shine some light in front of us, whereas the light of the soul is like a sun that illuminates everything around it. When the self has completely yielded to the soul within, the individual is illumined with insights, inspirations and the delights of wellbeing. There are numerous levels of folly and stupidity; the most dangerous one is a lack of belief and faith in the need to submit to God.

Revelations and scriptures link the infinite *Absolute* with the finite and relative. The Qur'an in particular provides that seamless connection. There are two levels of knowledge: one is when you come to know how things connect with each other at a base level; the other is when you review a situation from the point of view of knowing it from the inside. Its light then appears differently and so has a different effect.

Historically and traditionally, the patterns of reality that connect the unseen with the seen, the visible with the invisible, were revealed by great beings who were awakened to them. This revelation is often called the "Book." Everything is within that book because it is interconnected. Those who read the book and understand it are saved from all the darkness that accompanies the light in time and space.

Those who believe and have faith in it, who live it, and do good that is beyond their immediate benefit, will have a reward that is beyond the limit, implying the eternal God.

11-17

ثُمَّ ٱسْتَوَىٰٓ إِلَى ٱلسَّمَآءِ وَهِىَ دُخَانٌ فَقَالَ لَهَا وَلِلْأَرْضِ ٱئْتِيَا طَوْعًا أَوْ كَرْهًا قَالَتَآ أَتَيْنَا طَآئِعِينَ ۝ فَقَضَىٰهُنَّ سَبْعَ سَمَٰوَاتٍ فِى يَوْمَيْنِ وَأَوْحَىٰ فِى كُلِّ سَمَآءٍ أَمْرَهَا وَزَيَّنَّا ٱلسَّمَآءَ ٱلدُّنْيَا بِمَصَٰبِيحَ وَحِفْظًا ذَٰلِكَ تَقْدِيرُ ٱلْعَزِيزِ ٱلْعَلِيمِ ۝ فَإِنْ أَعْرَضُوا۟ فَقُلْ أَنذَرْتُكُمْ صَٰعِقَةً مِّثْلَ صَٰعِقَةِ عَادٍ وَثَمُودَ ۝ إِذْ جَآءَتْهُمُ ٱلرُّسُلُ مِنۢ بَيْنِ أَيْدِيهِمْ وَمِنْ خَلْفِهِمْ أَلَّا تَعْبُدُوٓا۟ إِلَّا ٱللَّهَ قَالُوا۟ لَوْ شَآءَ رَبُّنَا لَأَنزَلَ مَلَٰٓئِكَةً فَإِنَّا بِمَآ أُرْسِلْتُم بِهِۦ كَٰفِرُونَ ۝ فَأَمَّا عَادٌ فَٱسْتَكْبَرُوا۟ فِى ٱلْأَرْضِ بِغَيْرِ ٱلْحَقِّ وَقَالُوا۟ مَنْ أَشَدُّ مِنَّا قُوَّةً أَوَلَمْ يَرَوْا۟ أَنَّ ٱللَّهَ ٱلَّذِى خَلَقَهُمْ هُوَ أَشَدُّ مِنْهُمْ قُوَّةً وَكَانُوا۟ بِـَٔايَٰتِنَا يَجْحَدُونَ ۝ فَأَرْسَلْنَا عَلَيْهِمْ رِيحًا صَرْصَرًا فِىٓ أَيَّامٍ نَّحِسَاتٍ لِّنُذِيقَهُمْ عَذَابَ ٱلْخِزْىِ فِى ٱلْحَيَوٰةِ ٱلدُّنْيَا وَلَعَذَابُ ٱلْآخِرَةِ أَخْزَىٰ وَهُمْ لَا يُنصَرُونَ ۝ وَأَمَّا ثَمُودُ فَهَدَيْنَٰهُمْ فَٱسْتَحَبُّوا۟ ٱلْعَمَىٰ عَلَى ٱلْهُدَىٰ فَأَخَذَتْهُمْ صَٰعِقَةُ ٱلْعَذَابِ ٱلْهُونِ بِمَا كَانُوا۟ يَكْسِبُونَ ۝

Then He turned to the sky, which was smoke – He said to it and the earth, 'Come into being, willingly or not,' and they said, 'We come willingly.' Then He ordained seven heavens in two days, and inspired each heaven with its disposition. And We adorned the lowest heaven with lanterns, and for protection. Such was the devising of the Almighty, All-Knowing. If they turn away, say: 'I warn you of a thunderbolt like the thunderbolt of 'Ad and Thamud.' When the Messengers came unto them from before them and from be- hind them, saying, 'Serve none but Allah,' they said, 'Had our Lord willed, surely, He would have sent down angels; so, we disbelieve in the Message you were sent.' As regards the people of 'Ad, they grew arrogant on earth, unjustly, saying: 'Who is mightier than us?' Did they not observe that Allah Who created them is mightier than them? And they reviled Our revelations. So, We hurled at them a howling wind in ill-omened days, to make them taste the torment of humiliation in this present life. Yet the torment of the hereafter is more humiliating – nor shall they find any to support them. As regards Thamud, We conferred guidance upon them, but they chose blindness over guidance, and there seized them a thunderbolt of abasing torment because of what they earned.

11-17 Whatever there is in our earth, including our cellular and molecular structure, connects and resonates with our environment and all other surrounding energies. Whatever exists reveals aspects of its nature and transmits what it contains. As human beings we too, knowingly or otherwise, transmit an aspect of our friendliness or enmity. It is in our nature to try and hide what is culturally considered unacceptable or bad behaviour. When you know that God knows whatever you harbour, you may begin to change your attitude, letting more goodness into your intentions and actions. Our life on earth is balanced between dualities at every level – physical, mental, and spiritual. Indeed, on earth we are in between the limited, visible, and mentally discernible earthly realities and the infinite unknown.

It is in our nature to seek individual identity and understand our experiences at a mental level. The truth is that our soul is heavenly and celestial, but we try at all times to understand things at the earthly level. For that reason, much suffering and destruction takes place.

Creation had occurred in numerous steps and stages over billions of years, stabilizing materials that are important for us as humans to interact with, live by, improve on, and thereby exercise skills to raise our intelligence. According to the books of reality, whatever there is, seen and unseen, is insignificant if we do not realise that all this interaction is for us to marvel at the immensity of *Truth* and to be humble.

18-26 وَنَجَّيْنَا ٱلَّذِينَ ءَامَنُوا۟ وَكَانُوا۟ يَتَّقُونَ ۝ وَيَوْمَ يُحْشَرُ أَعْدَآءُ ٱللَّهِ إِلَى ٱلنَّارِ فَهُمْ يُوزَعُونَ ۝ حَتَّىٰٓ إِذَا مَا جَآءُوهَا شَهِدَ عَلَيْهِمْ سَمْعُهُمْ وَأَبْصَـٰرُهُمْ وَجُلُودُهُم بِمَا كَانُوا۟ يَعْمَلُونَ ۝ وَقَالُوا۟ لِجُلُودِهِمْ لِمَ شَهِدتُّمْ عَلَيْنَا ۖ قَالُوٓا۟ أَنطَقَنَا ٱللَّهُ ٱلَّذِىٓ أَنطَقَ كُلَّ شَىْءٍ وَهُوَ خَلَقَكُمْ أَوَّلَ مَرَّةٍ وَإِلَيْهِ تُرْجَعُونَ ۝ وَمَا كُنتُمْ تَسْتَتِرُونَ أَن يَشْهَدَ عَلَيْكُمْ سَمْعُكُمْ وَلَآ أَبْصَـٰرُكُمْ وَلَا جُلُودُكُمْ وَلَـٰكِن ظَنَنتُمْ أَنَّ ٱللَّهَ لَا يَعْلَمُ كَثِيرًۭا مِّمَّا تَعْمَلُونَ ۝ وَذَٰلِكُمْ ظَنُّكُمُ ٱلَّذِى ظَنَنتُم بِرَبِّكُمْ أَرْدَىٰكُمْ فَأَصْبَحْتُم مِّنَ ٱلْخَـٰسِرِينَ ۝ فَإِن يَصْبِرُوا۟ فَٱلنَّارُ مَثْوًۭى لَّهُمْ ۖ وَإِن يَسْتَعْتِبُوا۟ فَمَا هُم مِّنَ ٱلْمُعْتَبِينَ ۝ وَقَيَّضْنَا لَهُمْ قُرَنَآءَ فَزَيَّنُوا۟ لَهُم مَّا بَيْنَ أَيْدِيهِمْ وَمَا خَلْفَهُمْ وَحَقَّ عَلَيْهِمُ ٱلْقَوْلُ فِىٓ أُمَمٍۢ قَدْ خَلَتْ مِن قَبْلِهِم مِّنَ ٱلْجِنِّ وَٱلْإِنسِ ۖ إِنَّهُمْ كَانُوا۟ خَـٰسِرِينَ ۝ وَقَالَ ٱلَّذِينَ كَفَرُوا۟ لَا تَسْمَعُوا۟ لِهَـٰذَا ٱلْقُرْءَانِ وَٱلْغَوْا۟ فِيهِ لَعَلَّكُمْ تَغْلِبُونَ ۝

And We saved those who had faith and were cautiously aware. A Day shall come when the enemies of Allah shall be herded into the Fire, all held in tight order, until, arriving there, their own ears, eyes and skins shall testify as to what they used to do. They shall say to their skins: 'Why did you testify against us?' And these shall answer: 'Allah gave us speech, He Who gave speech to all things. It was He Who created you the first time, and to Him you have been returned. Nor were you discreet lest your ears and eyes and skins might testify against you; instead, you imagined that Allah does not know most of what you do. That then, the thought you thought about your Lord, has destroyed you, and therefore you find yourselves this morning among the losers.' Then if they persist, the Fire shall be a lodging for them; and if they ask amends yet no amends shall be made to them. To them We had assigned accomplices who embellished their actions, present and past, in their eyes. So, the Word came true upon them, as among other nations past, of humans and Jinn, that they were the losers. The unbelievers say: 'Do not listen to this Qur'an, and trifle with it; perhaps you will win the dispute.'

18-26 A person will experience quality of life and progress along higher consciousness with belief and trust in purpose and direction of life. With deep reflection one may realise the cosmic interconnectedness between all that exists. What we think or how we behave affects every cell within our body and will have an influence on our immediate environment. It is the dark side of the light in existence that causes distraction, loss, and confusion; this light is what the Qur'an reflects, in order for us to discriminate in our actions and choose appropriately.

The purpose of human life is to reconcile the temporariness of space-time with the *Source* of life itself, which is eternal and boundless. This is the reason for duty, responsibility, and accountability.

A most challenging revelation is that all of our senses, which connect our soul or spirit – the divine *Presence* – with the outer world, are aware of the truth. They are aware of us trying to hide what we are doing or what we are intending. Every cell bears witness to our folly and hypocrisy.

27-35

فَلَنُذِيقَنَّ ٱلَّذِينَ كَفَرُواْ عَذَابًا شَدِيدًا وَلَنَجْزِيَنَّهُمْ أَسْوَأَ ٱلَّذِى كَانُواْ يَعْمَلُونَ ۝ ذَٰلِكَ جَزَآءُ أَعْدَآءِ ٱللَّهِ ٱلنَّارُ لَهُمْ فِيهَا دَارُ ٱلْخُلْدِ جَزَآءًۢ بِمَا كَانُواْ بِـَٔايَٰتِنَا يَجْحَدُونَ ۝ وَقَالَ ٱلَّذِينَ كَفَرُواْ رَبَّنَآ أَرِنَا ٱلَّذَيْنِ أَضَلَّانَا مِنَ ٱلْجِنِّ وَٱلْإِنسِ نَجْعَلْهُمَا تَحْتَ أَقْدَامِنَا لِيَكُونَا مِنَ ٱلْأَسْفَلِينَ ۝ إِنَّ ٱلَّذِينَ قَالُواْ رَبُّنَا ٱللَّهُ ثُمَّ ٱسْتَقَٰمُواْ تَتَنَزَّلُ عَلَيْهِمُ ٱلْمَلَٰٓئِكَةُ أَلَّا تَخَافُواْ وَلَا تَحْزَنُواْ وَأَبْشِرُواْ بِٱلْجَنَّةِ ٱلَّتِى كُنتُمْ تُوعَدُونَ ۝ نَحْنُ أَوْلِيَآؤُكُمْ فِى ٱلْحَيَوٰةِ ٱلدُّنْيَا وَفِى ٱلْءَاخِرَةِ وَلَكُمْ فِيهَا مَا تَشْتَهِىٓ أَنفُسُكُمْ وَلَكُمْ فِيهَا مَا تَدَّعُونَ ۝ نُزُلًا مِّنْ غَفُورٍ رَّحِيمٍ ۝ وَمَنْ أَحْسَنُ قَوْلًا مِّمَّن دَعَآ إِلَى ٱللَّهِ وَعَمِلَ صَٰلِحًا وَقَالَ إِنَّنِى مِنَ ٱلْمُسْلِمِينَ ۝ وَلَا تَسْتَوِى ٱلْحَسَنَةُ وَلَا ٱلسَّيِّئَةُ ٱدْفَعْ بِٱلَّتِى هِىَ أَحْسَنُ فَإِذَا ٱلَّذِى بَيْنَكَ وَبَيْنَهُۥ عَدَٰوَةٌ كَأَنَّهُۥ وَلِىٌّ حَمِيمٌ ۝ وَمَا يُلَقَّىٰهَآ إِلَّا ٱلَّذِينَ صَبَرُواْ وَمَا يُلَقَّىٰهَآ إِلَّا ذُو حَظٍّ عَظِيمٍ ۝

So, We shall let the unbelievers taste a terrible chastisement, and shall recompense them with the worst of what they were working. That is the recompense of Allah's enemies – the Fire, wherein they shall have the Abode of Eternity as a recompense, for that they denied Our signs. And the disbelievers shall say, 'Our Lord, show us those that led us astray, both jinn and human, and we shall set them underneath our feet, that they may be among the lower ones.' As for those who say 'Our Lord is Allah' and are upright in deed, angels shall be made to descend upon them: 'Fear not, and do not grieve. Here are glad tidings of the Garden which you were promised. We are your guardians in this life and the next. In it you shall have all that your selves desire, all that you pray for hospitably received by One All-Forgiving, Compassionate to each.' And who speaks fairer than he who calls unto Allah and does righteousness and says, 'Surely I am of them that surrender'? A virtuous deed is not the equal of a sinful deed. Repay injury with conduct more becoming and, behold, the person with whom you are at enmity becomes like an intimate friend. None can attain this except the steadfast; None can attain it except the most fortunate.

27-35 Suffering on earth, as well as our love for comfort, ease, and a good life, may lead us to accept the spiritual path with its boundaries and limitations. Much of our transgression can be remedied and put right by repentance and good actions, but on some occasions serious wrong actions cannot be remedied or healed. Allah is All-Forgiving and most generous, but at the physical and material levels there are processes that cannot be reversed. With good thoughts, good speech, and good action we are ready to embrace the way of the prophet, which is illumined by the divine light that can lead us to full awakening. If the great fortune of enlightenment is not attained on earth, it will be known after death.

Pain, suffering, and sorrow simply indicate a deviation from the intended path of awakening. It is only those who want to experience the light and joy of their faith and belief who will come to know that they are guarded and guided toward the eternal garden.

Everything we experience as humans is in dualities, including our awareness of ourselves and the environment. There is the so-called day-to-day world and then the experience that we will share and go through after death. It is then that everything will be revealed to us – all that we hid and our hypocrisy. The divine light declares that if you connect with the *Origin*, with the divine, your life on earth will go smoothly, and your more everlasting life after death will be perfection itself. For this you need to have patience and high expectations of Allah.

36-43 وَإِمَّا يَنزَغَنَّكَ مِنَ ٱلشَّيْطَٰنِ نَزْغٌ فَٱسْتَعِذْ بِٱللَّهِ ۖ إِنَّهُۥ هُوَ ٱلسَّمِيعُ ٱلْعَلِيمُ ۝ وَمِنْ ءَايَٰتِهِ ٱلَّيْلُ وَٱلنَّهَارُ وَٱلشَّمْسُ وَٱلْقَمَرُ ۚ لَا تَسْجُدُواْ لِلشَّمْسِ وَلَا لِلْقَمَرِ وَٱسْجُدُواْ لِلَّهِ ٱلَّذِى خَلَقَهُنَّ إِن كُنتُمْ إِيَّاهُ تَعْبُدُونَ ۝ فَإِنِ ٱسْتَكْبَرُواْ فَٱلَّذِينَ عِندَ رَبِّكَ يُسَبِّحُونَ لَهُۥ بِٱلَّيْلِ وَٱلنَّهَارِ وَهُمْ لَا يَسْـَٔمُونَ ۝ وَمِنْ ءَايَٰتِهِۦٓ أَنَّكَ تَرَى ٱلْأَرْضَ خَٰشِعَةً فَإِذَآ أَنزَلْنَا عَلَيْهَا ٱلْمَآءَ ٱهْتَزَّتْ وَرَبَتْ ۚ إِنَّ ٱلَّذِىٓ أَحْيَاهَا لَمُحْىِ ٱلْمَوْتَىٰٓ ۚ إِنَّهُۥ عَلَىٰ كُلِّ شَىْءٍ قَدِيرٌ ۝ إِنَّ ٱلَّذِينَ يُلْحِدُونَ فِىٓ ءَايَٰتِنَا لَا يَخْفَوْنَ عَلَيْنَآ ۗ أَفَمَن يُلْقَىٰ فِى ٱلنَّارِ خَيْرٌ أَم مَّن يَأْتِىٓ ءَامِنًا يَوْمَ ٱلْقِيَٰمَةِ ۚ ٱعْمَلُواْ مَا شِئْتُمْ ۖ إِنَّهُۥ بِمَا تَعْمَلُونَ بَصِيرٌ ۝ إِنَّ ٱلَّذِينَ كَفَرُواْ بِٱلذِّكْرِ لَمَّا جَآءَهُمْ ۖ وَإِنَّهُۥ لَكِتَٰبٌ عَزِيزٌ ۝ لَّا يَأْتِيهِ ٱلْبَٰطِلُ مِنۢ بَيْنِ يَدَيْهِ وَلَا مِنْ خَلْفِهِۦ ۖ تَنزِيلٌ مِّنْ حَكِيمٍ حَمِيدٍ ۝ مَّا يُقَالُ لَكَ إِلَّا مَا قَدْ قِيلَ لِلرُّسُلِ مِن قَبْلِكَ ۚ إِنَّ رَبَّكَ لَذُو مَغْفِرَةٍ وَذُو عِقَابٍ أَلِيمٍ ۝

If a provocation from Satan should provoke you, seek refuge in Allah; He is the All-Hearing, the All-Knowing. Among His signs are the night and day, the sun and moon. Bow not to the sun or moon, but bow to Allah Who created them, if it is Him you worship. And if they wax proud, yet those who are with your Lord do glorify Him by night and day, and grow not weary. And of His signs is that you see the earth humble; then, when We send down water upon it, it quivers, and swells. Surely, He who quickens it is He who quickens the dead; surely, He is powerful over everything. Those who deviate Our signs are not concealed from Us. So, is he who is cast into the Fire better or he who comes secure on the Day of Resurrection? Do whatever you will; indeed, He is Seeing of what you do. Those who disbelieve in the Remembrance when it comes to them, and surely it is a Book Sublime. Falsehood comes not to it from before it nor from behind it; a sending down from One All-Wise, All-Laudable. Naught is said to thee but what already was said to the Messengers before you. Surely your Lord is a Lord of forgiveness and of painful retribution.

36-43 No one on earth is spared from being afflicted by difficult situations and the suffering that comes from darkness and confusion. It is through humbleness, trust, and reliance upon God that everything will pass, and one may be given another chance to be more aware, reflective, and committed to God's mercy and guidance. One of the biggest pitfalls in human conduct is pride, arrogance, and the illusion of independence or separation from God's governance. Even the darkness and difficulties we suffer have within them the potential to give us additional strength and wisdom for better steadiness in future. Every sign points to its origin and *Source* – Allah. With a clear mind and pure heart, a human being is given the ultimate gift of being enchanted by prevailing cosmic *Oneness* during a short earthly journey.

Divine governance and control over the whole universe can be seen wherever you look. This leads one to conclude that there is a rise in consciousness and a direction in life towards the original *Essence*. Life emerged upon the dead earth, and it is life that will prove life – the divine sacredness – itself.

A human being's consciousness can be exposed to magnificent lights and delights, as well as to shadows, darkness, lower elementals, and suffering. When that happens, we need to stop, repent, and try to clean our minds and hearts of this darkness. Then we can respond properly to the environment around us, balancing the seen and the unseen. Over a long period, awakened beings and prophets have repeatedly reminded people that they have a purpose in life to acknowledge life's supremacy, to be humble, honest, cheerful, joyful, and do their best.

44-50 وَلَوْ جَعَلْنَٰهُ قُرْءَانًا أَعْجَمِيًّا لَّقَالُوا۟ لَوْلَا فُصِّلَتْ ءَايَٰتُهُۥٓ ءَا۬عْجَمِىٌّ وَعَرَبِىٌّ قُلْ هُوَ لِلَّذِينَ ءَامَنُوا۟ هُدًى وَشِفَآءٌ وَالَّذِينَ لَا يُؤْمِنُونَ فِىٓ ءَاذَانِهِمْ وَقْرٌ وَهُوَ عَلَيْهِمْ عَمًى

أُو۟لَٰٓئِكَ يُنَادَوْنَ مِن مَّكَانٍۭ بَعِيدٍ ۝ وَلَقَدْ ءَاتَيْنَا مُوسَى ٱلْكِتَٰبَ فَٱخْتُلِفَ فِيهِ ۚ وَلَوْلَا كَلِمَةٌ سَبَقَتْ مِن رَّبِّكَ لَقُضِىَ بَيْنَهُمْ ۚ وَإِنَّهُمْ لَفِى شَكٍّ مِّنْهُ مُرِيبٍ ۝ مَّنْ عَمِلَ صَٰلِحًا فَلِنَفْسِهِۦ ۖ وَمَنْ أَسَآءَ فَعَلَيْهَا ۗ وَمَا رَبُّكَ بِظَلَّٰمٍ لِّلْعَبِيدِ ۝ إِلَيْهِ يُرَدُّ عِلْمُ ٱلسَّاعَةِ ۚ وَمَا تَخْرُجُ مِن ثَمَرَٰتٍ مِّنْ أَكْمَامِهَا وَمَا تَحْمِلُ مِنْ أُنثَىٰ وَلَا تَضَعُ إِلَّا بِعِلْمِهِۦ ۚ وَيَوْمَ يُنَادِيهِمْ أَيْنَ شُرَكَآءِى قَالُوٓا۟ ءَاذَنَّٰكَ مَا مِنَّا مِن شَهِيدٍ ۝ وَضَلَّ عَنْهُم مَّا كَانُوا۟ يَدْعُونَ مِن قَبْلُ ۖ وَظَنُّوا۟ مَا لَهُم مِّن مَّحِيصٍ ۝ لَّا يَسْـَٔمُ ٱلْإِنسَٰنُ مِن دُعَآءِ ٱلْخَيْرِ وَإِن مَّسَّهُ ٱلشَّرُّ فَيَـُٔوسٌ قَنُوطٌ ۝ وَلَئِنْ أَذَقْنَٰهُ رَحْمَةً مِّنَّا مِنۢ بَعْدِ ضَرَّآءَ مَسَّتْهُ لَيَقُولَنَّ هَٰذَا لِى وَمَآ أَظُنُّ ٱلسَّاعَةَ قَآئِمَةً وَلَئِن رُّجِعْتُ إِلَىٰ رَبِّىٓ إِنَّ لِى عِندَهُۥ لَلْحُسْنَىٰ ۚ فَلَنُنَبِّئَنَّ ٱلَّذِينَ كَفَرُوا۟ بِمَا عَمِلُوا۟ وَلَنُذِيقَنَّهُم مِّنْ عَذَابٍ غَلِيظٍ ۝

Had We revealed the Qur'an in a foreign tongue, they would have said: 'If only its verses were made clear! What? Foreign and Arabic?' Say: 'To those who believe, it is Guidance and Remedy. But those who do not believe have heaviness in their ears, and to them it is blinding. These shall be called as though from a remote place.' We brought Moses the Book, but disputes arose concerning it. Were it not that a Word had already passed from your Lord, judgment would have been pronounced between them. And yet they are in perplexing doubt about it. Whoso does righteousness, it is to his own gain, and whoso does evil, it is to his own loss. Your Lord wrongs not His servants. To Him must knowledge of the Hour be referred. No fruits issue from their sheaths, and no female bears or delivers except with His knowledge A Day shall come when He shall call out to them: 'Where are My partners?' and they shall answer: 'We declare to You that none of us can testify to this.' And away from them shall go what they called upon before, and they shall know for certain that there is no escape for them. Man wearies not from praying for good, but if evil touches him, he grows desperate and dismayed. Yet whenever We let him taste some of Our grace after hardship has visited him, he is sure to say, 'This is but my due! and, I do not think that the Last Hour will ever come: but if I should indeed be brought back unto my Lord, then, behold, the ultimate good awaits me with Him!' We shall most certainly give those who disbelieved full understanding of all that they ever did, and shall most certainly give them a taste of suffering severe.

44-50 All genuine prophetic revelations have come to show us the meaning, purpose, and direction of life, according to the cultures of the people to whom they were revealed. No two prophets or messengers were the same in the outer sense, but the essence of their message was the same. Some of these great beings had a big impact upon humanity, whereas many were little known even amongst their own people. The most common prophetic reminder is that the purpose of human life is to perfect worship and awakening to God, whose presence is in every heart as a spirit or a soul. We need to learn to improve our attention, intentions, and actions so that we enter a zone of easy flow guided by higher consciousness. The illusion of separation from *Oneness* causes much of our suffering and confusion. In order to awaken to this truth, we need to reflect upon the signs that are all around us in the world as well as within ourselves. We are given limited sight and hearing so that we can practice deeper insights and listening. Indeed, human beings can be most fortunate if they live with total honesty and faith.

Every intelligent human being seeks benefit and success in life; the ultimate victory is to know that life itself is eternal and that one's own personal life is inseparable from that eternal nature. Whatever real goodness we do is for ourselves, but the ultimate goodness is to be at one with the source of all goodness – Allah.

We are all driven by good expectations, desiring goodness. The pattern of revealed knowledge repeatedly shows us that we are driven to do good for our own sake. If you do goodness, it is for your own self and soul. If you do wrong, you have wronged yourself. Due to the nature of the animal in us, whenever things are easy and good, we become arrogant and vain. Whenever things are not easy, we blame and claim and continue in our distraction.

51-54 وَإِذَآ أَنْعَمْنَا عَلَى ٱلْإِنسَٰنِ أَعْرَضَ وَنَـَٔا بِجَانِبِهِۦ وَإِذَا مَسَّهُ ٱلشَّرُّ فَذُو دُعَآءٍ عَرِيضٍ ۝ قُلْ أَرَءَيْتُمْ إِن كَانَ مِنْ عِندِ ٱللَّهِ ثُمَّ كَفَرْتُم بِهِۦ مَنْ أَضَلُّ مِمَّنْ هُوَ فِى شِقَاقٍۭ بَعِيدٍ ۝ سَنُرِيهِمْ ءَايَٰتِنَا فِى ٱلْءَافَاقِ وَفِىٓ أَنفُسِهِمْ حَتَّىٰ يَتَبَيَّنَ لَهُمْ أَنَّهُ ٱلْحَقُّ أَوَلَمْ يَكْفِ بِرَبِّكَ أَنَّهُۥ عَلَىٰ كُلِّ شَىْءٍ شَهِيدٌ ۝ أَلَآ إِنَّهُمْ فِى مِرْيَةٍ مِّن لِّقَآءِ رَبِّهِمْ أَلَآ إِنَّهُۥ بِكُلِّ شَىْءٍ مُّحِيطٌ ۝

Whenever We are gracious to man, he goes away haughtily, but, as soon as evil touches him, he turns to prolonged prayer. Say: 'Consider. If it is from Allah and you then scorn it, who can be more lost than one sunk deep in discord?' We shall show them Our signs on all horizons and in their very selves, until it becomes obvious to them that it is the Truth. Does it not suffice that your Lord is a witness of all things? And yet they are in doubt about the encounter with their Lord, though it is He Who encompasses all things.

51-54 As humans, who are in the cocoon of separateness and isolation from the *Oneness*, we have the illusion of independence and the ability to change and interact without reference to the *Source* from which all energies and patterns emerge. These are the signs that we need to reflect upon within our own selves and the macro world, that there is no other *Source* which is cosmic, far beyond distance, yet closer than closeness. This is the purpose of our life: to reflect and reach the point of the highest intellect, so that we may begin to read with insight and our innermost heart.

Divine signs appear everywhere and at all levels, including the physical and material, as well as signs on the horizon and within our own selves. What is needed is to move from uncertainty to complete certainty of the divine *Presence* and guidance.

Due to human nature, whenever we are flowing with goodness and success, we try to attribute it to ourselves. And whenever we are not, we try to find reasons and excuses. So, we maintain the illusion that we are never wrong. It is a natural human tendency to think that you are more intelligent and can do better than anyone else around you. Whereas the one who has faith and trust in the purpose of this short journey knows that there are signs upon signs upon signs, some emanating from the pure divine light and others ending up on the other extreme as the darkness of hell.

17. Surah 44 Ad-Dukhan (Smoke)

Human life makes progress by advancing from darkness and ignorance to light, knowledge and higher illumination. The soul carries the complete divine imprint; its lower, shadow-self points to the light that illumines it. Turning away from the shadow, one faces the light.

بِسْمِ اللَّهِ الرَّحْمَٰنِ الرَّحِيمِ

1-17 حم ۝ وَالْكِتَابِ الْمُبِينِ ۝ إِنَّا أَنزَلْنَاهُ فِي لَيْلَةٍ مُّبَارَكَةٍ إِنَّا كُنَّا مُنذِرِينَ ۝ فِيهَا يُفْرَقُ كُلُّ أَمْرٍ حَكِيمٍ ۝ أَمْرًا مِّنْ عِندِنَا إِنَّا كُنَّا مُرْسِلِينَ ۝ رَحْمَةً مِّن رَّبِّكَ إِنَّهُ هُوَ السَّمِيعُ الْعَلِيمُ ۝ رَبِّ السَّمَاوَاتِ وَالْأَرْضِ وَمَا بَيْنَهُمَا إِن كُنتُم مُّوقِنِينَ ۝ لَا إِلَٰهَ إِلَّا هُوَ يُحْيِي وَيُمِيتُ رَبُّكُمْ وَرَبُّ آبَائِكُمُ الْأَوَّلِينَ ۝ بَلْ هُمْ فِي شَكٍّ يَلْعَبُونَ ۝ فَارْتَقِبْ يَوْمَ تَأْتِي السَّمَاءُ بِدُخَانٍ مُّبِينٍ ۝ يَغْشَى النَّاسَ هَٰذَا عَذَابٌ أَلِيمٌ ۝ رَّبَّنَا اكْشِفْ عَنَّا الْعَذَابَ إِنَّا مُؤْمِنُونَ ۝ أَنَّىٰ لَهُمُ الذِّكْرَىٰ وَقَدْ جَاءَهُمْ رَسُولٌ مُّبِينٌ ۝ ثُمَّ تَوَلَّوْا عَنْهُ وَقَالُوا مُعَلَّمٌ مَّجْنُونٌ ۝ إِنَّا كَاشِفُو الْعَذَابِ قَلِيلًا إِنَّكُمْ عَائِدُونَ ۝ يَوْمَ نَبْطِشُ الْبَطْشَةَ الْكُبْرَىٰ إِنَّا مُنتَقِمُونَ ۝ وَلَقَدْ فَتَنَّا قَبْلَهُمْ قَوْمَ فِرْعَوْنَ وَجَاءَهُمْ رَسُولٌ كَرِيمٌ ۝

In the name of Allah, the Merciful to all, the Compassionate to each!
Ha Mim. By the Clear Book! We sent it down on a blessed night – We have warned! Therein every wise affair is made distinct, at Our command – We have sent a messenger! A mercy from your Lord – All-Hearing, All-Knowing is He! Lord of the heavens and earth and what lies between, if your faith is firm. There is no Allah but He, He gives life and deals death, Your Lord is He, and Lord of your ancient forebears. And yet, in their doubt, they dally. So be on the watch for a day when heaven shall bring a manifest smoke. Covering the people; this is a painful chastisement. 'Our Lord, draw away this torment from us, for we are believers.' But how will remembering help them when a messenger, undeniable, had already come to them. And they had turned their backs on him, saying: 'He is tutored and crazed'? 'Behold, We are removing the chastisement a little; behold, you revert!' A Day shall come when We shall

deliver the Great Blow – We shall exact vengeance. Already before them We tried the people of Pharaoh, and a noble Messenger came unto them,

1-17 Human life is based upon connecting strands of past experiences with contemporary ones, relating them to the flow of life experienced according to the level of each created being. Life is nourished by visible earthly processes as well as subtle and powerful energies that can barely be discerned. The whole universe appeared from nowhere and will vanish again into a smoke of uncertainty back to its infinite origin.

The miracle of creation emerged from the boundless, unseen cosmic power. Originating from cosmic energy, everything we perceive in creation became visible and tangible. In the same manner that everything emerged, the universe will also return to its origin.

If you look around deeply you find that most people just move from day to day and year to year without trying to discover the absolute truth that is transmitted from their own hearts. The absolute *Truth* is that we are in this world, a transition zone from the unseen-unknown through the illusion of separation and individuality, back to the conclusion of the unitive *Reality* that encompasses all. A beautiful description of what was before the creational state was that it was like a smoke or energy field in which nothing could be discerned. The same thing would come to us after death unless we have awakened before then.

18-28 نْ أَدُّوٓا۟ إِلَىَّ عِبَادَ ٱللَّهِ إِنِّى لَكُمْ رَسُولٌ أَمِينٌ ۝ وَأَن لَّا تَعْلُوا۟ عَلَى ٱللَّهِ إِنِّىٓ ءَاتِيكُم بِسُلْطَٰنٍ مُّبِينٍ ۝ وَإِنِّى عُذْتُ بِرَبِّى وَرَبِّكُمْ أَن تَرْجُمُونِ ۝ وَإِن لَّمْ تُؤْمِنُوا۟ لِى فَٱعْتَزِلُونِ ۝ فَدَعَا رَبَّهُۥٓ أَنَّ هَٰٓؤُلَآءِ قَوْمٌ مُّجْرِمُونَ ۝ فَأَسْرِ بِعِبَادِى لَيْلًا إِنَّكُم مُّتَّبَعُونَ ۝ وَٱتْرُكِ ٱلْبَحْرَ رَهْوًا إِنَّهُمْ جُندٌ مُّغْرَقُونَ ۝ كَمْ تَرَكُوا۟ مِن جَنَّٰتٍ وَعُيُونٍ ۝ وَزُرُوعٍ وَمَقَامٍ كَرِيمٍ ۝ وَنَعْمَةٍ كَانُوا۟ فِيهَا فَٰكِهِينَ ۝ كَذَٰلِكَ وَأَوْرَثْنَٰهَا قَوْمًا ءَاخَرِينَ ۝

saying: 'Deliver Allah's worshippers into my hands, for I am a trustworthy messenger to you. Do not uplift yourselves above Allah for I come to you with clear authority. I seek refuge in my Lord and yours against your insults! But if so be that you believe me not, go you apart from me!' So, he prayed to his Lord: 'These are a wicked people.' [Allah said,] 'Set out at night with My worshippers, but you will surely be pursued. And leave the sea behind you calm and still, for they are a troop that will surely be drowned.' They left how many gardens and fountain sown fields, and how noble a station, and what prosperity they had rejoiced in! Even so; and We bequeathed them upon another people.

18-28 Great spirits amongst humankind have always existed who connected the visible world with the vast unknown. Human experience on earth can provide a metaphor relating to what we aspire for – such as security, knowledge, comfort, love, and so on. Our own soul transmits all these desirable attributes to body, mind, and emotions. The more we reflect upon them, and the human drive towards contentment and happiness, the more our belief and faith deepens. These insights lead us to surrender to *Truth*, with its security and utter goodness. It is a dim intellect that denies the truth that there is another version of life after death and that human death is in fact the beginning of a second and more important birth.

The most perplexing paradox and challenge in life is that human beings are given the apparent ability to decide and act as though they are independent whereas, in truth, it is God who provides the energy and the action. If we do not respond to the light of *Truth*, then our experiences will remain flimsy and we may experience disillusionment.

Through the reason and rationality that we can share with others, we sometimes reach a point of inspiration beyond reason and rationality. For this reason, once you are fully living the moment you are tuned to that which is infinite and boundless and so unlikely to make irreversible mistakes. Look back at how many cultures were destroyed, how many people lost what was developed over millennia through warfare and animosities. Those who will inherit the *Truth* live by the *Truth*, with no fear or sorrow.

29-38 فَمَا بَكَتْ عَلَيْهِمُ ٱلسَّمَآءُ وَٱلْأَرْضُ وَمَا كَانُوا۟ مُنظَرِينَ ۞ وَلَقَدْ نَجَّيْنَا بَنِىٓ إِسْرَٰٓءِيلَ مِنَ ٱلْعَذَابِ ٱلْمُهِينِ ۞ مِن فِرْعَوْنَ إِنَّهُۥ كَانَ عَالِيًا مِّنَ ٱلْمُسْرِفِينَ ۞ وَلَقَدِ ٱخْتَرْنَٰهُمْ عَلَىٰ عِلْمٍ عَلَى ٱلْعَٰلَمِينَ ۞ وَءَاتَيْنَٰهُم مِّنَ ٱلْءَايَٰتِ مَا فِيهِ بَلَٰٓؤٌا۟ مُّبِينٌ ۞ إِنَّ هَٰٓؤُلَآءِ لَيَقُولُونَ ۞ إِنْ هِىَ إِلَّا مَوْتَتُنَا ٱلْأُولَىٰ وَمَا نَحْنُ بِمُنشَرِينَ ۞ فَأْتُوا۟ بِـَٔابَآئِنَآ إِن كُنتُمْ صَٰدِقِينَ ۞ أَهُمْ خَيْرٌ أَمْ قَوْمُ تُبَّعٍ وَٱلَّذِينَ مِن قَبْلِهِمْ أَهْلَكْنَٰهُمْ إِنَّهُمْ كَانُوا۟ مُجْرِمِينَ ۞ وَمَا خَلَقْنَا ٱلسَّمَٰوَٰتِ وَٱلْأَرْضَ وَمَا بَيْنَهُمَا لَٰعِبِينَ ۞

Neither heaven nor earth wept for them, nor were they respited; and, indeed, We delivered the children of Israel from the shameful suffering. At the hands of Pharaoh: he was a tyrant who exceeded all bounds. And We chose them, out of a knowledge, above all beings, and gave them signs wherein there was a manifest trial. But now these people say: 'There is nothing but our first death, and we shall not be resurrected. Bring back to us our forebears, if you speak the truth.' Are they better or the people of Tubba and those before them? We destroyed them, for surely, they were guilty. We created not the heavens and earth, and all that between them is, in play;

29-38 The light of the soul reflects the divine origin, and the shadow of the soul brings upon us suffering and distractions. Ignorant and egotistic leaders can cause greater damage to humanity than mere confused individuals. Much of human distraction is due to the denial of total accountability in this life, as well as in the hereafter. No intention, thought, or action goes without a counter-response and reaction. Goodness begets goodness, and so does wrongdoing. A feeble mind may argue that powerful, evil leaders have left the world without being punished. Our life's experience encompasses our earthly transition as well as what comes after death. Ghosts and tortured souls give us hints as to what may come later. It is only when the collective consciousness of a people or nation live and work within boundaries and strive toward higher consciousness with full accountability that goodness prevails on earth.

The purpose of creation is for us to evolve by intention and action to realise the cosmic light that governs all. Through this process of a rise in consciousness, we will realise that life is forever and individual life is not separate from timeless life itself. Most people, however, remain within conditioned consciousness.

These basic principles – the need to have a clear mind and a pure heart and to apply them – have been tested for millennia now. They have proven that, if we are vigilant, diligent, and refer back to the ultimate light in the heart, both individually and collectively, our passage will be magnificent. Otherwise, suffering will prevail.

39-59 مَا خَلَقْنَٰهُمَآ إِلَّا بِٱلْحَقِّ وَلَٰكِنَّ أَكْثَرَهُمْ لَا يَعْلَمُونَ ۝ إِنَّ يَوْمَ ٱلْفَصْلِ مِيقَٰتُهُمْ أَجْمَعِينَ ۝ يَوْمَ لَا يُغْنِى مَوْلًى عَن مَّوْلًى شَيْـًٔا وَلَا هُمْ يُنصَرُونَ ۝ إِلَّا مَن رَّحِمَ ٱللَّهُ إِنَّهُۥ هُوَ ٱلْعَزِيزُ ٱلرَّحِيمُ ۝ إِنَّ شَجَرَتَ ٱلزَّقُّومِ ۝ طَعَامُ ٱلْأَثِيمِ ۝ كَٱلْمُهْلِ يَغْلِى فِى ٱلْبُطُونِ ۝ كَغَلْىِ ٱلْحَمِيمِ ۝ خُذُوهُ فَٱعْتِلُوهُ إِلَىٰ سَوَآءِ ٱلْجَحِيمِ ۝ ثُمَّ صُبُّوا۟ فَوْقَ رَأْسِهِۦ مِنْ عَذَابِ ٱلْحَمِيمِ ۝ ذُقْ إِنَّكَ أَنتَ ٱلْعَزِيزُ ٱلْكَرِيمُ ۝ إِنَّ هَٰذَا مَا كُنتُم بِهِۦ تَمْتَرُونَ ۝ إِنَّ ٱلْمُتَّقِينَ فِى مَقَامٍ أَمِينٍ ۝ فِى جَنَّٰتٍ وَعُيُونٍ ۝ يَلْبَسُونَ مِن سُندُسٍ وَإِسْتَبْرَقٍ مُّتَقَٰبِلِينَ ۝ كَذَٰلِكَ وَزَوَّجْنَٰهُم بِحُورٍ عِينٍ ۝ يَدْعُونَ فِيهَا بِكُلِّ فَٰكِهَةٍ ءَامِنِينَ ۝ لَا يَذُوقُونَ فِيهَا ٱلْمَوْتَ إِلَّا ٱلْمَوْتَةَ ٱلْأُولَىٰ وَوَقَىٰهُمْ عَذَابَ ٱلْجَحِيمِ ۝ فَضْلًا مِّن رَّبِّكَ ذَٰلِكَ هُوَ ٱلْفَوْزُ ٱلْعَظِيمُ ۝ فَإِنَّمَا يَسَّرْنَٰهُ بِلِسَانِكَ لَعَلَّهُمْ يَتَذَكَّرُونَ ۝ فَٱرْتَقِبْ إِنَّهُم مُّرْتَقِبُونَ ۝

We created them not save in truth; but most of them know it not. Verily, the Day of Distinction is the term appointed for all of them. A Day when no patron can avail his client in any wise, nor will they be succoured, except such as Allah has shown mercy to, for He is Almighty, Compassionate to each. The Tree of Bitterness is the food of the guilty. Like molten brass, boiling in stomachs like boiling water. Take him, and thrust him into the midst of Hell, then pour over his head a torment of boiling water. 'Taste it, you who are mighty and noble! This is that concerning which you were doubting.' Surely those who are reverent are in a secure place, amidst gardens and springs, clothed in silk and brocade, face to face. Thus, shall it be. And We shall pair them with companions pure, most beautiful of eye. In that they shall claim all the fruits, resting in security; therein they do not taste death, except for the first death, and He has spared them the torment of hell, a bounty from your Lord; that is the mighty triumph. We have indeed made it easy by your tongue; perhaps they will remember. So be on the watch; they too are on the watch.

39-59 The entire creation emanates from a source of perfect justice, and if we do not accept this essential, important foundation, we wrong ourselves and others. The descriptions of hellfire or paradise after death have been revealed to us to demonstrate that if we do not realise the magnificence of the soul within the heart during our earthly experience, we will know it after death with regret and sorrow. The powers of Allah are inexplicably immense and operate at numerous levels, most of which are indiscernible and subtle. Our scientific knowledge merely reveals certain aspects that are peripheral to the cosmic forces that govern the universe. Everything emanates from, is sustained by, and returns to Allah. The fountainhead of *Reality* is the godhead, and from it emanates countless realities, culminating in what we consider normal, comprehensible, earthly transactions.

Only a few people awaken to the *Truth* whilst still active and alive in this world. Everyone will experience the cosmic lordship and prevalence of Allah after death. According to one's state at the point of death, one either goes through the turmoil of purification followed by quality life forever, or total disintegration and what is defined as hell.

Apart from a clear mind and a pure heart, we need to be constantly cautious about slipping into a zone that is not justifiable by any of these reasons or faculties. For this reason, if a situation comes wherein, we lose our caution and our ability to repent, we may be heading towards a big disaster.

18. Surah 46 Al-Ahqaf (The Dunes)

The absolute *Truth* or divine *Reality* reveals itself through various stages and levels that connects the infinite with the finite. The mystery of life is indeed the greatest of all miracles, enabling matter and energy to sing, in unison, the praise of *Oneness*.

بِسْمِ اللَّهِ الرَّحْمَٰنِ الرَّحِيمِ

1-8 حمٓ ۝ تَنزِيلُ ٱلْكِتَٰبِ مِنَ ٱللَّهِ ٱلْعَزِيزِ ٱلْحَكِيمِ ۝ مَا خَلَقْنَا ٱلسَّمَٰوَٰتِ وَٱلْأَرْضَ وَمَا بَيْنَهُمَآ إِلَّا بِٱلْحَقِّ وَأَجَلٍ مُّسَمًّى ۚ وَٱلَّذِينَ كَفَرُوا۟ عَمَّآ أُنذِرُوا۟ مُعْرِضُونَ ۝ قُلْ أَرَءَيْتُم مَّا تَدْعُونَ مِن دُونِ ٱللَّهِ أَرُونِى مَاذَا خَلَقُوا۟ مِنَ ٱلْأَرْضِ أَمْ لَهُمْ شِرْكٌ فِى ٱلسَّمَٰوَٰتِ ۖ ٱئْتُونِى بِكِتَٰبٍ مِّن قَبْلِ هَٰذَآ أَوْ أَثَٰرَةٍ مِّنْ عِلْمٍ إِن كُنتُمْ صَٰدِقِينَ ۝ وَمَنْ أَضَلُّ مِمَّن يَدْعُوا۟ مِن دُونِ ٱللَّهِ مَن لَّا يَسْتَجِيبُ لَهُۥٓ إِلَىٰ يَوْمِ ٱلْقِيَٰمَةِ وَهُمْ

عَن دُعَآئِهِمْ غَٰفِلُونَ ۞ وَإِذَا حُشِرَ ٱلنَّاسُ كَانُوا۟ لَهُمْ أَعْدَآءً وَكَانُوا۟ بِعِبَادَتِهِمْ كَٰفِرِينَ ۞ وَإِذَا تُتْلَىٰ عَلَيْهِمْ ءَايَٰتُنَا بَيِّنَٰتٍ قَالَ ٱلَّذِينَ كَفَرُوا۟ لِلْحَقِّ لَمَّا جَآءَهُمْ هَٰذَا سِحْرٌ مُّبِينٌ ۞ أَمْ يَقُولُونَ ٱفْتَرَىٰهُ قُلْ إِنِ ٱفْتَرَيْتُهُۥ فَلَا تَمْلِكُونَ لِى مِنَ ٱللَّهِ شَيْـًٔا هُوَ أَعْلَمُ بِمَا تُفِيضُونَ فِيهِ كَفَىٰ بِهِۦ شَهِيدًۢا بَيْنِى وَبَيْنَكُمْ وَهُوَ ٱلْغَفُورُ ٱلرَّحِيمُ ۞

In the name of Allah, the Merciful to all, the Compassionate to each!

Ha Mim. The sending down of the Book is from Allah, the All-Mighty, the All-Wise. We have not created the heavens and the earth, and what between them is, save with the truth and a stated term; but the unbelievers are turning away from that they were warned of. Say: 'Have you considered that you call upon apart from Allah? Show me what they have created of the earth; or have they a partnership in the heavens? Bring me a Book before this, or some remnant of a knowledge, if you speak truly.' And who is further astray than he who calls, apart from Allah, upon such a one as shall not answer him till the Day of Resurrection? Such as are heedless of their calling. And when mankind is mustered, they shall be their enemies, and shall renounce their worship of them. And when Our signs are recited to them, clear signs, the unbelievers say to the truth when it has come to them, 'This is manifest sorcery.' Or do they say: 'He fabricated it?' Say: 'If I have fabricated it, you can do me no good at all against Allah. He knows best your constant haranguing concerning it. Let it suffice as witness between me and you.' He is All-Forgiving, Compassionate to each.

1-8 *Ha meem.* Any letter of a language implies the building block of a word. Every word constitutes *ha* or *meem*, is like to *Ha meem*, as in *Hamd* (Praise), and *Rahman* (All-Compassionate). These letters are connected to this ayah and surah. The book communicates beams of energies that are composed of such letters and their meanings. From a simple sound arises communication, which can connect or disconnect us to higher levels of meaning and consciousness. Everything emanates from the simple, basic nothingness and explodes into everything. The power of Allah contains all that is known and unknown. The intelligent human being will accept that these signals, signs, and symbols point to the immense, boundless perfection of them all. The seeker floats on these rafts towards the illumined destiny.

Creation occurs in numerous steps and stages, and the inner light of the *Truth* penetrates through them regularly in different ways and formats, including by way of prophetic revelations and sacred books. Only a believing heart will be energised and illumined by the higher level of revelation.

Our life on earth is based on duality, stretched between numerous subtle or definable causes and their effects. So, we are between the ultimate source of divine light and the lowest of shadow-plays. For this reason, the more often we can stop our mind, thoughts, intentions and actions, the more we are at the point of the transmitted light from the divine *Presence* in our own soul. The more often we do this, the less likely we are to suffer the consequences of being confused and at a loss.

9-15 قُلْ مَا كُنتُ بِدْعًا مِّنَ ٱلرُّسُلِ وَمَآ أَدْرِى مَا يُفْعَلُ بِى وَلَا بِكُمْ ۖ إِنْ أَتَّبِعُ إِلَّا مَا يُوحَىٰٓ إِلَىَّ وَمَآ أَنَا۠ إِلَّا نَذِيرٌ مُّبِينٌ ۝ قُلْ أَرَءَيْتُمْ إِن كَانَ مِنْ عِندِ ٱللَّهِ وَكَفَرْتُم بِهِۦ وَشَهِدَ شَاهِدٌ مِّنۢ بَنِىٓ إِسْرَٰٓءِيلَ عَلَىٰ مِثْلِهِۦ فَـَٔامَنَ وَٱسْتَكْبَرْتُمْ ۖ إِنَّ ٱللَّهَ لَا يَهْدِى ٱلْقَوْمَ ٱلظَّٰلِمِينَ ۝ وَقَالَ ٱلَّذِينَ كَفَرُوا۟ لِلَّذِينَ ءَامَنُوا۟ لَوْ كَانَ خَيْرًا مَّا سَبَقُونَآ إِلَيْهِ ۚ وَإِذْ لَمْ يَهْتَدُوا۟ بِهِۦ فَسَيَقُولُونَ هَٰذَآ إِفْكٌ قَدِيمٌ ۝ وَمِن قَبْلِهِۦ كِتَٰبُ مُوسَىٰٓ إِمَامًا وَرَحْمَةً ۚ وَهَٰذَا كِتَٰبٌ مُّصَدِّقٌ لِّسَانًا عَرَبِيًّا لِّيُنذِرَ ٱلَّذِينَ ظَلَمُوا۟ وَبُشْرَىٰ لِلْمُحْسِنِينَ ۝ إِنَّ ٱلَّذِينَ قَالُوا۟ رَبُّنَا ٱللَّهُ ثُمَّ ٱسْتَقَٰمُوا۟ فَلَا خَوْفٌ عَلَيْهِمْ وَلَا هُمْ يَحْزَنُونَ ۝ أُو۟لَٰٓئِكَ أَصْحَٰبُ ٱلْجَنَّةِ خَٰلِدِينَ فِيهَا جَزَآءًۢ بِمَا كَانُوا۟ يَعْمَلُونَ ۝ وَوَصَّيْنَا ٱلْإِنسَٰنَ بِوَٰلِدَيْهِ إِحْسَٰنًا ۖ حَمَلَتْهُ أُمُّهُۥ كُرْهًا وَوَضَعَتْهُ كُرْهًا ۖ وَحَمْلُهُۥ وَفِصَٰلُهُۥ ثَلَٰثُونَ شَهْرًا ۚ حَتَّىٰٓ إِذَا بَلَغَ أَشُدَّهُۥ وَبَلَغَ أَرْبَعِينَ سَنَةً قَالَ رَبِّ أَوْزِعْنِىٓ أَنْ أَشْكُرَ نِعْمَتَكَ ٱلَّتِىٓ أَنْعَمْتَ عَلَىَّ وَعَلَىٰ وَٰلِدَىَّ وَأَنْ أَعْمَلَ صَٰلِحًا تَرْضَىٰهُ وَأَصْلِحْ لِى فِى ذُرِّيَّتِىٓ ۖ إِنِّى تُبْتُ إِلَيْكَ وَإِنِّى مِنَ ٱلْمُسْلِمِينَ ۝

Say: 'I am not a novelty among messengers. I know not what is to be done to me or you. I merely follow what is revealed to me. I am nothing but a manifest warner.' Have you considered? If it be from Allah, and you disbelieve in it, and a witness from among the Children of Israel bears witness to its like, and believes, and you were arrogant, Allah guides not the people of the evildoers. And those who disbelieve say of those who believe, 'If it had been good, they would not have preceded us to it.' And when they are not guided by it, they will say, 'This is an ancient falsehood.' Before it there was the Book of Moses, a guide and a mercy; and this is a Book that confirms it, in the Arabic tongue, to warn the wicked and bring glad tidings to the righteous. Those who say: 'Our Lord is Allah,' and are upright, no fear shall come upon them, nor shall they grieve. They are the inhabitants of the Garden, Dwelling therein forever, As a reward for their deeds. We enjoined upon man to be kind to his parents. His mother bore him in hardship, and delivered him in hardship; His bearing and his weaning are thirty months. Until, when he is fully grown and reaches forty years, he says: 'My Lord, inspire me to be thankful for Your blessings, which You bestowed on me and my parents, and that I act in virtue, pleasing to You. Grant me a virtuous progeny; I have sincerely repented before You, And I have sincerely embraced Islam.'

9-15 In the same way that basic letters and sounds have come to us, we have the gift of beings more spiritually evolved or awakened in terms of consciousness, such as prophets and messengers. The lower self and ego (*nafs*) perpetuates itself and will therefore hear the message but not allow it to interact with the mind's past values and bring about relevant change. When the Moses of mercy appears to Pharaoh, who is in denial and arrogance, his message goes unheeded; the situation continues until a breakdown occurs. Whatever exists interacts with others like itself. As human beings, we acknowledge our earthly origin, parentage, and culture, but we are encouraged to move on to the spiritual realisation that is beyond form and culture.

It is natural for human beings to desire, hope, and strive towards lasting goodness and benefit. It is through diligent good work and accountability that one begins to experience inner bliss and the light of the spirit within. Through gratitude and good works without expectations we move swiftly along the prophetic path.

Intelligence will begin to rise and flow along the path of evolution when we accept the idea that we are here to perfect our trust in the infinite, while doing our best in the finite with accountability, transparency, and honesty. The more often we refer back to the *Truth* and *Haqq*, the more likely we are to deter the lower self and ego from indiscretion and loss.

16-22

أُو۟لَٰٓئِكَ ٱلَّذِينَ نَتَقَبَّلُ عَنْهُمْ أَحْسَنَ مَا عَمِلُوا۟ وَنَتَجَاوَزُ عَن سَيِّـَٔاتِهِمْ فِىٓ أَصْحَٰبِ ٱلْجَنَّةِ ۖ وَعْدَ ٱلصِّدْقِ ٱلَّذِى كَانُوا۟ يُوعَدُونَ ۝ وَٱلَّذِى قَالَ لِوَٰلِدَيْهِ أُفٍّ لَّكُمَآ أَتَعِدَانِنِىٓ أَنْ أُخْرَجَ وَقَدْ خَلَتِ ٱلْقُرُونُ مِن قَبْلِى وَهُمَا يَسْتَغِيثَانِ ٱللَّهَ وَيْلَكَ ءَامِنْ إِنَّ وَعْدَ ٱللَّهِ حَقٌّ فَيَقُولُ مَا هَٰذَآ إِلَّآ أَسَٰطِيرُ ٱلْأَوَّلِينَ ۝ أُو۟لَٰٓئِكَ ٱلَّذِينَ حَقَّ عَلَيْهِمُ ٱلْقَوْلُ فِىٓ أُمَمٍ قَدْ خَلَتْ مِن قَبْلِهِم مِّنَ ٱلْجِنِّ وَٱلْإِنسِ ۖ إِنَّهُمْ كَانُوا۟ خَٰسِرِينَ ۝ وَلِكُلٍّ دَرَجَٰتٌ مِّمَّا عَمِلُوا۟ ۖ وَلِيُوَفِّيَهُمْ أَعْمَٰلَهُمْ وَهُمْ لَا يُظْلَمُونَ ۝ وَيَوْمَ يُعْرَضُ ٱلَّذِينَ كَفَرُوا۟ عَلَى ٱلنَّارِ أَذْهَبْتُمْ طَيِّبَٰتِكُمْ فِى حَيَاتِكُمُ ٱلدُّنْيَا وَٱسْتَمْتَعْتُم بِهَا فَٱلْيَوْمَ تُجْزَوْنَ عَذَابَ ٱلْهُونِ بِمَا كُنتُمْ تَسْتَكْبِرُونَ فِى ٱلْأَرْضِ بِغَيْرِ ٱلْحَقِّ وَبِمَا كُنتُمْ تَفْسُقُونَ ۝ وَٱذْكُرْ أَخَا عَادٍ إِذْ أَنذَرَ قَوْمَهُۥ بِٱلْأَحْقَافِ وَقَدْ خَلَتِ ٱلنُّذُرُ مِنۢ بَيْنِ يَدَيْهِ وَمِنْ خَلْفِهِۦٓ أَلَّا تَعْبُدُوٓا۟ إِلَّا ٱللَّهَ إِنِّىٓ أَخَافُ عَلَيْكُمْ عَذَابَ يَوْمٍ عَظِيمٍ ۝ قَالُوٓا۟ أَجِئْتَنَا لِتَأْفِكَنَا عَنْ ءَالِهَتِنَا فَأْتِنَا بِمَا تَعِدُنَآ إِن كُنتَ مِنَ ٱلصَّٰدِقِينَ ۝

Those are they from whom We shall accept the best of what they have done, and We shall pass over their evil deeds. They are among the inhabitants of Paradise – the promise of the very truth, which they were promised. But he who says to his father and his mother, 'Fie upon you! Do you promise me that I shall be brought forth, when already generations have passed away before me?' While they call upon Allah for succour – 'Woe upon you! Believe; surely Allah's promise is true'; then he says, 'This is naught but the fairy tales of the ancients.' Upon such people shall the Word come true, as it did among nations before them of both Jinn and humans. They were indeed lost. For all there are stations, in accordance with their deeds. He will pay them in full for their works, and they shall not be wronged. A Day shall come when the unbelievers shall be paraded before the Fire: 'You wasted the good things in your present life and had full enjoyment of them. Today, you shall be rewarded with an abasing torment because you grew arrogant on earth, unjustly, and because of your debauchery. Remember the man from 'Ad, when he warned his people, amidst the rolling sands, and when warners had passed away before and after him: 'Worship none but Allah. I fear for you the torment of a mighty Day.' They answered: 'Have you come to lure us away from our Gods? Bring upon us what you threaten, if you speak the truth.'

16-22 When we connect with the higher *Reality*, which is in resonance with our soul, we are in touch with our material, biological, and subtler connectedness as well with our inseparability from Allah. If we do not experience this state, we have missed the gift of perpetual life. There are countless degrees of evolution and awakening to higher truth. Most people remain at a basic level; others may be endowed with ability to rise higher in their experience and live according to higher knowledge – that *Truth* is ever-there, timeless. This surah is entitled 'sandy hills'. The people who dwelt in the 'sandy hills' were warned by the Prophet of Ad and those before and after him. Ancient peoples' main concern was survival, and evolution towards the higher spiritual levels was in its early stages.

Divine grace and goodness are seamless and include every situation in which we find ourselves, even though we experience pain and confusion. We need to act upon whatever goodness is recognized and trust that the origin of everything is divine. The story of life is about tuning one's mind and action with the divine light and direction.

Creation is within space and time; therefore, everything happens according to a measure and a degree. The more we excel in doing our best for its own sake, towards its ultimate arrival at the point of eternal light, the easier and more cheerful our lives will be. We cannot have any good news unless it has in it the potential of darkness and bad news. Most of the warning is to do with losing the opportunity to do our best accountably and honestly, while blaming the lower self rather than other people for mistakes.

23-29 قَالَ إِنَّمَا ٱلْعِلْمُ عِندَ ٱللَّهِ وَأُبَلِّغُكُم مَّآ أُرْسِلْتُ بِهِۦ وَلَٰكِنِّىٓ أَرَىٰكُمْ قَوْمًا تَجْهَلُونَ ۝ فَلَمَّا رَأَوْهُ عَارِضًا مُّسْتَقْبِلَ أَوْدِيَتِهِمْ قَالُوا۟ هَٰذَا عَارِضٌ مُّمْطِرُنَا ۚ بَلْ هُوَ مَا ٱسْتَعْجَلْتُم بِهِۦ ۖ رِيحٌ فِيهَا عَذَابٌ أَلِيمٌ ۝ تُدَمِّرُ كُلَّ شَىْءٍۭ بِأَمْرِ رَبِّهَا فَأَصْبَحُوا۟ لَا يُرَىٰٓ إِلَّا مَسَٰكِنُهُمْ ۚ كَذَٰلِكَ نَجْزِى ٱلْقَوْمَ ٱلْمُجْرِمِينَ ۝ وَلَقَدْ مَكَّنَّٰهُمْ فِيمَآ إِن مَّكَّنَّٰكُمْ فِيهِ وَجَعَلْنَا لَهُمْ سَمْعًا وَأَبْصَٰرًا وَأَفْـِٔدَةً فَمَآ أَغْنَىٰ عَنْهُمْ سَمْعُهُمْ وَلَآ أَبْصَٰرُهُمْ وَلَآ أَفْـِٔدَتُهُم مِّن شَىْءٍ إِذْ كَانُوا۟ يَجْحَدُونَ بِـَٔايَٰتِ ٱللَّهِ وَحَاقَ بِهِم مَّا كَانُوا۟ بِهِۦ يَسْتَهْزِءُونَ ۝ وَلَقَدْ أَهْلَكْنَا مَا حَوْلَكُم مِّنَ ٱلْقُرَىٰ وَصَرَّفْنَا ٱلْـَٔايَٰتِ لَعَلَّهُمْ يَرْجِعُونَ ۝ فَلَوْلَا نَصَرَهُمُ ٱلَّذِينَ ٱتَّخَذُوا۟ مِن دُونِ ٱللَّهِ قُرْبَانًا ءَالِهَةًۢ ۖ بَلْ ضَلُّوا۟ عَنْهُمْ ۚ وَذَٰلِكَ إِفْكُهُمْ وَمَا كَانُوا۟ يَفْتَرُونَ ۝ وَإِذْ صَرَفْنَآ إِلَيْكَ نَفَرًا مِّنَ

$$\text{ٱلْجِنِّ يَسْتَمِعُونَ ٱلْقُرْءَانَ فَلَمَّا حَضَرُوهُ قَالُوٓاْ أَنصِتُواْ فَلَمَّا قُضِىَ وَلَّوْاْ إِلَىٰ قَوْمِهِم مُّنذِرِينَ ۝}$$

He said, 'Knowledge is only with Allah, and I deliver to you the Message with which I was sent; but I see you are an ignorant people.' Then, when they saw it as a sudden cloud coming towards their valleys, they said, 'This is a cloud, that shall give us rain!' 'Not so; rather it is that you sought to hasten – a wind, wherein is a painful chastisement, which will destroy everything by its Lord's command.' In the morning there was nothing to see except their dwellings: this is how We repay the guilty. And We had established them in that wherein We have not established you, and We appointed for them hearing, and sight, and hearts; and yet their hearing, their sight and their hearts availed them nothing, since they denied the signs of Allah, and they were encompassed by that they mocked at. And We destroyed the cities about you, and We turned about the signs, that haply they would return. Then why did those not help them that they had taken to themselves as mediators, deities apart from Allah? Not so; but they went astray from them, and that was their calumny, and what they had been forging. Remember when We steered towards you a small band of Jinn to listen to the Qur'an. When they arrived, they said: 'Listen!' When it was finished, they returned to their people, carrying a warning.

23-29 All our senses point to and are metaphors for higher senses and spiritual lights. As children, we begin with outer senses. As we evolve, we move on to the inner subtler senses, until we connect with the innermost soul within the heart, which itself connects cosmic *Reality* and our personal, short-lived reality. Higher knowledge, creativity, and comprehension emanate from the inner heart. If the mind is cluttered and the body is ill, we are unlikely to realise the high intensity and energy of the heart. We need to contain and discipline the lower self and the *nafs* until we are in touch with our inner heart and its lights; at that point, earthly death will become a natural experience of transfer. There are many other entities in existence, which are not the same as human beings, with their own evolutionary processes and changes.

We seek all the great attributes, such as acting with excellence and awareness as well as demonstrating knowledge, efficiency, and accountability every moment. Our senses and intellect exist to keep us on the narrow path of being in the world but not of the world. If we are distracted from our human duty, then all kinds of affliction and destruction are likely to affect us, which are all still part of the divine *Mercy*.

The amazing composition of human beings is such that through all the senses, and all of our other numerous, intricate faculties, we can rise above whatever is short-term to the essence that is ever-present and timeless. The more frequently we can touch this zone, the more likely that our life based on causality, will be agreeable and cheerful. This does not only apply to us human beings, but also to those living entities that are like us in composition and direction, which we call *jinn*.

30-35 قَالُوا۟ يَٰقَوْمَنَآ إِنَّا سَمِعْنَا كِتَٰبًا أُنزِلَ مِنۢ بَعْدِ مُوسَىٰ مُصَدِّقًا لِّمَا بَيْنَ يَدَيْهِ يَهْدِىٓ إِلَى ٱلْحَقِّ وَإِلَىٰ طَرِيقٍ مُّسْتَقِيمٍ ۝ يَٰقَوْمَنَآ أَجِيبُوا۟ دَاعِىَ ٱللَّهِ وَءَامِنُوا۟ بِهِۦ يَغْفِرْ لَكُم مِّن ذُنُوبِكُمْ وَيُجِرْكُم مِّنْ عَذَابٍ أَلِيمٍ ۝ وَمَن لَّا يُجِبْ دَاعِىَ ٱللَّهِ فَلَيْسَ بِمُعْجِزٍ فِى ٱلْأَرْضِ وَلَيْسَ لَهُۥ مِن دُونِهِۦٓ أَوْلِيَآءُ أُو۟لَٰٓئِكَ فِى ضَلَٰلٍ مُّبِينٍ ۝ أَوَلَمْ يَرَوْا۟ أَنَّ ٱللَّهَ ٱلَّذِى خَلَقَ ٱلسَّمَٰوَٰتِ وَٱلْأَرْضَ وَلَمْ يَعْىَ بِخَلْقِهِنَّ بِقَٰدِرٍ عَلَىٰٓ أَن يُحْۦِىَ ٱلْمَوْتَىٰ بَلَىٰٓ إِنَّهُۥ عَلَىٰ كُلِّ شَىْءٍ قَدِيرٌ ۝ وَيَوْمَ يُعْرَضُ ٱلَّذِينَ كَفَرُوا۟ عَلَى ٱلنَّارِ أَلَيْسَ هَٰذَا بِٱلْحَقِّ قَالُوا۟ بَلَىٰ وَرَبِّنَا قَالَ فَذُوقُوا۟ ٱلْعَذَابَ بِمَا كُنتُمْ تَكْفُرُونَ ۝ فَٱصْبِرْ كَمَا صَبَرَ أُو۟لُوا۟ ٱلْعَزْمِ مِنَ ٱلرُّسُلِ وَلَا تَسْتَعْجِل لَّهُمْ كَأَنَّهُمْ يَوْمَ يَرَوْنَ مَا يُوعَدُونَ لَمْ يَلْبَثُوٓا۟ إِلَّا سَاعَةً مِّن نَّهَارٍۭ بَلَٰغٌ فَهَلْ يُهْلَكُ إِلَّا ٱلْقَوْمُ ٱلْفَٰسِقُونَ ۝

They said, 'Our people, we have heard a Book that was sent down after Moses, confirming what was before it, guiding to the truth and to a straight path. O our people! Accept the Divine Caller and believe in Him, He will forgive you of your faults and protect you from a painful punishment.' Whoso answers not him who calls to Allah cannot escape His power on earth, nor has he any patrons apart from Him. Such people are in manifest error. Do they not realize that Allah, Who created the heavens and earth, and did not grow weary from their creation, is capable of reviving the dead? Yes indeed, He has power over all things. Upon the day when the unbelievers are exposed to the Fire: 'Is not this the truth?' They shall say, 'Yes, by our Lord!' He shall say, 'Then taste the chastisement of your unbelief!' So, remain steadfast, as other resolute messengers had stood fast. Seek not to bring it quickly upon them. It will be as if, when they witness the Day they are promised, They had been on earth a mere hour of a day. That is the message! Will any be destroyed but the dissolute?

30-35 The *jinn*, who are unseen entities with life similar to us humans, have heard the Qur'an and confirm that it gives guidance to *Truth* and awakening to *Reality*. Like human beings, some respond to the message and evolve to the higher and some do not. Whoever refers to the higher zone, beyond space-time, will naturally be on a trajectory of wellbeing and success. We understand patience within space-time, whilst doing our utmost to live in the light of consciousness. The ultimate advice to the Prophet and his followers is to be patient, steadfast, and committed to the path of enlightenment.

Allah is all forgiving, beyond all the ups and downs to which creation is exposed. Through true faith and accountable, good action we will reach a point where we are truly guided by the divine light transmitted from the soul. Patience leads ultimately to timelessness, and this is the nature of our own soul, our biggest treasure within ourselves.

We can only survive and exist in this world through the mediumship of the lower self and the ego. Therefore, we have no option other than trying to groom, purify, and deal with it in a balanced way. This is what we call wise – patience. Invariably, every one of us will be tested by having a situation in which, even though you have done your best with kindness and generosity, you will find that you are challenged and may get to the point of anger or disappointment. Here we can rise in consciousness above the skirmish, not dismissing or responding to it, not being subjected to all of the usual enmity that is the norm in our world. We acknowledge all of the changes whilst deferring and referring to the point from which they all emerged: pure consciousness.

19. Surah 50 Qaf (Qaf)

Wherever the letter *qaf* appears, as in the Arabic words *Qadr* (able), *Qahr* (the power that overcomes all), *Qadeem* (ancient beyond time) or *Qareeb* (that which is ever near), these are indicators of the higher qualities and attributes of Allah. Reflecting on the combination of letters, words and sentences, along with understanding a culture and its language, bring us to a situation whereby we are looking at the mirror of reflection of someone else who has journeyed on this path toward *Haqq*, towards Allah.

بِسْمِ اللَّهِ الرَّحْمَٰنِ الرَّحِيمِ

1-13 قٓ ۚ وَٱلْقُرْءَانِ ٱلْمَجِيدِ ۝ بَلْ عَجِبُوٓا۟ أَن جَآءَهُم مُّنذِرٌ مِّنْهُمْ فَقَالَ ٱلْكَٰفِرُونَ هَٰذَا شَىْءٌ عَجِيبٌ ۝ أَءِذَا مِتْنَا وَكُنَّا تُرَابًا ۖ ذَٰلِكَ رَجْعٌۢ بَعِيدٌ ۝ قَدْ عَلِمْنَا مَا تَنقُصُ ٱلْأَرْضُ مِنْهُمْ ۖ وَعِندَنَا كِتَٰبٌ حَفِيظٌۢ ۝ بَلْ كَذَّبُوا۟ بِٱلْحَقِّ لَمَّا جَآءَهُمْ فَهُمْ فِىٓ أَمْرٍ مَّرِيجٍ ۝ أَفَلَمْ يَنظُرُوٓا۟ إِلَى ٱلسَّمَآءِ فَوْقَهُمْ كَيْفَ بَنَيْنَٰهَا وَزَيَّنَّٰهَا وَمَا لَهَا مِن فُرُوجٍ ۝ وَٱلْأَرْضَ مَدَدْنَٰهَا وَأَلْقَيْنَا فِيهَا رَوَٰسِىَ وَأَنۢبَتْنَا فِيهَا مِن كُلِّ زَوْجٍۭ بَهِيجٍ ۝ تَبْصِرَةً وَذِكْرَىٰ لِكُلِّ عَبْدٍ مُّنِيبٍ ۝ وَنَزَّلْنَا مِنَ ٱلسَّمَآءِ مَآءً مُّبَٰرَكًا فَأَنۢبَتْنَا بِهِۦ جَنَّٰتٍ وَحَبَّ ٱلْحَصِيدِ ۝ وَٱلنَّخْلَ بَاسِقَٰتٍ لَّهَا طَلْعٌ نَّضِيدٌ ۝ رِّزْقًا لِّلْعِبَادِ ۖ وَأَحْيَيْنَا بِهِۦ بَلْدَةً مَّيْتًا ۚ كَذَٰلِكَ ٱلْخُرُوجُ ۝ كَذَّبَتْ قَبْلَهُمْ قَوْمُ نُوحٍ وَأَصْحَٰبُ ٱلرَّسِّ وَثَمُودُ ۝ وَعَادٌ وَفِرْعَوْنُ وَإِخْوَٰنُ لُوطٍ ۝

In the name of Allah, the Merciful to all, the Compassionate to each!
Qaf, and by the Glorious Qur'an! But nay – they deem it strange that a warner should have come unto them from their own midst; and so, these deniers of the truth are saying, 'A strange thing is this! What, when we are dead and

become dust? That is a far returning!' We know indeed what the earth diminishes of them, and with Us is a writing that preserves. In fact, they cried lies to the Truth when it came to them, and are thus in perplexity. Have they not observed the sky above them and how We erected it and decked it out, how free of cracks it is? And the earth – We stretched it forth, and cast on it firm mountains, and We caused to grow therein of every joyous kind. A eye-opener is this, and a remembrance to every servant turn in repentance. From the sky We sent down blessed water, Wherewith We caused gardens to flower and grains for the harvest. Soaring palm trees bearing serried clusters provision for the servants, and thereby We revived a land that was dead. Even so is the coming forth. Cried lies before them the people of Noah and the men of Er-Rass, and Thamud, and 'Ad, and Pharaoh, and Lot's brethren,

1-13 Many of us miss the crucial point of accepting daily conditioned consciousness along with the necessity to constantly touch the zone of the highest consciousness. Our life is due to the light of the soul, and unless we are in constant reference to that light, we remain insecure and unhappy.

The most universal challenge to all human beings is the issue of death and life after death. The revealed messages constantly remind us that for Allah everything is possible. The unseen and the seen seamlessly connect. We are here as part of a process of preparation for the immensity of life after death.

The soul or spirit is a divine reality whose nature is beyond the limitation of space and time as well as beyond our mind to comprehend. For the soul to connect with the world as we experience duality, you need the intermediate state of a mind, which physically, is based upon the brain, but is much more a field of energy that can also be limited or defined. Through intelligence the mind can move higher and higher until it touches the zone of the soul within the heart. Due to the mind's intermediary stage, we have all kinds of doubts, uncertainties, and confusion. Faith and trust in the afterlife are something that the mind cannot comprehend, since it is an issue of the heart and the soul. The mind rejects the proposition that after death you will come to live again and after this, there is a second death and the ultimate awakening of life.

14-29 وَأَصْحَٰبُ ٱلْأَيْكَةِ وَقَوْمُ تُبَّعٍ كُلٌّ كَذَّبَ ٱلرُّسُلَ فَحَقَّ وَعِيدِ ۝ أَفَعَيِينَا بِٱلْخَلْقِ ٱلْأَوَّلِ بَلْ هُمْ فِى لَبْسٍ مِّنْ خَلْقٍ جَدِيدٍ ۝ وَلَقَدْ خَلَقْنَا ٱلْإِنسَٰنَ وَنَعْلَمُ مَا تُوَسْوِسُ بِهِۦ نَفْسُهُۥ وَنَحْنُ أَقْرَبُ إِلَيْهِ مِنْ حَبْلِ ٱلْوَرِيدِ ۝ إِذْ يَتَلَقَّى ٱلْمُتَلَقِّيَانِ عَنِ ٱلْيَمِينِ وَعَنِ ٱلشِّمَالِ قَعِيدٌ ۝ مَّا يَلْفِظُ مِن قَوْلٍ إِلَّا لَدَيْهِ رَقِيبٌ عَتِيدٌ ۝ وَجَآءَتْ سَكْرَةُ ٱلْمَوْتِ بِٱلْحَقِّ ذَٰلِكَ مَا كُنتَ مِنْهُ تَحِيدُ ۝ وَنُفِخَ فِى ٱلصُّورِ ذَٰلِكَ يَوْمُ ٱلْوَعِيدِ ۝ وَجَآءَتْ كُلُّ نَفْسٍ مَّعَهَا سَآئِقٌ وَشَهِيدٌ ۝ لَّقَدْ كُنتَ فِى غَفْلَةٍ مِّنْ هَٰذَا فَكَشَفْنَا عَنكَ غِطَآءَكَ فَبَصَرُكَ ٱلْيَوْمَ حَدِيدٌ ۝ وَقَالَ قَرِينُهُۥ هَٰذَا مَا

لَدَىَّ عَتِيدٌ ۝ أَلْقِيَا فِى جَهَنَّمَ كُلَّ كَفَّارٍ عَنِيدٍ ۝ مَّنَّاعٍ لِّلْخَيْرِ مُعْتَدٍ مُّرِيبٍ ۝ ٱلَّذِى جَعَلَ مَعَ ٱللَّهِ إِلَٰهًا ءَاخَرَ فَأَلْقِيَاهُ فِى ٱلْعَذَابِ ٱلشَّدِيدِ ۝ قَالَ قَرِينُهُۥ رَبَّنَا مَآ أَطْغَيْتُهُۥ وَلَٰكِن كَانَ فِى ضَلَٰلٍۭ بَعِيدٍ ۝ قَالَ لَا تَخْتَصِمُوا۟ لَدَىَّ وَقَدْ قَدَّمْتُ إِلَيْكُم بِٱلْوَعِيدِ ۝ مَا يُبَدَّلُ ٱلْقَوْلُ لَدَىَّ وَمَآ أَنَا۠ بِظَلَّٰمٍ لِّلْعَبِيدِ ۝

the People of the Thicket and of Tubba. Each had cried lies to messengers, and the divine threat came true upon them. What, were We wearied by the first creation? No indeed; but they are in uncertainty as to the new creation. And certainly, We created man, and We know what his mind suggests to him, and We are nearer to him than his life-vein. When the two receivers receive, sitting on the right and on the left. Not a word he utters, but by him is an observer ready. And the stupor of death shall come with the Truth – this is what you tried to avoid. And the Trumpet shall be sounded: that shall be the Day of Menace. And every soul shall come, and with it a driver and a witness. 'You were heedless of this; therefore, We have now removed from you your covering, and so your sight today is piercing.' And his comrade shall say, 'This is what I have, made ready.' Do cast into hell every ungrateful, rebellious one, every persistent denier of virtue, every aggressor, every doubter, as also him who set up another Allah alongside Allah. Hurl him into the terrible torment. And his comrade shall say, 'Our Lord, I made him not insolent, but he was in far error.' He shall answer: 'Do not squabble in My presence after having sent you a threat. My word is unchanging, nor am I ever unjust to My servants.'

14-29 Throughout human history, there have been people who have ignored anything to do with the meaning and the purpose of life. Their actions caused havoc to their people and those around them. If our minds are tarnished and our actions and intentions are confused, if the inner light is veiled by *nafs* and the lower self, confusion will continue until death, which will include suffering and loss. Those on the path of higher consciousness realise that sight will lead to greater insight, and that there is always a reference point within us that is like our companion. The more we refer to the higher companion within us, the closer we are to being able to see things with the light of our soul. Prophetic beings, who are fully exposed to the ultimate *Truth* and continue to function as human beings with all the necessary responsibilities towards the body, mind, and heart, have the most challenging task to convey that the *Absolute* is ever-connected with the relative.

We can only appreciate and connect with the soul and its divine light through its shadow, which is the lower self. We must accept the elusive nature of the animal self, try to groom it, and transcend it, following it to its origin and root, the soul or the spirit within. There is always an apparent dispute between the lower self and the soul.

When we lose the body, the mind, and the illusion of individuality and personality, what is left is the power that is driving the self and the *nafs* towards its highest point in consciousness. Within that, there is a pure witnessing faculty that sees things for what they are and not as we imagined, wished, or hoped they would be. For this reason, with death we awaken from the stupor that we have had on this earth. We are like in another sleep zone in this world, and when we die, we wake up from it also.

30-45 يَوْمَ نَقُولُ لِجَهَنَّمَ هَلِ ٱمْتَلَأْتِ وَتَقُولُ هَلْ مِن مَّزِيدٍ ۝ وَأُزْلِفَتِ ٱلْجَنَّةُ لِلْمُتَّقِينَ غَيْرَ بَعِيدٍ ۝ هَٰذَا مَا تُوعَدُونَ لِكُلِّ أَوَّابٍ حَفِيظٍ ۝ مَّنْ خَشِيَ ٱلرَّحْمَٰنَ بِٱلْغَيْبِ وَجَآءَ بِقَلْبٍ مُّنِيبٍ ۝ ٱدْخُلُوهَا بِسَلَٰمٍ ذَٰلِكَ يَوْمُ ٱلْخُلُودِ ۝ لَهُم مَّا يَشَآءُونَ فِيهَا وَلَدَيْنَا مَزِيدٌ ۝ وَكَمْ أَهْلَكْنَا قَبْلَهُم مِّن قَرْنٍ هُمْ أَشَدُّ مِنْهُم بَطْشًا فَنَقَّبُوا۟ فِى ٱلْبِلَٰدِ هَلْ مِن مَّحِيصٍ ۝ إِنَّ فِى ذَٰلِكَ لَذِكْرَىٰ لِمَن كَانَ لَهُۥ قَلْبٌ أَوْ أَلْقَى ٱلسَّمْعَ وَهُوَ شَهِيدٌ ۝ وَلَقَدْ خَلَقْنَا ٱلسَّمَٰوَٰتِ وَٱلْأَرْضَ وَمَا بَيْنَهُمَا فِى سِتَّةِ أَيَّامٍ وَمَا مَسَّنَا مِن لُّغُوبٍ ۝ فَٱصْبِرْ عَلَىٰ مَا يَقُولُونَ وَسَبِّحْ بِحَمْدِ رَبِّكَ قَبْلَ طُلُوعِ ٱلشَّمْسِ وَقَبْلَ ٱلْغُرُوبِ ۝ وَمِنَ ٱلَّيْلِ فَسَبِّحْهُ وَأَدْبَٰرَ ٱلسُّجُودِ ۝ وَٱسْتَمِعْ يَوْمَ يُنَادِ ٱلْمُنَادِ مِن مَّكَانٍ قَرِيبٍ ۝ يَوْمَ يَسْمَعُونَ ٱلصَّيْحَةَ بِٱلْحَقِّ ذَٰلِكَ يَوْمُ ٱلْخُرُوجِ ۝ إِنَّا نَحْنُ نُحْىِۦ وَنُمِيتُ وَإِلَيْنَا ٱلْمَصِيرُ ۝ يَوْمَ تَشَقَّقُ ٱلْأَرْضُ عَنْهُمْ سِرَاعًا ذَٰلِكَ حَشْرٌ عَلَيْنَا يَسِيرٌ ۝ نَّحْنُ أَعْلَمُ بِمَا يَقُولُونَ وَمَآ أَنتَ عَلَيْهِم بِجَبَّارٍ فَذَكِّرْ بِٱلْقُرْءَانِ مَن يَخَافُ وَعِيدِ ۝

A Day shall come when We shall say to hell: 'Are you full?' and it shall answer: 'Can there be more?' And the Garden shall be drawn near to the pious, not far at all. 'This is what you were promised – this is for everyone who turned often and kept Him in mind, who held the Most Gracious in awe, though He is unseen, who comes before Him with a heart turned to Him in devotion. Enter it in peace! This is the Day of Eternity.' Therein they shall have whatever they will; and with Us there is yet more. How many a generation We destroyed before them! They were greater than them in prowess, and traversed the earth – but was there any escape? Most surely there is a reminder in this for him who has a heart or he gives ear and is a witness. We created the heavens and earth and what lies between in six days, and no weariness touched Us. Bear patiently what they say, and glorify the praises of your Lord, Before sunrise and before sunset. In the night, glorify Him, as too after prostration. And listen you for the day when the caller shall call from a near place. On the day they hear the Cry in truth, that is the day of coming forth. It is We Who give life and deal death, and to Us is the journey's end. Upon the day when the earth is split asunder from about them as they hasten forth; that is a mustering easy for Us. We know best what they say, and you are not one to compel them; therefore, remind him by means of the Qur'an who fears My threat.

30-45 Our love for goodness and wellbeing shows itself in a myriad of ways in our earthly behaviour. We love perfumed flowers, gardens, and birdsong. The dark side of each garden is as the dark side of hell. If we are to benefit from the experience of transitory, earthly gardens as a metaphor for the celestial garden beyond time, we require a pure heart and the best expectations of the Creator of it all. Every moment is connected with the flow of time as well as timelessness. If we can be fully attentive and focused in the now, we are at the threshold of timelessness. Everything in the physical world is within space and time, thus in perpetual change journeying toward a destiny. Our love for higher consciousness is an immense gift that drives us to be ready for the next phase of life after death.

If you are at one with your soul, then you are already in the garden. If you have remained in the darkness of the lower self, then a process of purification (referred to as punishment) needs to take place before the light of your own soul shines throughout.

If you have been diligent in this life about what will come next and have prepared yourself through discipline and constant reference to the *Absolute*, then your death is a big gift and a relief, because you were in conscious awareness and lived by the light of your own soul and accepted the limitations and the shadows of the ego-self. Therefore, with death you enter into the ultimate peace, without the hindrances of the shadow plays of other creatures. Through living the promises of the path, through caring for and sharing with others who are less fortunate, through realising that you do not own anything and that the *Truth* is transmitted from your own divine soul, then your transition is glorious.

20. Surah 52 At-Tur (The Mount)

On earth we seek the securities of solid homes and relationships, whereas in truth what we pray for and want belongs to the zone beyond space and time. Our earthly life is but a practice for our next abode.

بِسْمِ اللَّـهِ الرَّحْمَـٰنِ الرَّحِيمِ

1-18 وَالطُّورِ ۝ وَكِتَـٰبٍ مَّسْطُورٍ ۝ فِى رَقٍّ مَّنشُورٍ ۝ وَالْبَيْتِ الْمَعْمُورِ ۝ وَالسَّقْفِ الْمَرْفُوعِ ۝ وَالْبَحْرِ الْمَسْجُورِ ۝ إِنَّ عَذَابَ رَبِّكَ لَوَاقِعٌ ۝ مَّا لَهُۥ مِن دَافِعٍ ۝ يَوْمَ تَمُورُ السَّمَآءُ مَوْرًا ۝ وَتَسِيرُ الْجِبَالُ سَيْرًا ۝ فَوَيْلٌ يَوْمَئِذٍ لِّلْمُكَذِّبِينَ ۝ الَّذِينَ هُمْ فِى خَوْضٍ يَلْعَبُونَ ۝ يَوْمَ يُدَعُّونَ إِلَىٰ نَارِ جَهَنَّمَ دَعًّا ۝ هَـٰذِهِ النَّارُ الَّتِى كُنتُم بِهَا تُكَذِّبُونَ ۝ أَفَسِحْرٌ هَـٰذَآ أَمْ أَنتُمْ لَا تُبْصِرُونَ ۝ اصْلَوْهَا فَاصْبِرُوٓا۟ أَوْ لَا تَصْبِرُوا۟ سَوَآءٌ عَلَيْكُمْ ۖ إِنَّمَا تُجْزَوْنَ مَا كُنتُمْ تَعْمَلُونَ ۝ إِنَّ الْمُتَّقِينَ فِى جَنَّـٰتٍ وَنَعِيمٍ ۝ فَـٰكِهِينَ بِمَآ ءَاتَىٰهُمْ رَبُّهُمْ وَوَقَىٰهُمْ رَبُّهُمْ عَذَابَ الْجَحِيمِ ۝

20. Surah 52 At-Tur (The Mount)

In the name of Allah, the Merciful to all, the Compassionate to each!

I swear by the Mountain, and a Book inscribed, in a parchment unrolled, by the frequented House, and the roof uplifted, and the sea swarming. Your Lord's torment shall surely fall. Nothing can repel it. The Day when heaven shall heave in turmoil, and the mountains shall scurry in haste, woe on that Day to those who deny the Truth, who amuse themselves with idle chatter: that Day they shall be hustled to hell – and what hustling! 'This is the fire that you used to deny. What is this magic, or is it you that do not see? Burn in it. it makes no difference whether you bear it patiently or not. You are only being repaid for what you have done.' Surely, the reverent shall be in gardens and bliss, enjoying what their Lord has given them, for their Lord has spared them the torment of hell.

1-18 Our human perception distinguishes, amongst other things, between solids, fluids, touch, and sound, without realising that all of them emanate from the celestial ocean of *Oneness* in which such factors do not exist. Our perception of individuation is only a starting point to take us back to the original *Oneness*. If we do not rise to this level of higher consciousness before death, we will only regret the lost opportunity after it. Those who have tasted the experience of boundlessness describe it as paradise. Indeed, we live within the confinement of space and time to prepare us for the infinite domain of the next birth – also called death.

It is natural for us to seek everlasting security and peace. Our earthly experiences exist to challenge us to stop looking in the outer world and rather give in to our own soul and the divine *Presence* therein. The Adamic creation was in the perfect garden, but for the offspring of Adam to return to the garden, we need to be in the turmoil of earthly challenges.

Whatever there is in creation indicates the miracle of its inception, our interaction with it, and its return to its origin. With the rise in intelligence, we will deduce clearly that there is a cosmic Master behind anything we see or do not see. We are given very little leeway to interact courteously so that we practice the art of correct flow and justice in everything that interconnects.

19-35 كُلُوا۟ وَٱشْرَبُوا۟ هَنِيٓـًٔۢا بِمَا كُنتُمْ تَعْمَلُونَ ۝ مُتَّكِـِٔينَ عَلَىٰ سُرُرٍ مَّصْفُوفَةٍ ۖ وَزَوَّجْنَـٰهُم بِحُورٍ عِينٍ ۝ وَٱلَّذِينَ ءَامَنُوا۟ وَٱتَّبَعَتْهُمْ ذُرِّيَّتُهُم بِإِيمَـٰنٍ أَلْحَقْنَا بِهِمْ ذُرِّيَّتَهُمْ وَمَآ أَلَتْنَـٰهُم مِّنْ عَمَلِهِم مِّن شَىْءٍ ۚ كُلُّ ٱمْرِئٍۭ بِمَا كَسَبَ رَهِينٌ ۝ وَأَمْدَدْنَـٰهُم بِفَـٰكِهَةٍ وَلَحْمٍ مِّمَّا يَشْتَهُونَ ۝ يَتَنَـٰزَعُونَ فِيهَا كَأْسًا لَّا لَغْوٌ فِيهَا وَلَا تَأْثِيمٌ ۝ وَيَطُوفُ عَلَيْهِمْ غِلْمَانٌ لَّهُمْ كَأَنَّهُمْ لُؤْلُؤٌ مَّكْنُونٌ ۝ وَأَقْبَلَ بَعْضُهُمْ عَلَىٰ بَعْضٍ يَتَسَآءَلُونَ ۝ قَالُوٓا۟ إِنَّا كُنَّا قَبْلُ فِىٓ أَهْلِنَا مُشْفِقِينَ ۝ فَمَنَّ ٱللَّهُ عَلَيْنَا وَوَقَىٰنَا عَذَابَ ٱلسَّمُومِ ۝ إِنَّا كُنَّا مِن قَبْلُ نَدْعُوهُ ۖ إِنَّهُۥ هُوَ ٱلْبَرُّ ٱلرَّحِيمُ ۝ فَذَكِّرْ فَمَآ أَنتَ بِنِعْمَتِ رَبِّكَ بِكَاهِنٍ وَلَا مَجْنُونٍ ۝ أَمْ يَقُولُونَ شَاعِرٌ نَّتَرَبَّصُ بِهِۦ رَيْبَ ٱلْمَنُونِ ۝ قُلْ تَرَبَّصُوا۟

فَإِنِّى مَعَكُم مِّنَ ٱلْمُتَرَبِّصِينَ ۝ أَمْ تَأْمُرُهُمْ أَحْلَـٰمُهُم بِهَـٰذَآ أَمْ هُمْ قَوْمٌ طَاغُونَ ۝ أَمْ يَقُولُونَ تَقَوَّلَهُۥ بَل لَّا يُؤْمِنُونَ ۝ فَلْيَأْتُوا۟ بِحَدِيثٍ مِّثْلِهِۦٓ إِن كَانُوا۟ صَـٰدِقِينَ ۝ أَمْ خُلِقُوا۟ مِنْ غَيْرِ شَىْءٍ أَمْ هُمُ ٱلْخَـٰلِقُونَ ۝

Eat and drink in delight for the deeds you have done. They are comfortably seated on couches arranged in rows; We pair them with beautiful-eyed maidens. We unite the believers with their offspring who followed them in faith – We do not deny them any of the rewards for their deeds: each person is in pledge for his own deeds. We provide them with any fruit or meat they desire. They pass around a cup which does not lead to any idle talk or misdeed. And there go round them youths, their own, as if they were hidden pearls. And they shall turn to one another and wonder. 'When we were still with our families we used to live in fear. But Allah has favored us, and spared us the torment of the scorching wind. We would once pray to Him – He is All-Generous, Compassionate to each.' Therefore, remind. You are not, by grace of your Lord, a soothsayer or a mad man. If they say, 'He is only a poet: we shall await his fate.' Say, 'Wait if you wish; I too am waiting.' Does their reason really tell them to do this, or are they simply insolent people? If they say, 'He has made it up himself' – they certainly do not believe. Let them produce one like it, if what they say is true. Or were they created out of nothing? Or are they the creators?

19-35 When reflection does not go beyond our mind and identity, we are boxed in. Consequently denial, lies, and hypocrisies arise. Those who see through the lens of *Oneness* experience inner contentment and the continuity of the moment. Whoever calls people towards this awakening is considered odd, strange, or even mad. Our conditioned consciousness is so limiting that it forces us to reject anything that is more creative or at a higher level of consciousness. Human discord, rejection, and rebellion relate to the nature of the lower self and ego. With awakening to the light of the inner soul, the darkness of the ego vanishes. The progress towards awakening is the ultimate threat to the lower self and ego. The ego-self makes one doubt oneself and reject the prophetic message regarding the purpose of life on earth.

It is through reason, intellect, and higher intelligence that we move from the zone of rationality to the pure lights of spirituality. The enlightened being would not deny the earthly human needs and the usefulness of a healthy mind, yet they acknowledge and perpetually refer to the perfect cosmic light.

With the exercise of cautious awareness in our interactions, we enter into the zone of physical reality as human beings with limitations, with trust in and understanding of a boundless, eternal *Truth* and *Reality* that encompasses it all. Through this interaction, we know that nothing is separate from the *Creator* and that the creating principle emanates from the divine *Source* itself.

20. Surah 52 At-Tur (The Mount)

٣٦-٤٩ أَمْ خَلَقُوا السَّمَاوَاتِ وَالْأَرْضَ ۚ بَل لَّا يُوقِنُونَ ۝ أَمْ عِندَهُمْ خَزَائِنُ رَبِّكَ أَمْ هُمُ الْمُصَيْطِرُونَ ۝ أَمْ لَهُمْ سُلَّمٌ يَسْتَمِعُونَ فِيهِ ۖ فَلْيَأْتِ مُسْتَمِعُهُم بِسُلْطَانٍ مُّبِينٍ ۝ أَمْ لَهُ الْبَنَاتُ وَلَكُمُ الْبَنُونَ ۝ أَمْ تَسْأَلُهُمْ أَجْرًا فَهُم مِّن مَّغْرَمٍ مُّثْقَلُونَ ۝ أَمْ عِندَهُمُ الْغَيْبُ فَهُمْ يَكْتُبُونَ ۝ أَمْ يُرِيدُونَ كَيْدًا ۖ فَالَّذِينَ كَفَرُوا هُمُ الْمَكِيدُونَ ۝ أَمْ لَهُمْ إِلَٰهٌ غَيْرُ اللَّهِ ۚ سُبْحَانَ اللَّهِ عَمَّا يُشْرِكُونَ ۝ وَإِن يَرَوْا كِسْفًا مِّنَ السَّمَاءِ سَاقِطًا يَقُولُوا سَحَابٌ مَّرْكُومٌ ۝ فَذَرْهُمْ حَتَّىٰ يُلَاقُوا يَوْمَهُمُ الَّذِي فِيهِ يُصْعَقُونَ ۝ يَوْمَ لَا يُغْنِي عَنْهُمْ كَيْدُهُمْ شَيْئًا وَلَا هُمْ يُنصَرُونَ ۝ وَإِنَّ لِلَّذِينَ ظَلَمُوا عَذَابًا دُونَ ذَٰلِكَ وَلَٰكِنَّ أَكْثَرَهُمْ لَا يَعْلَمُونَ ۝ وَاصْبِرْ لِحُكْمِ رَبِّكَ فَإِنَّكَ بِأَعْيُنِنَا ۖ وَسَبِّحْ بِحَمْدِ رَبِّكَ حِينَ تَقُومُ ۝ وَمِنَ اللَّيْلِ فَسَبِّحْهُ وَإِدْبَارَ النُّجُومِ ۝

Did they create the heavens and the earth? No! They do not have faith. Or is it that they possess the treasures of your Lord? Or are they the ones in supreme control? Do they have a ladder to climb, in order to eavesdrop Let their eavesdropper produce clear proof. Or has He daughters while you have sons? Or you demand payment from them that would burden them with debt? Or is the Unseen in their keeping, and so they are writing it down? Or desire they to outwit? The unbelievers, they are the outwitted. Or do they have a god other than Allah? Glory be to Allah far above what they associate with Him! Even if they see missiles raining down from the sky, they would say: 'Massed clouds!' Then leave them, till they encounter their day wherein they shall be thunderstruck. A Day when their guile shall avail them nothing, and they shall be without support. Another punishment awaits the evil-doers, though most of them do not realize it. Wait patiently for your Lord's judgement: you are under Our watchful eye. Celebrate the praise of your Lord when you rise. Glorify Him at night and at the fading of the stars.

36-49 Whatever appears, has an origin and may have a discernible reality that is either physical or energetic. It contains subtler patterns that indicate its connectedness to a higher beginning and meaning. Allah's plan is complete and total; Allah's commands are for all creation to orient towards its origin and to be loyal and honest, as a true reflector of that unfathomable *Oneness*. As for those who remain in the darkness, they will remain in it until they realise that there is no possibility to mend anything from this shadow, since the nature and habit of humanity is to perpetuate what it has become used to. As for those who want to awaken, there is a path with associated rules, which implies acceptance of boundaries that lead to awareness of *Truth*.

As humans we seek the divine attributes of power, knowledge, wealth, and all other great qualities of Allah. Equally, we know that we cannot attain any of these for any durable period of time, because we are within the limitations of space-time on earth. Yet our own soul is heavenly, both eternal and limitless.

Higher intelligence will lead us to accept the duality that we experience in this world: one of which is our human nature, expecting the best, acting towards the best with limitations and hopes. The other side of us, the spirit or the soul in our heart, is the ultimate guide. So, we do not regret what we do. We do not have any guilt or anything other than the good flow of nature, from the Creator of nature.

21. Surah 53 An-Najm (The Star)

Our life on earth reveals a fraction of the unseen, and unless we reflect upon and try to transcend our limitations, we will be confused and at a loss. This surah confirms that what was revealed to the Prophet is from the lights of the divine.

بِسْمِ اللَّـهِ الرَّحْمَـٰنِ الرَّحِيمِ

وَالنَّجْمِ إِذَا هَوَىٰ ۝ مَا ضَلَّ صَاحِبُكُمْ وَمَا غَوَىٰ ۝ وَمَا يَنطِقُ عَنِ الْهَوَىٰ ۝ إِنْ هُوَ إِلَّا وَحْيٌ يُوحَىٰ ۝ عَلَّمَهُ شَدِيدُ الْقُوَىٰ ۝ ذُو مِرَّةٍ فَاسْتَوَىٰ ۝ وَهُوَ بِالْأُفُقِ الْأَعْلَىٰ ۝ ثُمَّ دَنَا فَتَدَلَّىٰ ۝ فَكَانَ قَابَ قَوْسَيْنِ أَوْ أَدْنَىٰ ۝ فَأَوْحَىٰ إِلَىٰ عَبْدِهِ مَا أَوْحَىٰ ۝ مَا كَذَبَ الْفُؤَادُ مَا رَأَىٰ ۝ أَفَتُمَارُونَهُ عَلَىٰ مَا يَرَىٰ ۝ وَلَقَدْ رَآهُ نَزْلَةً أُخْرَىٰ ۝ عِندَ سِدْرَةِ الْمُنتَهَىٰ ۝ عِندَهَا جَنَّةُ الْمَأْوَىٰ ۝ إِذْ يَغْشَى السِّدْرَةَ مَا يَغْشَىٰ ۝ مَا زَاغَ الْبَصَرُ وَمَا طَغَىٰ ۝ لَقَدْ رَأَىٰ مِنْ آيَاتِ رَبِّهِ الْكُبْرَىٰ ۝ أَفَرَأَيْتُمُ اللَّاتَ وَالْعُزَّىٰ ۝

In the name of Allah, the Merciful to all, the Compassionate to each!

By the Star when it plunges, your companion has not strayed; he is not deluded; nor is he giving voice to his fancies. It is but an inspiration, inspired, taught him by one immense in power, daunting. very strong; he stood poised, on the highest horizon. Then drew near and hung suspended, until he was two bow-lengths away or even closer. And He revealed to His servant what He revealed. The yearning heart did not distort what it saw. What, will you dispute with him what he sees? And certainly, he saw him in another descent, by the lote-tree of the farthest limit. Near the Garden of Restfulness. When that which covers covered the lote-tree; the eye did not waver, nor yet did it stray. And he saw some of the greatest signs of his Lord. Have you, then, ever considered Al-Lat and Al-Uzza.

1-19 When the lights of inspiration descend upon us, numerous levels of epiphanies, signs, and signals come from the unseen within the creative fields and imaginative openings. This gift of connectedness can only be acknowledged and praised with gratitude and humility. The purpose of this life is to realise and experience the total connectedness between the seen and unseen, as well as between the *Absolute* and the relative. When this happens to an awakened or prophetic being, their inner heart confirms this realisation of truth. Amongst the signs that come to humanity is this great and unique connectedness. This surah is entitled 'star', and each living entity in a way resembles a heavenly star in the ways it is illuminated and can be illuminating.

The miracle of human life echoes the miracle of the universe with all its galaxies and stars. The light we see in the night sky shone billions of years ago; it existed then but may not now.

Whatever occurs or arises will also disappear. Our little earth is part of the incredible expansion of galaxies in the universe. All that we observe and try to measure indicate that whatever has occurred is according to patterns and designs that interlink from the infinite unknown, through a short period of material or chemical presence, back again to the unknown. We human beings are given the capacity to connect the world of change and material interaction with the origin of the divine spirit, which is beyond the mind to comprehend.

20-31 وَمَنَوٰةَ ٱلثَّالِثَةَ ٱلْأُخْرَىٰ ۝ أَلَكُمُ ٱلذَّكَرُ وَلَهُ ٱلْأُنثَىٰ ۝ تِلْكَ إِذًا قِسْمَةٌ ضِيزَىٰٓ ۝ إِنْ هِيَ إِلَّآ أَسْمَآءٌ سَمَّيْتُمُوهَآ أَنتُمْ وَءَابَآؤُكُم مَّآ أَنزَلَ ٱللَّهُ بِهَا مِن سُلْطَٰنٍ إِن يَتَّبِعُونَ إِلَّا ٱلظَّنَّ وَمَا تَهْوَى ٱلْأَنفُسُ وَلَقَدْ جَآءَهُم مِّن رَّبِّهِمُ ٱلْهُدَىٰٓ ۝ أَمْ لِلْإِنسَٰنِ مَا تَمَنَّىٰ ۝ فَلِلَّهِ ٱلْءَاخِرَةُ وَٱلْأُولَىٰ ۝ وَكَم مِّن مَّلَكٍ فِى ٱلسَّمَٰوَٰتِ لَا تُغْنِى شَفَٰعَتُهُمْ شَيْـًٔا إِلَّا مِنۢ بَعْدِ أَن يَأْذَنَ ٱللَّهُ لِمَن يَشَآءُ وَيَرْضَىٰٓ ۝ إِنَّ ٱلَّذِينَ لَا يُؤْمِنُونَ بِٱلْءَاخِرَةِ لَيُسَمُّونَ ٱلْمَلَٰٓئِكَةَ تَسْمِيَةَ ٱلْأُنثَىٰ ۝ وَمَا لَهُم بِهِۦ مِنْ عِلْمٍ إِن يَتَّبِعُونَ إِلَّا ٱلظَّنَّ وَإِنَّ ٱلظَّنَّ لَا يُغْنِى مِنَ ٱلْحَقِّ شَيْـًٔا ۝ فَأَعْرِضْ عَن مَّن تَوَلَّىٰ عَن ذِكْرِنَا وَلَمْ يُرِدْ إِلَّا ٱلْحَيَوٰةَ ٱلدُّنْيَا ۝ ذَٰلِكَ مَبْلَغُهُم مِّنَ ٱلْعِلْمِ إِنَّ رَبَّكَ هُوَ أَعْلَمُ بِمَن ضَلَّ عَن سَبِيلِهِۦ وَهُوَ أَعْلَمُ بِمَنِ ٱهْتَدَىٰ ۝ وَلِلَّهِ مَا فِى ٱلسَّمَٰوَٰتِ وَمَا فِى ٱلْأَرْضِ لِيَجْزِىَ ٱلَّذِينَ أَسَٰٓـُٔوا۟ بِمَا عَمِلُوا۟ وَيَجْزِىَ ٱلَّذِينَ أَحْسَنُوا۟ بِٱلْحُسْنَى ۝

And Manat the third, the other? Are you to have the male and He the female? This indeed is an unjust division! These are nothing but names you have invented yourselves, you and your forefathers. Allah has sent no authority for them. These people merely follow guesswork and the whims of their souls, even though guidance has come to them from their Lord. Is man to have everything he wishes for? When the present life and the life to come belong only to Allah? There are many angels in heaven whose intercession will be of no use until Allah gives permission to those He will, whose words He will accept. Those who deny the life to come give the angels female names. They have no knowledge to base this on: they merely follow guesswork. Guesswork is of no value against the Truth. So, ignore those who turn away from Our revelation, who want only the life of this world. Such is the extent of their knowledge. Your Lord knows best who has strayed from His path, and knows best who has found guidance. Everything in the heavens and earth belongs to Allah. He will repay those who do evil according to their deeds, and reward, with what is best, those who do good.

20-31 When spiritual openings take place clearly and repeatedly, we come to understand that such events are intended to help human beings rise from identification with matter and temporality towards the realisation of pure energies as well as those that emanate from the spiritual centre of the entire universe, the sacred zone of Godhood. Most people confine themselves to the limitations of space-time and so tend to doubt and reject these utterances and revelations. It is human nature to fear what is unknown and unfamiliar. As such, this tendency limits our progress, both in the conscious world as well as in the spiritual realm. Progress requires faith and trust in the divine *Presence*, the source and destiny of all that is known and unknown.

Whatever we experience moves within space and time and is never constant. The finite and infinite all emanate from Allah. It is our duty to try to reconcile what is relative and changeable with that which is permanent.

Because of the dominating influence of our minds and bodies, we try to justify most of the things that we do not know. A lot of our notions of the unknown or the unseen are just sheer speculation, which does not help us in understanding this world or the origin from which they have all emerged. For that reason, we have to do what we can where the cause and effect of rationality prevails and then trust in the rest.

32-49 ٱلَّذِينَ يَجْتَنِبُونَ كَبَٰٓئِرَ ٱلْإِثْمِ وَٱلْفَوَٰحِشَ إِلَّا ٱللَّمَمَ إِنَّ رَبَّكَ وَٰسِعُ ٱلْمَغْفِرَةِ هُوَ أَعْلَمُ بِكُمْ إِذْ أَنشَأَكُم مِّنَ ٱلْأَرْضِ وَإِذْ أَنتُمْ أَجِنَّةٌ فِى بُطُونِ أُمَّهَٰتِكُمْ فَلَا تُزَكُّوٓا۟ أَنفُسَكُمْ هُوَ أَعْلَمُ بِمَنِ ٱتَّقَىٰٓ ۝ أَفَرَءَيْتَ ٱلَّذِى تَوَلَّىٰ ۝ وَأَعْطَىٰ قَلِيلًا وَأَكْدَىٰٓ ۝ أَعِندَهُۥ عِلْمُ ٱلْغَيْبِ فَهُوَ يَرَىٰٓ ۝ أَمْ لَمْ يُنَبَّأْ بِمَا فِى صُحُفِ مُوسَىٰ ۝ وَإِبْرَٰهِيمَ ٱلَّذِى وَفَّىٰٓ ۝ أَلَّا تَزِرُ وَازِرَةٌ وِزْرَ أُخْرَىٰ ۝ وَأَن لَّيْسَ لِلْإِنسَٰنِ إِلَّا مَا سَعَىٰ ۝ وَأَنَّ سَعْيَهُۥ سَوْفَ يُرَىٰ ۝ ثُمَّ يُجْزَىٰهُ ٱلْجَزَآءَ ٱلْأَوْفَىٰ ۝ وَأَنَّ إِلَىٰ رَبِّكَ ٱلْمُنتَهَىٰ ۝ وَأَنَّهُۥ هُوَ أَضْحَكَ وَأَبْكَىٰ ۝ وَأَنَّهُۥ هُوَ أَمَاتَ وَأَحْيَا ۝ وَأَنَّهُۥ خَلَقَ ٱلزَّوْجَيْنِ ٱلذَّكَرَ وَٱلْأُنثَىٰ ۝ مِن نُّطْفَةٍ إِذَا تُمْنَىٰ ۝ وَأَنَّ عَلَيْهِ ٱلنَّشْأَةَ ٱلْأُخْرَىٰ ۝ وَأَنَّهُۥ هُوَ أَغْنَىٰ وَأَقْنَىٰ ۝ وَأَنَّهُۥ هُوَ رَبُّ ٱلشِّعْرَىٰ ۝

As for those who avoid grave sins and foul acts, though they may commit small sins, your Lord is ample in forgiveness. He has been aware of you from the time He produced you from the earth and from your hiding places in your mothers' wombs, so do not assert your own goodness: He knows best who is mindful of Him. Have you considered him who turned away? Who gave a little and then withheld? Has he the knowledge of the unseen so that he can see? Or was he not apprised of what is in the scrolls of Moses and of Abraham, who fulfilled his duty: that no soul shall bear the burden of another; that man will only have what he has worked towards; that his labour will be seen. Then He shall reward him with the most ample reward, and to your Lord is the final destination. That it is He Who causes laughter and weeping; who brings about death and life; and He created the pairs, male and female, from a sperm drop, when discharged; that it is He Who shall undertake the Second Creation; that it is He who gives wealth and possessions; that He is the Lord of Sirius.

32-49 It is understandable that human beings seek stability and reliability at physical, mental, and other levels. Therefore, it is easy to dismiss what we are not familiar with and pay the price for a lack of acceptance and openness to higher reality. Whatever we strive for will be realised sooner or later. Great beings of the past have struggled in the way of awakening to higher consciousness and God when they realised that it is God who is the beginning and the end, and who causes our experiences to occur. This amazing creation was born from nothingness and cosmic void in order to reveal the magnificent universes we are exposed to and wonder about.

Our constant duty is to experience visible, tangible reality and relate it to its meaning and origin. It is our duty to be accountable for whatever we think and do and to be aware that a much longer period of life begins after our earthly death.

The human experience can be challenging in most situations. Yet, with a bit of cautious awareness, reflectiveness, and trust in the direction that we are on, our mistakes can be easily remedied and we can return to a neutral position along with the flow of nature. Therefore, outer effort, with the rise of intelligence, with renewing our determination to do our utmost to be in direct connection and resonance with our soul, will put us in the best situation we can hope for on earth.

50-62 وَأَنَّهُۥٓ أَهْلَكَ عَادًا ٱلْأُولَىٰ ۝ وَثَمُودَا۟ فَمَآ أَبْقَىٰ ۝ وَقَوْمَ نُوحٍ مِّن قَبْلُ إِنَّهُمْ كَانُوا۟ هُمْ أَظْلَمَ وَأَطْغَىٰ ۝ وَٱلْمُؤْتَفِكَةَ أَهْوَىٰ ۝ فَغَشَّىٰهَا مَا غَشَّىٰ ۝ فَبِأَىِّ ءَالَآءِ رَبِّكَ تَتَمَارَىٰ ۝ هَٰذَا نَذِيرٌ مِّنَ ٱلنُّذُرِ ٱلْأُولَىٰٓ ۝ أَزِفَتِ ٱلْءَازِفَةُ ۝ لَيْسَ لَهَا مِن دُونِ ٱللَّهِ كَاشِفَةٌ ۝ أَفَمِنْ هَٰذَا ٱلْحَدِيثِ تَعْجَبُونَ ۝ وَتَضْحَكُونَ وَلَا تَبْكُونَ ۝ وَأَنتُمْ سَٰمِدُونَ ۝ فَٱسْجُدُوا۟ لِلَّهِ وَٱعْبُدُوا۟ ۩ ۝

And He Who destroyed ancient 'Ad, and Thamud, leaving no trace of them, and before them the people of Noah who were even more unjust and insolent; that it was He who brought down the ruined cities. And enveloped them in the punishment He ordained for them? Which then of your Lord's blessings do you deny? This is a warning just like the warnings sent in former times. The Imminent Event is at hand! [Although] none but Allah can unveil it. So, is it this discourse that you find so strange? And do you laugh, and do you not weep. Why do you pay no heed? Bow down before Allah and worship.

50-62 All peoples and facets of creation follow cyclical patterns. Whatever appears will also disappear, except for that which existed before appearance, the original divine light gifted to us as a soul. To trust in this reality and submit to it is an act of faith, wisdom, and higher understanding; this act brings about true prostration and higher connectedness through adoration and worship. The human drive for higher knowledge and awakening leads us through numerous veils and covers, from utter darkness to perfect light and from temporariness and doubts to constant certainty. The ultimate fuel for this journey is to be in constant awareness of the moment and in real prostration in heart.

As humans, we are often distracted by frivolous entertainment and short-term pleasures, which usually end in regret. If we are constantly aware of the soul's nature, and accountable for our actions, then we may experience earthly joys as a prelude to paradisiacal joys.

With a bit of historical reflection and evaluation, we find that if individuals, groups, or nations were flowing along this path of dealing with what is knowable, understandable, and shareable, with justice and humility, while trusting in the perfect divine justice, they would emerge as decent and happy people instead of being decimated by suspicions and warfare as is often the case.

22. Surah 54 Al-Qamar (The Moon)

In numerous ways the Qur'an reminds us that the end of time is already here but is veiled by the illusion of time. For us to recalibrate our understanding and knowledge, we need to prostrate and transcend earthly limitations. Our earthly consciousness is a veil that can only be pierced through meditation, devotion and transcendence.

بِسْمِ اللَّهِ الرَّحْمَٰنِ الرَّحِيمِ

1-15 اقْتَرَبَتِ السَّاعَةُ وَانشَقَّ الْقَمَرُ ۝ وَإِن يَرَوْا آيَةً يُعْرِضُوا وَيَقُولُوا سِحْرٌ مُّسْتَمِرٌّ ۝ وَكَذَّبُوا وَاتَّبَعُوا أَهْوَاءَهُمْ وَكُلُّ أَمْرٍ مُّسْتَقِرٌّ ۝ وَلَقَدْ جَاءَهُم مِّنَ الْأَنبَاءِ مَا فِيهِ مُزْدَجَرٌ ۝ حِكْمَةٌ بَالِغَةٌ فَمَا تُغْنِ النُّذُرُ ۝ فَتَوَلَّ عَنْهُمْ يَوْمَ يَدْعُ الدَّاعِ إِلَىٰ شَيْءٍ نُّكُرٍ ۝ خُشَّعًا أَبْصَارُهُمْ يَخْرُجُونَ مِنَ الْأَجْدَاثِ كَأَنَّهُمْ جَرَادٌ مُّنتَشِرٌ ۝ مُّهْطِعِينَ إِلَى الدَّاعِ يَقُولُ الْكَافِرُونَ هَٰذَا يَوْمٌ عَسِرٌ ۝ كَذَّبَتْ قَبْلَهُمْ قَوْمُ نُوحٍ فَكَذَّبُوا عَبْدَنَا وَقَالُوا مَجْنُونٌ وَازْدُجِرَ ۝ فَدَعَا رَبَّهُ أَنِّي مَغْلُوبٌ فَانتَصِرْ ۝ فَفَتَحْنَا أَبْوَابَ السَّمَاءِ بِمَاءٍ مُّنْهَمِرٍ ۝ وَفَجَّرْنَا الْأَرْضَ عُيُونًا فَالْتَقَى الْمَاءُ عَلَىٰ أَمْرٍ قَدْ قُدِرَ ۝ وَحَمَلْنَاهُ عَلَىٰ ذَاتِ أَلْوَاحٍ وَدُسُرٍ ۝ تَجْرِي بِأَعْيُنِنَا جَزَاءً لِّمَن كَانَ كُفِرَ ۝ وَلَقَد تَّرَكْنَاهَا آيَةً فَهَلْ مِن مُّدَّكِرٍ ۝

22. Surah 54 Al-Qamar (The Moon)

In the name of Allah, the Merciful to all, the Compassionate to each!

The Hour has drawn near, and the moon is split! Yet if they see a sign they turn away, and they say, 'A continuous sorcery!' They lie, and follow their whims, but every matter shall reach its proper end. There came to them news in which was remonstrance, and consummate Wisdom; but how will warners avail them? So, leave them alone. A Day shall come when the caller shall call to a thing they now deny, and their eyes shall be downcast, as they come out of their tombs, like spreading locusts, running with outstretched necks to the Caller. The unbelievers shall say, 'This is a hard day!' The people of Noah cried lies before them; they cried lies to Our servant, and said, 'A man possessed!' And he was rejected. And so, he called upon his Lord, 'I am defeated: help me!' So, We opened the gates of the sky with torrential water, and caused the earth to burst forth with springs, so that the waters met for a purpose preordained. And We bore him on that which was made of planks and nails, that floated under Our watchful eye, a reward for the one who had been rejected. We have left this as a sign: will anyone take heed?

1-15 Cosmic *Reality* is not restricted to space-time, and those whose consciousness has evolved to be closer to *Reality* will realise that miracles are natural, even though they will be considered abnormal by most people. Yet, like Prophet Noah, they will float on the ocean of truth and light in the same way that his ark floats during the flood. Beginnings and endings are ever together.

Our soul is ever-constant, timeless, and not subject to change. As a result, we are often shocked and deny major changes that we may experience. We have evolved over billions of years during which major events have taken place on earth. The deep memory of disasters remains within our consciousness, which can serve as a reminder of the end of our earthly journey.

Human beings have evolved and grown in consciousness by being on earth, part of the solar system, the most important influence upon us being the moon. As things began from early creation – coalescing from pure cosmic energy – they will also deteriorate and break down. The moon, which is held together by all kinds of forces, mainly gravitational, will also begin to disintegrate. One of the first things that would give us a sign that this is the end of the end is when the moon cracks and breaks down. Then those who have been practising being a soul or spirit will realise that whatever exists as mass or matter must yield to its origin, as must all human beings. As such, they will remember the incredible gift of life – for us to be in the presence of eternal life itself.

16-34 فَكَيْفَ كَانَ عَذَابِى وَنُذُرِ ۝ وَلَقَدْ يَسَّرْنَا ٱلْقُرْءَانَ لِلذِّكْرِ فَهَلْ مِن مُّدَّكِرٍ ۝ كَذَّبَتْ عَادٌ فَكَيْفَ كَانَ عَذَابِى وَنُذُرِ ۝ إِنَّآ أَرْسَلْنَا عَلَيْهِمْ رِيحًا صَرْصَرًا فِى يَوْمِ نَحْسٍ مُّسْتَمِرٍّ ۝ تَنزِعُ ٱلنَّاسَ كَأَنَّهُمْ أَعْجَازُ نَخْلٍ مُّنقَعِرٍ ۝ فَكَيْفَ كَانَ عَذَابِى وَنُذُرِ ۝ وَلَقَدْ يَسَّرْنَا ٱلْقُرْءَانَ لِلذِّكْرِ فَهَلْ مِن مُّدَّكِرٍ ۝ كَذَّبَتْ ثَمُودُ بِٱلنُّذُرِ ۝

فَقَالُوٓاْ أَبَشَرًا مِّنَّا وَٰحِدًا نَّتَّبِعُهُۥٓ إِنَّآ إِذًا لَّفِى ضَلَٰلٍ وَسُعُرٍ ۞ أَءُلْقِىَ ٱلذِّكْرُ عَلَيْهِ مِنۢ بَيْنِنَا بَلْ هُوَ كَذَّابٌ أَشِرٌ ۞ سَيَعْلَمُونَ غَدًا مَّنِ ٱلْكَذَّابُ ٱلْأَشِرُ ۞ إِنَّا مُرْسِلُواْ ٱلنَّاقَةِ فِتْنَةً لَّهُمْ فَٱرْتَقِبْهُمْ وَٱصْطَبِرْ ۞ وَنَبِّئْهُمْ أَنَّ ٱلْمَآءَ قِسْمَةٌۢ بَيْنَهُمْ كُلُّ شِرْبٍ مُّحْتَضَرٌ ۞ فَنَادَوْاْ صَاحِبَهُمْ فَتَعَاطَىٰ فَعَقَرَ ۞ فَكَيْفَ كَانَ عَذَابِى وَنُذُرِ ۞ إِنَّآ أَرْسَلْنَا عَلَيْهِمْ صَيْحَةً وَٰحِدَةً فَكَانُواْ كَهَشِيمِ ٱلْمُحْتَظِرِ ۞ وَلَقَدْ يَسَّرْنَا ٱلْقُرْءَانَ لِلذِّكْرِ فَهَلْ مِن مُّدَّكِرٍ ۞ كَذَّبَتْ قَوْمُ لُوطٍۭ بِٱلنُّذُرِ ۞ إِنَّآ أَرْسَلْنَا عَلَيْهِمْ حَاصِبًا إِلَّآ ءَالَ لُوطٍ نَّجَّيْنَٰهُم بِسَحَرٍ ۞

So how do you find My torment and My warnings? We have made it easy to learn lessons from the Qur'an: will anyone take heed? 'Ad denied. How then were My chastisement and My warnings? We released a howling wind against them on a day of terrible disaster. It swept people away like uprooted palm trunks. For, how severe is the suffering which I inflict when My warnings are disregarded! We have made it easy to learn lessons from the Qur'an: will anyone take heed? Thamud denied to the warnings. And said, 'What, shall we follow a mortal, one out of ourselves? Then indeed we should be in error and insanity. Was the Remembrance revealed to him – of all people here? No indeed! He is a puffed-up liar.' They will know soon enough who is the puffed-up liar! For We shall send them a she-camel to test them: so, watch them and be patient. Tell them the water is to be shared between them each one should drink in turn. But they summoned their companion, and he ventured and cruelly slaughtered, and how severe was the suffering which I inflicted when My warnings were disregarded! Behold, We let loose upon them one scream and they became like the dried-up, crumbling twigs of a sheepfold. We have made it easy to learn lessons from the Qur'an: will anyone take heed? The people of Lot cried lies to the warnings. And We sent them a hail-storm, All except the family of Lot, Whom We saved at dawn,

16-34 The miracle of revelation is that it encompasses all human life on earth as well as the mysterious sacredness of the one *Reality*. The Qur'an expounds this truth in many ways, because the mind cannot comprehend boundlessness and infinity. The numerous symbols, metaphors, and signs are given to us so that we will be willing to go beyond our mind and enter another zone of consciousness, one resonating with the higher *Reality*. Therefore, most humans are suspicious of people who experience this transcendent state. This package of knowledge has been revealed numerous times to different people and places on earth. Yet rejection, doubt, and suspicion about these revelations occurs throughout history and continues.

With intelligence, deep reflection, and meditation, we may realise that our limited, conditioned consciousness is only part of the higher and boundless full consciousness. This deep awareness and remembrance enables us to put our life's experiences into the appropriate perspective.

22. Surah 54 Al-Qamar (The Moon)

Intelligence often rises by learning, until such time that there is no more discernible learning. What remains is simply trust in the *Source* of all knowledge, the Light of lights, the divine *Essence* itself. As such, you will know that the nature of the ego-self is to deny. It wants to assert itself as being the master, whereas it is nothing more than a shadow of the soul or the spirit. It tries to postpone the reflection and meditation upon its own nature. It is the light that produces that shadow that we seek and want to be in reference to. The Qur'an shows us the different versions or colours of this divine light.

35-55 نِعْمَةً مِّنْ عِندِنَا ۚ كَذَٰلِكَ نَجْزِى مَن شَكَرَ ۝ وَلَقَدْ أَنذَرَهُم بَطْشَتَنَا فَتَمَارَوْا۟ بِٱلنُّذُرِ ۝ وَلَقَدْ رَٰوَدُوهُ عَن ضَيْفِهِۦ فَطَمَسْنَآ أَعْيُنَهُمْ فَذُوقُوا۟ عَذَابِى وَنُذُرِ ۝ وَلَقَدْ صَبَّحَهُم بُكْرَةً عَذَابٌ مُّسْتَقِرٌّ ۝ فَذُوقُوا۟ عَذَابِى وَنُذُرِ ۝ وَلَقَدْ يَسَّرْنَا ٱلْقُرْءَانَ لِلذِّكْرِ فَهَلْ مِن مُّدَّكِرٍ ۝ وَلَقَدْ جَآءَ ءَالَ فِرْعَوْنَ ٱلنُّذُرُ ۝ كَذَّبُوا۟ بِـَٔايَٰتِنَا كُلِّهَا فَأَخَذْنَٰهُمْ أَخْذَ عَزِيزٍ مُّقْتَدِرٍ ۝ أَكُفَّارُكُمْ خَيْرٌ مِّنْ أُو۟لَٰٓئِكُمْ أَمْ لَكُم بَرَآءَةٌ فِى ٱلزُّبُرِ ۝ أَمْ يَقُولُونَ نَحْنُ جَمِيعٌ مُّنتَصِرٌ ۝ سَيُهْزَمُ ٱلْجَمْعُ وَيُوَلُّونَ ٱلدُّبُرَ ۝ بَلِ ٱلسَّاعَةُ مَوْعِدُهُمْ وَٱلسَّاعَةُ أَدْهَىٰ وَأَمَرُّ ۝ إِنَّ ٱلْمُجْرِمِينَ فِى ضَلَٰلٍ وَسُعُرٍ ۝ يَوْمَ يُسْحَبُونَ فِى ٱلنَّارِ عَلَىٰ وُجُوهِهِمْ ذُوقُوا۟ مَسَّ سَقَرَ ۝ إِنَّا كُلَّ شَىْءٍ خَلَقْنَٰهُ بِقَدَرٍ ۝ وَمَآ أَمْرُنَآ إِلَّا وَٰحِدَةٌ كَلَمْحٍۭ بِٱلْبَصَرِ ۝ وَلَقَدْ أَهْلَكْنَآ أَشْيَاعَكُمْ فَهَلْ مِن مُّدَّكِرٍ ۝ وَكُلُّ شَىْءٍ فَعَلُوهُ فِى ٱلزُّبُرِ ۝ وَكُلُّ صَغِيرٍ وَكَبِيرٍ مُّسْتَطَرٌ ۝ إِنَّ ٱلْمُتَّقِينَ فِى جَنَّٰتٍ وَنَهَرٍ ۝ فِى مَقْعَدِ صِدْقٍ عِندَ مَلِيكٍ مُّقْتَدِرٍۭ ۝

as a favour from Us: this is how We reward the thankful. For he had truly warned them of Our punishing might; but they stubbornly cast doubt on these warnings. Even his guests they had solicited of him; so, We obliterated their eyes, saying, 'Taste now My chastisement and My warnings!' And early in the morning a punishment seized them that still remains – 'Taste now My chastisement and My warnings!' We have made it easy to learn lessons from the Qur'an: will anyone take heed? The people of Pharaoh also received warnings. They rejected all Our signs so We seized them with all Our might and power. 'Are your disbelievers any better than these? Were you given an exemption in the Scripture?' Do they perhaps say, 'We are a great army and we shall be victorious'? Their forces will be routed and they will turn tail and flee. But the Hour is their appointed time – the Hour is more severe and bitter: truly the wicked are misguided and quite insane on the Day when they are dragged on their faces in Hell. 'Feel the touch of Hell.' We have created all things in due measure; when We ordain something it happens at once, in the blink of an eye; We have destroyed the likes of you in the past. Will anyone take heed? Everything they do is noted in their records: every action, great or small, is recorded. The reverent are securely among Gardens and rivers, in a seat of truth, in the presence of a Sovereign who determines all things.

35-55 Allah's generosity is infinite and ever continuous. The subtle unveilings continue, which can only be confirmed by personal experience and conviction, but so does the denial of people and their turning away from this message. Most people will experience annihilation and an end to their waywardness. Those who are in cautious awareness realise that whatever they experience is according to a measure, whereas the truth of *Reality* is immeasurable. Reflective beings yearn for peace and lasting goodness, for the realisation of the Garden and the bliss of paradise. God's lights are immeasurable, but what we comprehend with our senses is within the limitations and boundaries of conditioned consciousness.

It is through spiritual intelligence that we refer our limited experiences to that which is boundless; revelations and scriptures enhance this process. Nothing ever exists unless it is limited and will pass, yet the light that enables us to realise this fact emanates from an ever-existent *Source*. That light is what we seek in our journey on earth, and awakening to it is our purpose in life.

Our duty as human beings is to bring lasting goodness and reduce suffering, ignorance, abusiveness, and injustice. We all have to accept a certain measure of guardianship or stewardship upon those entities whose abilities and consciousness are less than ours. If you do not care for the other, you will not be able to care for the only so-called you. Because in truth, there is *Oneness*. You and otherness have a lot in common. We all hope and pray for the same thing, which is the best of ends. People on this path will realise that without cautious awareness at all times, we will remain at the lower end of humanity and will not be illumined by the light of divinity.

23. Surah 55 Ar-Rahman (The Merciful to All)

The last ayah of the previous surah declares that those who had lived in correct worship are in the Garden and being honoured by the governor of the universe, the All-Merciful who brought the knowledge of the Qur'an to humanity.

بِسْمِ اللَّهِ الرَّحْمَٰنِ الرَّحِيمِ

1-19 ٱلرَّحْمَٰنُ ۝ عَلَّمَ ٱلْقُرْءَانَ ۝ خَلَقَ ٱلْإِنسَٰنَ ۝ عَلَّمَهُ ٱلْبَيَانَ ۝ ٱلشَّمْسُ وَٱلْقَمَرُ بِحُسْبَانٍ ۝ وَٱلنَّجْمُ وَٱلشَّجَرُ يَسْجُدَانِ ۝ وَٱلسَّمَآءَ رَفَعَهَا وَوَضَعَ ٱلْمِيزَانَ ۝ أَلَّا تَطْغَوْا۟ فِى ٱلْمِيزَانِ ۝ وَأَقِيمُوا۟ ٱلْوَزْنَ بِٱلْقِسْطِ وَلَا تُخْسِرُوا۟ ٱلْمِيزَانَ ۝ وَٱلْأَرْضَ وَضَعَهَا لِلْأَنَامِ ۝ فِيهَا فَٰكِهَةٌ وَٱلنَّخْلُ ذَاتُ ٱلْأَكْمَامِ ۝ وَٱلْحَبُّ ذُو ٱلْعَصْفِ وَٱلرَّيْحَانُ ۝ فَبِأَىِّ ءَالَآءِ رَبِّكُمَا تُكَذِّبَانِ ۝ خَلَقَ ٱلْإِنسَٰنَ مِن صَلْصَٰلٍ كَٱلْفَخَّارِ ۝ وَخَلَقَ ٱلْجَآنَّ مِن مَّارِجٍ مِّن نَّارٍ ۝ فَبِأَىِّ ءَالَآءِ رَبِّكُمَا تُكَذِّبَانِ ۝ رَبُّ ٱلْمَشْرِقَيْنِ وَرَبُّ ٱلْمَغْرِبَيْنِ ۝ فَبِأَىِّ ءَالَآءِ رَبِّكُمَا تُكَذِّبَانِ ۝ مَرَجَ ٱلْبَحْرَيْنِ يَلْتَقِيَانِ ۝

23. Surah 55 Ar-Rahman (The Merciful to All)

In the name of Allah, the Merciful to all, the Compassionate to each!
The All-Merciful! Taught the Qur'an. He created man. He taught him eloquence. The sun and the moon follow their calculated courses. Prostrate themselves the stars and the trees. He has raised up the sky. He has set the balance. Transgress not in the Balance, weigh with justice and do not fall short in the balance. And earth – He set it down for all beings, with its fruits, its palm trees with sheathed clusters, its husked grain, its fragrant plants. Which, then, of your Lord's blessings do you both deny? He created mankind out of dried clay, like pottery; and He created the jinn of a smokeless fire. Which, then, of your Lord's blessings do you both deny? He is Lord of the two risings and Lord of the two settings. Which, then, of your Lord's blessings do you both deny? He brought the two seas together.

1-19 Mercy and compassion are the connecting forces within the fabric of existence, including that of humanity. Our human consciousness is based on balance, reason, rationality, and stability, which all come about by connecting cause and effect. It is our duty to maintain balance in all we do and in all our transactions. Everything manifests in duality. There are humans and *jinn*, there are emanations and returns. Numerous creations and meanings become apparent and then vanish. This is due to the nature of conditioned earthly life, which is only an aspect of perpetual consciousness. These two oceans, mercy and compassion, connect infinite *Reality* with short-term realities through the knowing soul. It is the energy of mercy and compassion that brings together entities that share empathy and love.

Mercy is eternal connectedness, the source of all patterns, the foundation of existence. Due to this cosmic reality and the intricate balances that govern the universe, we are driven to experience and witness the perfection of all.

The great gift of divine mercy upon all of us is manifest by the numerous teachings that are intrinsically transmitted from our own hearts. We want a delightful presence. We want to know about the best possible future. We want to be certain that all is better than the "well that ends well." Therefore, we are reassured that it is through the revelation of the Qur'an that we can rise from base consciousness to the highest level of consciousness within us. We know that there is a balance in our outer human existence, and if we disturb that balance, we will also disturb ourselves and have suffering and regrets.

20-37 بَيْنَهُمَا بَرْزَخٌ لَّا يَبْغِيَانِ ۝ فَبِأَيِّ ءَالَآءِ رَبِّكُمَا تُكَذِّبَانِ ۝ يَخْرُجُ مِنْهُمَا اللُّؤْلُؤُ وَالْمَرْجَانُ ۝ فَبِأَيِّ ءَالَآءِ رَبِّكُمَا تُكَذِّبَانِ ۝ وَلَهُ الْجَوَارِ الْمُنشَـَٔاتُ فِى الْبَحْرِ كَالْأَعْلَٰمِ ۝ فَبِأَيِّ ءَالَآءِ رَبِّكُمَا تُكَذِّبَانِ ۝ كُلُّ مَنْ عَلَيْهَا فَانٍ ۝ وَيَبْقَىٰ وَجْهُ رَبِّكَ ذُو الْجَلَٰلِ وَالْإِكْرَامِ ۝ فَبِأَيِّ ءَالَآءِ رَبِّكُمَا تُكَذِّبَانِ ۝ يَسْـَٔلُهُ مَن فِى السَّمَٰوَٰتِ وَالْأَرْضِ كُلَّ يَوْمٍ هُوَ فِى شَأْنٍ ۝ فَبِأَيِّ ءَالَآءِ رَبِّكُمَا

تُكَذِّبَانِ ۝ سَنَفْرُغُ لَكُمْ أَيُّهَ ٱلثَّقَلَانِ ۝ فَبِأَيِّ ءَالَآءِ رَبِّكُمَا تُكَذِّبَانِ ۝ يَٰمَعْشَرَ ٱلْجِنِّ وَٱلْإِنسِ إِنِ ٱسْتَطَعْتُمْ أَن تَنفُذُوا۟ مِنْ أَقْطَارِ ٱلسَّمَٰوَٰتِ وَٱلْأَرْضِ فَٱنفُذُوا۟ لَا تَنفُذُونَ إِلَّا بِسُلْطَٰنٍ ۝ فَبِأَيِّ ءَالَآءِ رَبِّكُمَا تُكَذِّبَانِ ۝ يُرْسَلُ عَلَيْكُمَا شُوَاظٌ مِّن نَّارٍ وَنُحَاسٌ فَلَا تَنتَصِرَانِ ۝ فَبِأَيِّ ءَالَآءِ رَبِّكُمَا تُكَذِّبَانِ ۝ فَإِذَا ٱنشَقَّتِ ٱلسَّمَآءُ فَكَانَتْ وَرْدَةً كَٱلدِّهَانِ ۝

yet there is a barrier between them they do not transgress. Which, then, of your Lord's blessings do you both deny? From both come forth pearl and coral. Which, then, of your Lord's blessings do you both deny? His too are the ships that run, raised up in the sea like landmarks. Which, then, of your Lord's blessings do you both deny? All who are upon it shall perish. And there remains the face of your Lord, Majestic and Noble. Which, then, of your Lord's blessings do you both deny? All in the heavens and earth beseech Him; He is ever engaged upon some matter. Which, then, of your Lord's blessings do you both deny? We shall apply Ourselves to you, you two great masses of creation! Which, then, of your Lord's blessings do you both deny? Species of Jinn and humans, if you can make your escape from the regions of the heavens and earth, escape! You shall not escape except by divine authority. Which, then, of your Lord's blessings do you both deny? A flash of fire and smoke will be released upon you and no one will come to your aid. Which, then, of your Lord's blessings do you both deny? And when the heaven is rent asunder, and then becomes red like red hide.

20-37 We can only act either as a human being or as the light of Truth. One of them is the equivalent of a particle, which has a beginning and an end, and the other is like a continuous wave function, eternal. These are the truths behind the human challenge. Whatever we have and whatever we perceive emanates from one facet or its equivalent complementary side. As for reality itself, it permeates all. We cannot say that Allah is now in this and that – Allah is in all and always. If we are to get out of the box of duality, we need to transcend our identity and mental conditioning. In order to enter the heavenly abodes of infinity, we need to stop our self-identifications bounded in time; then that which has always been there will become manifest as boundless and timeless.

Human consciousness is contained and limited within the boundaries of space-time. It has arisen from the infinite supreme consciousness, which is boundless. These two realities – one temporary, one permanent – are seamlessly connected through the human soul.

There are two zones of our existence. One is the creational one from which the human self and animal self have evolved over billions of years. The other one is the Light of lights that encompasses the boundless universe. These two major oceans of consciousness meet in us. Therefore, whenever I am confronted with a situation in the outer world – whether a fire, abuse, or injustice – I have to try and address that or help in it first, with constant reference to the perfect justice that is beyond the mind, body, time, and space – divine justice itself. So, I am here acting as a minor steward representing divine justice.

38-56 فَبِأَيِّ ءَالَآءِ رَبِّكُمَا تُكَذِّبَانِ ۝ فَيَوْمَئِذٍ لَّا يُسْـَٔلُ عَن ذَنۢبِهِۦٓ إِنسٌ وَلَا جَآنٌّ ۝ فَبِأَيِّ ءَالَآءِ رَبِّكُمَا تُكَذِّبَانِ ۝ يُعْرَفُ ٱلْمُجْرِمُونَ بِسِيمَٰهُمْ فَيُؤْخَذُ بِٱلنَّوَٰصِى وَٱلْأَقْدَامِ ۝ فَبِأَيِّ ءَالَآءِ رَبِّكُمَا تُكَذِّبَانِ ۝ هَٰذِهِۦ جَهَنَّمُ ٱلَّتِى يُكَذِّبُ بِهَا ٱلْمُجْرِمُونَ ۝ يَطُوفُونَ بَيْنَهَا وَبَيْنَ حَمِيمٍ ءَانٍ ۝ فَبِأَيِّ ءَالَآءِ رَبِّكُمَا تُكَذِّبَانِ ۝ وَلِمَنْ خَافَ مَقَامَ رَبِّهِۦ جَنَّتَانِ ۝ فَبِأَيِّ ءَالَآءِ رَبِّكُمَا تُكَذِّبَانِ ۝ ذَوَاتَآ أَفْنَانٍ ۝ فَبِأَيِّ ءَالَآءِ رَبِّكُمَا تُكَذِّبَانِ ۝ فِيهِمَا عَيْنَانِ تَجْرِيَانِ ۝ فَبِأَيِّ ءَالَآءِ رَبِّكُمَا تُكَذِّبَانِ ۝ فِيهِمَا مِن كُلِّ فَٰكِهَةٍ زَوْجَانِ ۝ فَبِأَيِّ ءَالَآءِ رَبِّكُمَا تُكَذِّبَانِ ۝ مُتَّكِـِٔينَ عَلَىٰ فُرُشٍۭ بَطَآئِنُهَا مِنْ إِسْتَبْرَقٍ وَجَنَى ٱلْجَنَّتَيْنِ دَانٍ ۝ فَبِأَيِّ ءَالَآءِ رَبِّكُمَا تُكَذِّبَانِ ۝ فِيهِنَّ قَٰصِرَٰتُ ٱلطَّرْفِ لَمْ يَطْمِثْهُنَّ إِنسٌ قَبْلَهُمْ وَلَا جَآنٌّ ۝

Which, then, of your Lord's blessings do you both deny? So, on that day neither man nor jinni shall be asked about his misdeeds. Which, then, of your Lord's blessings do you both deny? The criminals shall be known by their outward visage, and they shall be seized by forelocks and feet. Which, then, of your Lord's blessings do you both deny? This is the Hell the guilty deny. They shall wander between it and water, fiercely boiling. Which, then, of your Lord's blessings do you both deny? And for him who fears to stand before his Lord are two gardens. Which, then, of your Lord's blessings do you both deny? Both covered with foliage. Which, then, of your Lord's blessings do you both deny? In it are two running springs. Which, then, of your Lord's blessings do you both deny? In it are, of every fruit, two kinds. Which, then, of your Lord's blessings do you both deny? They will sit on couches upholstered with brocade, the fruit of both gardens within easy reach. Which, then, of your Lord's blessings do you both deny? There will be maidens restraining their glances, untouched beforehand by man or jinn.

38-56 How can we deny that every entity lives and experiences life according to its potential ability, conditioned by all the lenses and filters within its physical, mental, and spiritual make-up? Everything we have assumed to have importance or value will be shown to us from an entirely different viewpoint. Whoever enters that higher state of consciousness will experience two states of bliss, two Gardens. One is terrestrial and limited; the other is celestial and boundless.

Our human duty and honour lie in consciously attempting to rise in consciousness: to realise that the nature of the soul is infinite and that the nature of earthly experience is finite and short-lived.

Earthly experience leads to the eternal life of the hereafter, once the illusory identity of body and mind unravels.

If I know that I straddle double zones of consciousness, then with cautious awareness and true worship, as well as the taste, knowledge, and the presence of *tawhid* in me, I will experience the garden on earth. The pattern of whatever comes is perfect, whether I like it or not. Therefore, if we taste *tawhid* we will experience the garden of perfection on this earth and the eternal garden after we leave the body. Goodness also occurs in doubles: one is human goodness, kindness, and generosity for others; the other goodness connects to the *Source* of generosity and goodness, which is *ihsan* itself.

57-78 فَبِأَىِّ ءَالَآءِ رَبِّكُمَا تُكَذِّبَانِ ۝ كَأَنَّهُنَّ ٱلْيَاقُوتُ وَٱلْمَرْجَانُ ۝ فَبِأَىِّ ءَالَآءِ رَبِّكُمَا تُكَذِّبَانِ ۝ هَلْ جَزَآءُ ٱلْإِحْسَٰنِ إِلَّا ٱلْإِحْسَٰنُ ۝ فَبِأَىِّ ءَالَآءِ رَبِّكُمَا تُكَذِّبَانِ ۝ وَمِن دُونِهِمَا جَنَّتَانِ ۝ فَبِأَىِّ ءَالَآءِ رَبِّكُمَا تُكَذِّبَانِ ۝ مُدْهَآمَّتَانِ ۝ فَبِأَىِّ ءَالَآءِ رَبِّكُمَا تُكَذِّبَانِ ۝ فِيهِمَا عَيْنَانِ نَضَّاخَتَانِ ۝ فَبِأَىِّ ءَالَآءِ رَبِّكُمَا تُكَذِّبَانِ ۝ فِيهِمَا فَٰكِهَةٌ وَنَخْلٌ وَرُمَّانٌ ۝ فَبِأَىِّ ءَالَآءِ رَبِّكُمَا تُكَذِّبَانِ ۝ فِيهِنَّ خَيْرَٰتٌ حِسَانٌ ۝ فَبِأَىِّ ءَالَآءِ رَبِّكُمَا تُكَذِّبَانِ ۝ حُورٌ مَّقْصُورَٰتٌ فِى ٱلْخِيَامِ ۝ فَبِأَىِّ ءَالَآءِ رَبِّكُمَا تُكَذِّبَانِ ۝ لَمْ يَطْمِثْهُنَّ إِنسٌ قَبْلَهُمْ وَلَا جَآنٌّ ۝ فَبِأَىِّ ءَالَآءِ رَبِّكُمَا تُكَذِّبَانِ ۝ مُتَّكِـِٔينَ عَلَىٰ رَفْرَفٍ خُضْرٍ وَعَبْقَرِىٍّ حِسَانٍ ۝ فَبِأَىِّ ءَالَآءِ رَبِّكُمَا تُكَذِّبَانِ ۝ تَبَٰرَكَ ٱسْمُ رَبِّكَ ذِى ٱلْجَلَٰلِ وَٱلْإِكْرَامِ ۝

Which, then, of your Lord's blessings do you both deny? Like rubies and brilliant pearls. Which, then, of your Lord's blessings do you both deny? Shall the reward of good be anything but good? Which, then, of your Lord's blessings do you both deny? There are two other gardens below these two. Which, then, of your Lord's blessings do you both deny? Over-shadowing. Which, then, of your Lord's blessings do you both deny? Therein two fountains of gushing water. Which, then, of your Lord's blessings do you both deny? In both are fruits and palms and pomegranates. Which, then, of your Lord's blessings do you both deny? In them are maidens, virtuous and beautiful. Which, then, of your Lord's blessings do you both deny? Dark-eyed, sheltered in pavilions. Which, then, of your Lord's blessings do you both deny? Man has not touched them before them nor Jinni. Which, then, of your Lord's blessings do you both deny? They will all sit on green cushions and fine carpets. Which, then, of your Lord's blessings do you both deny? Blessed be the name of your Lord, Majestic and Noble!

57-78 Different entities emerge from different roots, yet of the same origin. When we rise in our consciousness, we will realise that not only are we following a map of *Reality*, progressing towards higher levels of knowledge and lights, we are also unable to act in any way other than through the perfect light that has contained all. Those who are awakened cannot but act with grace, goodness, and unconditional love. Our human consciousness resides within the limitations of dualities; we need to reckon with these dualities, since they not only confine us within physical, emotional, and spiritual states but also lead us towards the effulgent *Source* of their unity. Our relentless drive is to experience the vast pure consciousness, whose essence resides in our soul.

Our earthly zone of consciousness is based on dualities and pluralities emanating from *Unity*, which is the light that illumines our life. A being awakened to this truth will naturally reveal its magnificence and generosity.

Duality is the norm in our earthly life. Human beings and *Jinn* also represent dualities, one visible, one not. Both are subject to the laws of creation, birth and death. Our experiences lead us to a zone of consciousness that will be the reality after death, and the removal of distractions of body and mind. The search for the perfect partner is natural due to the fact that your soul is your mate – without it you have no life.

24. Surah 56 Al-Waqiah (The Inevitable)

The most important event, as far as human beings are concerned, is the state in which normal conditioned consciousness no longer dominates. There is also a collective event that reflects this notion, regarding all other living creatures, including the earth and the universe. When all visible and sensory realities vanish, then every entity faces past intentions and actions clearly.

بِسْمِ اللَّـهِ الرَّحْمَـٰنِ الرَّحِيمِ

1-19 إِذَا وَقَعَتِ ٱلْوَاقِعَةُ ۝ لَيْسَ لِوَقْعَتِهَا كَاذِبَةٌ ۝ خَافِضَةٌ رَّافِعَةٌ ۝ إِذَا رُجَّتِ ٱلْأَرْضُ رَجًّا ۝ وَبُسَّتِ ٱلْجِبَالُ بَسًّا ۝ فَكَانَتْ هَبَآءً مُّنۢبَثًّا ۝ وَكُنتُمْ أَزْوَٰجًا ثَلَـٰثَةً ۝ فَأَصْحَـٰبُ ٱلْمَيْمَنَةِ مَآ أَصْحَـٰبُ ٱلْمَيْمَنَةِ ۝ وَأَصْحَـٰبُ ٱلْمَشْـَٔمَةِ مَآ أَصْحَـٰبُ ٱلْمَشْـَٔمَةِ ۝ وَٱلسَّـٰبِقُونَ ٱلسَّـٰبِقُونَ ۝ أُوْلَـٰٓئِكَ ٱلْمُقَرَّبُونَ ۝ فِى جَنَّـٰتِ ٱلنَّعِيمِ ۝ ثُلَّةٌ مِّنَ ٱلْأَوَّلِينَ ۝ وَقَلِيلٌ مِّنَ ٱلْـَٔاخِرِينَ ۝ عَلَىٰ سُرُرٍ مَّوْضُونَةٍ ۝ مُّتَّكِـِٔينَ عَلَيْهَا مُتَقَـٰبِلِينَ ۝ يَطُوفُ عَلَيْهِمْ وِلْدَٰنٌ مُّخَلَّدُونَ ۝ بِأَكْوَابٍ وَأَبَارِيقَ وَكَأْسٍ مِّن مَّعِينٍ ۝ لَّا يُصَدَّعُونَ عَنْهَا وَلَا يُنزِفُونَ ۝

In the name of Allah, the Merciful to all, the Compassionate to each!

When that which is coming arrives, no one will be able to deny it has come, bringing low and raising high. When the earth is shaken violently. And the mountains are broken down, crumbling, and turn to scattered dust, you shall be of three kinds. The companions of the Right – wondrous are the companions of the Right! The Companions of the Left: what of the Companions of the Left? And those in front – ahead indeed! These shall be the nearest. In the Gardens of Bliss. Many from the past, and a few from later generations. On lined couches, reclining on them, facing one another. Immortal youths will wait upon them, with glasses, flagons, and cups of a pure drink, causing them neither ache nor intoxication.

1-19 The greatest event of all is when the universe returns to its origin of divine light. This is the most significant cosmic event, when matter reveals itself as energy states and when human souls admit and realise the truth: that they are only there to sing the praise of the cosmic soul, Allah, and unify with the centre of all unities. People who realise this before death or resurrection will have experienced paradise within their hearts; this is where the soul was born or created and this is its home environment. Most of our experiences have beginnings and endings, and the entire universe will also come to this inevitable end event. *Truth* and God are beyond all events and are the cause of all temporary manifestations as well as their end.

Every beginning has an end, and so does our universe. There will come a time when our solar system and galaxy will vanish. The pure energy source is eternal and will reveal some of the traces of the spirits that pass through.

The most crucial event is that which reveals *Reality* and *Truth*: everlasting, divine, constant, before and after any event. So, this is the issue of the human quest and challenge. The event is that only the *Source*, which remains constant in timelessness, causes countless events. This is the nature of our soul. For this reason, the human being is a carrier of a light or trust that is beyond measure. Those who realise this are already in gardens beyond measure.

20-41 وَفَٰكِهَةٍ مِّمَّا يَتَخَيَّرُونَ ۝ وَلَحْمِ طَيْرٍ مِّمَّا يَشْتَهُونَ ۝ وَحُورٌ عِينٌ ۝ كَأَمْثَٰلِ ٱللُّؤْلُؤِ ٱلْمَكْنُونِ ۝ جَزَآءًۢ بِمَا كَانُوا۟ يَعْمَلُونَ ۝ لَا يَسْمَعُونَ فِيهَا لَغْوًا وَلَا تَأْثِيمًا ۝ إِلَّا قِيلًا سَلَٰمًا سَلَٰمًا ۝ وَأَصْحَٰبُ ٱلْيَمِينِ مَآ أَصْحَٰبُ ٱلْيَمِينِ ۝ فِى سِدْرٍ مَّخْضُودٍ ۝ وَطَلْحٍ مَّنضُودٍ ۝ وَظِلٍّ مَّمْدُودٍ ۝ وَمَآءٍ مَّسْكُوبٍ ۝ وَفَٰكِهَةٍ كَثِيرَةٍ ۝ لَّا مَقْطُوعَةٍ وَلَا مَمْنُوعَةٍ ۝ وَفُرُشٍ مَّرْفُوعَةٍ ۝ إِنَّآ أَنشَأْنَٰهُنَّ إِنشَآءً ۝ فَجَعَلْنَٰهُنَّ أَبْكَارًا ۝ عُرُبًا أَتْرَابًا ۝ لِّأَصْحَٰبِ ٱلْيَمِينِ ۝ ثُلَّةٌ مِّنَ ٱلْأَوَّلِينَ ۝ وَثُلَّةٌ مِّنَ ٱلْءَاخِرِينَ ۝ وَأَصْحَٰبُ ٱلشِّمَالِ مَآ أَصْحَٰبُ ٱلشِّمَالِ ۝

And such fruits as they shall choose, the meat of any bird they like. And maidens, eyes large and dark, like hidden pearls. A reward for what they used to do. They will hear no idle or idle talk there, only the saying Peace, Peace. The companions of the Right – wondrous are the companions of the Right! They are among thornless lote trees, and acacia in clusters, with spreading shade, and flowing water, and abundant fruits, unfailing, unforbidden, and upraised couches. Perfectly We formed them, perfect. Making them intact virgins. Loving, equals in age, for those on the Right. Many from the past. And many from later generations. But those on the Left, what people they are.

24. Surah 56 Al-Waqiah (The Inevitable)

20-41 In the heavenly paradise, there are no needs or desires for those in that state. There is for them perfect peace. The second group are those who are completing the return journey via the grace and perfection of the perfect cosmic soul – Allah. The third group have not realised their potential, and their souls are covered by their egos, with the illusions of duality and multiplicity, cause and effect, and birth and death. They are caught in the dark clouds of lower consciousness, as is the usual earthly experience. Most human beings are in this third group, where there is a perpetual struggle to experience durable goodness and balance. Our consciousness on earth is subject to this constant change and uncertainty, which leads us to reflect on our purpose as well as our distraction from it. The soul can transcend the sensory to the zone of pure consciousness and perfection within.

Human life on earth will be followed by an experience in the hereafter, which will deal with all unfulfilled desires and hopes, as well as the fears and sorrows that we experience on earth. The soul will emerge free of these encumbrances of mind and body.

If you have moved away from changes – appearing, disappearing, physical reality, dream reality – and gone into the zone touching the absolute timelessness, then you have done your duty. As such, you are in the highest levels of paradise.

42-61 فِى سَمُومٍ وَحَمِيمٍ ۝ وَظِلٍّ مِّن يَحْمُومٍ ۝ لَّا بَارِدٍ وَلَا كَرِيمٍ ۝ إِنَّهُمْ كَانُوا۟ قَبْلَ ذَٰلِكَ مُتْرَفِينَ ۝ وَكَانُوا۟ يُصِرُّونَ عَلَى ٱلْحِنثِ ٱلْعَظِيمِ ۝ وَكَانُوا۟ يَقُولُونَ أَئِذَا مِتْنَا وَكُنَّا تُرَابًا وَعِظَٰمًا أَءِنَّا لَمَبْعُوثُونَ ۝ أَوَءَابَآؤُنَا ٱلْأَوَّلُونَ ۝ قُلْ إِنَّ ٱلْأَوَّلِينَ وَٱلْءَاخِرِينَ ۝ لَمَجْمُوعُونَ إِلَىٰ مِيقَٰتِ يَوْمٍ مَّعْلُومٍ ۝ ثُمَّ إِنَّكُمْ أَيُّهَا ٱلضَّآلُّونَ ٱلْمُكَذِّبُونَ ۝ لَءَاكِلُونَ مِن شَجَرٍ مِّن زَقُّومٍ ۝ فَمَالِـُٔونَ مِنْهَا ٱلْبُطُونَ ۝ فَشَٰرِبُونَ عَلَيْهِ مِنَ ٱلْحَمِيمِ ۝ فَشَٰرِبُونَ شُرْبَ ٱلْهِيمِ ۝ هَٰذَا نُزُلُهُمْ يَوْمَ ٱلدِّينِ ۝ نَحْنُ خَلَقْنَٰكُمْ فَلَوْلَا تُصَدِّقُونَ ۝ أَفَرَءَيْتُم مَّا تُمْنُونَ ۝ ءَأَنتُمْ تَخْلُقُونَهُۥٓ أَمْ نَحْنُ ٱلْخَٰلِقُونَ ۝ نَحْنُ قَدَّرْنَا بَيْنَكُمُ ٱلْمَوْتَ وَمَا نَحْنُ بِمَسْبُوقِينَ ۝ عَلَىٰٓ أَن نُّبَدِّلَ أَمْثَٰلَكُمْ وَنُنشِئَكُمْ فِى مَا لَا تَعْلَمُونَ ۝

In hot wind and boiling water, in the shadow of black smoke, neither cool nor refreshing. Before, they overindulged in luxury. And persisted in great violation, always saying, 'What? When we are dead and have become dust and bones, shall we then be raised up? And our earliest forefathers too?' Say, 'The earliest and latest generations, will indeed be gathered together at an appointed time on a Day known. And you who have gone astray and denied the truth. Most surely eat of a tree of Bitterness, filling your bellies with it, and drink on top of that boiling water lapping it like thirsty camels.' This will be their welcome on the Day of recompense. It was We who created you: will you not believe? Consider what you discharge; do you create it yourselves or are We the Creator? We ordained death to be among you. Nothing could *stop Us, that We may exchange the likes of you, and make you to grow again in a fashion you know not.*

42-61 The third group experiences the all-too-usual difficulties, fears, sorrow, and misery, as symbolised by the eternal fire. With intelligent reflection and contemplation, we eventually admit that there is divine mastery and perfect governance behind all that is known and unknown. Individuals and people will emerge on earth, but also vanish. In the same way that creation emerged from nothingness, it will return to the zone of pure consciousness and infinitude. With serious reflection, meditation, prayer, and grace we realise that this magnificent creation is intricately interconnected, under perfect governance in the visible sense as well as in all the subtle, non-discernible states that lead it to its ultimate destiny.

After death, the soul will be purged from all the sediments and precipitations with which it burdened itself. This is akin to the purgatory period, described by many religions and ancient revelations.

We are driven to leave the earthly morass of darkness and catch a glimpse of the cosmic light. Deep within our souls lies the knowledge of the first creation. If you forget everything else, lose all movement inwardly and outwardly, you may realise that your reality is the divine light captured for a while within space and time to appreciate the miracles of all the events that are here, the amazing nature of water, earth, fire, and air. Once you enter that zone of miracles, then you have connected your physical, material, and human reality with your cosmic origin. If you do not do this, then when the soul is about to depart, you will feel your throat closing and be perplexed as to what is going on. If you have done your duties before, death is the biggest gift and relief. If not, you know there will be questioning and whatever it takes for you to lose everything except the original light that was given to you to experience all.

62-81 وَلَقَدْ عَلِمْتُمُ ٱلنَّشْأَةَ ٱلْأُولَىٰ فَلَوْلَا تَذَكَّرُونَ ۝ أَفَرَءَيْتُم مَّا تَحْرُثُونَ ۝ ءَأَنتُمْ تَزْرَعُونَهُۥٓ أَمْ نَحْنُ ٱلزَّٰرِعُونَ ۝ لَوْ نَشَآءُ لَجَعَلْنَٰهُ حُطَٰمًا فَظَلْتُمْ تَفَكَّهُونَ ۝ إِنَّا لَمُغْرَمُونَ ۝ بَلْ نَحْنُ مَحْرُومُونَ ۝ أَفَرَءَيْتُمُ ٱلْمَآءَ ٱلَّذِى تَشْرَبُونَ ۝ ءَأَنتُمْ أَنزَلْتُمُوهُ مِنَ ٱلْمُزْنِ أَمْ نَحْنُ ٱلْمُنزِلُونَ ۝ لَوْ نَشَآءُ جَعَلْنَٰهُ أُجَاجًا فَلَوْلَا تَشْكُرُونَ ۝ أَفَرَءَيْتُمُ ٱلنَّارَ ٱلَّتِى تُورُونَ ۝ ءَأَنتُمْ أَنشَأْتُمْ شَجَرَتَهَآ أَمْ نَحْنُ ٱلْمُنشِـُٔونَ ۝ نَحْنُ جَعَلْنَٰهَا تَذْكِرَةً وَمَتَٰعًا لِّلْمُقْوِينَ ۝ فَسَبِّحْ بِٱسْمِ رَبِّكَ ٱلْعَظِيمِ ۝ فَلَآ أُقْسِمُ بِمَوَٰقِعِ ٱلنُّجُومِ ۝ وَإِنَّهُۥ لَقَسَمٌ لَّوْ تَعْلَمُونَ عَظِيمٌ ۝ إِنَّهُۥ لَقُرْءَانٌ كَرِيمٌ ۝ فِى كِتَٰبٍ مَّكْنُونٍ ۝ لَّا يَمَسُّهُۥٓ إِلَّا ٱلْمُطَهَّرُونَ ۝ تَنزِيلٌ مِّن رَّبِّ ٱلْعَٰلَمِينَ ۝ أَفَبِهَٰذَا ٱلْحَدِيثِ أَنتُم مُّدْهِنُونَ ۝

You know all about the first creation – will you not remember and reflect? Have you considered what you sow? Is it you who make them grow or We?

If We wished, We could turn your harvest into chaff and leave you to wail, We are burdened with debt. Nay! We are deprived. Have you considered the water you drink? Was it you who brought it down from the raincloud or We? If We wanted, We could make it bitter: will you not be thankful? Have you ever considered the fire which you kindle? Is it you who make the wood for it grow or We? We have made it to be a reminder – and, too, a comfort to hungry travelers. So, [Prophet] glorify the name of your Lord, the Supreme. I swear by the positions of the stars. A mighty oath, if you only knew. That this is truly a noble Qur'an. In a protected Record. That only the purified can touch, sent down from the Lord of all being. How can you scorn this statement?

62-81 Through deep reflection and contemplation we may realise our drive to discover our origin and the beginning of everything, whether this relates to our personal ancestral origins, humanity itself, or life on earth. Allah, the origin of all, the primal cause, remains constantly the same, attributed with many desirable sacred names and qualities from which opposites emerge and to which they submerge. This zone is so powerful and immense that it is described as a singularity, the most unimaginable, dense beginning and cause of the universe. If we contemplate the physical universe, stars, and galaxies, we see how this incredible creation cannot be pinned down, even the position of a star is impossible to ascertain. When one sees the sun rising above the horizon, it has actually arisen several minutes before. All our experiences are influenced by the relativity of space-time. Our life on earth is based on so many uncertainties, yet we always seek absolute certainty during our short journey. That absoluteness resides within the sacred soul.

It is natural for human beings to seek what is constant and unchanging, though everything that we experience within space-time has no constancy. Only the light of the soul is steady, for its origin is beyond space and time.

We search for knowledge to connect different aspects of life. In reality, we are floating in the ocean of lights in order to abandon our self-consciousness into the immensity of wonderment. How does everything begin and morph into other realities? Only with a pure and present heart, do we realise that the soul within our heart is eternal and divine. This is what we need to follow and obey.

82-96 وَتَجْعَلُونَ رِزْقَكُمْ أَنَّكُمْ تُكَذِّبُونَ ۝ فَلَوْلَا إِذَا بَلَغَتِ ٱلْحُلْقُومَ ۝ وَأَنتُمْ حِينَئِذٍ تَنظُرُونَ ۝ وَنَحْنُ أَقْرَبُ إِلَيْهِ مِنكُمْ وَلَٰكِن لَّا تُبْصِرُونَ ۝ فَلَوْلَا إِن كُنتُمْ غَيْرَ مَدِينِينَ ۝ تَرْجِعُونَهَا إِن كُنتُمْ صَٰدِقِينَ ۝ فَأَمَّا إِن كَانَ مِنَ ٱلْمُقَرَّبِينَ ۝ فَرَوْحٌ وَرَيْحَانٌ وَجَنَّتُ نَعِيمٍ ۝ وَأَمَّا إِن كَانَ مِنْ أَصْحَٰبِ ٱلْيَمِينِ ۝ فَسَلَٰمٌ لَّكَ مِنْ أَصْحَٰبِ ٱلْيَمِينِ ۝ وَأَمَّآ إِن كَانَ مِنَ ٱلْمُكَذِّبِينَ ٱلضَّآلِّينَ ۝ فَنُزُلٌ مِّنْ حَمِيمٍ ۝ وَتَصْلِيَةُ جَحِيمٍ ۝ إِنَّ هَٰذَا لَهُوَ حَقُّ ٱلْيَقِينِ ۝ فَسَبِّحْ بِٱسْمِ رَبِّكَ ٱلْعَظِيمِ ۝

And how, in return for the livelihood you are given, can you deny it? Wait till your soul reaches your throat while you gaze on. We are nearer to him than you, though you do not see Us. Why, if you are not to be recompressed? Then bring it back, if you are telling the truth! Then, if he be of those brought near. There shall be repose and ease, and a Garden of Delight; and if he be a Companion of the Right: Peace be upon you, Companion of the Right! But if he is one of those who denied and went astray. He will be welcomed with scalding water. He will burn in Hell. This is the certain truth. [Prophet], glorify the name of your Lord the Supreme.

82-96 To look for absolute certainty is a natural, primal drive within us; however, we look incorrectly in the zone of time and space. Certainty exists within the soul, but to experience this we need to exclude all other ideas and experiences until we unify the inner light of the soul with the outer lights and shadows that come through our eyes and perception. Due to the limitations of our humanity, we identify our experiences with our mind and biography. We pursue goodness for ourselves, without referring to the ultimate goodness, which is stillness, contentment, and inner joy. That is the state in the Garden on earth, as well as in the hereafter. Those who have not read this map travel with increased confusion, fears, and sorrow in this life and as an almost ongoing experience after death.

Ultimate honesty reveals the truth that the soul does not belong to us, but to the divine, and that 'we' experience life because of the soul. Perfections in life will be experienced because of one's humility, loyalty, and honesty. Truth will always prevail, but for one to realise it, one must surrender all other notions, which are transitory.

The barrier to light and knowledge is the assumption and illusion that the self or ego can lead and rule. In reality, it can only mislead. The path of awakening is landmarked by reminders to be present in the now – that is the nature of the eternal soul. Your material and spiritual health is dependent on the quality and frequency of touching the light of your own heart.

25. Surah 57 Al-Hadid (Iron)

The last ayah of Surah Waqîah declares that the purpose of life is to be certain about the master of all, with whom we can only connect fully by glorification and worship. The first ayah of Surah Hadid enjoins upon us to be in a state of true adoration and glorification towards the One, who controls all.

بِسْمِ اللَّهِ الرَّحْمَٰنِ الرَّحِيمِ

سَبَّحَ لِلَّهِ مَا فِي السَّمَٰوَٰتِ وَٱلْأَرْضِ وَهُوَ ٱلْعَزِيزُ ٱلْحَكِيمُ ۝ لَهُۥ مُلْكُ ٱلسَّمَٰوَٰتِ وَٱلْأَرْضِ يُحْىِۦ وَيُمِيتُ وَهُوَ عَلَىٰ كُلِّ شَىْءٍ قَدِيرٌ ۝ هُوَ ٱلْأَوَّلُ وَٱلْءَاخِرُ وَٱلظَّٰهِرُ وَٱلْبَاطِنُ وَهُوَ بِكُلِّ شَىْءٍ عَلِيمٌ ۝ هُوَ ٱلَّذِى خَلَقَ ٱلسَّمَٰوَٰتِ وَٱلْأَرْضَ فِى سِتَّةِ أَيَّامٍ 1-7

25. Surah 57 Al-Hadid (Iron)

ثُمَّ ٱسْتَوَىٰ عَلَى ٱلْعَرْشِ يَعْلَمُ مَا يَلِجُ فِى ٱلْأَرْضِ وَمَا يَخْرُجُ مِنْهَا وَمَا يَنزِلُ مِنَ ٱلسَّمَآءِ وَمَا يَعْرُجُ فِيهَا وَهُوَ مَعَكُمْ أَيْنَ مَا كُنتُمْ وَٱللَّهُ بِمَا تَعْمَلُونَ بَصِيرٌ ۝ لَّهُۥ مُلْكُ ٱلسَّمَٰوَٰتِ وَٱلْأَرْضِ وَإِلَى ٱللَّهِ تُرْجَعُ ٱلْأُمُورُ ۝ يُولِجُ ٱلَّيْلَ فِى ٱلنَّهَارِ وَيُولِجُ ٱلنَّهَارَ فِى ٱلَّيْلِ وَهُوَ عَلِيمٌۢ بِذَاتِ ٱلصُّدُورِ ۝ ءَامِنُوا۟ بِٱللَّهِ وَرَسُولِهِۦ وَأَنفِقُوا۟ مِمَّا جَعَلَكُم مُّسْتَخْلَفِينَ فِيهِ فَٱلَّذِينَ ءَامَنُوا۟ مِنكُمْ وَأَنفَقُوا۟ لَهُمْ أَجْرٌ كَبِيرٌ ۝

In the name of Allah, the Merciful to all, the Compassionate to each!
Everything in the heavens and earth glorifies Allah – He is the Almighty, the Wise. His is the dominion over the heavens and the earth; He grants life and deals death; and He has the power to will anything. He is the First and the Last; the Outer and the Inner; He has knowledge of all things. It was He who created the heavens and earth in six Days and then established Himself on the throne. He knows what enters the earth and what comes out of it; what descends from the sky and what ascends to it. He is with you wherever you are; He sees all that you do. To Him belongs sovereignty of the heavens and earth, and to Allah all matters shall revert. He makes night merge into day and day into night. He knows what is in every heart. Believe in Allah and His Messenger, and give out of what He has made pass down to you: those of you who believe and give will have a great reward.

1-7 One of the most powerful forces in existence is the continual rise in consciousness and awareness, reaching the point of vast, pure, and boundless awareness. Whatever we admire and seek is along this direction. We glorify that which is endless, perpetual, and beyond the mind, which is an important gift from Allah, to Whom all that is known and unknown belongs. Allah is the unfathomable *Reality* who is beyond any beginning or end, who appears in greater clarity than all that appears, except to the inner eye of the soul. Otherwise, He is the most hidden. All that is within space-time is contained and controlled by Him. All conditioned and limited consciousness is within this vast infinity of pure consciousness.

The universe has emanated from the supreme *Reality*, which radiates truth and the light of knowledge of *Oneness*. This *Reality* is before everything, within everything, and encompasses everything. It is through intelligence and deep reflection that each one of us will come to realise this magnificent truth and live by it contentedly and serenely.

Whatever is in the heavens and earth is resonating, responding, and reflecting the *Source* that has given it life. That source of life is the beginning and the end, the evident and the hidden. As such, if we consciously live this purpose and direction of life with higher intelligence, not just believing, then we have to exert whatever power, knowledge, and wealth we have to enhance that evolvement back to the *Origin*. That is why generosity is vital.

8-13 وَمَا لَكُمْ لَا تُؤْمِنُونَ بِٱللَّهِ وَٱلرَّسُولُ يَدْعُوكُمْ لِتُؤْمِنُوا۟ بِرَبِّكُمْ وَقَدْ أَخَذَ مِيثَٰقَكُمْ إِن كُنتُم مُّؤْمِنِينَ ۝ هُوَ ٱلَّذِى يُنَزِّلُ عَلَىٰ عَبْدِهِۦٓ ءَايَٰتٍۭ بَيِّنَٰتٍ لِّيُخْرِجَكُم مِّنَ

ٱلظُّلُمَٰتِ إِلَى ٱلنُّورِ وَإِنَّ ٱللَّهَ بِكُمْ لَرَءُوفٌ رَّحِيمٌ ۝ وَمَا لَكُمْ أَلَّا تُنفِقُوا۟ فِى سَبِيلِ ٱللَّهِ وَلِلَّهِ مِيرَٰثُ ٱلسَّمَٰوَٰتِ وَٱلْأَرْضِ لَا يَسْتَوِى مِنكُم مَّنْ أَنفَقَ مِن قَبْلِ ٱلْفَتْحِ وَقَٰتَلَ أُو۟لَٰٓئِكَ أَعْظَمُ دَرَجَةً مِّنَ ٱلَّذِينَ أَنفَقُوا۟ مِنۢ بَعْدُ وَقَٰتَلُوا۟ وَكُلًّا وَعَدَ ٱللَّهُ ٱلْحُسْنَىٰ وَٱللَّهُ بِمَا تَعْمَلُونَ خَبِيرٌ ۝ مَّن ذَا ٱلَّذِى يُقْرِضُ ٱللَّهَ قَرْضًا حَسَنًا فَيُضَٰعِفَهُۥ لَهُۥ وَلَهُۥٓ أَجْرٌ كَرِيمٌ ۝ يَوْمَ تَرَى ٱلْمُؤْمِنِينَ وَٱلْمُؤْمِنَٰتِ يَسْعَىٰ نُورُهُم بَيْنَ أَيْدِيهِمْ وَبِأَيْمَٰنِهِم بُشْرَىٰكُمُ ٱلْيَوْمَ جَنَّٰتٌ تَجْرِى مِن تَحْتِهَا ٱلْأَنْهَٰرُ خَٰلِدِينَ فِيهَا ذَٰلِكَ هُوَ ٱلْفَوْزُ ٱلْعَظِيمُ ۝ يَوْمَ يَقُولُ ٱلْمُنَٰفِقُونَ وَٱلْمُنَٰفِقَٰتُ لِلَّذِينَ ءَامَنُوا۟ ٱنظُرُونَا نَقْتَبِسْ مِن نُّورِكُمْ قِيلَ ٱرْجِعُوا۟ وَرَآءَكُمْ فَٱلْتَمِسُوا۟ نُورًا فَضُرِبَ بَيْنَهُم بِسُورٍ لَّهُۥ بَابٌۢ بَاطِنُهُۥ فِيهِ ٱلرَّحْمَةُ وَظَٰهِرُهُۥ مِن قِبَلِهِ ٱلْعَذَابُ ۝

Why should you not believe in Allah when the Messenger calls you to believe in your Lord, and He has already made a pledge with you, if you have faith? It is He Who has sent down clear revelations to His Servant, so that He may bring you from the depths of darkness into light; Allah is truly kind and merciful to you. Why should you not give for Allah's cause when Allah alone will inherit what is in the heavens and earth? Those who gave and fought before the triumph are not like others: they are greater in rank than those who gave and fought afterwards. But Allah has promised a good reward to all of them: Allah is fully aware of all that you do. Who will make Allah a good loan? He will double it for him and reward him generously. On the Day when you see the believers, both men and women, with their light streaming out ahead of them and to their right, 'The good news for you today is that there are Gardens graced with flowing streams where you will stay: that is truly the supreme triumph!' On the same Day, the hypocrites, both men and women, will say to the believers, 'Wait for us! Let us have some of your light!' They will be told, 'Go back and look for a light.' A wall with a door will be erected between them: inside it lies mercy, outside lies torment.

8-13 It is natural for the intellect to want a map that is handy and reliable, that guides us from ignorance to knowledge, from fear and sorrow to joy and contentment. This guidance can only come about by realising that the cause of our misery is nothing more than the illusion of separation, which we describe as the lower self and ego. This idea is like a seed, which has to be planted to grow. The more we refer to the soul, the more we realise that it is a light that leads us to the perfect destiny. If we are not enlightened by will and effort in this life, we will experience loss and misery after death and in the hereafter. Our orientation towards truth becomes more focused if we remember the hereafter. If we leave this earth as an enlightened soul, there will be few shocks or surprises after death. In fact, death then becomes a great gift of liberation from earthly limitations, fears, and sorrow.

It is in human nature to desire local knowledge as well as that which is celestial and eternal. The drive to have faith and belief is in every human heart, but because of the limitations of identity and other mental veils, one's direction is lost in survivalist concerns.

When you truly know that God is in charge and you are given roles in different situations to make the flow in the direction of the higher, better, and easier, then a minor representative of the *Creator*, your light will lead you to the original light.

14-20 يُنَادُونَهُمْ أَلَمْ نَكُن مَّعَكُمْ قَالُواْ بَلَىٰ وَلَـٰكِنَّكُمْ فَتَنتُمْ أَنفُسَكُمْ وَتَرَبَّصْتُمْ وَٱرْتَبْتُمْ وَغَرَّتْكُمُ ٱلْأَمَانِىُّ حَتَّىٰ جَآءَ أَمْرُ ٱللَّهِ وَغَرَّكُم بِٱللَّهِ ٱلْغَرُورُ ۝ فَٱلْيَوْمَ لَا يُؤْخَذُ مِنكُمْ فِدْيَةٌ وَلَا مِنَ ٱلَّذِينَ كَفَرُواْ مَأْوَىٰكُمُ ٱلنَّارُ هِىَ مَوْلَـٰكُمْ وَبِئْسَ ٱلْمَصِيرُ ۝ أَلَمْ يَأْنِ لِلَّذِينَ ءَامَنُوٓاْ أَن تَخْشَعَ قُلُوبُهُمْ لِذِكْرِ ٱللَّهِ وَمَا نَزَلَ مِنَ ٱلْحَقِّ وَلَا يَكُونُواْ كَٱلَّذِينَ أُوتُواْ ٱلْكِتَـٰبَ مِن قَبْلُ فَطَالَ عَلَيْهِمُ ٱلْأَمَدُ فَقَسَتْ قُلُوبُهُمْ وَكَثِيرٌ مِّنْهُمْ فَـٰسِقُونَ ۝ ٱعْلَمُوٓاْ أَنَّ ٱللَّهَ يُحْىِ ٱلْأَرْضَ بَعْدَ مَوْتِهَا قَدْ بَيَّنَّا لَكُمُ ٱلْأَيَـٰتِ لَعَلَّكُمْ تَعْقِلُونَ ۝ إِنَّ ٱلْمُصَّدِّقِينَ وَٱلْمُصَّدِّقَـٰتِ وَأَقْرَضُواْ ٱللَّهَ قَرْضًا حَسَنًا يُضَـٰعَفُ لَهُمْ وَلَهُمْ أَجْرٌ كَرِيمٌ ۝ وَٱلَّذِينَ ءَامَنُواْ بِٱللَّهِ وَرُسُلِهِ أُوْلَـٰٓئِكَ هُمُ ٱلصِّدِّيقُونَ وَٱلشُّهَدَآءُ عِندَ رَبِّهِمْ لَهُمْ أَجْرُهُمْ وَنُورُهُمْ وَٱلَّذِينَ كَفَرُواْ وَكَذَّبُواْ بِـَٔايَـٰتِنَآ أُوْلَـٰٓئِكَ أَصْحَـٰبُ ٱلْجَحِيمِ ۝ ٱعْلَمُوٓاْ أَنَّمَا ٱلْحَيَوٰةُ ٱلدُّنْيَا لَعِبٌ وَلَهْوٌ وَزِينَةٌ وَتَفَاخُرٌۢ بَيْنَكُمْ وَتَكَاثُرٌ فِى ٱلْأَمْوَٰلِ وَٱلْأَوْلَـٰدِ كَمَثَلِ غَيْثٍ أَعْجَبَ ٱلْكُفَّارَ نَبَاتُهُۥ ثُمَّ يَهِيجُ فَتَرَىٰهُ مُصْفَرًّا ثُمَّ يَكُونُ حُطَـٰمًا وَفِى ٱلْأَخِرَةِ عَذَابٌ شَدِيدٌ وَمَغْفِرَةٌ مِّنَ ٱللَّهِ وَرِضْوَٰنٌ وَمَا ٱلْحَيَوٰةُ ٱلدُّنْيَآ إِلَّا مَتَـٰعُ ٱلْغُرُورِ ۝

The hypocrites will call out to the believers, 'Were we not with you?' They will reply, 'Yes. But you allowed yourselves to be tempted, you were hesitant, doubtful, deceived by false hopes until Allah's command came – the Deceiver tricked you about Allah. Today no ransom will be accepted from you or from the disbelievers: your home is the Fire – that is where you belong – a miserable destination!' Is it not time for believers to humble their hearts to the remembrance of Allah and the Truth that has been revealed, and not to be like those who received the Scripture before them, whose time was extended but whose hearts hardened and many of whom were law-breakers? Remember that Allah revives the earth after it dies; We have made Our revelation clear to you so that you may use your reason. Charitable men and women who make a good loan to Allah will have it doubled and have a generous reward. Those who believe in Allah and His messengers are the truthful ones who will bear witness before their Lord: they will have their reward and their light. But those who disbelieve and deny Our revelations are the inhabitants of Hell. Bear in mind that the present life is just a game, a diversion, an attraction, a cause of boasting among you, of rivalry in wealth and children. It is like plants that spring up after the rain: their growth at first delights the sowers, but then you see them wither away, turn yellow, and become stubble. There is terrible punishment in the next life as well as forgiveness and approval from Allah; the life of this world is only an illusory pleasure.

14-20 If we do not regret our wrong actions and confused intentions in this life, we will suffer from this neglect after death, when we can no longer make amends for past mistakes. If our heart allows the light of the soul within it to shine and bring about higher discrimination, our awareness of right and wrong or of darkness and light becomes more intense. The hardened heart veils the light of the soul. Every individual who awakens and realises that there is an inner guidance that connects with outer wisdom, will have an orchard that grows and yields on earth. Our life on this earth is like being in a kindergarten, where we compete and experience pleasure, pain, success, and failure. If this leads to higher awareness, pain and pleasure will become wisdom and goodness, competition will become cooperation, fear and anxiety will become willingness to serve the less fortunate.

Duality covers every aspect of existence including two zones of life: one temporary and earthly and the other permanent. Every human being will experience this after death, a few through awakening and enlightenment on earth.

The key issue in our need to groom the *nafs* and the ego is to have the heart and the light of the soul shine and lead us towards the original light itself. We need to have a soft and gentle heart and do our utmost in the outer world to help and serve whomever else is needy along the path. Otherwise, we will be deluding ourselves in the transitory world.

21-26

سَابِقُوٓا۟ إِلَىٰ مَغْفِرَةٍ مِّن رَّبِّكُمْ وَجَنَّةٍ عَرْضُهَا كَعَرْضِ ٱلسَّمَآءِ وَٱلْأَرْضِ أُعِدَّتْ لِلَّذِينَ ءَامَنُوا۟ بِٱللَّهِ وَرُسُلِهِۦ ۚ ذَٰلِكَ فَضْلُ ٱللَّهِ يُؤْتِيهِ مَن يَشَآءُ ۚ وَٱللَّهُ ذُو ٱلْفَضْلِ ٱلْعَظِيمِ ۝ مَآ أَصَابَ مِن مُّصِيبَةٍ فِى ٱلْأَرْضِ وَلَا فِىٓ أَنفُسِكُمْ إِلَّا فِى كِتَٰبٍ مِّن قَبْلِ أَن نَّبْرَأَهَآ ۚ إِنَّ ذَٰلِكَ عَلَى ٱللَّهِ يَسِيرٌ ۝ لِّكَيْلَا تَأْسَوْا۟ عَلَىٰ مَا فَاتَكُمْ وَلَا تَفْرَحُوا۟ بِمَآ ءَاتَىٰكُمْ ۗ وَٱللَّهُ لَا يُحِبُّ كُلَّ مُخْتَالٍ فَخُورٍ ۝ ٱلَّذِينَ يَبْخَلُونَ وَيَأْمُرُونَ ٱلنَّاسَ بِٱلْبُخْلِ ۗ وَمَن يَتَوَلَّ فَإِنَّ ٱللَّهَ هُوَ ٱلْغَنِىُّ ٱلْحَمِيدُ ۝ لَقَدْ أَرْسَلْنَا رُسُلَنَا بِٱلْبَيِّنَٰتِ وَأَنزَلْنَا مَعَهُمُ ٱلْكِتَٰبَ وَٱلْمِيزَانَ لِيَقُومَ ٱلنَّاسُ بِٱلْقِسْطِ ۖ وَأَنزَلْنَا ٱلْحَدِيدَ فِيهِ بَأْسٌ شَدِيدٌ وَمَنَٰفِعُ لِلنَّاسِ وَلِيَعْلَمَ ٱللَّهُ مَن يَنصُرُهُۥ وَرُسُلَهُۥ بِٱلْغَيْبِ ۚ إِنَّ ٱللَّهَ قَوِىٌّ عَزِيزٌ ۝ وَلَقَدْ أَرْسَلْنَا نُوحًا وَإِبْرَٰهِيمَ وَجَعَلْنَا فِى ذُرِّيَّتِهِمَا ٱلنُّبُوَّةَ وَٱلْكِتَٰبَ ۖ فَمِنْهُم مُّهْتَدٍ ۖ وَكَثِيرٌ مِّنْهُمْ فَٰسِقُونَ ۝

So, race for your Lord's forgiveness and a Garden as wide as the heavens and earth, prepared for those who believe in Allah and His messengers: that is Allah's bounty, which He bestows on whoever He pleases. Allah's bounty is infinite. No misfortune can happen, either in the earth or in yourselves, that was not set down in writing before We brought it into being – that is easy for Allah. So that you may not grieve for what has escaped you, nor be exultant at what He has given you; and Allah does not love any arrogant boaster: as for those who are stingy, and enjoin others to be stingy, or those who turn away – Allah is All-Sufficient, All-Praiseworthy. We sent Our messengers with clear signs, the Scripture and the Balance, so that people could uphold justice: We also sent iron, with its mighty strength and many uses for mankind, so that Allah could mark out those who would help Him and His messengers though they cannot see Him. Truly Allah is Powerful, Almighty. We sent Noah and Abraham, and gave prophethood and scripture to their offspring: among them there were some who were rightly guided, but many were lawbreakers.

21-26 For this awakened state, everyone needs to be determined to follow the map of *Reality*, to be weary of downfalls and danger, to remain on the course of vigilance, accountability, and higher referencing, and to be certain that what comes to us is part of the perfect design of cause and effect contained in the Book of *Reality* that encompasses all. This course guides the diligent follower who is free from any arrogance and confusion that could be caused by it. We all make the mistake of imagining the joy we may have from attaining something. Often circumstances change and the potential joy we sought is no longer attainable. Everything known and unknown has descended from the unseen divine effulgence. All material entities have emerged from the primordial energies and elements, including what emerged later as iron – the name of this chapter.

An intelligent being strives to awaken to the highest level of consciousness and to witness how everything on earth flows according to higher patterns. The origin of everything is heavenly and seamlessly connects the visible and the invisible.

Competition and cooperation are natural phenomena in human nature. But for us to compete as to who excels more in inner tuning and responding to the divine decree, that is where we try to excel as much as possible. Otherwise, no matter what we experience, it is part of a pattern that has already been designed as part of the beginning of creation. We have repeatedly experienced this during the past few thousand years amongst the enlightened and awakened people and all the prophets.

27-29 ثُمَّ قَفَّيْنَا عَلَىٰ ءَاثَٰرِهِم بِرُسُلِنَا وَقَفَّيْنَا بِعِيسَى ٱبْنِ مَرْيَمَ وَءَاتَيْنَٰهُ ٱلْإِنجِيلَ وَجَعَلْنَا فِى قُلُوبِ ٱلَّذِينَ ٱتَّبَعُوهُ رَأْفَةً وَرَحْمَةً وَرَهْبَانِيَّةً ٱبْتَدَعُوهَا مَا كَتَبْنَٰهَا عَلَيْهِمْ إِلَّا ٱبْتِغَآءَ رِضْوَٰنِ ٱللَّهِ فَمَا رَعَوْهَا حَقَّ رِعَايَتِهَا فَـَٔاتَيْنَا ٱلَّذِينَ ءَامَنُوا۟ مِنْهُمْ أَجْرَهُمْ وَكَثِيرٌ مِّنْهُمْ فَٰسِقُونَ ۝ يَٰٓأَيُّهَا ٱلَّذِينَ ءَامَنُوا۟ ٱتَّقُوا۟ ٱللَّهَ وَءَامِنُوا۟ بِرَسُولِهِۦ يُؤْتِكُمْ كِفْلَيْنِ مِن رَّحْمَتِهِۦ وَيَجْعَل لَّكُمْ نُورًا تَمْشُونَ بِهِۦ وَيَغْفِرْ لَكُمْ وَٱللَّهُ غَفُورٌ رَّحِيمٌ ۝ لِّئَلَّا يَعْلَمَ أَهْلُ ٱلْكِتَٰبِ أَلَّا يَقْدِرُونَ عَلَىٰ شَىْءٍ مِّن فَضْلِ ٱللَّهِ وَأَنَّ ٱلْفَضْلَ بِيَدِ ٱللَّهِ يُؤْتِيهِ مَن يَشَآءُ وَٱللَّهُ ذُو ٱلْفَضْلِ ٱلْعَظِيمِ ۝

We sent other messengers to follow in their footsteps. After those We sent Jesus, son of Mary: We gave him the Gospel and put compassion and mercy into the hearts of his followers. But monasticism was something they invented – We did not ordain it for them, only to seek Allah's pleasure, and even so, they did not observe it properly. So, We gave a reward to those of them who believed, but many of them were lawbreakers. O believers, be cautiously aware of Allah and believe in His Messenger and He will double your share of His compassion, and shine His light upon the path you tread, and forgive you. God is All-Forgiving, Compassionate to each. The People of the Book should know that they have no power over any of Allah's grace and that grace is in the hand of Allah alone: He gives it to whoever He will. Allah's grace is truly immense.

27-29 The process of creation continues and so does the process of reminders and inspired teachings. Trust and love for those who are living the *Truth* is a necessary condition to take on their imprints, which will connect with our soul within. We are bracketed between the seen and the unseen. We have light from within us, which provides sight as well as insight. Humanity and divinity are in constant resonance. All of this will lead to what already was at the beginning and is due only to the grace of Allah. All goodness is in Allah's hand. All we need to do is to dismiss the illusion that we are independent, that we can do things, attain things, and be self-sustaining. The more we refer to the original *Source*, the more our actions will have visible, long-lasting goodness. The soul is permanent, the self is temporary.

Due to evolution over the last few thousand years, awakened beings and prophets have shown the need to restrict one's lower animal tendencies and be dutifully loyal to the divine light within. These revelations have often appeared as scriptures and holy books.

For one's own sake one likes to awaken increasingly in self-awareness and awareness of awareness. We are led by the inner light as we move in this short life experience to better states until we know the true giver is Allah and what stops that grace and mercy is the lower self and the ego shadow. To remove and reduce this, then there is only the divine grace.

26. Surah 62 Al-Jumu'ah (Friday)

In truth, whatever exists in heaven and on earth, aims to connect and continue within the limits of space and time. Our human duty is to connect the visible and apparently diverse with that which is invisible and all-encompassing. We can only perfect worship if we follow the spiritual light and avoid all earthy shadows, including the shadows of identity and individuality.

بِسْمِ اللَّهِ الرَّحْمَٰنِ الرَّحِيمِ

1-7 يُسَبِّحُ لِلَّهِ مَا فِي السَّمَٰوَٰتِ وَمَا فِي ٱلْأَرْضِ ٱلْمَلِكِ ٱلْقُدُّوسِ ٱلْعَزِيزِ ٱلْحَكِيمِ ۝ هُوَ ٱلَّذِى بَعَثَ فِى ٱلْأُمِّيِّـۧنَ رَسُولًا مِّنْهُمْ يَتْلُواْ عَلَيْهِمْ ءَايَٰتِهِۦ وَيُزَكِّيهِمْ وَيُعَلِّمُهُمُ ٱلْكِتَٰبَ وَٱلْحِكْمَةَ وَإِن كَانُواْ مِن قَبْلُ لَفِى ضَلَٰلٍ مُّبِينٍ ۝ وَءَاخَرِينَ مِنْهُمْ لَمَّا يَلْحَقُواْ بِهِمْ وَهُوَ ٱلْعَزِيزُ ٱلْحَكِيمُ ۝ ذَٰلِكَ فَضْلُ ٱللَّهِ يُؤْتِيهِ مَن يَشَآءُ وَٱللَّهُ ذُو ٱلْفَضْلِ ٱلْعَظِيمِ ۝ مَثَلُ ٱلَّذِينَ حُمِّلُواْ ٱلتَّوْرَىٰةَ ثُمَّ لَمْ يَحْمِلُوهَا كَمَثَلِ ٱلْحِمَارِ يَحْمِلُ أَسْفَارًۢا بِئْسَ مَثَلُ ٱلْقَوْمِ ٱلَّذِينَ كَذَّبُواْ بِـَٔايَٰتِ ٱللَّهِ وَٱللَّهُ لَا يَهْدِى ٱلْقَوْمَ ٱلظَّٰلِمِينَ ۝ قُلْ يَٰٓأَيُّهَا ٱلَّذِينَ هَادُوٓاْ إِن زَعَمْتُمْ أَنَّكُمْ أَوْلِيَآءُ لِلَّهِ مِن دُونِ ٱلنَّاسِ فَتَمَنَّوُاْ ٱلْمَوْتَ إِن كُنتُمْ صَٰدِقِينَ ۝ وَلَا يَتَمَنَّوْنَهُۥٓ أَبَدًۢا بِمَا قَدَّمَتْ أَيْدِيهِمْ وَٱللَّهُ عَلِيمٌۢ بِٱلظَّٰلِمِينَ ۝

26. Surah 62 Al-Jumu'ah (Friday)

In the name of Allah, the Merciful to all, the Compassionate to each!

Whatever is in the heavens and whatever is in the earth declares the glory of Allah, the King, the Holy, the Mighty, the Wise. It is He who raised a messenger, among the people who had no Scripture, to recite His revelations to them, to make them grow spiritually and teach them the Scripture and wisdom – before that they were clearly astray to them and others yet to join them. He is the Almighty, the Wise: such is Allah's favour that He grants it to whoever He will; Allah's favour is immense. Those who have been charged to obey the Torah, but do not do so, are like asses carrying books: how base such people are who disobey Allah's revelations! Allah does not guide people who do wrong. Say, 'You who follow the Jewish faith, if you claim that out of all people you alone are friends of Allah, then you should be hoping for death if you are truthful.' But because of what they have stored up for themselves with their own hands they would never hope for death – Allah knows the wrongdoers very well.

1-7 All existence, seen and unseen, is forever connected to the origin via countless patterns and designs that express loyalty to and contentment with what holds them and gives them existence. Everything is self-declaring. When we express discontent, it is a sign that we miss the energy of ever-present perfection, the soul within the heart. Many people do their utmost to reach balance and equanimity by better intentions and selfless, outer action. However, there are a few who constantly witness the presence of the perfect Truth and light. This grace results from the abandonment of the lower self in order to live by the light of the higher self or soul. People who are at the gate of the Ka'ba yearn for the completion of their journey and moving on to the next phase after death. Most people fear death, because they have not had proof of the magnificent state that comes to the purified heart after death.

Allah's governance and control encompasses all that is known and unknown; as such, everything that exists flows according to a natural pattern. The biggest gift upon human beings is to realise that everything emerged from a perfect, unitive state flowing towards a short-term destiny on earth. We love gatheredness, which is our origin.

The desire to connect and continue is deep in human consciousness. The qualities of connection and continuation emerge from the original unity before the emergence of duality and multiplicity. We are here to practise that we are not just this body, mind, and identity: the source of our life is a divine spirit. Acceptance of death with no fear or anxiety will enable us to live wholesomely in this life and depart without fuss.

8-11 قُلْ إِنَّ ٱلْمَوْتَ ٱلَّذِى تَفِرُّونَ مِنْهُ فَإِنَّهُۥ مُلَٰقِيكُمْ ۖ ثُمَّ تُرَدُّونَ إِلَىٰ عَٰلِمِ ٱلْغَيْبِ وَٱلشَّهَٰدَةِ فَيُنَبِّئُكُم بِمَا كُنتُمْ تَعْمَلُونَ ۝ يَٰٓأَيُّهَا ٱلَّذِينَ ءَامَنُوٓا۟ إِذَا نُودِىَ لِلصَّلَوٰةِ

مِن يَوْمِ ٱلْجُمُعَةِ فَٱسْعَوْا۟ إِلَىٰ ذِكْرِ ٱللَّهِ وَذَرُوا۟ ٱلْبَيْعَ ذَٰلِكُمْ خَيْرٌ لَّكُمْ إِن كُنتُمْ تَعْلَمُونَ ۞ فَإِذَا قُضِيَتِ ٱلصَّلَوٰةُ فَٱنتَشِرُوا۟ فِى ٱلْأَرْضِ وَٱبْتَغُوا۟ مِن فَضْلِ ٱللَّهِ وَٱذْكُرُوا۟ ٱللَّهَ كَثِيرًا لَّعَلَّكُمْ تُفْلِحُونَ ۞ وَإِذَا رَأَوْا۟ تِجَٰرَةً أَوْ لَهْوًا ٱنفَضُّوٓا۟ إِلَيْهَا وَتَرَكُوكَ قَآئِمًا قُلْ مَا عِندَ ٱللَّهِ خَيْرٌ مِّنَ ٱللَّهْوِ وَمِنَ ٱلتِّجَٰرَةِ وَٱللَّهُ خَيْرُ ٱلرَّٰزِقِينَ ۞

So say, 'The death you run away from will come to meet you and you will be returned to the One who knows the unseen as well as the seen: He will tell you everything you have done.' O you who believe! when the call is made for prayer on Friday, then hasten to the remembrance of Allah and leave off trading; that is better for you, if you know. But when the prayer is ended, then disperse in the land and seek of Allah's grace, and remember Allah much, that you may be successful. Yet they scatter towards trade or entertainment whenever they observe it, and leave you standing there. Say, 'Allah's gift is better than any entertainment or trade: Allah is the best provider.'

8-11 The intelligent person realises the inevitability of death as well as its gift of reminding us to be prepared for it by rejecting the illusion of identification with body and mind. The real challenge is the fact that we are dying but do not want to die. The answer is to be the real you, the soul that does not die. Just as our life on this earth lies between the two extremes of birth and death, it also lies between gatheredness and dispersion. After we have dived into the inner light through prayer and have transcended our outer humanity on earth with its lower nature, we experience the lights of God-consciousness with its infinite dimensions that cannot be described or defined.

In our worldly experience, we strive to discover what is durable, and what will have a bigger impact on our life so that we can give it more attention. In reality, whatever comes into this world will also exit. If we focus on the meaning and reality of death, we may find some respite. After death, there is nothing anyone of us can do, add, or subtract. Our account will include what we have done in this life as well as the darkness or the goodness that has emanated from it. When we revert to a zone of no identity, the pure realities of the energies from which the so-called identity can emerge.

We have emerged from absolute Unity to duality. Outer rituals such as communal prayers and Friday gatherings are helpful to remind us that all human beings are essentially challenged in the same way. We want quality life on earth and the abode of the Garden after death. All other human activities can help us in our earthly journey if we refer to the state after death.

27. Surah 63 Al-Munafiqun (The Hypocrites)

The lower self is a shadow of the soul, and as such, it is a lie. It is not unnatural for humans to lie, deny and try to exonerate themselves from errors or falsehood. Whoever is a hypocrite, if they reflect deeply, they will find a touch of the realisation of their hypocrisy and lies. In the hereafter, this state will become clear to all. The darkness of a lie contains a spark of truth, and a hypocrite denies this fact.

بِسْمِ اللَّهِ الرَّحْمَٰنِ الرَّحِيمِ

1-7 [Arabic verses 1–7]

In the name of Allah, the Merciful to all, the Compassionate to each!

When the hypocrites come to you, they say: 'We bear witness that you are most surely Allah's Messenger;' and Allah knows that you are most surely His Messenger, and Allah bears witness that the hypocrites are surely liars. They use their oaths as a cover and so bar others from Allah's way: what they have been doing is truly evil. That is because they believed, then disbelieved, and so their hearts are sealed and they cannot understand. When you see them, you are impressed by their outward appearance, and when they speak, you listen to their words. But they are like wooden stilts: every shout they hear they imagine to be the enemy. So be on your guard against them. May Allah strike them down! How they pervert the truth! And if told to come so that the Messenger of Allah might ask forgiveness for you, they twist their heads, and you see them saunter off in arrogance. It is all the same if you seek or do not seek forgiveness for them, for Allah shall not forgive them. Allah guides not a people who are depraved. They are the ones who say, 'Give nothing to those who follow Allah's Messenger, until they abandon him,' but to Allah belong the treasures of the heavens and earth, though the hypocrites do not understand this.

1-7 The last ayah of Surah Jumu'ah describes superficial believers who prefer worldly gain to higher consciousness and enlightenment. Having noted their lies and denial, this ayah connects with the first ayah of Surah Munafiqun. Hypocrisy implies a contradictory behaviour emanating from the same person at the same time: what is said is not what is meant. It reveals a discordance and disconnectedness at a deep level, in opposition to the purpose of the human journey to increase connectedness and Oneness. Life emanates from one Source, which constantly points to the oneness of its reality. People who are two-faced are sick and do whatever possible to maintain their behaviour.

Lack of clarity and confusion can cause much suffering and darkness. Hypocrisy is a handicap along the path, which only enhances our own confusion and hinders clarity. When it becomes a habit, then hypocrisy casts a dark shadow on one's thoughts and actions; as such, one is far away from the path of clarity and oneness.

Hypocrisy is a very complex issue with many connotations; the foundation of it is lies, denial, and perversion of truth. It also comes with a certain measure of arrogance and haughtiness so that the lower self maintains that state of hypocrisy. Hypocrisy is a serious aspect that humans can fall into as part of a wider range of ignorance and darkness.

8-11 يَقُولُونَ لَئِن رَّجَعْنَآ إِلَى ٱلْمَدِينَةِ لَيُخْرِجَنَّ ٱلْأَعَزُّ مِنْهَا ٱلْأَذَلَّ وَلِلَّهِ ٱلْعِزَّةُ وَلِرَسُولِهِۦ وَلِلْمُؤْمِنِينَ وَلَٰكِنَّ ٱلْمُنَٰفِقِينَ لَا يَعْلَمُونَ ۝ يَٰٓأَيُّهَا ٱلَّذِينَ ءَامَنُوا۟ لَا تُلْهِكُمْ أَمْوَٰلُكُمْ وَلَآ أَوْلَٰدُكُمْ عَن ذِكْرِ ٱللَّهِ وَمَن يَفْعَلْ ذَٰلِكَ فَأُو۟لَٰٓئِكَ هُمُ ٱلْخَٰسِرُونَ ۝ وَأَنفِقُوا۟ مِن مَّا رَزَقْنَٰكُم مِّن قَبْلِ أَن يَأْتِىَ أَحَدَكُمُ ٱلْمَوْتُ فَيَقُولَ رَبِّ لَوْلَآ أَخَّرْتَنِىٓ إِلَىٰٓ أَجَلٍ قَرِيبٍ فَأَصَّدَّقَ وَأَكُن مِّنَ ٱلصَّٰلِحِينَ ۝ وَلَن يُؤَخِّرَ ٱللَّهُ نَفْسًا إِذَا جَآءَ أَجَلُهَا وَٱللَّهُ خَبِيرٌۢ بِمَا تَعْمَلُونَ ۝

They say, 'Once we return to Medina the powerful will drive out the weak,' but power belongs to Allah, to His Messenger, and to the believers, though the hypocrites do not know this. Believers, do not let your wealth and your children distract you remembering Allah: those who do be the ones who lose. Give out of what We have provided for you, before death comes to one of you and he says, 'My Lord, if You would only reprieve me for a little while, I would give in charity and become one of the righteous.' Allah does not reprieve a self when its turn comes: Allah is fully aware of what you do.

8-11 The hypocrite's thought patterns and actions are discordant, producing confusion with a certain measure of cynicism, imbalance, and injustice. This life is a journey towards awakening, to a zone that is constant, perpetual and the source of contentment and total security. The shadow reflection of this journey is being fully distracted by earthly, temporary connections and pleasures, which are often accompanied by displeasure. Excess concern about provisions and power will distract one from the main purpose of life: to unify one's personal life with eternal life itself. Those who are on the path of awakening will naturally tend to give that which they want to keep themselves. Liberating oneself from desires and attachments are key steps toward liberation from the lower self.

Like everything else that we experience, life is at two levels: one is basic sentience and the other is awakening to cosmic life itself. Life at the base level may or may not connect with cosmic life, which is perpetual. The foundation of a quality earthly life is to know that it is preparing us for a higher zone of consciousness after death.

It is natural for us in this world to be affected by what concerns us in our relationships and our comfort, ease, and security. Most of these concerns can cause us to be distracted from and lose our commitment to what we are responsible for on this earth – to reconnect by will and by intelligence to the Source of life within us. It is an urgent issue for us to accept the mind, clear it, purify the heart, and listen to what is transmitted from the soul within the heart.

28. Surah 67 Al-Mulk (Sovereignty)

It is a big gift for any human being to acknowledge that everything known and unknown in the heavens and earth belongs to God and is under God's governance. At best, human beings are short-term custodians or stewards on earth during their lifetime. None of us own or control anything other than in a short-term, approximate manner. This knowledge liberates us from the myth of being in charge or in control.

بِسْمِ اللَّهِ الرَّحْمَٰنِ الرَّحِيمِ

9-1 تَبَارَكَ الَّذِي بِيَدِهِ الْمُلْكُ وَهُوَ عَلَىٰ كُلِّ شَيْءٍ قَدِيرٌ ۝ الَّذِي خَلَقَ الْمَوْتَ وَالْحَيَاةَ لِيَبْلُوَكُمْ أَيُّكُمْ أَحْسَنُ عَمَلًا وَهُوَ الْعَزِيزُ الْغَفُورُ ۝ الَّذِي خَلَقَ سَبْعَ سَمَاوَاتٍ طِبَاقًا مَّا تَرَىٰ فِي خَلْقِ الرَّحْمَٰنِ مِن تَفَاوُتٍ فَارْجِعِ الْبَصَرَ هَلْ تَرَىٰ مِن فُطُورٍ ۝ ثُمَّ ارْجِعِ الْبَصَرَ كَرَّتَيْنِ يَنقَلِبْ إِلَيْكَ الْبَصَرُ خَاسِئًا وَهُوَ حَسِيرٌ ۝ وَلَقَدْ زَيَّنَّا السَّمَاءَ الدُّنْيَا بِمَصَابِيحَ وَجَعَلْنَاهَا رُجُومًا لِّلشَّيَاطِينِ وَأَعْتَدْنَا لَهُمْ عَذَابَ السَّعِيرِ ۝ وَلِلَّذِينَ كَفَرُوا بِرَبِّهِمْ عَذَابُ جَهَنَّمَ وَبِئْسَ الْمَصِيرُ ۝ إِذَا أُلْقُوا فِيهَا سَمِعُوا لَهَا شَهِيقًا وَهِيَ تَفُورُ ۝ تَكَادُ تَمَيَّزُ مِنَ الْغَيْظِ كُلَّمَا أُلْقِيَ فِيهَا فَوْجٌ سَأَلَهُمْ خَزَنَتُهَا أَلَمْ يَأْتِكُمْ نَذِيرٌ ۝ قَالُوا بَلَىٰ قَدْ جَاءَنَا نَذِيرٌ فَكَذَّبْنَا وَقُلْنَا مَا نَزَّلَ اللَّهُ مِن شَيْءٍ إِنْ أَنتُمْ إِلَّا فِي ضَلَالٍ كَبِيرٍ ۝

In the name of Allah, the Merciful to all, the Compassionate to each!

Blessed is He in Whose hand is sovereignty, Who holds power over all things! Who created death and life that He may try you – which of you is best in deeds; and He is the Mighty, the Forgiving, Who created the seven heavens one above another; you see no incongruity in the creation of the Beneficent Allah; then look again, can you see any disorder? Look again! And again! Your sight will turn back to you, weak and defeated. And We adorned the lower heaven with lamps, and made them things to stone Satans; and We have prepared for them the chastisement of the Blaze. And to those who blasphemed their Lord there awaits the torment of hell – and a wretched destiny it is! When they are cast into it they will hear it sighing, the while it boils. Almost bursting for fury. Whenever a group is cast into it, its keeper shall ask them: Did there not come to you a warner? They will reply, 'Yes' a warner did come to us, but we did not believe him. We said, 'Allah has sent down nothing: you are greatly misguided.'

1-9 Blessings and grace emanate from one Essence, the Source from which all known and unknown creations and existences have emanated. From that infinite unknown, countless beams of lights and packages of energies and entities have emerged. These can be discerned as heavenly objects, earthly material objects, the sub-atomic world, and the astrophysical entities. These creations have their boundaries, relations, and interactions. Matter is balanced with anti-matter and good with bad. Benign, angelic energies are balanced by Shaytanic and destructive forces. Perfection prevails over everything in existence, and any local or temporary imperfection, when viewed through the light of higher consciousness, will be recognised as having its own perfection.

The universe is governed by the most efficient, perfect Governor of all. It is from this Source that our experiences emanate and move in time as dualities or pluralities. It is only through insight that we see the ever-perfect Oneness of it all.

Intelligent human beings seek grace, ease, and flow in their lives and remember that the entire cosmic governance emanates from a Source that is beyond our ability to appreciate its power, justice, and magnificent dominance. Whenever we feel the situation is not quite right, we need to stop ourselves from that judgment and look at the whole thing from its inception. Then we will realise that even the worst injustices have come about because of numerous links between cause and effect, and there is always perfection in this as well.

10-21

وَقَالُواْ لَوْ كُنَّا نَسْمَعُ أَوْ نَعْقِلُ مَا كُنَّا فِىٓ أَصْحَٰبِ ٱلسَّعِيرِ ۝ فَٱعْتَرَفُواْ بِذَنۢبِهِمْ فَسُحْقًا لِّأَصْحَٰبِ ٱلسَّعِيرِ ۝ إِنَّ ٱلَّذِينَ يَخْشَوْنَ رَبَّهُم بِٱلْغَيْبِ لَهُم مَّغْفِرَةٌ وَأَجْرٌ كَبِيرٌ ۝ وَأَسِرُّواْ قَوْلَكُمْ أَوِ ٱجْهَرُواْ بِهِۦٓ إِنَّهُۥ عَلِيمٌۢ بِذَاتِ ٱلصُّدُورِ ۝ أَلَا يَعْلَمُ مَنْ خَلَقَ وَهُوَ ٱللَّطِيفُ ٱلْخَبِيرُ ۝ هُوَ ٱلَّذِى جَعَلَ لَكُمُ ٱلْأَرْضَ ذَلُولًا فَٱمْشُواْ فِى مَنَاكِبِهَا وَكُلُواْ مِن رِّزْقِهِۦ وَإِلَيْهِ ٱلنُّشُورُ ۝ ءَأَمِنتُم مَّن فِى ٱلسَّمَآءِ أَن يَخْسِفَ بِكُمُ ٱلْأَرْضَ فَإِذَا هِىَ تَمُورُ ۝ أَمْ أَمِنتُم مَّن فِى ٱلسَّمَآءِ أَن يُرْسِلَ عَلَيْكُمْ حَاصِبًا فَسَتَعْلَمُونَ كَيْفَ نَذِيرِ ۝ وَلَقَدْ كَذَّبَ ٱلَّذِينَ مِن قَبْلِهِمْ فَكَيْفَ كَانَ نَكِيرِ ۝

أَوَلَمْ يَرَوْا إِلَى ٱلطَّيْرِ فَوْقَهُمْ صَـٰٓفَّـٰتٍ وَيَقْبِضْنَ ۚ مَا يُمْسِكُهُنَّ إِلَّا ٱلرَّحْمَـٰنُ ۚ إِنَّهُۥ بِكُلِّ شَىْءٍۭ بَصِيرٌ ۝ أَمَّنْ هَـٰذَا ٱلَّذِى هُوَ جُندٌ لَّكُمْ يَنصُرُكُم مِّن دُونِ ٱلرَّحْمَـٰنِ ۚ إِنِ ٱلْكَـٰفِرُونَ إِلَّا فِى غُرُورٍ ۝ أَمَّنْ هَـٰذَا ٱلَّذِى يَرْزُقُكُمْ إِنْ أَمْسَكَ رِزْقَهُۥ ۚ بَل لَّجُّوا۟ فِى عُتُوٍّ وَنُفُورٍ ۝

And they shall say: 'Could we but hear or understand, we would not be among the dwellers of the Blaze.' They will confess their misdeeds. Away with the inhabitants of the blazing fire! But they who fear their Lord in the Unseen shall obtain forgiveness and a great reward. Be secret in your speech, or proclaim it, He knows the thoughts within the breasts. How could He who created not know His own creation, when He is the Most Subtle, the All Aware? He it was Who made the earth subservient to you, so roam its byways and eat of His provisions; to Him is the Resurgence. Or are you confident that He Who is in heaven would not cause the earth to collapse beneath you, as it heaves in turmoil? Do you feel secure that He who is in heaven will not loose against you a squall of pebbles, then you shall know how My warning is? Those who went before them also disbelieved – how terrible was My condemnation! Have they not observed the birds above them, with wings outstretched or clasped? None can restrain them but the All-Merciful. He sees full well all that exits. Who is it who can act as your troops, to bring you aid, apart from the All-Merciful? The unbelievers are merely living in illusion. Or who is it who can provide for you if He withholds His provision? They have assuredly sunk deep in obstinacy and aversion from truth.

10-21 The heart connects the soul with the faculty of intellect and reason. We require a clear mind and a pure heart to function at both the material and subtler levels. We live in a discernible world through our senses and hope for states and situations in the unseen that will give us a continuation of wellbeing, contentment, and happiness. There is no certainty in outer existence. There is, however, a constant desire to be certain of a good outcome. We yearn for lasting security and the assurance of contentment and happiness. The powers that bring about what we hope and pray for are numerous, but only a few are discernible to us. The vast unknown is far greater than whatever can be known.

Through intelligent observation, we reach the conclusion that our consciousness and reading of a situation are not complete until we observe with higher insight and the light of Oneness. If we are not on this path, then there is much suffering.

It is in human nature to blame and claim without apportioning to ourselves the appropriate measure of ignorance and hastiness. All that will be remedied if we calibrate our time regularly by being in the moment, reflecting, and meditating. This is easy to do when you divert your attention to the amazing, natural phenomena that govern our daily life.

22-30 ﴿٢٢﴾ فَمَن يَمْشِى مُكِبًّا عَلَىٰ وَجْهِهِۦٓ أَهْدَىٰٓ أَمَّن يَمْشِى سَوِيًّا عَلَىٰ صِرَٰطٍ مُّسْتَقِيمٍ ﴿٢٣﴾ قُلْ هُوَ ٱلَّذِىٓ أَنشَأَكُمْ وَجَعَلَ لَكُمُ ٱلسَّمْعَ وَٱلْأَبْصَٰرَ وَٱلْأَفْـِٔدَةَ قَلِيلًا مَّا تَشْكُرُونَ ﴿٢٤﴾ قُلْ هُوَ ٱلَّذِى ذَرَأَكُمْ فِى ٱلْأَرْضِ وَإِلَيْهِ تُحْشَرُونَ ﴿٢٥﴾ وَيَقُولُونَ مَتَىٰ هَٰذَا ٱلْوَعْدُ إِن كُنتُمْ صَٰدِقِينَ ﴿٢٦﴾ قُلْ إِنَّمَا ٱلْعِلْمُ عِندَ ٱللَّهِ وَإِنَّمَآ أَنَا۠ نَذِيرٌ مُّبِينٌ ﴿٢٧﴾ فَلَمَّا رَأَوْهُ زُلْفَةً سِيٓـَٔتْ وُجُوهُ ٱلَّذِينَ كَفَرُوا۟ وَقِيلَ هَٰذَا ٱلَّذِى كُنتُم بِهِۦ تَدَّعُونَ ﴿٢٨﴾ قُلْ أَرَءَيْتُمْ إِنْ أَهْلَكَنِىَ ٱللَّهُ وَمَن مَّعِىَ أَوْ رَحِمَنَا فَمَن يُجِيرُ ٱلْكَٰفِرِينَ مِنْ عَذَابٍ أَلِيمٍ ﴿٢٩﴾ قُلْ هُوَ ٱلرَّحْمَٰنُ ءَامَنَّا بِهِۦ وَعَلَيْهِ تَوَكَّلْنَا فَسَتَعْلَمُونَ مَنْ هُوَ فِى ضَلَٰلٍ مُّبِينٍ ﴿٣٠﴾ قُلْ أَرَءَيْتُمْ إِنْ أَصْبَحَ مَآؤُكُمْ غَوْرًا فَمَن يَأْتِيكُم بِمَآءٍ مَّعِينٍۭ

What! Is he who goes prone upon his face better guided or he who walks upright upon a straight path? Say: 'It is He Who brought you into being, Who provided you with hearing, sight and hearts, but little thanks do you give.' Say: 'He it is Who multiplied you in the earth and to Him you shall be gathered.' They say, 'When shall this promise come to pass, if you speak truly?' Say: 'The knowledge thereof is only with Allah and I am only a plain warner.' But when they see it coming near, the faces of unbelievers will grow sorrowful, and it shall be said: 'This is what you asked for.' Say: 'Consider this. Should Allah make me perish, along with those who are with me, or else should He show us His mercy, Who shall offer refuge to the blasphemers from a painful punishment?' Say: 'He is the All-Merciful. We believe in Him, and in Him we put all our trust. Assuredly, you will soon, know who is in manifest error.' Say, 'Consider this. If your water is swallowed up by the earth, who will bring you water from a spring that is pure?'

22-30 Those who have awakened to their soul and higher Reality differ from those who are muddling through in the confusion of conditioned consciousness and the limitations of body and mind. Those who deny the message that full and complete life begins after death are in constant doubt and cynicism about life in general. As for those who have awakened to this truth, their earthly life is experienced smoothly, since they are in constant awareness of the timeless Reality itself. The seekers along the prophetic path will benefit greatly from reflecting upon the infinite ways that mercy and generosity are bestowed upon us, sometimes not as we expect. With deep reflection one realises that even past errors and mishaps were, at that time, good for one. With humility and repentance, one returns to the path with renewed energy and receptibility.

It is the light of the All-Merciful that enables us to recalibrate our understanding of a situation through the higher light of our own soul. Our senses are preliminary stages of higher vision and sensing than are accessible via the purely physical state.

The more you refer to the All-Merciful, and the grace that emanates from it to all of us, the more you will see how glorious this life is in all of its aspects, rather than only when you feel good, comfortable, and at ease. Goodness pervades everything, including what you and I judge as not being agreeable or acceptable. Even within this, lies perfection in relationships, cause, and effect.

29. Surah 74 Al-Muddathir (The Cloaked)

Prophets and spiritual teachers will naturally meet with resistance from ignorant people. Those who are patient and know that perpetual joy lies in transcending earthly limitations as well as in the hereafter will understand and accept these challenging resistances.

بِسْمِ اللَّهِ الرَّحْمَـٰنِ الرَّحِيمِ

1-19 يَـٰٓأَيُّهَا ٱلْمُدَّثِّرُ ۝ قُمْ فَأَنذِرْ ۝ وَرَبَّكَ فَكَبِّرْ ۝ وَثِيَابَكَ فَطَهِّرْ ۝ وَٱلرُّجْزَ فَٱهْجُرْ ۝ وَلَا تَمْنُن تَسْتَكْثِرُ ۝ وَلِرَبِّكَ فَٱصْبِرْ ۝ فَإِذَا نُقِرَ فِى ٱلنَّاقُورِ ۝ فَذَٰلِكَ يَوْمَئِذٍ يَوْمٌ عَسِيرٌ ۝ عَلَى ٱلْكَـٰفِرِينَ غَيْرُ يَسِيرٍ ۝ ذَرْنِى وَمَنْ خَلَقْتُ وَحِيدًا ۝ وَجَعَلْتُ لَهُۥ مَالًا مَّمْدُودًا ۝ وَبَنِينَ شُهُودًا ۝ وَمَهَّدتُّ لَهُۥ تَمْهِيدًا ۝ ثُمَّ يَطْمَعُ أَنْ أَزِيدَ ۝ كَلَّآ إِنَّهُۥ كَانَ لِـَٔايَـٰتِنَا عَنِيدًا ۝ سَأُرْهِقُهُۥ صَعُودًا ۝ إِنَّهُۥ فَكَّرَ وَقَدَّرَ ۝ فَقُتِلَ كَيْفَ قَدَّرَ ۝

In the name of Allah, the Merciful to all, the Compassionate to each!

O you who are cloaked. Arise and warn. Proclaim the greatness of your Lord. And your garments do purify, and abandon impurity. Give not, thinking to gain greater. And for your Lord, be patient. When the Trumpet is blown; that, at that time, shall be a difficult day, for the unbelievers not easy. Leave Me and him whom I created alone, and give him vast riches, and sons by his side, making everything easy for him. Yet he still hopes I will give him more. No! He has been stubbornly hostile to Our signs. I shall inflict a steep ascent upon him. He reflected and determined – curse him how he determined!

1-19 As we perceive aspects of the truth of Reality, we tend to want to share them with others and expound upon them. Occasionally, we may experience a measure of reticence and reserve in delivering the news that we are here to discover the Reality of life itself. This discovery is the good news; it is accompanied by a caution that, if this news is not realised, we will have regrets all the time, since no matter how successful we may be on earth, it will be lost at death. The majority of people are concerned with survival and existential issues. Few are keen to discover the art of transcending mundane earthly experience.

Much of human life on earth has to do with grooming the lower self and reducing the distractions of our ego tendencies, which have to do with acquisition of power and wealth. No doubt we need a certain measure of security, comfort, and ease, but once this becomes our main objective, then we are at the edge of being destroyed.

Part of our protection is to be cloaked or clothed in a way that enables our body with all the amazing organs and faculties in it to continue functioning efficiently. Therefore shelter, clothing, and food are the most essential aspects of our basic health. Immediately after these come our relationships with whatever is around us – plants, trees, animals, and other humans. As a result, we are often challenged and require wisdom, understanding, and patience until we know that whatever we are given is appropriate for us in our immediate state of evolution.

20-34

ثُمَّ قُتِلَ كَيْفَ قَدَّرَ ۝ ثُمَّ نَظَرَ ۝ ثُمَّ عَبَسَ وَبَسَرَ ۝ ثُمَّ أَدْبَرَ وَٱسْتَكْبَرَ ۝ فَقَالَ إِنْ هَٰذَآ إِلَّا سِحْرٌ يُؤْثَرُ ۝ إِنْ هَٰذَآ إِلَّا قَوْلُ ٱلْبَشَرِ ۝ سَأُصْلِيهِ سَقَرَ ۝ وَمَآ أَدْرَىٰكَ مَا سَقَرُ ۝ لَا تُبْقِى وَلَا تَذَرُ ۝ لَوَّاحَةٌ لِّلْبَشَرِ ۝ عَلَيْهَا تِسْعَةَ عَشَرَ ۝ وَمَا جَعَلْنَآ أَصْحَٰبَ ٱلنَّارِ إِلَّا مَلَٰٓئِكَةً ۙ وَمَا جَعَلْنَا عِدَّتَهُمْ إِلَّا فِتْنَةً لِّلَّذِينَ كَفَرُوا۟ لِيَسْتَيْقِنَ ٱلَّذِينَ أُوتُوا۟ ٱلْكِتَٰبَ وَيَزْدَادَ ٱلَّذِينَ ءَامَنُوٓا۟ إِيمَٰنًا ۙ وَلَا يَرْتَابَ ٱلَّذِينَ أُوتُوا۟ ٱلْكِتَٰبَ وَٱلْمُؤْمِنُونَ ۙ وَلِيَقُولَ ٱلَّذِينَ فِى قُلُوبِهِم مَّرَضٌ وَٱلْكَٰفِرُونَ مَاذَآ أَرَادَ ٱللَّهُ بِهَٰذَا مَثَلًا ۚ كَذَٰلِكَ يُضِلُّ ٱللَّهُ مَن يَشَآءُ وَيَهْدِى مَن يَشَآءُ ۚ وَمَا يَعْلَمُ جُنُودَ رَبِّكَ إِلَّا هُوَ ۚ وَمَا هِىَ إِلَّا ذِكْرَىٰ لِلْبَشَرِ ۝ كَلَّا وَٱلْقَمَرِ ۝ وَٱلَّيْلِ إِذْ أَدْبَرَ ۝ وَٱلصُّبْحِ إِذَآ أَسْفَرَ ۝

And curse him again how he assessed. Then he considered. Then he frowned and scowled, and turned away and behaved arrogantly. And said, 'This is just old sorcery. Nothing but human speech.' I shall scorch him in Saqar. But how can you know what is Saqar? It spares nothing and leaves nothing; a scorcher for flesh, upon it stand nineteen. We assigned only angels to rule over the Fire, and made their tally to be only an ordeal to the unbelievers, that those granted Scripture may grow certain, and the believers may increase in belief, and that neither those granted Scripture nor the believers should be in doubt, and that they in whose hearts is sickness, and the unbelievers too, might say: 'What did Allah intend by this as a parable?' Thus does Allah lead astray whom He wills, and guides whom He wills. None knows the troops of your Lord save He, and it is nothing but a Reminder to mankind. Ah no! By the moon! And the night when it departs, and by the morning when it dawns!

20-34 There are two zones of reason. One is mental and intellectual wisdom; the other is intuitive and spiritual wisdom. Humans require both as these two states are inseparable. In the early developmental period, human beings required development of the body and mind as well as clarity in conduct and character, followed by the need to delve deeper into the meaning of such development, and more importantly, to experience transcending the limitations of the senses. The condition of the Garden is that of transcending limitations; that of the fire is of sinking deeper into limited, restricted, and stifling experience. Our higher nature is that of the boundless spirit,

The early stages of being confused and lost, which bring about suffering, can be corrected with higher awareness and constant referencing to the soul within. The danger is when one gets used to stupid and selfish activities, this can take one to an irreversible point of darkness. Many human beings can be considered as dead before they die.

It is natural for all of us to measure the situation we are in as to how it would affect the future, because we are all obsessed with the best ending for our earthly experience. We are full of hope about what comes tomorrow and how our ending will be. So, we struggle towards attaining what is better, until such time we know that the Master of it all is compassionate and considerate. If you turn your sight to insight, you will see that whatever situation you are experiencing is the best for you, and then you will be truly content. The more frequently you remember that, like every human being, you will give up your body and mind, this calibration will reduce anxieties, fears, desires, sorrows, and suffering.

35-56 إِنَّهَا لَإِحْدَى ٱلْكُبَرِ ۝ نَذِيرًا لِّلْبَشَرِ ۝ لِمَن شَآءَ مِنكُمْ أَن يَتَقَدَّمَ أَوْ يَتَأَخَّرَ ۝ كُلُّ نَفْسٍ بِمَا كَسَبَتْ رَهِينَةٌ ۝ إِلَّآ أَصْحَٰبَ ٱلْيَمِينِ ۝ فِى جَنَّٰتٍ يَتَسَآءَلُونَ ۝ عَنِ ٱلْمُجْرِمِينَ ۝ مَا سَلَكَكُمْ فِى سَقَرَ ۝ قَالُوا۟ لَمْ نَكُ مِنَ ٱلْمُصَلِّينَ ۝ وَلَمْ نَكُ نُطْعِمُ ٱلْمِسْكِينَ ۝ وَكُنَّا نَخُوضُ مَعَ ٱلْخَآئِضِينَ ۝ وَكُنَّا نُكَذِّبُ بِيَوْمِ ٱلدِّينِ ۝ حَتَّىٰٓ أَتَىٰنَا ٱلْيَقِينُ ۝ فَمَا تَنفَعُهُمْ شَفَٰعَةُ ٱلشَّٰفِعِينَ ۝ فَمَا لَهُمْ عَنِ ٱلتَّذْكِرَةِ مُعْرِضِينَ ۝ كَأَنَّهُمْ حُمُرٌ مُّسْتَنفِرَةٌ ۝ فَرَّتْ مِن قَسْوَرَةٍ ۝ بَلْ يُرِيدُ كُلُّ ٱمْرِئٍ مِّنْهُمْ أَن يُؤْتَىٰ صُحُفًا مُّنَشَّرَةً ۝ كَلَّا بَل لَّا يَخَافُونَ ٱلْءَاخِرَةَ ۝ كَلَّآ إِنَّهُۥ تَذْكِرَةٌ ۝ فَمَن شَآءَ ذَكَرَهُۥ ۝ وَمَا يَذْكُرُونَ إِلَّآ أَن يَشَآءَ ٱللَّهُ هُوَ أَهْلُ ٱلتَّقْوَىٰ وَأَهْلُ ٱلْمَغْفِرَةِ ۝

It is one of the mightiest things. A warning to mankind, to any of you who wish to come forward, Or lag behind. Every soul shall be pledged for what it has earned, save those who shall have attained to righteousness. In gardens, they shall ask each other. About the guilty: What has brought you into hell? They shall say: 'We were not of those who prayed; and we used not to feed the poor; and we waded into blasphemy with those who waded. And we used to call the day of recompense a lie; till certainty overtook us.' No intercessor's plea will benefit them now. What is with them? Why do they turn away from the warning, as though they were terrified asses that had fled from a lion? No, every man of them desires to be given scrolls unrolled. No indeed; but they do not fear the Hereafter. No indeed; surely it is a Reminder; Whoso wills can remember it; But they shall not remember unless Allah wills. Worthy is He of piety! Worthy is He to forgive!

35-56 The truth is that life on earth is a necessary step in human evolution; it is important to realise this, since every self – be it human, animal, or other – is held by what it desires, intends and acts upon. We are constrained by our attachments and desires. We are caught and trapped by how we perceive life and what our foundation of consciousness is. By transcending our senses, we can experience the expansive, timeless state for which we yearn. If we realise that the self is only a shadow indicating the light of the soul, we will naturally look for the correct map, which may lead us to the realisation of the supremacy of the soul. We also then realise that the shadowy self is a product of the soul and exists because of it.

Actions and reactions are opposites in perfect balance. Whatever we think, say, or do, will have a repercussion. It is for this reason that we require constant reflection and review of our mental and physical activities. With constant self-correction, we may be led to awareness of the infinite moment that touches our immortal soul.

In our daily life, we spend a lot of time and effort concerned about tomorrow, but what about the hereafter? This is missing in most of our lives, until such time you know that the only provision you have for the next life are your intentions and actions whilst you had the illusion of choice on earth. The nations before us, pre-Pharaonic and others, have always cared for provisions after death, but our cultures nowadays do not seem to give it prominence. All of this calibration is based on touching the state of the hereafter, where we have no power, ability, mind, or choice. The more we remember this point in time, which is timeless, the healthier our journey on earth will be.

30. Surah 75 Al-Qiyamah (Resurrection)

When life as we know it comes to an end – on the earth, on other planets and in the universe – then the resurrection and collection of all souls will be a major event in the unseen. In that state, everyone will come with what they have earned and will be compensated accordingly.

بِسْمِ اللَّهِ الرَّحْمَٰنِ الرَّحِيمِ

لَا أُقْسِمُ بِيَوْمِ ٱلْقِيَٰمَةِ ۝ وَلَا أُقْسِمُ بِٱلنَّفْسِ ٱللَّوَّامَةِ ۝ أَيَحْسَبُ ٱلْإِنسَٰنُ أَلَّن نَّجْمَعَ عِظَامَهُۥ ۝ بَلَىٰ قَٰدِرِينَ عَلَىٰٓ أَن نُّسَوِّىَ بَنَانَهُۥ ۝ بَلْ يُرِيدُ ٱلْإِنسَٰنُ لِيَفْجُرَ أَمَامَهُۥ ۝ يَسْـَٔلُ أَيَّانَ يَوْمُ ٱلْقِيَٰمَةِ ۝ فَإِذَا بَرِقَ ٱلْبَصَرُ ۝ وَخَسَفَ ٱلْقَمَرُ ۝ وَجُمِعَ ٱلشَّمْسُ وَٱلْقَمَرُ ۝ يَقُولُ ٱلْإِنسَٰنُ يَوْمَئِذٍ أَيْنَ ٱلْمَفَرُّ ۝ كَلَّا لَا وَزَرَ ۝ إِلَىٰ رَبِّكَ يَوْمَئِذٍ ٱلْمُسْتَقَرُّ ۝ يُنَبَّؤُاْ ٱلْإِنسَٰنُ يَوْمَئِذٍ بِمَا قَدَّمَ وَأَخَّرَ ۝ بَلِ ٱلْإِنسَٰنُ عَلَىٰ نَفْسِهِۦ بَصِيرَةٌ ۝ وَلَوْ أَلْقَىٰ مَعَاذِيرَهُۥ ۝ لَا تُحَرِّكْ بِهِۦ لِسَانَكَ لِتَعْجَلَ بِهِۦٓ ۝ إِنَّ عَلَيْنَا جَمْعَهُۥ وَقُرْءَانَهُۥ ۝ فَإِذَا قَرَأْنَٰهُ فَٱتَّبِعْ قُرْءَانَهُۥ ۝ ثُمَّ إِنَّ عَلَيْنَا بَيَانَهُۥ ۝ 1-19

30. Surah 75 Al-Qiyamah (Resurrection)

In the name of Allah, the Merciful to all, the Compassionate to each!

Yes indeed! I swear by the Day of Resurrection! Nay! I swear by the self-accusing soul. Does man imagine We shall not reassemble his bones? Yea! We are able to make complete his very fingertips. But man wishes to persist in his debauchery. He asks when the Day of Resurrection shall come. But when the sight is dazed. And the moon is eclipsed, and the sun and the moon are brought together, on that Day man will say, 'Where can I escape?' Truly, there is no refuge. With your Lord alone shall on that day be the place of rest. Man shall on that day be informed of what he sent before and (what he) put off. But man is a clear witness against himself, even though he offers his excuses. Move not your tongue with it, seeking to hasten it along; up to Us is its collection and recitation. When We recite it, follow its recitation, then it is up to Us to expound it.

1-19 An important landmark in the human journey is death, which opens the door for higher consciousness and the hereafter. To imagine the Day of Reckoning, we need to enter a zone of non-space and non-time where there is no movement or change. In that state no clearly defined celestial or territorial entities exist. We can experience a touch of this state on earth when we desire to prolong and transcend natural consciousness by experiencing higher connectedness, floating in the boundless zone of celestial lights and delights.

Our natural desires to know and discover are easy when they deal with our earthly zone of life, as long as we use the conscious referencing of our reason and mind. The gift of prophetic revelation is the completion of the story of life, telling us that we will experience a higher zone of consciousness without the interference of body or mind after death.

The biggest challenge in human life is not only to accept and understand the meaning of the hereafter but also to constantly use it as a calibrating point along our earthly journey. The nafs is always argumentative and therefore finds a reason to deny it, postpone it, or say we are not sure anymore. Those who are tuned to the higher light within their souls know there is no escape. Every person will die, and every person will be resurrected. And then there will be an end of life again, after all of that. We have to go deeper and deeper into the original light from which life has emerged. It is also from there that the wisdom and the lights of the Qur'an have emerged.

20-40 كَلَّا بَلْ تُحِبُّونَ ٱلْعَاجِلَةَ ۞ وَتَذَرُونَ ٱلْءَاخِرَةَ ۞ وُجُوهٌ يَوْمَئِذٍ نَّاضِرَةٌ ۞ إِلَىٰ رَبِّهَا نَاظِرَةٌ ۞ وَوُجُوهٌ يَوْمَئِذٍ بَاسِرَةٌ ۞ تَظُنُّ أَن يُفْعَلَ بِهَا فَاقِرَةٌ ۞ كَلَّا إِذَا بَلَغَتِ ٱلتَّرَاقِيَ ۞ وَقِيلَ مَنْ رَاقٍ ۞ وَظَنَّ أَنَّهُ ٱلْفِرَاقُ ۞ وَٱلْتَفَّتِ ٱلسَّاقُ بِٱلسَّاقِ ۞ إِلَىٰ رَبِّكَ يَوْمَئِذٍ ٱلْمَسَاقُ ۞ فَلَا صَدَّقَ وَلَا صَلَّىٰ ۞ وَلَٰكِن كَذَّبَ وَتَوَلَّىٰ ۞ ثُمَّ ذَهَبَ إِلَىٰ أَهْلِهِۦ يَتَمَطَّىٰ ۞ أَوْلَىٰ لَكَ فَأَوْلَىٰ ۞ ثُمَّ أَوْلَىٰ لَكَ فَأَوْلَىٰ ۞ أَيَحْسَبُ ٱلْإِنسَٰنُ أَن يُتْرَكَ سُدًى ۞ أَلَمْ يَكُ نُطْفَةً مِّن مَّنِيٍّ يُمْنَىٰ ۞ ثُمَّ كَانَ عَلَقَةً

$$\text{فَخَلَقَ فَسَوَّىٰ ۝ فَجَعَلَ مِنْهُ ٱلزَّوْجَيْنِ ٱلذَّكَرَ وَٱلْأُنثَىٰ ۝ أَلَيْسَ ذَٰلِكَ بِقَٰدِرٍ عَلَىٰ أَن يُحْيِىَ ٱلْمَوْتَىٰ ۝}$$

No indeed; but you love the hasty world, and neglect the hereafter. Upon that day faces shall be radiant, to their Lord their eyes are lifted; and on that Day there will be the sad and despairing faces. Knowing a back-breaker shall befall them. No indeed; when it reaches the clavicles and it is said, 'Who is an enchanter?' And he thinks that it is the parting. And affliction is combined with affliction; on that day he will be driven towards your Lord. But he neither believed nor prayed. Instead, he denied and departed; walking back to his people with a conceited swagger. Closer and closer it comes to you. Closer and closer still. Does man think he shall be abandoned to futility? Was he not a sperm drop, to be discharged. Then he was a clinging clot, that He created and formed, and made from it a pair, male and female? Is not He, then; able to bring the dead back to life?

20-40 Human nature is designed to experience the now and anticipate what is immediately likely to come next. We give far more importance to our present moment than what comes later. If we practice silence and transcend our normal consciousness, the process of death becomes easy; wisdom and spiritual openings increase. All dualities in life point to unity, and we are given a will to exercise the awakening state. With constant reflection and prayers, the divine grace will reveal itself in numerous ways, more specifically in the truth that divine presence is the Reality itself at all its levels, and that there is no excuse for any human being not to be dedicated to that realisation and its awesomeness.

Our duty in this life is to unveil the divine light transmitted from our own soul and through it to deal with dualities in constant reference to cosmic unity. With this practice, death becomes the most natural opening to the vastness of the unseen world, which was veiled by body and mind.

It is human nature to want the next moment to be good. It is also human nature to postpone what happens next year, or what happens after death. The more you are able to touch the now, the more you are drawing energy from that amazing miracle that is eternally present. The danger, of course, is that the nafs will prevail and will bring about a veil of arrogance such that we remain alive but not truly living. Then we do not remember how we started or how life began in the womb, nor can we visualise the hereafter. Instead, we need to remember that from that point of absolute Oneness, dualities have emerged and all of them seek the reassurance of unity in the now.

31. Surah 76 Al-Insan (Humankind)

This surah is a great reminder that the real origin of human beings is a timeless soul. Our earthly manifestation carries with it some darkness, denial, and rejection, just as it does some gratitude and contentment.

بِسْمِ اللَّهِ الرَّحْمَـٰنِ الرَّحِيمِ

1-15 هَلْ أَتَىٰ عَلَى ٱلْإِنسَـٰنِ حِينٌ مِّنَ ٱلدَّهْرِ لَمْ يَكُن شَيْـًٔا مَّذْكُورًا ۞ إِنَّا خَلَقْنَا ٱلْإِنسَـٰنَ مِن نُّطْفَةٍ أَمْشَاجٍ نَّبْتَلِيهِ فَجَعَلْنَـٰهُ سَمِيعًۢا بَصِيرًا ۞ إِنَّا هَدَيْنَـٰهُ ٱلسَّبِيلَ إِمَّا شَاكِرًا وَإِمَّا كَفُورًا ۞ إِنَّآ أَعْتَدْنَا لِلْكَـٰفِرِينَ سَلَـٰسِلَا۠ وَأَغْلَـٰلًا وَسَعِيرًا ۞ إِنَّ ٱلْأَبْرَارَ يَشْرَبُونَ مِن كَأْسٍ كَانَ مِزَاجُهَا كَافُورًا ۞ عَيْنًا يَشْرَبُ بِهَا عِبَادُ ٱللَّهِ يُفَجِّرُونَهَا تَفْجِيرًا ۞ يُوفُونَ بِٱلنَّذْرِ وَيَخَافُونَ يَوْمًا كَانَ شَرُّهُۥ مُسْتَطِيرًا ۞ وَيُطْعِمُونَ ٱلطَّعَامَ عَلَىٰ حُبِّهِۦ مِسْكِينًا وَيَتِيمًا وَأَسِيرًا ۞ إِنَّمَا نُطْعِمُكُمْ لِوَجْهِ ٱللَّهِ لَا نُرِيدُ مِنكُمْ جَزَآءً وَلَا شُكُورًا ۞ إِنَّا نَخَافُ مِن رَّبِّنَا يَوْمًا عَبُوسًا قَمْطَرِيرًا ۞ فَوَقَـٰهُمُ ٱللَّهُ شَرَّ ذَٰلِكَ ٱلْيَوْمِ وَلَقَّىٰهُمْ نَضْرَةً وَسُرُورًا ۞ وَجَزَىٰهُم بِمَا صَبَرُوا۟ جَنَّةً وَحَرِيرًا ۞ مُّتَّكِـِٔينَ فِيهَا عَلَى ٱلْأَرَآئِكِ لَا يَرَوْنَ فِيهَا شَمْسًا وَلَا زَمْهَرِيرًا ۞ وَدَانِيَةً عَلَيْهِمْ ظِلَـٰلُهَا وَذُلِّلَتْ قُطُوفُهَا تَذْلِيلًا ۞ وَيُطَافُ عَلَيْهِم بِـَٔانِيَةٍ مِّن فِضَّةٍ وَأَكْوَابٍ كَانَتْ قَوَارِيرَا۠ ۞

In the name of Allah, the Merciful to all, the Compassionate to each!
Surely there came upon man a span of time, when he was a thing not worth remembering! We created man from a drop of mingled fluid to put him to the test; We gave him hearing and sight; We guided him upon the way, be he grateful or ungrateful. Surely, We have prepared for the unbelievers chains and shackles and a burning fire. But the righteous shall drink from a cup mixed with choicest fragrance, A spring for Allah's servants, which flows abundantly at their wish. They fulfil vows and fear a day the evil of which shall be spreading far and wide. And they give food out of love for Him to the poor and the orphan and the captive: we only feed you for Allah's sake; we desire from you neither reward nor thanks: For we fear from our Lord a frowning day, inauspicious. So, Allah shall spare them the evil of that Day, and grant them splendour and joy. And reward them, because they were patient, with garden and silk, they shall recline therein on couches, and therein shall experience neither burning sun nor piercing cold. With its shades spread above them and clusters of fruit hanging close at hand. They will be served with silver plates.

1-15 As humans, we assume that there was a time that we did not exist as a defined entity. In the unseen knowledge beyond space and time, however, everything existed. Life's journey, and a rise in consciousness, takes us to a position in which we either apply a certain vision or faith or remain in denial regarding Truth itself. The path of spiritual awakening brings bliss and joy in this world and more consistently after death.

Miraculously, our human composition contains all the provisions and guidance needed for our journey on earth. We have a responsibility towards our personal safety and maintenance. We have a greater duty towards awakening to the original light of the Creator – which governs the entire universe. We love paradise, since it allows us a state of effulgent tranquillity and joy.

Our human composition is an intimate unity between the energy and light that are before time, mingling with matter, energy, and other forces that have produced, after billions of years of evolution, our physical, material, and mental reality. We have emerged from the unseen and are returning to that original zone propelled by the extent of our rise in consciousness, purification, and reference to the timeless light in our hearts.

16-31

قَوَارِيرَا۟ مِن فِضَّةٍ قَدَّرُوهَا تَقْدِيرًا ۝ وَيُسْقَوْنَ فِيهَا كَأْسًا كَانَ مِزَاجُهَا زَنجَبِيلًا ۝ عَيْنًا فِيهَا تُسَمَّىٰ سَلْسَبِيلًا ۝ وَيَطُوفُ عَلَيْهِمْ وِلْدَٰنٌ مُّخَلَّدُونَ إِذَا رَأَيْتَهُمْ حَسِبْتَهُمْ لُؤْلُؤًا مَّنثُورًا ۝ وَإِذَا رَأَيْتَ ثَمَّ رَأَيْتَ نَعِيمًا وَمُلْكًا كَبِيرًا ۝ عَٰلِيَهُمْ ثِيَابُ سُندُسٍ خُضْرٌ وَإِسْتَبْرَقٌ وَحُلُّوٓا۟ أَسَاوِرَ مِن فِضَّةٍ وَسَقَىٰهُمْ رَبُّهُمْ شَرَابًا طَهُورًا ۝ إِنَّ هَٰذَا كَانَ لَكُمْ جَزَآءً وَكَانَ سَعْيُكُم مَّشْكُورًا ۝ إِنَّا نَحْنُ نَزَّلْنَا عَلَيْكَ ٱلْقُرْءَانَ تَنزِيلًا ۝ فَٱصْبِرْ لِحُكْمِ رَبِّكَ وَلَا تُطِعْ مِنْهُمْ ءَاثِمًا أَوْ كَفُورًا ۝ وَٱذْكُرِ ٱسْمَ رَبِّكَ بُكْرَةً وَأَصِيلًا ۝ وَمِنَ ٱلَّيْلِ فَٱسْجُدْ لَهُۥ وَسَبِّحْهُ لَيْلًا طَوِيلًا ۝ إِنَّ هَٰٓؤُلَآءِ يُحِبُّونَ ٱلْعَاجِلَةَ وَيَذَرُونَ وَرَآءَهُمْ يَوْمًا ثَقِيلًا ۝ نَّحْنُ خَلَقْنَٰهُمْ وَشَدَدْنَآ أَسْرَهُمْ وَإِذَا شِئْنَا بَدَّلْنَآ أَمْثَٰلَهُمْ تَبْدِيلًا ۝ إِنَّ هَٰذِهِۦ تَذْكِرَةٌ فَمَن شَآءَ ٱتَّخَذَ إِلَىٰ رَبِّهِۦ سَبِيلًا ۝ وَمَا تَشَآءُونَ إِلَّآ أَن يَشَآءَ ٱللَّهُ إِنَّ ٱللَّهَ كَانَ عَلِيمًا حَكِيمًا ۝ يُدْخِلُ مَن يَشَآءُ فِى رَحْمَتِهِۦ وَٱلظَّٰلِمِينَ أَعَدَّ لَهُمْ عَذَابًا أَلِيمًا ۝

Crystal-like silver, perfectly proportioned, and they will be given a drink infused with ginger, from a spring called Salsabil. And round about them shall go youths never altering in age; when you see them you will think them to be scattered pearls. And when you see there, you shall see blessings and a great kingdom. Upon them shall be garments of fine green silk and thick silk interwoven with gold, and they shall be adorned with bracelets of silver, and their Lord shall make them drink a pure drink. This shall be as a reward to you: Your venture was worthy of all praise. Surely, We have sent down the Qur'an to you descended in portions. So, bear your Lord's verdict with patience, and obey not the unbeliever or wicked among them. And pronounce your Lord's name, morning and evening, and part of the night; bow down before Him and magnify Him through the long night. These people love the fleeting world, and turn their backs upon a weighty Day. Yet We created them; We strengthened their constitution; if We please, We can replace such people completely. This is a Reminder. Whoso wishes may follow a path to his Lord; and you cannot so wish unless Allah wishes. Allah is All-Knowing, All-Wise. For He admits into His mercy whomsoever He will; as for the evildoers, He has prepared for them a painful chastisement.

16-31 The description of the Garden varies according to what gives maximum, constant contentment and satisfaction to the seeker. We can understand a state of goodness that we cannot increase. That state of consciousness is more regularly touched on by practice, repetition, and passion, since it has to do with the soul within the heart. The inner heart burns in passion with its obsession with Reality itself. This path is a reminder that there is a direction, but a person must choose and embrace that direction and apply and live by it until timelessness is experienced and oblivion is tasted. The ultimate mercy is to experience the continuity and perpetuity of life itself.

By turning away from worries and concerns that cannot be changed, we maintain our connection with higher consciousness within. We have no option other than caring for the emotional and physical sides of our life, but equally we need to experience the light within our heart and its vast domain.

If we have managed to calibrate constantly with the divine light within us, then we have already moved to the state of paradise and the garden. If not, then the soul has been tarnished on its journey on earth and needs to be purified; this is the meaning of purgatory and what comes after. There are two zones of memory: one is to remember short-term and long-term, and the other is to remember before the advent of individuality, creation, and what we call normal memory. If we are in the right state of worship, then that pre-memory memory will kick in and will connect us to the divine within us.

32. Surah 78 An-Naba' (The Event)

It is natural for human beings to enquire about the meaning of life as well as how it began and how it ends. The last ayah of the previous surah outlines the doubts and insecurities of human beings, which are answered in this surah.

بِسْمِ اللَّهِ الرَّحْمَٰنِ الرَّحِيمِ

1-19 عَمَّ يَتَسَآءَلُونَ ۝ عَنِ ٱلنَّبَإِ ٱلْعَظِيمِ ۝ ٱلَّذِى هُمْ فِيهِ مُخْتَلِفُونَ ۝ كَلَّا سَيَعْلَمُونَ ۝ ثُمَّ كَلَّا سَيَعْلَمُونَ ۝ أَلَمْ نَجْعَلِ ٱلْأَرْضَ مِهَٰدًا ۝ وَٱلْجِبَالَ أَوْتَادًا ۝ وَخَلَقْنَٰكُمْ أَزْوَٰجًا ۝ وَجَعَلْنَا نَوْمَكُمْ سُبَاتًا ۝ وَجَعَلْنَا ٱلَّيْلَ لِبَاسًا ۝ وَجَعَلْنَا ٱلنَّهَارَ مَعَاشًا ۝ وَبَنَيْنَا فَوْقَكُمْ سَبْعًا شِدَادًا ۝ وَجَعَلْنَا سِرَاجًا وَهَّاجًا ۝ وَأَنزَلْنَا مِنَ ٱلْمُعْصِرَٰتِ مَآءً ثَجَّاجًا ۝ لِنُخْرِجَ بِهِۦ حَبًّا وَنَبَاتًا ۝ وَجَنَّٰتٍ

أَلْفَافًا ۝ إِنَّ يَوْمَ ٱلْفَصْلِ كَانَ مِيقَٰتًا ۝ يَوْمَ يُنفَخُ فِى ٱلصُّورِ فَتَأْتُونَ أَفْوَاجًا ۝ وَفُتِحَتِ ٱلسَّمَآءُ فَكَانَتْ أَبْوَٰبًا ۝

In the name of Allah, the Merciful to all, the Compassionate to each!

What is it that they question each other about? The momentous announcement about which they differ? No indeed; they shall soon know! Again, no indeed; they shall soon know! Did We not make the earth smooth, and the mountains as pegs? And We created you in pairs, give you sleep for rest, the night as a cover, and the day for your livelihood? Did We not build seven strong above you, and have placed a lamp full of blazing splendour? And We send down from the clouds water pouring forth abundantly, that We may bring forth thereby grain and plants, and gardens intertwined? A time has been appointed for the Day of Decision: the Day when the trumpet is sounded and you all come forward in multitudes; and when the skies are opened and become gates.

1-19 The most important news, revelation, insight, or intuition is that there is only Oneness or eternal Unity, which encompasses all that is known and unknown. From the unseen, all of creation emanated in every possible design, form, and connectivity, all sustained by that Oneness. The Truth cascades from pure light into creational realities as energies, matter, solids, gas, and liquids. We can witness manifested glimpses of such creational dynamics in the formation of the stars, solar systems, and galaxies, as well as in the fact that we can only physically survive by consuming what grows from the earth whilst seeking meaning and the purpose of existence beyond it. Surrender or acceptance of that Presence will also occur when creation returns to its origin on the Day of Reckoning.

The source of human life is timeless and boundless, yet we live our daily lives on earth accepting limitations and boundaries. The inner knowledge of Reality is in every heart, but outer distractions veil the heart, causing many distractions and confusion. It is through prayers and the ability to stop thoughts and clear the mind that we touch upon the Source of life within our heart.

The most powerful human drive is to know our end and what comes after death: to know whether we will be in a garden, a hell, or another state. Every one of us is driven to know. No story is complete except at its end. So, we all want to know what is this thing we are promised in the hereafter? This question will be answered if we truly see the state we are in now, in creation, and that this earth has samples of everything – gardens, hells, in-betweens, suspense, all the possible good and all the possible bad, tragedies, and mistakes. So, it is by trust that we accept that an end will come.

وَسُيِّرَتِ ٱلْجِبَالُ فَكَانَتْ سَرَابًا ۝ إِنَّ جَهَنَّمَ كَانَتْ مِرْصَادًا ۝ لِّلطَّٰغِينَ مَـَٔابًا ۝ لَّٰبِثِينَ فِيهَآ أَحْقَابًا ۝ لَّا يَذُوقُونَ فِيهَا بَرْدًا وَلَا شَرَابًا ۝ إِلَّا حَمِيمًا وَغَسَّاقًا ۝

جَزَآءً وِفَاقًا ۞ إِنَّهُمْ كَانُوا لَا يَرْجُونَ حِسَابًا ۞ وَكَذَّبُوا بِـَٔايَـٰتِنَا كِذَّابًا ۞ وَكُلَّ شَىْءٍ أَحْصَيْنَـٰهُ كِتَـٰبًا ۞ فَذُوقُوا فَلَن نَّزِيدَكُمْ إِلَّا عَذَابًا ۞ إِنَّ لِلْمُتَّقِينَ مَفَازًا ۞ حَدَآئِقَ وَأَعْنَـٰبًا ۞ وَكَوَاعِبَ أَتْرَابًا ۞ وَكَأْسًا دِهَاقًا ۞ لَّا يَسْمَعُونَ فِيهَا لَغْوًا وَلَا كِذَّٰبًا ۞ جَزَآءً مِّن رَّبِّكَ عَطَآءً حِسَابًا ۞ رَّبِّ ٱلسَّمَـٰوَٰتِ وَٱلْأَرْضِ وَمَا بَيْنَهُمَا ٱلرَّحْمَـٰنِ لَا يَمْلِكُونَ مِنْهُ خِطَابًا ۞ يَوْمَ يَقُومُ ٱلرُّوحُ وَٱلْمَلَـٰٓئِكَةُ صَفًّا لَّا يَتَكَلَّمُونَ إِلَّا مَنْ أَذِنَ لَهُ ٱلرَّحْمَـٰنُ وَقَالَ صَوَابًا ۞ ذَٰلِكَ ٱلْيَوْمُ ٱلْحَقُّ فَمَن شَآءَ ٱتَّخَذَ إِلَىٰ رَبِّهِۦ مَـَٔابًا ۞ إِنَّآ أَنذَرْنَـٰكُمْ عَذَابًا قَرِيبًا يَوْمَ يَنظُرُ ٱلْمَرْءُ مَا قَدَّمَتْ يَدَاهُ وَيَقُولُ ٱلْكَافِرُ يَـٰلَيْتَنِى كُنتُ تُرَٰبًا ۞

When the mountains will vanish like a mirage. Hell lies in ambush, For the insolent a resort. In it shall they remain for a long time. Therein they taste neither coolness nor anything to drink, save boiling water and pus for a suitable recompense. They indeed hoped not for a reckoning, and they rejected Our messages as lies. But We have placed on record every single thing. So, taste it! For We shall only increase you in torment. Surely, for those who are cautiously aware is achievement, Gardens and vineyards, companions, shapely and alike of age, and an overflowing cup. No empty talk will they hear in that nor any lie. A reward from your Lord, a gift according to a reckoning: From the Lord of the heavens and earth and everything between, the Lord of Mercy. They will have no authority from Him to speak. The day on which the spirit and the angels shall stand in ranks; they shall not speak except he whom the Beneficent Allah permits and who speaks the right thing. That is the Day of Truth. So, whoever wishes to do so should take the path that leads to his Lord. We have warned you of imminent torment, on the Day when every person will see what their own hands have sent ahead for them, when the disbeliever will say, 'If only I were dust!'

20-40 All physical matter will disintegrate and return to its sub-atomic origin and subsequent nothingness. We live in space-time and are eager to discover what lies beyond the boundaries that we experience. Whatever appears is linked to and interconnected with everything else, and one day this will all vanish and return to its origin. Whoever witnesses light, the spiritually constant light, is at the door of deep contentment and realisation of the Truth. In this zone, there is only pure cosmic consciousness, which is divine light and Reality, the experience of which will give every seeker the most hoped-for state and station. If we are not preparing for transcending our mundane, conditioned consciousness, then we are heading towards the shock of death and the hereafter.

Through higher consciousness we realise that real life is eternal, and that we shall enter it upon death. All our intentions and actions and whatever we have hidden in this life will be made evident to us. The souls that have practiced the Truth will experience the eternal garden. Those who need to be completed in realising consciousness will have their treatment prepared for them.

It is by trust we know that the entire universe will collapse, and all these amazing billions of galaxies will return to the state from which they emerged. As for the completion of our own story, when the end of this human journey comes, then all that remains is the soul or the spirit with a hint of what it has done. Therefore, on the Day of Reckoning, every being will know whether they have given up the illusion of being separate from the One or be begging and crying for and doing their utmost to be in timelessness with the One and only who is eternal.

33. Surah 85 Al-Buruj (The Constellations)

The infinite Absolute connects to the relative and finite through countless stages and steps, which all emanate from the primal tablet of divinity.

بِسْمِ اللَّهِ الرَّحْمَٰنِ الرَّحِيمِ

73-82 وَالسَّمَاءِ ذَاتِ الْبُرُوجِ ۝ وَالْيَوْمِ الْمَوْعُودِ ۝ وَشَاهِدٍ وَمَشْهُودٍ ۝ قُتِلَ أَصْحَابُ الْأُخْدُودِ ۝ النَّارِ ذَاتِ الْوَقُودِ ۝ إِذْ هُمْ عَلَيْهَا قُعُودٌ ۝ وَهُمْ عَلَىٰ مَا يَفْعَلُونَ بِالْمُؤْمِنِينَ شُهُودٌ ۝ وَمَا نَقَمُوا مِنْهُمْ إِلَّا أَن يُؤْمِنُوا بِاللَّهِ الْعَزِيزِ الْحَمِيدِ ۝ الَّذِي لَهُ مُلْكُ السَّمَاوَاتِ وَالْأَرْضِ ۚ وَاللَّهُ عَلَىٰ كُلِّ شَيْءٍ شَهِيدٌ ۝ إِنَّ الَّذِينَ فَتَنُوا الْمُؤْمِنِينَ وَالْمُؤْمِنَاتِ ثُمَّ لَمْ يَتُوبُوا فَلَهُمْ عَذَابُ جَهَنَّمَ وَلَهُمْ عَذَابُ الْحَرِيقِ ۝ إِنَّ الَّذِينَ آمَنُوا وَعَمِلُوا الصَّالِحَاتِ لَهُمْ جَنَّاتٌ تَجْرِي مِن تَحْتِهَا الْأَنْهَارُ ۚ ذَٰلِكَ الْفَوْزُ الْكَبِيرُ ۝ إِنَّ بَطْشَ رَبِّكَ لَشَدِيدٌ ۝ إِنَّهُ هُوَ يُبْدِئُ وَيُعِيدُ ۝

In the name of Allah, the Merciful to all, the Compassionate to each!

By the sky, with its constellations! And the promised day, by a witness and what is witnessed! Perish the People of the Trench, the fire abounding in fuel, as they sat above it, witnessing what they did to the faithful! Their only grievance against them was their faith in Allah, the Mighty, the Praiseworthy, Allah to whom belongs the Kingdom of the heavens and the earth, and Allah is Witness over everything. For those who persecute believing men and women, and do not repent afterwards, there will be the torment of Hell and burning. Those who believe, and do righteous deeds, for them await gardens underneath which rivers flow; that is the great triumph. Surely the might of your Lord is great. It is He who brings people to life, and will restore them to life again –

1-13 We continually evolve in consciousness towards enlightenment. So does our capacity to witness clearly as well as to understand and awaken to the truth of the All-Encompassing universal soul (Allah). When our direction and destination is to move out of darkness towards light, then confusion and sorrow will be replaced with contentment and happiness. Good actions that lead to the state of paradise prove to us that there is one Source of all actions; at best we are here as its stewards and joyful slaves.

The entire universe is totally interconnected, experienced on different levels of clarity as well as various stages along the path of evolution. Over the past billions of years, life began and developed in the simplest and most basic forms. Now human beings are exposed to the cosmic powers as well as to the realisation of human needs for survival and arrival.

We are carrying a consciousness that spans infinite boundlessness down to the point of our awareness of the immediate situation through our senses and feelings. It is natural for us to realize that everything we experience is in cycles with beginnings and ends.

14-22 وَهُوَ ٱلْغَفُورُ ٱلْوَدُودُ ۝ ذُو ٱلْعَرْشِ ٱلْمَجِيدُ ۝ فَعَّالٌ لِّمَا يُرِيدُ ۝ هَلْ أَتَىٰكَ حَدِيثُ ٱلْجُنُودِ ۝ فِرْعَوْنَ وَثَمُودَ ۝ بَلِ ٱلَّذِينَ كَفَرُوا۟ فِى تَكْذِيبٍ ۝ وَٱللَّهُ مِن وَرَآئِهِم مُّحِيطٌۢ ۝ بَلْ هُوَ قُرْءَانٌ مَّجِيدٌ ۝ فِى لَوْحٍ مَّحْفُوظٍۭ ۝

and He is the All-Forgiving, the All-Loving, the Glorious Lord of the Throne, He does whatever He wills. Has the story of the troops reached you? Of Pharaoh and Thamud? And yet the unbelievers continue to deny, Allah surrounds them all. Nay, but it is a glorious Qur'an, in a guarded tablet.

14-22 Truth encompasses everything that moves within spacetime. This includes any beginning and ending, as well as all that appears and all that is veiled. Everything happens according to the magnificent, glorious divine will within the field of infinity. If we deny this ultimate, all-prevailing truth, we cause injustice towards our self and others. This Reality and truth are permeated by knowledge of it. This knowledge is called the Qur'an, which gathers all and reveals it all. It is the most sacred Reality that discloses itself in every state of its appearance, both subtle and hidden. What is needed is sincerity, humbleness, and trust in the Qur'an's divine authenticity.

If we look back into our recent history, we will realise that through honest reflection, modesty, and servitude, we will enable ourselves to go higher in consciousness and trust that Allah is indeed in charge of all.

Allah prevails upon all. Whatever exists has been touched by the divine power, and the outer manifestation of events are all due to divine acceptance. Even if it causes suffering, it is to show that we are participating, to a certain extent, in the immediate events that we like or dislike. The divine light penetrates all, and this has been shown to us through reflection and meditation with the Qur'an and all the revealed knowledge.

34. Surah 87 Al-A'la (The Most High)

The supreme Lord governs the known and the unknown through numerous powers and realities, which bring about all visible, changing experiences.

بِسْمِ اللَّهِ الرَّحْمَٰنِ الرَّحِيمِ

سَبِّحِ اسْمَ رَبِّكَ الْأَعْلَى ۝ الَّذِي خَلَقَ فَسَوَّىٰ ۝ وَالَّذِي قَدَّرَ فَهَدَىٰ ۝ وَالَّذِي أَخْرَجَ الْمَرْعَىٰ ۝ فَجَعَلَهُ غُثَاءً أَحْوَىٰ ۝ سَنُقْرِئُكَ فَلَا تَنسَىٰ ۝ إِلَّا مَا شَاءَ اللَّهُ ۚ إِنَّهُ يَعْلَمُ الْجَهْرَ وَمَا يَخْفَىٰ ۝ وَنُيَسِّرُكَ لِلْيُسْرَىٰ ۝ فَذَكِّرْ إِن نَّفَعَتِ الذِّكْرَىٰ ۝ سَيَذَّكَّرُ مَن يَخْشَىٰ ۝ وَيَتَجَنَّبُهَا الْأَشْقَى ۝ الَّذِي يَصْلَى النَّارَ الْكُبْرَىٰ ۝ ثُمَّ لَا يَمُوتُ فِيهَا وَلَا يَحْيَىٰ ۝ قَدْ أَفْلَحَ مَن تَزَكَّىٰ ۝ وَذَكَرَ اسْمَ رَبِّهِ فَصَلَّىٰ ۝ بَلْ تُؤْثِرُونَ الْحَيَاةَ الدُّنْيَا ۝ وَالْآخِرَةُ خَيْرٌ وَأَبْقَىٰ ۝ إِنَّ هَٰذَا لَفِي الصُّحُفِ الْأُولَىٰ ۝ صُحُفِ إِبْرَاهِيمَ وَمُوسَىٰ ۝ 1-19

In the name of Allah, the Merciful to all, the Compassionate to each!

Glorify the name of your Lord, the Most High, Who creates, then makes complete, Who determined and guided, Who brought forth the pasturage, then made it dark debris. We shall make you recite and you will not forget. Save what Allah wills; surely, He knows what is spoken aloud and what is hidden. We shall show you the easy way. So, remind, if reminding will help. And he who fears shall remember, but it will be ignored by the most wicked. He who shall be scorched by the great Fire, wherein he will neither die nor remain alive. He indeed shall be successful who purifies himself, and mentions the Name of his Lord, and prays. Yet you prefer the life of this world, though the hereafter is better and more lasting. All this is in the earlier scriptures, the scriptures of Abraham and Moses.

1-19 From the point of view of the soul and Truth, all that appears has come about in accordance with its destiny and cycle. What we need to remember is indelibly written in our souls. The original light as the ever-prevailing Reality can never be forgotten. Whoever is not content with transient realities, whoever is in cautious awareness regarding what the ultimate Reality is, will benefit from reminders of the path emanating from that light. A big distraction is our desire to control the outer world, which will lead to the ultimate shock of losing it all, if not before death, then upon it. Whoever has purified their self from self-illusion can progress towards higher consciousness and awakening. However, normally the human tendency is to prefer the immediate and to fear the loss of life and property. This state has accompanied human beings from prehistoric times.

Our earthly experiences are based on duality. Likewise, human nature is based upon the divine soul and its shadowy, earthly self.

The prophetic path takes us higher in consciousness towards full awakening. To refer constantly to the divine light within the heart allows us to progress spiritually from this basic transactional life to cosmic life itself.

The whole process of our earthly journey is that of returning to the origin of intelligence, which is the intrinsic memory of the beginning of existence. The more we refer to this, the more we can transcend all the fears, anxieties, and distractions that surround us. So, by the remembrance of the presence of the supreme Lord of all we can transcend the pitfalls of being engrossed in the lower world. And this has been revealed over many millennia to seekers of truth.

35. Surah 88 Al-Ghashiyah (The Overshadowing Event)

The Qur'an is a great reminder that our life on earth is a mere prelude to the hereafter and, as such, instructs and guides us to be ready for the inevitable event after death.

بِسْمِ اللَّهِ الرَّحْمَٰنِ الرَّحِيمِ

1-19 هَلْ أَتَاكَ حَدِيثُ ٱلْغَٰشِيَةِ ۝ وُجُوهٌ يَوْمَئِذٍ خَٰشِعَةٌ ۝ عَامِلَةٌ نَّاصِبَةٌ ۝ تَصْلَىٰ نَارًا حَامِيَةً ۝ تُسْقَىٰ مِنْ عَيْنٍ ءَانِيَةٍ ۝ لَّيْسَ لَهُمْ طَعَامٌ إِلَّا مِن ضَرِيعٍ ۝ لَّا يُسْمِنُ وَلَا يُغْنِى مِن جُوعٍ ۝ وُجُوهٌ يَوْمَئِذٍ نَّاعِمَةٌ ۝ لِّسَعْيِهَا رَاضِيَةٌ ۝ فِى جَنَّةٍ عَالِيَةٍ ۝ لَّا تَسْمَعُ فِيهَا لَٰغِيَةً ۝ فِيهَا عَيْنٌ جَارِيَةٌ ۝ فِيهَا سُرُرٌ مَّرْفُوعَةٌ ۝ وَأَكْوَابٌ مَّوْضُوعَةٌ ۝ وَنَمَارِقُ مَصْفُوفَةٌ ۝ وَزَرَابِىُّ مَبْثُوثَةٌ ۝ أَفَلَا يَنظُرُونَ إِلَى ٱلْإِبِلِ كَيْفَ خُلِقَتْ ۝ وَإِلَى ٱلسَّمَآءِ كَيْفَ رُفِعَتْ ۝ وَإِلَى ٱلْجِبَالِ كَيْفَ نُصِبَتْ ۝

In the name of Allah, the Merciful to all, the Compassionate to each!

Has there come unto thee the tiding of the Overshadowing Event? Faces on that day humbled, labouring, toil worn, scorched by a blazing Fire, made to drink from a boiling spring. With no food for them except bitter dry thorns. Which will neither fatten nor avail against hunger. On that Day there will also be faces radiant with bliss, with their striving well-pleased, in a lofty garden, where they will hear no idle talk, with a flowing spring, therein uplifted couches and drinking-cups ready placed, cushions set in rows, and fine carpets outspread. Will they not then consider the camels, how they are created? How the sky was uplifted? And the mountains, how they are firmly fixed,

1-19 During our lifetime, we experience certain states that overcome previous states, for example sleep overcomes wakefulness, or severe sickness or hallucination covers up the state of coherence, or pain overcomes pleasure. Ultimately, there is a state that does away with all the illusions and shadows that accompany dualities and life on earth. This can happen to different degrees or in various stages in this life, as well as after death. The few who have managed to transcend the box of space-time have touched upon higher consciousness and real happiness and joy. As for those who have missed this opportunity due to distractions, there is nothing for them other than flowing with the destiny of the whole universe, as everything returns back to its origin. As human beings, we have the potential for higher consciousness, and whoever has attained it is saved.

Before the emergence of the universe, there was total cosmic Reality without manifestation. Then creation emerged, which helps those who are reflective to trace its origin to the absolute, infinite and eternal One. Whoever realises this truth can access the inner eternal garden and will always be able to touch the source of goodness on earth.

We are reminded in many ways that our earthly experiences will end but lead to life after death. The more open and loyal we are to the eternal Truth, the less will be our shock of death and what comes after it. If we are honest, we realise that all we have is given to us to be tested: how accountable we are, how much we are living the intensity of the moment. Then our journey will be with ease and dignity; the humbler our human side is, the more illumined our spiritual light will be.

20-26 وَإِلَى ٱلْأَرْضِ كَيْفَ سُطِحَتْ ۞ فَذَكِّرْ إِنَّمَآ أَنتَ مُذَكِّرٌ ۞ لَّسْتَ عَلَيْهِم بِمُصَيْطِرٍ ۞ إِلَّا مَن تَوَلَّىٰ وَكَفَرَ ۞ فَيُعَذِّبُهُ ٱللَّهُ ٱلْعَذَابَ ٱلْأَكْبَرَ ۞ إِنَّ إِلَيْنَآ إِيَابَهُمْ ۞ ثُمَّ إِنَّ عَلَيْنَا حِسَابَهُم ۞

how the earth is spread out? Therefore, do remind, for you are only a reminder. You are not there to control them. As for those who turn away and disbelieve, him Allah shall torment with the greatest of torments. It is to Us they will return, and then it is for Us to call them to account.

20-26 The more we reflect on how everything has emerged from a non-existent, pure Essence or source, the more we will move towards experiencing our eventual return to this origin. As human beings, if this process is accompanied by awakened awareness, we are on the path of attaining life's objective. Otherwise, we will fall into darkness akin to a black hole, where everything is lost.

A healthy practice is to reflect upon and remember that anything that begins will also end as well as that the Truth is not subject to space-time. It is by the light of Truth that we are alive, and to it we will all return. After death, everyone will realise what they have earned on earth.

It took many billions of years for the earth to stabilize and be able to accept this great miracle of life. Then after more millions of years of evolution, we have come to the point of a highly sophisticated human being, with many levels of intelligence and the most complex physical reality that almost resonates in a cosmic way with whatever there is in existence. If we do not reflect upon these amazing phenomena and simply get carried away by delusion and distraction, we will only have regrets and suffering after death.

36. Surah 90 Al-Balad (The City)

The natural desire of human beings to be in a state of happiness and live in a tranquil abode is preceded by the last four ayat of the previous surah. When the self is completely subdued, it can enter the complete perfection of the inner garden of the soul.

بِسْمِ ٱللَّهِ ٱلرَّحْمَٰنِ ٱلرَّحِيمِ

1-20 لَا أُقْسِمُ بِهَٰذَا ٱلْبَلَدِ ۝ وَأَنتَ حِلٌّ بِهَٰذَا ٱلْبَلَدِ ۝ وَوَالِدٍ وَمَا وَلَدَ ۝ لَقَدْ خَلَقْنَا ٱلْإِنسَٰنَ فِى كَبَدٍ ۝ أَيَحْسَبُ أَن لَّن يَقْدِرَ عَلَيْهِ أَحَدٌ ۝ يَقُولُ أَهْلَكْتُ مَالًا لُّبَدًا ۝ أَيَحْسَبُ أَن لَّمْ يَرَهُۥٓ أَحَدٌ ۝ أَلَمْ نَجْعَل لَّهُۥ عَيْنَيْنِ ۝ وَلِسَانًا وَشَفَتَيْنِ ۝ وَهَدَيْنَٰهُ ٱلنَّجْدَيْنِ ۝ فَلَا ٱقْتَحَمَ ٱلْعَقَبَةَ ۝ وَمَآ أَدْرَىٰكَ مَا ٱلْعَقَبَةُ ۝ فَكُّ رَقَبَةٍ ۝ أَوْ إِطْعَٰمٌ فِى يَوْمٍ ذِى مَسْغَبَةٍ ۝ يَتِيمًا ذَا مَقْرَبَةٍ ۝ أَوْ مِسْكِينًا ذَا مَتْرَبَةٍ ۝ ثُمَّ كَانَ مِنَ ٱلَّذِينَ ءَامَنُوا۟ وَتَوَاصَوْا۟ بِٱلصَّبْرِ وَتَوَاصَوْا۟ بِٱلْمَرْحَمَةِ ۝ أُو۟لَٰٓئِكَ أَصْحَٰبُ ٱلْمَيْمَنَةِ ۝ وَٱلَّذِينَ كَفَرُوا۟ بِـَٔايَٰتِنَا هُمْ أَصْحَٰبُ ٱلْمَشْـَٔمَةِ ۝ عَلَيْهِمْ نَارٌ مُّؤْصَدَةٌۢ ۝

In the name of Allah, the Merciful to all, the Compassionate to each!

No indeed! I swear by this City. While you live in this City! By a begetter and what he begot! We have created man in hardship. Does he imagine that none can over-power him? He says, 'I have squandered great wealth.' Does he think none has seen him? Did We not give him two eyes? A tongue and two lips? And point out to him the two clear ways. Yet he has not attempted the steep path. What will explain to you what the steep path is? It is to free a slave. Or feeding, in time of famine. An orphan near in kin. Or a poor person in distress. Then he is of those who believe and charge one another to show patience, and charge one another to show compassion. Such are they that have attained to righteousness; whereas those who disbelieve Our signs they are such as have lost themselves in evil. Fire closing in upon them.

1-20 Humanity's evolution of consciousness has led us to conjure up incredible ways to create a better quality of life on earth, with less disease and suffering and fewer needs. We love cities and towns where there is law, order, and justice. The same applies to the body and mind. When our organs function well, we are poised towards a higher level of consciousness. Yet, the nature of human beings is to be under some stress, because we need to strive to get out of the box of space-time and its limitations, including our personal identity. Shadows indicate the light, and the heart of our personal "town" is that light, the innermost heart, which resonates with its origin in the divine light of Allah. Our awareness of the human makeup enables the self to surrender to the soul, to be at ease and content, since the soul is ever-loyal, resonating with Allah. If this surrender does not happen, we run the danger of being lost in the darkness of the lower self.

Our magnificent world challenges us regularly at numerous levels of dualities. Our earthly consciousness looks for reliability, safety, and a comfortable environment. We change houses or migrate for that purpose, when in fact we carry our own city, the human body, with us. Physical human needs can be understood intellectually, but the spiritual need is to break through all discernible entities and situations – transcendence.

With reflection and meditation, we find that our ultimate duty is to be liberated from the lower self-ego and its ever-changing images and shadows. For this liberation, we need to completely abandon the idea of duality and separation. That can only happen by serving and giving until such time there is no profile of identity. What remains is cosmic Reality and its lights.

37. Surah 93 Adh-Duha (Morning Brightness)

The divine light permeates all that is known and unknown. It is the darkness of the lower self and ego that is a barrier between us and it. This surah assures us that we are in this world to be prepared for the hereafter.

بِسْمِ اللَّـهِ الرَّحْمَـٰنِ الرَّحِيمِ

1-11 وَالضُّحَىٰ ۝ وَاللَّيْلِ إِذَا سَجَىٰ ۝ مَا وَدَّعَكَ رَبُّكَ وَمَا قَلَىٰ ۝ وَلَلْآخِرَةُ خَيْرٌ لَّكَ مِنَ الْأُولَىٰ ۝ وَلَسَوْفَ يُعْطِيكَ رَبُّكَ فَتَرْضَىٰ ۝ أَلَمْ يَجِدْكَ يَتِيمًا فَآوَىٰ ۝ وَوَجَدَكَ ضَالًّا فَهَدَىٰ ۝ وَوَجَدَكَ عَائِلًا فَأَغْنَىٰ ۝ فَأَمَّا الْيَتِيمَ فَلَا تَقْهَرْ ۝ وَأَمَّا السَّائِلَ فَلَا تَنْهَرْ ۝ وَأَمَّا بِنِعْمَةِ رَبِّكَ فَحَدِّثْ ۝

In the name of Allah, the Merciful to all, the Compassionate to each!
By the morning brightness and the night when it settles your Lord has not forsaken you nor disdains. And surely what comes after is better for you than that which has gone before. Your Lord is sure to give you so much that you will be well satisfied. Did He not find you an orphan and give you shelter? Did He not find you lost and guide you? Did He not find you in need and make you self-sufficient? Therefore, as for the orphan, do not oppress and as for him who asks, do not chide and talk about the blessings of your Lord.

1-11 Our life is bracketed between beginnings and ends, light and darkness, and when the light of the soul shines upon the self (nafs) it drives us towards our destiny. Allah's way is that we are turning from one opposite to another, held within the divine grace. If there was no darkness, we could not recognise light taking us to a point where we reach contentment of the soul within. We acknowledge that this guidance was always from Allah, through our souls via our hearts, and that this grace was and is always there. We each have experienced aspects of being orphans or being needy. The more we express gratitude, the more likely we are to be in touch with perpetual grace and its divine Origin. This life is a mere preparation for the hereafter, where real fulfilment is promised for the awakened ones.

We are indeed given the ultimate grace to experience dualities in order to choose what is best for our durable contentment and happiness. We have always experienced shortages, including that of health. Ultimately what will give us true contentment is the knowledge of the divine soul within the heart – the ultimate blessing.

Divine control and governance is total in all situations, for whatever exists, even for our personal difficulties and disturbances. Whatever is good may contain a bit of what is considered bad and vice versa. So, we have to practice equanimity, gentleness, and generosity, since the power of generosity has engulfed us always.

38. Surah 94 Ash-Sharh (The Expanding)

During one's lifetime, there are invariably situations in which one experiences great constriction and difficulty. This surah reminds us that all earthly events will eventually pass, and that difficulties always appear together with ease.

بِسْمِ اللَّهِ الرَّحْمَٰنِ الرَّحِيمِ

1-8 أَلَمْ نَشْرَحْ لَكَ صَدْرَكَ ۝ وَوَضَعْنَا عَنكَ وِزْرَكَ ۝ ٱلَّذِىٓ أَنقَضَ ظَهْرَكَ ۝ وَرَفَعْنَا لَكَ ذِكْرَكَ ۝ فَإِنَّ مَعَ ٱلْعُسْرِ يُسْرًا ۝ إِنَّ مَعَ ٱلْعُسْرِ يُسْرًا ۝ فَإِذَا فَرَغْتَ فَٱنصَبْ ۝ وَإِلَىٰ رَبِّكَ فَٱرْغَب ۝

In the name of Allah, the Merciful to all, the Compassionate to each!

Have We not expanded for you your breast. And taken off from you your burden. That weighed so heavily on your back, and raise your reputation high? So truly where there is hardship there is also ease. Truly where there is hardship there is also ease. When your work is done, turn to devotion, and turn to your Lord for everything.

1-8 All mature human beings have experienced, on occasion, ease and expansion of the breast accompanied by wider horizons and higher consciousness. This is to do with the prevalence of the lights and delights of the soul. Otherwise, like most people, we feel stressed and oppressed, carrying our worries on our backs. Through wisdom we see that ease and difficulty alternate. The Source of all life is "ease" itself, that is always being emitted through our hearts. Whenever we are at points of ease, having attended to the visible, physical, earthly needs that tend to dominate, we are at the door of higher consciousness, of lights and delights beyond the senses. High quality prayers and meditation follow with ease after one has dispensed with earthly duties and responsibilities.

We have all experienced stress and difficulties that weigh us down. This is all part of the training that we must undertake to make better and better choices in our life, until such time we learn to choose that which will not bring us sorrow, grief, or regret. This means to be at one with the eternal light of the One in our own hearts.

Whenever we stop concern with the good and bad, the up and down, the healthy and ill – only in that neutrality are we at the edge of transcendence, beyond any duality, touching the zone of the Oneness from which everything has emerged.

39. Surah 97 Al-Qadr (Determination)

Within our experiences of time and space, there are occasions when the power and impact of an event are far more than we could imagine. This is the impact of the Night of Power.

بِسْمِ اللَّهِ الرَّحْمَٰنِ الرَّحِيمِ

1-5 إِنَّا أَنزَلْنَاهُ فِى لَيْلَةِ ٱلْقَدْرِ ۝ وَمَآ أَدْرَىٰكَ مَا لَيْلَةُ ٱلْقَدْرِ ۝ لَيْلَةُ ٱلْقَدْرِ خَيْرٌ مِّنْ أَلْفِ شَهْرٍ ۝ تَنَزَّلُ ٱلْمَلَٰٓئِكَةُ وَٱلرُّوحُ فِيهَا بِإِذْنِ رَبِّهِم مِّن كُلِّ أَمْرٍ ۝ سَلَٰمٌ هِىَ حَتَّىٰ مَطْلَعِ ٱلْفَجْرِ ۝

In the name of Allah, the Merciful to all, the Compassionate to each!

We sent it down in the Night of Determination. But how can you know what is the Night of determination? The Night of determination is better than a thousand months. In it the angels and the Spirit are sent down, by their Lord's leave, attending to every command. Peace it is, till the rising of dawn.

1-5 The last ayah of the previous surah indicates the unison between the message and the messenger, leading to the actual event of the descent of the Qur'an to humanity. Everything in existence is according to a measure and a cycle of beginnings and ends. The essence of all that has come about is embedded in the unseen. This essence is also reflected in the human soul. The rest is manifestation and descent, which bring about the physicality of this world for a while. The most powerful event in existence is when the essence of the unseen reveals its earthly connection.

Our love for power, which is the soul's possession, is such that a rise in consciousness often comes to us as parcels of light and knowledge. You may be praying and trying for months when suddenly a flash of insight changes your entire outlook and understanding. For the believer on the path, the experience of the Night of Power is real.

Earthly evolution and the rise in consciousness over the last few billions of years occur in continuous slow motion except for occasions when certain bursts take place. During these major movements you find many species become extinct and others transform into what we consider now to be key. We need to reflect upon this changing stability within an ocean of containment and contentment.

40. Surah 112 Al-Ikhlas (Sincerity)

Every ayah describes a unique attribute of God, not shared with any other being.

بِسْمِ اللَّهِ الرَّحْمَـٰنِ الرَّحِيمِ

1-4 قُلْ هُوَ اللَّهُ أَحَدٌ ۝ اللَّهُ الصَّمَدُ ۝ لَمْ يَلِدْ وَلَمْ يُولَدْ ۝ وَلَمْ يَكُن لَّهُ كُفُوًا أَحَدٌ ۝

In the name of Allah, the Merciful to all, the Compassionate to each!
Say: 'He is Allah, Unique, Allah, Self-sufficient. Neither begetting nor begotten. And none can be His peer.'

1-4 Say, confess, read, and know that Allah is one, and that Allah is the only Reality that is self-sustaining, self-effulgent, and not subject to cause and effect or comings and goings. This Reality is supreme and incomparable. Most desirable human qualities are rooted in divine attributes, and sincerity, honesty, and loyalty are in the forefront. If your ultimate reference is God, whose light radiates from your heart, then you do not fear criticism or disappointment, nor will you experience much regret or anger. Your sincerity to the light of timelessness brings about a tranquillity and contentment that transcends all the usual, normal human emotions, feelings, or desires.

Allah is the most unique, not one as it relates to other numbers, for Allah is the only self-perpetuating, self-sufficient, bestower of all powers according to Allah's own wisdom and designs. None other than Allah governs the universe.

From this Oneness, the entire universe of plurality and dualities has emanated. And everything returns to that Oneness when the universe ends.

41. Surah 113 Al-Falaq (Break of Dawn)

Human life is a movement from darkness to light. In this journey, we need to exercise the utmost caution and courtesy not to slip into arrogance and self-deception.

بِسْمِ اللَّهِ الرَّحْمَٰنِ الرَّحِيمِ

قُلْ أَعُوذُ بِرَبِّ ٱلْفَلَقِ ۝ مِن شَرِّ مَا خَلَقَ ۝ وَمِن شَرِّ غَاسِقٍ إِذَا وَقَبَ ۝ وَمِن شَرِّ ٱلنَّفَّٰثَٰتِ فِى ٱلْعُقَدِ ۝ وَمِن شَرِّ حَاسِدٍ إِذَا حَسَدَ ۝   1-5

In the name of Allah, the Merciful to all, the Compassionate to each!
Say: 'I seek refuge in the Lord of the dawn, from the evil of what He has created, and from the evil of the utterly dark night when it comes, and from the evil of the blowers in knots, from the evil of the envier when he envies.'

1-5 The awakened person on the path of awakening to the Real, remains cautious about shadows and distractions, avoiding any deviation from being at one with the One. Avoidance of evil includes all aspects of wrongdoing as well as any distractions from the path of surrender and unity with higher consciousness. There are different levels to human mischief, which include the paranormal as well as magic. It is sufficient for an intelligent person to try to deal with the challenges of duality that we experience at all times. Surely, it is enough for an individual to watch out for the trickery of the lower self and to be in constant reference to higher consciousness in order to recalibrate one's intentions and actions to be present at this moment in time.

With early intelligence we become cautious as to what we are planning and doing, because we do not want to suffer, nor do we want to end up in a situation that is not reversible. We like to be safe from natural darkness and mischief, including that which is perpetrated by other creatures. Unless we are reasonably safe and stable, we cannot grow in consciousness towards awakening.

To travel on this earth with contentment and the least serious obstacles and troubles, one has to be cautious of the destructive energies, visible and otherwise, which are always there. This includes jealousy, hatred, and many other negative emotions.

42. Surah 114 Al-Nas (Mankind)

The biggest challenge is relationships with other people, most of whom are ignorant about their purpose and direction in life.

بِسْمِ اللَّهِ الرَّحْمَٰنِ الرَّحِيمِ

قُلْ أَعُوذُ بِرَبِّ ٱلنَّاسِ ۝ مَلِكِ ٱلنَّاسِ ۝ إِلَٰهِ ٱلنَّاسِ ۝ مِن شَرِّ ٱلْوَسْوَاسِ ٱلْخَنَّاسِ ۝ ٱلَّذِى يُوَسْوِسُ فِى صُدُورِ ٱلنَّاسِ ۝ مِنَ ٱلْجِنَّةِ وَٱلنَّاسِ ۝   1-6

In the name of Allah, the Merciful to all, the Compassionate to each!
Say: 'I seek refuge with the Lord of mankind, King of mankind, Allah of

mankind, against the harm of the slinking whisperer. Who whispers in the hearts of mankind, of Jinn and mankind.'

1-6 It is natural for ordinary human beings to be jealous and covetous, to prefer what they think is good for themselves over anything else, until the lower self is restricted and contained. It is a big gift to avoid human mischief and treachery. The last ayah of the previous surah confirms this in terms of its warning of the evil eye. Honest people reveal what is in their hearts by their tongues. They are cautious to avoid mischief, a trait prevalent in all creation. Believers are those on the middle path, between arrival to the Truth and deviation and distraction. We need to be cautious regarding both visible mischief and the invisible path of darkness that can be more dangerous. The act of announcing, pronouncing, and declaring that we want to be saved from the onset of mischief and wrongdoing is the beginning of protection.

It is natural for us to pray and hope that we ward off distractions that can harm us and cause affliction. Human mischief in all kinds of varieties is perhaps amongst the worst from which we can suffer. To be wary of this and to pray to be saved is a most intelligent endeavour and supplication.

Amongst the greatest obstacles are mental doubts about others and constant inner whisperings regarding the dishonesty, unreliability, or negative states of other people. It is a great hope and expectation to be spared from the mischief of other living entities, both humans and *Jinn*.

www.ingramcontent.com/pod-product-compliance
Lightning Source LLC
Chambersburg PA
CBHW011953150426
43197CB00020B/2944